Dressing the Part

A HISTORY OF COSTUME FOR THE THEATRE

REVISED EDITION

Dressing the Part

A HISTORY OF COSTUME FOR THE THEATRE

BY FAIRFAX PROUDFIT WALKUP

School of the Theatre ~ Pasadena Community Playhouse

✳ ✳ ✳

New York   Appleton-Century-Crofts, Inc.   *1950*

PN
2067
.W3

FOREWORD

It gives me very real pleasure to introduce this book to its readers. Fairfax Proudfit Walkup, the author of *Dressing the Part,* comes to her subject through the teaching of history, and is thoroughly conversant with the historic background of costuming. She has long been accepted as an authority on the material of which she writes, and has lectured extensively before colleges and universities on the subject of costume. She has written of it previously, and has been Instructor in Costume at the Pasadena Playhouse School of the Theatre since its founding.

Mrs. Walkup has costumed various Pasadena Playhouse productions and her practical knowledge of the possibilities and limitations of the stage has proved invaluable. Her long experience in theatrical work has taught her to adapt a costume, historically correct, to the needs of the actor, so that his clothes may not hamper him in any way nor conflict with his characterization. Instead, she knows how to make material and ornament, line and color, reinforce and high-light the actor's art until the costumes, in some subtle manner, become a part of the play, helping to clarify its meaning, intensify its mood, and increase the emotional response it arouses. This is the work of an artist, but Mrs. Walkup's ability is not confined to artistry. She thoroughly understands the limitations imposed by the production budget, and her experience with color and materials has given her an uncanny knack of seeming to turn budget liabilities into production assets.

In *Dressing the Part,* Mrs. Walkup is sharing with you, its readers, as much of her hardly earned experience, her fine technique and art of designing, as it is possible to get between the covers of a book. Like the true theatre worker that she is, she makes her contribution freely and graciously, that her own attainments may be of service to others in the theatre who have the responsibility of "dressing the part."

Gilmor Brown

Pasadena Playhouse
Pasadena, California

ACKNOWLEDGMENTS

I wish to express my appreciation to the staff of the Henry E. Huntington Library and Art Gallery at San Marino for their interest and scholarly aid in matters of research. Valuable also was the help of Dr. Margaret Carhart, of the University of California at Los Angeles, in planning the structure of this book.

Thanks are due in generous measure to Eugart Yerian, Director of the Memphis Little Theatre, for his able assistance in preparing the drawings and patterns; to my first student, Miss Wilma Leithead, designer for Twentieth Century-Fox Studios, for the end sheets and for many practical details; and to the artist, Albert Stockdale, who designed the figures on the title page. At this time I wish to express my gratitude for the several drawings contributed by the late Robert Redington Sharpe.

To Norman Mennes, of the Pasadena Playhouse, I am greatly indebted for various drawings; and to Marian Johnson, also of the Playhouse, who created the children's costumes.

I value sincerely the excellent suggestions given by Andrew J. Campbell and Fred Carl Huxley, of the Pasadena Playhouse staff, concerning make-up and lighting respectively. And to DeWitt Bodeen I express my warmest thanks for his untiring devotion to the task of assembling, typing, and checking material for *Dressing the Part*.

For aid in assembling material for the years 1937–1950, I am indebted to Marvyn Harbert, Art Director of the Old Globe Theatre, San Diego, for certain full-page drawings; to Miss Peggy Kellner, my assistant at the University of Arizona, for the small detailed drawings; to Professor Peter Marroney, Head of the Drama Department, Professor Robert Burroughs, Art Director of the Drama Department, and Captain Robert D. Dwan, U. S. Army, of the University of Arizona; to Dr. C. Lowell Lees, Head of the Department of Drama, University of Utah, Dr. Harold Folland, University of Utah; to Dr. Hector Lee, Dean of Humanities, Chico College; and to Professor Hunton D. Sellman, San Diego State College. These valued friends and co-workers made the task easier, with their voluntary contributions of specific data and source material.

FAIRFAX P. WALKUP

TABLE OF CONTENTS

INTRODUCTION

Clothes do not make the man, but they do much to explain him. As an old trunk in the attic may open up the past, so the clothes of another day may recreate a period. Who can look upon the rhythmic draperies of the "Winged Victory" without feeling once more the sweeping simplicity of the Greeks?

The story of dress is an old one – as old as the story of civilization. The known history of man is coincident with the history of dress. Does not the Bible state that Adam had no sooner eaten of the fruit of the tree of knowledge than he began to clothe himself? This desire for adornment is in itself a manifestation of man's social policy. It shows his eagerness to be not merely a material mass of flesh and bones, but also the symbol of an idea. This idea is Beauty. Costume is, then, man's attempt to embellish nature with art.

Dress is the art most closely associated with man. The Parthenon, the "Hermes," the "Mona Lisa," the *Decameron,* the Parsifal legend, express man objectively; the art of adornment exists only in connection with the body of man. It covers his body, and it also reveals his personality.

It seems quite certain that dress evolved, not primarily to fulfill a need for warmth or decency, but for ornament, to express an inward love of beauty. To trace dress to a need for warmth only is to give it but passing significance. True enough, in some ancient and chilly age, man found that the skins of animals gave pleasing warmth. It must have been a thrilling experience when prehistoric man first draped the furry skins about him. One can see him adjusting them, tunic fashion, front and back, tying the two pelts together on the shoulders by means of the paws. Perhaps he wrapped them around his loins with another skin laid over his shoulder, shawl fashion. Thus adorned, the primitive Beau Brummel paraded before his fellow tribesmen, accepting complacently their grunts of admiration at this, the first Spring Fashion Show. It meant more than mere display. It heralded the first development of man's individual taste – his first evidence of artistic selectiveness.

Having chosen and arranged skins in a design which proved pleasing, primitive man further enhanced his attractiveness by tattooing and cicatrice; having no clothes to embroider, he (as Gautier said) embroidered himself! Red and yellow ochre, blue woad, green malachite added color to man's person. Woman, later, usurped this prerogative, not by power of might, but just because she had the cheek to do it!

From furs, man progressed to the use of fiber beaten to a pulp and made into matted cloth or felts; and finally he wove woolen strands into cloth. Linen, cotton, and silk followed in an ever-increasing variety of weights, textures, and patterns.

Macaulay has said that a revolution in dress is as pregnant in meaning as a revolution in political power. It is significant that one almost always influences the other.

ix

History has its direct effect on clothes. Trousers, for example, were adopted by the Greeks through contact with the barbarians to the north and east; this modern symbol of man's masculinity is, in reality, only a relic of barbarism. So the outer covering of man – the "vestigial tissue," as Carlyle calls it – became richer and finer as man rose from the savage state to that of a civilized creature. Dress not only kept pace with man's development, but also shadowed any radical change in his condition. On the other hand, dress has influenced history. The extravagant dress of Marie Antoinette's court furnished a definite grievance only silenced by the guillotine.

There is a distinct psychology in clothes. Every woman knows that a fit of the blues may be dispelled by donning a becoming frock. Mark Twain, it is said, wrote best in a nightgown. Wagner deliberately wore rich colors and draped his room in warm materials when composing the "Ring of the Nibelung." Chopin said that it rested him, after a day at the piano, to put on formal evening clothes. Monarchs dress young princelings in military costume, that they may early get the feel of domination. The judge's powdered wig recalls the gay court of the French Louis; the coachman's cockade is a vestige of the headdress of the fourteenth century; the epaulet is the last remnant of medieval chain mail. Thus the life and romance of bygone days are carried about, perhaps unconsciously, in a hundred small details of daily dress. Bit by bit each is the outward and visible sign of a once dominant urge; vanity is the heritage of all the ages.

Fashions change; new designs in dress arise; new experiences lead to new creations. So man weaves endless patterns, each bearing his impress. Perhaps the whole pattern of life is but the silhouette of eternity.

Dressing the Part

A HISTORY OF COSTUME FOR THE THEATRE

TO MY SON JOHN
TO DOROTHY
AND TO DENNIS

CHAPTER I

EGYPT

IMPORTANT PEOPLE AND EVENTS

ARCHAIC PERIOD (4500–2980 B. C.) *

July 19, 4241 B. C.: Origin of the Egyptian calendar – first authentic date.

First Dynasty: Menes. . . . First great ruler or "Pharaoh" (which means "great house"). . . . Founded Memphis, capital of Lower Egypt.

OLD KINGDOM (2980–2475 B. C.)

Third Dynasty: Pyramid Kings. . . . Khufu (Cheops) built the Great Pyramid of Gizeh. . . . Khafre built the Lesser Pyramid and the Sphinx. . . . Menkure completed the Third Pyramid. . . . Ptah-Hotep wrote *The Book of Moral Precepts*. . . . Imhotep, a great physician and also an architect.

MIDDLE KINGDOM (2160–1788 B. C.)

Eleventh Dynasty: Sesostris I built a temple at Heliopolis, canals, and pyramids. . . . Worked copper and malachite mines. . . . Sesostris III conquered Nubia. . . . Hyksos, or Shepherd Kings, invaded and conquered Egypt. . . . Horses introduced into Egypt. . . . Geometry used to re-establish field boundaries after Nile floods. . . . Gold used as money. . . . Books on astronomy written. . . . Science of embalming perfected. . . . Writing on stone and papyrus was at its height. . . . Hieroglyphics or picture writing. . . . The Hyksos were driven out of Egypt by Ahmose. . . . Calendar of twelve months, three hundred sixty-five days, perfected.

NEW KINGDOM (1600–800 B. C.)

Eighteenth Dynasty: First Empire (1580–1350 B. C.). . . . Feudal age. . . . Thutmose III (a sort of Egyptian Alexander the Great) and Queen Hatshepsut, his sister-wife, built obelisks at Thebes. . . . Great Temple of Karnak. . . . Thutmose conquered Palestine, Phoenicia, and Syria. . . . Egyptian art at its height. . . . Amenhotep III and Tiy, his wife. . . . Colossal statues of Memnon constructed at Thebes. . . . Amenhotep IV, later called Akhenaten. . . . Worship of Aten, or one God. . . . Tell-el-Amarna letters – the first international correspondence. . . . Joseph, and also Jacob and his other sons, in Egypt. . . . Tutankhamen restores worship of Amen.

Nineteenth Dynasty: Second Empire (1350–1150 B. C.). . . . Seti I, great organizer. . . . Ramses II. . . . Oppressor of Hebrews. . . . War against the Hittites. . . . Exodus of the Hebrews from the land of Egypt. . . . The Ten Commandments. . . . Joshua led the Hebrews into Canaan. . . . Fall of Troy.

SAITE PERIOD (663–525 B. C.)

Twenty-sixth Dynasty: Psammetichus opened the kingdom to foreign trade. . . . Assyrians under Sennacherib overran Egypt. . . . Phoenicians circumnavigated Africa. . . .

* See pages 373–383 for information as to the sources of the dates, names, and other historic facts included in this work.

Egypt devastated by Nebuchadnezzar of Babylon. . . . 525 B. C., Egypt
conquered by Cambyses. . . . Became a Persian province.

332 B. C.   Egypt conquered by Alexander the Great. . . . Ptolemaic Dynasty founded
by one of Alexander's generals, Ptolemy.

30 B. C.   Egypt became a Roman province under Augustus Caesar, at the death
of Cleopatra and Mark Antony.

The oldest display of coquetry in dress is presented by the Sphinx. For six thousand
years she has been setting her cap at the world. The folds of the headdress are a bit
frayed, and the face under the cap is somewhat seamed by time. A mere fleck of paint
remains on the right cheek. Yet the charm of this mysterious individual persists, and
men, even the Caesars and Napoleons, bow low before her.

This recognition is only natural. Egypt has a perennial allure. She has the distinction of being the oldest country in the world – and the youngest. She is the oldest,
since her civilization dates back authentically to 4241 B. C. She is the youngest because
each year she is reinvigorated, her life essence recharged, by the inundation of the
Great River. Herodotus long ago called this country "the gift of the Nile," a gift re-
newed each birthday. Is not this the perpetuity of youth?

The historian Rawlinson likened Egypt to a lotus with a crooked stem. The cup
of the flower is the delta, bending over into the Mediterranean. The stem is the sinuous
line of the Nile, without a single tributary branch for a thousand miles.

It is no wonder that the people in this narrow, isolated land were a reserved race,
withdrawn into themselves. It is no wonder that life acquired a distinct outward form,
a fixed rule and order. Had not Egypt put on the cerements of immortality when
the rest of the world was in swaddling clothes? There is a certain sophistication that
comes of being "with yesterday's seven thousand years." It is the unmistakable air of
the aristocrat of time.

To such an aristocrat, freedom or carelessness in person or dress would be distasteful.
Tradition gave the standard. Yet this very stability of fashion has a certain freshness.
A thing that never changes can never grow old.

Today, a few weeks may bring in a revolution in the shape of a sleeve or the length
of a skirt. In Egypt, style in the days of Cheops, the pyramid builder, was identical
with that of the time of Cleopatra. The garments of the men differed little from
those of the women. It was an easy matter for Hatshepsut, the "Queen Elizabeth" of
Egypt, to assume masculine garb, as she did. Especially was it easy to assume the
beard – for this, even with the men, was always false, as all the ancient records show.
Yet in spite of the fact that costume was undeviating, it was still quite satisfactory.
Why, queried the Egyptians, change what has proved pleasing, simple, and adequate?

Because they had geometrically trained minds, the lines of dress were simple and
exact. Unnecessary use of material was discouraged. This economy of effect was
embellished with great wealth of color and richness of jeweled ornament. The materials used were the simple products of the Nile-drenched fields – the fiber of the
cotton, thread of the flax, or wool of the flocks.

The colors were the elementary but glowing spectrum of the world about them –

green of the grasses, blue of the sky, red and purple of the setting sun, yellow of the noonday, orange of the dawn, and brown of the Nile's muddy stream. Blue, especially, was used extensively. It was the color sacred to Amen, the god of gods, and many of the figures of this god are painted blue. The color itself was obtained from indigo, or from copper, a metal with which the Egyptians were early acquainted, found at Sinai, or obtained from the island of Cyprus (the Greek name for copper).

The jewels that bedecked the straight bodies of the Egyptians were flecks of hidden fire, captured and held precious by these men as their tribute to beauty. The mountains that lined the Nile valley were rich in agate, jasper, chalcedony, rock crystal, carnelian, and lapis lazuli; emeralds could be found in the region round about Mount Zabara (Jebel). Gold, of course, was plentiful; it was obtained in great quantities from Nubia, whose name means the "Land of Nut Gold." Silver was much scarcer and therefore more valuable; it was not imported until late, and then from the country round about Cilicia.

Treasure, then, was abundant; and the Egyptians took care to store it away for use in the important future life beyond the short span which so quickly passed in the narrow, rock-enclosed valley. To house this treasure – and themselves – they lovingly built, not their temporal homes, which were of wood or plaster, soon decayed, but their spiritual homes. Here, in the tombs, they lived, moved, and had their being. Here, in carved or pictured form, they carried on their daily occupations, so that when the three thousand years' probation prescribed by Osiris was ended, they could take up the thread of life at the very point where it was snipped from their linen-swathed bodies.

COSTUME

GENERAL CHARACTERISTICS

With few exceptions, all classes of Egyptians wore the same general styles of dress. Difference in rank was evidenced by finer materials, more elaborate ornaments and accessories, and also by a few more elaborate types of garments.

Certain general aspects show little or no variation. These, applicable to the costume of both men and women, are as follows: (1) Sheathlike tunics, long or short, (2) radiation of fullness (gathered or pleated) from center front, (3) the use of sheer, transparent materials, (4) the use of diagonal lines, (5) the use of circular collars, (6) the use of primary and secondary colors, and (7) the use of wigs.

Materials

These were linen, cotton, and (rarely) wool. The linen woven at Chemmis measured five hundred threads to the inch, and was as transparent as modern organdy. King Solomon ordered much of his household linen from Chemmis. Threads of real gold or silver were woven into the cloth for royal garments. Since silver came from Cilicia, it was often more expensive than gold, which came from near-by Nubia. Priests were forbidden to wear anything but linen next their bodies; the leopard skins they wore for ritualistic occasions, and their woolen cloaks, rarely used, were lined

Fig. 1

with linen. Cotton was used by the middle and lower classes. Both linen and cotton had patterns woven in, painted, printed, or embroidered on the material. Woolen cloth was dyed or embroidered. The Egyptian bodies, varying in color from light cream brown to deep red brown, offered a splendid background for the brilliantly colored or transparent materials.

Underclothes

Neither men nor women paid serious heed to underclothes. A scant loincloth sufficed, wrapped tightly about the hips, one end passed between the legs and fastened behind. The other end, perhaps fringed, might hang down in front. Rarely, women added a short tight tunic beneath a fuller one, but this was by no means considered necessary.

COSTUME FOR MEN

Tunic

The short, hip-length tunic graced the men of Egypt (Fig. 2) in three different styles: the straight edge (D 1), the rounded edge (D 2), and the diagonal edge (D 3). Poor people wore only the short tunic with the loincloth underneath. Older men wore longer tunics reaching to the ground (Fig. 3 A D   Fig. 26 C).

Robe

This type of garment was used by older men, by men of rank, by priests and other dignitaries. It consisted of a rectangle twice the height of the wearer, shoulder to ground (Fig. 4 A C). A wide sash (Fig. 4 A D) confined the material at the waist. Another method of arrangement was to pull the front panel toward the center, then lap the back panel over the front until the edges met, center front (Fig. 4 B). A cord or sash held this in place. Usually a very sheer linen material was used for the robe. It might be gathered or pleated.

Skirt and Cape

Another type of garment worn by older men, kings, and other dignitaries was the skirt and cape. The skirt was made of a rectangular piece threaded at the waist with a cord (Fig. 6 B   Fig. 28 B). The cape was a rectangle, twisted, draped, and tied in a knot, center front, underneath the collar. Sometimes the two ends of the cape were drawn down into the waistband center front, thus forming a kimono-sleeve effect over the arms.

Mantle

The mantle, draped like a shawl about the neck, was longer behind than in front, and might be rectangular or circular about the bottom edge (Fig. 3 A B   Fig. 26 C).

Shawl

The shawl (not shown) was about fifteen feet long, about five feet wide, and was draped about the body, over the shoulders, and belted about the waist somewhat like a Hindu sari.

Corselet

The corselet for warriors, of quilted linen or leather, was covered with metal tabs or rings (Fig. 2 C   Fig. 26 F). A more ornamental type, for young men of rank, was

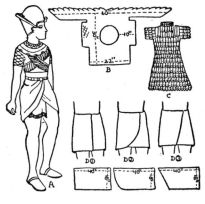

Fig. 2

made of quilted linen or leather patterned like a short jacket, with two wing-shaped ends folding over the chest in imitation of the protecting wings of Horus, god of valor (Fig. 2 A B   Fig. 15).

Collar

This was an indispensable part of Egyptian dress. The collar was circular and fastened in the back. It was made of stiffened linen, painted leather, beads, or precious stones (Fig. 6 D   Fig. 26 C).

Sash or Girdle

When a simple cord did not suffice, the more ornamental sash was used. This consisted of a piece of material, about a hundred inches long by twenty-four inches wide, wrapped twice about the hips and tied in front. One end (which might be fringed) was looped up under the sash, the loop showing above the waistline (Fig. 4 A D). This loop formed a pouch in which small accessories, such as seals, valuables, and the like, might be carried.

Belt

A belt, two or three inches wide, of painted linen or leather, was worn with the tunic or robe (Fig. 2 A   Fig. 3 A C), especially when the triangular bronze shield or the royal apron was used. For royal use the shield was made of gilded bronze, engraved and painted; for ordinary men it was of stiff leather or bronze (Fig. 3 A C). Slaves were not allowed to wear the shield. The royal apron, the insignia of highest rank, was worn only by the Pharaoh or heir apparent. It consisted of a striped pendant of linen or leather, about six inches wide at the base, and bordered with a row of serpent heads. On either side of this pendant were folds of striped cloth, arranged pyramid fashion. Perhaps the entire apron was of leather painted to imitate folds. (The stylized method of Egyptian painting makes it impossible to determine certain matters of dress and detail clearly.)

Footwear

Until the Fifth Dynasty, people of all classes, even the Pharaohs themselves, went barefoot. After that time sandals were adopted; they were made of leather lined with cloth, or of linen, or of woven palm leaves, papyrus stalks, or bark (Fig. 11 A B Fig. 12 B). The earliest sandals were flat, with a supporting piece at the side (of leather or metal), and a strap between the big toe and the second (Fig. 11 A Fig. 8 M). By the time of the Eighteenth Dynasty, sandals with curved toes (Fig. 12 A) were in vogue. These were often elaborately jeweled and otherwise decorated. An amusing custom was that of painting the figure of an enemy or slave in the sole of the sandal, so that the wearer might have the pleasure of trampling on him at every step (Fig. 8 L). A beautiful pair of sandals adorned with rosettes was found in the tomb of Tutankhamen.

Hair

Various and intricate arrangements were made of the hair. In earliest times, the hair was worn either long or short, and was often curled. From the time of the Pyramid Kings (Third Dynasty), elaborate arrangements developed. The hair might be cropped short in front, curving down to shoulder length behind, the whole arranged in horizontal rows of curls; or it might be arranged in two masses, one at either side of the face, with a third portion behind (Fig. 4 A). A more intricate arrangement was obtained by separating the hair into numerous strands, and twisting or braiding them in rows about the head. The hair on the crown of the head was curled or left smooth. Wigs were sewed to a net skullcap, carefully arranged to provide for ventilation to the scalp. The line over the forehead was horizontal and low.

An interesting arrangement was that used by the prince, or heir apparent to the throne. When appearing with shaven head (as he often appeared in battle), or with a wig, the prince always wore the "prince-lock." This was a broad braid of hair extending over the side of the face and curved at the end (Fig. 1 B Fig. 28 B). The prince-lock was often encased in gold. Horus, as son of Osiris, is often represented with the prince-lock.

Ritual demanded that priests shave their heads every day (Fig. 26 A). Poor people greased their hair and arranged it in the simpler fashions followed by the wealthy (Fig. 9).

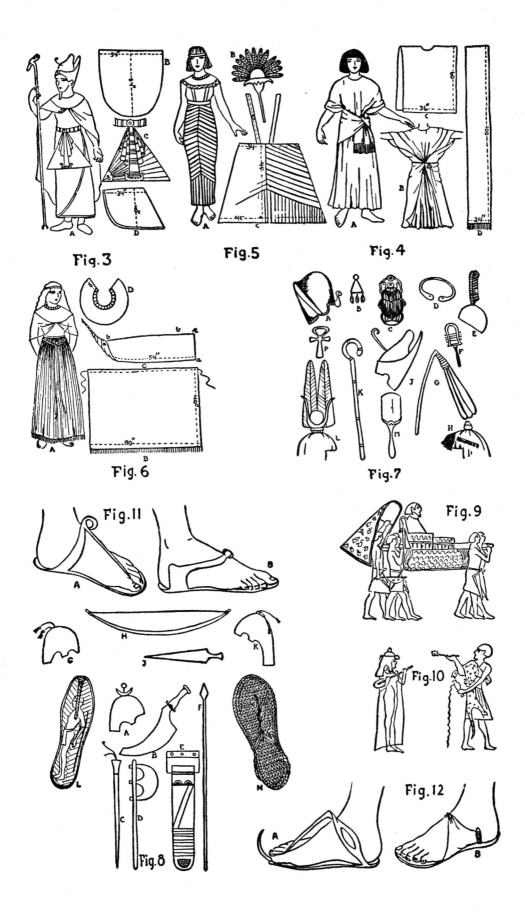

Fig. 3

Fig. 5

Fig. 4

Fig. 6

Fig. 7

Fig. 11

Fig. 9

Fig. 10

Fig. 8

Fig. 12

Beards

The shape of the beard indicated the rank of the wearer. Slaves and the lower classes went smooth-shaven (a curved bronze razor was used), as did also the priests. Merchants, landed proprietors, and the upper classes wore beards about two inches long; the Pharaohs wore them from four to six inches long (Fig. 1 C   Fig. 3 A   Fig. 26 C). The gods were represented as wearing beards of about the same length, but curved at the ends (Fig. 1 D). All beards were false; they were made of tufts of hair held in place by cords looped back over the ears (Fig. 1 D   Fig. 26 C). Inasmuch as the Pharaohs were regarded as gods after death, they too were often depicted with curved beards (Fig. 1 D).

Headdress

The Egyptians were very fond of headdresses. The earliest type, to be seen on the Sphinx, was a striped cloth bound about the temples, the folds falling forward on either side of the face, and over the shoulders (Fig. 1 C   Fig. 26 F). Priests wore skullcaps with no decoration (Fig. 10) except when the priest also held the office of scribe, in which case he wore a single feather upright on the cap (Fig. 7 E   Fig. 26 E). A similar type of skullcap, made of leather or quilted linen, was worn by soldiers. It varied in shape about the bottom edge, and was often decorated with tassels, crescents, and other ornaments (Fig. 8 A G K). The plain skullcap was also worn as a protection under the metal helmet. The metal helmet (Fig. 7 A   Fig. 28 C) was introduced by Thutmose III. It was tall, round in front, and squared off at the back; the surface was plain or studded with metal scales or rings. A leather helmet topped with feathers (Fig. 1 D) was another type of military headdress that was much used.

Symbolic Headdress

The most used type of symbolic headdress was the *pschent,* or crown of Upper and Lower Egypt, worn by the Pharaohs (Fig. 7 J   Fig. 3 A   Fig. 26 C). It consisted of the Red Crown of Lower Egypt, with a long point in the back, and the White Crown of Upper Egypt, resembling a fat tenpin but curved at the top. The tendril (*lituus*) protruding in front was red, and belonged to the Red Crown. The *uraeus,* or serpent, poised over the forehead, was always a symbol of royalty. Since the Egyptians recognized some seventy major divinities, and also many minor ones, symbolic headdresses were many and varied. The principal divinities are listed toward the close of this chapter. (See pages 13–15.)

Ornaments and Accessories

Egyptian ornaments consisted of armlets, bracelets (Fig. 7 D), rings, earrings, and pectorals. The latter were made of painted cloth or leather, or of glazed pottery for the lower classes. For the more wealthy, jewels, gold and silver, and enamelwork, or cloisonné, were used. The armlets and bracelets were painted or otherwise ornamented with intricate geometric or floriated patterns. The rings were either plain circlets, or scarabs, or flat or bezeled seals, or jewels set in gold or silver. The type of ring denoted the rank of the wearer. Rings were worn on all the fingers, as well as on the thumb.

Fig. 27

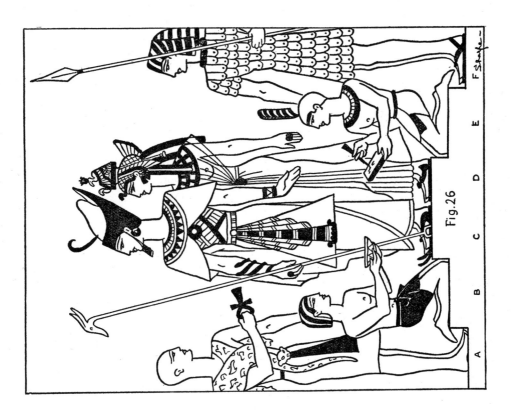

Fig. 26

Earrings, either looped over the ear or suspended from the pierced ear lobe, were fashioned of metal or of enamelwork, in the forms of animals or flowers, or were simple pendants of pearls or other jewels (Fig. 7 B). Gentlemen of rank carried a long and slender walking stick that was topped by a lotus or by a dog's head similar in type to that of a greyhound. Other accessories included a parasol (sunshade), carried by slaves to shield their masters from the sun (Fig. 9); a small writing tablet, with a stylus or pen; and a kind of fan made of one ostrich feather. The priest carried a long incense pipe, for ritualistic occasions, and also a small vase for libations (Fig. 10).

Symbolic Accessories

Among the symbolic accessories most frequently used were the following: the *ankh* (Fig. 7 P   Fig. 26 A), emblem of life and immortality, usually carried in the right hand; the crook (Fig. 7 K), symbol of mercy; the flail (Fig. 7 G), symbol of punishment; the Nilometer, symbol of stability, a long, dog-headed staff, having four horizontal bars about six inches below the dog's head, and with the crook and the flail branching out on either side some six inches below this (Fig. 20); the feather, symbol of writing, of knowledge, of the intellect (Fig. 7 E); the scarab (Fig. 7 C), symbol of immortality, of the creative process [The scarab, or beetle, lays its eggs and encases them in mud balls which it then rolls up above the high-water line of the Nile, thus insuring a new generation]; the uraeus, or serpent, symbol of royalty, insignia sacred to Lower Egypt, as were also the papyrus tuft and the bee (which was later adopted by Napoleon after his sojourn in Egypt); the lily plant or lotus, sacred to Upper Egypt.

Make-up

Men used kohl, or stibnite, to accent their eyebrows and eyelids. The lines were drawn out to the temples. Sometimes a green or blue line accentuated the aquiline nose, and the lips were reddened.

Weapons

The warrior might carry any one or several of these accouterments: the bow (Fig. 8 H); the quiver or bow case (Fig. 8 E); the straight sword (Fig. 8 J); the falchion (Fig. 8 B); the javelin (Fig. 8 C); the battle-ax (Fig. 8 D); and the spear (Fig. 8 F).

Mourning

Mourning was indicated by the wearing of black clothes. Though men ordinarily shaved their heads, they let their hair grow during the mourning period.

COSTUME FOR WOMEN

Tunic

The oldest and simplest type of dress was the tunic (Fig. 5   Fig. 27 B), a scant rectangle, ankle length, wrapped about the body, overlapping in the back, or sewed. The material slanted diagonally outward from the top to the bottom edge; often this effect was heightened by painted or woven diagonal stripes that radiated from a center front line, or by a narrow front panel running from the top to the bottom of the skirt. Sometimes vertical stripes about the bottom edge simulated a ruffle, though a pleated ruffle was often added to give fullness about the ankles. The tunic might fall from the waist only, and there be confined by a belt, or it might fall from just below the armpits. In the latter case, the belt might or might not be worn. Shoulder straps were commonly used with all types of tunic (Fig. 5 A C), though they were not necessary.

Robe

Another type of dress was the robe, which was worn on more elaborate occasions (Fig. 4 Fig. 26 D). (See the description of men's robes on page 4.) Though this garment was much used by ladies of rank and by priests, it was also used, in its simplest and sheerest form, undraped and hanging loosely both in front and at the back, by such widely different individuals

Fig. 28

A   B   C   Sharpe—

as the god Osiris and the ordinary dancing girl (Fig. 10   Fig. 28 A). The dancing girl, however, might wear only a narrow belt and bits of jewelry!

Skirt and Cape

The skirt consisted of a rectangle. In length it reached from waist to instep; the width was about one and one-half times or twice the length (Fig. 6 A B   Fig. 27 A). The material was gathered or pleated, and perhaps also fringed at the bottom edge (Fig. 6 A). The fullness was held in about the waist with a cord, or by means of a wide sash. The cord, passed twice about the waist, was usually tied low in front (Fig. 6 A). The shawl, or cape, was a narrower rectangle, about twenty inches wide and fifty-four inches long; the ends were twisted up under the collar so that a rounded cape effect was achieved (Fig. 6 A C). This shawl was often pleated also.

Collar

The collar fitted close to the neck, opened at the back, and was made of stiffened linen, leather, beads, or intricate jewelwork (Fig. 6 D). The chief decorative elements used in painting or ornamenting the collar were the lotus flower or lotus bud, the papyrus tuft, the scarab, triangle, disk, and rosette (Fig. 27 A).

Footwear

Sandals, worn more for dress than out of necessity, were of stiffened linen, leather (lined with linen), fiber, plaited palm leaves, or other material, often with curved bronze tips (after the Eighteenth Dynasty), reinforced and decorated with metalwork at the sides or over the instep and toe, and further enriched with beads or precious stones.

Hair

The hair was always carefully arranged; the arrangement reflected the taste and often the rank of the wearer. Even slaves wore wigs of coarse hair or wool, dyed black (Fig. 27 C). The simplest type shows bangs straight across the forehead, the rest of the hair being arranged about the head, chin-length or longer, with a straight bottom edge (Fig. 4   Fig. 27 B). The hair was often left quite long behind (Fig. 6), however, and the portion brought forward over the shoulders was either shortened or disposed in flat, square-cut arrangement (Fig 10   Fig. 28 A). An example of this is the head-dress of Nefertari-Aahmes. Other more elaborate arrangements show a mass of curls on the crown of the head, or tight long curls or braids about the head. These braids were decorated along the bottom edge with beads of wood, faïence, precious stones, or even (among the very poor) clay (Fig. 1 E   Fig. 27 C). Like the men's wigs, these were also carefully made on reticular frames in order to insure ventilation. A woman of quality usually possessed many wigs of various styles; black was the most common color, but blue wigs were by no means uncommon, and sometimes red, yellow, green, or brown ones were worn.

Headdress

These were many and varied. The simplest adornment was a fillet of colored cloth about the forehead, tied behind (Fig. 1 E), sometimes with the ends flowing. This band might be wrapped with a serpentlike coil of gold or silver. If of royal birth, the woman wore the sacred uraeus, usually jeweled, over her forehead. The fillet might also be adorned with fresh or jeweled flowers. For entertainments, banquets, and similar functions, women wore a perfumed cone on the crown of the head (anointed with fresh perfume several times during the evening by slaves), and also a lotus, arranged with the blossom directly over the forehead and the stem back over the head. In addition, a comb was often placed on the side of the coiffure (Fig. 7 H   Fig. 28 A). The most magnificent headdress was that used by queens and princesses of the blood royal; it was called the *klaft,* or vulture headdress, and was sacred to Maut, the mother goddess, wife of Amen. It covered the head and was shaped like a bird, having the sacred uraeus over the forehead, in addition to the small head of the bird; the wings stretched down past the ears to the shoulders; the tail of the bird extended toward the back (Fig. 1 A   Fig. 14   Fig. 21   Fig. 27 A). The headdress was of linen or leather, sometimes painted, or of gilded metal, or of gold and faïence, or of enamelwork in blue, green, yellow, or red (Fig. 21, see also page 9).

Symbolic Headdress

Egypt had many gods, and each of these was characterized by one or more religious or symbolic headdresses. The principal gods were the following:

Osiris (Fig. 13) – "Lord of Life," "Beneficent Spirit," "Lord of the Underworld" (Amentet). Osiris was god of the setting sun, of resurrection, and of judgment after death. He was worshipped at Abydos or Dendereh. His symbolic headdress consisted of the White Crown of Upper Egypt, with one lateral feather at either side. Osiris usually carried a flail and crook (Fig. 7 G K), or an ankh (Fig. 7 P).

Isis (Fig. 14) – Sister and wife of Osiris, goddess of married women, and of faithful devotion. She was the defender and avenger of wrongs done Osiris. She was worshipped at Philae or Bubastis. Her symbolic headdress consisted of a step-crown on a rail-pedestal. Sometimes the step-crown surmounted the horns and disk (of Hathor).

Horus (Fig. 15) – Son of Isis and Osiris, brother and husband of Hathor. Lord of the Rising Sun, "Helper of His Father," the god of youth and valor. Horus was worshipped at Heliopolis. His symbolic headdress was a hawk cap surmounted by the pschent, or double crown (Fig. 3 A   Fig. 7 J   Fig. 15   Fig. 26 C). In Fig. 26 C the shaded portion is red, for Lower Egypt, the white portion white, for Upper Egypt. Sometimes the prince-lock was worn at the side.

Hathor (Fig. 16) – Daughter of Isis and Osiris, sister and wife of Horus. Goddess of youthful love, of the moon and night, "Lady of Dance and Mirth." Hathor was worshipped at Thebes. Her symbolic headdress was the moon disk and cow horns. She usually carried the ankh in the right hand.

Nephthys (Fig. 17) – Sister of Isis and Osiris, sister and wife of Set. The "Benevolent Sister" who helped Isis find Osiris. Her symbolic headdress was a house with a door, and a basket above.

Ra (Fig. 18) – The sun god, the "Master of Light." Ra was worshipped at Heliopolis and also at Thebes, where he was associated in worship with Amen about the

Fig. 13   Fig. 14   Fig. 15   Fig. 16   Fig. 17   Fig. 18

Fig. 19

Fig. 20   Fig. 21   Fig. 22   Fig. 23   Fig. 24   Fig. 25

Eighteenth Dynasty. Ra's symbolic headdress was the sun disk surmounted by the uraeus.

Aten (Fig. 19) – Also the sun god. Aten was later raised to supreme power by Akhenaten. He was worshipped at Akhetaten. His symbolic headdress, if any, was ornamented with the sun disk, around whose bottom edge projected six or more rays that terminated in small hands.

Pthah (Fig. 20) – The demiurge, or creator, of the material universe. Pthah was worshipped at Memphis. His symbolic headdress was like that of a mummy with a cloth hood, but the hands were free to hold the scepter and also the Nilometer, emblem of stability. A lotus flower, or bent lotus bell, was placed at the nape of the neck.

Maut (Fig. 21) – "The Mother," the passive principle in nature. Maut was worshipped at Thebes. She wore the vulture cap, with wings stretched down over the ears and surmounted by the pschent.

Set or Typhon (Fig. 22) – Brother of Isis and Osiris, husband of Nephthys, and wicked slayer of Osiris. His symbolic headdress was an ibis head with two tabs diagonally erect.

Anubis (Fig. 23) – Guardian of the dead, embalmer of Osiris, conductor of spirits to Osiris. His symbolic headdress was a dog's head with long snout and tall, erect ears.

Thoth (Fig. 24) – God of wisdom, "Lord of Truth," who noted and recorded the deeds of men that were weighed in the balance before Osiris. He composed the *Ritual of the Dead*. Thoth was worshipped at Hermopolis. His symbolic headdress consisted of an ibis head, surmounted by a crescent and disk, with one ostrich feather upright as a symbol of truth. He usually carried a tablet and pen.

Amen or Ammon (Fig. 25) – "King of Gods," "The Concealed." Amen was worshipped at Thebes. His symbolic headdress consisted of two tall parallel feathers, plain or striped, surmounting a warrior cap. Two blue streamers from the headdress hung down behind. His symbol was later combined with that of Ra, the sun god, or with that of Hathor (Fig. 7 L).

Ornaments and Accessories

These were varied and beautiful. Egyptian women wore many rings on all the fingers, and also on the thumb. They were made of faïence, base metals, and gold, were jeweled, or were carved with the scarab and lotus. Hieroglyphics were carved on seals, on scarabs, and on twining snake rings. Bracelets and armlets were also made of metal or faïence, and were enameled and jeweled. Common elastic snake bracelets, often fashioned with enameled scales, little iridescent wings, and flexible bodies, were in great favor. Earrings, though not extensively worn, probably on account of the thick wigs, were beautifully executed in gold and enamelwork in various natural and geometric designs (Fig. 7 B). Anklets of wide or narrow bands were used by women from the highest to the lowest rank. Necklaces of jewels, carved gold, enamelwork, and other precious materials were much favored. Intricately carved pectorals of exquisite workmanship added an important touch to more elaborate toilettes. Fans made of palm leaves or painted linen, or the more elaborate ones of ostrich plumes, were indispensable accessories in the hot climate of Egypt (Fig. 5 B). Slaves used long-handled fans to waft breezes to their masters. A walking stick topped with the lotus flower was used by women of high rank. The bronze mirror (Fig. 7 M) was another feminine necessity. So, too, were the kohl box, the alabaster ointment jar, perfume bottles, the jewel box, and the comb. The *sistrum* (Fig. 7 F Fig. 28 A), used by dancing girls, was a bronze musical instrument made by stringing rings on wires. These jingled when the sistrum was shaken. Pins and needles made of bone and bronze, hairpins, and brooches of all kinds were used.

Make-up

The make-up was elaborate. Due to the dryness of the atmosphere, much oil was used to soften the skin tissue. Olive, almond, lettuce, and palm oils were favored. Kohl, or stibnite (a black substance), was used to darken the eyes and eyebrows. These lines were usually drawn out to the temple, thus giving an oriental cast to the face. Green malachite might also be added along the nose to emphasize the straight aquiline features that were characteristic of the purest Egyptian type. Blue was also used for this purpose. The lips of the women were carmined; the palms of the hands were hennaed.

Mourning

This was indicated by black clothing, for both men and women. In addition, women showed many outward evidences of grief, such as scratching the face, pouring ashes on the hair, and a general disarray of garments and features.

Costume for Children

Both little boys and girls went quite naked, with no suggestion of embarrassment. Later they wore the same types of dress as their elders, usually the simple tunic or robe (Fig. 5 Fig. 4 C). Children of higher rank wore clothing more generally than did those of the other classes.

Costume for the Lower Classes

A simple loincloth (Fig. 2) and shaven heads or simple wigs were used by men, whether they were peasants, workers, or slaves (Fig. 26 B). Sometimes headdresses (Fig. 1 C) were also used. Women wore plain or striped tunics (Fig. 5 Fig. 27 B), or robes (Fig. 4 C Fig. 28 A), with simple wigs. Ornaments, consisting of beads, rings, bracelets, and anklets, were made of glass, wood, or glazed pottery.

Modern Adaptations

Egyptian dress fabrics can be imitated in modern materials by using unbleached domestic or Japanese crepe for the opaque textiles. Fine muslin is best for transparent garments. Modern Egyptian wedding shawls, made of hammered silver on net, are excellent for costumes. They drape well and the white net takes dye to advantage. The pattern can be painted on the material. If the pattern is first outlined with wax crayon, the paint (poster paint or oil paint) is less likely to run. For the clinging or pleated types of garments, metaline is an excellent fabric. It is cheap, takes dye well, and simulates accordion pleating if treated in the following manner: Dye the material first. While it is still wet, twist it tightly, knot it securely, and then bake it. Take out and undo. A tightly curled accordion pleating is the result. Chiffon is also excellent for thin, clinging garments, but it is more expensive. Rayon tubing is excellent for sheathlike tunics. Buy it by the pound. It has the advantage of not raveling when it is cut.

For heavy clothing, use unbleached muslin, dyed or painted, or Osnaburg (desert cloth), which comes in rich, brilliant shades. Japanese crepe also comes in good colors, but it does not have so smooth a surface for designs or painting. Canvas or denim, dyed, is excellent for soldiers' tunics. For mantles, canton flannel, duvetyn, or terry cloth can be used. The last two take design especially well.

For accessories: House insulation sheeting is excellent for headdresses. Use the kind that is silvered on both sides. If it has to be glued onto another surface, however, use the kind that is silvered on one side only. Papier-mâché may be used for molding headdresses. Plastic wood and gesso may be used for building up designs.

For beads or beaded decorations: Colored wooden nursery beads show up well on the stage. So also do colored china beads.

For feathers: Use turkey wings or cock feathers that may be got from any poultry market. Old ostrich plumes, always in demand, are also very effective.

For jeweled effects: Apply flitter over the area to be embellished. Also use silver, gold, red, green, or blue metallic paper, folded or pleated in cuplike shapes and sewed onto the garment. Such surfaces catch the light and gleam like jewels. These cups may also be glued on. If time presses, flat squares of metallic paper glued on show up very well.

For wigs: The cost of wigs is usually prohibitive. For making Egyptian wigs, however, and all other types that can be more or less stylized, the following process is well worth knowing. Wigs made in the fashion described below cost only a few cents apiece, and may be used for a long time.

The process, which requires only about half an hour for the simpler styles, is as follows: (1) Place a piece of tissue paper over the actor's head, sufficiently large to cover it completely. (2) Next, place a band of adhesive tape, three-fourths of an inch wide, around the head. Then pass bands of the tape across the head from front to back, and also from side to side. Next, crisscross other pieces of the tape, and fasten the ends to the headband until the whole head is thoroughly covered. (3) While the tapes are still on the head, mark the hair line, the position of the ears, and all other necessary notations on the head form. (4) Lift the head form off, and trim the edges. Write the name of the actor on the inside, and also write the words *front* and *back* at the proper positions on the head form. (5) Put the head form back on the head of the actor in order to check it for size. (6) Remove the head form, and hold it in one hand while you continue to crisscross pieces of tape until very little light shines through the headform. It should then be of good substantial shape. (7) Now begin to apply hair, consisting of hempen rope, cotton rope, raffia, spun glass, or whatever else is to be used.

One may use common floor mops that may be purchased in white, brown, or black. Dye the white ones the required color; for Egyptian wigs, black or blue; for other wigs, natural hair colors. One may also use (*a*) raffia, (*b*) cellophane, (*c*) spun glass (a glistening, ribbonlike material used as a Christmas tree decoration), (*d*) thin strips of rubber from old tires, (*e*) thin strips of silvered house insulation sheeting wound into curls, (*f*) metallic gold, silver, or colored Christmas ribbon curled on a hot curling iron, (*g*) pieces of sponge, (*h*) yarn or string, or (*i*) frayed hempen rope. Arrange the hair material on the head form in a stylized pattern, that is, the part, the knot, bangs, waves, curls, and so on. Glue in place. One may use a few stitches, but not many. When the wig is complete, try it on again. Shellac the inside of the head form so that perspiration may not penetrate it and soften the glue that holds the hair, thus ruining the wig.

To make waves, pompadours, marcels, or other ornamental coiffures, pad the head form with cotton or frayed rope before the hair material is applied, then carefully arrange the hair material and glue it onto the padding. To simulate a bald head, cover the desired bald area with cheap voile and glue it smoothly onto the head form. The actor may then put make-up on the bald spot so that it will blend into that on his face and forehead. When making wigs, any number of combinations of materials may be used for hair. For example, rope may be combined with raffia, spun glass with white cotton, insulation material with sponge, and so on.

Ornamental headdresses, crowns, diadems, turbans, towers, and similar decorative adjuncts may easily be affixed, since these wigs fit the head snugly. The symbolic head-dresses of Hathor, Osiris, and the other deities, the double crown of Upper and Lower Egypt, and similar decorative accessories may be made out of molded papier-mâché, then properly painted and affixed to the wigs.

BABYLONIA

ASSYRIA

PERSIA

HEBREW

PLATE I   CHAPTER II

GREEK
CHLAMYS

GREEK
IONIC CHITON

GREEK
DORIC CHITON

GREEK WARRIOR

PLATE II   CHAPTER III

CHAPTER II
MESOPOTAMIA
AND ASIA MINOR

IMPORTANT PEOPLE AND EVENTS

5000 B. C. The Sumerian kingdom (non-Semitic) in the "Land of Shinar." . . . Patesi, or priest-kings, at Ur, Lagash, and Babylon. . . . Building of the temple to En-lil, god of the air, at Nippur. . . . The tree-of-life motif created. . . . The making of stone seals. . . . The Gilgamesh Epic.

2870 B. C. The kingdom of Akkad. . . . Sargon I conquered the Elamites. . . . Building of the temple to Bel (Babel). . . . Origins of the story of the Deluge. . . . First use of copper helmets.

2200 B. C. Establishment of the Babylonian (or Chaldean) Empire. . . . Hammurabi made Babylon the leading city. . . . The study of astrology, a pseudo-science of divination. . . . The building of canals. . . . Hammurabi wrote his code of laws. . . . Cuneiform writing perfected. . . . The development of the arch and tower. . . . Nimrod, a "mighty hunter before the Lord," to whom the foundation of Babylonia and Assyria is ascribed. . . . The patriarch Abraham left Ur of the Chaldees. . . . His family, Isaac and Jacob, followed him. . . . The worship of Marduk and Ishtar (Astarte). . . . Nineveh was built by Asshur.

2000 B. C. Semiramis, a wise and beautiful queen, ruled and beautified Babylon. . . . India, Lybia, and Ethiopia were invaded. . . . The horse was introduced. . . . Schools were founded.

1700 B. C. The Tell-el-Amarna letters. . . . Joseph was brought down to Egypt. . . . Exodus of the Hebrews out of Egypt under the leadership of Moses. . . . The expedition of the Argonauts.

1276 B. C. Founding of the Assyrian empire. . . . Tiglath-pileser I conquered the lands from Bagdad and Babylon westward to the Mediterranean Sea. . . . Iron was used for weapons. . . . The winged sun disk, the triple arch, glazed brick, and human-headed bulls were used in art. . . . The fall of Troy. . . . Saul was in Jerusalem. . . . The story of David. . . . The revolt of Absalom. . . . Zoroaster (Zarathustra) taught in Persia. . . . Solomon built the temple of Jerusalem.

900 B. C. The Assyrians invaded Persia. . . . The reign of Ashurnasirpal (Sardanapalus). . . . Cotton was used.

722 B. C. Sargon II conquered and carried away the Ten Tribes of Israel. . . . Conquered Media, Babylonia, and Damascus. . . . United the two great kingdoms and organized them into an empire. . . . Satrapies were set up. . . . A system of royal post roads was established. . . . Sennacherib conquered the Hebrews and the Egyptians. . . . The palace of Dur Sharrukin was built. . . . A palace was built at Nineveh. . . . Sennacherib destroyed Babylon. . . . Plundered Greek cities of Asia Minor. . . . 776 B. C., first Greek Olympiad opened. . . . Traditional founding of Rome by Romulus is dated 753 B. C.

681 B. C. Sennacherib murdered by two of his sons, and Esarhaddon became king of Assyria.

669 B. C. Ashurbanipal lost Egypt. . . . Conquered Lydia and Elam. . . . Great libraries — cuneiform (wedge-shaped) characters impressed on clay tablets — began to be founded.

19

625 B. C.   Rise of the late Chaldean or Babylonian empire. . . . Nabopolassar reigned.

604 B. C.   Nebuchadnezzar built the Hanging Gardens and the Ishtar Gate at Babylon. . . . Destroyed Jerusalem. . . . Babylonian captivity of the Jews began. . . . Jeremiah "prophesied against the city." . . . "Belshazzar the king made a great feast." . . . The story of Daniel. . . . "Mene, Mene, Tekel, Upharsin" ("Thy kingdom is divided and given to the Medes and the Persians"). . . . Fall of Chaldea.

547 B. C.   Cyrus, king of Persia, conquered King Croesus of Lydia. . . . Conquered all Babylonia. . . . New capital established at Susa. . . . Canals constructed and a palace built at Persepolis. . . . The winged bull and the horse-headed column used as decorative elements. . . . Temple at Jerusalem rebuilt for the Jews. . . . 568 B. C., Buddha born in India. . . . 551 B. c., Confucius born in China. . . . 594 B. c., Solon gave the Greeks laws.

525 B. c.   Cambyses, king of the Medes and the Persians, conquered Egypt.

522 B. c.   Darius, king of the Persians, organized his empire into satrapies. . . . Conquered Thrace. . . . 490 B. c., Greeks defeated the Persians on the Plain of Marathon.

484 B. c.   Xerxes defeated the Greeks. . . . 480 B. c., Battle of Thermopylae. . . . At the Battle of Salamis (September 21, 480 B. c.) the Greeks decisively defeated the Persian hosts.

From time immemorial the desert has been a challenge to man – to conquer or to be conquered. There are no half measures, as there is no twilight to the desert day.

Man, like the keen arc of a scimitar, warily circled the edge of the shining crescent, and appropriated the area of habitable verdure for his own. In this slender slice he built up one great civilization after another – the kingdoms of the Sumerians, Babylonians, and Hittites, of the Lydians, Assyrians, and Elamites, of the Phoenicians, the Hebrews, and the Medes, the kingdom of the Persians. Beyond, the vacant eye of the desert kept scornful watch.

In the presence of natural supremacy man became boastful and proud, out of self-protection. His clothing was pompous, rich, and rippling – fashioned of heavy woolen cloth, deep-dyed in the dull red of ripe wine, the black purple of night, the dark green of ancient boughs, the deep blue of dead seas, the dull brown and old gray of weary earthen things. Man wrapped himself in these woolen garments against the stealthy cold of desert nights. His struggle, a sober one, was reflected in the hues of his materials. Oriental splendor was at bottom a bold gesture of defiance in the bland face of defeat.

Belshazzar, in his palace that blazed with brilliant tiles, terrible with gigantic, stone, human-headed bulls, knew too well that the foundations of his glory were sand and sun-baked brick. His banquet table was laden with the richest meats, the sweetest fruits, the headiest wines, but before him burned the handwriting on the wall – "and the winds blew, and beat upon that house; and it fell: and great was the fall of it."

COSTUME

GENERAL CHARACTERISTICS

These may be summed up as follows: (1) The use of heavy materials, (2) the use of fringe from two to twenty inches deep, (3) the predominance of long garments having straight lines that emphasized the bulky, almost rotund figures, (4) the use of rich, dark colors, and (5) bushy hair and heavy full beards.

Fig. 29

Materials

As with all nomadic races, wool was the staple material for garments. A roughly-woven material of the natural shade of wool, or dyed either a dull brown or gray, was worn by slaves and very poor people, though they also used coarse linen. Wealthier classes used finely woven, soft woolen cloth, both light and heavy and of various textures. This was dyed in a wide range of colors, maroon, blue, purple, rust, olive, and the like. Kings and great nobles preferred embroidered robes of wool and fine linen, shot through with threads of gold and silver. The best linen was woven at Borsippa. Cotton came into general use around 900 B. C.

Underclothes

Men wore the loincloth draped tightly about the thighs, the ends being passed between the legs and fastened behind. Women added a tight band about the breasts, and a plain, scant tunic beneath the outer garment, particularly if a linen garment was worn.

Costume for Men

SUMERIANS AND CHALDEANS

Tunic

This was similar to that of the Egyptians (page 10). It extended from armpits to ankles, and was sewed down the back. A single strap on the left shoulder held it in place (Fig. 30 A B). A fringe from six to twelve inches deep (Fig. 30 C) began at the bottom edge of the tunic and extended in a spiral up to the armpits, thence over the left shoulder, to form a diagonal line at the top, leaving the right shoulder free (Fig. 30 A). Priests are usually represented as wearing this type of dress, as may be seen in engravings on the signet cylinders of kings of Uruk. Women also wore this garment.

Surplice

This garment, which is to be seen in many early drawings, was edged all round with fringe from two to six inches deep (Fig. 31 A). The surplice might be shorter in front than in the back (Fig. 31 D), or rounded in front with a straight edge in the back (Fig. 31 C), or rounded both in front and at the back (Fig. 31 B). It was not belted. The surplice was worn over a snug tunic having short, tight sleeves (Fig. 33 B). Women also wore this garment.

Fringed Wrap-around

This simple type of dress consisted of a rectangle of material edged all about with fringe from four to ten inches deep (Fig. 32 A B). It was drawn tightly about the body twice, beginning under the left armpit, then across the front, and under the right armpit. It was fastened on the right shoulder, usually by tying the fringe of the front end to a strand of fringe at the back. Sometimes the draping was reversed, the garment then being fastened on the left shoulder. Women also wore this garment.

Hair

The archaic style of hairdressing may be studied in Fig. 30 A and Fig. 32 A. The hair of both men and women was brought smoothly back to the nape of the neck and held in place by a fillet. The little loop at the back was turned up and then passed under the fillet, the end of the loop falling over. This arrangement, to be seen in other archaic drawings also, was later used by the early Cretans and Greeks.

Headdress

Fig. 30 A shows a ceremonial headdress – three graduated rolls (perhaps a spiral) surmounted by a crescent – worn with the coiffure just described. This was probably the priestly crown of the moon god. Another type of headdress was the round, open crown with feathers (Fig. 29 A). Still another was a caplike miter that graduated toward the top (Fig. 31 A).

Military Dress

Warriors wore short, fringed, knee-length tunics. (Slaves wore the same garments, but without fringe.) Warriors were armed with spears, arrows, and flint knives. The feet were almost always bare, though occasionally plain sandals were worn.

Ornaments

These consisted of heavy bracelets, rings, cylindrical seals, and looped earrings.

ASSYRIANS AND BABYLONIANS

The types of costume described above were adopted by both the Assyrians and Babylonians. These peoples, however, later added certain additional styles. There were the following:

Short-sleeved Tunic

This type is shown in Fig. 33 B. A deep, knotted fringe about sixteen inches wide was draped about the bottom (Fig. 33 C), and another piece, from sixteen to twenty inches wide, was worn at a low waistline level. This fringe was draped from right to left around the front, and from left to right across the back, and then diagonally across the front from right to left. The end was thrown over the left shoulder, thus leaving the end of the fringe to hang down behind (Fig. 33 B).

Tunic and Apron

This style tunic (Fig. 34) had a wide or narrow knotted fringe at the bottom edge. Across the back of the tunic was a square, fringed apron having two long, tasseled

Fig. 30

Fig. 31

Fig. 32

Fig. 33

Fig. 34

Fig. 39

Fig. 35

Fig. 36

Fig. 37

Fig. 41

cords, one of which hung down at either side (Fig. 34 A B). A double belt held this in place. The broad belt was of leather or linen, the narrow one usually of red leather. Three buckles and straps fastened it (Fig. 34 A C). Two daggers were often placed side by side, diagonally, in the narrow belt. Women did not wear this type of garment.

Shawl

This was a long, elaborate garment, fringed all round and draped about the body several times. The fringe made diagonal patterns similar to flounces. This type, not illustrated here, is an elaboration of the garment shown in Fig. 32, with the addition of a belt.

Footwear

This item of dress was well designed and ornate. Simple sandals, constructed so as to enclose the heel in leather and leave the toes bare, were held on the feet by

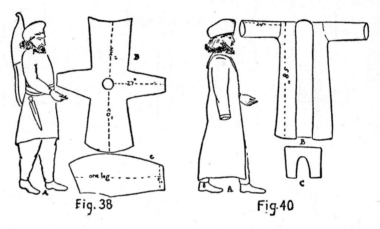

Fig. 38   Fig. 40

means of straps crisscrossed above the instep (Fig. 42 E). Other sandals had straps that passed straight across the instep (Fig. 42 D). Ankle-high boots (Fig. 42 C) were worn, as were also knee-high ones (Fig. 35 A). These were made of either natural-colored or painted leather. More elaborate sandals were pierced or painted in elaborate designs. Sometimes the soles were graduated in thickness from toe to heel.

Hair

Both Assyrians and Babylonians had thick, bushy hair which they curled elaborately by means of heated bronze curlers. The hair stood out behind, at the nape of the neck, as shown by Fig. 29 A D E. Beards of natural hair, eked out with false tresses, were also elaborately curled, perfumed, and oiled. Older men and kings wore longer beards (Fig. 33 A   Fig. 34 A). Women's hair was dressed much as men's was, though the back hair was frequently arranged in fat, regular ringlets confined with a fillet or low crown.

Headdress

Headdresses consisted of plain or decorated fillets (Fig. 32 A) or of others shaped high in front (Fig. 33 A   Fig. 34 A). The latter were often tied behind, the ends of the ties falling down the back. A more elaborate type, worn by kings and other high dignitaries, was the miter, a tall, cone-shaped cloth or felt cap, usually red, yellow, or white in color (Fig. 29 E). This headdress was decorated in zones, and often had a fillet added about the bottom edge. A smaller truncated cone was added at the top. Another type of headdress, used by the Babylonians, consisted of a round miter made of leather, painted in intricate designs, and edged at the top with a row of feathers (Fig. 29 A). Still another type was a pleated miter made of stiffened linen (Fig. 29 D).

Military Dress

Warriors wore a plain or fringed short tunic or kilt (Fig. 35 A C). The narrow pendant at the front (Fig. 35 A D) was a separate item similar to the Scotch sporran. This type of costume was commonly worn by light-armed archers. Heavy-armed archers wore, in addition, a short-sleeved or sleeveless coat of mail made of scales, bands, or rings (Fig. 35 A B). Infantrymen and cavalrymen wore similar types of armor, and, in addition, short or long, plain or patterned tunics.

Ornaments and Accessories

These were heavy, elaborately carved, and highly colored. Belts, necklaces, armlets, bracelets, and earrings seem to have been most favored. The necklace (Fig. 41 F) might consist of twisted gold wires, a string of delicately carved lozenge-shaped beads, a broad band, or a string of small, sacred, emblematic objects. These included the crescent of the moon god, Sin, the four-rayed disk of the sun god, Shamash, the forked lightning emblem of En-lil, god of the upper air. Armlets were plain bands or circlets of twisted metal, whose ends sometimes overlapped. The ends were often carved like animal heads. Bracelets were usually wide bands, and were sometimes patterned in rosettes and geometric designs (Fig. 41 B). Earrings were of various types: the long drop (Fig. 29 D E), a sort of Maltese cross (Fig. 29 A), and ear loops adorned with heads of animals or birds. Women also wore jewelry similar to that worn by men. Accessories included daggers (Fig. 36 D), swords (Fig. 36 K), seals (Fig. 41 G), tear bottles (Fig. 41 H), parasols (Fig. 41 L – allowed only to kings), fly swatters (Fig. 41 J), drinking horns (Fig. 41 E), plain, long walking sticks, and fans. The sword, elaborately carved, was worn in a horizontal position at the waistline. Objects of symbolic significance were the sacred basket (Fig. 41 D), representing eternity; the sacred tree of life (Fig. 41 K); and the winged disk of Ishtar (Astarte) (Fig. 41 C). Art motifs most commonly used included the rosette, the winged disk, the human-headed bull, the horse, the circle, the cross, the tree of life, and the pomegranate.

Make-up

The eyebrows, which were very bushy, almost met above the bridge of the nose (Fig. 29 A D E). Lips were carmined, beards and hair were dyed black if necessary, and mustaches were waxed.

Military Dress

Besides sword and dagger, warriors carried various sorts of light and heavy shields (Fig. 36 P). These were made of wood or wicker, reinforced with leather. They were oblong and convex, parted and curved at the top, and ranged in height from two to six feet. A round shield was also used (Fig. 36 G). Other implements of war included the bow (Fig. 36 B), arrows and quiver (Fig. 36 F), the archer's arm guard (Fig. 36 N), the spear (Fig. 36 H), the ax (Fig. 36 E), and the mace (Fig. 36 L). Helmets were of various shapes. Usually they were made of leather, felt, or metal, shaped like a cone, and had chain-mail lappets at the side (Fig. 36 M). Some had loops, crescents, or other ornaments at the peak (Fig. 36 A C J).

Costume for Children

Children wore clothes plainer in detail, but similar to those of their elders (Fig. 43 Fig. 44).

Fig. 43   Fig. 44

Costume for the Lower Classes

Lower classes wore shorter garments, similar to those already described, but with no fringe; they went barefooted and bareheaded.

HEBREWS

Among the ancient Hebrews, both men and women wore garments similar to those already described. According to the Mosaic law, the fringes on their garments had to be blue (Numbers 15:38). At a later period the Hebrews adopted the sleeved coat of the Persians (Fig. 40 A B). The high priest wore the sacerdotal garments (Fig. 37), first made for Aaron at the behest of Moses, as the Lord commanded (Exodus 28:4–43; 39:1–31). These included a long, white, tight-sleeved robe that was usually made of wool. Over this a shorter tunic was worn. It was made of "fine blue linen," and had "pomegranates of blue, and of purple, and of scarlet" embroidered on the hem. Suspended from the edges of the garment, a little golden bell hung between every two designs. Over this tunic was worn the ephod (Fig. 37 A B), a sacred sleeveless tunic "of gold, of blue, and of purple, of scarlet, and fine twined linen," heavily embroidered with threads of fine gold. A breastplate about nine inches square, set with twelve semi-precious stones arranged in four rows of three each, each stone engraved with the name of one of the Twelve Tribes of Israel, was suspended on the high priest's breast by means of two gold chains pendant from two brooches, one on either shoulder of the ephod. The breastplate was held in place by means of blue laces that bound it to the front of the ephod. A linen miter, to which blue laces secured "a plate of pure gold" bearing the words "Holiness to the Lord," completed the high priest's garb.

Tunic and Trousers

These were made of linen, wool, or leather. The long-sleeved tunic fitted snugly about the neck, was of knee length, and had a slightly diagonal bottom edge (Fig. 38 A B). The trousers were long and full, but fitted snugly around the ankle (Fig. 38 A C).

Coat

A woolen coat was often worn over the tunic and trousers (Fig. 40 A B). Slung over the shoulders, it was held in place by cords that tied in front. The sleeves of the coat, which was made either with or without a collar, hung loose (Fig. 40 C). The coat might also be worn over the long plain tunic, which resembled that used by the Assyrians and Babylonians (Fig. 33 B).

Median Robe

This garment, known as a *candys,* was originally worn by the Medes and later adopted by the Persians (Fig. 39 A B). It was a long, full, loose robe, the sleeves of which were formed by belting the garment at the waist. The resulting capelike sleeves fell in graceful ripples from each shoulder. From the waist down, the sides of the robe were sewed together to form other deep and graceful folds on the side.

Mantle

Occasionally a rectangular or rounded mantle was used with the candys, as also with the other garments described in this section.

Footwear

The ancient Persians wore sandals similar in type to those of the Assyrians and Babylonians, but turned up at the toes and more highly ornamented (Fig. 42 A B).

Hair

The principal change in hairdressing consisted in the use of a more rounded coiffure at the back. Beards were longer and flatter and often augmented with false hair. The Persians perfumed and greased their hair and elaborately curled it (Fig. 29 B Fig. 38 Fig. 39 Fig. 40).

Headdress

A specially shaped cap was favored by the Persians. It was made of linen, felt, or

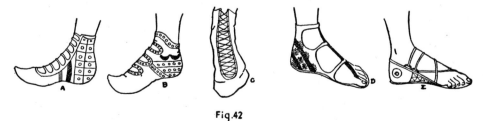

Fig. 42

leather, was high in the crown, and projected in a rounded peak at front (Fig. 29 B Fig. 38 A Fig. 40 A). Another type of headdress, adopted from the Assyrians, is shown in Fig. 29 D. The crown (Fig. 39 A C) was later adopted by European royalty as a definite symbol of rank. Women wore bushy hair, and the crown (Fig. 29 C), if of royal station.

Ornaments and Accessories

Jewelry and other adornments were similar to those worn by the Babylonians and Assyrians. Persians were fond of scent bottles (Fig. 41 A); in these they kept their precious attar of roses and other perfumes. They carried long canes (Fig. 39 A), some of which had a knob at the head.

Make-up

The "adorner," or barber, made up the Persian men elaborately. The hair was curled, oiled, and scented; eyelids were touched up with blue black to make the eyes seem larger; the lips were rouged.

Military Dress

Persian men-at-arms carried weapons similar to those already described. They were specially famed as archers. Young Persian boys were taught three things: to ride horseback, to handle the bow, and to tell the truth. Persian bows were very tall, the arrows long, the bow case (Fig. 38 A) elaborately decorated.

Mourning

Among all the peoples mentioned in this chapter, a state of mourning was indicated by the wearing of somber-colored or black garments, and by dishevelled hair. Ornaments were dispensed with during the period.

Costume for Women

Little or nothing is known about women's dress among the ancient Persians, since women seem to have rarely been depicted on the monuments. It was probably similar to the costume worn by men, and perhaps longer and wider in the skirted parts.

Costume for Children

Children wore modified versions of their elders' garments, with little or no ornament.

Costume for the Lower Classes

Common people wore simple tunics. These were often short, were not ornamented, and were of a dull color.

Modern Adaptations

For heavy garments, duvetyn (cotton broadcloth) or monk's cloth is best and gives the richest effect; canton flannel, terry cloth, and cotton jersey are, however, quite satisfactory. If a brocaded or embroidered material must be simulated, use drapery fabrics having an allover design, especially those that are deeply colored. Striped materials are well suited for making Hebrew garments. Osnaburg (desert cloth) and ratiné, which dye well, are also satisfactory materials.

Costumes for royal personages are most satisfactory when made of corduroy or costume velveteen, though these fabrics are costly. Sateen, which dyes well, is effective in the deeper shades.

Burlap may be used for slave or peasant costumes.

Belts may be made out of leather, patent leather, oilcloth, or webbing.

Felt is the most satisfactory material for making the fringes that are so characteristic of the costumes described in this chapter. It does not ravel, hangs straight, and adds needed weight to a costume. Scissors should be used for fringing. Tassels may be made of cotton or woolen string. Fold the string into skeins of such size that when cut the tassel will be of the proper weight and length. Tie the skeins at one end, cut at the other, then sew through.

Materials suggested in the preceding chapter (pages 16–18) may be used for making the ornaments, jewelry, and other decorative items necessary for supplementing the costumes just described.

CHAPTER III

GREECE

IMPORTANT PEOPLE AND EVENTS

2800–1000 B. C.	Aegean civilization. . . . Achaeans in northern Greece. . . . Aeolians in eastern Greece. . . . Dorians mingled with Ionians on the Peloponnese. . . . Crete, a land "of a hundred cities" and many nations, but by 1200 B. C. the Achaeans were the ruling people of Crete. . . . The three ages of Minos in Crete (2700 B. C.–1240 B. C.). . . . Age of Bronze. . . . Cretan art, influenced by Egypt, in vases, jewelry, architecture. . . . Cnossus palace and the two gold cups of Vaphio. . . . The legend of the Minotaur. . . . Commerce with Phoenicians (*circa* 1500 B. c.), who introduced the chiton from Babylonia, iron ore from the Hittites, and furniture and jewelry from Egypt and Mesopotamia. . . . 1183(?) B. c., Fall of Troy. . . . Great sea power established by the Cretans, who were known in Egypt as the "Peoples of the Sea." . . . An early tribe from Crete supposedly migrated to Asia Minor, settled in Philistia, and thus originated the race known as the Philistines. . . . Rise of the city-states in Greece – Argos, Mycenae (the Lion Gate, the Shaft Graves, the Treasury of Atreus – one of the wonders of the world). . . . Thebes (founded by Cadmus, *circa* 1313 B. c.). . . . Age of Iron, 1000 B. c.
Ninth Century B. c.	Age of Kings. . . . Lycurgus and social laws. . . . The period of epic poetry – Homer, "the blind old man of Scio's rocky isle," to whom are attributed the *Iliad* and the *Odyssey*. . . . Phoenician alphabet gained supremacy. . . . Elijah, the prophet. . . . 822(?) B. c., traditional founding of Carthage by Dido.
Eighth Century B. c.	Rise of Athens and Sparta. . . . 776 B. c., the first Olympiad. . . . Syracuse and other Greek colonies in Sicily. . . . 753 B. c., Romulus founded Rome. . . . Age of aristocracies. . . . The archons. . . . Hesiod sang of the life of the people. . . . Money coined in Lydia and Ionia. . . . Great Assyrian supremacy. . . . Transparent glass at Nineveh. . . . Sculpture of the Dying Lioness. . . . Amos, Isaiah, prophets of Israel.
Seventh Century B. c.	Thales fixed year at three hundred sixty-five days and calculated eclipses. . . . Sappho and Alcaeus. . . . Brilliant period of Greek vases (red on black, black on red). . . . 621 B. c., strict reforms of Draco. . . . Zoroaster (Zarathustra). . . . 612 B. c., destruction of Nineveh. . . . Numa (715–673 B. c.) and the seven kings of Rome.
Sixth Century B. c.	Age of the Seven Sages of Greece. . . . Lydia and the Age of the Tyrants. . . . 594 B. c., Solon, made archon, established a wise code of laws. . . . 560 B. c., Peisistratus, a good tyrant, built a theater at Athens, and encouraged drama. . . . Spread of coined money in Greece proper. . . . Rise of commerce. . . . Rise of democracy. . . . Croesus, rich king of Lydia. . . . 539 B. c., Cyrus the Persian conquered Babylonia. . . . 525 B. c., Cambyses conquered Egypt. . . . Dionysian revels developed into drama. . . . Thespis of Icaria, who first won the prize for *tragedy* ("goat-singing") in 534 B. c.

508 B. C., the reforms of Cleisthenes, the lawgiver. . . . Aesop's fables. . . . Buddha. . . . Marble first used for statues. . . . Pythagoras, the philosopher. . . . Pindar, the poet of Thebes. . . . Doric column. . . . Map makers in Miletus declared the earth round. . . . Anacreon, the Ionian poet. . . . 509 B. C., the Roman Republic.

Fifth Century B. C. Greco-Persian Wars. . . . Darius invaded Greece. . . . Miltiades' victory at Marathon in 490 B. C. . . . Pheidippides, the Greek runner who ran from Athens to Sparta in forty-eight hours. . . . 480 B. C., defeat of Leonidas, the Spartan, at Thermopylae. . . . Victory of Themistocles over Xerxes at Salamis. . . . Final Greek victories at Plataea and Mycale. . . . 487(?) B. C., the prize for *comedy* first won by Chionides. . . . The Athenian Empire. . . . The Delian League. . . . The Periclean democracy, "the Golden Age of Greece," 461–431 B. C. . . . Architecture: Parthenon, Erechtheum, Theseum. . . . Sculpture: Myron's "Discobolus," Polyclitus' (the sculptor of men) "Doryphorus," Phidias' (the sculptor of gods) "Athena." . . . Painting: Polygnotus' "The Painted Porch," Apollodorus' "Venus" (Apollodorus, "the shadow-painter," who made a systematic study of light and shade). . . . History: Herodotus, Thucydides. . . . Philosophy: Socrates, Plato, the Sophists. . . . Drama: Aeschylus (*The Oresteia, Prometheus Bound*), Sophocles (*Oedipus Rex, Antigone*), Euripides (*Iphigenia in Tauris, Electra*), Aristophanes, the writer of comedy (*The Clouds, Lysistrata*). . . . Development of the Doric and Ionic columns. . . . Peloponnesian Wars, 431–404 B. C. . . . Nicias and the failure of the Sicilian expedition. . . . Alcibiades, the general. . . . Aspasia and Pericles. . . . Long walls, built by Pericles, torn down after Athenian defeat at Aegospotami (404 B. C.). . . . Growth of banking and manufacturing. . . . Cotton was used.

Fourth Century B. C. Supremacy of Sparta. . . . Dionysius, tyrant of Syracuse. . . . Rule of Thirty at Athens. . . . Epaminondas won supremacy of Thebes at Leuctra. . . . Demosthenes' orations against Philip of Macedon, who conquered Greece at Chaeronea (338 B. C.). . . . Praxiteles' "Hermes." . . . Mencius in China (372–289 B. C.). . . . Alexander the Great conquered Asia, formed greatest empire of classic times. . . . His conquests introduced into the Mediterranean world new patterns, materials (silk, cotton), customs from India and Persia. . . . The philosopher Aristotle, tutor of Alexander, and his encyclopedia of science. . . . Development of the Corinthian column. . . . The Mausoleum (built for Mausolus by his widow, Artemesia, at Halicarnassus). . . . The "Laocoön," which Agesander created with his two sons, Polydorus and Athenodorus. . . . Apelles was acclaimed the greatest of the Greek painters, but fourth-century Greek painting has completely disappeared. . . . Licinian laws at Rome. . . . Alexander's death (June 13, 323 B. C.) broke up the empire. . . . His general Ptolemy founded a kingdom in Egypt. . . . Hellenistic culture was cultivated at Alexandria. . . . Growth of the celebrated library. . . . Parks. . . . Science. . . . Medicine. . . . Euclid's geometry. . . . Archimedes' (287–212 B. C.) lever at Syracuse. . . . Stoic philosophy. . . . Epicurus and the Epicurean philosophy. . . . The poet Theocritus, "Father of Pastoral Poetry." . . . 146 B. C., Greece was finally conquered by Rome, at Corinth. . . . Corinth was burnt and art treasures were destroyed or carried to Rome. . . . The end of the Achaean League. . . . The end of the glory that was Greece.

Freedom sprang, like Athena, full-grown from the mind of Hellas. There is a clean wind that blows from the Argive Sea; it washes away the memory of massive Egyptian temples, of boastful Mesopotamian palaces. Egypt was likened to a lotus; Greece, in shape, is like a graceful hand, laving its sensitive fingers in the blue waters of the tideless Mediterranean.

In the groves of Greece, maidens tossed their bright veils in a dusk of dancing to the pipes of Pan, good friend to mortals. The neighboring slopes of Mount Olympus brought all the gods near to man, but not too near to hamper the rational growth of democratic individualism. Gods and men met – and often – on common ground, encircled by the magic restraint of beauty.

This union of mortal and immortal, this grace of loveliness and strength of freedom, was reflected in every sweeping fold of Grecian dress. It was caught in the rhythmic line of Nike binding her sandal; it swathed the dignity of Sophocles. On analysis, one finds in all Greek garments a startling simplicity of line, repeated in the incidental sway of delicate fabric revealing perfect form beneath.

Delicate also was the choice of color: soft green of young leaves, shell pink, ripeness of corn, olive of sacred groves. The more somber hues showed definite and refined shading. The borders, sole decoration for most garments, were distinct but not intrusive. They repeated the motifs of Greek architecture – the horizontal and vertical shafts of the stern Doric; the honeysuckle, the key, the egg and dart of the Ionic entablature; the foliated wreath of the Corinthian capital. The balance was exact, the rhythm of line continuous. The intelligence that guided the pattern was one with the sensitivity that created the design. In clothing, as in every other manifestation of Greek genius, there was simplicity, regularity, and inspired charm. Mind, body, and soul were directed consciously and harmoniously toward a goal in which the part was perfectly related to the whole, in which intellect and spirit merged in ideal beauty.

Just as the gods of Greece live on in sculptured story and inspired song, so, too, did the men and women of Greece also achieve immortality. Phidias was doubtless thinking of this when he adorned the walls of his perfect Parthenon with the imperishable frieze of Athenian men and maidens; they are in truth worthy of being admitted into the presence of the Most High. Here, turned to marble – not by the wicked sorcery of Medusa but by the precious magic of Phidias – these Attic shapes live on in mute but expressive ecstasy, "forever panting and forever young."

COSTUME

GENERAL CHARACTERISTICS

The predominating characteristic of classic Greek dress was simplicity and charm. (1) Fundamentally, each costume simply consisted of a rectangle; the secret of its beauty lay in the draping. (2) All garments brought the back over the front fold, on the shoulders. (3) All garments had the same dip in front over the chest, the same downward slope over the hips. (4) All garments had borders along one or more edges of the rectangle. (5) All outer garments were so draped that the right arm could be freed.

Materials

From earliest times, both coarse and fine linen were universally used. One very thin and glistening variety, mentioned in the *Odyssey* as being "fine as a filmy web . . . that dazzled like a cloudless sun," was probably treated with a solution that made it glossy. The island of Amorgos became famous for this weave. The Ionic *chiton* was usually of linen. The cloth was almost always made in the home. Flax was spun into thread with a distaff. The thread was sometimes woven into cloth by slaves, the mistress superintending the execution of finishing touches and embroidery. She also supervised the making of the garment, an activity carried on in the large living room, or *gyneconitis,* reserved for the women of the household. As Grecian women were closely kept at home, they found in these occupations a pleasant and profitable way of passing time.

Wool was also used by the Greeks from earliest times. Their own flocks furnished the wool (Arcadian sheep grew the finest), and deft hands wove the patterns. Coarse woolen cloth was used by slaves, peasants, and poor people. Finer textured woolens were made into Doric chitons, men's garments, *himations,* and traveling cloaks.

Silk brought from China was used by the Greeks from the fourth century B. C. on; though it had been known earlier, the price had been prohibitive. Silk was expensive even in the days of Alexander the Great, a pound of it being sometimes worth a pound of gold. Silk cloth manufactured from imported raw silk was first made on the island of Cos; half the threads used were silk, the other half, linen.

Cotton came into use after Alexander's campaigns, but was never highly esteemed. The clothing of peasants and slaves was made of felt, which was also used for headgear, sandals, and heavy wraps.

Designs were either woven into the material or embroidered on it; less commonly they were printed. Allover designs, including stars, sprigs, dots, palmetto, and meandering patterns, were worked into the ground of the material, and in richer stuffs the designs were accentuated by means of gold and silver threads. Greek women were famed for both their weaving and their needlework. The fair-haired Helen, "weaving the Trojan wars, herself the prize," or Penelope, unraveling each night the pattern made that day for Laertes' robe, typify the high esteem in which these arts were held.

Colors

Colors, predominatingly light of hue, were obtained from vegetable dyes. Women were especially fond of them. Pinks, blues, yellows, greens, and lavenders, all pastel shades, were chiefly used for fabrics of lighter texture. Men's clothing was usually of darker shades, among which were olive green, maroon, saffron, corn, mustard, purple blue, scarlet, tawny orange, dark blue, "a color like an unripe grape," brown, gray, and black. Outer wraps were always of darker shades, as were also the garments of the lower classes. Purple was usually reserved to kings in the earlier times, and for use on state occasions during the age of the democracies.

Underclothes

Men used a loincloth, and sometimes a short chiton was worn under the outer garment. Philosophers used no underclothing at all, and often omitted the outer gar-

Fig. 45

ment. Affecting great hardihood, some of them appeared in the himation only, as did Socrates when on the expedition to Potidaea, as Plato tells. On occasion, perhaps at the Olympic games, young warriors also seem to have worn only the *chlamys*.

Underneath the outer dress, women wore the *strophion,* or bandeau, about the breasts; a zone, tightly wrapped about the hips, to confine the abdomen; and sometimes a shield about the armpits to absorb perspiration. In addition, a plain slip (Ionic chiton) was worn beneath the outer chiton. As time went on, women kept increasing the number of undergarments until finally, in 594 B.C., Solon, the Athenian sage and lawgiver, issued a sumptuary edict limiting women to three garments. Another of his laws read: "Let not the corpse be buried with above three garments." Except for the greaves men wore in battle, both sexes let their legs go bare. Sandals were a matter of choice, and going about barefoot was quite customary.

COSTUME FOR MEN

HOMERIC AGE

The usual costume was the long-sleeved tunic, or Phrygian dress, made familiar to the Greeks during their trips back and forth to Asia Minor. It consisted of a short, knee-length, woolen garment having an allover pattern of circles or dots. The sleeves were long and tight, the neck rather low and rounded, the fullness of the neck confined by a broad flat belt (Fig. 46 A B C). Bands about the neck, the cuffs, and the hem of the garment were often decorated with classical designs. The sleeve was sometimes made in two pieces, then seamed at front and back. With this type of dress the Phrygian cap (Fig. 46 D) was used. This also had an allover pattern. Used later to denominate the freedman in Rome (the cap when used for that purpose being red in color), it was in 1789 adopted by the French revolutionists as the red cap of liberty. Paris, the Trojan prince who stole far-famed Helen, was usually depicted in Phrygian dress. Sometimes he wore with it the long, rather loose trousers popular in Asia Minor and north of the Euxine Sea. During the Alexandrian Age, a long-sleeved garment similar to the Phrygian dress was favored.

CLASSICAL AGE

Chiton

The Ionic chiton, a rectangle of linen or woolen cloth, was the usual dress. (The word *chiton* means "linen garment.") For the sleeveless type that was worn by young men, boys, workers, and slaves, the width of the material used for a garment was double the distance from elbow to elbow when the arms were akimbo (Fig. 47 B). The length of the garment depended upon the age and occupation of the wearer. Young boys, young men, workers, peasants, and slaves wore the chiton at about knee length, slightly bloused at the waist (Fig. 47 A C). To allow for blousing, the length was from the shoulder to a point two inches below the knee. Older men and those engaged in dignified professions wore a chiton measuring from shoulder to instep, plus an allowance of about two inches for blousing. For the sleeved type of chiton, which was either pinned at intervals along the upper arm or gathered, as shown by the statue of the "Bronze Charioteer" at Delphi, the width of the material used for the garment was twice the distance from wrist to wrist of the outstretched arms (Fig. 51 A B). In all cases the Ionic chiton was sewed up at the side, usually at the right side, as shown by the bottom line of Fig. 47 B. A border about two inches wide might run across the upper edge of the chiton, and another about six or more inches wide across the lower edge. The two borders were not necessarily of the same pattern; they might be simple bands of color or elaborate floriated or geometrical designs. Favorite patterns were the fret (Fig. 55, bottom) and the scroll (Fig. 55, top).

In use, the chiton was slipped over the head, then centered both in front and at the back with the seam at the right side, as shown by Fig. 52. Next the back top edge of the garment was grasped at a point shoulder-distant from its center, folded over the front top edge, and secured with a pin or brooch. This operation was then repeated at the other shoulder (Fig. 52 D E Fig. 53 C D). The front of the garment fell loosely at the neck, and so disclosed the throat (Fig. 52 B C Fig. 53 A). After fastening as described, the remainder of the top at either side was allowed to fall so that the arms would be free, thus forming graceful folds at the wearer's sides. The right side of the sleeveless chiton could be dropped, thus completely baring that side of the torso.

With the Ionic chiton, men wore a cord or ribbon about the waist, tied in front or at the side. A more elaborate type of girdling is to be seen on the statue of the "Bronze Charioteer." As shown there, in order to confine the fullness of the gathered long sleeve, a cord about four yards long was used, and arranged as shown in Fig. 52 A B C. It was first centered in a V shape at the back (Fig. 52 A). Next it was brought up over either shoulder, then down the sides in front (Fig. 52 B), and then back under the arms and through the V in the back. Finally, it was again brought round to the front, where the ends were tied (Fig. 52 B).

Kolobion

This is the type of garment, "without seam, woven from the top throughout," that Jesus wore to his crucifixion, and for which the soldiers afterward cast lots. It had been worn by men of the Greek regions since the time of Alexander the Great. The kolobion was usually woven of wool, more rarely of linen, preferably in an allover pattern. It consisted of a single piece of cloth, woven round, as is the modern knitted sweater. A slit for the head was left at the center of the top; others, for the arms, were left at either side, below the top edge (Fig 48 B). Sometimes long sleeves were added. Measurements varied according to the size of the wearer, but an average-size kolobion measured about forty inches around and was about thirty-eight inches in length.

Mantle

When out-of-doors, men wore the himation, the chlamys, and several varieties of circular cape having a hood attached. The himation was the kind most in use (Fig. 54 A). It was usually made of woolen cloth, though linen ones were often worn during hot weather. The himation was rectangular in shape, about six yards long and from five to six feet in width. The four edges were bordered. Since the himation was woven in a single piece, the selvaged edges caused it to drape easily and gracefully.

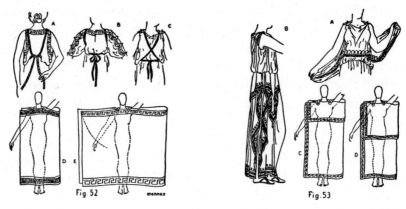

Fig 52   Fig 53

The corners of the garment were usually weighted to insure that the folds would fall nicely and remain in place.

Proper draping of the himation was important. The several steps that had to be taken in adjusting it to the wearer were as follows: (1) Beginning at the left foot, the material was draped over the left front of the body and caught together in the hand at the left shoulder. Enough material had to be left ungathered to reach midway between elbow and wrist. The left arm was held outstretched, shoulder-high, to insure proper draping. (2) When the garment was draped on the left shoulder, the material was next draped diagonally down across the back with the right hand, while at the same time the left hand smoothed the top bordered edge into place. (3) At hip length the material was passed under the right arm and diagonally upward across the chest to the left shoulder, the bordered edge being kept smoothly in place. (4) With the left arm still outstretched, the material was again gathered partly on the shoulder, with enough left ungathered to reach midway between elbow and wrist. This time, however, care was taken to gather the material diagonally toward the back. This allowed proper play for the arms. (5) The himation was then draped down the left back, almost to the ground. The diagonal draping on the shoulder resulted in a fine zigzag effect of folds down the back.

The method of draping just described was the customary one. For the sake of variety, however, other methods were also used. (6) After the first step, which was always the same, step (2) and part of step (3) were also performed, except that the garment was now thrown across the left forearm instead of being carried up to the left shoulder. Or, (7) the material was pleated along the top edge and then tucked into the girdle at the front. Again, (8) at step (3) the himation was pulled forward over the head to form a head covering. It could also be held tightly across the breast in front, thus completing the shawl effect. Or, (9) the shawl, or wrap, effect could be achieved by holding the right edge of the himation tightly across the breast without covering the head. This sort of draping may be seen on the statue of Sophocles. The Tanagra figurines chiefly show styles (6), (7), (8), and (9). Entirely different was style (10), which favored both ends of the himation hanging down on either side in front, the back being draped in a deep V. This type of draping was effective for occasions that demanded a show of dignity on the part of the wearer. (It is excellent for stage use.)

For mourning, the himation was made of black or dark gray. It may be noted here that the himation is another garment said to have been worn by Jesus.

Chlamys

The *chlamys* was a shorter cloak, preferred by young men to the himation, and used when traveling or riding (Fig. 48 A C). It was rectangular in shape, some seven feet wide and from three and a half to six feet long. The shorter length was used for horseback riding, the longer for traveling, for cold weather, or for rain.* Like the himation, it was bordered on all four sides.

To drape the chlamys, the material was fastened on the right shoulder, the left shoulder being underneath the cloak. The points front and back, so fastened, might be the corners of the chlamys or points about fifteen inches from the corners. A pin or round brooch was usually used to hold these points together, though they were occasionally tied. In the latter case, the greater length (six feet) was necessary. While riding, or during any other activity, the front drape was thrown back over the left shoulder, thus leaving both arms free. The procession of horsemen in the frieze of the Parthenon shows this arrangement and illustrates the graceful flow of the drapery. When traveling, or during cold weather, the long chlamys, drawn closely about the shoulders, hung down straight at both front and back. Mercury – a traveler by profession and a liar by choice – is usually shown wearing the chlamys. Military men favored a red chlamys. The darker shades were common for general wear.

The circular cloak, with or without the hood, was made of thick, coarse wool or of felt. Though occasionally used by the better classes, it was the ordinary cold-weather garb of the peasant. It reached to the shins or ankles and was tied with thongs or strings under the chin.

Footwear

The feet were usually bare, especially indoors. The Greeks prided themselves, however, on the variety and fine workmanship of their sandals. These were made of felt, linen, leather, or matting. The soles were either of the same materials or of wood or cork. The simplest style consisted of a sole with a piece of leather or other material encasing the heel, and having a strap across the instep with perhaps another connect-

* Measurements of the chlamys (Fig. 48 C) should be changed from 252″ x 126″ to 84″ x 60″.

ing with the sole alongside the great toe (Fig. 56 A E F). Straps were crisscrossed, pierced, or otherwise elaborated. Sometimes the lacings were continued up the leg, with a strip of leather in the back to hold the lacings in place. This type of footwear was known as the *ypodemata* (Fig. 56 D). The *buskin,* worn by comedians (Fig. 56 B), was a soft, flat sandal which fully enclosed the foot to ankle height. The *cothurnos,* or boot (Fig. 56 C), made of leather, was fitted to the foot and leg and reached halfway to the knee or higher. At the front it was laced with leather thongs. The soles were made of wood or cork. The tragic actor, who adopted this style of boot, increased the thickness of the sole to twelve or more inches, and so increased his height. The cothurnos was sometimes lined with the fur of a cat or other small animal, and often the creature's head and claws were left hanging over the top edge of the boot.

Sandals and boots were painted, pierced, gilded, and sometimes jeweled. Dandies invented new styles which were given their names; one such style was the "Alcibiades sandal." Tan and black were the colors most commonly used. Red leather sandals were a mark of distinction.

Hair

The Greeks wore heavy heads of hair and usually went bareheaded. Homer considered hair a great element of masculine beauty. Among the Spartans a boy's hair was closely cropped till he became an ephebus; after that the hair was allowed to grow. Spartan men usually took little pains with their hair except on the eve of battle, at which time it was carefully arranged. At Athens in the time of Pericles, a boy wore his hair long until he became an ephebus, whereupon the locks were cut off and presented to the Delphic Apollo or some other god as a votive offering. Slaves wore their hair cropped short. Athenian gentlemen wore it fairly long, curled at the ends behind and in rows across the forehead (Fig. 45 C). The curls were never stiff, but instead were soft and rather loosely grouped. Philosophers commonly wore their hair shoulder length.

The barbershop was the favorite meeting place of men; it was "a symposium without wine." As shown by busts of Zeus and Homer, full beards and mustaches were worn in Homeric times. During the Periclean age the face was smooth-shaven. Later, during the Alexandrian age, a patch of hair in front of the ears was in fashion. The Greeks never favored mustaches without beards. A mustache without a beard was the mark of the barbarian.

Since most Greeks were of dark complexion, fair hair was a much-esteemed sign of beauty. Homer mentions the blond locks of Achilles and of Menelaus. According to Euripides, Dionysos was a blond.

Fig. 56

Headdress

A simple band or fillet around the head was the usual headdress (Fig. 47 A). It was placed high over the forehead, just above the hairline. Garlands were worn at festivals. A wreath of myrtle was worn in honor of Aphrodite; this was a favorite garland for symposia (banquets). A wreath of laurel was worn for Apollo, an olive wreath for Athena, one of oak for Zeus, an ivy or grape-leaf one for Dionysos. The archon wore a wreath of myrtle as symbol of his dignity, as did also the orators when addressing the people.

Victors of the Olympic games were awarded a wreath or crown of wild olive. At the Pythian games the award was a wreath of bay leaves plucked by a boy whose parents were still alive. At the Isthmian (Corinthian) games the prize was a wreath of dried celery. Wealthy gentlemen of fashion wore golden bands or fillets. Some of them had golden wreaths made of imitation leaves, flowers, or ears of corn. The dead were crowned with wreaths of fresh myrtle or of ivy.

As an ordinary head covering, the Greeks wore the himation pulled up over the head, as has been explained, or the hood of the circular cape. Travelers, soldiers, hunters, and all who were exposed to wind, rain, and cold used the *petasos* (Fig 48 A). This was a hat made of felt, leather, or weasel skin. Whether its brim was broad, round, or four-cornered, it had a low, round crown. The brim was either turned up at the front or the back, or slit at the sides and then turned up or down. The petasos was tied under the chin by means of cords or thongs. When not in use, it was allowed to hang down behind, secured by these cords. Mercury is usually pictured as wearing the petasos. For valor, a Greek general was awarded a red petasos. (This was the origin of the cardinal's hat of later times.)

Another Greek headdress was the *pilos,* a conical, close-fitting cap made of felt. Sailors, smiths, and workers in general used this. Ulysses, a sailor of vast experience, is commonly pictured wearing the pilos.

Ornaments and Accessories

In classic times Greek gentlemen wore comparatively little jewelry. They wore signet rings of fine workmanship, for use as seals rather than for adornment (Fig. 55 D). During the Hellenistic period lavish use of rings indicated the general love of luxury and display. Glass, precious stones, cameos, and other materials were employed as settings, in striking contrast to the broad, massive armlets and bracelets used by the hardier, simpler men of Homeric times.

Men carried walking sticks, though not highly ornamented ones. Other accessories were seldom used. A *rhyton,* or drinking horn (Fig. 55 E), was at times carried to banquets.

Make-up

Only in Corinth did some of the dandies indulge in the extreme fashion of artificially accentuating the features with paint and other aids. The Greeks always perfumed themselves, however, for banquets and other festive occasions. They also oiled their bodies, especially before athletic events.

Military Dress

The ordinary soldier wore the short Ionic chiton. He might also wear a leather jacket and a linen, leather, or bronze helmet. Metal plates reinforced the leather jacket, and leather tabs studded with metal guarded the abdomen. Greaves of leather or metal protected the shins. He might wear sandals or not, as he chose. He carried a round or oblong shield to protect his body. His weapons were a spear, or javelin, or bow and arrows.

The officer was more elaborately garbed. Over the short Ionic chiton (rather full and often decorated with a red border), he wore a bronze or steel corselet, engraved or chased in intricate designs (Fig. 49 A B). Sometimes these designs were washed in gold. In rare instances, the corselet was of gold, etched in fanciful designs. Leather straps, faced with metal to protect the shoulders, were attached to the corselet at both front and back. Suspended from the waist was a row of leather tabs six or eight inches long, with metal facings. Metal greaves covered the shins, and sandals, the feet. The officer had a round or oblong shield, and a sword, which was a sign of his rank. Greek swords were rather short, and either rounded or pointed at the end. An armor-bearer usually carried the shield, the sword (in its finely wrought case), and other accouterments; in active engagement, the sword, in its case, was belted about the officer's waist.

Originally, according to Homer, a close-fitting leather cap made of the raw hide of an animal and designed without crest or knob, was worn by the young warrior. This developed into the casque of metal, semi-globular in shape, and made of brass. As time went on, the helmet (Fig. 45 E) became an actual work of art, with such additions made to the original simple casque as front, back, and cheek pieces, visors and demi-visors, and crests to protect the skull. In the group of the Aeginetai at Munich, the bowman Teukros is depicted wearing a helmet to which have been added a neck-piece about five inches wide and a narrow front-piece. In the same group, Telamon's helmet shows a piece of metal to cover the nose as having been added to the front-piece. Movable flanges protected the jaw, and on some helmets cheek-pieces were added by hinges to the sides of the helmet; when these were turned up, the helmet looked as if it were winged. The most graceful helmet design is that worn by Athena in the Villa Albani sculpture. In this helmet the neck-piece was separated from the front-piece by an incision, and the front-piece was developed into a complete visor with small slits for the eyes. In battle, the visor was pulled down to protect the face, leaving the skull protected by the metal cap; out of battle, the helmet was pushed back over the neck, and the visor left resting on top of the head. The common soldier's helmet was without ornament, but the officer's helmet was elaborately decorated with figures or patterns, the cap, visor, and stephane being literally covered with them. An officer also frequently wore a brilliant crest of either horsehair or feathers, as is told by Homer and as is shown in vase-paintings of the day. A crest of horsehair, dyed a brilliant scarlet, often extended from the forehead to the nape of the neck in a cropped ridge, and then terminated in a long, wavy tail of red horsehair. No wonder Hector's baby was frightened by such an apparition! Another type of helmet (shown in the statues of Pericles and also in the actual helmet found in the river Alpheios, near Olympia) was cast in one piece, with slits for the eyes (Fig. 49 A).

Mourning

For mourning, men wore clothing with little or no decoration, either dark gray or black in color. The hair was cut short, and the shorn locks were presented as a votive offering at the tomb.

Costume for Children

Children wore essentially the same types of dress as their elders, but with little or no decoration. For outer wraps, they usually wore the circular cape and hood, as is shown in the figure of little Telesphorus.

Costume for the Lower Classes

Peasants and slaves, while actively engaged in work, wore scant Ionic chitons of wool or coarse linen, fastened generally on the left shoulder only. Older men, in cold weather, wrapped their legs in oxhides or woolen cloth, gartered with thongs. The forearms might also be so covered. The peasant, unable to afford trips to the barber, let his beard grow (Fig. 47 C).

Modern Adaptations

For ordinary Greek costume, Japanese crepe can be used, as it comes in good shades and can be dyed. Its surface, however, is rather too crinkled to take designs well, and unbleached muslin is better for general use. The himation or the chlamys can be made of these materials, or of canton flannel, or cotton duvetyn. These heavy materials do not take designs any too well, but thick poster paint will adhere fairly well. Gold and aluminum are the most difficult to apply.

For borders, a stencil should be made, and the paint should be applied with a fairly thick brush; poster paint is cheaper than oil paint. Where large quantities are needed, kalsomine powder is more economical than poster paint, as it can be bought by the pound and mixed with water as needed. The light shades are cheaper than the dark shades. Red is one of the most expensive shades. A border of the same color, but of a darker shade than the body of the garment, is always effective.

For the warrior's corselet, Col-o-tex is best; gold or silver oilcloth is fairly effective. Sandals of chamois skin or painted cloth serve for temporary use; many modern commercial sandals will be found satisfactory. The petasos can be made of an old, flat-brimmed hat.

Costume for Women

HOMERIC AGE

Costumes of the Homeric period seem, from vase paintings, to have followed Asiatic styles. The type usually shown is a close-fitting robe, with rounded neck, long sleeves, and snug belt. Another costume, the *peplos,* was a tight-fitting tunic with a bib, or overfold, at the top. The peplos was usually made of wool, embroidered or woven in allover design.

The *crinkled chiton* was another early form of dress. The crinkled chiton (Fig. 50 A B) was a short-sleeved, hip-length garment worn over a long, full undergarment. The crinkled effect was probably obtained by pleating the material, which had first been immersed in a starchlike substance, into fine accordion pleats; this long line of pleats was then accordion-pleated crosswise (Fig 50 C). Over the crinkled chiton was sometimes draped, diagonally, a pleated ruffle or draping, which accentuated the zigzag lines (Fig. 50 D).

CLASSICAL AGE

In the classic period there was developed a distinct type of dress. This was the rectangular chiton, Ionic or Doric. The Ionic was usually of linen; the Doric, of wool.

The Ionic Chiton

The length of this garment was two inches more than the distance from shoulder to ground. This allowed a slight blousing at the waist. The width, for the narrow, sleeveless variety, was double the measure from elbow to elbow when the arms were akimbo (Fig. 52 D). For the long-sleeved variety (pinned or gathered), the width was double the measure from wrist to wrist, with arms outstretched (Fig. 52 E Fig. 51 A B).

The material was sewed up the right side. The borders were at the top and bottom edges. The width of the top border was about two inches; that of the bottom border might be six inches or more. The designs of the two borders were not necessarily alike; the wide bottom border might consist of a combination of several designs.

The method of adjusting the Ionic chiton is shown in Fig. 52 D E. With the arms held free, the front and back edges were pinned together at the shoulders. To do this, the back edge was held tightly, while the front edge was held loosely to allow for a graceful fold-over of about two inches, center front. The back edges were pointed and pinned *over* the front edges. In early days, sharp pins, with the points upward, were used. These were later forbidden by law, and brooches or a species of safety pins came into use.

Girdling

Three ways of girdling the chiton were employed: (1) A cord, or ribbon, about two yards long, was tied about the waist, the ends left to fall loosely at the front or the sides (Fig. 53 B). (2) A cord about four yards long was centered at the middle back, and held there by the thumb. Each end was then passed over a shoulder and back under an arm; both ends were threaded through the V, center back, and brought around to the front, where they were tied (Fig. 52 A B). (3) A cord about five yards long was centered, as before, at the middle back; the ends were passed over the shoulders, and then crossed over the breast in front. The ends were then brought back and threaded through the V, and tied in front, as described above (Fig. 52 A C). After the

Fig. 46

Fig. 47

Fig. 48

Fig. 49

Fig. 50

Fig. 51

Fig. 54

Fig. 55

cord was tied (whichever method had been used), the front of the chiton was pulled slightly upward and bloused. Thus the sides hung somewhat lower than the front. This downward curve was called the *kolpos,* and was indispensable to a perfect draping (Fig. 52 A B C).

The Amazons were represented as wearing a short variety of the Ionic chiton. A second girdle, low about the hips, served to free the limbs still further, and is frequently shown in representations of Artemis, the huntress.

The Doric Chiton

This type of chiton was usually woven in one piece, of fine wool. Like the Ionic chiton, it was a rectangle, but it was bordered on all four sides. In width it was double the measure from elbow to elbow when the hands were on the hips. The length was two inches more than the distance from shoulder to ground, *plus* the length of the overfold (Fig. 53 C D). This overfold distinguished the Doric chiton from the Ionic. The Doric also could be (and usually was) left open on the right side (sometimes, more rarely, the opening is shown on the left). The open edge was caught with pins at intervals, but from the knee to the ground it was left unfastened. The overfold varied from eight to thirty-six inches. The usual length, however, was to the waist – about twelve inches (Fig. 53 C).

The method of adjusting the Doric chiton was the same as the first method described for the Ionic. A cord, tied in front or at the sides (Fig. 53 A B), held in the material at the waist. The border on a Doric chiton was usually about two inches wide. It ran along all four sides of the open Doric chiton, and the two bordered edges at the side produced more elaborate and beautiful effects than could be achieved with the Ionic chiton (Fig. 53 A B). A deeper border might be added about the bottom edge; sometimes two or three different borders were applied, one above the other. The draping showed the same kolpos as that of the Ionic chiton.

Though younger women tended to wear the shorter overfold, and older women the longer, hip-length type, this was by no means an unvarying rule. Athena is usually shown with the hip-length type (Fig. 53 B).

Mantle

Greek women wore the himation, but not the chlamys. The himation had to be worn on the rare occasions when women went out-of-doors. It was a rectangle (Fig. 54 A B) with a border all around, measuring approximately 540" x 72". Although they were usually made of wool, those worn in warm weather were sometimes of heavy linen. Women's himations were adjusted in the same way as men's (see pages 36–37).

Veil

The *predemnon* was a short veil, about a yard square, worn over the head. Worn often in conjunction with the himation, it indicated a journey or an excursion out-of-doors. Penelope, when asked to choose between remaining with her father or going away as the bride of Ulysses, signified her decision by dropping the predemnon over her face.

Footwear

Women wore the same types of sandals as men (Fig. 56 A D E F). Those which enclosed the heel were called *pedilla*. Women's sandals were more delicately made, had more decoration, fitted the foot perfectly, and, for elegant use, were colored or gilded. Cork or matting soles were preferred. The cothurnos was seldom, if ever, used by women.

Hair

Greek women were proud of their hair, and took great care in arranging it. In Homeric and archaic times, the hair was parted in the middle, waved down over the temples in set curves, or arranged in tight curls about the forehead (Fig. 45 A). Long corkscrew curls fell on either shoulder and behind. A band or fillet held the coiffure in place.

In classic times, the hair was arranged in a variety of ways. Young girls wore their hair flowing, with one or more fabric bands or chaplets of flowers about the head. Women wore their hair parted and waved over the forehead and down over the ears. It was then drawn back and knotted high on the neck (Fig. 45 B D). Often a few curled ends protruded from the knot (Fig. 45 B). Sometimes a net held up the knot in the back (Fig. 45 B); sometimes a band of cloth or a kerchief folded triangularly served the same purpose. A second kerchief was occasionally added to the coiffure. It was likewise folded in a triangle, and was adjusted bandeau-fashion over the forehead, back of the ears, and under the knot at the nape of the neck.

Three bands or windings of ribbon, equally spaced on the crown of the head and converging under the knot, were favorite (and easy) devices for hairdressing (Fig. 45 D). A more elaborate style employed the *stephane,* a crown placed rather high on the forehead back of the hairline. The ends of the stephane touched the ears. Two cords tied underneath the hair knot held it in place. The stephane was of very stiff fabric or of metal; gold ones were not uncommon, carved, engraved, or jeweled (Fig. 45 B).

Headdress

In addition to the stephane, which was part of the hair arrangement, Greek women wore, for outdoor use and travel, the petasos. There was also a broad-brimmed sun hat of straw, called *tholia,* which had a conical, pointed crown, six to eight inches high, and which was tied with ribbons under the chin. This type of hat is often seen in the Tanagra statuettes.

Ornaments and Accessories

Hairpins of bronze, gold, or silver, sometimes carved or jeweled, were worn in the coiffure. Brooches of many types, from simple pins with carved heads to elaborately fashioned safety pins and exquisitely engraved cameos, were popular. Earrings were much prized. They might be simple gold circlets, pendants of jewels or gold beads, or carved figures suspended on thin gold chains (Fig. 55 C). Bracelets were thin bands or coiled flexible snakes (Fig. 55 J), and were carved or enameled. Necklaces of beads, pearls, or gold trinkets (acorns, flowers, crescents) were favorite adornments (Fig.

55 H). Rings of glass, of precious stones, cameos, intaglios, and signets were in demand (Fig. 55 D).

Fans were widely used (Fig. 55 B). They were usually leaf-shaped and made of palm leaves, linen, feathers, or wings of birds. In warm weather, slaves carried long-handled fans while attending their mistresses.

Sunshades (Fig. 55 A) were also used. They could be folded; the most usual color was green. A type of handkerchief was also carried. The polished bronze mirror (Fig. 55 F), with or without a cover, was useful for the lady of fashion when arranging the toilette. The small, oval, metal mirror was also the indispensable insignia of the courtesan, or *hetaira*. A rectangular jewel box with a hinged cover, a toilet box (pyxis), pin box, ointment jar, comb (single- or double-toothed), ear pick and toothpick, strigil (for scraping powder and perspiration off the body), and workbasket were some of the accessories desired and used by women. Vases (Fig. 55 G K) were used for various purposes.

Make-up

Grecian women were adept in the art of make-up. They used white lead to whiten the complexion; red minium or a root preparation was used for rouge on cheeks and lips; pulverized antimony or fine soot was employed to blacken the eyebrows and lashes. Powder of various shades was used; there were also ointments, perfumes, creams, tooth powders (probably ground roots, like the orris). Bronze spatulae were used for mixing and applying cosmetics. Dipping rods of bronze or glass were used for applying perfumes.

Mourning

For mourning, women wore dark gray or black and dispensed with jewelry and ornamentation. They sheared their hair, depositing the locks on the tomb as a votive offering. (Electra is shown engaged in this ceremony; her hair is cut quite short.) Women were forbidden by law to scratch their faces or display excessive grief at funerals or near the obsequies.

COSTUME FOR CHILDREN

Little girls wore simplified versions of the garments generally worn by women. Their hair was worn flowing.

COSTUME FOR THE LOWER CLASSES

Women of the lower classes wore the simple Ionic chiton of coarse linen or wool. The hair was left down or drawn back in a simple knot. For outer wrap they wore the circular cloak of felt, rarely the himation.

MODERN ADAPTATIONS

Silk was a late development in Greek costume, and is therefore not authentic for the classic type of dress, unless it is intended to represent the shiny type of fine linen spoken of in the classics. For stage use, however, silk or its substitutes is permissible.

To produce the crinkled chiton, dip material (metaline or other thin fabrics are pre-ferred) in a starch solution; pleat and press; then accordion-pleat the other way and press. If a wavy wrinkled line is desired, dip the fabric in the starch, twist and tie it in a tight knot, and leave it thus till it dries.

A stencil should be made for the borders. If the outline of the pattern is traced on the fabric with wax crayon, the paint is less likely to run. Both kalsomine and poster paint are economical and easy to apply. Paint or dye the cord the same deep shade as the border. Gold and silver paper borders, with glued backs, are sometimes available at paint and paper stores.

For the himation, canton flannel, broadcloth, or heavy crepe is good. For the stephane, patented household insulation materials are excellent. They are made in silver finish and are as stiff as pasteboard but bend like tin. Cord for girdling is made, usually, in black and white, is called cording, and is quite inexpensive; it can be dyed.

For most garments, rayon tubing is excellent. It is purchasable (in white only) by the pound, takes dye well (use only silk dyes on it), and drapes in beautiful folds. Cheap crepe silk, heavily loaded, is next best. For thinner textures, cheap China silk is good; it can be dyed in cold silk dyes. Silkaline is very good; it has more body than China silk and comes in good colors; it is, however, wiry and will not stay pleated.

Raw silk is good for Doric chitons, as it looks like wool, but it has a tendency to cling to non-fabric objects. It may be successfully used for the chlamys, himation, or other type of cloak. Canton flannel or duvetyn can also be used.

Japanese crepe, rayon crepe, chiffon, georgette, and pussy willow all are excellent; chiffon takes accordion pleating well. If panne satin can be afforded, it well repays the cost, as it has a beautiful sheen and a nice weight.

For accessories and wigs, see previous chapters.

Make sandals of felt or unbleached muslin, laced up with strips of muslin. The soles should be of felt or of several layers of heavy canvas. For peasants, wrap burlap or sacking about the legs, and, if desired, about the forearms.

For an ordinary soldier's tunic, use heavy unbleached muslin, dyed, or burlap, canvas, or denim. For bronze or silver corselets, Col-o-tex is better than gold or silver oilcloth, as it is softer and does not crack. It comes in silver, gold, and a few colors.

Special Types

Some of the Greek and Roman gods and lesser deities have a special dress.

Zeus (Jupiter) wears a long chiton and himation, and carries a handful of thunder-bolts. His hair is in deep curls, and he wears a long, curly beard (Fig. 45 C).

Athena (Minerva) wears the long Doric chiton with the hip-length overfold. Over her breast is the aegis, or breastplate, with the Gorgon's (Medusa's) head and snakes on it. She wears a helmet, and carries a round shield and a spear.

Hermes (Mercury) wears a short Ionic chiton, a short chlamys or traveling cloak, and the petasos, or traveling hat. He carries the caduceus, or wand of healing, wreathed in serpents. Both his hat (sometimes small, like a cap) and his sandals are winged.

Artemis (Diana) wears a short Ionic chiton with two girdles, one about the waist, the other about the hips. She has a crescent (moon) in her hair, and she carries a bow and arrow.

Aphrodite (Venus) wears a scant Ionic chiton, sleeveless, and the cestus or wide girdle sacred to her (said to inspire love). She is accompanied by a swan or a dove, and she wears a garland of myrtle or violets about her head.

Ares (Mars) wears full armor, with helmet, shield, and sword.

Phoebus (Apollo) wears the short Ionic chiton, a chlamys about his shoulders, and sandals. He wears a laurel wreath on his curly hair, and carries a lyre.

Demeter (Ceres) wears a long, full Ionic chiton and a himation, has a stephane (or diadem) on her head, and carries a cornucopia.

Hera (Juno) has no special insignia, but is robed like Demeter; so also is Hestia (Vesta, goddess of the hearth).

Hephaestus (Vulcan) wears a short Ionic chiton, leather apron (he was a forger of metal), and unkempt hair and beard. He is lame in one foot.

The Muses and Graces are dressed like any young maidens. The Fates are dressed like older women of rank.

Dionysos (Bacchus) wears a short chiton and a wreath of ivy or grape leaves about his head.

Heracles (Hercules) wears a short Ionic chiton, with a leopard or lion skin over his shoulders. His hair is rather long and curly, and he wears a thick, curly beard; he is of muscular appearance, and carries a large wooden club. He wears high, laced boots.

Although Paris was not himself divine, his figure appears usually in company with the immortals. His costume influenced dress, in certain details, through the ages. He wears a short tunic of figured material fitted to the body, with round neck and long sleeves. With this he wears long, tight trousers of the same figured material, and medium-high laced boots. These trousers, Asiatic in origin, were to influence barbarian dress, particularly that of the Gauls. On his head is a cap of figured material with rounded peak curved over the forehead. This type of cap was adopted by the Romans, becoming the badge of the freed slave; when worn as such a badge, it was red. Later, in the eighteenth century, it was adopted by the French Revolutionists as the "Cap of Liberty." His hair is long and curly. He is sometimes represented carrying the golden apple.

CHAPTER IV

ROME

IMPORTANT PEOPLE AND EVENTS

753 B. C.	Rome founded (traditionally) by Romulus. . . . Seven kings of Rome, the last, Tarquin the Proud. . . . Period of Etruscan pottery, bronze and iron ware.
509 B. C.	The Republic established. . . . Institution of two annual consuls – the praetors. . . . Struggle of plebs for equal rights.
494 B. C.	First secession of plebs. . . . Tribunes appointed in their place.
486–266 B. C.	Wars – with Aequians, Volscians (Coriolanus), Samnites (Camillus), Latins, and the city of Tarentum ("Pyrrhic victory"); all Italy finally united under Rome.
457 B. C.	Cincinnatus, dictator.
449 B. C.	Twelve Tables of laws. . . . Second secession of plebs won them partial legislative rights.
390 B. C.	Rome sacked by the Gauls.
367 B. C.	Licinian Law – provided that one consul should be a pleb.
287 B. C.	Hortensian Law – all political offices opened to plebs. . . . Building of famous Roman roads – Appian Way, Flaminian Way, etc.
278–270 B. C.	The Septuagint (translation of the Old Testament into Greek).
264–201 B. C.	Punic Wars. . . . Regulus, Hamilcar Barca. . . . Sicily gained for Rome.
218 B. C.	Hannibal crossed the Alps. . . . Fabius, dictator. . . . Hannibal spared Rome.
216 B. C.	Defeat of Romans at Cannae.
202 B. C.	Hannibal defeated by Scipio at Zama.
146 B. C.	Destruction of Carthage, also of Corinth. . . . Africa and Macedonia made Roman provinces. . . . Cato. . . . Archimedes announced the principle of the lever. . . . Silver money used in Rome. . . . Plautus (*Menaechmi*). . . . Terence (*Andria*). . . . The poet Ennius.
133–123 B. C.	Reforms of the Gracchi. . . . Free grain. . . . Attalus of Pergamum. . . . Vellum (calfskin) and parchment (sheep and goat skin) used for writing. . . . First library at Rome.
119–66 B. C.	Marius. . . . Drusus. . . . Sulla, dictator. . . . Lucullus. . . . Cruel proscriptions.
101 B. C.	Wars with Teutons and Cimbri. . . . (Han dynasty in China.)
88 B. C.	Mithridatic wars. . . . Rome traded with India. . . . Gladiatorial combats.
60 B. C.	First Triumvirate – Caesar, Crassus, Pompey.
59 B. C.	Julius Caesar, consul.
58–50 B. C.	Conquest of Gaul, invasion of Britain. . . . Caesar reformed the calendar. . . . Pompey's defeat. . . . Caesar's wise legislation.
44 B.C.	Caesar assassinated by Brutus and the senators (March 15).
43 B.C.	Second Triumvirate – Octavius Caesar (Augustus), Antony, and Lepidus.
31 B.C.	Antony and Cleopatra defeated by Octavius at Actium. . . . End of republican era. . . . Great writers – Sallust, Cicero, Lucretius.
31 B. C.–14 A. D.	Augustus Caesar made emperor. . . . "Golden Age" of Rome. . . . Egypt became a Roman province. . . . Herod in Jerusalem. . . . Birth of Jesus. . . . System of provincial government reformed. . . . Initiation of postal service.

... Fire and police protection installed. ... Buildings – Basilica Julia, Altar of Peace, aqueducts, bridges. ... 22 B. C., the dance introduced on Roman stage. ... Writers – Vergil (*Aeneid, Eclogues*), Horace (*Odes*), Livy (history), Ovid (*Metamorphoses*).

14–37 A. D. Tiberius – and his villa at Capri. ... Earthquakes in Asia Minor. ... 33 A. D., Crucifixion of Jesus. ... Caligula (the "mad emperor"), 37–41 A. D. ... Claudius, 41–54 A. D. ... Kind treatment of slaves. ... Claudian aqueducts. ... Southern Britain conquered by Claudius, 43 A. D.; capture of Caractacus, the British chieftain. ... Theater of Marcellus. ... 42 A. D., St. Peter and St. Paul at Rome.

54–68 A. D. Nero ordered the murder of Agrippina (his mother), his two wives (Octavia and Poppaea), his brother (Britannicus), Seneca (his tutor), Petronius, Lucan, and countless others. ... 61 A. D., revolt of Boadicea in Britain. ... 64 A. D., Rome burned. ... Persecution of the Christians, accused of burning Rome. ... The Golden House and its great statue of Nero as the colossus of the sun.

70–79 A. D. Vespasian. ... 70 A. D., destruction of Jerusalem.

Circa 75–126 A. D. Pliny the Elder, Pliny the Younger. ... Josephus. ... Tacitus (*On the Germans*). ... Plutarch (*Lives*). ... Pausanius (*Tour of Greece*). ... The Gospels of the Apostles, and the Epistles

79–81 A. D. Titus. ... Destruction of Pompeii and Herculaneum by Vesuvius (August 24, 79 A. D.). ... Colosseum completed.

81–96 A. D. Domitian. ... Britain conquered by Agricola. ... Wall built across northern Britain. ... Persecution of Christians continued.

96–98 A. D. Nerva (first of the Good Emperors). ... Galen (study of medicine and anatomy). ... The philosopher Epictetus. ... Use of the magnifying glass and of glass windows. ... Sculpture of sarcophagi, triumphal arches, etc.

98–117 A. D. Roman empire attained its greatest extent under Trajan. ... Slaves protected by laws. ... Christians persecuted. ... The letters of Pliny the Younger described the struggles with, and persecution of, the Christians in Asia Minor. ... Trajan's Column.

117–138 A. D. Hadrian. ... Good government of provinces. ... Great wall in Britain. ... Pantheon rebuilt. ... Hadrian's tomb. ... Juvenal.

161–192 A. D. Marcus Aurelius (*Meditations*). ... Commodus murdered (Dec. 31, 192 A. D.).

200–300 A. D. Rome under the rule of the Barrack Emperors. ... Period of confusion. ... Caracalla. ... Aurelian's Wall. ... Zenobia conquered by the Emperor Aurelian, and her kingdom of Palmyra added to the Roman Empire.

284–305 A. D. Diocletian. ... Crown of jewels for Emperor. ... Continued persecution of Christians ("era of martyrs"). ... Longinus (*On the Sublime*). ... Baths of Diocletian.

312–337 A. D. Constantine the Great. ... 325 A. D., Council of Nicaea. ... Christianity adopted by the empire. ... 321 A. D., seat of imperial government removed from Rome to Byzantium. ... Constantinople founded. ... Library, Arch of Constantine, early Christian basilica (St. Paul's without the Walls). ... Julian the Apostate.

364 A. D. Roman empire divided into Eastern and Western (legal separation came in 438 A. D.).

368 A. D. Visigoths at Adrianople. ... Ulfilas translated the Bible into Gothic. ... St. Martin, St. Ambrose, St. Jerome.

410 A. D. Rome sacked by Visigoths under Alaric (August 24). ... Stilicho, one of Rome's ablest statesmen and generals. ... St. Augustine wrote *The City of God*. ... 438 A. D., Theodosian Code promulgated.

432–461 A. D. St. Patrick in Ireland.

449 A. D. Angles and Saxons invade Britain. ... Legends of Vortigern and Hengest and Horsa.

452 A.D.	Attila and his Huns checked in Italy by Pope Leo the Great.
455 A.D.	Rome sacked by the Vandals, under their king Gaiseric.
476 A.D.	Fall of Rome.

It is man's love of conquest that makes history. The story of a peaceful people is cheerful, but it is uninteresting. Ordinary men go their way and vanish into obscurity; the heel of the conqueror leaves an indelible mark.

Rome's primary characteristic is suggested by the mere geographical outline of Italy. Its shape is that of a huge military boot, poised to make an impress on the western world. Rome was so busy conquering and exploiting new territory that she had little time to develop national taste. So she accepted her clothes ready-made from the Greeks, as she accepted her architecture, sculpture, literature, and religion – worshiping, in the Latin tongue, the gods of Olympus in Greco-Roman temples upon the Capitoline Hill.

One garment, however, Rome did originate, to flaunt along the Appian Way; one garment she fashioned to symbolize the Roman citizen in all his pride of dominance. This garment was woven into the very warp and woof of Roman history; its segment marks the far-flung arc of Roman conquest. This garment was the *toga*. When, on the fatal Ides of March, Mark Antony draped the many-gashed form of Julius Caesar with the toga picta, symbol of victory, he swept the destiny of a nation into its circling folds.

The Golden Age of Augustus marked the advent of success – and of surfeit, which led to interior decay. Emperors, with their inordinate lust for display, eschewed the simple toga and the plain customs of their fathers. They overloaded dress with the spoils of their many victories. They boasted of their deeds in heavy, huge monuments that arched the Roman roads; they reared spacious basilicas to hoard the spoils of captured provinces. They expanded with pride, to burst finally with folly.

Rome, that could discipline the world and lay down laws for countless generations to follow, could not restrain her own vanity. Rome, mistress of the world, was supine before her own personal desires. Indulgence was the order of the day; the password was pleasure. Games, which the Greeks used to refine the body and honor the gods, became the pastime of a population crazed for sensationalism. Not the noblest youth of the land, but hired brutes and slaves were the gladiators who, in the vast Colosseum, cried out prophetically, "We who are about to die salute thee, O Caesar!"

COSTUME

GENERAL CHARACTERISTICS

These may be summed up as follows: (1) adoption (and adaption) of the Greek chiton (*tunica*), himation (*pallium*), chlamys (*paludamentum* and *sagum*), kolobion (*colobium*); (2) use of Etruscan ornament and symbols, to embellish costume; (3) use of special markings to indicate social status; (4) use of toga, in various styles, by Roman citizens only; (5) use of armor (similar to Greek), carefully designed more for use than for beauty; (6) general lavishness in the late empire.

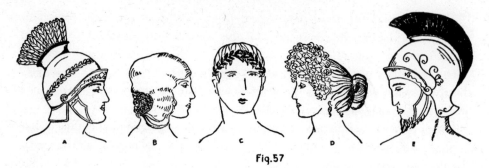

Fig.57

Materials

Wool was more commonly used in Rome than in Greece, as Rome's climate was cooler. Linen, however, was still used in abundance, cotton in later times (from 180 B. C. on), and silk from the first century B. C. Emperors led the fashion for extravagance in dress and materials; silks became most popular.

Colors

Romans preferred white until the second century A. D. Men then took to using natural linen and wool colors, beige, sand, brown, and the like. Allover patterns and more vivid colors marked the decadent period of Rome's domination.

Underclothes

These included essentially the same garments as those worn by the Greeks. The *subligaculum* was a loincloth worn under the tunic or by itself by athletes, workers, etc. In the days of the empire, men used more underclothing. One or two, or more, *subucula* or under-tunics were common; these were often of wool, though linen was also used.

COSTUME FOR MEN

Tunic

The *tunica alba* was an adaptation of the Ionic chiton. It was a little wider than the Greek chiton. In early times, one side was left open halfway up the thigh. Older men of dignity and rank wore the *tunica talaris*. It measured somewhat longer than the distance from shoulder to ground. A girdle (*cinctura*) about the waist held it in place; a slight blouse was usual. About the time of Commodus the tunica talaris for general use developed long sleeves, and became known as the *tunica manicata* (Fig. 58). It had previously been worn as part of the regular wardrobe of officiating priests and of actors.

The tunica talaris (used as a wedding garment, in addition to its use by older men, men of rank, etc.) was further distinguished by the following insignia:

(1) The *latus clavus,* a broad stripe about two fingers wide, adopted from the Etruscans about the seventh century B. C. It was purple (a term which in those times might mean any shade from scarlet through crimson, claret, violet, to deep blue) and was sewed or woven down the front and back center of the tunic. It denoted the rank of senator.

(2) The *angustus clavus*, two narrow stripes, each about one finger wide. This was adopted from the official dress of the "Camilli," the group of youths and maidens who assisted in religious ceremonials. The angustus clavus was also purple and was sewed or woven down either side, front and back, of the tunic, passing over the shoulders (Fig. 58). It denoted equestrian rank.

(3) The *tunica palmata* was embroidered in gold with palm branches. It was a long tunica talaris, worn by victorious generals when making the triumphal progress along the Sacred Way to the Capitoline Hill, where they made sacrifices to Jupiter. With the tunica palmata the general wore the toga picta of purple. On his head was a laurel wreath; in his right hand he carried a laurel bough, and in his left hand an ivory scepter tipped with an eagle's head.

When the tunica talaris was decorated in any of the above ways, it was usually worn without a girdle, although, as Quintilian remarks, it was "not so convenient."

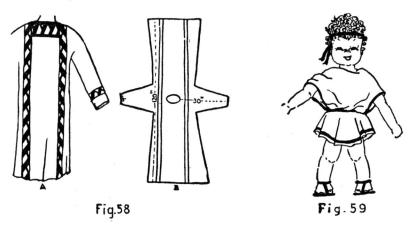

Fig. 58   Fig. 59

The tunica talaris was never worn without an outer covering (usually the toga, if the wearer were a Roman citizen), if the wearer had any pretensions to social position.

Workmen, peasants, and slaves, however, wore the tunic alone, or even the subligaculum alone.

Colobium

This was a type of dress adopted by the Romans from the Etruscans, about the fourth century B. C. It was essentially the same garment as the kolobion of the Greeks, from whom the name was derived. It was, however, usually wider than the kolobion, so that the upper part formed a kimono-type sleeve halfway to the elbow, very loose, but with a fairly small armhole. The colobium had a rounded neck and a plain line border about the bottom edge, and it was girdled about the waist with a cord or belt (Fig. 59).

Dalmatica

This garment was adopted by the Romans about 190 A. D. from Asia Minor (by way of Dalmatia), where it had been in use for several centuries. It differed from the colobium in that it had long, loose sleeves. It was often worn as an outer garment over the colobium. Heliogabalus made a public appearance in this garment about 218

A. D. In its Oriental form it was reminiscent of the Persian sleeved coat (see chapter II, Fig. 40 A B), and was probably open down the front and worn over another garment. As time went on, however, it grew in favor with the general public, who used it in the form shown in Fig. 62 III, closed, with straight neckline; the two angusti clavi were added for those of proper rank. The wide sleeves were usually joined to the straight garment. The color was the natural color of the material, wool, linen, or cotton; no girdle or belt was worn with the dalmatica.

Mantles and Cloaks

The Romans wore a variety of outer wraps on account of the climate, the extensive traveling of the populace, and the many military campaigns. Some of these were as follows:

Pallium

This was the Latin name for the Greek himation (see chapter III, Fig. 54 A B), which the Romans adopted and draped in the same manner as the Greeks (Fig. 62 A). Roman philosophers in the empire period copied the custom of the Greek philosophers in favoring this mantle, though they usually wore it over a tunic, rather than by itself, as many Greek philosophers had done. By the fourth century A. D. it had become an official badge of office in the state. When used for this purpose, it was not worn as a mantle but was folded lengthwise to a width of a half yard or less (something like the Mexican serape), and draped about the body like the original himation (Fig. 62 B).

Later, when the *paenula* (see below) was worn for real warmth and the pallium became merely a badge of office, it was found more convenient to drape the pallium over the right shoulder rather than under it. This made a loop about the neck (Fig. 62 C). The sumptuary Lex Vestiaria, 382 A. D., decreed this type of pallium draping for senatorial officers. The folds were discarded and the pallium was reduced to a scarf about a foot wide. This type of pallium was adopted by the later Byzantines. Another adaptation will be mentioned later (see p. 87).

Abolla

This was the Roman type of the Greek chlamys (see chapter III, Fig. 48 A C). It was usually of wool, and red in color. It was tied or pinned on the right shoulder; sometimes it was fastened on either shoulder with large round brooches.

Paludamentum

This was a mantle like the chlamys, but of larger proportions; it was used as a military cloak. The paludamentum was usually pinned or tied on the right shoulder, and was of purple, dark blue, green, or occasionally brown. It was the official cloak for generals on campaigns, for lictors, and for certain magistrates.

Paenula

This was a circular cape adapted from the circular cape of felt worn by Greek peasants. It was in general use by all classes in Rome, for traveling and for inclement or cold weather. It was of wool or (for the peasants) of felt; it was, in shape, a semicircle, split down the front (Fig. 62 va); a hood (*cucullus*) might be attached to the

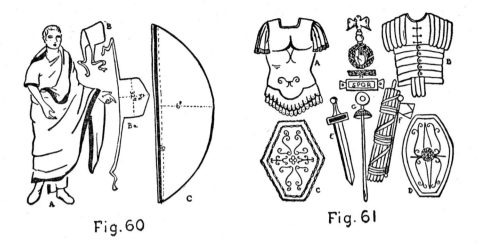

Fig. 60

Fig. 61

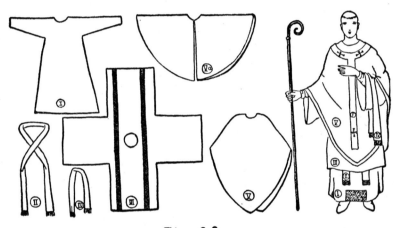

Fig. 62

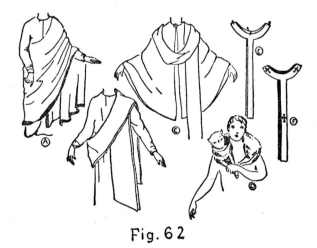

Fig. 62

Fig. 64

neckline. Dark shades were used for this cloak, brown, black, dark gray, etc. Rarely, it was fastened together down the front. Other wraps in use were the *lacerna* (like the abolla but with rounded edges), the *byrrus,* with a hood, and the *laena,* a sort of oblong woolly shawl.

Toga

This outer wrap is the one garment created by the Romans and used by them as the official symbol of the Roman citizen; no slaves, criminals, or foreigners could wear it. In shape it was the segment of a circle, fifteen or eighteen by six feet at the widest point. It was draped exactly like the himation (Fig. 60 A C), except that the part under the right arm could be turned over to form a fold, or "sinus"; also, the long front drape, over the left foot, could be pulled up to form a pouch, or "umbo." This was often used as a pocket for the right hand. The toga, like the himation, could be pulled up over the head and right shoulder for warmth or protection.

There were several different types and colors of the toga:

(1) The *toga praetexta* was originally worn by kings only; in republican times it was the distinctive mark of curule magistrates and was assumed by noble youths, on attaining manhood, at the Feast of the Liberalia, on March 17. The toga praetexta was awarded as a mark of distinction and was then called the *toga ornamentum.* In both its ancient and its republican forms it was of the natural color of the wool (lower classes of Roman citizens used coarse linen or felt) with a purple stripe about three inches wide along the straight edge (Fig. 60 C).

(2) The *toga pura* was the symbol of a Roman citizen from the third century B. C. It was a natural wool color with no band.

(3) The *toga candida* was worn by candidates for office and was bleached white (to emphasize the candidate's purity of purpose). It was worn also by clients (usually when seeking favors of their patrons).

(4) The *toga virilis* was assumed by Roman youths of less than noble rank at the Feast of the Liberalia. It was of plain wool, natural color, and had no band.

(5) The *toga trabea* was worn by priests (Salii) and augurs, and measured four or five feet at the widest point. It was striped white or red, with a purple border around both the curved and the straight edges.

(6) The *toga picta* was originally worn by Etruscan priests and state officials. The Romans adopted it about the third century B. C. in a simpler form than the ornate Etruscan one, which had an allover painted pattern (*picta* means "painted"). The first type used by the Romans had an embroidered border, and the woolen cloth was a deep purple in color. About the time of Sulla the usual fabric was silk. It became the official robe for generals making triumphal entries into Rome, and for magistrates in the processions to the Circensian Games; it was also worn by praetors and governors of provinces. Julius Caesar was awarded, not only both consular offices, but also the privilege of wearing the toga picta for general use. For state occasions it was usually worn over the tunica palmata.

(7) The *toga pulla* was worn for mourning and was of black.

After the establishment of the empire, the toga gradually became a less indispensable part of a Roman citizen's costume. Business, wars, and constant travel made the simpler and more compact garments favored.

Footwear

The Romans adopted Greek sandals and boots, but they also favored Etruscan models, especially those which had straps or laces up the leg above the ankle (Fig. 63 A). The equivalent of the Greek sandal was the *solea,* worn by both men and women in their own homes. The *crepida* had a sole of wood, cork, or leather, with heel enclosed and straps across the ankle (Fig. 63 E). The *udo,* or low shoe, of felt, covering the ankles, was favored for indoor as well as outdoor use. *Perones* were crude sandals of untanned leather.

When the covering extended farther up the leg, like a boot, the shoe was called the *calceus;* it usually had no lacing, but was slit on the side, or otherwise adapted to the foot, and fastened with a strap about the ankles (Fig. 63 D).

High boots (*campagi*) were used by soldiers. Often they were lined with fur, the head and claws of an animal hanging over and ornamenting the top edges (Fig. 63 B C). Patricians wore a boot of untanned leather with four black straps. Senators wore red leather boots with a *C* on the instep. The *C,* Roman numeral for one hundred, was symbolic of the senator's descent from the first one hundred patricians, a noble order organized by Romulus.

The *caliga* (from which Caius Caesar received his nickname of Caligula) were thick-soled, strong shoes, fastened with thongs. They were worn by common soldiers, both in camp and on the march.

Fig. 63

Hair

Romans wore their hair, in general, like the Greeks (Fig. 57 C), but more closely cropped. After the third century it was usually brushed straight front, though gentlemen of fashion curled it all over the head. Romans used the razor after the fourth century B. C., and were clean-shaven until the second century A. D., when beards, with or without mustaches, came into favor (Fig. 57 E).

Slaves wore their hair long and their beards unshaven.

Headdress

A simple fillet about the forehead, below the hairline, was in general use for adornment. As head covering in bad weather or for traveling, the cucullus, or hood, was used (Fig. 60 B Ba). Soldiers wore helmets of leather or metal (Fig. 57 A E).

In addition, there were several symbolic headdresses:

(1) The *corona etruscan* was used for the triumphal march of a general, being held over his head by an official. It was a wreath of gold leaves set with jewels.

(2) The *corona navalis,* made of miniature prows of ships, was presented to one who had distinguished himself in naval enterprises. Similarly, the *corona muralis,* of miniature turrets on a gold band, was the award for distinguished services during a siege.

(3) The *corona radiata,* of sun-rays, was adopted by Nero and his successors.

(4) The *corona triumphalis* (Fig. 57 C) was a laurel crown awarded to generals returning home from some great victory. In the beginning it was woven of real laurel leaves, but was later wrought in gold. After Julius Caesar's time, it became the diadem of all Roman emperors.

(5) The *corona myrtea,* made of myrtle leaves, was awarded to generals to wear at their *ovatio,* or small-triumph. It is also known as the *corona ovalis.*

(6) The *corona civica,* made of oak leaves, was given as an acknowledgment of bravery in rescuing a Roman citizen from death on the battlefield.

(7) The *corona graminea* was a crown of grass and was the highest military decoration possible. It was given only to a soldier or leader who had performed what amounted to almost a miracle of heroism on the battlefield. Other awards were made by a general, but the *corona graminea* was given only by unanimous consent of the entire army. Pliny says of this decoration, "It was also called 'crown of siege' [*corona obsidionalis*] in case a whole camp had been delivered from a siege or dishonorable terms. It was composed of green herbs picked on the spot where the besieged had been delivered."

Ornaments and Accessories

Rings were the one ornament in common use by men. In the early days of the republic they were of iron, plain or with a seal. The ring of gold was the special insignia of state officials, and was awarded to military leaders as an honor. Gold rings were highly prized and willed to descendants. During the second century B.C., the gold ring became the insignia of the equites or knights. (At the battle of Cannae, 216 B.C., Hannibal's army collected a bushel of gold rings from dead and captive Romans, to be sent to Carthage.) Earrings were used by men in and after the third century A.D.

A wand of office was used by certain officers. Lictors carried the *fasces,* a bundle of rods and an ax (the ax had to be removed inside the city limits) (Fig. 61 F). Each Roman legion had an elaborate *standard,* topped by an eagle (Fig. 61 G). A handkerchief (*sudarium*) was also carried. At the games, an *orarium,* or large napkin, was carried to be waved in token of applause. Oraria might be distributed gratuitously to audiences. Another type of napkin, used at table, was the *mappa.*

Make-up

Roman men used no artificial make-up until the later and more dissolute period of the empire, when dandies used paint to heighten their color and features.

Military Dress

Roman armor followed the general Greek types. Over a tunic or colobium of wool, the officer wore a leather jacket, which had rows of leather straps, dyed or gilded, about the armholes and the waist (Fig. 61 B). Sometimes there were two rows about the waist. These straps might be further ornamented with metal tabs, and fringed. Over this jacket was the corselet of bronze, fitted to the body. It was called the *lorica,* and was often engraved or embossed. It was hinged on the right side and fastened with straps and buckles on the left side. Metal straps over the shoulder (Fig. 61 A), and sometimes a colored scarf tied around the waist, helped to hold the lorica in place.

A helmet (usually of bronze) had an ornamental tuft of red feathers or red horsehair on the top (Fig. 57 A). Sometimes this extended down the back of the helmet (Fig. 57 E). A visor, a neck-piece, and a neck flange gave further protection. Boots completed the costume.

Another type of corselet was made of metal scales fastened to the leather jacket. For additional ornament, *phalera,* or large medallions, engraved or embossed, might be placed over the front of the corselet.

The ordinary soldier wore a leather jacket over which were four or more bands of bronze or iron; it was fastened in front, like a corset. Several of these metal bands were adjusted over the shoulders front and back to hold the corselet in place. The soldier's helmet was a plain, rounded covering with a jaw piece, visor, and neck flange, and perhaps a knot on top. Soldiers wore sandals and sometimes *braccae,* or trousers below the knee.

The shield was round, oblong, oval, hexagonal, or octagonal, and might be plain or engraved (Fig. 61 C D). The sword was short and rather wide (Fig. 61 E). Various types of spears, javelins, maces, battle-axes, and other weapons were used.

Mourning

Men let their hair grow and wore black garments and the toga pulla (if citizens) when in mourning.

COSTUME FOR CHILDREN

Little boys wore no clothing at all, or else the tunic, or a colobium in the simplest form (Fig. 59). About their necks they wore, on a cord or chain, the *bulla,* a locket given young children on the eighth day after birth and kept by them throughout life as a lucky charm. Though they put away the bulla when they assumed the toga virilis, they took pains to wear it again in moments of triumph (like the triumphal procession) to ward off envy and revenge.

COSTUME FOR THE LOWER CLASSES

These wore the subligaculum and the tunic or colobium. Their hair was worn long and shaggy; perones covered the feet, and felt cloaks and hoods were used for additional covering. The colors were dull.

COSTUME FOR WOMEN

The Grecian dress was adopted by Roman women with little change but with much enrichment and ornamentation. The *camisia,* a narrow under-tunic, was used over the loincloth, and a band was used to confine the breasts.

Stola

This garment was the Ionic chiton (rarely the Doric) with the long sleeve line (see chapter III, Fig. 51 A B   Fig. 52). It was sewed or fastened with pins at intervals up the arms. A simple cord might girdle the waist, though a cross-girdle was preferred. Several under-tunics were not unusual. In empire days, the cross-girdle was often of beads or jewels.

Dalmatica

This was a garment like the men's (Fig. 62 III), used after the third century A. D. For women it reached about ten inches, or less, from the ground. It was unbelted. Sleeves were decorated with bands, and the angusti clavi, of embroidery, were worn down the sides, as the rank demanded. About the fourth century A. D., the dalmatica was cut with outward-sloping lines in skirt and sleeve, which added grace to the garment. With this style a belt was used.

Mantles and Cloaks

The *palla* was the Roman version of the himation, and was draped like the Grecian wrap (Fig. 62 A). It was usually of wool. It went out of fashion about the third century A. D., but was revived in the fourth century. The *paenula* was a circular cloak which frequently had a cucullus, or hood, attached. The *ricinum,* or veil, was worn as a head covering. It was of various colors, sometimes shot with gold threads and fringed. In pagan times the bride wore a flame-colored or orange veil for the ceremony. The early Christian bride wore a purple and white veil.

Footwear

Women's shoes were similar to men's, but more delicately fashioned; they might be gilded or painted, and, in the empire period, they were frequently studded with jewels.

Hair

Fashions in hairdressing were many and varied. The general type of Greek coiffure was adopted, but elaborated. A favorite style consisted of many rows of curls piled high over the forehead, and small braids carried back into a large knot at the nape of the neck (Fig. 57 D). The hair was also worn parted and elaborately waved and coiled at the back (Fig. 57 B). Crowns like the stephane, but taller and thickly jeweled, were fashionable. Ladies used gold dust to powder their hair. After the first century B. C. they also dyed the hair red, in imitation of the Germans. Pads, false curls, and braids were profusely used.

Headdress

Besides the crowns, rows of pearls or beads were twined in the hair. For covering, the palla, the ricinum, the cucullus, or a sort of sun hat like the Greek one, was customary.

Ornaments and Accessories

These were many and often expensive. Rings, brooches, bracelets, hairpins, necklaces, cameos, intaglios, and especially earrings, were very popular. Seneca once complained that a Roman lady carried a fortune in her ear. Pearls were used for rings, brooches, pins, and, arranged in long strands, were wound about the neck and arms and even served as cross-girdles. Amber necklaces were also in great demand, and were very expensive, as they had to be imported from the Baltic Sea. Diamonds were also worn by fine ladies.

Roman ladies carried the sudarium, or handkerchief, and the orarium, to wave at the circus. They also carried balls of amber in gold or silver net bags; these they warmed by rubbing the hands, in order to enjoy the delicate fragrance. They also carried balls of crystal to keep the hands cool in hot weather. In the empire period, as a result of increased contact with northern barbarian tribes, furs were used for garments. Toilet boxes and jewel boxes, of carved wood or ivory, were in great demand.

Make-up

Roman women learned many arts of make-up. Ointments, cosmetics, and paints, rouges, eye-black, gold dust, and powders, and other aids to beauty were used.

Mourning

The hair was simply arranged; black garments and absence of ornament marked the mourning period.

COSTUME FOR CHILDREN

Little girls wore simple, short garments, shaped like the stola or dalmatica. No ornament was added.

COSTUME FOR THE LOWER CLASSES

As with the men, the dress consisted of the simplest versions of ordinary garments, made of coarse materials in dull colors.

EVOLUTION OF SACERDOTAL DRESS

With the adoption of Christianity at the Council of Nicaea (325 A.D.), the development of ecclesiastical garments followed. The priests, bishops, and other officers of the church adopted Greek and Roman garments, and gave meanings to certain vestments. Thus, the tunica talaris or tunica alba became the *alb* (Fig. 62 1), being originally white, but later being made in darker colors. A long, white woolen scarf, called the *orarium*, draped about the neck and falling almost to the feet, was adopted by the church. It was originally carried over the left shoulder by servants and slaves, a sort of towel for wiping vessels while serving. In Christian use it was worn by the deacon of the church over the left shoulder to clean vessels used at the Eucharist. In time it came to be folded into a long strip and in this form was called the *stole*. It was crossed on the breast to symbolize the crucifixion. Later, it was worn (directly over the alb) in various colors other than white, at the different religious seasons (Fig. 62 ii).

Next was worn the *dalmatic,* an adaptation of the dalmatica, over the stole and alb. It was of white, undecorated (Fig. 62 iii). It was adopted by the Christians because St. Cyprian, the martyr, wore a dalmatica at his death.

Next was worn the *maniple,* originally a handkerchief, or *sudarium,* used by the priest during celebration of high mass to wipe away the tears when overcome by the emotion of the ordeal. Folded, then later reduced to a narrow, short scarf, it became a purely symbolic part of the ecclesiastical dress (Fig. 62 iv).

Over the dalmatic for mass the priest might wear the *chasuble* (Fig. 62 v), or the *cope.* The chasuble was like the paenula, unopened down the front, and at first was worn with the hood. The cope was open down the front. Undoubtedly the custom of wearing several garments, one over the other, can be traced to the fact that the early Christians held their religious services in the catacombs or in cold basilicas, where many garments gave warmth; outer wraps (like the chasuble) were welcome additions.

The evolution of the himation or pallium (Fig. 62 A) in ecclesiastical dress is equally interesting. It was first adopted because Christ wore one; it evolved, as described above, to a strip about a foot wide wrapped around the body (Fig. 62 B); then, since it was so often worn over the circular paenula, it was wrapped about the neck (Fig. 62 C). It was seen to be similar in draping to the ewe lamb carried about the shoulders of the Good Shepherd (Fig. 62 D); therefore church authorities decreed that the pallium should be made of lamb's wool ("Agnus Dei"), blessed by the head of the church, ornamented with five crosses (symbolic of the five wounds of Christ), and cut in a circle about the shoulders with the long straight piece front and back center (Fig. 62 E F). This was the pallium presented to bishops as part of their investiture. The Investiture Conflict of the twelfth century was partly over this item of dress.

MODERN ADAPTATIONS

The same adaptations may be used as were suggested for Greece, with emphasis on richer fabrics, more jewelry, and finer accessories.

ROMAN WOMAN

ROMAN SENATOR

ROMAN KNIGHT

ROMAN GENERAL

PLATE III   CHAPTER IV

GOTH

CELTIC CHIEFTAN

VIKING

TEUTONIC

PLATE IV   CHAPTER V

CHAPTER V

THE DARK AGES

IMPORTANT PEOPLE AND EVENTS

400–500 A. D. 476, Fall of Rome. . . . 488, Theodoric the Ostrogoth conquered Italy, having slain Odovacar at Ravenna.

500–600 500, Buddhism introduced into Japan. . . . 507, Frankish kingdom founded by Clovis after his victory over the Visigoths at Poitiers. Through Chlotilde, his wife, he adopted Christianity; Clovis founded the Merovingian dynasty. . . . Fredegund, Brunhild. . . . 527–565, Justinian the Great at Byzantium, with Theodora, his wife. . . . Belisarius conquered the Goths and the Vandals. . . . Procopius, the historian. . . . Justinian Code promulgated. . . . Sancta Sophia rebuilt. . . . Period of highest Byzantine art . . . St. Ambrose introduced eight-note musical scale. . . . *Circa* 524, Boethius wrote *The Consolation of Philosophy*. . . . 529, Benedictine Order founded by St. Benedict. . . . 550, silkworms brought from China to Justinian by Nestorian monks; silk industry started at Byzantium. . . . Sidonius Apollinaris, Bishop of Clermont. . . . Bells made in France. . . . Quills used as pens. . . . 565, St. Columba, sent to Iona, Scotland, founded monastery. . . . 568, Lombards invaded Italy; Avars invaded Europe. . . . Pope Gregory the Great (590–603) sent St. Augustine (first Archbishop of Canterbury) and forty monks to Kent, England, where they converted the English king, Aethelberht. . . . Mass celebrated in England, June, 597. . . . Gregory of Tours wrote *History of the Franks*. . . . 593, block printing invented by Chinese. . . . 600, paper made from cotton in China. . . . Gregorian chant. . . . Isidore, Bishop of Seville, wrote of the Visigoths.

600–700 622, the Hegira, or flight of Mahomet. . . . Dagobert's bronze, gilded and jeweled throne. . . . 660, organ first used. . . . Caedmon and the English sacred songs. . . . "The Venerable Bede." . . . Beginning of T'ang dynasty in China. . . . 697, first Doge of Venice.

700–800 711, Tarik and Moors invaded Spain at strait dominated by a great rock – called Gib el Tarik (Gibraltar). . . . Saracens conquered Spain. . . . 718, St. Boniface went to Germany. . . . Bede's Ecclesiastical History (finished in 731). . . . 732, Charles Martel saved remainder of Europe from the Moors at Battle of Tours (or Poitiers). . . . 751, Pepin the Great founded Carolingian dynasty. . . . Pepin defeated the Lombards, bestowed lands in Italy on the pope, thus founding the Papal Estates. . . . 768–814, Charlemagne (Charles the Great, Carolus Magnus, Karl der Grosse) conquered many tribes, including the Lombards and the Moors; fought the Saxons, united the Frankish kingdom, encouraged art and learning. . . . The "Palace School," with Alcuin, an Anglo-Saxon, as teacher. . . . Charlemagne became friend of Haroun al Raschid, and rival of the Empress Irene at Byzantium. . . . His famous friend, Roland, killed at Roncesvalles. . . . Knowledge of Arabian studies in geography and astronomy disseminated in Europe. . . . Cynewulf, the rune-poet. . . . Benedict Biscop, educational work and church music. . . . Japanese capital at Kyoto. . . . In China, Ming Huang and famous beauty, Yang Kuei-Fei, and Li Po the poet. . . . 789, Northmen in Britain. . . . Anglo-Saxon Chronicle. . . . "From the fury of the Northmen, good Lord, deliver us!" . . . December 25, 800, Charlemagne crowned Emperor of Holy Roman Empire.

A Short Survey of Various Barbarian Tribes

I. Celts

Origin: probably Asia. First known in Europe in the sixth century B. C. The Greeks originally referred to all fair-haired peoples north of the Alps as *Keltoi*.

They settled in what are now France and Great Britain, though Gauls had first gone to southeastern Europe and to Asia Minor, where they settled in Galatia (the "foolish Galatians," to whom St. Paul wrote). In France, the Gauls settled over the entire area – north, middle, south, southeast, and southwest. The Bretons settled in northwestern France, the Belgae in northeastern France and in Belgium. The Bretons and Belgae both settled over most of England; the Picts settled in Scotland; and the Scots settled in northwestern Ireland before making Scotland their home. The Irish Celts were firmly ensconced in Ireland by 250 B. C. (Contemporary sources: Irish and Welsh songs and poems; church writings; Scotch songs and stories. For Gauls: Caesar, Tacitus, Strabo, Pliny, Plutarch.)

II. Teutons

Origin: Gothland or Gotaland, the southern part of the Scandinavian peninsula.

The different branches of the Teutons scattered, going southeast to the areas now called Russia and Germany, then west to what are now called France, northern Germany, Denmark, and England.

A. Cimbri and Teutons came down into the southeastern part of modern France; they were defeated by Marius and the Romans at Aquae Sextiae (102 B. C.) and at Vercellae (101 B. C.).

B. Goths settled along the Vistula in the first century A. D. About 250 A. D., they settled in Thrace. Here they were held in check by Aurelian and Constantine. Finally they crossed the Danube. They divided into East or Ostrogoths, and West or Visigoths.

    1. The Visigoths, after defeating Valens at Adrianople, went west and with Alaric as their leader, sacked Rome, 410 A. D. They continued westward and settled in Spain.

    2. The Ostrogoths, under Theodoric, moved west and controlled all Italy by 476 A. D.

C. The Germans settled in modern Germany, along the Rhine. They fought the Romans, defeating Varus and his legions at Teutoburg Forest, 9 A. D. They long held Roman civilization at bay. (Contemporary sources: Caesar, Pliny, Tacitus, Strabo, Plutarch, Ulfilas.)

D. Angles, Saxons, and Jutes settled between the rivers Rhine and Weser. In 449 A. D., under Hengest and Horsa, they invaded and settled England. About 800 A. D. they combined and were called Anglo-Saxons, under Egbert, a Saxon king. Charlemagne clashed with European Saxons at the end of the eighth century A. D. (Contemporary sources: St. Boniface, Bede's Ecclesiastical History, Beowulf, Caedmon, Alfred the Great.)

E. The Vandals overran Gaul and Spain, and settled in Africa. Under Gaiseric (or Genseric) they sacked Rome in 455 A. D.

F. The Burgundians migrated from the Rhine to the Rhone, and established a kingdom which lasted until 534 A. D.; later, revived as a dukedom, it flourished, particularly under its great leader, Charles the Bold, who was finally conquered by Louis XI and the Swiss legions in the fifteenth century.

G. The Lombards settled in the Po valley, in northern Italy, and after long conflict with the Romans, were conquered by Pepin the Frank in the eighth century A. D.

H. The Franks migrated from the shores of the Baltic to Gaul. They united under Clovis (481–511 A. D.). Charles Martel, Mayor of the Palace, conquered the Moors at Tours, 732 A. D., checking the Mohammedan invasion. Pepin conquered the Lombards in 751 A. D. and was made king. Charlemagne fought the Moors at Roncesvalles, and was crowned as head of the Holy Roman Empire by Pope Leo III, Christmas Day, 800 A. D., in Rome. (Contemporary sources: Gregory of Tours, Sidonius Apollinaris, Agathias.)

I. The Vikings (Northmen, Norsemen, Normans) migrated from Gothland to England and Iceland. In the ninth century they went to Russia (Novgorod), 862 A. D. Canute, a Dane, ruled England, 1017 A. D. Danes visited North America under Leif Ericsson, 1000 A. D. Normans settled in northern France, 911 A. D. Under William the Conqueror they invaded and conquered England, 1066 A. D. Normans settled in Sicily, 1017 A. D. (Contemporary sources: Viking Edda and sagas – Heimskringla, Eyrbyggia, Voluspa, etc; Anglo-Saxon Chronicle; Bayeux tapestry.)

III. Byzantines

Origin: A mixture of Greek, Roman, and Asia Minor peoples. They rose to great heights under Justinian (527–565 A. D.). Belisarius, his general, drove the Ostrogoths from Italy, and the Vandals from Africa. Justinian built hospitals, forts, churches (among them, Sancta Sophia), and aqueducts; he codified the law (Justinian Code). Later, the Byzantine Empress Irene ruled at the same time Charlemagne ruled in Europe. (Contemporary source for Justinian: Procopius.)

IV. Mohammedans (Moors)

Origin: Originally a religious sect of Arabs, led by Mahomet, who fled from Mecca to Medina (the Hegira) in 622 A. D. His followers (Moors) conquered Syria and Egypt, and crossed at Gibraltar (meaning "Rock of Tarik," the leader), and conquered Spain in 711 A. D. They were checked in their circle of conquest by Charles Martel at Tours, 732 A. D. They remained in Spain, however, until the last of the Moors were driven from Granada in 1492. (Contemporary sources: The Koran; Gregory of Tours.)

V. Huns

Origin: Doubtful, but probably Asia. Entered Europe about 372 A. D. They were defeated at Chalons, 451 A. D., and dispersed soon after.

The warriors of Rome no longer trod, heavy-footed, the western world; the cothurnus had shrunk to the loose buskin; the shield had become a mirror in which to gaze and forget. Byzantium, last heir to the glory of Greece and the grandeur of Rome, abandoned herself to admiration of her own image, until the view was obscured by a dark cloud sweeping down from the north.

Out of this cloud emerged a new and lusty force – an infant force which pushed its way through the gloom of forest and interlacing branches; for it was itself as absorbing as night, as stout as the rugged tree-trunks which marked its passage.

This force was the family of barbarian conquerors, the Goths, Vandals, Teutons, Saxons, Franks, Celts – these infants of a new order, as numerous as the branches of the forest. They had to learn their letters, humbly, from the classic sources, Greece and Rome; they had to learn manners and the rules of decorum from regal Byzantium; they had to learn the catechism of Christian faith from the Patriarchs of Antioch, of Byzantium, of Rome; but in their own homes, the nurseries of future European nations, they kept their own ways, their own salutary discipline.

These barbarians were frugal, they were brave, they were romantic. Their dress reflected these qualities. Girded as they were for constant struggle against the elements and mankind, they evolved a costume that was close-fitting, that was sturdy, that displayed their physical fitness. They brought into use a new trimness, a durability, and an economy of material that, in its spiritual significance, was to save a decadent world.

COSTUME

GENERAL CHARACTERISTICS

The barbarians were a nomadic group and wandered much from place to place. The country they frequented was rather cold, with much rain, and was deeply forested with dense undergrowth, through which they had to make their way. Their clothing, therefore, had these general characteristics: (1) crude materials, though warm and durable, with trim-fitting lines; (2) general use of trousers, or braccae, for the men; (3) short, snug tunics; (4) close-fitting sleeves; (5) subdued, but elementary, coloring; (6) extensive use of metallic jewelry.

Materials

The use of leather skins, or hides of wild beasts, with or without the fur or hair, was common among most barbaric tribes. Wool from their own flocks was woven into coarse or fine cloth. Linen, of various textures, was a staple cloth. Silk did not come into use until the eighth century.

Colors

Subdued colors were used. The natural color of the wool or linen sufficed for many garments. Natural vegetable dyes were used to produce deep saffron, dark and light blue, olive green, red, brown, gray, and similar shades. Red, blue, and green were the favorite colors. White was little worn.

Underclothes

It seemed to be a general custom for the men to wear an undershirt with short sleeves, and perhaps a type of short drawers. The women wore a long undershirt like a chemise. In cold weather women added one garment on top of another, so that a person might wear one, two, or even three shirts, or long tunics, as the temperature demanded. The outer garment usually had wider sleeves than the undergarments.

CELTS

(GAULS, BRITONS, PICTS, SCOTS, BRETONS, BELGAE)

COSTUME FOR MEN

According to Pliny and Diodorus Siculus, the Gauls in France and the Britons used fine wool dyed purple, scarlet, saffron, and other bright colors. It was woven into stripes or checks, for lightweight or summer garments. This cloth, called *breach,* or *brycan,* is probably the origin of the Scotch plaid or tartan, called "the garb of old Gaul." The word *tartan* was probably derived from the Gaelic *tarstin* or *tarsuin,* meaning "across." For winter, plain fabrics, leather, or hides with the skin on were used.

Tunic

The tunic, with either short or long sleeves, reached halfway to the knee, for younger men; for older men, the tunic was fuller and longer – about to the calf of the leg. In battle, the torso was bared and often painted blue with woad. A short wrap-around garment, similar to a short petticoat, was called the *phillibeg* (Gaelic *feile-beag*), or *kelt* (Lowland Scotch *kilt*).

Trousers

With the tunic were worn trousers, or braccae (Fig. 69 A), of plain or checked material, usually tied in about the ankles with leather thongs. The predominating color of the tunic and braccae was red. Sometimes a longer tunic was worn, and the legs were left bare, or painted with woad, or pricked with designs in woad.

Mantle

Over the body garments was worn the *sagum,* or mantle (from *saic,* a skin or hide, the original cloak), a short rectangle about three by five feet; it was usually of a solid color, blue, black, or crimson. Chieftains, however, might wear longer sagums, lined inside or out with fur (Fig. 75). Priests wore certain emblematic colors. The *druids,* those of highest rank, wore "proud" white, with a garland of oak leaves; the *bards,* or poets, wore blue, emblematic of peace; the *vates,* or professors of astronomy and medicine, wore green, the prevailing tone of nature.

Footwear

Shoes or sandals were of leather with flat soles. In some types the leather covered the toes and arch only (Fig. 88 A D). Another type, with a seam up the center, covered

Fig. 65

the entire foot (Fig. 88 B). In another type, the leather was gathered about the ankle with thongs (Fig. 88 E).

Hair

The usual arrangement consisted of loose locks about the forehead and long curls over the nape of the neck. Men of rank shaved their chins, but favored uncouth mustaches of great length and thickness. Common men wore beards. The Gauls were usually blond or red-haired.

Headdress

Though they usually went bareheaded, the Gauls and Britons often wore a conical cap (from *cab,* a hut).

Ornaments and Accessories

The Gauls wore rings on the middle finger, bracelets, and armlets. *Torques* (Fig. 87 M) were worn only by men of rank; they were of twisted wires of gold, silver, brass, or even iron. Beads and ornaments of coal have been found. Round brooches were used to pin the sagum, usually on the right shoulder, or at center front.

Make-up

The Celtic tribes had a curious custom of painting their torsos or entire bodies with woad. In fact, the Picts were so called by the Romans from their custom of "picturing" their bodies with woad – a whitish, sticky substance, derived from the leaves of the woad, or pastel plant. When it is properly prepared, it takes on a deep blue color.

Military Dress

The Gauls wore helmets of leather or brass (Fig. 86 D), with metal spikes or animal horns decorating those of the chieftains (Fig. 75   Fig. 86 A). Breastplates or gorgets of gold and brass (Fig. 86 G), or sometimes of scales or rings (Fig. 75) were used. For weapons they carried the dagger (Fig. 86 K), javelin, spear, and a long, broad sword (*spatha*) (Fig. 86 J). The Britons carried a leaf-shaped sword, of mixed metal. The Gallic shield was round, oval, or hexagonal. The British shield was round or oblong. The *celt,* a small bronze or iron ax or hatchet, was an indispensable part of the warrior's outfit. The word *Celt* was adopted later as the group name.

COSTUME FOR CHILDREN

A Celtic boy wore a simple adaption of his elders' styles (Fig. 66).

Costume for Women

British and Gallic women wore the tunic long, to the ankles; over this, women of higher rank wore a shorter tunic (*gwyn* or *gown*, Fig. 67), short-sleeved and perhaps of checked material; over the gown was worn, for warmth, a cloak of coarse, heavy material, fastened with a *fibula*, or brooch. Boadicea was fond of garments dyed saffron (an orange color, obtained from the stigmas and styles of the crocus). Sandals, similar to the men's, covered the feet. The hair, especially of the upper classes, was worn long and flowing. The color was blond or red.

Ornaments

The torque (Fig. 87 M) of gold was the favorite ornament of women of rank.

Fig. 66

Fig. 83

In addition, rings (Fig. 87 D), bracelets, and other ornaments affected by the men, were common.

Costume for the Lower Classes

Animal skins, with or without the hair, bearskins, sheepskins, or coarse, dull-colored cloth, were the materials used by the common people, men and women. Instead of ornamented pins, they used thorns for fastening tunics and cloaks. Bare feet or crude sandals marked them also.

TEUTONS OR GERMANS

CIMBRI, TEUTONS

Little is known of the costumes of these early Germans, who swept down from the Baltic and fought the Romans at Vercellae and Aquae Sextiae, 101 B. C. In monumental drawings they are shown wearing short tunics, braccae, and cloaks on the right shoulder.

GOTHS

Costume for Men

Both Ostrogoths and Visigoths, while still in the barbaric state, wore essentially the same type of costume. Later, when they mingled with Byzantines or other groups, Ostrogoths and Visigoths adopted the styles of the older civilizations.

Tunic

The tunic was of homespun linen of a dun or fawn color (Fig. 68). It had sleeves so long they could be pulled over the hands for warmth, or shoved back over the wrist. The tunic opened in front, lapping over on a diagonal. Neck, opening, and lower edge might be edged with fur, goat, lamb, marten, etc. The tunic reached more than halfway to the knee. A belt held it in at the waist.

Trousers

Braccae, or loose trousers, were worn, tied in at the ankles. Often these were cross-gartered with cord.

Footwear

Shoes of leather covered foot and instep and were tied about the ankle.

Hair

The hair was worn long, over the nape of the neck; the beard was cut round or square, and mustaches were universal.

Headdress

A hood not unlike the Phrygian cap, but extending down over the nape of the neck, was general (Fig. 65 E Fig. 68).

Military Dress

Gothic arms consisted of shields, oval or hexagonal (Fig. 68), arrows and bow, spear, knife, and long, pointed sword.

Costume for Women

Little is known of the costume of Gothic women. On Trajan's Column and on sculptured monuments in Mayence, Bordeaux, Nîmes, Lincoln, Chester, etc., the women are shown in long tunics similar to the Romans' dress, but much simpler in cut and arrangement. The jewelry, heavy and barbaric in type, indicated the origin of the wearer.

FRANKS

Costume for Men

A. Early Franks:

Tunic

The early Merovingian Franks (around 450 A. D.) in battle often left the torso bare, though at other times they wore snug-fitting tunics which almost reached the knee (Fig. 69 B). These tunics had short sleeves and were girdled with a fairly wide belt studded with metal disks. Sometimes a striped material was used. Another tunic, of fur (otter, marten, etc.), might be worn by men of higher rank, over or under the ordinary tunic (Fig. 69 B).

Braccae

Slender braccae, tied at the ankles, covered the legs (Fig. 88 B), though these were often left bare.

Mantle

The cloak, or mantle, was a rectangle fastened in front or on the right shoulder. It was of woolen cloth, plain or horizontally striped and was called a sagum (Fig. 69 B). Sidonius Apollinaris described a cloak of green with a scarlet border.

Footwear

Footwear consisted of sandals of soft leather, rolled up over the ankles (Fig. 88 B) or else cut out over the instep (Fig. 88 D). *Pedules,* or cross-wrappings up to the calf of the leg, were popular (Fig. 88 C D). They were sometimes wrapped bandage-fashion (Fig. 86 E).

Hair

These early Franks wore their hair fairly long. It was fastened on top of the head, so that the ends cascaded like a fountain (Fig. 65 A Fig. 69 B). Chieftains wore the hair long, and often braided (Fig. 65 B). Other characteristics were long, drooping mustaches, shaven chins, and shaven napes.

Military Dress

They carried a two-edged ax, called the *francisque,* suspended by a loop from the wrist; in addition, a long spear and a round shield with a sharp-pointed knob in the middle (Fig. 69 B). In battle, they twirled the shields rapidly, to terrify the enemy. A dagger might be worn at the right side; at the left, suspended from a baldric, was the long sword (Fig. 69 B).

Ornaments and Accessories

Ornaments were many and elaborate. The Franks were expert craftsmen. Their fibulae (Fig. 87 G K L) were especially beautiful, of bronze, brass, gold, or other metals, gilded, enameled, and set with stones. Rings, armlets, bracelets (on the right arm) (Fig. 87 F), earrings of gold or bronze, necklaces of glass beads or gold, and buckles (Fig. 87 C J) of many sizes and shapes, some enameled and some jeweled, were in general use.

Make-up

Except for tattooing and the occasional use of woad, artificial make-up was not indulged in.

B. Later Franks:

The later Franks, in the time of Charlemagne (800 A. D.), wore, on ordinary occasions, a linen or wool tunic, cut full (Fig. 71 A B). The sleeves were long, and wide at the armhole but close-fitting at the wrist (Fig. 71 A E). A belt confined the tunic at the waist, which was slightly bloused. The skirt of the tunic was full and reached almost to the knees. About the bottom edge might run a colored border of another material, or one embroidered in silk.

Braccae

Braccae (or *braies*) covered the legs (Fig. 69 A   Fig. 71 A F); these might be cross-gartered to the knees with leather thongs, often studded with metal disks. It was customary to leave the legs entirely bare, or to the knees with the lower portion cross-gartered. An under-tunic of linen might be worn (Fig. 71 A).

Mantle

A cloak, or sagum, of wool lined with silk or fur, circular along the lower edge, was fastened on the right shoulder with a fibula or brooch (Fig. 71 A). This cloak might be striped – the *saga Fresonica* (Fig. 69 B). For extra warmth, a fur tunic might be worn over this mantle, in the early Frankish way. Charlemagne wore a Venetian mantle, green or blue, and rectangular. For court or state dress, Charlemagne and others after him adopted Byzantine dress (see below for descriptions).

Footwear

Footwear was more elaborate than in the early period. The leather was painted or set with stones and embroidered in colors. White wool pedules, cross-gartered, were popular (Fig. 88 C E).

Hair

The hair was worn fairly short, and brushed back of the ears, forming a frame for the face.

Headdress

A favorite type of headgear was a round cap with a high, raised front, ornamented with an embroidered band (Fig. 71 A C).

Ornaments and Accessories

Ornaments were, if possible, richer than in the earlier period. Mosaics were very popular. St. Eloi of Cadillac (588–659) was famous for his goldsmith work. He made two jeweled chairs of gold for Clotaire II, besides numerous brooches, buckles, fibulae (Fig. 87 A C G H J K L P), and the like for both Clotaire and Dagobert. St. Eloi is the patron saint of goldsmiths. Heavy collars of gold plaques set with jewels were worn by great nobles.

Crowns were adopted, probably from the Byzantines (Fig. 71 A D). A pouch, or pocket, was worn at the belt. It usually contained a short eating knife, money, comb (Fig. 87 O), knife-sharpener, and other necessities. Gloves (called *wanti*), with the thumb separate, were made of skins, with the fur inside.

Military Dress

Later Franks carried the same types of armor as the earlier Franks, with the addition of certain Byzantine items. The long lance was one addition; so also was the heavy type of Greco-Roman sword (Fig. 86 J). Leather jackets, plain or scaled with leather or gilded horn, were distinctively Frankish. The helmets also were the four-cornered, basin-shaped ones worn by many of the Teutonic tribes (Fig. 65 D). A large dagger, called a *scramasaxe,* was carried at the right side of the belt.

Fig. 67

Fig. 69   A   B

FRONT   BACK

Fig. 68

Fig. 70

Fig. 78

Fig. 84

Fig. 85

Fig. 79

Mourning

Mourning was expressed by dull or black garments and general disarray.

Costume for Children

Children wore the simplest of tunics. For wraps they used cloaks with hoods attached.

Costume for the Lower Classes

The simple linen or leather tunic sufficed for ordinary people, with braies of the same; however, the latter were usually cross-gartered far up the leg. Sleeveless fur jackets or sheepskins were also worn. A long, loose cloak, with or without a hood, was worn for warmth. Shoes were of untanned leather, gathered up over the instep. The hair was cut short about the forehead. Beards and mustaches were allowed to grow fairly long.

Costume for Women

A. Early Franks:

Early Frankish women wore linen garments, often dyed purple. The skirt was a rectangle gathered about the waist. The waist was sleeveless; it might, indeed, consist of nothing more than a sort of suspender arrangement, leaving the breasts bare (Fig. 70). Later, the women wore the *camisia* (chemise), an under-tunic retained as a sleeping garment at night; sometimes (as was Queen Radegund's) it was embroidered in gold. Over the camisia might be worn the sleeveless tunic.

Mantle

Capes or cloaks similar to the men's, but longer, were worn by the women.

Footwear

Women adopted a type of boot or buskin which encased the ankle and the lower part of the leg.

Hair

Hair and hairdress were very important to Frankish women. A free woman always wore her hair long (Fig. 70). It was a grave offense to cut off a woman's hair; under some circumstances even the death penalty might be incurred. Unmarried girls had to wear their hair loose and flowing, without ornament. Married women might braid their hair and adorn it with ribbons or garlands. They also wore a sort of cap or coif called an *obbo*. (If a man disarranged this obbo, he could be fined fifteen solidi.)

Ornaments

Rings, brooches, necklaces, fibulae, and other ornaments used by the men were adopted by the women, in even richer form (Fig. 87).

B. Later Franks:

Later Frankish women (of the Carolingian period) adopted more elaborate dress. Roman costume was copied, with the addition of the barbaric type of jewelry. Two tunics were usually worn. The under-tunic was long and scanty, with long, tight sleeves; the outer tunic was short and full, with elbow-length sleeves cut wide and full. Often the edges of the tunics were banded with contrasting colors. The belt was wide and shaped in front. The hair was done in Greco-Roman fashion, and covered with a veil, which often reached almost to the ground and concealed much of the hair.

Mourning

Mourning was evidenced by black garments.

Costume for Children

Children wore simple tunics with no ornamentation, and cloaks like the women's.

Costume for the Lower Classes

Women of the lower classes wore simple skirts, suspender waists or sleeveless tunics, and braided hair (or flowing, if unmarried).

SAXONS, VIKINGS, LOMBARDS, ANGLES, JUTES

Costume for Men

Early Saxon dress was very similar to that of the Franks and other Teutonic tribes. As time went on, the costume came to consist of a tunic of linen or wool (often scarlet in color) with short sleeves. When inflamed with the frenzy of battle, the Vikings tore off this tunic, or shirt, which they called *serk,* and went stripped, or *berserk.* The Vikings called the tunic the *kyrtil* (Fig. 74 Fig. 75). Over this was worn a leather corselet with scales of horn or metal, sometimes gilded. This corselet, called by the Vikings a *bryngia,* extended below the hips, and was frequently held in by a broad leather belt with bosses of metal (Fig. 75). From this belt knives, daggers, and other small weapons were suspended. Scabbards were of wood covered with skin. The Lombards were fond of ornamenting their tunics with embroidery in varied colors.

A mantle of wool or an animal skin was fastened about the neck (Fig. 69 B Fig. 75). The legs were left bare or were covered with wrappings, cross-gartered to the knee; or braccae (*braeke*) were worn, gathered in at the ankle only (Fig. 69 A B), or cross-gartered (Fig. 75).

The Saxon dress is shown in Fig. 74 and Fig. 75.

Footwear

Footwear consisted of skin or leather shoes gathered over the instep (Fig. 88 D).

Hair

The hair was worn long and flowing; drooping mustaches, with or without beards, were worn; the hair of these tribes was usually golden yellow or red. Beards were respected; like the Mohammedans, the Saxons touched the beard when making an oath. (The Lombards wore unusually long beards, from which they got their Latin name, *Langobardi,* or Long-beards.)

Headdress

In battle, a helmet (Viking *hjalm*) of metal was worn; it was four-cornered, with flaps of metal, and a ridge or other ornament on top (Fig. 65 D). Sometimes it was a round helmet with a ridge (Fig. 74), or with a ridge and side-flaps (Fig. 74 inset). Often two horns of animals, one on either side, gave a ferocious air to the helmet

Fig.74

Fig.75

(Fig. 65 B   Fig. 75). The Vikings' helmets were adorned with the black wings of the raven, a bird sacred to them. The Saxons also wore these wings (Fig. 74).

Ornaments and Accessories

The torque, or necklace, was in general use (Fig. 74), as were also armlets, wide bracelets, brooches, and fibulae of many types (Fig. 87). Jeweled circlets of gold were worn by rulers, who also carried scepters.

Military Dress

Viking arms consisted of iron-headed spears, with very long shafts; of axes, single- or double-bladed, often suspended from the belt by a loop (Fig. 86 C); of iron swords in skin-covered wooden scabbards; of shields, round or oblong, of metal or of wood or rushes covered with hides, and decorated with varying designs (Fig. 86 H). Spiked clubs (Fig. 86 B) were also carried. The *seax,* or *saxe,* a short sword (Fig. 86 F), gave the tribal name to the Saxons.

Costume for Women

In the earlier periods, Saxon women wore hempen garments similar to the Roman tunica. They were fairly wide, extended to the ankles, and were long-sleeved or sleeveless (Fig. 76 A B). The lower edge of the garments might have a band of contrasting color.

Later on, women of the upper classes adopted the custom of wearing two garments, one over the other. The under-tunic was long, with short sleeves. The over-tunic reached below the knee, was split up the sides, and fastened on either shoulder. A narrow belt confined it at the waist. A hip belt was placed at low hip level; the belt was wide and profusely ornamented. From this belt hung a purse (Fig. 76 A C), a dagger, and housewifely accessories such as scissors, keys, and the like (Fig. 77).

Women of the lower classes wore a short woolen, leather, or linen jacket, with short sleeves; the jacket fastened in front with brooches (Fig. 78 and pattern). Sometimes the jacket was of fur, turned inside, with the lower edge turned over to make a trimming. The skirt, a rectangle, was gathered about the waist, and held in place by a broad leather belt ornamented with small metal bosses (Fig. 78); from the belt hung the dagger.

Mantle

Mantles of cloth or fur were fastened over the shoulder.

Footwear

Soft sandals gathered over the instep were worn; they might be of fine or coarse material, according to the station of the wearer.

Hair

Ladies of rank wore their hair flowing, with bands of twisted gold or silver wires about their heads (Fig. 77). The lower classes usually braided the hair to hang down on either side (Fig. 76).

Ornaments and Accessories

Rings, bracelets, armlets, necklaces, earrings, collars, brooches, pins, and other ornaments were popular. Even the poorer classes wore armlets, collars, and brooches (Fig. 87).

Mourning

Early illuminations show funerals, but the mourners are not clothed in any particular fashion or color. "Widows' garments" are mentioned in Saxon records, but these seem to be given no definite characteristics. Probably somber hues and absence of decoration contrasted them with the highly embroidered garments of ordinary life. With the Vikings this was not true. Black was a favorite, if not a general, color with them; because of this they were called "black Danes," or the "black army." In the Danish ballad, *Child Dyring,* the hero is represented as riding to the bridal feast in "black sendell." It is to be remembered that their national standard bears a black raven.

In general, the costumes of the Vandals and Burgundians did not differ markedly from those of the other Teutonic tribes discussed above.

By the seventh and eighth centuries peoples in Britain, known as Anglo-Saxons, developed a distinct garb, combining features of the Roman, early Saxon, British, Frankish, and other contributing influences.

COSTUME FOR MEN

Adhelm, Bishop of Sherborne, writing in the seventh century, indicated that woolen cloth was the most commonly used material; however, linen was in general use, and silk (*seolc*) and other valuable materials of foreign manufacture had been introduced by the eighth century. Adhelm also mentioned the passion of the English for weaving cloth of red, purple, blue, green, and other bright colors. However, very few accurate descriptions or pictorial representations of costume existed until about the tenth century. At that time the costume was as follows:

Underclothes

Those in general use were of linen, cut tunic style.

Tunic

Over the under-tunic, in summer, was worn a linen tunic (Aglo-Saxon *roc* – Fig. 79); in winter, a woolen one, with ornamental borders. The rounded neck was slit four or five inches down the front, so that the garment might be easily donned. Embroidery or banding emphasized the slit and the rounded neckline. The sleeves were long and snug, and were wrinkled, or shoved back over the forearm from wrist to elbow. In the crude pictures of the time, these lines often look like bracelets (Fig. 80 A C). Perhaps one bracelet was worn at the wrist, but the rest of the lines were folds of the sleeve. The custom of using such long sleeves probably arose from the comfort to be obtained in cold weather by pulling the sleeve down over the hand, as a sort of mitten. The roc, or tunic (Fig. 79), was often ornamented around the neck and hem (as mentioned above) with colored borders, woven or embroidered in designs; these borders might be of silk. The tunic might have the two angusti clavi of the Romans, signifying a gentleman of rank. As worn by kings, the roc was longer, of richer material, and wider in the skirt than were those worn by ordinary men (Fig. 79 and pattern).

Trousers

The legs were covered with long drawers or *brech,* also called *hosa.* Over the hosa were wrapped bands (called *scanc-beorg,* or leg guards) of wool, linen, or leather, to the knee (Fig. 79); these were rolled like the ordinary modern soldier's puttees (Fig. 86 E), or else cross-gartered, sandal-wise. Kings wore leg guards of gold. Men of

Fig.71

Fig.72

Fig.73

Fig.76

Fig.80

Fig.81

Fig.82

Fig.86

action wore hosa of leather (*scin-hosa*). Sometimes the hosa reached only to the knee and were met by stockings or socks (see below).

Mantle

The *mantle* (*mentil* or *mantil*) was worn by warriors and men of rank. It was similar to the Roman abolla and the Gallic sagum, and was fastened sometimes on the breast, sometimes on one or both shoulders, with brooches or fibulae. A fastening much favored by the English was a ring, through which the cloth was drawn (Fig. 80 D). Peculiar to the Anglo-Saxons was the custom of removing the cloak over the head, leaving the fastening intact.

Footwear

Socks (*socca*) of wool or coarse linen were worn, as well as long hose; some long hose had ornamental borders, and when cross-gartered looked rather like modern golf stockings. The Saxon shoe (*sceo*) was usually painted black, with an opening down the center, secured by a leather lacing. The shoes seem to have had soft soles.

Hair

The hair was worn parted in the middle, and long, beyond the nape of the neck (Fig. 79), or even shoulder length, despite the fact that priests inveighed against long hair. Beards, which seem to have been usually forked, were worn by elderly men. Younger men's faces were clean-shaven.

Headdress

Men usually went bareheaded, even the clergy; sometimes a cap similar to the Phrygian was used. Kings, however, wore jeweled circlets of gold, or more elaborate square crowns, such as the one worn by King Edgar (Cotton MS., Tiberius, A III) (Fig. 81). In battle, of course, helmets were worn.

Ornaments and Accessories

Besides wearing the crown or diadem, kings carried scepters. Men (and women) wore gloves (Anglo-Saxon *glof*); sometimes the glove was called *hand-sceo*, "hand-shoe." Men ornamented their belts with metal decorations and with gold and jewels. They wore gold and silver chains, crosses (after their conversion by St. Augustine, 597 A. D.), strings of amber or other beads, and elaborately wrought rings, brooches, and buckles. Metal ornaments were often beautifully enameled. One such ornament – of gold, enameled and inscribed "Aelfred me haet gewercan" (Alfred ordered me to be made) – was found in the Isle of Athelney, the refuge of Alfred the Great, and was probably the top of a scepter or staff. King Athelwulf's ring is also extant, in the British Museum.

Make-up

Anglo-Saxons still practiced tattooing, an art learned from the early Britons; a law passed against it in 785 A. D. is evidence of its late survival. Strutt also mentions the fact that, in early Anglo-Saxon manuscripts, hair is often painted blue; this may or may not infer the custom of tinting or dyeing the hair. It is very doubtful, however, as the censorious priests would certainly have attacked such a custom.

Military Dress

As warfare was a principal occupation of the men, the military dress was in constant use. Either the linen roc or tunic was worn, with perhaps a metal collar or breast-guard (Fig. 86 G); or a leather corselet; or a coat of mail or iron rings, called *gehrynged byrn*. Adhelm had a famous enigma (seventh century) about chain mail; many illustrations of armor with chain (or later, ringed) mail are seen in manuscripts of that time and later. Often these mailed coats were split front and back, for riding horseback.

In battle, the Anglo-Saxons wore a cloth or leather helmet shaped very much like the Phrygian cap (sometimes banded with metal). Conical helmets of leather or metal were also used (Fig. 86 D).

Shields were oval and convex, with a metal *umbo,* or boss. They were faced with gilt, or were painted with circles, usually on a white ground. Some were small; others were large enough to protect the entire body. The body of the shield was of leather.

Weapons were of iron and included long broadswords, two-edged daggers, javelins, long spears (often barbed), long-handled axes called *bills,* and double axes; also used was the curved sword-dagger, called *seax* (Fig. 86 K). Spurs without rowels were used by the Anglo-Saxons.

Ecclesiastical Costume

At the separation of the Latin and Greek churches (ninth century), ecclesiastical costume became uniform through Christian Europe. The *casula,* or chasuble, by the sixth century was regularly worn; St. Augustine mentions it particularly. The dalmatic, adopted and made obligatory by Pope St. Sylvester (fourth century), was worn by women, saints, and martyrs, as well as men. The *stola,* or stole – often with fringed ends – and the maniple, as well as the alb, were in general use. The pallium, by the ninth century, was embroidered with crosses. The miter is shown as early as the tenth century.

Costume for Women

Anglo-Saxon women wore several garments, one over the other. The short *cemes,* or chemise, never shown in illustrations, was described by contemporary writers. Over this was the *tuneca,* like the Roman tunic. It was long and full, with long, tight sleeves, often shoved back in rolls like the men's sleeves, confined at the wrist by bracelets or by a band of embroidery (Fig. 80 A C). Over this was worn the *gwyn* (or *gunna,* gown), with loose, elbow-length sleeves; it was often short, reaching about halfway from the knees to the ground. The gunna was usually ornamented with a border about the neck, sleeves, and lower edge, embroidered or woven in bright colors, in patterns of rings, flowers, sprigs, and stars; sometimes the border was emphasized with gold threads. (Anglo-Saxon women were famous for their superior skill in spinning, weaving, and embroidering; in the *Gesta Gulielmi ducis,* p. 211, it is said that "English women excell all others in needlework, and in the art of embroidering with gold.") Later, the bottom edge was not straight, but on a downward diagonal from right to left (Fig. 80 A B). Often this border was drawn tight, the material of the gunna being gathered into it (not unlike the overskirt popular in 1910). A panel of the same decoration, up the center front, was adopted about the tenth century. There was also a kyrtil,

Fig. 77

or kirtle, which may have been an outer or inner garment, short or long. As it is usually described as white, it probably was an under-tunic, a sort of petticoat.

Mantle

The mantle was similar to the Roman palla. Often it was draped low front and back, like a chasuble.

Footwear

Sosa, or *socca,* as well as hose, or long stockings, were probably worn by women, but the long gowns concealed them. The shoes, when visible, were generally painted black, though occasionally other colors were also used. They were pointed at the toes, fastened at the instep by a thong, and, for ladies of noble rank, they were stamped or punched in various patterns. Otherwise they were not dissimilar in shape and make to the men's.

Hair

As the head was always covered, it is impossible to judge from illustrations what styles of hair arrangement were used. Adhelm, however, described a wife as having long, flowing hair, curled by a heated iron; in the Anglo-Saxon poem *Judith* the maid has "twisted" (curled?) locks. The Lady Godiva (eleventh century), as a noblewoman, had long hair. In fact, long, flowing hair was a sign of freedom and rank. Braiding in two long plaits was allowed, but on her wedding day the bride always unbraided her tresses and wore her hair rippling free over her shoulders as a sign of her rank as well as of her virginity. After marriage, early Anglo-Saxon ladies cut their hair short, as a symbol of servitude to their husbands. Later, however, this custom was abandoned, and the bride was required only to wind the hair closely about the head. The veil over the head was called the headrail (*heafod-hroegel*) (Fig. 80 A). It was of linen or silk draped over the head and sometimes carried around under the chin and over the left shoulder.

Gold head bands, or circlets, were sometimes worn over the headrail, especially in later centuries (Fig. 80 A).

Make-up

Adhelm mentions the custom of ladies curling their hair and painting their cheeks red with stibnite. Blue hair is shown in many illuminations (but see above, pp. 80–81).

Mourning

Black garments were in general use by both men and women for mourning; during the mourning period embroidery and other decorations were not worn.

COSTUME FOR CHILDREN

Children of both sexes of the middle and lower classes went naked until about six years old. Children of rank were clothed like their elders except that the mantle, or cloak, was usually much shorter.

COSTUME FOR THE LOWER CLASSES

Both men and women are represented as never going barefooted, though often barelegged. However, in Harleian MS. No. 603, women gossips are shown barefooted, and the children in their arms are naked.

BYZANTINES
500–800 A. D.

Born of Greece, stepbrother of Rome, and cousin to the Germans and to the Orient, Byzantium displayed its mixed heritage in its costume, a mingled galaxy of colors and styles and precious ornaments, like the mosaics in which its culture is best revealed. The height of its power was in the sixth century A. D. Byzantium was, however, the center of fashion from the fall of Rome until the Crusades. Materials ranged from wool to the sheerest silk. Colors included most of the definite shades, red, blue, green, and the like.

COSTUME FOR MEN

The principal garment was the tunica, similar to the Roman garment. It had long, close-fitting sleeves, with bands of embroidery or other decoration at the wrists. On the shoulders were appliquéd ovals or squares of embroidery; other such pieces adorned the lower part of the tunic (Fig. 82 A B). Except for old men, or men of rank on ceremonial occasions (when the tunic was worn long), it was usual to wear the tunic just a little more than knee length. It was belted low about the waist, with a slight blouse, and was often slit up the sides to the hip (Fig. 82 B). The slit was emphasized by a band of embroidery, coming to a point at the hip. The neck was either rounded or square. Over the shoulders were bands of embroidery ending in points above the waist – angusti clavi reduced to mere shoulder straps. The dalmatica, with short, wide sleeves, was also worn, though it was not so highly decorated as the tunic.

Though the earlier Byzantines had gone barelegged, by the sixth century the custom of wearing leg coverings had been introduced, probably as a result of contacts with barbarian Ostrogoths and Visigoths who wore the braccae, and also with the Persians, who wore tight leg-coverings of silk. Justinian adopted snug-fitting hosa of rich silk (Fig. 82 A B). Men of consular position wore the tunica talaris, long-sleeved, and another embroidered tunic, with wide sleeves, over it. Over this they wore the toga picta, folded and draped like the pallium. As the pallium proved easier to drape, it gradually replaced the toga. At first the pallium was left wide at the end, which was draped over the arm; finally, it was reduced to a long narrow strip and draped as shown in Fig. 72 A B C. After the consular office was abolished in the sixth century A. D., this strip was called the *lorum;* it became part of the regular garb of the emperor after the eighth century A. D. (Fig. 72 A B C D).

Mantle

For outer covering, the Roman paludamentum, an adaptation of the Greek chlamys, was most in favor with men of rank. It was about six by seven feet, fastened on the right shoulder with a fibula or brooch, and often decorated with an allover design embroidered in silk or gold thread (Fig. 82 A C). Emperors wore a purple paludamentum, encrusted with jewels (pearls were the favorite); only emperor and empress could wear purple. As distinct from the Roman garment, the Byzantine paludamentum had diagonal or sloping sides. Along each of these diagonal sides (which met on the right shoulder or in front) was placed a square or oblong decoration called the *tablion.* For royalty this was richly embroidered and ornamented with pearls, emeralds, and other jewels; men of rank wore less ornamented tablions (Fig. 82 A C).

Other cloaks of Greek or Roman design were used, but the paludamentum was most common.

Footwear

Sandals of leather, red and other colors, were fastened over the instep with straps secured by buckles (Fig. 88 F). Men of rank and rulers wore elaborate shoes studded with jewels on the toes and over the instep. A favorite design covered toes and heels and was fastened high over the instep (Fig. 88 E). Ordinary shoes were of soft leather or skin, snug about the ankles and rolled down over the top edge. This type of shoe was laced down the front or fastened at the side. Sometimes the toes were left bare. Workmen wore this type extending high up the leg, like boots.

Hair

The Roman style was usually followed, though Byzantines let the hair grow somewhat longer than the Romans had done. The fashion seems to have been to brush the hair down from the crown of the head, so that it formed a thick aureole about the face and neck. The face was clean-shaven (Fig. 82 A); beards and mustaches were worn only by older men of the upper classes, or by men of the middle and lower classes (Fig. 72 A).

Headdress

Men usually went bareheaded, or wore a simple fillet, like the Greeks and Romans. The emperor wore an elaborate fillet (Fig. 82 A), and on state occasions a crown of hinged plaques set with jewels and edged with pearls. From either side of the crown depended ropes of pearls.

Ornaments and Accessories

Byzantine jewelry was famous. Rings, bracelets, earrings, belts studded with precious stones, fibulae, and brooches in exquisite mosaic patterns or set with jewels, were

Fig. 87

lavishly used. A favorite brooch for fastening the paludamentum was circular and set with jewels, with several ropes of pearls pendant. Rings were engraved with monograms, the cross, and other insignia, and were used for engagements and weddings, and as gifts in general. Some were locket-fashion, enclosing sacred relics (Fig. 87 A N P). Pectorals of the locket type, often in the shape of a cross, were adopted and used extensively.

Military Dress

The Roman type of protective armor was used, as were also the Roman weapons.

COSTUME FOR WOMEN

Byzantine women wore a costume similar to the Greek chiton, or to the kolobion, cut wide so that the part over the arms extended far down over the forearm. It was long and was belted tightly at a high waistline. Under this wide garment was often worn another, with long tight sleeves; sometimes this tight-sleeved garment, richly embroidered, was worn alone (Fig. 84). If worn by a lady of rank, the dress was embroidered with the angusti clavi in elaborate designs. An adaptation of the dalmatica was also worn, belted or unbelted at the waist. By the sixth century the dress consisted of a stola, usually white, with long tight sleeves banded about the wrist. Angusti clavi might be embroidered down the front; or the garment might be outlined at the hems and up the sides by bands of embroidery ending in ornamental points near the knees.

Mantle

Over this dress was worn, for out-of-doors, the palla, in allover design or plain, draped in classic fashion, but often held in at the waist by another belt. The palla could be pulled up over the head for cold or inclement weather. In sixth-century use, a bit of the palla was pulled forward over the right shoulder and tucked into the belt; the rest of it was draped, as usual, under the right arm and over the left shoulder. This made a fairly complete covering. A semicircular mantle was also worn (Fig. 84); this mantle might be lined.

Footwear

Women's sandals resembled men's, except that they were more delicately made.

Hair

The hair was piled up on the head in a soft knot, and confined with a circlet or fillet of ribbon or metal; ladies of rank wore circlets of gold and jewels. The hair was often, however, completely hidden by the headdress.

Headdress

The Byzantine headdress was peculiar; it resembled a roll or turban (the design was probably influenced by the Orient). A tight-fitting cap with a circular roll completely enveloped the head, allowing only occasional wisps of hair to escape over the ears. For ladies of rank, the roll was of richest silk, ornamented at regular intervals with narrow strips edged with pearls (Fig. 65 C   Fig. 84). As time went on, the strips were reduced in number but not in richness of adornment. The roll also dipped over the forehead. For empresses, the color of the roll was black, red, or purple. Often a veil was draped over the back. Ropes of pearls depended at either side from the roll over the ears (Fig. 65 C).

Ornaments and Accessories

Jewelry was essentially the same for women as for men, except that the articles for women were more delicate and exquisite in shape. Earrings of gold, jewels, enamel-work, or mosaic were much in demand; so also were rings of all types, including intaglios, cameos, seals, and reliquaries. The cross on a pendant was a great favorite.

Most important and typical of the time was the Byzantine collar, worn from the fifth century (Fig. 65 C   Fig. 84). It was similar to the Egyptian collar, except that it was not so closely fitted to the neck. Of linen, ornamented with jeweled plaques, outlined often in pearls, and with pearl pendants, it was a gorgeous addition to the costume.

Mourning

Byzantines followed the Roman custom in regard to mourning, though they adapted it to Christian usage and symbolism.

COSTUME FOR CHILDREN

Children wore simplified forms of the garments worn by their elders (Fig. 83).

Fig. 88

Costume for the Lower Classes

Women wore usually the dalmatica, plain and ungirdled. Under this, frequently, they wore a tunic with long, tight sleeves. If a cap were worn, it was of plain linen with an unornamented roll about the hair. For a wrap, they wore a plain palla, often draped over the head.

Eighth Century

About the time of Charlemagne, the imperial costume consisted of a dalmatica, richly embroidered and lined, over a tunic with long sleeves. Embroidery at neck and hem, and sometimes about the sleeves, emphasized the richness of the costume, especially when the embroidery was studded with jewels and accentuated with jeweled belts (Fig. 72).

Mantle

Later, the lorum was added, a stylization of the old Greek himation or the Roman pallium (Fig. 72 A B C D). The lorum was brought up from left center front (Fig. 72 Ba), then passed over the right shoulder (b) and under it again (c), brought up front over the left shoulder (d), passed across the back and around under the right shoulder (e), across the front, and ended over the left forearm (f g). The lorum was often studded with jewels. The neck was outlined with a jewel-studded collar. Men of ordinary rank wore tunics (short for younger men, long for older men) cut like the tunica talaris, but snug-fitting to the waistline and cut wide in the skirt. The neckline was slit, with the opening in front. Besides the lorum, the paludamentum with embroidered and jeweled tablion was worn.

Ornaments and Accessories

The crown was taller and more elaborate; it was a linked series of plaques set with jewels, the tallest at center front and surmounted by a cross (Fig. 72 A Fig. 73). Additional royal insignia were the scepter and the orb. The mappa, a sort of handkerchief, was carried, and was used at the Hippodrome to give the signal for the games to begin. Consuls had carried the mappa for this purpose in earlier times.

Women of rank wore the same elaborate type of dalmatica, embroidered and jeweled. A paludamentum with tablion and a rich collar completed the costume. If the wearer were of imperial rank, lavishness of decoration distinguished the dress. The crown was heavy, domed at the top, and set with large jewels. It rested within the roll cap (Fig. 65 C).

The lower classes wore simplified versions of the costumes described above.

MOHAMMEDANS (MOORS)

The Mohammedan dress was somewhat similar to that of the Hebrews and other peoples of Asia Minor.

HUNS

Costume for Men

These Asiatic people, who overran Europe in the fifth century, wore tunics woven from the hair of the Bactrian camel, the dromedary, or the yak; or they wore linen materials or cloth made from sheep and goat wool. They also sewed together skins of field mice for tunics. Their cloth was usually the natural color of the material. As the Huns were a people of slovenly habits, their clothing, once donned, was not taken off to be cleaned but was worn until it fell off in rags.

Tunic

The Hunnish tunic was a loose, shapeless garment resembling the Roman colobium. Usually the tunics were belted low (Fig. 85). Kings, chieftains, and men of high rank probably wore tunics of silk obtained from China. These were embroidered with colored borders.

Mantle

Mantles were made of the hides of animals, or of furs sewn together, or of coarse woolen or hairy material (Fig. 85).

Footwear

The Huns wore clumsy shoes of hide, laced up the front, the toes painted and curved upwards. Sometimes they were worn with the hair of the animals outward. Frequently, the legs were wrapped in hides, twined about with thongs (Fig. 85).

Hair

Their long, coarse, shining black hair was allowed to hang in unkempt strands over their shoulders. The general custom among the younger men was to go clean-shaven, though occasionally a drooping mustache was worn. Older men, and some branches of the race, wore beards (Fig. 85).

Headdress

A brightly colored cap, round or square, with a peak in the center and a roll of fur around the edge, was worn on the head (Fig. 85).

Ornaments

Little jewelry was worn. A bracelet or two and an occasional earring were used, but in general the Huns went without adornment.

Military Dress

The Huns carried long bows, spears ornamented with yaks' hair, round shields of wood or wicker covered with hides of animals, and knives and long daggers in scabbards on a leather strap hung over the right shoulder.

Costume for Women

Little is known of their costume, but it was probably semi-oriental in character.

Costume for Children and the Lower Classes

Children and the lower classes dressed in skins or coarse garments, without decoration.

Modern Adaptations

In general, the costumes of the barbarians should be made of thick, coarse materials. Colors should be the dark, rich shades. Leather tunics can be simulated with unbleached muslin, dyed a dun shade (without being wetted first). Scaled armor can be painted with aluminum or gold paint, or cut in strips of cloth, painted and sewed on the tunic. Byzantine costumes should be made of heavy materials and in richer colors.

For the barbarian garments, in general, use flannel, canton flannel, duvetyn, terry cloth, Osnaburg, unbleached muslin, and patent leather. Use felt for appliqué work in various patterns, squares, etc. For very heavy, rough clothing, use gunny sacking, burlap, potato sacking. Soft monk's cloth is clinging, and is good for stately garments; so is velveteen, if the budget will allow it.

There is no substitute for fur, which is so essential for costumes of this period. Fur cloth (leopard, zebra, etc.) can be used, but it is not effective. The best procedure is to hunt in such places as old-clothes stores and Salvation Army stores for old coats with fur collars, or old fur pieces, and use the fur.

For jewelry, use the kinds previously described. For Byzantine jewels, get colored ten-cent-store jewelry.

For footwear, make sandals out of felt or unbleached muslin; lace up with strips of muslin. The soles should be of felt or of several layers of heavy canvas. For peasants, wrap burlap or sacking about the legs and, if desired, about the forearms. Where the sandal is to come up over the foot, use duvetyn, flannel, or Osnaburg, as these are softer than canvas to shape.

CHAPTER VI

THE MIDDLE AGES (800-1300 A.D.)

IMPORTANT PEOPLE AND EVENTS

	ITALY	GERMANY
	Popes	*Emperors*
Ninth Century	Leo III (795–816)	Charlemagne (768–814) Louis the Pious (814–840)
Tenth Century	John XII (955–963)	Otto I (the Great) (936–973)
Eleventh Century	Gregory VII (Hildebrand) (1073–85) Urban II (1088–99)	Conrad II (the Salic) (1024–39) Henry III (1039–56) Henry IV (1056–1106)
Twelfth Century	Hadrian IV (1154–59) Alexander III (1159–81) Innocent III (1198–1216)	Frederick I (1152–90) Otto IV (1198–1218)
Thirteenth Century	Gregory IX (1227–41) Boniface VIII (1294–1303)	Frederick II (1218–50) Conrad IV (1250–54) Rudolf of Habsburg (1273–91)

	FRANCE	ENGLAND
	Kings	*Kings*
Ninth Century	Charles the Bald (840–877)	Egbert, King of the West Saxons (802–839) Alfred the Great (871–901)
Tenth Century	Hugh Capet (987–996) Robert (996–1031)	Athelstan (925–940)
Eleventh Century	Henry I (1031–60) Philip I (1060–1108)	Canute the Dane (Knut) (1017–35) Edward the Confessor (1042–66) Harold (1066)

		William I (the Norman) (1066–87)
		William II (1087–1100)
Twelfth Century	Louis VI (1108–37)	Henry I (1100–35)
	Louis VII (1137–80)	Stephen (1135–54)
	Philip II (Augustus) (1180–1223)	Henry II (Plantagenet) (1154–89)
		Richard I (1189–99)
		John (1199–1216)
Thirteenth Century	Louis VIII (1223–26)	Henry III (1216–72)
	Louis IX (1226–70)	Edward I (1272–1307)
	Philip III (1270–85)	
	Philip IV (1285–1314)	

NINTH CENTURY

800, Charlemagne crowned Emperor of Holy Roman Empire. . . . Rurik the Norseman (Viking) became Grand Prince of Russia (*circa* 850). . . . Alfred the Great encouraged learning; Anglo-Saxon Chronicle. . . . Candle clock devised. . . . Witan established.

TENTH CENTURY

911, Rollo, with his Northmen, settled in France, founded Normandy. . . . Monasteries founded at Cluny (910) and at Citeaux. . . . Cotton grown in Spain. . . . Arabic numerals adopted. . . . 977, St. Mark's, Venice, begun. . . . 978, London Bridge built. . . . *Quem Queritis,* first Mystery Play. . . . Tang, Chow dynasties in China. . . . 987, Hugh Capet (so called from monk's hood he wore as abbot of St. Martin's of Tours) made King of France, founder of Capetian dynasty.

ELEVENTH CENTURY

Thousands made pilgrimage to Rome, thinking end of world near. . . . Truce of God. . . . Norsemen settled in southern Italy and in Sicily. . . . Norsemen visited North America. . . . *Beowulf.* . . . Danes in England. . . . Danelaw. . . . Rodrigo (Ruy) Diaz de Vivar, the Cid, in Spain. . . . Power of Holy Roman Empire at height under Henry III of Germany. . . . Edward the Confessor's good laws. . . . Westminster Abbey built. . . . 1066, Harold the Saxon defeated by William the Conqueror at Hastings. . . . Bayeux tapestry. . . . Domesday Book (1087). . . . Curfew. . . . Celibacy required of priests. . . . Investiture Conflict between popes and emperors. . . . 1077, Gregory VII (Hildebrand) humbled Emperor Henry IV at Canossa. . . . Tower of London built. . . . Omar Khayyám, Persian poet and astronomer. . . . Romanesque and Norman architecture flourished. . . . Musical intervals (the gamut, etc.) introduced. . . . First Crusade, 1095, led by Raymond of Toulouse, Robert of Normandy, Bohemond of Taranto (with his nephew Tancred), Godfrey de Bouillon. . . . Capture of Jerusalem, July 15, 1099.

TWELFTH CENTURY

Rise of universities at Salerno (medicine), Bologna (law), Paris (theology). . . . Oxford, Cambridge. . . . Henry I of England granted Charter of Liberties. . . . Abelard's books burned.

... 1122, Concordat at Worms settled Investiture Conflict, reconciling the Empire and the papacy. ... Silk brocades made in Sicily. ... *Circa* 1135, Geoffrey of Monmouth's *Historia Regum Britanniae*. ... *Song of Roland*. ... *Aucassin and Nicolette*. ... Chansons de Geste, Laies, Fabliaux. ... Hafiz, the Persian poet. ... Moorish tiles introduced into Italy. ... Cathedral at Pisa built. ... Notre Dame de Paris begun. ... Tournaments introduced. ... 1147–49, the Second Crusade. ... Sugar brought from the Holy Land. ... Art of painting on glass developed. ... 1159, Bank of Venice founded. ... Henry II of England quarreled with Thomas à Becket, Archbishop of Canterbury, and instigated his murder (December 29, 1170). ... Rise of the jury system. ... Scutage. ... Eleanor of Aquitaine, on her marriage to Henry II, brought large dowry of French territory. ... 1177, Frederick I humbled himself to Pope Alexander III. ... Third Crusade, 1189–92, led by Richard I (the Lion-Hearted) of England, Philip II (Augustus) of France, Frederick I (Barbarossa) of Germany. ... The Sultan Saladin. ... 1189, siege of Acre. ... Windmills – idea imported from the Orient. ... Chateau Gaillard. ... Innocent III struggled with King John of England, also with Philip Augustus. ... Papal power at its height. ... Rise of Gothic art and architecture. ... Cathedral of Chartres begun. ... *Circa* 1190, original composition of the *Nibelungenlied*.

THIRTEENTH CENTURY

1201–04, Fourth Crusade; plundering of Constantinople, April 13, 1204. ... 1216, St. Dominic founded the Dominican Order. ... Genghiz Khan founded the Mongol Empire. ... Troubadours, trouvères. ... *Tristram and Iseult*. ... *Cycle de Bretagne*. ... *Roman de la Rose*. ... The *Brut* of the Anglo-Norman author Wace. ... Marie de France. ... King Arthur and his Round Table. ... 1208, Albigensian Crusade. ... Chrétien de Troyes and the *Perceval* poems, later developed into the Parsifal and the Grail legends. ... 1212, Children's Crusade. ... June 15, 1215, Magna Carta sealed at Runnymede. ... 1219, the Fifth Crusade. ... Frederick II's Sicilian reforms. ... St. Francis of Assisi founded the Franciscan order, which was confirmed by Pope Honorius III in 1223. ... Louis IX (St. Louis), 1226–70, abolished trial by combat. ... The Inquisition established. ... Height of Gothic art, to be seen in the cathedrals of Notre Dame de Paris, Reims, Amiens, etc. ... Great Interregnum in Germany, 1250–73. ... 1265, Simon de Montfort's Parliament. ... House of Commons established. ... Roger Bacon (died 1294), Thomas Aquinas (*circa* 1225–74), and Scholastic thought. ... Dante (1265–1321) and the *Divine Comedy*. ... Teutonic Knights acquired East Prussia from the Slavs. ... Kublai Khan. ... Marco Polo. ... Edward I of England conquered Scotland, seized the Stone of Scone (reputedly Jacob's pillow); also conquered Wales (first Prince of Wales was Edward's son). ... Wallace's revolt. ... Robert Bruce. ... Rudolf of Habsburg, king of the Romans. ... Artists: Cimabue, Giotto, Guido of Siena.

The medieval period was an age of youth – youth that is hard and cruel and materialistic, youth that is mystical and romantic and chivalrous. Youth prefers to see the world, not as it is, but reflected in a magic mirror, in which, like the mirror of the Lady of Shalott "that hangs before her all the year, Shadows of the world appear." Magic does tricks with truth; that is the price of delving in the black arts.

In the Middle Ages, astrology represented science; chivalry, the art of war; Courts of Love, the art of life; all used symbols, for fear of touching the naked truth. Even the Church, the heart and soul of medieval Europe, the inspiration of its faith, its art, its wars, its commerce – most of all, indeed, the Church used symbols. It carved them in enduring fantasies of lace-light stone. It reflected them through its rose windows – not light-pools of red and blue and gold, but the blood of martyrs, the infinity of Heaven, the radiance of Truth.

The garments of the time also showed magic curves; they expressed beauty in a thousand hidden meanings. They expressed the romance of the new Western nations, as well as that of the ancient Orient; the magic rose grew behind castellated walls as richly as it did beside the perfumed fountains of Arabia.

Three things are proof against all alchemy – Courage and Honor and Love. Youth, in his crusade against an intolerant age, armed himself with these three – with Courage, which overcame his fear; with Honor, which protected his ideals; with Love, which affirmed his happiness and pledged his immortality.

Youth, the Green Knight, sheathed himself in this shining armor and so rode forth, with banners flying, to capture the rich wonder of the world.

COSTUME

GENERAL CHARACTERISTICS

Dress underwent little vital change from barbaric times until the eleventh century. Then, due to the Crusades, to chivalry, and to the elaborations of the feudal system, refinements crept into costume. Foremost among these were: (1) the use of richer materials, many of which were imported from the Orient; (2) the development of long, loose sleeves, lined and embroidered; (3) the tendency toward sheathlike garments, a reflection of the close-fitting armor; (4) the elaboration of hoods, veils, and other head coverings, including helms; (5) the refinement of footwear; (6) the general use of long mantles.

Although in the Middle Ages there arose a diversity of nations, such as England, France, and Germany, the Church tended to unify them, not only spiritually, but in details of daily living and customs. The Crusades brought Oriental products and customs back to all the European countries; ecclesiastical conceptions not only standardized churchly vestments for centuries to come, but insensibly influenced the very colors, lines, and arrangement of lay dress. The symbolic blues and reds of the Madonna's dress, the pious veiling, were copied; even the sway-backed walk of medieval ladies aped the enceinte Virgin, to accentuate which illusion small pads were placed over the stomach.

France led the fashions throughout the period.

Materials

Linen was still in general use by high and low. A patterned type was called *damask,* like the silk of that name. Another variety of linen was called *moleskin.* Wool was also woven into many fabrics – serge, homespun, and others, including *cameline,* woven of camel's hair, very warm (another importation from the Orient). Cotton was introduced into France in the twelfth century, under the name of *bombax.* Some of the popular cotton weaves were *isambrun,* a brown cloth; *bonnette,* a green cloth; *brunette* and *galebrun,* brown or russet-brown; *fustian,* used first by the clergy, later adopted by the middle classes; and *buckram,* of which little is known except that it probably came originally from Bokhara. For warmth, the lower classes wore leather, sheepskin, straw wrappings, and even felt.

Silks, however, were in high favor, and were of many weaves. *Cendal* was similar to modern taffeta, and was woven in rich and varied colors, scarlet being most popular. Sometimes the cendal was striped. *Ciclatoun* (or *siglatoun*), first used in the thirteenth century, was especially prized for headrails. *Samite,* a thick, closely woven, heavy silk, of Chinese origin, was much used by kings, bishops, and the highest nobility. St. Louis wore a robe of samite; Excalibur (King Arthur's sword), when thrown into the lake, was caught by an arm clothed in samite. *Brocade* was a patterned silk, which frequently had gold or silver threads woven into it. *Damask,* first made in Damascus, was also woven in designs. *Baudekyn,* first made at Baldeck (Bagdad), was a stiff texture shot with gold, used for the canopy over a king or a pope; *paile* or *pall* was similar in weight and was also used for canopies; from these fabrics come the modern words *baldechin* and *pall,* meaning covering. *Frise* was cloth of gold, very precious; its origin was probably Phrygia. Brocade, paile, and frise were in use from the fifth century. *Crepe silk* was first used in the twelfth century. *Sarcenet* (from *Saracen*) was a thin silk, usually of a plain color, used for robes, veils, and linings; it was used from the thirteenth century on. *Pourpre* was of rich quality, made at Tyre (it took its name from the Tyrian purple) and at Venice, in shades of purple, vermilion, indigo, crimson, violet, and the like; it also was in use from the thirteenth century on. *Velvet,* a silken fabric with looped surface or cut (the Latin name was *pannus vellosus*) was known in the thirteenth century, but was not generally used until the fifteenth century.

The Sicilian weavers of the eleventh and twelfth centuries were famous for their brocades and patterned silks. In France, Beauvais, Étampes, Chartres, and Tours were large manufacturing centers for silk, wool, and linen weaves.

Colors

The clear, bright hues of stained glass windows were reflected in medieval garments. Deep blue, rich red, ruby, emerald green, purple, saffron, light apple green, yellow, gold, crimson, indigo, brown, gray, white, and silver were some of the shades.

Underclothes

Men wore the linen *serte* or shirt (also called a *just-au-corps*), next the skin; it descended to the knee and was slit up the side like an old-fashioned nightshirt; about the neck it was embroidered with colored or black wool. Long drawers were worn under the long tunic and sometimes under the long hose. Under the short tunic, drawers, somewhat like loosely wrapped diapers, were worn; these were visible when the tunic was looped up at the sides. The hose were held up by straps or tapes sewed to the front of the hose, above the knee, and fastened or tied to the waistband, like modern suspenders. Hose (also called *chausses*) were made of linen for summer, wool for winter, and were laced up behind. The poorer classes wore leather hose. Only the very poorest went barelegged.

Women wore the *camise,* or chemise, a long garment of linen, short- or long-sleeved, as the weather demanded. In very cold weather, several chemises were worn, as well as several pairs of hose with the necessary suspenders; knee-length drawers, similar to those worn by the men, were also used. At night, women slept in the chemise, though

Fig. 89

men usually went to bed naked. In the twelfth century, women wore a short vest or jacket of fur, called a *plisson* (or *pelisse*), between the chemise and the outer garment. It was fastened at the side, under the arm.

COSTUME FOR MEN

ELEVENTH CENTURY

Tunic

For civil dress in the eleventh century, the short tunic (Fig. 90 A) was used by all classes except kings, ecclesiastics, great nobles, and elderly men. The tunic was sometimes slit on the sides, and was usually girdled at the waist. Some had long sleeves, which might be wrinkled back from the wrist, or turned back over the wrist like cuffs (Fig. 90 A C). Another type of sleeve reached the forearm only; it was wide, with embroidered edges both inside and outside. This type of sleeve showed the under-sleeve of the just-au-corps. The neck was round, square, or V-shaped, with a band of embroidery to accentuate the line. The opening was usually center front. Long hose were worn underneath; these hose were often cross-gartered to the knee. They were attached to the belt beneath the tunic.

Mantle

The mantle was rectangular or semicircular. It reached below the knees, and was usually fastened on the right shoulder or at center front. The fastening was a brooch, or metal ring, or cord (Fig. 92 A C).

Footwear

Leather or thick cloth sandals were worn, ankle height or low, with straps across the instep (Fig. 96 E), or slits at the side (Fig. 96 F). Toward the end of the century, a "debauched fellow named Robert 'Cornard,' at the court of William Rufus," stuffed the pointed toes until they curled up like rams' horns – to the great disgust of William of Malmesbury.

Hair

The Bayeux tapestry shows the Norman custom of shaving the back of the head. However, the Normans admired the long hair of the Saxons so much that they speedily adopted it. Toward the end of the century, pictures show Anglo-Normans parting their hair, as described by Ordericus Vitalis: "from the crown of the head on either side of the forehead, and letting their locks grow long, like women. . . . The forepart of their heads is bare, like thieves, while behind they nourish long hair, like harlots. . . . Their locks are curled with irons, and instead of wearing caps, they bind their hair with fillets."

Headdress

In addition to the fillets and the skirted hood (Fig. 90 A B), the Phrygian cap was still in vogue (Fig. 89 E). There was also a plain, round skullcap without a brim, as well as a third type, also brimless, but conical in shape.

Military Dress

The Bayeux tapestry, woven by Matilda, wife of William the Conqueror, shows the types of armor worn at the Battle of Hastings. Both Normans and Saxons wore a *hauberk* (*haven,* to cut, *berg,* a defense). This was a sheathlike garment (Fig. 91) with no visible division, like a union suit (some authorities, like Planché, claim that it is a tunic, slit up the front). The sleeves are elbow length, and the garment is knee length. A very much longer type, reaching the ankles, is seen on certain figures, perhaps of older men. The hauberk was of leather, covered with iron rings sewed flat in rows, interlaced, or threaded through leather strips. "Tegulated," "trellised," "mascled," "banded," "scaled," "imbricated," "meshed" — these are some of the descriptions of the many types used. William the Conqueror probably wore a hauberk of interwoven rings, and no doubt a tunic type, as it is said he put it over his head, in his haste, wrong side before, thus half-covering his face with the attached hood, and had to make himself known to his men because they had feared him killed.

Under the hauberk were a long, close-fitting tunic and long, tight hose crisscrossed or gartered with tight leather bands. The feet were covered with pointed leather shoes; sometimes the shoes were mailed and spurred. Attached to the hauberk the Normans wore the *cowl,* or *capuchin,* made in the same fashion and coming well up on the chin in front.

Both Normans and Saxons wore conical *helms* covering only the head. A broad nasal guard protected the nose (Fig. 91).

The Norman shield was kite-shaped, long and slender, bowed (Fig. 94 A B) or flat. It was of leather-covered wood, or of iron, and frequently had a device, such as a dragon, a lion, a band, or other emblem upon it. This device was later transferred from the shield to the surcoat, and became the basis of heraldic design. The Saxon shield was usually round with a boss or spike in the center.

The Normans carried the lance (Fig. 91), with a flag or pennon attached (Fig. 94); this flag was called a *gonfanon* (or *gonfalon*). The Saxons carried lances also; Harold's gonfanon had upon it the figure of a man, embroidered in gold and encrusted with precious stones.

The bow and arrow were favorite weapons with the Saxons; it was a strange twist of fate that Harold was killed by an arrow through his brain.

The crown of William the Conqueror is shown in Fig. 98.

Fig. 90

Fig. 91

Fig. 92

Fig. 93

Fig. 95

Fig. 98

Fig. 99

Fig. 100

Fig. 101

Fig. 102

Fig. 103

Fig. 104

Tunic

In the twelfth century, men's tunics were more carefully cut. They were wider in the skirt, and were often tucked up at the sides, showing the undershirt and drawers beneath. In some illustrations, these drawers seem to be merely the tails of the split undershirt, brought between the legs and tucked up into the waistband. Older men and dignitaries wore ankle-length tunics, full-skirted, and richly embroidered about the neck, wrists, and hem. Sleeves were either long and tight, or open and full. A buckled belt, usually of wide leather, confined the tunic at the waist.

Long Tunic

This type was used by older men, royalty, and dignitaries. The sleeves were cut as part of the tunic, full at the shoulder, tapering at the wrist (Fig. 92 A D). Over this was worn a sleeveless *surcoat,* or *tabard,* or *cyclas,* or *scapular* (all these names are used, unfortunately), as is shown in Fig. 92 A B. The long tunic, especially when worn by the clergy as an undergarment or foundation, was sometimes called a *cassock.*

Hair

The hair was generally worn long, to the shoulders, and curled up at the ends (Fig. 92 A). Kings and high dignitaries wore their hair twisted into four tight curls, or "tails," behind, and one over either shoulder in front. Curling irons were used to "crisp" the hair and also the short but carefully tended beard. The beard was usually shaped like that on the peasant in Fig. 89 E. Mustaches were in general favor throughout the century, though not universally worn.

The crown of Richard I is shown in Fig. 99.

Military Dress

The hauberk was longer than those of the eleventh century; it was slit either front and back, or at the sides, and sometimes it was not slit at all. It was almost always chain mail, of fine mesh and workmanship.

By the end of the twelfth century, chain mail had become the standard dress of the warrior and knight. The complete dress of a young knight would be as follows:

1. The just-au-corps, or undershirt. For initiation into knighthood, it was black, signifying death, which Christ endured for all.

2. The camise, of white linen, signifying Christian purity.

3. The *gambeson,* a quilted garment with long sleeves, either of leather padded with wool or of buckskin padded with cotton, sometimes called the *aketon.* (Fig. 93 B). Common soldiers wore only the gambeson.

4. Over the gambeson was worn the *plastron de fer,* an iron plate to protect the chest from blows.

5. Next, the hauberk, of chain mail, soft, pliable, conforming to the figure, yet very heavy, with all the weight on the shoulders. It was slit up the sides, or front and back. It had crescents of leather under the arms (Fig. 93 D). The long sleeves

ended in gloves woven as part of the sleeve, but slit so that they might be pushed back when not needed. The gloves, or *gauntlets,* were also made separately, with leather palms (Fig. 93 F). The hauberk signified the fortress of the soul against evil. The gauntlet was a pledge of loyalty.

6. The *chausses* or leg coverings of chain mail were laced up the back of the leg to the knee (Fig. 96 A); the feet were woven in one with the legs. The waist was gathered onto a leather band, and leather crescents covered the seat of the garment (Fig. 93 E). The knees were further protected by knee guards (called *genouillières*) of *cuirbouilli* – leather boiled in oil (Fig. 93 A H).

7. A cowl, or hood, of chain mail, covered the head and extended down over the neck. An opening was left for the face (Fig. 93 C). It might be thrown back (like a cloth cowl) when not needed.

8. The *surcoat* was a sleeveless tunic of linen or silk, fairly full, and belted. It reached below the knees, almost to the ankles, in 1180; later, it became shorter and shorter, especially in front; by the middle of the fourteenth century it had almost disappeared. The surcoat was slit up the front and back, for horseback riding (Fig. 93 A); later, it was slit on the sides. Its purpose was to protect the chain mail from the heat of the sun and from rain (which rusted the iron). The distinguishing arms of the knight were later put on the front of the surcoat. The Hospitalers, or Knights of St. John, used a white cross on a black surcoat; the Knights Templars used a red cross on a white surcoat; the Teutonic Knights, a black cross on a white surcoat. Untried knights had to wear a green surcoat until they had won their spurs. Spurs, also called *pryck-spurs* (Fig. 96 A), were three-pointed, and, for special reward, were of gold. A belt (Fig. 93 A) of leather, low-hung, held the sword, the hilt of which was in the form of the cross, to which it was dedicated.

Over the cowl of chain mail, another head covering was sometimes worn – the *barrel-helm,* of solid metal (Fig. 93 A). This was a round, flat-topped piece, with an *ocularium,* or vision-slit, in front.

Other accessories of the knight were the *misericorde,* or dagger, with which to dispatch the enemy – to give the *coup de grace,* the "'mercy of God" (!). A ten-foot lance was also used, with a lozenge-shaped point (Fig. 94 A) of iron, symbol of strength; a *main-gauche,* or left-handed dagger; and a ring of gold, symbol of knighthood and of the allegiance due the suzerain.

Knights in action are shown in Fig. 94. A *baldric,* of colored silk or of leather, was often slung over the right shoulder and beneath the left arm; it usually supported the sword, but might be worn merely for ornament.

Fig. 94.

Ecclesiastical Dress

The clergy standardized their vestments in the twelfth century. The general type of robe was the long dalmatica, with full, long sleeves, over an alb. A hood, or capuchin, pointed at the back, was attached to the robe, and could be thrust down on the neck when not in use. The head was tonsured, or shaved on top (Fig. 95). The Benedictines wore a white cassock, black robe, and a black hood – often a circular cape, or *pelerine*, was worn over the shoulders; kings copied this custom. The *crozier* and the miter were necessary adjuncts to a bishop.

THIRTEENTH CENTURY

Tunic

Little change was made in the tunic itself, except to make it more elegant; but the hose beneath were continued up to the waistline, and became the equivalent of modern tights. They were fastened about the waist with cords. They were also parti-colored, the several seams running lengthwise down the leg (Fig. 96 B E).

Mantle

In this century, the hood was usually added to the mantle, or *cloak,* as it was beginning to be called. The hood acquired a long point (Fig. 90 A B).

Footwear

More elaborate shoes came into use, with patterns crisscrossed, or of circles, etc.; the shoes fitted snugly up over the ankle (Fig. 96 D). One type was cut out in a circle over the instep and buttoned (Fig. 96 B); another was decorated with rayed straps, and buttoned high over the instep (Fig. 96 C).

Hair

The hair was worn short, just below the ears, but waved and curled so that it puffed out gracefully at the sides. Mustaches and short beards from chin to ear were worn.

Headdress

Former styles were elaborated and refined; hoods were more pointed; caps were of finer material.

The crown of Edward I is shown in Fig. 100. A crown of the Holy Roman Empire, 900 A. D., is shown in Fig. 101. A papal tiara of the eleventh century is shown in Fig. 102.

Military Dress

The dress of the Crusaders was continued, with embellishments. The surcoat was shortened. The helmet was made smaller, with a movable visor (Fig. 89 A), and to it was attached the gorget of chain mail. Greaves of *cuirbouilli* became more elaborate

Fig. 96

and covered the shins completely. The surcoat was also often embroidered in many-colored designs. *Roundlets* at elbow and shoulder gave added protection.

Ecclesiastical Dress

The Mendicant Orders arose in the thirteenth century; the Dominicans, or Black Friars, instituted by St. Dominic de Guzman, in 1216; and the Franciscans, or Gray Friars (also called Cordeliers, from their girdles of rope), were established in 1209. Later, the Carmelites, or White Friars, appeared, and the Augustinians, also called Gray Friars (Fig. 95).

The Dominicans wore a white woolen dalmatica, white and black mantle or cloak, with black hood or capuchin. The Franciscans wore a gray dalmatica without a scapular, and a gray mantle and hood. With these was worn a gray cord about the waist. The Carmelites wore white; the Augustinians, gray.

Mourning

Men wore black for mourning. Other marks of mourning were wearing hose with insteps cut out, and wearing garments wrong side out.

COSTUME FOR CHILDREN

Children wore garments similar to those of their elders, but usually of plainer materials, decoration, and cut. A general type for boys is seen in Fig. 97.

COSTUME FOR THE LOWER CLASSES

The costume shown in Fig. 90 was fairly typical. Coarse, warm materials, such as homespun, leather, sheepskin, and moleskin, were used. Those who had no long chausses wore wrappings of straw or cloth.

COSTUME FOR WOMEN

ELEVENTH CENTURY

Tunic or Robe

This was a loose gown, long or reaching just below the knees. The sleeves were wide and fairly short – evidently an adaptation of the Roman dalmatica. The under-tunic, with long skirt and long, tight sleeves, was usually of another color and intended to be seen. The edges of the sleeves, neck, and hem of the over-tunic were banded with embroidery; the under-tunic was usually plain. Beneath these two was worn a third garment, the camise, or chemise, and short, loose drawers (described above). Hose were fastened to the waistband by tapes sewed above the knee. The outer tunic was girdled with a rather wide belt, richly embroidered or jeweled.

Toward the end of the century, the *super-tunic,* also called *bliau,* became form-fitting to the hips, then full and rippling to the feet (Fig. 103 A D). A *train* was added behind. The sleeves were elongated until they fell to or below the knee, but a slit at the wrist left the hand free. Another and more popular type of sleeve was the diagonal style of dalmatic sleeve, elongated until the points touched or trailed on the floor (Fig.

103 A B). The long types of sleeves were lined and the edges were sometimes embroidered. In the Cotton MS., Nero C, IV, Fol. 18, there is a picture of Satan dressed in an extravagant caricature of a gown with sleeves and train both knotted up elaborately, and the front of the dress laced to suffocation-point, showing that lacing was used for slenderizing effect as well as for fastening (Fig. 103 A C). The neck was a V or round.

Mantle

A semicircular mantle was worn, fastened in front by a brooch or cords. Sometimes the mantle had decorations of metal plaques set with pearls and precious stones, with cords (or chains) attached, which could be loose or tightened to insure an open or snug effect to the mantle. Fur was used, both for trimming and for lining the entire garment.

Hair

The hair was worn coiled close about the head, under the veil or *couvre-chef* (kerchief) (Fig. 89 B). Some early illuminations, however, show the hair parted, and braided or coiled in one or two ropes behind, without a veil (as seen in the MS. of the Douce collection, Oxford). A *snood,* or band of silk, held the veil on (Fig. 89 B).

Headdress

This was the veil, or kerchief. It might be short, or it might extend to the bottom of the dress in back. It was also worn draped under the chin and back over the left shoulder, like the Greek himation; this draping was much used in representations of the Virgin Mary and other saintly women (Fig. 89 B).

Footwear, ornaments and accessories, and make-up will be discussed in general for the entire period, as the changes were small.

TWELFTH CENTURY

Importation of silks from the Orient, as a result of the Crusades, added color and variety to women's dress. Cotton stuffs were used, as were also fur linings. The statue of Queen Clotilda, wife of Clovis (although she lived in the sixth century, her effigy is in the costume of the sculptor's time), shows the dress of the period. It was a long, loose tunic or bliau, the upper part made of a ribbed mesh similar to the Crusader's chain mail. The neck was a V, outlined with embroidery and fastened with a round brooch. The sheath effect ended at the hips, where a circular skirt was attached, falling in many ripples about the feet (Fig. 104 A B C). The girdle (Fig. 104 A) was passed about the natural waistline, crossed in back, and knotted low in front, outlining the lower edge of the sheath. The ends of the girdle fell almost to the hem of the garment. The sleeves were long and pendant, with serrated edges. Another sleeve of this period is shown in Fig. 104 A D. A band at the waist dropped down and was lined to accentuate its decorative value. The *chainse* was a lighter form of the bliau.

Mantle

In addition to the circular mantle, which was much like that of the eleventh century

(Fig. 92 C), the women wore a type of fur jacket imported from Persia. It had wide, loose sleeves, was fastened by one clasp at the waistline in front, and reached to the knees.

Hair

The hair was confined under a close-fitting coif, or cap, with a stiff, wide, upstanding band about the forehead, often decorated and jeweled (Fig. 89 D Fig. 104 A). To hold the cap in place, a chin band was attached to the cap at the temples. Another, more elaborate, way of dressing the hair was to part it in the middle, braid or roll each part, and interwine the long coils with ribbons, ropes of pearls, or other ornaments (Fig. 89 C). Often false hair was used to eke out the long braids. The ends of the braids were tufted, or encased in pointed metal casings.

Headdress

In addition to the tight cap and chin band mentioned above, the crown, chaplet, and veil (short or long), were used. The crown was now a wide band ornamented with knobs, leaves, and jewels; it might be worn by nobles of many degrees (Fig. 89 C).

THIRTEENTH CENTURY

The important differences in dress between this century and the twelfth were the increased use of rich stuffs, the multiplicity of garments, one over the other, and the preference for tight coifs. The tunics were still cut tight about the waist and hips, flaring at the bottom, lying six inches or more on the ground, both front and back; often a long train was in evidence. The dress was held up in front, to show the undergarment, and a sway-back walk was affected. No girdle was worn with the tight dress. It was sometimes laced at the sides or down the front. The neck was round or square.

Mantle

Mantles were similar to those of the twelfth century, but perhaps longer and fuller.

Footwear

Elaborate shoes, embroidered, jeweled, and elongated into points, were worn by the better classes, though they were usually hidden by the long skirts. Shoes of Cordovan leather, from Spain, were highly prized, red being the favorite color. No heels were used.

Hair

Young girls, as was customary throughout the Middle Ages, wore their hair long and flowing, ornamented with chaplets of flowers or narrow metal, gold, or silver bands. The tight coif, chin band, crown, and veil continued to be worn, but the long braids of hair almost disappeared.

Headdress

Headdresses, an integral part of the hair arrangement, continued as in the former century; but reticulated styles, with bands and metalwork, grew in favor.

Ornaments and Accessories

Pins, brooches, buckles, enamel and repoussé work on clasps, jeweled girdles, fillets, crowns, rings, chains, and jeweled shoe clasps were used. Beryls, amethysts, and chrysolites were favored, as well as the always popular pearls.

Short walking sticks, ornamented with the heads of birds and beasts, were much favored for walking in the gardens or ruling in the Courts of Love. A *chatelaine*, or *aumonière*, or *pouch*, pendant from the low girdle, held scissors, keys, etc. Gloves, with or without fingers, were carried thrust in ladies' belts, or worn when riding or hunting or when engaged in falconry. Rosaries, instituted by the Dominican order, became another indispensable item of a lady's outfit.

Make-up

The use of cosmetics was decried by all the priests, with the usual results. Vermilion, saffron, white chalk, and soot (for the eyes) were in common use. A little quick-

Fig. 97   Fig. 105

silver (!) was added to the vermilion and chalk to give a proper glow to the complexion. Guy de Provence, in despair, declared that the saints in heaven rebelled against the women's excessive use of color, and that they complained that there was no color left to paint the holy images in the churches. A prescription guaranteed to bring the bloom of youth to the cheek consisted of a poultice of boiled and mashed beans, with arrowroot and fennel added; this was reduced to a paste with a liquid of sour cream and asses' milk. It was to be applied when retiring; next morning, the skin must be washed in white wine and mares' milk.

Mourning

Black indicated mourning, as also did simple, undecorated clothing. Long and heavy veils were worn; they were in the sable shades.

Costume for Children

Types of garments similar to their elder's were worn by the children, but these garments were more simply cut. A full robe, long but plain, was usual for little girls; the hair was left to hang loose and flowing (Fig. 105).

Costume for the Lower Classes

The women confined their hair in *wimples* of coarse linen. Serving maids often wore horizontal-striped garments, and, rarely, aprons are shown in illustrations.

Modern Adaptations

(For the Middle Ages and the Fourteenth Century)

For the long tunics for men, terry cloth, Osnaburg, flannel, monk's cloth, and ratiné give the effect of heavy woolen cloth. Raw silk has no sheen and drapes beautifully. Flannel can occasionally be obtained in deep shades; it is excellent for this period. So, too, is cotton both in stripes and in plaids (if Scotch plays are being costumed – *Macbeth,* etc.). Cotton duvetyn is excellent and has a rich appearance.

Canvas is good for men's clothes that must stand wear and tear. For light linens and cottons, voile, celanese voile, and batiste are best. For thin silks, use rayon, metaline, or China silk – the latter, though, is expensive.

For the thinner materials, also use paper cambric; it is slick and shiny, and it cuts and holds shape well for a few performances, although it is not good for continuous use. Sateen, taffeta (especially for the fourteenth century), and velveteen are excellent. Use pure silk taffeta; it is stiff, and holds its shape well. Rayon taffeta has too much body for this type of garment, will not crinkle well, and does not hold its shape.

For the thin veils, use China silk, thin rayon, or raw silk.

For the clinging type of garments, especially those of the fourteenth century, use cotton or silk jersey, or rayon tubing.

Fur, as suggested above, is a necessary adjunct to costumes of this period.

For gold or silver materials, use gold or silver lamé, or Kasai cloth. There are also novelty cloths, like jewel cloths, embossed duvetyn, lahm, sparkle satins, cire metal cloth, metallic cloth, satin brocade, etc.

For heavy, leatherlike tunics, use heavy sheeting muslin. Crinkle it while dry; dye without wetting first; the result will be a mottled effect, like a leather jerkin. On the tunic may be fixed roofing caps, to simulate the warrior's mailed tunic. Place one cap on either side of the material, and put through and bend back a tack to hold them on.

Jewels may be imitated as explained previously.

Chain Mail

This can be imitated satisfactorily only by a knitted garment. (1) For knitting needles, use two No. 4 doweling sticks (½″); have them pointed at the lumber mill and wax the points with beeswax, to keep them from catching in the wool. (2) Get office string by the pound, cast about 50 stitches or more and knit and knit and knit. (3) Be careful to knit the garment large enough, as it will shrink at least one third its size when dyed. (4) Dye the finished garment in desired basic color (gray, tan, black, brown, blue, copper, silver, etc.). (5) Stretch it while wet; if necessary, make a wide wooden frame, outline with large nails, and stretch the garment on this. Five or six garments can be stretched on one frame (like the old-fashioned lace-curtain frame). (6) Just before the garment is dry, take it off the frame and paint it with the desired color. Use a powdered-metal paint mixed with gum arabic and glue (heated). (7) Paint the knitted garment with a large brush so that it brushes the top of the stitches. (8) Before it is completely dry, hammer the entire garment over and over with a large wooden mallet, preferably on a concrete floor (at any rate, far from protesting neighbors). (9) This will result in a flat, metallic surface, properly dulled, and not resembling knitting. For the metal helmet, make a cast, mold in papier-mâché, paint steel, silver, or gold color. For the fourteenth-century helmet, plumes may be added, if desired.

Patterns (Middle Ages and Fourteenth Century)

For women's dress, use a princess petticoat pattern or else a long, princess evening dress pattern. For sleeves, use a plain, tight-sleeve pattern, add long, pointed sleeves, or tippet as shown in costume patterns. Always lay a bias to a straight edge in putting in godets (for extra fullness around bottom of trains, etc.). For military tunic, tight breeches, etc., use a union-suit pattern.

For the fourteenth-century long waist effect (cote-hardie) use the same princess pattern smoothly fitted, belt low. Set in godets on circular skirt.

For houppelande, use a man's or woman's dressing-gown pattern.

KNIGHT
TEMPLAR

MIDDLE AGES
1150

ARCHER

ENGLISH
10TH C

PLATE V   CHAPTER VI

14 TH C.

14 TH C.

14 TH C.

14 TH C.

PLATE VI   CHAPTER VII

CHAPTER VII

THE FOURTEENTH CENTURY

IMPORTANT PEOPLE AND EVENTS

ITALY
Popes
Babylonian Captivity
  (1305–77)
Great Schism
  (1378–1417)

Artists and Writers
Duccio
Simone Martini (or
  Menini)
Taddeo Gaddi
Orcagna (Andrea di
  Cione)

Fra Angelico (Gio-
  vanni Guido)
Andrea del Castagno
Paolo Uccello (Paolo di
  Dono)
Giovanni Boccaccio
Francesco Petrarch

ENGLAND
Kings
Edward II
  (1307–27)
Edward III
  (1327–77)

Richard II
  (1377–99)
Henry IV (Lancas-
  trian)
  (1399–1413)

GERMANY
Emperors
Charles IV
  (1347–78)

FRANCE
Kings
Louis X
  (1314–16)

Philip V
  (1316–22)
Charles IV
  (1322–28)
Philip VI (Valois)
  (1328–50)
John II
  (1350–64)
Charles V
  (1364–80)
Charles VI
  (1380–1422)

1302, Philip IV (le Bel) called the first Estates-General in France. . . . 1305–77, Babylonian Captivity of Popes at Avignon. . . . Knights Templars condemned, De Molay burned. . . . Bruce won battle at Bannockburn and was crowned King of Scots. . . . Sir John Mandeville traveled widely. . . . 1315, Swiss won their independence at Morgarten. . . . Valois line founded. . . . "Salic Law" established. . . . 1337, Hundred Years' War began between England and France. . . . Edward III claimed French crown. . . . 1346, Battle of Crécy; first important military use of cannon. . . . Disputes between France and England over possession of Calais. . . . Circa 1348, Order of the Garter instituted by Edward III – "Honi soit qui mal y pense." . . . 1348–50, terrible ravages of the Black Death. . . . Rienzo ruled a short time in Rome, as "Tribune of the People." . . . Petrarch wrote sonnets, odes. . . . 1355–56, Charles IV of Germany issued Golden Bull. . . . The Black Prince captured John II at Poitiers. . . . 1360, Treaties of Calais and Bretigny. . . . 1362, William Langland wrote *Piers Plowman*. . . . 1363, English sumptuary laws. . . . English made the official language of Parliament. . . . Decay of feudalism. . . . Revolt of the Jacquerie in France. . . . Dante (1265–1321), Boccaccio (*Decameron*). . . . German universities founded at Erfurt and Heidelberg. . . . Ming Dynasty in China, period of great art and high culture. . . . 1376, the Good Parliament in England. . . . Poll tax. . . . Timur the Lame (Tamberlane) revived the Mongol Empire. . . . William of Wykeham planned buildings at Oxford and Windsor. . . . 1378, John Wyclif translated the Bible into English. . . . 1381, Peasants' Revolt against Richard II, led by Wat Tyler and John Ball. . . . 1390(?), Geoffrey Chaucer wrote *The Canterbury Tales*. . . . 1399, Richard II deposed. . . . Henry IV (1399–1413), first Lancastrian king. . . . Great age of art in Italy. . . . Taddeo Gaddi, Orcagna (painter, sculptor, architect), Fra Angelico, Castagna, Uccello, Veneziano. . . . Guelfs (Pope's party) and Ghibellines (Emperor's party) carried their differences into the dress, the habits, and even the art of Italy. . . . Rise of the middle classes to political power and economic affluence. . . . With decay of feudalism, power of the nobles lessened; the power of the Church over all Europe diminished, and the power of local and national heads increased. . . . Commerce flourished. . . . Rise of the guilds.

Man is born with wonder in his eyes. As he grows up, he investigates the cause of this wonder. Man, even common man, comes to know beauty; in attempting to catch this beauty, he girdles the earth and makes contact with the stars.

In the fourteenth century, he looked down to earth, into the mire of travail, for even here he found reflected beauty; even in the darkest hour of the Black Death, the bell of the order of the Misericordia summoned aid and comfort to the pestilence-ridden. Romance was stricken, but common sense – and the common man – carried on with satisfying zeal.

France, the battleground of the Hundred Years' War, showed of this released energy but faint gleams. The independent Italian cities, though disturbed by the constant bickerings of Guelfs and Ghibellines, found time to mold, at fever heat, imperishable treasures of art which to this day retain the warmth of the fire of creative genius.

England, far from the flaming circle of Dante, warmed herself in the rude glow of Chaucer's familiar hearth-fire. It was this tradesman by lineage (*Chaucer,* or *Chaussière,* means "hose-maker") who fashioned homespun creations which kings were proud to own.

It was the English foot soldier at Crécy who, with his good yew bow, shot into the air his clothyard shaft, which was to shatter the feudal castle to its very foundations.

It was the English burgher who learned to wear the cloak of affluence – and the cloak was fleece-lined. Wool brought revenue to English kings, but it brought power and respectability to English merchants. Dick Whittington and his fellow citizens learned the feel of ermine. The doors of Parliament were opened to them – Parliament, where the Lord Chancellor sat upon a woolsack and where good honest English, and not French, was at last, by royal decree, the official language of lord and commoner.

COSTUME

General Characteristics

This century brought some radical changes and many refinements of styles begun in the previous era. Among the notable points of fourteenth-century costume were these: (1) the tight bodice; (2) the low belt line; (3) the use of buttons, both for fastening and for trimming; (4) the use of fur for trimming and lining – an evidence of the general desire for warmth and comfort; (5) the elaboration of the hood into liripipe, etc.; (6) the exaggeration of the pointed shoe; (7) the use of reticulated headdresses for women; (8) the use of parti-colored, or pied, garments; (9) the transition from chain mail to plate armor (partial, not complete); (10) the edges of garments dagged, scalloped, and otherwise elaborately cut and fashioned.

Materials

To the rich Oriental and Sicilian silks were added several new weaves, among which were *gauze,* a thin silk, and *zatonic,* a kind of satin. Furs were an integral part of dress materials, whole bodices being made of marten, fox, weasel, and other furs. Ermine and miniver and lettice (a gray fur) were for royalty or very high nobility, and were used to trim court costumes, robes of state, and the like. Linen was used in vast quantities, and wool (the leading export from England) was woven in many textures and designs in England, Flanders, and elsewhere. *Kendal* was a coarse woolen cloth much used by huntsmen, foresters, and country squires. *Fustian,* a cotton cloth, first used by the clergy for chasubles, became a staple cloth for durable garments. *Folding* was a coarse cloth used by the poor for heavy service. The use of warm materials was the most outstanding characteristic of the time.

First Italy, then France, led the fashions for this century. England, however, showed a certain sureness and independence of style, especially along the lines of comfort and solid richness of apparel.

Colors

Rich, bright colors were still popular – *sangwin,* a rich red, and *pers,* a deep blue, were the favorite shades. Russets, Kendal greens, grays, and browns were favored by the middle classes, which were becoming influential and prominent.

Underclothes

Quilted tunics or *doublets* (so called because the cloth was doubled, sometimes being padded between) of linen, fustian, and other cloths were in demand for use in cold weather and for protection against the stiff chain mail and plate armor. Garters were commonly used by men (to hold up the tips of the absurdly long shoes) and by women (as evidenced by the incident of the Countess of Salisbury's garter in 1347). Drawers, shirts, and chemises, under-tunics for women, fur-lined bodices – all showed an increasing number of garments worn, as well as a sensible appreciation of the value of dress. The fourteenth century may not have been the smartest, but it was certainly a most comfortable age.

COSTUME FOR MEN

Cote-hardie

This garment superseded the long robe and tunic formerly in favor. For young men it had a tight-fitting body to the hips. Here it ended; or, as variation, a short skirt, eight or ten inches long, was added. The cote-hardie buttoned all the way down the front, or to the skirt which was added at the low belt line. A broad belt was worn about the hips at the lower edge of the cote-hardie. This belt was of leather or cloth, buckled or clasped in front, sometimes elaborately jeweled (Fig. 107 A). A cote-hardie used for military costume was called a *jupon,* and was frequently padded. Sometimes, too, the civilian type was stuffed and padded over the chest.

The sleeves were long (or elbow length) and tight. If elbow length, the sleeve of the under-tunic, long and often buttoned from elbow to wrist, showed. Above the elbow of the cote-hardie sleeve was a band, from which depended a *tippet,* or narrow piece of cloth, originally white (Fig. 107 A C). The tippets became more elaborate, scalloped along the edges, and cut in one with the short sleeve (Fig. 115 B). Some-

Fig. 106

times the tippet was simply a cord with tassels or bells at intervals as trimming. For older men, the cote-hardie was worn with a long skirt to the ankles.

Houppelande

Next to the cote-hardie, the *houppelande* was the most popular garment in this century, although it did not come into general use until near the close of the period, and continued in use through the fifteenth century. The name was probably derived from the Spanish *hopalanda,* a long, fur-lined gown worn by students. It was buttoned close about the neck, even to the ears at times (Fig. 108 D), and down the front, or at least part way. Snug-fitting about the shoulders, it flared out at the bottom (Fig. 108 A B). The sleeves were long and snug, or loose and flowing (Fig. 108 A C). Not only was the houppelande often lined with fur, but it was edged with fur about the neck and sleeves. It was usually unbelted. Charles VI of France is said to have introduced the style when he hastily donned a houppelande one morning to go to the rescue of his constable.

Tabard

The *tabard* (sometimes called a surcoat) was probably derived from the dalmatic. In its simplest form, it was an oblong with a hole in the center for the head (Fig. 92 A B). Older men wore it over a long tunic or cote-hardie. The ploughman, in the *Canterbury Tales,* wore a tabard. ("Tabard," as may be recalled, was also the name of the inn.) Lawyers preferred the tabard to other garb.

Cyclas

This was another sleeveless garment with curved portions cut out under the arms (Fig. 116 A B). It was worn over a long tunic or cote-hardie, and often it was decorated with pockets or slits cut vertically in front.

Pelisse

This was a type of garment which resembled a circular cape. It fell to the ankles, but was slit up each side, forming a sort of full circular tabard. Smooth-fitting about the neck and shoulders, it fell in many folds about the feet. It was often bordered with a deep band of fur, and frequently it was fur-lined. Later, the slit was reduced to a mere armhole, and a sleeve was inserted.

Chausses

With all short garments, and usually with long ones also, the men wore chausses, or long hose (Fig. 107 A Fig. 109). At first of a solid color, they were later made of a different color for each leg; later still, each leg was striped in two or more colors, lengthwise (Fig. 111 D F) or horizontally (Fig. 111 B). The chausses were put on and held up like tights. Frequently a ribbon (or garter) was tied about each leg of the chausses, below the knee, to prevent wrinkling and sagging. Many Renaissance artists, like Taddeo Gaddi, Benozzo Gozzoli, and Ghirlandaio, show details of gartering. An instance of unlacing is shown in Bicci di Lorenzo's picture of St. Nicholas of Bari, where the red chausses are being unlaced at bedtime.

Mantle

The mantle was long, semicircular, and fastened on the right shoulder or in front with buttons or a band (Fig. 117 A B). The garment was essentially the same for men and women alike. A capuchin or hood was often fastened to the mantle; it was allowed to fall back when not in use. The word *cloak* was used more frequently than *mantle.*

Court-pie

This was a short mantle, or cloak, for cold weather. It was never more than three-fourths the length of the wearer's body, and was usually somewhat shorter. It was cut in a perfect circle, with a hole in the center for the head. The sides were slit a short distance. The *court-pie* was always in two colors, hence the name – *court,* short, *pie,* two-toned. It was very similar to the pelisse.

Footwear

As the century progressed, shoes became more and more elaborate. Designs were cut out of the instep (Fig. 111 B); horizontal stripes were used (Fig. 111 C); straps, buckles, and dotted designs added distinction (Fig. 111 D); the rose window of St. Paul's Gothic church was perpetuated on the instep of a shoe (Fig. 111 E); finally, the toes grew longer and more pointed, until the foot looked like a pointed tail (Fig. 111 F). The pointed shoes were called *poleyns* and, more rarely, *chopines;* in England they were called *cracows,* from the home of Anne of Bohemia, queen of Richard II. In France, by royal decree of Philip le Bel, peasants could wear shoes six inches long; bourgeois, twelve inches long; lords, twenty-four inches long – and so on! The king, and the dandies who aped royal caprices, fastened the tips of the shoes up to the leg, or garter, with fine chains. *Clogs* or *poleyns* (the same name was applied to the undershoe as to the shoe) were used to keep the delicate footwear off the muddy ground (see next chapter for details). *Buskins,* or short, laced boots, were also used, especially by soldiers, travelers, and the lower classes. *Cordevain* (Cordova leather) was excellent for making the shoes.

Fig. 111

Hair

At the beginning of the century, beards were worn. Mustaches were also popular, and both mustache and beard were carefully curled. The hair was cut square across the forehead and brushed back of the ears in curls, "as if they were laid in press." Younger men, however, preferred the hair to be rolled or tucked under, close about the head, like short hair; they also went clean-shaven, or with a mustache only. The French preferred pointed beards, and the English copied them; toward the end of the century, forked beards became fashionable, and the hair was worn long and flowing.

Headdress

The capuchin or hood, separate or attached to a mantle, was much in evidence, and persisted as the common head covering of monks through the centuries. The separate hood (Fig. 107 A B) was a staple article of dress for men. Many varieties were worn, and the skirts to them were zigzagged, scalloped, and cut in many different designs. The hood acquired a tail, or *liripipe,* an elongation of the point of an earlier time (Fig. 106 E   Fig. 107 A B). The liripipe was worn hanging down the back, or wound about the neck, or carried gracefully over the wrist or in the hand. The hood was fastened under the chin or on the right shoulder with buttons or lacings (Fig. 107 A). Sometimes a row of five or six buttons was used. A *cap,* like a baby's cap, tied under the chin, was used by all classes; other headdresses might be worn over this cap.

The *abacot* was a variety of hat which was much worn in this and succeeding centuries. It was of felt, leather, or beaver (introduced from Flanders, as a result of the Hundred Years' War), and might be parti-colored – the crown of white, the brim of red (or any other combination of colors). The crown was conical or round; the brim was turned up front or back; the sharp peak, back or front, was a distinctive feature. The brim might be plain, or cut in scallops or sharp points (Fig. 106 A   Fig. 113 A). A feather, perched upright in front, added a saucy touch to the hat. A small, round cap, with a point on top, like a Hun's cap, was also used.

The *sugar loaf* was a tall, conical, or round-topped hat of leather, felt, or beaver, much affected by hunters, travelers, and the like (Fig. 124 D   Fig. 131 A). It was brimless, but might have a feather worn upright, front or back.

The *chaperon* was a type of hat used in France toward the end of the century, and by dandies in England. It will be fully described in the next chapter.

In addition, fillets, chaplets, and coronets were worn, especially indoors. Hats, however, were not necessarily doffed indoors, but were worn at table and at indoor gatherings.

A crown of Richard II is shown in Fig. 121.

Ornaments and Accessories

The sumptuary laws of England indicate the luxuries of the toilet. Ermine and lettice, as well as pearls, were strictly forbidden to all who did not possess a thousand

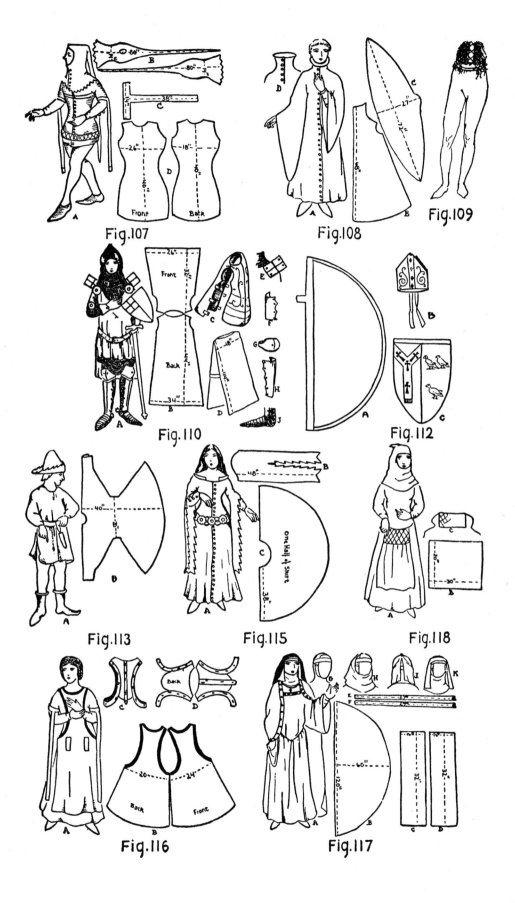

Fig.107

Fig.108

Fig.109

Fig.110

Fig.112

Fig.113

Fig.115

Fig.118

Fig.116

Fig.117

pounds yearly income. Cloth of gold and silver, jewel embroidery, and miniver and other furs were forbidden to those not having a yearly income of four hundred marks. Ribbons, girdles, embroidered garments, jeweled belts, rings, buckles, jeweled pouches, jeweled chaplets – all these were permitted only to persons having stated incomes. Gartering acquired rich and jeweled trimmings.

Pouches or purses, called *gypcières,* hung at the girdle; in these pouches was often thrust an *anelace* or knife. (The franklin in the *Canterbury Tales* wore such a pouch and knife.) Gold and silver buttons, daggers, little bells (on tunic and hood, and pendant from the jeweled belt) were used. Pilgrims carried a *staff* and a *scrip* (or bag).

Military Dress

The addition of plate armor to chain mail was gradual but steady during this era. *Brassarts* or plates connected the shoulder with the elbow pieces (Fig. 110 F). The hauberk began to have pieces of plate armor over the chain mail; *greaves* of plate protected the shins (Fig. 110 H). Instead of leather *genouillières,* metal ones were used (Fig. 110 G). *Ailettes* (Fig. 110 A E) were worn at the shoulder. Pieces of plate – *sollerets* – covered the feet (Fig. 110 J Fig. 111 A). Finally, the hauberk ceased to be of chain mail, except for a bit front and back; occasionally a light chain mail hauberk was worn under another hauberk (or *jupon*) of solid plate. The solid hauberk was usually put on over a quilted cloth or leather jacket (also called *jupon*). The hauberk of solid plate was fitted to the body, hinged at the sides, and buckled together (Fig. 110 C). The surcoat became shorter in front than in back, and finally disappeared altogether (Fig. 110 A B). Heralds wore a sort of tabard, like a modern sandwich-board (Fig. 110 D); on this tabard were embroidered the arms of the person or nation represented.

The helm, called a *basinet,* was a round metal head covering, usually fastened to the chain mail hood or gorget (Fig. 106 D Fig. 110 A). Another type of helm came to be worn; it was very ornate and was topped with a large crest, design, or plume.

The weapons carried were the sword, the *bill* or *gisarme* (like a scythe on a long pole), a triangular or pear-shaped shield, a poleax, a scimitar, a bow and arrows. The *clothyard shaft* (tipped with gray goose feather), which won the day at Crécy, was so called because it measured a cloth-yard in length. The measure of a yard was standardized by Henry II, who "smelled a yard," i. e., measured the length from his nose to the tip of his finger.

Ecclesiastical Dress

Figure 112 shows the cape, miter, and heraldic shield of Thomas à Becket, murdered at Canterbury Cathedral in 1170. Priests in this time wore about the same vestments they had worn during the Middle Ages, though the miter was somewhat more elaborate, and the chasuble was worn with a point front and back. Monastic robes, and also nuns' robes, were thoroughly regulated, with few changes.

Pilgrims who were bound for Jerusalem wore a white cross, if from England; a red cross, if from France (probably in honor of St. Denis, whose oriflamme was scarlet); a green cross, if from Flanders. If they completed the pilgrimage to Jeru-salem, they were privileged to wear a palm branch, and were called *palmers;* if they went to Rome on a pilgrimage, they could wear the crossed keys of St. Peter, or the *vernicle,* in honor of St. Veronica; if they made a pilgrimage to Santiago di Compostella (St. James's shrine), they could wear a scallop shell. If they went to the shrine of St. Thomas à Becket at Canterbury, they could wear the Canterbury bells, or carry an *ampulla* with some of the holy saint's blood (much diluted) in it.

A papal crown of the fourteenth century is shown in Fig. 120.

Mourning

In the writings of this century occur many definite allusions to mourning garb. Chaucer describes Palamon appearing at Arcite's funeral "in clothes black"; another mark of mourning was to have the face clean-shaven. The entire household of a nobleman wore black for the mourning period, the nobleman or family furnishing the garments.

COSTUME FOR CHILDREN

Children wore simplified adaptations of their elders' clothes (Fig. 107 Fig. 113). Babies were wrapped in swaddling clothes and strapped to boards with cross-gartering. Boys wore the hood, a short tunic (Fig. 113 A B Fig. 114), and loose shoes. The abacot was also worn, and the liripipe. The use of the liripipe led to the game of "blind man's buff." In this game, as then played, the victim groped, with the hood put over his head backward, thus blinding him, as the others, eluding his grasp, whipped him with the skirted tips of their own liripipes.

COSTUME FOR THE LOWER CLASSES

These wore the smock-frock, or full tunic, of canvas, fustian, russet, galebrun, or other coarse material. A type of tunic is shown in Fig. 113 A B; this illustration shows also the kind of high, rolled shoes, or buskins, used by the peasants and lower classes. It also shows one way the abacot was worn. Cowls or hoods (Fig. 106 E) were favorite headgear for the lower classes; they also wore wide hats of felt or straw, or caps tied under the chin. The blacksmith wore a leather apron over the tunic. Jews were obliged to sew two woolen tablets of different colors, two fingers broad and four fingers long, on the breasts of their garments.

COSTUME FOR WOMEN

Cote-hardie

This garment was worn as frequently by women as by men. For the women it was made very long, tightly buttoned down the front to the hips; the buttons might even extend to the hem. The neckline was high, buttoned tightly up to the chin, or low and round about the shoulders, Victorian style. The low hip-belt was used, either of plain leather, buckled, or made of square or round metal clasps, variously decorated. The sleeves were long and tight, with tippets, plain or serrated, above the elbows; or the same type of full, pendant sleeve was used as in the Middle Ages (Fig. 115 A B). The pattern shows that to the form-fitting waist was attached a circular skirt, full and rippling (Fig. 115 A C).

Sometimes the dress might be cut princess-style, widely flared at the bottom. There was no belt around the natural waistline of this type of dress, but often a girdle was draped low over the hips, and the excessively long skirt bloused over this girdle. Some skirts were remarkably wide: Occleve mentions a skirt of scarlet twelve yards wide.

Cyclas (or Surcoat)

Another type of dress was the *cyclas,* sometimes called the surcoat. This was a sleeveless over-dress, or super-cote-hardie, with the armholes cut out in a deep curve. If the cyclas were long, to the ankles, the bottom edge flared moderately; pockets or slits placed vertically in front formed the decoration (Fig. 116 A B). The rounded

Fig. 114

Fig. 119

neck and rounded armholes were decorated with bands of contrasting material, or of fur.

In its shorter form, the cyclas or surcoat reached only to the hips. It was cut straight around at the bottom edge, or in deep scallops, front and back (Fig. 116 C D). Around the neck and armholes and down the front might be bands of contrasting material or fur. Always worn over the cote-hardie or other type of long gown, this garment assumed the appearance of a jacket, especially as it might be lined with fur throughout.

Houppelande

Occasionally older women wore the houppelande.

Nuns affected the loose dalmatic with wide sleeves (Fig. 117 A).

All types of dress might have long trains – so long that women of the time were compared by the preaching friars to magpies, trailing their tails in the dirt.

In the fourteenth century, women began to emblazon their arms on their dresses. The insignia of the woman's own family was on her cote-hardie or other type of gown; that of her husband was on her mantle.

Mantle

The semicircular mantle, fastened with a band across the breast, was worn also by women (Fig. 117 A B). It might be cut out a little at the back of the neck, to insure a better fit.

Footwear

Women's shoes followed the fashions of men's, although they did not affect extremely pointed toes, probably because the very long skirts hid the feet.

Hair

The fourteenth century was an age eager for new fashions in hairdressing. The two braids that had characterized twelfth-century hair arrangement were still worn, but were now coiled on either side of the head; sometimes a high, wired gorget (Fig. 106 C) partly concealed them; sometimes they were wound about the

Fig. 120

Fig. 121

head, coronet fashion. Often they were tucked into cylinders of wire mesh at the side of the head, as will be described later.

Young girls still wore their hair long and flowing, with chaplets of flowers, or metal circlets of gold or silver.

Headdress

In addition to the hood (sometimes the hood and liripipe), the women wore the wimple and gorget, snugly draped. As this type of headdress was in use so long and was the basis for many headdresses, it will be carefully explained.

In Fig. 117 C D are the two pieces of white cloth (linen was the material used by nuns) used for wimple and gorget. Though these rectangles drape nicely, better results may be obtained by using two squares, in which instance the designer must double the width given (instead of 32″ x 16″, use 32″ x 32″). Strips E and F (each about one inch wide) are fastened, E about the forehead, F about the chin, care being taken to follow the tip of the chin (Fig. 117 G). Pin securely; also pin at temples where the two strips cross. Next adjust the gorget, C. Fold the square C on the bias, center bias edge at chin, follow line of chin strap F, and lap over on top (Fig. 117 H J). Next lay the wimple (square D) over the head, centering front edge at middle of forehead, pinning to band E. Pin the straight edge of D carefully to the temples at either side, where E and F cross. The veil will then fall in graceful folds down either side of the face (Fig. 117 K). Over the white gorget and wimple was often worn a second, longer veil of white or black or blue; the color designated the religious order of the wearer.

This type of headdress was not confined to women in religious orders; it will be remembered that the Wife of Bath wore a wimple which weighed "ten pound."

The most elaborate headdress was the *crespin and caul* (Fig. 106 B). The *crespin* was a circlet or chaplet of metal, wire, gold, or silver. Sometimes it was an elaborate crown, with points, leaves, jewels, etc. Attached to it at each side, over the ear, was a *caul,* a cagelike cylinder of wire mesh. The shapes of the cauls varied from oblong to round, but the purpose was the same, to encase the braids or rolls of hair. The cauls were sometimes set with pearls and other stones. The wimple was often added to this headdress. (The lady in Fig. 106 B is wearing both.) Crespins and cauls were so valuable that they were often mentioned as heirlooms in wills.

Turbans, reminiscent of the Orient, were affected by ladies of fashion. These were wrapped about the head in various manners, and were often decorated with pearls. A sort of *net turban* covered the coiled braids and entire hair, like a large hair net.

The chaplets or crowns worn by ladies of rank became wider and more ornate. They were usually worn over the wimple (Fig. 106 C). Wimples, in their earliest form, went out of fashion in 1360, except for widows, nuns, and middle-class women – but variations were used for centuries afterwards.

For travel, a flat-brimmed, low, round-crowned hat (similar to the Greek petasos), tied under the chin with cords, was used.

Ornaments and Accessories

Besides the crespin and caul, chaplets, crowns, rings, bracelets, brooches, gold and silver buttons, and gold and silver girdles (often jeweled) were among the ornaments most in demand. Buckles were decorated and jeweled, and even gloves were jeweled. Jet was supposed to possess certain virtues, and was therefore in great demand for jeweled ornaments.

The gypcière, or pouch, suspended from the girdle, was often of rich silk or leather, lined and jeweled. Aprons, embroidered or plain, were worn on domestic occasions by ladies of rank and by other classes as ordinary garb. Gloves were worn by ladies of quality. A *pomander* or spherical scent ball was carried, not only for the perfume, but also for (supposed) protection against the plague.

Since ladies' sleeves were used as pennants by faithful knights, on their lances, the fashion prevailed of making them separate from the dress, even of a different color. Several pairs of sleeves might be made for one gown; ladies gave them as favors (and seemed always prepared). The edges of the sleeves were "indented," "dagged," "barred," "paled," "bended," or "serrated."

Make-up

The same extravagance in make-up continued. Paint, powder, and eye-black were heavily used. Taddeo Gaddi said that the Florentine women were the best painters in the world.

Mourning

Black was still the color of mourning. Chaucer describes Cressid as being "in widow's habit black," although she is also described as wearing a widow's habit of "samite brown."

Costume for Children

A plain tunic (Fig. 116 A) was usual for girls. It was made with buttons down the front; over this might be worn an apron, or a long cyclas with pockets. The hood was worn with this. A dress for a young child is shown in Fig. 119.

Costume for the Lower Classes

These wore the loose or full gown, ankle length, with or without the apron, or *barme-cloth* (Fig. 118 A B C), as they called it. Sometimes a cyclas was worn. A hood for cold weather wear, a full wimple, a circular cloak — all helped to keep the goodwife or the peasant woman warm and comfortable (Fig. 118 A). Linen, fustian, linsey-woolsey, galebrun, russet, buckram, and other stuffs were used. Short hose, cross-gartered, were the usual leg coverings.

Modern Adaptations

For materials, the same suggestions hold true for this century as for the period preceding. A little more pattern in the materials, more brocaded designs, more gold and silver threadwork in the patterns – these things accentuate the richness and material prosperity of this period. Especially were the sleeves brocaded. A good way to bring out the pattern, which is best painted on the material (as appliqué is apt to ravel after a few performances), is to outline the design with cord, gilded, silvered, or plain white. Anything which raises up the pattern is good for this period.

The pieces of plate armor added to the chain mail are best simulated by gold or silver oilcloth, or else by oilcloth turned wrong side out and painted (the right side does not take paint easily and cracks immediately), or by heavy unbleached muslin painted with aluminum. The material should be lined, with canvas if possible, so it will hold its shape.

CHAPTER VIII

THE FIFTEENTH CENTURY

IMPORTANT PEOPLE AND EVENTS

ITALY

Popes

Martin V
  (1417–31)
Alexander VI
  (1431–1503)

Artists

Tommaso dei Masaccio
Benozzo Gozzoli
Fra Filippo Lippi
Sandro Botticelli
Domenico Ghirlandaio
Filippino Lippi
Antonio Pollaiuolo
Andrea del Verrocchio
Piero della Francesca
Perugino (Pietro Van-
  nucci)
Pinturicchio
  (Bernardino Betti)
Andrea Mantegna
Bartolomeo Montagna
The Bellini
  (Jacopo, father; Gio-
  vanni and Gentile,
  sons)
Vittore Carpaccio
Il Francia
  (Francesco Raibo-
  lini)
Donatello di Niccolò
Lorenzo Ghiberti

Luca della Robbia
Filippo Brunelleschi
Leonardo da Vinci

Notable People

Angelo Poliziano
Manuel Chrysoloras
Marsilio Ficino
Nicolò di Machiavelli
Girolamo Savonarola

Notable Families

The Borgias
The de' Medicis
The Pazzis
The Riccardis
The Rucellais
The Pittis
The Strozzis
The Tuornabuonis
The Sforzas
The Orsinis
The Malatestas

Explorers

Amerigo Vespucci
Christopher Columbus

ENGLAND

Kings

Henry IV (Lancaster)
  (1399–1413)

Henry V
  (1413–22)
Henry VI
  (1422–61)
Edward IV (York)
  (1461–83)
Edward V
  (1483)
Richard III
  (1483–85)
Henry VII (Tudor)
  (1485–1509)

Notable People

William Caxton
William Tyndale
Thomas Malory

GERMANY

Emperors

Maximilian I
  (1493–1519)

Artists

Michael Wolgemuth

SPAIN

Kings

Ferdinand of Aragon
  and Isabella of Cas-
  tile (married in
  1469)

FLANDERS

Artists

Hubert and Jan van
  Eyck
Rogier van der Wey-
  den
  (de la Pasture)
Hans Memling
Quinten Massys
Jan van Mabuse
  (Jan Gossart)

FRANCE

Kings

Charles VI (Valois)
  (1380–1422)
Charles VII
  (1422–61)
Louis XI
  (1461–83)
Charles VIII
  (1483–98)
Louis XII
  (1498–1515)

Artists

René of Anjou
Jean Fouquet

Notable People

François Villon
St. Joan of Arc

The fifteenth century centered in Italy, where (it may be said) began the great Renaissance of art. The age was profusely sprinkled with painters like Masaccio and Botticelli, sculptors like Donatello and Verrocchio, architects like Brunelleschi, men of letters like Poliziano, and men of affairs like the de' Medicis. Soon the frenzy of inspiration spread beyond the Alps to Flanders, where the Van Eycks and others labored; to France and (only by way of the Church and its liturgical dramas and the first printers) to England.

The Church was having a struggle to maintain its own dignity. . . . Schisms led to Church councils (at Basel, Pisa, Constance) and to the burning of John Hus. . . , Gutenberg invented movable type (*circa* 1450), opening the way for Caxton (1477) and the great age of printing – Aldine, Stephani, and Froben presses.

Wars continued in France and England. . . . 1415, Henry V of England won victory at Agincourt. . . . 1420, Treaty of Troyes. . . . Henry V married Catherine, daughter of Charles VI of France (she later, when widowed, married Owen Tudor). . . . 1429, siege of Orleans. . . . 1431, Joan of Arc burned. . . . 1453, Hundred Years' War ended.

1453, Turks captured Constantinople, thus ending the Eastern Roman Empire. . . . University of Salamanca founded. . . . Wars of the Roses in England, 1455–85, between Houses of Lancaster and York. . . . Tudors won at Bosworth Field, and Henry VII, a Tudor, was crowned, 1485. . . . 1477, Charles the Bold of Burgundy was killed by Swiss at Nancy; his daughter Mary married Maximilian of Austria. . . . 1469, Isabella of Castile married Ferdinand of Aragon. . . . Ivan III founded the first united Russian monarchy at Moscow. . . . Jesus Christ was made King of Florence in 1492 – "Rex regium et Dominus Dominantium" carved over Palazzo Vecchio. . . . 1494, Savonarola made Florence a republic, driving out the Medicis, burning all "vanities" in an auto-da-fé. . . . 1498, Savonarola burned as a heretic.

Great age of discovery. . . . 1486, Diaz discovered the Cape of Good Hope. . . . 1492, Ferdinand and Isabella sent Columbus to find route to Indies; he found America. . . . 1497, Henry VII sent Cabot westward; he discovered the mainland of America. . . . 1498, Vasco da Gama discovered all-water route to India.

1492, expulsion of Moors from Spain. . . . Silk factory established at Lyons, France. . . . Tapestries made at Arras. . . . Plate armor reached height of perfection. . . . Period of development of guilds, arts and crafts.

The Renaissance was not an event, but an ecstasy. It glowed from the quickened spirit of an awakened people. From that quickening were produced the marvels of Botticelli, Ghiberti, and Leonardo da Vinci that still delight the world. There also came into being men who, by their virile personalities, left indelible imprints on their own and future times. Some of these men were saints, like Fra Angelico and Savonarola; some were devils, like Ludovico Sforza and Alexander Borgia; some were neither saint nor devil, but very human, like Cosimo and Lorenzo de' Medici. Although the Renaissance was an intellectual passion, it by no means neglected the physical world.

Florence, "city of the lily," called by Dante the most beautiful and famous daughter of Rome, drew to her bosom the genius of the Renaissance. She who had been fed on the milk of human greatness and the manna of freedom nourished in turn the exponents of emancipation. Eagerly she breathed in the invigorating air of the early Renaissance while the rest of Europe was still in its medieval trance. Louis XI was shivering in his astrologer's tower; York and Lancaster were reddening the bosom and whitening the cheek of England in the name of a Rose.

The Holy Roman Emperors twisted and racked the tenets of Christianity to fit an ironbound fanaticism; the tortured smile of John Hus raised a question to which the printing presses of Gutenberg were to thunder a reply. In the East, Ivan the Great, at Moscow, founded the first united Russian monarchy, and Sultan Mohammed II brought to an end the last Roman Empire at Constantinople. In the West, Ferdinand of Aragon balanced the victory of Mohammed by the expulsion of the Moors. He and Isabella, however, were to find their real fame in the rash loan of a few royal trinkets to a persuasive Genoese sailor.

This extension of credit, which stretched man's horizon halfway round the earth, was typical of the Renaissance, and particularly of the Renaissance at Florence. The greatness of the city rested on the credit of her merchant princes – men to whom half of Europe was financially debtor, to whom all the world was to be debtor aesthetically. The hand that balanced the scales of commerce weighed out beauty for mankind.

These Florentine merchants, like their fellow citizens, were a highly practical, intensely curious, strongly imaginative people. Being traders, they had vision, that psychic sense of future values which has helped to label the Hebrews Oriental mystics. Art and industry were inseparable – and invaluable so. The Calimala brought rough cloth from Flanders, refined it, and sold it at triple the price to the unimaginative Northerners.

Politics was another tool of the trade. No one was eligible for political preferment who was not enrolled in one of the twenty-one guilds, or *Arti*. Dante belonged to the guild of Doctors or Apothecaries – the same *Arti* to which the de' Medicis belonged, as the pills or *palle* on their coat of arms showed (the same pills, in threes, that today swing before the pawnbroker's shop).

Dress was a prime business of the guilds; the Renaissance brought a self-consciousness which expressed itself in a thousand new inventions of taste. The same craftsmen who designed a necklace or a headdress might be limning a Madonna or carving a saint; the sure touch of genius quickened all into the beauty which still fires the imagination of the world.

COSTUME

GENERAL CHARACTERISTICS

This great century of the Renaissance reflected its glory, its richly fertile imagination in the costume of the time. (1) Materials were costly and varied; (2) furs were in general use as trimming; (3) the parts of costume (particularly sleeves) were duplicated in different designs; (4) hair and headdresses were intricate in arrangement; (5) plate armor reached its highest development; (6) jewelry and accessories were artistic in the extreme and exquisite in workmanship.

The patterns of cloth reflected mythological and classic designs and heraldic insignia. The universality of such patterns showed the tremendous influence of Italy, home of the Renaissance, on costume and creative design. Burgundy, however, during the rule of Philip the Good, became conspicuous by the lavishness and richness of its dress. France became the center for new and unusual headdresses and also for plate armor; England, torn with the wars, gave little thought to dress until Richard II gave too much thought to it – and was, as a result, relieved of his other cares.

Materials

The establishment of a silk factory at Lyons by Louis XI (Louis, while probably one of the worst-dressed kings, was not averse to profiting by the vanity of others) in 1466 led to the production of many domestic patterns and weaves. Brocades in varied designs were produced, and also samite in a six-thread tissue, figured and flowered, with interweaving designs. Velvet became one of the favored textiles for the wealthy, as did also gold and silver tissue and satin. Cendal, sarcenet, taffeta, and other silks continued in vogue. Linen, cotton, and wool were still the staple cloths for the middle and lower classes. Woolen cloth, as refined by the Calimala, became almost as soft and fine in texture as silk. Fustian was used for rough wear.

From the sumptuary laws we learn that the following materials were denied the middle classes: cloth of gold, velvet, damask, satin, and certain furs – miniver, biche, ermine, lettice, and sable. Ordinary folk could wear fox, coney, and marten. But they could not wear clothes elaborately dagged, or cut in the form of letters or rose leaves or *posies,* as certain embroidered mottoes, much in fashion, were called. One example of the posy was provided by Charles, Duke of Orleans, who had the words and music of a song embroidered in gold thread and pearls on one of his houppelandes.

Colors

Green, yellow, gold, silver, purple, orange, red, garnet, crimson ("sangwin"), blue ("pers"), violet, and all rich shades were in favor. Beatrice, Duchess of Milan, wore a cloth of gold and silver tissue over a green velvet petticoat and on her head wore a crimson felt hat trimmed with blue ribbons.

Underclothes

Long drawers, fashioned on the pattern of chapter VII, Fig. 109, were worn for warmth beneath the long, loose robes of the men, and perhaps also beneath the women's dresses, though there are no proofs of this. Undershirts for men, chemises (or *shifts*) for women were commonly used. A snug-fitting robe or kirtle with tight sleeves was worn under the outer robe and was shown generously when the outer skirt was lifted in front, as was the custom in walking.

An under-jacket (or doublet) was often worn by men under a loose outer jacket. The accusation of Joan of Arc enumerates her masculine garments – shirts, breeches (drawers), hose, under-jacket, long jacket, and chaperon. The shirt, for men and women alike, was made of fine material, as it was revealed at the shoulder joinings of the sleeves, a bit about the neck, and under the outer garments when puffs and slashes became fashionable.

Short, slightly puffed trunks were worn over or under the long hose, as the hose were often worn separately and not sewed together at the top.

Costume for Men

Houppelande

The popularity of this garment increased. Variations came in; instead of a houppelande with a high, tightly buttoned collar, for instance, there was substituted one with a roll collar of the same or contrasting material or of fur (Fig. 124 C), turned back to a deep V in front; or a standing collar might be used (Fig. 124 D Fig. 129 C Fig. 130 C Fig. 131 A). The sleeve also came in for elaboration. It was puffed and stuffed at the shoulders (Fig. 124 D); it was very long, styled perhaps with a slit at the elbow, and trimmed with fur (Fig. 129 C Fig. 133 K L). The sleeve might be puffed at the shoulder, slit, and laced across, with a loose, wrinkled cuff at the wrist (Fig. 124 D Fig. 133 F G); or it might be tight, or pendant in a long V, with plain or serrated edges, as in the preceding century. An infinite variety of forms embellished this detail of dress.

The houppelande was ankle length at least and often swept the ground. It might, however, be slit to the knee for ease in walking, or even worn short, calf length, over a jacket. Fur bandings – on sleeves, collar, bottom edge, and front – were common; for outdoor use, the entire garment might be lined, and used as a cloak. Old and young wore the houppelande, although it was most favored by the more sedate members of society.

Gown

A long, unbelted gown, snug about the upstanding neckband, moderately full, usually unbelted, with open sleeves, was fashionable in Italy, and was adopted by professional men in other lands.

Jacket

Pourpoint, jacquette, doublet, jupon – all these designations were used in various countries for the short type of garment of various designs.

One type of this garment resembled the houppelande – in fact, it might be called a short houppelande; it was smooth-fitting at the neck and radiated out into regularly-laid pleats at the waistline and below (Fig. 125 A C). The sleeve was puffed at the shoulder; below, it might be pendant and open (Fig. 125 B Fig. 130 C), or closed (Fig. 129 C Fig. 133 K L). Often the jacket had a band of fur about the neck, sleeves, and bottom edge. Examples of this type of dress are seen in Gozzoli's figure of Lorenzo de' Medici in the "Journey of the Magi," in Fabriano's "Adoration of the Magi," in Francesca's "Queen of Sheba." In some instances, the jacket was fulled about the neck in gathers or pleats.

Another type of the jacket came to the middle of the thighs, and had a turn-back collar and revers of fur down the front. Sleeves similar to the styles described above were worn. This type of jacket is associated with Louis XI. Often under it was worn a plain, belted tunic.

Very Short Jacket

This type (Fig. 127 A) was condemned by the sumptuary laws of the time; it was cut almost circular, falling in many folds at the waist, unbelted. In Fig. 127 is the pattern, along the plain edge and inner circular line. A longer version with diagonal front edge is shown in Fig. 127 B, and pattern along heavy edge with outside circular line.

Fitted Jacket

This type, fitted to the body, stuffed and padded, like a pouter pigeon, is shown in Fig. 126 C D E. The front might be slashed to reveal the white shirt beneath,

Fig. 122

Fig. 123

Fig. 125

Fig. 124

CAPE

Fig. 126

FRONT
BACK

Fig. 127

Fig. 128

WAIST-FRONT
BACK
BELT
FRONT SKIRT

Fig. 134

SLEEVE
FRONT
BACK

Fig. 133

Fig. 137

Fig. 138

with lacing across (Fig. 126 C). The skirt to the jacket was sometimes cut separately. Sleeves of the new slashed and puffed type are shown (Fig. 126 E, and in pattern, Fig. 133 M N). This type was also worn without the skirt, as shown in Pinturicchio's "Pageant of Calisto III."

Surcoat or Tabard

The surcoat was still worn, cut very short front and back, and usually of brocade. It was lined, had no sleeves, and the sides were either straight or flared out diagonally.

Other types of the short jacket are shown in Fig. 129 A, Fig. 130 C, Fig. 131 B D.

Leg Coverings

The chausses or long hose of cloth continued to be worn. The pattern is shown in chapter VII, Fig. 109, with the method of attaching them to the doublet or underjacket by means of eyelets, through which were threaded *points* or *aiguillettes* (laces tipped with pointed metal caps). Points were used not only to fasten nether to upper garments, but also to fasten sleeves to the body of the garment (chapter VII, Fig. 109). The shirt beneath the doublet showed between the fastenings.

The long hose were also worn under the long robe (Fig. 124 D). Parti-colored hose, each leg a different color, developed striped, zigzagged, and floriated patterns (Fig. 126 A). The hose were full-fashioned, the foot in one with the leg portion; or they were funnel-shaped, with a strap beneath the instep. Rarely, they were worn without other foot covering, stiff soles being attached to the hose themselves.

The hose, at first two separate pieces, were later joined together at the top, when short jackets became the mode. A *codpiece,* or separate bag or pouch, was fastened in front to the hose and waistband by points or laces. It was sometimes ornamented with small bows. This was the forerunner of the modern fly or front trouser-flap.

Mantle

A circular cloak served as extra outer wrap. The fur-lined houppelande also was used for this purpose, with a capuchin, or hood, added; the hood was thrown back when not needed. A shorter variety of cape is shown in Fig. 126 A B. This type of cape was worn with or without a collar, which might be flat or rolled.

Footwear

The pointed shoes (poleyns or cracows) of the fourteenth century were still in fashion; they were made of leather, velvet, or thick cloth. Dandies held up the extremely long points with thin, fine chains to a garter just below the knee (Fig. 127 A Fig. 130 C Fig. 136 C), or to the top of the shoe itself (Fig. 126 A). A wooden clog (called *poleyn, cracow,* or *chopine*) was used to keep the long-toed shoes off the ground (Fig. 131 D Fig. 136 B).

The shoes were shaped like the earlier types, and were either slit at the sides (Fig. 125 A Fig. 129 A Fig. 136 C), or buckled at the ankle (Fig. 131 B). In addition, boots came into favor as a result of the wars, the interest in tournaments, and the general esteem paid the fighting class. The boots were of soft leather, usually turned over at the top (Fig. 136 D), and wrinkled a bit on the leg. They were pulled on by means of loops at the top (Fig. 136 D), or were laced up the sides (Fig. 136 B). The usual type of spurs is shown in Fig. 136 D.

Hair

The hair was worn longer in Italy, France, Flanders, and Germany (in the order named) than in England. The general fashion was to wear the hair to the nape of the neck and curled slightly upward at the lower edge (Fig. 131 B). Usually there were bangs across the forehead, or the hair was parted and brushed low over the forehead. Occasionally, the hair was worn long and straight (Fig. 131 D). In England, it was generally cut much shorter. Mustaches (seldom worn at all) were quite small; beards likewise were small and pointed, but usually young men went beardless.

Headdress

The hood and liripipe, even before the end of the preceding century, had evolved into the chaperon (Fig. 129 C). The hood and liripipe (Fig. 127, two patterns) came to be adjusted differently. The face opening was used for the head opening. The cape of the hood was gathered up like a cock's comb (the edges usually scalloped, dagged, or otherwise designed); the liripipe was then twisted about it and around the head, and allowed to drape over the shoulder, over the forearm, or was brought up under the chin and fastened to the hood above (Fig. 127 A B).

At first the chaperon was draped each time it was put on; later, it was found to be much easier to fasten it permanently. A round roll about a snug crown made a headdress called a *roundlet* (Fig. 129 C). The chaperon was draped over this, with the cock's comb at either side, and the liripipe looped and arranged in any of the many ways. When not in use, the chaperon or roundlet was worn slung over the shoulder. A vestige of the chaperon is seen in the cockades of coachmen, on the right shoulder of the capes of Knights of the Garter, and on the headdress of the modern French lawyer.

The abacot was still worn (Fig. 131 D), usually with a feather before or behind. Felt or beaver was the ordinary material. The small *round cap,* used by pages, and worn with or without a feather, was also popular (Fig. 126 A Fig. 129 A). The tall, pointed hat (Fig. 126 E) was made of felt or beaver, or even heavy linen, and was worn by all classes. The sugar-loaf hat was similar to the last, but was rounded at the top (Fig. 124 D Fig. 131 A). The flat, low-crowned, wide-brimmed hat, familiar through the ages, still made its appearance; the brim was split at the sides

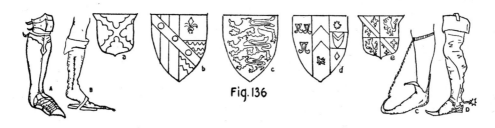

Fig. 136

Fig.131

A   B   C   D

and sometimes folded up over the crown. Simple fillets or chaplets of flowers, as well as crowns, continued to be worn by nobles, especially indoors.

Renaissance portraits and other pictures of the time furnish many illustrations of the headdresses above. Gozzoli's "Journey of the Magi," Maximilian of Austria's portrait (exhibited in Paris, 1874), and "The Money Changers" by Massys provide a few examples.

A crown of Henry V (Plantagenet) is shown in Fig. 137, one of Richard III (York) in Fig. 138, and one of Henry VII (Tudor) in Fig. 139.

Ornaments and Accessories

Men wore chains about their necks; these chains were fashioned of carved links with a plaque or pendant; both chains and plaques were plain, engraved, or studded with gems. Men also wore rings and pins. Brooches adorned headdresses, jackets, and cloaks. Dagger belts, daggers, and swords were carved and often jeweled. Chains to fasten the shoes were of gold or silver. Jewels in demand for ornament were amethysts (thought to ward off drunkenness), chrysolites (thought to lose brilliance in a cup of poison), and opals (reputedly endowed with the power to render the wearer invisible).

The *pouch* was almost universally worn (Fig. 124 B). It held money, seals, and other necessaries, and was square or rectangular, with rounded corners. Often a knife or dagger was thrust through the flap. The dagger was an ordinary accessory

Fig. 139

of civilian garb; it was worn on the side or directly in front, fastened to the belt; sometimes it was worn directly behind, dangling on a cord at the back of the neck, or slung on a strap or bandolier across the breast.

Gloves, combs, mirrors, and other aids to the toilet were carried, especially by the young dandies.

Make-up

Boncompagno states that some young dandies made up their faces with cosmetics and wore wigs. Horsehair was used for the wigs, the primary purpose of which was to conceal baldness.

Military Dress

This century was the finest period of plate armor. Plate armor was fashioned to ward off blows to the body from every possible direction. The plates were made thick over the more vulnerable areas, thin over the less vulnerable. Lines were engraved in the plates, not merely for decorative purposes, but to catch lance points and deflect them. The plates were pierced and attached to a leather jacket (also called gambeson or doublet), one plate overlapping the next, but so adjusted that they allowed freedom of movement. A full suit of plate armor consisted of about eighty plates. The principal parts of plate armor were these (Fig. 128   Fig. 130 A D):

1. The helm or helmet. The *basinet* (Fig. 128 B) was worn in this century. It had a beaked visor and fitted snugly about the chin. The *salade*, also worn, had a movable visor, a metal cape over the nape of the neck, and a separate chin piece

(called a *hausse col*), which protected the lower part of the face (Fig. 123 Fig.
130 A). A crest of feathers (*panache*) was attached to the helmet at the top or
at the base of the neck (Fig. 123 Fig. 130 D). Various crests or emblems were
cast in metal and placed on top of the helmet. Some of these were of tremendous
proportions and of eccentric design. They are shown in monumental brasses and
in effigies of knights and warriors of the time.

  2. The *cuirass* or breastplate was made in one or more pieces, shaped to the body;
usually the lower pieces overlapped the upper, front and back (Fig. 128 A D).
At the armpits might be *roundels* (Fig. 130 D), or disks, to protect these vulnerable points. The neck was protected with a gorget, like a bib (Fig. 128 B);
ailettes and *pauldrons* protected the shoulders (Fig. 128 A C Fig. 130 A D).
The arms were covered by overlapping plates, the *coude* at the elbow sometimes

Fig. 132   Fig. 135

being fan-shaped and protruding like a bat's wing (Fig. 128 A C). The lower
arm was covered with plates called *vambraces*. Gauntlets with small, overlapping plates on fingers, thumb, and the back of the hand, protected the hands.

  3. About the hips were overlapping plates called *tasses* with *tailles* depending
from them (Fig. 128 A D). The thighs had *cuisses* and *cuilles* covering them,
with *knee-caps* (or *genouillières*), also sometimes fan-shaped, protecting them
(Fig. 136 A).

  4. The shins were protected by *jambes,* hinged plates to the knees (Fig. 128 A
Fig. 130 A D   Fig. 136 A). The foot was covered with overlapping plates forming
the *solleret* (Fig. 128 A   Fig. 130 A D   Fig. 136 A).

  5. Over the armor might be worn the surcoat with the heraldic ornament, but
this was beginning to be discarded, except for ceremonial occasions.

  6. The shields were shaped like the bearers' heraldic designs (Fig. 136 a b c d e).
The smaller shields were used to guard the arm from dagger thrusts. Giorgione's
picture of the Madonna with Saint Francis and Saint Liberale shows the armor
of the late fifteenth century. It also shows the extreme length of the lance.

Heralds wore short tabards embroidered or painted with the arms of the family
represented.

Ecclesiastical Dress

Little change was made in monastic or priestly garb. St. Francis, in the Giorgione picture just mentioned, wears the gray robe of the order.

The Doge of Venice wore the cap made famous by Gentile and Giovanni Bellini in their portraits of the Doge Loredano. In shape, the cap was reminiscent of the old Egyptian headdress of Upper and Lower Egypt. Tintoretto's "Marriage of St. Catherine" shows the Doge in cap and robe.

Mourning

Mourning was expressed by simple, unadorned clothing of black or brown. A black cloak was worn over the somber garments. Men usually shaved their mustaches or beards in honor of the dead.

COSTUME FOR CHILDREN

Contemporary pictures seem to indicate that well-to-do children wore houppelandes, jackets, and other garments exactly like their elders'. Poor children wore simple tunics. Ghirlandaio's portrait of the old man and his grandson shows the child in sleeved jerkin, gathered doublet over this, low collar, round, brimless hat, and flowing hair.

A little boy in typical costume is shown in Fig. 132.

COSTUME FOR THE LOWER CLASSES

Simple tunics of fustian, coarse wool, and like materials were worn with long chausses and shoes. A hood or cowl was usually worn over the head. To the belt might be attached a roomy pouch. The hair was worn long and shaggy, with beard and mustache.

Often, over the chausses, a shirt was worn, the skirt of which was split up the sides. During work hours, it was tucked up into the waistband. As a protection against cold weather, leggings of cloth or felt were worn to the knee; these were wrapped or gartered with strips of fabric or leather. Aprons of cloth or leather were worn about the waist. Leather and felt jackets were added for the sake of warmth, and worn hip length or longer. As a cloak, a square of woolen cloth might be wrapped shawl-wise over the shoulders.

COSTUME FOR WOMEN

Gown

The long houppelande, belted high, was worn by women in the late fourteenth and early fifteenth centuries. The neck was buttoned high, or a standing collar was used. Sleeves were long and tight, or pendant with dagged edges.

V-Bodiced Gown

This, a great favorite, was made with a short-waisted bodice, having a collar, or revers, wide over the shoulders, and forming a deep V in front (Fig. 130 B Fig.

131 C). Sometimes the point of the V extended below the belt. Sometimes, too, the neck and bosom were bare to the waist; however, much of the V was usually filled with an under-body (later to develop into the stomacher). The V collar was often of fur. The skirt was circular (Fig. 134 pattern), gathered or pleated, and often had a train. It was worn long, often trailing the ground in front. A deep border of contrasting material or fur might edge the bottom of the skirt. The sleeves might be long and pendant, or of other fashions (Fig. 133). The sway-back walk, and the fashion of holding the skirt up in front (Fig. 133 A), was in honor of the enceinte Virgin Mary; in order to insure the effect, some of the ladies wore little pads over the stomach. An illustration of this fashion is seen in Fra Carnevali's "The Birth of the Virgin" (Metropolitan Museum of Art, New York City).

Laced-Bodice Gown

This type had a bodice laced in front, displaying the white chemise beneath. The sleeves were pendant or puffed at the shoulder (Fig. 133 A D). A slit at the elbow showed the sleeve of the chemise. The skirt was fashioned in one piece with the bodice (Fig. 133 C), or separate, and it flared at the bottom and might have a train. This type is seen in Ghirlandaio's "Birth of John the Baptist." It was popular in Germany for a long time, and is the type of costume associated with Marguerite in *Faust*. Another variety of this type is shown in Fig. 129 B.

Sleeves

Many varieties of sleeve were used; several types were made for a single dress. They were attached by points to the armhole, and so could be changed at will. Besides those already described, notice the sleeve in Fig. 133 J and its pattern H; this was worn either as a separate sleeve or over other types; often it was made of fur. Fig. 133 F, with pattern G, shows the sleeve slit lengthwise at the elbow. Fig. 133 E shows the pendant sleeve slit and laced over the upper arm. Fig. 133 K and pattern L show a pendant sleeve used for gown and cloak; it, too, was often trimmed with bands of fur. Fig. 133 N and pattern M show a puff at the shoulder, slashed. Other material was placed beneath M, to show through the slashes.

Many Renaissance pictures show clearly the patterns of the sleeve, the shoulder fastenings (Montagna's "Lady of Rank" shows the fastening very well), and other details of cut, make, and decoration.

Mantle

A semicircular cloak was worn for warmth. It was fastened with a double clasp or a band of cloth. It had a high collar or hood, fastening loosely on the shoulders and often trailing behind, like the cloak shown in Francesca's "Queen of Sheba."

Footwear

Women wore the same kind of pointed shoes as men, but not so exaggerated, because the shoes could not be seen under the long skirts.

Fig.130

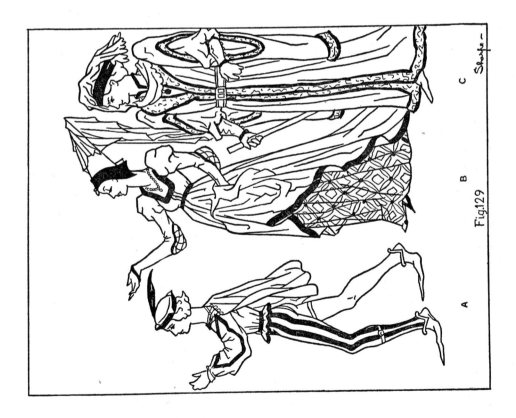

Fig.129

Hair

The hair was usually hidden from view by the headdress. In addition, it was plucked well back from the line of the forehead. The crespin and caul disclosed the braids they encased (Fig. 122). Veils were often draped over the back of the head, as in Fra Filippo Lippi's picture of the Virgin (Uffizi). Botticelli's "Calumny" shows hair arrangement excellently.

Young girls still wore their hair long and flowing. Leonardo da Vinci left many pencil sketches of intricate hair arrangements. Not only were eyebrows and the hair over the forehead plucked, but the back of the neck also was either plucked or shaved.

Headdress

This age abounded in intricate and exaggerated headdresses. Among the many types, the following stand out:

1. The *hennin*. This was a tall, cone-shaped or steeple headdress (Fig. 129 B Fig. 133 A B). It varied in height from six inches to three feet. Isabeau of Bavaria (wife of Charles VI of France) had to have the doors of her palace at Vincennes heightened, to accommodate her tall hennins. Thomas Connecte preached against them; Jean de Mehun and Geoffrey de la Tour Landry railed; yet the vogue continued. The hennin, according to Paradin, was a roll of stiffened linen, wired or pointed, fitted to the head, with a ring of metal, or frontlet, attached to the center front (Fig. 133 A), with which it might be jerked back into position should it lose its proper angle – forty-five degrees. Memling's "Marie Portinari" shows this ring clearly. Often a band of satin, velvet, or other material framed the face (Fig. 133 A). A veil of thin silk or gauze might hang from the tip of the hennin, or be draped over it. In addition, other varieties of headdress were made with the hennin as base. The *lampshade* was so called because it had a wired veil over a truncated hennin cone; the *butterfly,* so called because it had two wings over the cone; the *horned headdress,* so called because two horns, one on either side, sprouted from the cone, with points upward. Other varieties are to be seen in the pictures of the time. The *heart-shaped headdress* consisted of a heart-shaped roll over a low hennin cone, or a wired form. It was often placed on top of a crespin and caul (Fig. 131 C), and is familiar to readers as the headdress of the Duchess in *Alice in Wonderland*. Francesca's "Queen of Sheba" also wears this type.

2. The *caul and horns with veil* (Fig. 122) consisted of the crespin and caul, with wired horns, a veil, and a crown; this type was worn by the Countess of Arundel.

3. The *cloven-hoof headdress* was a stiff, wired arrangement of buckram and gauze, which was simple and yet effective.

4. The *roundlet,* similar to that worn by the men, was favored by the women, especially when heavily jeweled about the brim and worn with a veil.

5. The *Juliet cap,* a close-fitting mesh cap, is shown in Fig. 130 B.

6. The *turban* was imported from Turkey, by way of Venice. It may be seen in Andrea del Sarto's "Lucrezia Borgia," in Raphael's "Madonna della Sedia," and in Guido Reni's "Beatrice Cenci."

7. The *coif* or cap was favored by older women. It was like a baby hood, though often wired about the face. This remained in favor through succeeding generations, and served as a base for many styles. Caps were worn by many noblewomen, especially indoors. Beatrice of Milan wore caps at dinner.

8. Veils, or wimples, simply draped about the head and chin, were still in favor. The Madonnas are shown wearing them in countless representations. The older women in Ghirlandaio's "John the Baptist" wear them. Veils were sometimes draped very elaborately.

9. The *ferronnière* was a chain or ribbon about the head; it held a pendant or jewel at the center of the forehead. Sometimes other jewels were strung on the chain or ribbon at regular intervals about the head (Fig. 130 B). Examples of the ferronnière are seen in the portrait of Beatrice d'Este by Leonardo da Vinci, as well as in his "La Belle Ferronnière," and in Montagna's "Duchess Elizabeth Gonzaga." The pendant in the last-named portrait is a scorpion. The ferronnière continued in vogue for a long time.

Ornaments and Accessories

Necklaces of fine workmanship, rings, jeweled brooches (for shoulder joinings, caps, dresses, etc.), belt buckles, jeweled buttons, hair ornaments, pearl necklaces, bracelets, clasps, and other embellishments reflected the artistry and ingenuity of Renaissance craftsmen.

Accessories included jeweled belts, pouches, pomanders, illuminated missals (*Book of the Hours,* etc.), needlecases, scissors, ivory combs, gloves, jeweled head bands, jeweled caps, gold-wired mesh caps set with jewels ("Juliet" type), and muffs. The latter were made fashionable by Venetian ladies, who carried them not only for warmth, but also for snugly ensconcing therein their little pet dogs.

Savonarola's bonfire of "vanities" burned masses of hennins, gloves, jewels, perfumes, dresses, and the like – but, unfortunately, it also destroyed priceless paintings by Fra Bartolommeo and Botticelli, writings of Boccaccio and Petrarch, as well as the work of other artists – invaluable articles which no preaching could replace.

Make-up

Women painted their faces and plucked their eyebrows to a fine line; they plucked the hair back from the forehead line, rouged the lips, and employed every known artifice to heighten their charms. They used cosmetics, wore wigs to eke out their hair, laced and fasted to achieve the desired effect – a slender figure, wan face, aureole of hair, scarlet lips.

Mourning

Plain robes and a black cloak usually denoted mourning; for body garments, brown was also used. Little jewelry was worn, and caps and veils, rather than elaborate headdresses like hennins, were in good taste, though the latter were worn at court. Widows preferred black satin for fashionable mourning.

Costume for Children

Little girls wore garments cut in the style of their elders' (Fig. 135), unless they were poor; simple tunics then sufficed, and hoods for headgear. A very good illustration of dress for children is seen in Gozzoli's painting of St. Zenobius resurrecting a dead child.

Costume for the Lower Classes

Lower-class women wore simple tunics with tight or loose sleeves and a round or V neck. Usually an apron covered the dress, or the top skirt was tucked up into the waistband. A hood was the usual head covering, though caps and wimples, folded up over the head, were also worn.

Modern Adaptations

Brocaded patterns are best simulated by painting the designs on unbleached muslin; a stencil saves time. If the pattern is outlined with cable cord, or smaller cord which has been colored or gilded, the effect is much richer. Jewels of crushed gilt, of flitter, or of silver and colored tinsel are easy to sew on, and are very effective. Ten-cent-store jewels are always good.

The headdresses are made with buckram, wire, silvered insulation board, and pasteboard; or the process given in chapter I may be followed.

For corded headdresses, use gold or silver Christmas-tree cord.

For the tight sleeve of the fourteenth and fifteenth centuries, use the standard fitted sleeve pattern in two pieces. For the fitted tunic (for men and women) use the standard fitted lining or body pattern, fitted back and front. Cut it hip length for fourteenth-century garments.

A Russian blouse pattern is a good basic pattern for the loose tunics and coats of this period.

For the pleated coats and tunics, lay pleats in the material before cutting pattern.

For the houppelande, or long tunic, use a dressing gown (or hostess gown or cassock) pattern and flare at the bottom.

CHAPTER IX

THE SIXTEENTH CENTURY

IMPORTANT PEOPLE AND EVENTS

ITALY
Popes
Julius II
  (1503–13)
Leo X
  (1513–21)
Adrian VI
  (1522–24)
Clement VII
  (1523–24)
Paul III
  (1543–49)
Gregory XIII
  (1572–85)
Sixtus V
  (1585–90)

Artists
Michelangelo
  (Michel Angelo
  Buonarroti)
Raphael
  (Raffaeli Sanzio)
Andrea del Sarto
Il Sodoma
  (Giovanni Antonio
  Bazzi)
Giorgione
  (Giorgio Barbarelli)
Titian
  (Tiziano Vecellio)
Jacopo Tintoretto
Paolo Veronese
Bernardino Luini

Writers
Benvenuto Cellini
Giordano Bruno
Pietro Aretino
Torquato Tasso

Composer
Giovanni Palestrina

SPAIN
Rulers
Charles V
  (1517–56)

Philip II
  (1556–98)

Artists
Alonso Coello
El Greco
  (Domenico Theoto-
  copuli)

Writers
Lope de Vega
Miguel de Cervantes

Notable People
Ferdinand Magellan
Hernando Cortez
Francisco Pizarro
Ignatius Loyola

POLAND
Copernicus
  (Nicolaus Kopper-
  nigk)

INDIA
Akbar
  (Jellaladin Mahom-
  med)

GERMANY
Rulers
Charles V
  (1519–55)
Ferdinand I
  (1556–64)
Maximilian II
  (1564–76)
Rudolf II
  (1576–1612)

Notable People
Albrecht Dürer
Martin Luther

ENGLAND
Rulers
Henry VIII
  (1509–47)

Edward VI
  (1547–53)
Mary ("Bloody Mary")
  (1553–58)
Elizabeth
  (1558–1603)

Writers
Christopher Marlowe
William Shakespeare
Thomas Kyd
Ben Jonson
John Lyly
Francis Beaumont
John Fletcher
Sir Thomas Wyatt
Edmund Spenser
Sir Philip Sidney
George Chapman
Dean John Colet
Roger Ascham
Sir Francis Bacon
Sir Thomas More
Sir Walter Raleigh

Notable People
Lady Jane Grey
Sir John Hawkins
Sir Martin Frobisher
Sir Francis Drake
Robert Devereux, Earl
  of Essex
Cardinal Wolsey
John Knox
William Cecil, Lord
  Burghley
Mary, Queen of Scots

RUSSIA
Rulers
Ivan the Terrible
  (1547–84)
Boris Godunov
  (1598–1605)

THE NETHERLANDS
Notable People
William I (the Silent)
Desiderius Erasmus
Lucas van Leyden
Pieter and Jan Breu-
  ghel
Antonio Moro

SWITZERLAND
Notable People
Huldereich Zwingli
John Calvin

FRANCE
Rulers
Francis I
  (1515–47)
Henry II
  (1547–59)
Francis II
  (1559–60)
Charles IX
  (1560–74)
Henry III
  (1574–89)
Henry IV (Bourbon)
  (1589–1610)

Artists
François and Jean
  Clouet
Martin de Fréminet

Notable People
Michel de Montaigne
François Rabelais
Pierre de Ronsard
Marguerite de Valois
Diane de Poitiers
Catherine de' Medici
Le Chevalier Bayard
Le Duc de Guise
Le Duc de Condé

Explorations of Ferdinand Magellan, Jacques Cartier, Sir Francis Drake, and others in the New World. . . . Great Renaissance in Italy – Leonardo da Vinci, Michelangelo, Raphael, Titian, and others – centering in Rome, Venice, and Florence. . . . Golden age of English literature under Elizabeth's patronage – Shakespeare, Ben Jonson, Christopher Marlowe, etc.

1519, Martin Luther defied Church of Rome. . . . 1520, meeting of Henry VIII and Francis I, Field of the Cloth of Gold. . . . 1524, soap manufactured in London. . . . 1525, East Prussia became an hereditary principality of Brandenburg – the beginning of unified Germany under the Hohenzollerns, rulers of Brandenburg. . . . 1530, first portable clock. . . . Six wives of Henry VIII followed one another with varying success – Catherine of Aragon, Anne Boleyn, Jane Seymour, Anne of Cleves, Catherine Howard, Catherine Parr. . . . 1531, Henry VIII quarreled with Rome, issued Act of Supremacy by which he became supreme head of Church of England; this was followed in 1534 by the suppression of the monasteries. . . . 1534, Luther led the Protestant revolt; translated Bible into German. . . . 1534, Loyola founded the Jesuit Order. . . . Inquisition in full force in Spain, Italy, and the Netherlands. . . . 1543, Copernicus charted the solar system. . . . 1553, Lady Jane Grey, nine days' queen. . . . 1558, Queen Mary lost Calais. . . . 1569, coaches used in England.

1513, Machiavelli's *The Prince* published. . . . Cultivation of peaches (from Persia). . . . 1571, victory of Venetians against Turks at Lepanto. . . . 1572, Catherine de' Medici instigated Massacre of St. Bartholomew's Day. . . . 1573, tobacco introduced into England from America by Sir Walter Raleigh. . . . Colonization by Raleigh in North Carolina. . . . Dutch, under William the Silent, opposed tyrannous Duke of Alva; Union of Utrecht, 1579. . . . 1582, Dutch Republic founded. . . . 1587, execution of Mary, Queen of Scots. . . . 1588, defeat of Spanish Armada. . . . 1590, forks used. . . . 1598, Henry IV issued Edict of Nantes, establishing religious toleration in France.

New horizons opened before the earth-encircling sails of sixteenth-century galleons. More wonderful than the world beyond the waves and its continuous curve, laid bare by Magellan and Drake, was the marvel of men's minds. Copernicus disclosed a vast universe in which Bruno viewed humanity as dwellers on a star. Jacob Fugger, international banker, unlocked the gates of distant places and gave glimpses of man's daily life in Peking, in Persia, in Peru. In the news-letters written by Fugger's commercial agents all around the globe to the shrewd but generous creditor of Charles V, man was shown to be not a creature of heaven or hell, but one possessing attributes of both – vital, violent, skeptical, credulous, creative, destructive. Interpolated in businesslike accounts of rainfalls, crop reports, and general market conditions, were recounted the defeat of the Invincible Armada in 1588; the execution of the Cenci, September 11, 1599; the excommunication of Queen Elizabeth in February of 1570 by Pope Sixtus V, who promised Philip II the throne of England – if and when he could get it. Emanuel Tomascon, a Calvinist and an eyewitness to the beheading of Mary Stuart of Scotland, February 18, 1587, recorded that all her belongings were burned, even her dress (the legitimate fee of the executioner), "so that no superstitious practices could be carried on therewith"! Here also, in the day's work, was described in detail the gold saltcellar fashioned by Benvenuto Cellini, listed among the presents of a royal bride. The machinations of Catherine de' Medici on a certain St. Bartholomew's Eve were related to Fugger, along with an account of the birthday fete of a Turkish sultan. Drake's looting of a Spanish galleon off the Galapagos Islands shared interest with the murder of the Guises and the expulsion of Christian missionaries from the Sacred City of Peking.

The finding of Saint Cecilia, in 1599, was a nine days' wonder – "the body, with the scarf over the head, perfectly preserved, dressed as she went to her martyrdom, eight hundred years ago"!

Man, by his own accounts, was as many-sided as the Renaissance, and he was thoroughly conscious of his complexity. Indeed, his intense self-consciousness and self-confidence were responsible for the high pitch of expression. A quarrelsome stonecutter named Michelangelo painted the ceiling of the Sistine Chapel; a medical monk named François Rabelais pricked man's conceit with Gargantuan laughter; a tavern loiterer named Shakespeare caught the imagination of man in the net of God's infinity.

These marvels were not solely for the courts of kings, even such kings as Francis I and the virgin-monarch, Elizabeth; nor were they for the Church terrestrial, powerful patrons though the Popes were. The Renaissance and the Reformation were essentially mass movements; in the inevitable clash between ecclesiastical and civil powers, the weight of the masses inclined toward a national spirit. Luther and Henry VIII started not so much new religions as a new Germany, a new England. The Boy David flung his inkpot in protest against the churchly bars to individual freedom. Henry VIII, as personal "Defender of the Faith," claimed the divine right to judge connubial fidelity. He exercised this right by trying his successive wives.

This new faith in Man, this new confidence on land and sea, this acquisitiveness and aggression, made mankind reach out for new fashions to clothe his prosperity and power. The circumnavigating ruff flaunted its folds to the four winds; the wheeled farthingale boxed the compass about the citizen's wife as well as about the Queen – and with the same complacent ugliness. The peascod doublet and bombasted breeches were stuffed as tightly as the bulging hold of a freebooter's pinnace. Taste was a matter of display, of newness, of daring; styles were pirated from the seven seas of fashion. Yet the men and women who squeezed themselves into the stiffened modes were nationalists to the center of their being; their leaders were individualists who sailed the ship of state by the lodestar of their own destiny.

COSTUME

1500–1550

GENERAL CHARACTERISTICS

The tremendous scope of the sixteenth century – its aggressiveness, its assurance, its change of thought, ideals, and aims, its curiosity about new things – was reflected in the lines, color, and material of costume. (1) The sinuous grace of fifteenth-century line was replaced by squareness and breath; (2) materials of rich weave and texture, and combinations of several weaves, were massed together in one costume; (3) puffs and slashes drew added attention to the details of dress; (4) hose became exaggerated, and divorced from the lower leg-hose fitted to the leg; (5) the neck was not only set off by a shirt but was emphasized by a ruff which grew to enormous proportions; (6) hats, stiff and businesslike in line, superseded the more informal hood and cap;

(7) shoes spread out into broad surfaces which gripped the earth with firmness and assurance; (8) accessories were plentiful, lavish, and showy.

Italy, which dominated styles in the fifteenth century, handed her inspiration on to Spain, which added a stiff dignity to the conception and passed it on to France and England. These kingdoms, weary with mutual wars, grasped at this milder rivalry with relief, and added deft touches and honest amplifications of their own. Germany, nominally linked with Spain, protested outwardly as well as inwardly, and went to the same extremes of declaration in dress as she did in theology. Design began with Renaissance Italy and ended in Protestant Germany.

Materials

Velvet, trimmed or patterned, piled or pressed, cut or uncut, was the favored material for the imposing styles of the time. Cloth of gold or silver, satin damask, taffeta, silk camlet (a mixture of wool and silk), and other rich materials that demanded a full purse – sarcenet, cendal, samite, ciclatoun, and other of the older weaves – were now made with gold threads and other embellishments; for the weavers, driven out of Flanders by the Duke of Alva, set up looms in England, where they wove textures such as the world had never seen, and had all Europe vying for the new weaves. Bombazine (silk and cotton – first manufactured in England), wool, serge, linen, fustian (cotton and linen mixed), linsey-woolsey (coarse woolen stuff first manufactured at Linsey in Suffolk), frieze, and buckram were some of the imposing array of stuffs from which dress was evolved. Lace, a new trimming, grew in favor, spurred by the impetus given it by such designers as Michelangelo and Raphael (his designs for Francis I are famous, and some of his work can be seen today in the Cluny Museum). The Netherlands made Honiton and other laces popular; Pierre Quinty published a book on lace at Cologne in 1527, which further stirred interest in this item; Wedmoll and other laces became well known in England. At first, laces were of various colors; later, white came to be generally preferred.

Colors

These had a wide range. Racinet quotes an impressive array: "wine, turquoise, orange, orange-tawny, amaranth, gray, astral, rat-gray, peach, virgin-green, brown-green, vert-de-gris, pale yellow, Judas color, aurore, pearl, ox-blood, migraine, dying monkey, blue death, smoked beef, amorous desires, kiss-me-my-mignon"! Besides these, murray, goose-green, pease-porridge, popinjay-blue, crimson, scarlet, garnet, egg-yellow – all vied for favor. The Duke of Buckingham preferred all white or all yellow; Philip II of Spain and Don John of Austria favored black velvet almost exclusively, as did Mary, Queen of Scots, widowed more than once; Elizabeth, on the other hand (widowed never!), preferred white, yellow, and green – the colors of spring and of eternal hope. In her wardrobe of more than three thousand dresses, however, she included virtually all the range of color of the rainbow.

Underclothes

The shirt, in this era, became a visible part of the dress and ceased to be an item of underwear. Men, however, wore an undershirt; women wore a shift or chemise. In cold weather, women also wore long under-hose and a sort of drawers. Men wore trunks under the hose, and drawers under the more capacious garments. Garters held up the nether-hose, sometimes being wound about, below and above the knee and knotted, cross-garter fashion, as worn by Malvolio in *Twelfth Night*.

Under outer garments, especially under armor, jackets or doublets of chamois, leather, quilted cotton, or coarse linen, were worn.

Costume for Men

Houppelande

This garment continued to be worn; however, the broad, flat, turned-back collar was further exaggerated in width and the revers of fur were emphasized.

Loose Gown (*Academic*)

This type (Fig. 144 A) was favored by theologians, and was adopted by professional men. It had a square yoke without collar, to which the long, loose body of the gown was pleated or gathered; full, loose sleeves, slightly puffed at the shoulder and usually banded about the wrists with fur, and revers of fur down the front of the gown itself, were familiar characteristics. With the gown was usually worn a flat cap or a square, boxlike structure (Fig. 144 A). The flat cap evolved into the mortarboard of today, as the robe became the gown for academic use in modern times. Cranach, Huber, and Holbein show these types of headdress and gown over and over again; Holbein's "The Ambassadors" shows both types of headdress perfectly.

Gentlemen of this time wore several layers of garments. Fig. 142 A shows a typical costume, associated with Henry VIII and Francis I of France. In the order in which the garments were donned, they included hose, shirt or partlet, stomacher, doublet, and jerkin.

Hose

The hose were still the long cloth hose shaped to the leg, and laced up behind. By the end of the first quarter of the century, however, upper hose (*haut-de-chausses*) came into fashion; these were full, puffed trunks, of the bloomer type, favored by Henry VIII, and called *hose* – to the confusion of the modern mind. The full, pleated skirt attached to the doublet was equally popular, and many contemporary portraits show the skirted type (Fig. 143).

Shirt

The shirt was of fine linen or lawn, or of silk or taffeta, and was often called the *partlet*. It had a low band or frill at the neck (Fig. 142 A). The shirt was often embroidered with black, gold, or silver; it was sometimes worn open at the neck, with a turndown collar (Fig. 143). The sleeve was full and gathered in at the wrist with a frill. Shirts varied in type from plain, coarse linen to finest silk; the cost ranged from ten shillings to ten pounds. No wonder Falstaff had "but a shirt and a half in the company"!

Stomacher

Over the shirt was worn the *stomacher,* if the doublet were slit down the front. Sometimes the stomacher was worn without the doublet; in this case, it was to be distinguished from the latter only by the fact that it was low in the neck, which was usually rounded or square. It might be likened to a low-cut bodice, without sleeves. The ordinary purpose of the stomacher was to show under the opening of the doublet.

Doublet

The *doublet* was so named because it was usually of double thickness, quilted or padded. It was fastened up the front with buttons or lacings, had a close, standing collar, and fitted the figure snugly (Fig. 143). The waistline tapered down to a bodice-like point in front; this feature was exaggerated later in the century. A pleated skirt was sometimes attached to the doublet, or else the full *trunk hose* (like bloomers) were used. The doublet was richly designed, with puffs and slashes, jewels, and other ornamentations to enhance its charm.

The history of puffs and slashes goes back to the Battle of Nancy in 1477, when the Swiss patriots overcame the Duke of Burgundy. The duke, famous for his elaborate display of dress, had come to war with silken tents, chests of clothes, jewels, and the like. After his defeat (and his death), the Swiss seized the finery, and, in a rage, ripped the tents and the gorgeous vestments, wrapped them about their cold and ill-clad bodies, and slipped their own tattered garments, more holes than cloth, over the finery. Pulling the silk through the holes, puffing it in derisive display, they marched triumphantly back to receive the delighted acclaim of their friends – and to set a style that endured well into the seventeenth century.

The doublet, though usually fastened up the front to the neckline, was also worn open, cut away from the center front at the waistline to the shoulder line at the top. The resulting V-shaped opening was filled in by the stomacher. The outlines and size of this opening varied.

Jerkin

Over the doublet was sometimes worn the jerkin, a kind of coat. It was slit down the front, and occasionally had a deep collar and wide revers. The jerkin came to the knees, or to hip length. It sometimes had a pleated skirt attached. The sleeves were long and full, with horizontal zoned puffs and slashes. Sometimes the jerkin was sleeveless. The sleeves of the jerkin or doublet were either sewed into the garment or attached by points and laced to the armhole; if they were laced, the white puffings of the shirt showed through these openings.

Coat or Cloak

Usually the doublet or jerkin kept the wearer sufficiently warm. However, for cold or outdoor weather, a coat or cloak was worn. The coat was abnormally broad of shoulder, with deep collar and revers of velvet or fur (Fig. 142 A B C D Fig. 143). The usual length of the coat was about six inches below the knees (Fig. 142 B Fig. 143). For state occasions, or for older men, it was cut long, to the ground (Fig. 142 B, dotted

A   B   C   Fig.141

Fig.140

D
C   HALF
     COLLAR
B   E

SHORT

LONG   F

Fig.142   Fig.152

A   D

A   B   C

Fig.144

YOKE
SLEEVE   PUFF
BODICE
COLLAR

BELL
FARTHINGALE   SKIRT

A   B

Fig. 145

line). The coat had long sleeves, or puffed elbow-length sleeves (Fig. 143), or hanging sleeves (Fig. 142 A), or was sleeveless.

A long circular cloak was also worn at times.

It is recorded that it took thirteen yards of black damask cloth of gold to make a "double cloak" for Henry VIII. Holbein's portrait of him shows Henry in a white frilled shirt and a doublet of cloth of gold, enriched with jewels and buttoned up the front with jeweled buttons. Over this was a jerkin of crimson, elaborately embroidered with gold, beautifully lined, and graced by a broad, flat collar of ermine. Holbein's portrait of George Gisze shows a white shirt with ruffled collar, stomacher, doublet split down the front, and coat.

Hose (*Full Trunks*)

The hose, as has been said, became, during this century, separate from the long chausses or leg-hose. Hose were made full, but not at this period puffed or padded, and they reached to the knee. They were called *breeches-hose, top-hose,* or just *hose*. Leg-hose were of cloth until knit hose were introduced about the middle of the century. A few instances of knit hose are known as early as 1527; St. Fiacre of Scotland was made the patron saint of knitters about this date; however, Europe was slow to adopt the style.

Codpiece

The codpiece was still worn; indeed, in this century it reached the extreme of fashion, and was a prominent part of dress. The pouch was buttoned, laced, or otherwise fastened to the front of the hose; it was puffed, slashed, looped with ribbons; sometimes it was decorated with a huge bow of silk or velvet. German styles show the most grotesque developments of this item of dress (Fig. 143   Fig. 149).

Footwear

The excessively long-pointed shoes of the fifteenth century gave way to a flat, broad-toed shoe, made of leather, cloth, or velvet. At first the toes were square and fairly plain (Fig. 154 G); later, they became exaggerated and were puffed and slashed and so broad they were called *duck-bills* (Fig. 142 A   Fig. 154 E). They were also called *sabbatons*. Cardinal Wolsey, famous for his indulgence in dress, had one pair of sabbatons of silver gilt inlaid with pearls and diamonds.

Pantofles were originally overshoes for out-of-doors; they flapped as the wearer walked. They were made of wood or cork, with the sole thicker toward the heel (Fig. 154 J).

Chopines were a Venetian type of overshoe, raised high off the ground (Fig. 154 A). They were fashionable throughout the century.

Boots were also in demand – loose and high, of soft leather. Hotspur bemoans his having to go "home, bootless, in this foul weather!"

Rosettes were sometimes worn on the instep of the wide shoes (Fig. 154 B); they were made of lace or ribbon, adorned with spangles, gold threads, and jewels. The rosettes might be four or five inches in diameter.

Hair

At first, the hair was worn long, to the shoulder, and often curled up at the end (Fig. 140 B). Playing cards of today reflect the styles of the early sixteenth century, especially in the hair treatment and women's headdress. The King and Jack show the haircut used at the beginning of the century. Then Francis I sustained an injury to his head, cropped his hair, and so set the vogue. Henry VIII, angered at the fancied effeminacy of long hair, ordered all hair cropped – and it was. Better to have the hair cut off than the head!

Young men were clean-shaven, though they frequently wore mustaches. Older men wore beards of various types (Fig. 141 Fig. 144 A B). There were the "cathedral beard" for church dignitaries, of long and flowing cut; the justice's beard "of formal cut"; the military "spade" beard, square of outline; the "stiletto," pointed and small, with which was worn the pointed mustache; and the round beard, like Falstaff's – and like Henry VIII's (Fig. 143).

Headdress

The hood practically disappeared, for formal use, and was retained only by the lower classes. In its stead, caps came into fashion. A flat cap of cloth or velvet (Fig. 143) was worn, sometimes alone, sometimes in conjunction with the snug-fitting hooded cap, like a baby's bonnet, mentioned previously (Fig. 152). This hooded cap no longer had strings to fasten it under the chin, but was tapered off, or rounded into semicircular flaps at the side, or, if extended all about the head, the front corners were often rounded. The flat cap placed upon this hood was often slit in sections, threaded with ribbons, and otherwise decorated. In London, the so-called *City flat cap* distinguished the citizen, the apprentice, and the artisan.

Another type of cap, called the *Milan bonnet,* was gathered and puffed over the crown, with a brim slit in sections (Fig. 148 D), or laced with ribbons (Fig. 148 C), or folded up and about the crown with ribbon lacings to accentuate the effect (Fig. 140 B). Feathers were commonly added to all these styles (Fig. 142 A Fig. 143). The under-hood was most favored by older men and professional men. The Italian ambassador to Henry VIII wore a crimson velvet cap, its brim threaded with laces having gold-enameled tags.

A cap approaching hat shape is shown in Fig. 144 A – a soft crown with a four-sided stiff brim turned up to form a boxlike structure. This cap was favored by lawyers, doctors, and other professional men; it was called the *cap divine.* These styles, as well as the others mentioned, were made of beaver, popular because of its reputed value in curing deafness.

Headdresses were worn indoors as well as out; nor were they removed in the presence of ladies.

Ornaments and Accessories

Most prominent was the wide, heavily linked chain worn about the shoulders (not about the neck), with a pendant in front (Fig. 143). Holbein's portrait of Henry VIII shows such a chain. These chains were usually orders, and, as such, have remained part of ceremonial costume to the present day. Among the orders most in use at that time and continuing in use today are the following:

1. Order of the Golden Fleece (*La Toison d'Or*), founded by Philip the Good, Duke of Burgundy, 1429; it had steel and flint links, and the pendant was a golden sheep (Jason's "Golden Fleece").

2. Order of St. Michael, founded by Louis XI of France, 1469; it was fashioned of scallop shells, with St. Michael's image on the pendant. Under Charles IX, so many were given this award that it became vulgarly known as *"Le Collier à Toutes Bêtes"* (which may be freely translated as "The Order of All Fools").

3. Order of the Garter, founded by Edward III of England, *circa* 1348; this had links of gold-buckled garters and white and red roses, with St. George slaying the dragon on the pendant.

4. Order of St. Esprit, founded by Henry III of France, 1578; this consisted of fleurs de lis and links, with a pendant of cipher and trophy of arms. Henry founded this Order because of the disrepute into which the older St. Michael award had fallen.

5. Order of the Elephant, founded by Christian I of Denmark, 1462; the pendant shows an elephant, with a howdah and rider.

6. Collar of *S's*, England; the origin of this is uncertain; it is composed of feathered S's, with a pendant in the form of a Tudor rose (indicating origin about this specific era). This collar is seen on most portraits of important people of the late fifteenth and early sixteenth centuries, and it is still worn on state occasions by the Lord Mayor of London, the Chief Justices of England, and others.

Other types of chains might be worn with the wide, shoulder-draped collar. These other chains were worn about the neck, and hung lower in front than the shoulder chain.

Elaborately jeweled ornaments were worn in the caps of this period; jeweled buttons adorned the fronts of the stomachers; rosaries, rings, jeweled gloves, jeweled daggers, and spangles (or *paillettes*) added splendor and glitter to the costumes. Among the jewels used were carbuncles, rubies, diamonds, sapphires, emeralds, turquoises, beryls, garnets, agates, and pearls – the latter the most popular. A Tudor crown is shown in chapter VIII, Fig. 139.

Besides gloves and daggers, men carried pomanders (supposed to guard against infection) and handkerchiefs. Henry VIII issued a royal decree regulating the shape of handkerchiefs to a uniform squareness; round, oval, and rectangular ones had been equally in vogue before.

Make-up

Gallants used perfume – civet and musk – but, in general, this age was one of masculine force and vitality, and men eschewed effeminate effects.

Military Dress

The sixteenth century saw the last development of plate armor; cannon and

Fig.143

Fig.146

Fig.149

Fig.151

pistols made coats of mail useless. Armor was still worn for jousting, tournaments, and ceremonial occasions, but rarely were full suits of plate armor worn into battle.

Fifteenth-century plate armor, in many pieces, gave way to the ribbed plate armor molded in a few pieces (Fig. 144 D). The breastplate was in one piece; the skirt, or *lamboy,* was frequently fluted in a few large pieces, although it might also be made in three or four horizontal layers of plate. The *pauldrons* were quite large, heavy, and engraved or embossed, as was the fashion. *Pass-guards,* or plates of steel, like standing collars, warded off blows to the neck (Fig. 144 D).

Helmets were of various types in this century. A closed type, with a movable visor, was called an *armet.* Another type was the *burgonet* (or Burgundian helmet), with or without a visor (Fig. 144 D). The *morion,* a Spanish type without visor or beaver, but with upcurved brim (often pointed at front, back, and sides), was much used by men-at-arms. Cortez and other early discoverers and explorers are usually pictured in this kind of helmet. Crests and plumes were frequently added.

The sollerets, or foot coverings, were broad-toed, like civilian shoes (Fig. 144 D).

The suit of armor given Henry VIII by Maximilian I of Austria, on the occasion of Henry's marriage to Catherine of Aragon (the first of his six wives) is a splendid example of the armor of his age. It is fluted, highly embossed, engraved with re-poussé work; the badges of Henry and Catherine are on it, their initials united in a true-lover's knot. Also engraved are the lives of the saints. Here (ironically), cut in steel, is pictured the "martyrdom of St. Catherine"!

This age saw several types of military uniform established. The Swiss Guards of the Pope today wear the type of uniform designed for them by Michelangelo. The Beef-Eaters of the Tower of London wear the uniform designed for them in the time of Henry VIII (if not, as sometimes reputed, by him). These are scarlet, yellow, and black, with the golden Tudor rose on the chest and on the shoes.

Costume for Women

The women copied the works of Raphael, Michelangelo, Leonardo da Vinci, and others; and the great artists of the Renaissance were not above designing dresses and laces for the ladies of the day. Writers like Piccolomini and Castiglione urged feminine elegance, and appreciated taste in dress as in other expressions of creative art.

Robe

The robe (Fig. 145 A Fig. 146) consisted of bodice, sleeves, and skirt over a kirtle, or underskirt. The bodice was tight, with a wide, square-cut neck; it was fastened down the front or the back. The bodice might have an inserted V of different material in front; this was the beginning of the "stomacher." A high neck was achieved by a partlet, or yoke, of lawn, gathered into an upstanding band about the neck; this band was often finished with a narrow lawn ruffle or ruff (Fig. 145 B), which was to grow to prodigious proportions as the century progressed. The partlet might be of the same material as the bodice.

The sleeves were long and fairly full, with other sleeves – *manches volantes* (Fig. 145 A Fig. 146) – over them, these oversleeves being of contrasting material, or of fur, richly lined. Often several types of sleeve might be used on the same dress; since they were fastened by points, they could easily be changed. The pattern for the oversleeves is seen in chapter VIII, Fig. 133 H J. Another type of oversleeve was bell-shaped. Catherine Parr wore this type frequently. Other types of hanging sleeve are shown in Fig. 142 E F.

The skirt was a full, gathered one, or cut semicircular. It was usually parted in front in a ∧ arranged over the stiff bell *farthingale,* an arrangement of canvas and steel or whalebone hoops, bell-shaped and fastened about the waist (Fig. 145 pattern). The origin of the farthingale is vague. (The suggestion that the name came from *vertu-gardien* suggests a modest beginning; however, *vertugade,* farthingale, and other names were used. It probably evolved from the Spanish *verdugo,* meaning "rod" or "plait.") It was first used in France by Eleanor of Castile about 1530. Henry III, in 1563, restricted the width in France to an ell – one and a quarter yards wide. Spanish ladies generally wore the skirt fastened down the front, but occasionally even they parted it to show the rich kirtle beneath.

The kirtle showed beneath the skirt, and was of material as rich as – and sometimes richer than – the top skirt, especially that ∧ portion which showed down the front (Fig. 145 A, pattern).

Dutch women wore the skirt and kirtle without a train. Anne of Cleves, being Dutch, followed this fashion. She also favored a sleeve puffed above the elbow, and full and open below, over a white lawn undersleeve. In France, Italy, and England the train (on the skirt alone, not on the kirtle) indicated the rank of the wearer.

Another type of robe is shown in Fig. 145 B. The bodice was cut essentially like that in Fig. 145 A and pattern; the fastening was down the front and accentuated by two ornamental strips – a further step toward the stomacher. The square neck was filled in with a yoke of the same material as the bodice, or of brocaded stuff, or a partlet of linen or lawn. The upstanding band, or collar, might have a ruffled edge, and stood open at the neck in front (Fig. 145, pattern of collar Fig. 146). The bodice extended in a moderate curve over the skirt in front.

The sleeve (see pattern) was fairly tight, with, at the top, a puff slit to show the material beneath. The underpiece was cut on the same pattern. The puff was usually wired through the center, making the stiff, outstanding effect (Fig. 145 B and pattern).

The skirt was made like that in Fig. 145 A, divided over a kirtle, brocaded and perhaps quilted. Underneath was a *bell farthingale.* German women favored a bodice with a square neckline, full partlet, and sleeves puffed at the shoulder, showing the white undersleeve also at a split at the elbow (the type of bodice associated with Marguerite in *Faust*). The over-bodice might be cut with an off-shoulder line, low in front (sometimes a mere girdle), and filled in with full partlet, or shirt. The skirt was very full, not split down the front, or, if split, fastened at intervals down the opening. A peculiarity of the German and French styles (seldom seen in other countries) was to embroider the name of the wearer on the band of the neck-yoke, across the breast. Dürer followed this custom in his pictures. Italian women wore the square neckline; the armhole was accentuated by puffs and points, the white chemise or shirt (partlet) beneath showing between the fastenings. Jeweled brooches were used as fastenings on the richer garments.

Mantle or Cloak

The cloak was a circular one, cut long to the ankles, with a hood attached. Sometimes a cloak with wide revers and large sleeves, like the men's cloak (Fig. 142 A), was used by women.

Footwear

Women's shoes were fashioned much like men's, with square toes, plain or slashed (Fig. 154 E G). Later, women tired of this ugly style, and returned to the round-toed type, and gradually to the pointed toe. In this century, a gradual building up of the heel took place (Fig. 154 B). Pantofles with lifted heels, like those worn by the men, were worn (Fig. 154 J).

Hair

The hair was simply arranged, as it showed very little beneath the hoods. Usually it was parted in the middle, waved low over the ears, and knotted at the nape of the neck, or higher. The hair was also worn in braids, wound at either side behind the ears. Sometimes it was puffed out over the sides of the head.

Headdress

A type of headdress which appeared in various adaptations was the *French hood*. This was probably evolved from the wimple. The front edges were folded back, rounded or squared about the face; sometimes a black fold was added over the white; sometimes the hooded part was pointed into a diamond shape in front; it was then called the *diamond-shaped cap* or *pedimental cap*. Sometimes a roll of striped cloth was worn underneath this type; the headdress was wired into shape, and called the *pyramidal hood* (Fig. 146).

The back might be folded up over the crown of the head, as in Fig. 146; the sides might be similarly folded. Part of the side might be drawn up under the chin, and fastened to the side; or the hood might be accentuated, toward the back of the head, by a padded roll beneath. The hood might be made of linen, close-fitting, or of lawn; in fact, the variations were many, and differed in type in different countries. The Germans tended to wear the smooth white hood, with padded puffs at the back. Italians wore a simple form of cap hood, with black over-hood, or else the coif, with a flat, pancake effect on the top. The French and English favored more complex styles, as described above. The jeweled net cap (chapter VIII, Fig. 130 B) was favored by Italians and French. The jeweled ferronnière was worn with this type of cap. The large cap with upstanding brim, split into four sections, was still worn.

Ornaments and Accessories

Chain girdles, dropping to the hem of the skirt in front (Fig. 145 A B Fig. 146), were important in the more elaborate dresses; they were often jeweled, or were ropes of pearls or of velvet. Necklaces were another important item, though not so large and heavy as those of the fifteenth century. Brooches, jeweled buttons, rings, ferronnières, sleeves, brooches, buckles, cap ornaments, were all included in the ornaments of the time.

Accessories included pomanders, scent balls containing aromatics, metal balls with charcoal inside for warming the hands, handkerchiefs (Fig. 153 E), reticules (suspended on long chains or ribbons from the belt), rosaries, breviaries, gloves (perfumed and jeweled), and fans. The fans were most commonly of feathers, ostrich plumes being popular; they were usually fashioned in circular or oval styles, with a mirror in the center. Corsets of whalebone or canvas were worn beneath the dresses. Pins were made in the Netherlands (they were a Spanish invention), and needles were perfected; both were needed for ruffs and other decorative articles of dress.

Make-up

The face received the same attention as before, except that the hair was not so carefully plucked back from the forehead; however, the eyebrows were still a very narrow arch. Cheeks were rouged and powder was abundantly applied.

COSTUME FOR CHILDREN

Children wore garments similar to those of their elders (Fig. 147).

1550–1600

GENERAL CHARACTERISTICS

The broad, square lines gave way to close-fitting, well-padded ones. The individual parts of dress were changed or added to, in the following details, for men, (1) the ruff, (2) doublet and hose, (3) hats, (4) puffs and slashes; for women, (1) the farthingale, (2) the stomacher, (3) the ruff, (4) hose, (5) hats, (6) puffs and slashes.

The general effect of these details was to give richness and suavity to the costume. Their type and use varied in the different countries. The Italians still felt the influence of the Renaissance, and their innate artistry held them to slender lines and simplicity of design. The Spanish, influenced by the gloomy Philip II, maintained a somber dignity of line and color; the Dutch, in spite of their violent secession politically, acknowledged allegiance to Spain in matters of dress. The French and English expressed exuberance and release in their various adaptations, but even here the Spanish influence showed. What was said of an English dandy –

> Behold a most accomplished cavalier
> That the world's ape of fashion doth appear,
> Walking the streets, his humor to disclose
> In the French doublet and the German hose.
> The muff, cloak, Spanish hat, Toledo blade,
> Italian ruff, and shoes right Flemish made –

indicates the infinite variety needed for the "glass of fashion and the mold of form."

Materials

The complaint of Philip Stubbs, a Puritan writer, in 1583 recites many of the popular cloths: "I say nothing of what their doublets be made – some of satin, taffeta, silk, grograine, chamlet [camlet], gold, silver, and what not; jagged, cut, carved, pinched, and laced with all kinds of costly laces." Degrees of rank were indicated by the costliness of material. Velvet, purple, crimson, and black, was for the very exalted; those of lesser degree wore satins, woolens, frieze – in fact, they ran the gamut down to the coarsest materials. Lawn, "white as driven snow, and cypress black as e'er was crow" were in demand by widows particularly, although the general public favored lawn as a material.

COSTUME FOR MEN

Doublet

This period saw the rise of the doublet from a simple undergarment to the elaborate, puffed, slashed, jeweled, and pointed costume of the gallant (Fig. 148 A B   Fig. 149). The doublet was fitted tightly to the body, waist length; attached to this might be a flare or skirt (peplum) of the same material, cut in one piece or slashed into sections. The doublet (Fig. 148 A B, pattern) was often designed in parallel strips, vertical or horizontal; vertical, however, predominated. These strips might be plain, of contrasting color, or puffed and slashed until the effect was chaotic. The lines tended to taper from shoulder to waist, accentuating slenderness, although neither the rather broad shoulder nor the slim waist was exaggerated.

The doublet was fastened up the front, with buttons or laces. The point in front dipped more decidedly as the century advanced, until the "peascod-bellied' doublets evolved. These were stuffed, curved, and protruding, in the style kept familiar to this day by "Mr. Punch."

As the doublet was originally an extra garment, or vest, doubled or padded for warmth, it had no sleeves. In the sixteenth century, sleeves were added, often by means of points, laces, or tabs (Fig. 144 B). Often a stuffed roll of material, or a crescent, puffed, slashed, and even jeweled, accentuated the shoulder line, and emphasized the junction. Around the wrist was a small frill of lawn (Fig. 148 A).

Ruff

About the high, snug neck of the doublet was a ruffle or *ruff* of lawn which, from a small edging an inch or so in width, grew with the century's advance to a prodigious width, ten or twelve inches. The ruff is said to have been adopted by Henry II of France to hide a wen, though it is also said to have been of Spanish origin. It was at first only a small, narrow ruffle; then it grew to a wide, flapping, cambric collar; later, a wire *supertasse,* or *under-propper,* was added to hold it away from the neck. Another name for this was *peccadillo* or *piccadilly;* the street Piccadilly in London is said to have been so named because these accessories were sold there.

Gradually, the ruff came to be pleated in thick layers. For the pleating, goffering or poking sticks of wood or bone were inserted while the material was wet and left there until it dried. Later, steel poking sticks were used, and were heated to hasten the process.

In 1564, Mrs. Dinghen van der Plasse, wife of a Dutch coachman, brought with her to England the secret of starch (which the Puritan, Stubbs, called "the devil's liquor"). From then on, starched ruffs became popular. At first, colored starches were used – yellow (until Mrs. Turner, a murderess, wore a yellow ruff to her execution), blue, and other colors being favorites. Then white became universally popular. With the advent of starch to stiffen and hold out the pleats, the ruffs grew in width to twelve inches and more; the maximum was reached in 1580. Eighteen or nineteen yards of linen, cambric, or lawn were used to make the more elaborate ruffs. A man's head over a ruff resembled John the Baptist's head on a platter.

Lace

Later, as the vogue for lace developed, the ruff was edged with lace. This new accessory was also colored at first; some lace patterns designed by Raphael and still to be seen in the Cluny Museum were colored. In time, however, white came to be preferred.

Ruffs became objects of legislation. When Queen Elizabeth learned that London apprentices were putting lace on their collars, she issued orders that the next one caught so attired would be publicly whipped. She also stationed guards at the city gates to measure ruffs; if they were wider than the sumptuary laws allowed, they were snipped off.

Underclothes

The custom of wearing ruffs focused attention on linen. This material, starched or unstarched, became a necessity for the undershirt, drawers, chemise, shirt, and underskirt. The ruff also made short hair for men an inevitable development.

Hose – Breeches

In this period, the hose separated into breeches and stockings, though the old names continued to be used for some time. The *breeches*, or *trunk hose*, were sometimes called *galligascons*, or *slops*. Loose, full upper hose were affected by Francis I, Henry VIII, and others earlier in the century; later, the styles varied – there were French hose, as well as Venetian, Spanish, German, Burgundian, etc.

French hose were similar to moderately slender knee breeches. They were usually slashed, often puffed – sometimes in horizontal rows of puffs – (Fig. 148 B and pattern), and often ended in *canions* or *rolls* just below the knee. Another type, also called French hose, consisted of loose, baggy puffs reaching only midway to the knee, with strips of material, often puffed and slashed, over the puffs (Fig. 149). *Burgundian hose* were similar to the last, but were longer, bombasted, and stuffed to the proportions of huge melons (Fig. 144 B). *German hose* were long, full, and loosely hung, but elaborately puffed and slashed; these slashes were often lozenge- or crescent-shaped. *Venetian hose* resembled French hose (Fig. 148 B) and were fastened below the knee with points and laces, often gold-tipped. Various styles of puffs and slashes are shown at the top of Fig. 153. Trunk hose became so elaborate that strict sumptuary laws were passed to limit the cloth used, and the amount of bombast or stuffing.

Hose – Stockings

There is some doubt as to when worsted or silk *stockings,* as such, were first introduced. By 1575 they were known and used by the nobility; by the end of the century they were fairly common (partly as a result of the invention of a stocking frame in 1599 by William Lee, who later was driven from England to France). Many stockings were made at Milan, Italy, and at Lyons, France. Henry VIII had several pairs of Venetian hose "woven like a caul" – but he did not like them; his son Edward VI had a long Spanish pair, of silk, presented to him by Sir Thomas Gresham. Queen Elizabeth, presented with a pair in 1561, took a great fancy to them and no doubt hastened the vogue.

For those who could not afford silk hose, jersey was a good substitute. The long seams were set by a plumb line. There were often clocks about the ankle. Stockings were always matched in color, not parti-colored, as the former hose had been. The stockings reached above the knee, and were usually fastened up to the waistline by laces or points. There is a reason for Poins's speech in *King Henry IV, Part I:* "their points being broken, down fell their hose"!

Cloak

Although the coat was still worn over the doublet (Fig. 149), and was of waist or hip length, this was the age of the *Spanish cloak*. The usual shape was semicircular, short, waist or hip length; for travel or for older men, it might even be long, to the ankles. It was made with or without a collar, fastened with clasps or cords (Fig. 148 A B, pattern). The longer cloaks were also worn by professional men – and by brigands. Usually the collar was rather wide and rounded over at the top.

The shorter cloaks were worn open, to show the lining and the finery beneath. They were edged and faced with gold and silver lace and other trimmings. The front edge was often turned back to show the lining (Fig. 148 B). Cloth, silk, velvet, and taffeta were the favorite materials, velvet predominating in favor. The favorite colors were black, white, red, tawny, green, yellow, russet, and violet.

The cloak was a very important part of a gentleman's attire. He must know how to wear it carelessly but correctly, to throw it up over the shoulder, to use it in bowing, to drape it about him to the best effect. Sir Walter Raleigh used his cape to advantage!

Footwear

Shoes became much simpler in this age. Moderately rounded or pointed, they boasted a few puffs and slashes (Fig. 149). They were shaped with points over the instep, usually decorated with rosettes. The Dutch wooden shoe to some extent influenced footwear. The pantofle was still in fashion (Fig. 154 J). As Harrington, Queen Elizabeth's godson, said, "We wear cork soles to seem taller."

Leather, velvet, and felt were the usual materials for shoes.

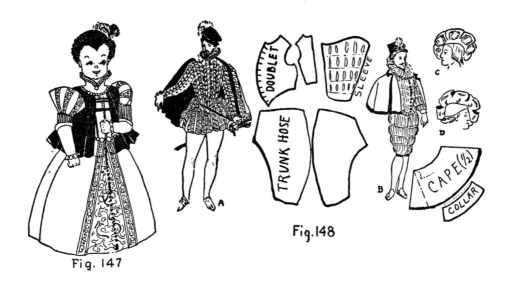

Fig. 147

Fig. 148

Fig. 150

Fig. 153

Fig. 155

Hair

Young men and gallants wore their hair short, with small, pointed beards; the pointed mustache was also small; the beard was not always worn. Beards were kept well trimmed (Fig. 140 C Fig. 148 A B Fig. 149). Older men wore beards of more formal cut, like Jaques' Justice. The soldier was "bearded like the pard"; at least, his was a fuller and more ragged beard than men of fashion favored (Fig. 141 Fig. 144 B).

Headdress

Caps were now relegated to the middle and lower classes, to professional men, and to children (Fig. 152). In 1571 a statute ordained that all above six years of age, except people of rank, should wear woolen caps "made in England." Though this law was later repealed, the cap was still "the sign of some degree." It was, of course, still worn by the clergy.

The Milan bonnet was still used. Another variety of bonnet had a small brim, often turned down, and a very high, puffed velvet crown, frequently decorated with a feather or tuft of feathers (Fig. 140 C Fig 148 A Fig. 149). Beaver hats, "of fine hair, from beyond the sea," became very popular, because (as has been said) they were supposed to restore a man's hearing, if steadily worn. There was a steeple hat, with a high, conical crown; a sugar loaf hat with a tall, rounded crown; and a hat with a square crown; brims to these were either narrow or wide. Another hat had a round, flat-topped crown and a narrow brim (Fig. 148 B). They were ornamented with a plume or plumes at the side; a hatband of ribbon, velvet, or metal was also worn, as well as a pin or brooch in the side of the crown. The fashion of wearing a lady's glove in the hatband is also seen in the pictures of this era. The high-crowned hat with broad brim was called a *capotain*, or "high-copt" hat. Hats were worn both indoors and out.

Ornaments and Accessories

Gold and jeweled hatbands, brooches, gold points, rings, chains, jeweled buckles, jeweled rosettes (Fig. 154 B), reflected the preference for decoration.

Gloves (Fig. 154 C H), handkerchiefs – with lace edges (Fig. 153 E), mirrors, combs, and garters (including the cross-garters fastened above and below the knee, and, in some instances, wrapped solidly up the leg from ankle to knee, as pointed out by Gage in the *Archaeologia*, Vol. 24, where the custom is traced to the early

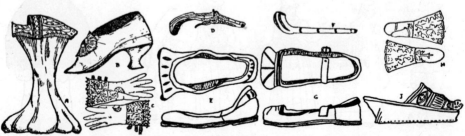

Fig. 154

Saxons) were a part of every gentleman's dress accessories. So also were daggers (Fig. 143) and swords – now worn by gallants and all people of rank as part of civil dress (Fig. 148 A Fig. 149). Walking canes were also used; a "staff tipped with horn" is mentioned in *Much Ado about Nothing*. Young gallants also slung musical instruments across the chest by ribbon sashes, or baldrics; the lute, viola, and other stringed instruments were especially popular. Watches, it is said, were first worn in Germany, and introduced into England (and presumably France) about 1580. The earlier type had one hand only, and thick oval or octagonal cases, elaborately carved. Pouches for carrying money were tucked into the belt; women, older men, and the working classes carried them at times suspended from the waist by a long ribbon or chain (Fig. 153 A). The new type of firearm called a *pistol* was carried by gallants and fighting men (Fig. 154 D). The *pipe,* for smoking the newly-introduced tobacco, was also used (Fig. 154 F).

Make-up

Dandies used perfumes, curled and oiled their hair, and waxed their mustaches. They carried little combs to keep their beards in trim.

Military Dress

Little remained of the elaborate plate armor. The corselet or steel breastplate was still worn over the doublet, and was plain or engraved (Fig. 144 B). Often, however, only the gorget, or neckpiece, was worn (Fig. 141); Fig. 144 B shows the gorget with breastplate. The morion or helmet, with projecting brim, had a high comb, or ridge, down the center of the crown (Fig. 141 Fig. 144 B), and a ridge covering the nape of the neck; it was often finely engraved, as shown. The burgonet was another type of helmet, with a chin piece; the upper rim fitted into the lower so that it presented a closed surface, with slits or a movable visor for the eyes (Fig. 144 D). Gauntlets were still necessary, and high, soft boots protected the legs; but the rest of the lower portion of the body was clad only in the bombasted breeches of the time. Occasionally pieces of plate armor were attached to the belt, covering the thighs, but this was not universally done.

Ecclesiastical Dress

Catholic vestments remained practically the same. The miter now had two arched points, front and back, and was very like the modern miter; the alb, dalmatic, stole, and maniple showed little change. The chasuble was now shortened on the sides to a fiddle shape, front and back; the cope was also shortened; buttons for the front fastening of the cope were designed by some of the great craftsmen of the Renaissance, chief among them being Cellini.

A cardinal (Wolsey, for example) wore a long cassock or alb, usually scarlet, with a moderate ruff; over that an *amice,* or circular cape reaching almost to the elbows, also of scarlet; and, at times, a long, circular cloak was worn for additional warmth. If ritual required, a white *cotta* or surplice, calf length, edged with lace, was added over the cassock. The cardinal's red hat, in the sixteenth century, had a low, rounded crown, a very wide brim, and cords at either side, ending in tassels. The number of tassels on each cord varied, apparently from three to fifteen; the latter is the number shown in the heraldic arms of cardinals, though Wolsey's individual arms show only six tassels.

The garb of Protestants was as reactionary as their tenets. Instead of the vestments sanctified by time and usage, the Protestant clergy substituted the soberer garb of the academic world. A long cassock, black, red, or purple, with tight sleeves, was worn; over that, a white *rochet,* or shorter tunic, low-necked and gathered, with full sleeves; over that, the *chimere,* or sleeveless gown, of black or some somber shade; about the neck, a soft *scarf* (the stole), usually black. On the head was worn either a flat cap with ear flaps or the four-pointed cap.

Costume for Children

Children and young boys of rank wore copies of their elders' clothes (Fig. 155); if of the middle or lower classes, they wore simple jerkins or doublets, loose hose or breeches, or perhaps, in the country, only the smock or tunic.

Christ's Hospital (founded by Edward VI in 1553 for orphans and foundlings) was later commonly called the Bluecoat School because its inmates wore long blue gowns buttoned from collar to waist with pewter or wooden buttons, yellow stockings, and broad black shoes; they went bareheaded. This type of dress, worn by Bluecoat boys up to modern times, with slight changes, was also the usual dress for London apprentices; these latter, however, wore flat caps.

Costume for the Lower Classes

Merchants – who became very prominent in the sixteenth century – wore substantial but plain clothes. Older men usually favored long robes, hooded or furred cloaks, leather jerkins, and wide beaver hats (or the square caps of the former era).

Workmen wore doublet or jerkin, the doublet often laced up the back; the doublets were usually slightly padded; if the jerkin were worn, it showed the full white sleeves of the shirt beneath. Long, loose-fitting, wool hose and loose breeches (Fig. 153 A) covered the legs, or else the older type of hose without breeches. Shoes were of soft leather with wooden soles, and they sometimes had straps over the ankles. A hood with a wide cape was worn, over which was worn, in addition, a wide-brimmed hat of the abacot type (Fig. 153 A).

The uncle of Will Somers (jester to Henry VIII), a plain old man, wore a russet jerkin, coarse but clean white linen shirt, close round breeches of russet wool, long stockings of white kersey, high shoes with yellow buckles, and a flat cap with flaps over the ears; these flaps could be buttoned up over the cap.

A countryman would wear, for instance, a sheepskin doublet, greasy felt hat, plain leather pouch, kersey stockings, and heavy shoes. For holiday attire, he would wear a russet doublet faced with red or some bright worsted, blue camlet sleeves, a row of pewter buttons down the front (usually left unbuttoned, however), gray kersey stockings, slop breeches, and a green hat.

Servants wore the arms, family crest, or insignia (sometimes called simply the *livery*), of their masters, embroidered in silver on their left arms. Lower servants wore blue coats, like the apprentices.

COSTUME FOR WOMEN

Underclothes

Women wore a shift or chemise, drawers, and stockings, held up by ribbon garters about the leg or by laces to the waistband. The story of Queen Elizabeth's garter (which she lost while boarding Drake's ship one day, and which was seized by the envoy of the Duke d'Alençon and returned only when she had promised it as a pledge to the Duke d'Alençon) shows that these garters were made of fine materials – in this instance, of purple and gold silk.

Corsets or *stays* (Fig. 150, pattern) with wooden stomachers in front and whalebone or steel stays were necessary to the tight-fitting bodices; petticoats were also worn underneath the kirtles and skirts to the robes. Shirts of fine lawn or linen, trimmed sometimes with lace, were worn under the bodices and showed sometimes at the neck and wrist.

The nightgown, or night rail (as distinct from the night gown, or evening costume), was introduced about this time. Formerly, women had slept without clothing of any kind, or else had worn a warm robe, like the modern dressing gown. The nightgown was of linen, lawn, cambric, or silk. Over it was worn, in very cold weather, the dressing robe. It is said that Elizabeth received the Spanish ambassador in a costume consisting of a thin lawn chemise, open down the front from collar to waist; over this, a white damask gown, like a princess petticoat, also open; and, over this, a black silk gown lined with crimson, with wide gold bands across it, likewise open down the front. This dressing gown revealed not only the two layers of white underclothes, but the body of the queen, to the waist. It was said that Elizabeth had a curious habit, while speaking, of throwing up her chin and with both hands casting open the collar of her dress – unless, as in this case, it was already open.

The use of many undergarments was furthered by the introduction of soap. Up to this time, clothes had been washed in plain water, beaten with wooden sticks or with stones, and then rubbed, scrubbed, and bleached in the sun. Soaps made of the bark of trees, of nettles, of hemlock, and other concoctions were used with varying success until soaps of wood ashes, lye, and animal fats were introduced. From this time on, the use of more undergarments and more white garments was possible. There was also an increase in the use of lace, ruffs, and starched materials. Incidentally, arsenic had to be put into the starch to keep the rats from eating it!

Bodice and Skirt

The usual dress after 1550 consisted of bodice and skirt (Fig. 150 Fig. 151). The bodice was cut along stiff lines, padded and boned, and worn over a stiff corset (Fig. 150, pattern). The front of the corset, consisting of a wooden piece, or stomacher, was curved outward in order to rest over the farthingale. The stays were tightly laced, so that the waist appeared very small. Catherine de' Medici prided herself on her thirteen-inch waist.

The bodice followed the lines of the corset. It also curved out in a projected V in front; this V was of different material from the bodice, and was also called a stomacher (Fig. 150 B). It was narrower than it had been in the first part of the century, and was boned and sometimes padded. The stomacher was much favored in Holland and Germany, continuing longer in vogue there than in France or England. Venetians wore a softer form of the stomacher.

The type of bodice and skirt shown in Fig. 145 B was still worn, with the sleeves changed to the newer type (see below). The partlet under the low-necked bodice was also worn. The high-necked bodice was finished with a ruff – which increased to a width of ten or twelve inches (Fig. 150 A   Fig. 151), or else had an upright collar with smaller ruffle. The low-necked bodice acquired, as a finish, a wide ruff, boned and wired upright over the shoulders and across the back of the neck (Fig. 150 B Fig. 151). This type lent itself to fanciful shapes; it was made round, or heart-shaped, or it was wired high up above the head. From Catherine de' Medici, who introduced the fashion in France, it was called the *de' Medici collar* (Fig. 150 B and pattern Fig. 151).

Young women's bosoms were bared fairly low, a custom begun by Catherine de' Medici and followed by Elizabeth. This low neck was worn out-of-doors as well as indoors.

Sleeves

The sleeves were stiff, crescent-shaped, and puffed and slashed in various ways, as was the bodice (Fig. 150 A B, pattern). They were stuffed or bombasted so much that the arms stood out awkwardly from the body, resting on the stiff farthingale. The sleeves were often laced into the armhole, and crescents, or pads of material, also puffed or slashed, were arranged over the shoulder line (Fig. 150 A). Other sleeves were sometimes worn over the stiff dress sleeves; the added sleeves might hang free from the shoulders, or from the elbows. This type of *manches volantes* was favored in the stiff Spanish and Flemish costumes of the time; the shape of the sleeve was often accentuated with an outline of braid. Fig. 150 A shows a sleeve favored by the French and English; it was split down the front, showing another sleeve underneath. At the wrist were worn lace ruffles, or cuffs turned back over the sleeve (Fig. 150 A B).

Ruff

The ruff was distinctly a sixteenth-century detail. It was made of linen, lawn, holland cambric, silk, gold and silver cloth, or lace – in fact, it dominated the costume, at least the upper part. Starched and lace-edged, it became more convoluted, wider and higher (Fig. 140 A). The de' Medici type expanded to great heights. The Hatfield portrait of Elizabeth shows her in a huge, heart-shaped collar (Fig. 151). Such a ruff made the wearer look small and almost dwarfed. The bourgeoisie favored the ruff opened and sewed along the edge of the square neck. In more elaborate form, this type was worn by the upper classes (Fig. 150 B). Sometimes the circular ruff was worn along with the de' Medici ruff (Fig. 151).

Skirt or Farthingale

The name of the contrivance which held out the skirt (farthingale) was given to the skirt also. The earlier form of bell-shaped farthingale was still in favor in France and Spain, as well as in Flanders and Germany and, to some extent, in England; however, the *wheel farthingale* superseded it in most fashionable English circles. This type consisted either of a roll like a huge sausage, tied about the hips, or of a steel framework hinged and fastened about the waist (Fig. 150, pattern Fig. 151). Over this the full pleated or gathered skirt was draped (Fig. 150, pattern). The skirt might be opened down the front, or draped over the kirtle beneath (Fig. 150 B) and held together at intervals with ribbons or buttons (Fig. 150 B). A second ruff, the width of the farthingale about the hips, was, toward the end of the century, superimposed over the skirt, and further added to the wide effect (Fig. 150 B Fig. 151). The result was that the legs seemed shortened to dwarfish proportions; the waist, with the long, pointed stomacher, seemed out of all proportion.

Queen Elizabeth (Fig. 151), starved throughout her neglected childhood for pretty clothes, indulged this craving when she was made queen. At her death, she had amassed a wardrobe of some three thousand dresses; it was said that she wore a different dress every day of the year. Among her famous costumes was the "eye and ear" gown, in which the Wimpole portrait of her is painted. It was so called because the skirt was patterned with representations of human eyes and ears; on the sleeves were embroidered serpents. A typical dress consisted of a stomacher, which was richly jeweled, and a brocaded skirt patterned in geometric design, studded with pearls; the sleeves of the dress consisted of lines of puffing divided by jewels, and at the wrists were deep, lace cuffs; strings of pearls were laced in the hair; single pendant pearls hung over the forehead; and a necklace of several rows of pearls surrounded the throat, while a high, lace ruff (de' Medici style) rose above the shoulders.

Robe

Another type of costume favored at this time, particularly in Spain and France, was the straight robe showing the petticoat and stomacher beneath. It might be fastened with a single button at the waist, or left entirely open down the front. The crescent pads might be attached over the shoulders; the hanging sleeves were fastened to the robe and fell over the regular sleeve from the elbow or from the shoulder. The robe was usually high-necked or had a turnover collar, often of fur.

Train

Most sixteenth-century dresses were worn long, but without trains. However, for court attire, trains were added. The longest train recorded was that worn by Isabeau of Bavaria on the occasion of her entry into Paris in 1571. Her train measured seventy feet. Moderate trains, varying in length from a few feet to several yards (the rank of the wearer determined the length) were worn for festive occasions; for dancing, trains were looped up by buttons or hooks.

Cloak

Over the dresses, a loose cloak or jerkin was worn; it was sometimes called a sur-coat. The length varied from hip length to knee length. The shorter type was fa-vored by the Dutch and Germans. Often these cloaks were sleeveless or had hanging sleeves, as the dresses beneath had such full, bombasted sleeves.

Circular cloaks with hoods were also still worn; velvet or wool was the favored material for these.

Footwear

Shoes of simple fashion, made of leather, velvet, silk, or cloth, were worn under the wide robes. Pantofles with thick soles (Fig. 154 J) were still worn; chopines were also popular for use in inclement weather. Venetian chopines, imported from Tur-key, had very high supports, sometimes twelve inches in height. (This explains the line in *Hamlet:* "Your ladyship is nearer heaven . . . by the altitude of a chopine.")

With the shoes, the women now wore the new silk or knit woolen hose. Mistress Montague gave Queen Elizabeth her first pair of silk stockings on New Year's Day, 1559; after that, they became very fashionable in England. Long hose were still worn by the majority of the populace.

Hair

The ruffs did away with low, elaborate arrangements of the hair. It was now brought up to the top of the head and knotted. It was curled (really frizzed) in close, fuzzy fashion, with frizzed bangs across the forehead. The hair was also worn brushed back from the forehead and puffed, pompadour style (Fig. 140 A   Fig. 144 C   Fig. 150 A B   Fig. 151). Occasionally, the hair was worn parted in the middle and drawn into a knot at the back. The pompadour might also be parted in the middle; this type was favored by Venetian ladies. Brides (who had not been married before) wore their hair long and flowing, as a symbol of their virginity.

If the hair were thin, false hair was added; if the hair were not of the proper shade, it was dyed – and as the fashion changed frequently, so did the hair. Many women in England dyed their hair red, in emulation of the queen. Elizabeth's own red hair faded and thinned as time progressed; she had made, in all, eighty wigs. Mary of Scotland dyed her hair so frequently that, at her execution, it showed a dozen different shades – including much gray underneath!

Hair for wigs was so much in demand that children with fine heads of hair were kept off the streets, as they might be kidnaped for their hair.

Headdress

The cap was still worn – especially the type called the *Mary, Queen of Scots* cap (Fig. 145 B   Fig. 147   Fig. 150 A). This was an adaptation of the earlier French hood. A lawn hood was worn, wired in the shape of a heart, with the peak in front. Often the peak was of black velvet, pointed over the forehead, while a veil, of white or black, was frequently allowed to hang down behind. This peak, when applied to the hair, and worn in order to accentuate a peak over the forehead, was called, after Queen Mary of Scotland, the "widow's peak."

The velvet bonnet with narrow brim, like the men's (Fig. 140 B), was worn also by the women; it was adorned with a plume or plumes, or with a jeweled brooch. The beaver hat, with high crown and medium or small brim, was also worn by women. It was decorated with a plume, buckle, rolled band, or jeweled brooch. The middle classes wore the beaver hat with tall crown and fairly wide brim (Fig. 153 D).

Ornaments and Accessories

Jewelry was much in evidence, especially pearls, singly or in strands. They were worn as necklaces, loops across stomachers (called *carcanets*); they were draped in the hair, over the forehead (Fig. 140 A); or they were worn as bracelets. In addition to the loops of pearls, single jewels were worn in the hair and on the costume; girdles of jewels, rings, brooches, bracelets, jeweled buttons, gold points, jeweled rosettes, and lockets aided in the rich effect of the costume. Diamonds, emeralds, rubies, and other colorful precious stones were used. Elizabeth was fond of the cat's-eye stone. "The Phoenix rising from the flames" was a favorite device of hers for any ornament. With the high-piled hair, earrings came back into favor, and were button shape, or pendants (Fig. 140 A). Shoe buckles, garter clasps, and jeweled hand mirrors were among the accessories in demand. The rings had "posies" or sentiments engraved in or on them. The ring which Elizabeth gave Essex was of gold, with the queen's portrait in jeweled headdress and ruff; it was designed by an Italian who had settled in England. The ring is now, after its tragic history, buried with Elizabeth in Westminster Abbey. The wedding ring was worn on the first finger instead of the third; in France, it graced the right hand; in England, the left hand.

Twisted girdles of silk, satin, velvet, and gold or jeweled fabrics, were used for the "cable hatbands" (Fig. 153 D). Small hand mirrors were carried at the end of ribbons or chains suspended from the waist (Fig. 150 A); they were also inserted in the center of the feather fans. Pouches or reticules also hung suspended from the waist, or were carried by a long loop (Fig. 150 A). The reticule held coins, scent, scissors, gay gilt knives, handkerchiefs, and other knickknacks.

Brides wore "bridelaces" or ribbons to tie up the sleeves; these they gave away afterward to their bridesmaids. Rosemary was the appropriate flower for brides.

Muffs, introduced by Venetian ladies, became fashionable; Velasquez' portrait of the Spanish Infanta shows her carrying a rectangular muff in her left hand. The Venetian ladies carried small dogs in their muffs – to keep their hands warm!

Masks were always worn out-of-doors by women of quality. They were usually of black silk or velvet, with or without a lace edge; they covered eyes and nose. The square, fan type on a stick was also used (chapter X, Fig. 165 F) toward the end of the century.

Watches, as mentioned above, came into vogue, but were only rarely worn by women.

Fans (introduced, it is said, by Catherine de' Medici, from Italy) were of ostrich or peacock feathers (Fig. 151); often a small mirror was in the center of the fan. They were sometimes worn suspended from the girdle by ribbons or chains.

Brushes, combs, needles, and pins were in high favor. Feathers (called "popinjay plumes") also had a great vogue, and were dyed many colors. Gloves were perfumed, embroidered, and jeweled. A pair given Elizabeth by Lady Mary Sidney had twenty-four gold buttons, each set with a diamond. Elizabeth was proud of her white hands, and carried her gloves with an air. Handkerchiefs of various colors, sometimes "garnished with gold," were carried; they were edged with lace, and perfumed (Fig. 153 E). Lace was a growing necessity, the best coming from Venice and Holland. English bone lace was used for less handsome clothing.

Autolycus, in *A Winter's Tale,* sings of the various whims of the day:

> Gloves as sweet as damask-roses;
> Masks for faces and for noses;
> Bugle-bracelet, necklace amber;
> Perfume for a lady's chamber;
> Golden quoifs and stomachers,
> For my lads to give their dears;
> Pins and poking-sticks of steel,
> What maids lack from head to heel.

Make-up

Artificial complexion aids were much sought after. Elizabeth had a sallow complexion, so her ladies swallowed ashes, gravel, and tallow to achieve a similar tint! Glue and powder were put on the hair to hold it in the high puffs fashion demanded, and also to shade it; the powder was of many hues. Paint was liberally applied to cheeks and lips; eyebrows were plucked to a thin, arched line, and blackened with soot. Hair was frizzed on hot curling irons.

A courtesan might wear a satin gown, lawn apron, velvet shoes, green silk stockings, and taffeta petticoat with gold fringe. She would be perfumed with hot civet, and always carried a fan. A distinguishing mark of her profession was the ring she wore on her middle finger; the ring was carved with a death's head.

Mourning

"Cypress black as e'er was crow" was the proper cloth for mourning – it was a thin material adaptable to bodices and veils. Widows were supposed to renounce all vanities, wear black garments, cover the hair completely, wear a veil over face and breast, and a circular cape like a shroud for outdoor wear. They had to assume a sad air when walking in public. In the house, they wore coifs completely covering the hair, as well as their black dresses. When they began to uncover their hair and put on a few ornaments, it indicated that the mourning period was waning. When a lady in mourning received a stranger, it was the custom for her to call in her gentlewomen and for all the ladies then to receive the stranger with black veils over their faces – thus, Olivia's conduct in *Twelfth Night,* when she receives Orsino's embassy.

COSTUME FOR CHILDREN

Children wore simple clothes – a smock or loose tunic, or a youthful version of their elders' dress, particularly the type shown in Fig. 144 C. Nobly-born children were dressed in the elegant fashion of the day (Fig. 147 Fig. 152) – at least, when having their portraits painted!

COSTUME FOR THE LOWER CLASSES

Fig. 144 C shows a woman costumed according to the general middle-class type. The bodice was cut along the very simple lines of the earlier period, with a partlet and turned-back collar or "band." The woman wore a large apron, with insets of lace bands. The skirt was full, over a moderate roll farthingale.

Fig. 153 B C shows the lower classes clad as in the preceding period. For the great middle and lower classes, styles changed slowly. Fig. 153 D, however, shows that a woman of the bourgeois, or tradesman, class in the city wore a somewhat clumsy imitation of the fashion of the day, even to the hat and the handkerchief. Only the absence of puffs and slashes, of much bombast, of extremely pointed bodices, of lace and ornamentation shows that the gown belongs to one not to the manor born. For practical purposes of work, skirts were tucked up, and aprons were worn for the same reason. Hoods, caps, and hats were all worn by the lower class, as was also a modified form of the wimple.

MODERN ADAPTATIONS

Materials

For brocades, use old-fashioned bedspreads, or dyed or rep curtains; also, decorators' fabrics that have a heavy, rich effect may be used. Beaded panels or relics of old evening dresses are most useful. Flitter may be applied on brocaded patterns. Lamé and all types of metallic cloth are excellent (see materials listed above for the medieval period). Upholsterers' velveteen is splendid for all the finer types of gowns.

When gold or silver designs are painted on any materials, mix gum arabic and glycerine (a teaspoonful to a can of gold paint) with the paint; this mixture will adhere better to the fabric.

Fur must be used to edge and trim garments.

Elizabethan Costume (Fig. 151)

Materials required:

1. Foundation:
    a. Eight yards of unbleached muslin for lining of the bodice, sleeves, and foundation of costume (underskirt).
    b. One pound of cotton batting for stuffing sleeves.
    c. Two yards of tarletan or starched cambric for under-ruffle on underskirt.

d. Two yards of featherboning for seams of bodice and for stomacher.

e. Belting for foundation skirt – to which farthingale is hung.

2. Dress:

a. Twelve yards of costume satin, brocade, or similar material.

b. Two yards of organdy ruffling for cuffs and collar.

c. Two yards of brocade for oversleeves (54″ material may be cut in two).

d. Jewels — as many as desired.

I. Wheel Farthingale (frame may be ordered at any shop which makes lampshades):

A. Obtain two circles of heavy wire, welded and reinforced with four spokes:

　1. Inner circle just large enough to go over the shoulders.

　2. Outer circle four to eight inches larger, as desired, for width of frame.

B. Wrap both inner and outer frames with tape or with strips (1″ wide) of unbleached muslin.

C. Sew muslin tabs (about 3″ long) to fitted belting and hang frame to these by sewing six or eight tabs to inner wire of frame.

II. Foundation Skirt:

A. Measure circumference of frame and make underskirt this width. (No fullness required for this foundation.)

　1. Sew selvage of muslin to the wrapping on the outer wire frame.

　2. Ascertain correct length of skirt (just to the floor) and stitch the underruffles around the bottom of the skirt:

　　a. The cambric or tarletan ruffle goes on first.

　　b. The silk ruffle goes over the stiffened one. (These ruffles should be from 12″ to 18″ deep.)

　3. Use a piece of muslin wide enough to extend a little below the edge of the wheel. It should be about one and a half times the measure of the circumference of the wheel. Gather it into a peplum that falls slightly over the edge of the frame after it is gathered and sewed onto the belting. After adjusting the gathers evenly, stretch this material out to the edge of the wire and sew it over the selvage of the foundation skirt. This will give the complete foundation for the skirt of the costume. If the top skirt is of lightweight material, a roll of cotton batting tacked along the edge of the hoop frame will soften the curve and eliminate the sharp, hoop effect.

III. Skirt (use same general plan as for foundation skirt):

A. Pleat or gather the satin around the edge of the frame and sew it on firmly all around, allowing for the fullness when the material is cut and seamed for the skirt.

B. Make a gathered ruffle or peplum, allowing about 5″ over the distance from the waist to the edge of the farthingale for a heading and a small piece to hang down over the skirt. Gather this peplum to the basque and stitch together (opening at the back).

   C. Sew waist down over the belting of the foundation by hand, using strong thread, thus joining the waist and skirt.

   D. Stretching the ruffle or peplum to the outer frame, adjust gathers evenly all around. Make a heading around the edge of the wheel and sew the peplum over the whole foundation, leaving a 3″ ruffle which hangs over the outer skirt of satin from the hoop.

   E. Sew fastenings down back of costume.

IV. Bodice (a square-necked, fitted basque, slightly below normal waistline):

   A. Cut and fit lining of basque waist, opening down back.

   B. Cut satin or brocade waist, by fitted lining, and sew this and the lining together – seaming and darting according to fitting.

   C. Fasten the featherboning to the lining on the side, side-back, and back seams.

   D. Face the square neck, sewing the facing to the lining by hand.

   E. Bind the bottom of the waist – this can be bias binding of satin, or it can be corded.

V. Stomacher:

   A. The stomacher is sewed on by hand at the neck and is tacked firmly at the waistline to hold it in place.

   B. The materials needed are:

      1. One-half yard of buckram.

      2. One to two yards of featherboning.

      3. One and one-half yards of covering material (preferably brocade).

   C. Cut the buckram to the desired length and width, and sew featherboning to each edge of the buckram base, reinforcing the point of the stomacher with several strips of featherboning.

   D. Cut the brocade ¼″ larger than the buckram base.

   E. Design a pattern on the brocade for the jewels, sew the jewels on, then sew the brocade onto the buckram, turning the excess material under.

   F. At the top of the stomacher sew a full strip of lace.

VI. Sleeves (the stuffed sleeve):

   A. Cut fitted foundation sleeve of heavy muslin, using tight-fitting foundation pattern.

   B. Tack cotton batting to foundation sleeve (the seams of which are left open until later), padding the sleeve, within the boundary of the underarm seams, the shoulder and cuff seams, to the desired fullness.

   C. Cover this padding with a slightly fuller foundation sleeve also made of muslin, and sew the underarm seams of the sleeve; stitch the two foundations together at the wrist.

   D. Make a long, gathered sleeve of the satin, with enough fullness to fit easily over the padded foundation. Place this sleeve, gathered at the cuff and the armhole, over the foundation and baste in place.

E. Finish with a 2″ cuff of white or of the dress material and sew sleeves into the bodice armholes. These sleeves can be crisscrossed with gold cord or ropes of jewels, like a latticework, or jewels may be sewed on the sleeve in any desired pattern either before the outer sleeve is put over the padded foundation or after the sleeve is completed and in the basque.

F. The oversleeves of damask are made by cutting the material down the middle, curving the ends that hang over the skirt, and curving and finishing the other straight side to fit around the armhole. Placing the material around the armhole, with the opening on top at the shoulder seam, sew this sleeve firmly to the shoulder and to the underarm seams of the bodice, and tack in two or three other places around the armhole. To finish the sleeve, sew a stuffed roll of the satin around the armhole (the stuffing is placed only across the top of the roll, which is cut on the bias so that it will fit easily around the sleeve).

VII. Collar:

A. Use wire to make the frame of the collar – dressmakers' wire or copper wire, preferably copper wire, because it is light in weight and still has body.

B. Take the wire and measure from the bust, in a diagonal line, to the shoulder. Bend the wire and measure, in a curved line, to the middle of the head – standing four inches above the head. Fold, and measure the other side of the collar by what you have already measured.

C. Shape the collar and reinforce with spokes of wire, one from the center of the neck to the top, one from the neck to the right shoulder, one from the neck to the left shoulder, and one from the left front around the neck to the right front.

D. Cover the frame with a lightweight lace. Then put brilliants or flitter on the lace. Iridescent sequins are ideal because they are very lightweight, and will catch any color of light.

E. Keep collar as light in weight as possible so as to give it a very delicate and elaborate appearance.

Lace

For sixteenth-century laces, use heavy lace. Put a little sugar in cold starch (about a teaspoonful to a pint of starch), till consistency is that of thick cream. Soak lace in this solution, iron it while wet with a very hot iron, and continue ironing until it is quite dry. The lace will then be very stiff; if pleated, the pleats will be very stiff also and will stay in; and the lace will not get limp or soiled throughout the run of an ordinary production.

Footwear

For fifteenth-century pointed shoes, make the soles of stiff canvas; cover and stuff the points. Do the same with the high boots. The boots can be of the same canvas, dyed, as was described for the jerkins in the previous period.

For sixteenth-century broad-toed shoes, puffed and slashed, use old bedroom slippers, and add broad, cushioned toes, slashed, with puffings in the slashes.

Patterns

The magazine *Vogue* has a series of patterns which are excellent for basic period designs. In addition, for the slender tights (or hose), use a union-suit pattern or *Vogue's* animal suit patterns. For a tight tunic, use a vest pattern. The pajama coat pattern is a good basic pattern for loose tunics, coats, etc.; one must allow for fullness, if necessary. For longer coats or cloaks, lengthen the pajama coat pattern. For the sixteenth-century pointed bodice and stomacher, use a fitted basque pattern, shown in the *Vogue* period patterns; or any Elizabethan fancy dress (or milkmaid or Spanish or shepherdess) pattern. The ruff is a plain strip, stiffly starched and folded in loops. To insure that the fold remains, tack each loop, top and bottom.

The sixteenth-century skirt should be built on a canvas foundation, with a petticoat and many muslin ruffles (see preceding pages). There should be a ruffle at the top, inside, to give extra fullness. The farthingale can be built of wire, as explained previously, or else made of canvas, stuffed and shaped like an automobile tire.

A bell farthingale can be made of wire and unbleached domestic; the wire is run through casings sewn in the petticoat.

A puffed sleeve, like that shown in Fig. 145 B, can be made of two circles, the lower one larger than the upper one. Holes for arms are cut off center, not in center. Sew the two circles together; the small upper one will hold the sleeve out.

For a very full skirt, an old ballet skirt is excellent. Use several petticoats over it.

For puffs and slashes, cut the slashes in the material, and put glue mixed with glycerine on the edges of the slashes, to keep them from raveling. For striped effect, use strips of material over sleeves, puffed breeches, etc.

CHAPTER X

THE SEVENTEENTH CENTURY

IMPORTANT PEOPLE AND EVENTS

FRANCE
Rulers
Louis XIII
 (1610–43)
Louis XIV
 (1643–1715)

Artists
Claude Lorrain
 (Gelée)
Pierre Mignard
 (Le Romain)
Nicolas Largillière
Hyacinthe Rigaud
Charles Le Brun
Nicolas Poussin
Jules Hardouin Mansart
François Mansart
 (Mansard)

Writers
Pierre Corneille
Jean Baptiste Racine
Molière
 (Jean Baptiste Poquelin)
La Rochefoucauld
 (François, duc de la Rochefoucauld)
François de Fénelon
René Descartes
Alain Le Sage
Saint-Simon
 (Louis de Rouvroy, duc de Saint-Simon)
Cyrano de Bergerac

Notable People
Cardinal Richelieu
 (Armand du Plessis, duc de Richelieu)

Jules Mazarin
Jean Baptiste Colbert
Vauban
 (Sébastien le Prestre, marquis de Vauban)
Sully
 (Maximilien de Béthune, duc de Sully)
René de La Salle
Samuel de Champlain
Maria Mancini
Henriette d'Orléans
Louise de la Vallière
Mlle de Fontanges
Mme de Maintenon
Ninon de Lenclos

SWEDEN
Gustavus Adolphus
 (1594–1632)
Christina
 (1632–52)
Charles XII
 (1697–1718)

ENGLAND
Rulers
James I (Stuart)
 (1603–25)
Charles I
 (1625–49)
The Commonwealth, under Oliver Cromwell
 (1649–60)
Charles II (Stuart)
 (1660–85)
James II
 (1685–89)
William and Mary
 (Orange-Stuart)
 (1689–1702)

Writers
Thomas Heywood
Philip Massinger
John Dryden
William Wycherley
William Congreve
Richard Lovelace
Robert Herrick
John Milton
John Donne
Sir Thomas Browne
John Punyan
Samuel Pepys
John Evelyn
Izaak Walton
Daniel Defoe
Jonathan Swift
John Locke
Sir Isaac Newton

Notable People
Henry Purcell
Sir Peter Lely
Sir Godfrey Kneller
Wenzel (Wenceslaus) Hollar
Inigo Jones
Sir Christopher Wren
Nell Gwyn

RUSSIA
Mikhail Feodorovich
 (first Romanoff)
 (1613–45)
Peter the Great
 (1689–1725)

INDIA
Aurungzebe
 (1658–1707)

AUSTRIA
Albrecht von Wallenstein
Johann von Tilly

THE NETHERLANDS
Artists
Franz Hals
Rembrandt van Rijn
Gerard Ter Borch
 (Terburg)
Jan Steen
Pieter de Hoogh
Vermeer
 (Jan van der Meer)
Peter Rubens
Sir Anthony Van Dyck
Justus Susterman

Notable People
Hugo Grotius
Baruch (Benedict) Spinoza
Fernando de Toledo, duke of Alva

ITALY
Popes
Innocent X
 (1644–55)

Artists
Guido Reni
Il Bronzino
 (Angelo Allori)
Michelangelo da Caravaggio
Salvator Rosa

Notable People
Galileo Galilei

PRUSSIA
Rulers
Frederick William
(the Great Elector)
(1640–88)
Frederick I
(1688–1713)

GERMANY
Rulers
Ferdinand II
(1618–37)

Ferdinand III
(1637–57)

Notable People
Gottfried von Leibnitz

SPAIN
Rulers
Philip III (Habsburg)
(1598–1621)
Philip IV
(1621–65)

Charles II
(1665–1700)

Artists
Diego Velásquez
Francisco Zurbaran
Bartolomé Murillo
Pedro Calderón de la Barca

THE AMERICAN
COLONIES
Sir Walter Raleigh

Captain John Smith
Pocahontas
John Winthrop
Captain Miles Standish
Peter Stuyvesant
Leonard Calvert
Roger Williams
William Penn
Sir Edmund Andros
Cotton Mather
John Eliot

FRANCE

1600, Sully's reforms. . . . 1610, Henry IV assassinated. . . . 1624–43, Richelieu destroyed feudalism, established central power of Louis XIII. . . . 1635, Richelieu founded French Academy. . . . 1643, Louis XIV and Mazarin. . . . 1648, Louis XIV founded Academy of Painting and Sculpture. . . . 1649, War of the Fronde. . . . 1667, wars with the Netherlands, Spain, Austria, etc. . . . 1681, La Salle explored the Mississippi and named the surrounding region Louisiana. . . . 1685, Revocation of Edict of Nantes. . . . Building of Versailles for Louise de la Vallière. . . . Colbert encouraged French mercantilism. . . . Champlain explored Great Lakes in America. . . . Age of court painters (Largillière, etc.), and court favorites (Madame de Montespan, etc.). . . . Great age of drama (Molière, etc.).

ENGLAND

1603, death of Queen Elizabeth and union of England and Scotland by accession of James I. . . . 1605, Gunpowder Plot. . . . 1609, Hudson's explorations. . . . 1629, Petition of Right. . . . 1640, Hollar published *Habits of English Women*. . . . 1642–49, Civil War between Cavaliers and Roundheads. . . . 1642, theaters closed. . . . 1649, beheading of Charles I, establishment of Puritan commonwealth. . . . 1660, restoration of Charles II. . . . After 1660, great era of Restoration drama; first actresses appeared in England – Mrs. Davenport, Nell Gwyn, etc. . . . 1665, Great Plague. . . . 1666, Great Fire. . . . 1679, Habeas Corpus Act. . . . 1688, Glorious Revolution. . . . 1689, Bill of Rights. . . . English trading stations established in India at Calcutta, Madras, Bombay. . . . Introduction of chocolate, coffee, tea. . . . 1694, Bank of England founded.

THE NETHERLANDS

Great age of painters (Rembrandt, etc.). . . . "Little Dutch Masters" portray home life. . . . 1618–48, Thirty Years' War. . . . Dutch independence recognized by Treaty of Westphalia, 1648. . . . Spinoza's philosophy.

OTHER COUNTRIES

Rise of Sweden under Gustavus Adolphus. . . . Sweden first developed concept of organized army. . . . Rise of Russia, founding of Romanoff dynasty. . . . Peter the Great westernized Russia. . . . Galileo's (1564–1644) astronomical discoveries. . . . Frederick William effected reforms in Prussia. . . . Great age of portrait painting in Spain (Velásquez, etc.). . . . 1607, Jamestown, Virginia, founded by Raleigh. . . . 1620, landing of Pilgrims. . . . Mayflower Compact. . . . 1636, Harvard founded. . . . 1664, New Amsterdam became New York. . . . Witchcraft at Salem. . . . 1682, Penn founded Pennsylvania. . . . 1693, College of William and Mary founded. . . . By 1700, all original thirteen colonies founded except Georgia, which was founded in 1733.

Gorgeousness tended to lapse into licentiousness; then the still small voice of conscience bored through the bombast of success. After the glaring midday splendor and spread of the sixteenth century came the shadowy softness of the early seventeenth century.

England, on the high, firm pinnacle where the Tudors had placed her, felt a giddiness in her soul; the divine right of kings was imperiled by the diviner right of man. The little island split diagonally; the gay, poetic Cavalier, with his lace and love knots, cut a dashing figure as opposed to the stolid Roundhead Puritan in "sad-colored" buff jerkin and stiff buckled hat. Van Dyck, imported from Holland, so caught the intriguing Stuart charm that later generations forgot the infamous adult career of the Baby Stuart, James II. Hollar, brought over to England about 1640 by the Earl of Arundel, caught the naïveté of London ladies in their transparent taffeta vizards.

France also had its internal struggles within the secret confines of palace walls. Philip de Champaigne, imported from Flanders, drew a three-sided portrait of the many-sided Richelieu; this arch-strategist, in his simple cardinal's robe, took precedence over silk-clad lords and ladies and made dupes of queens and generals.

Germany was drawn into the maelstrom of the Thirty Years' War – Germany, compact of many lands and faiths. At the end, the captains and the kings departed, and left the statesmen victors with their spoils.

Spain saw its arrogant sun sink into the New West; Velasquez draped the poverty-proud hidalgo in the somber cloak of his dignity and peopled a dwindling court with children and dwarfs.

Holland, secure behind its victorious dikes, put its house into the shining order reflected by Vermeer and dressed its prosperous burghers in the opulent style of Hals and Steen; but its everlasting fame lurked in the half-lit shadows of Rembrandt's impartial but imperious brush.

Italy, resting after the intense creative fury of the Renaissance, turned analytical and contemplative. The blind Galileo in his tower at Arcetri, a virtual prisoner of the Inquisition because he had seen too far into the universe, entertained and encouraged the young Englishman, John Milton – Milton, the far-sighted, who, one day, would vision Paradise after he, too, had lost his earthly sight.

By the middle of the seventeenth century, Protestantism had emerged triumphant in northern Germany, Holland, Sweden, Scotland, and England; the individual was assured of his right to personal redemption, and a New World beyond the seas echoed its assurance.

With the second half of the century, however, the reaction set in. Europe was a checkerboard, where kings controlled the nations held as pawns. Rulers like Frederick William, Charles II, and Peter the Great matched wits for individual power, not for national necessity. Charles II, weary of his long exile and of enforced piety, made his reign an era of lavishness and laxity. The theaters, opened after the Puritan interim, welcomed comedies of proper manners and improper morals, and on the stage women for the first time played their rightful parts.

It was an era when the people of each nation looked to their king to set the style in everything; and every king in Europe looked to Louis XIV, the Grand Monarch of fashion. Richelieu had reduced the feudal lords of France to servile courtiers who obsequiously applauded the king in his many dazzling triumphs. Louis gave glamor to his age but no true illumination. His dramatist ("by royal command"), Molière, his musician, Lulli, his architect, Mansart, his painter, Claude Lorrain, and other talented members of the Académie Française and of his newly-created Academy of Arts, furnished the real luster to his reign.

As patron of arts, Louis, of necessity, had to raise dress to a fine art. Sessions with his couturier, Langlée, were as important to him as conferences with Colbert; the cut of a coat was related to the body politic.

This arbiter of fashion was a true dictator. While Peter Romanoff was learning kingcraft in the marshes of the Neva, Louis was teaching it; while Charles II was learning obedience in London, Louis was demanding it. It is not strange, then, that his edicts concerning clothes were as solemnly obeyed as was the disastrous Revocation of the Edict of Nantes. If Louis XIV decreed red heels, all Europe followed in his footsteps. Events, indeed, might be timed by the tap-tapping of the Louis Quatorze heels down the mirrored corridors of Versailles.

COSTUME
1600–1660

GENERAL CHARACTERISTICS

The bombast, stiffness, and other characteristics reflecting the dominance of Spanish influence in sixteenth-century costume lasted until about 1620. Then changes began to appear. France led civil fashions, and Germany influenced military garb, probably because of its long involvement in the Thirty Years' War. There was a general softening of line and shape, of materials, of decoration. Specifically: (1) doublets lost their stuffed and padded appearance; (2) puffs and slashes were reduced to slits and strips; (3) waists became high and tended to lose the point in front; (4) breeches became soft and full, and skirts remained full, but the farthingale was discarded; (5) ruffs lost their stiffness, and finally became flat collars; lace became an indispensable part of costume, especially on collars and cuffs; (6) cloaks became longer and fuller; (7) the hair was worn soft and clinging about the shoulders by men and women alike; (8) sleeves were full but not stuffed. Italy, however, despite these changes elsewhere, retained its former styles to a great degree. Spanish styles showed a certain softening, but the farthingale, in a wide hoop style, was retained.

Materials

Materials covered a wide range. Broadcloth, serge, flannel, kersey, drugget, russet, duffel, worsted, and baize were used; so were buckskin and leather. Flowered patterns were worn, but plain fabrics were favored. Calico, dimity, and lawn were in great demand. Velvet, plush, satin, damask, and silk fabrics were woven in a great variety of ways; the thin silks, especially the taffetas, plain and watered, were very popular. Prunella, a coarse woolen stuff, and tabby, a watered silk, were favorite weaves. Lutestring, a bright or lustrous silk, was a less expensive material; so was holland linen. Other materials of the preceding century, still used, included frieze, fustian, camlet, and linsey-woolsey; string-linen was used, particularly for the lace-edged collars. Patterned materials continued in use in Italy, Spain, and Germany (last to adopt the new styles), whereas France, England, and Holland seemed to favor materials in plain but rich colors. For shirts and other white garments, holland linen (the finest, for elegant wear), buckram, dowlas, and even canvas were used for everyday wear. Buttons were of silver or pewter. The Puritan in England and America was distinguished by the plainness of his dress – somber coloring, simple, dull materials, and absence of lace, ornament, and ribbons.

Colors

During the first twenty-five years, pure white, peach, flame, orange-tawny, and pearl were favorite colors. Later came purple, russet, tawny, French green, De Boys brown (wood color), ginger-lyne, deer, fawn, leaf brown, orange, black, and Zebulah (a tan color). White was also much used, especially for collars, cuffs, sleeves, and aprons. Ter Borch's use of white satins is to be noted, as is also Van Dyck's emphasis on white collars and cuffs, edged with deep lace – Dutch, Venetian, English, or Flemish.

Underclothes

Underclothes were fairly well standardized. Women wore the chemise, corset, short drawers, underskirt, and stockings; hose were white, black, or red, though blue, green, and other colors were sometimes used. Flannel and silk petticoats were worn. Nightcaps (like Monmouth caps) with tasseled ends were worn. Dressing gowns of brocade, silk, or velvet, styled with loose sleeves and full-cut robe, became increasingly necessary. A turban cap or fur hood was worn with the dressing gown. For men, an undershirt, drawers, and stockings sufficed for underclothing; stockings, for the well-to-do, were of silk, and were blue, carnation, yellow, and other colors. The shirt with sleeves was now part of the outer dress.

COSTUME FOR MEN

1600–1620

The general type of Elizabethan dress continued in use, with a few changes (Fig. 157, pattern). The doublet lost some of its stiffness, but was still padded, and had puffs and slashes; tabs were added about the waist, like a skirt. The sleeves were slashed, but were not quite so full; the padded crescent was still worn over the shoulder. The lace-edged ruff was still in evidence; however, a stiffened, plain "band," flaring open at the throat, was also worn. Oversleeves often hung from the shoulders. The waist retained a slight point. Breeches were knee length, still often bombasted, but also worn very full, without stiffening (Fig. 157, pattern). There was a garter, trimmed with lace, or with a rosette, at each knee. This type of costume was

Fig.156

worn in America long after it was discarded in England, as is shown by ships' inventories of the time. Shoes were square-toed, and the rosettes were large. The cloak was circular, a bit longer than in the previous century. The beaver hat was almost a universal style; it had a tall crown and was ornamented with a buckled band or a twisted roll of brocade or other material. Feathers were worn at the side of the hat. Brims varied from wide to fairly narrow. Beards were pointed, in the Venetian manner. Boots were worn for riding. The sword was carried at the left side. The circular cape (Fig. 157, pattern) was worn over the shoulder and draped over the arms.

During this time, men spent fortunes on clothes. One outfit for the Duke of Buckingham cost £14,000; it was made of white uncut velvet, trimmed with diamonds and pearls, and worn with hat, stockings, etc.

1620–1660

Doublet and breeches – about 1625 (Fig. 158)

The doublet had lost some of its stiff padding, though it was still fitted rather closely to the body. Gentlemen wore corsets to give the effect of slender waists and puffed-out chests. The opening down the front of the doublet was fastened with a row of buttons close to the high waistline. The dip in front was retained, and a skirt was added, either in one piece or split into tabs (Fig. 158, pattern). About the waist, accentuating the waistline, was often placed a row of laces and points, tied in bow knots. The doublet might be solidly constructed, or the outer layer might be in strips (Fig. 158, pattern). The sleeves were full, but not padded or stuffed; the outer layer was in several strips (Fig. 158), or was split down the front seam to show the full white shirt beneath.

The crescent roll over the shoulder flattened into a flat fold or a semicircular series of tabs. The lace-edged ruff was still worn, though it tended to fall flatly over the doublet. A type of square, lace-edged collar, held out horizontally by wires or by much starching, was also frequently worn. Cuffs were plain or pleated, and were quite deep, usually edged with lace (the Vandyke cuff). The breeches were longer and looser than formerly. They were slashed down the outer seam, toward the knee, showing the lining; a row of buttons or loops provided fastening if desired. They sometimes fastened below the knees with a deep row of points or tabs about the breeches' opening. High, wide, soft leather boots were worn with this type of dress (Fig. 158).

The circular cape was still worn. This cape, together with the costume (as shown in Fig. 158), is usually associated with the figures of the Three Musketeers, d'Artagnan, and Cyrano de Bergerac.

Jerkin – about 1625

This was usually worn sleeveless, though at times snug sleeves were added. It was particularly popular in Germany and Holland. It might be made of velvet, satin, cloth, or leather. For military use it was usually of leather. The buff jerkin was cut rather long, hip length, loose, and semi-fitting, flaring out at the hips; it might be either in one piece (Fig. 159, picture), or in sections (Fig. 159, pattern), laced up the front. It was fastened up the front with buttons or cross lacing. A pad or a row of tabs was usually placed over the shoulder. A moderate ruff or a flat collar ("falling band") finished the neck.

The trunk hose or breeches (Fig. 159, pattern) were moderately large, and were fastened below the knee with ribbons and rosettes, or points and laces. This was the type of dress worn by Dutch burghers in pictures by Rembrandt, Hals, and others. It was also worn by French cavaliers at court, as is so splendidly portrayed in Meissonier's "Cavalier of the Time of Louis XIII" (Wallace Collection).

Straight doublet, long breeches – about 1640

This type (Fig. 160) was favored by Charles I of England. The doublet was cut on straight, plain lines (Fig. 160, pattern); for decoration, a series of horizonal trimmings, frogs, or braidings were used. The long, semi-fitted breeches might be similarly adorned (Fig. 160). They reached below the calf of the leg, usually being tucked into the soft boots. Vandyke collars and cuffs furnished a soft touch. The full sleeves had one or two lengthwise slashes, revealing the white shirt beneath. Another type of breeches might be worn with this jacket; this type was short, loose, knee length, with perhaps a row of tabs about the lower edge (Fig. 161 A E), or else gathered in below the knee (Fig. 161 B).

Plain, long, buttoned doublet and breeches – about 1645

This type (Fig. 161 A) was favored by the Puritans and by country people. It was of plain material and had no ornamention. The doublet was low hip length, buttoned down the front with large buttons, often of pewter or silver (Fig. 161 D). The sleeves were in one piece, medium-sized; the shirt was of plain linen, with falling band square-edged in front and unadorned with lace (Fig. 161 A C), and plain, turned-back cuffs. A long, low-hip-length circular cloak was often worn with it. (New England colonial types should wear this sort of costume.)

Shirt

At this time the shirt became important. It was made of white silk, taffeta, linen, or lawn, with long, full sleeves. The ruff had given way to the "falling band," or collar, cut circular with square front edges (Fig. 156 B). This type of collar and cuffs

CAPE

CAPE COLLAR

BACK

FRONT

SHOULDER

TRUNK HOSE

Fig. 157

A

SHOULDER

SLEEVE

COLLAR

BACK

TABS

TABS

Fig. 158

SLEEVE

TRUNK HOSE

CUFF

Fig. 159

Fig. 160

COLLAR

C

D

E

A

B

Fig. 161

Fig. 162

Fig. 163

CUFF

COLLAR

BODICE

FRONT BODICE OPEN

A

B

C

Fig. 165

D

E

F

G

were called *Van Dyck* (modern "Vandyke") after the painter who made them famous. These lace-trimmed collars were also called "bands" or *piccadilloes*.

Cloak

The very short circular cloak favored in the Elizabethan age, though occasionally worn, was now superseded by the larger, more capacious circular cloak or cape (Fig. 157, pattern). It might have either no collar or a deep collar. It was worn fastened about the neck, or thrown carelessly about the shoulders and held up, on occasion, with the right hand on the right hip (Fig. 157 A). It was also draped over the left shoulder only, and left to hang loose (Fig. 158). It might also be draped about the figure, up over the left shoulder, and might have a wide turn-back revers along the edge (Fig. 161 B). Cords fastened at either side of the collarband inside were used, if needed, to hold the cape in place. The *mandillion,* or cloak, was a loose sack, reaching midway down the thighs and fastened about the throat. The sleeves could be worn, but were usually left hanging free. The mandillion was of some warm woolen material, lined with silk or fustian.

Footwear

Between 1600 and 1625, shoes of velvet and satin, as well as leather, were worn. Boots were universally worn. They were knee length, of soft leather with moderate heels and a deep cuff at the top (Fig. 161 A B). The cuff was wide or narrow. The boots might be shorter and wider (Fig. 158 Fig. 160). (Fig. 167 C G shows the type called *French fall.*) Some boots were very wide and elaborate, with layers of lace on the boothose. Boothose (worn to protect the silk stockings) were of strong, thick linen edged with lace; they formed a lining to the boots. Gentlemen might wear two or three pair at a time. The lace edges were turned back over the boot-tops (Fig. 167 A E). The toes of the boots were medium-blunt; they became squarer toward the middle of the century. Over the instep, to protect the boot from the rubbing of the spur-strap, was a large leather pad or spur-leather, square or butterfly-shaped. Spurs were fastened high up on the heel, and were star-shaped. The very wide-topped boots made necessary a peculiar "straddling" walk which added to the swaggering air of the Cavalier and the musketeer.

Low shoes were also worn; they had low heels and squarish toes, like the boots. They were fastened across the instep with large rosettes (Fig. 157 A Fig. 159 Fig. 167 B D). The Puritans wore plain shoes, square-toed, with large, square buckles of silver or steel.

Hair

The hair was worn short, as were the beard and mustache, similar to the Elizabethan style, until about 1625 (Fig. 156 A Fig. 157 Fig. 159). Then the hair was worn long and flowing, to the shoulders (Fig. 156 B D Fig. 158 Fig. 160 Fig. 161 B). The front curls, one at each side of the face or one only on the left, were called *lovelocks,* and were often tied with ribbons, braided, or elaborately curled. The mustache grew smaller and sharper, and was turned up at the pointed tips (Fig.

156 B D Fig. 161 B). Beards ("appendices pruned") were still worn, but, except for older or professional men, were reduced to a tuft on the chin (Fig. 160 Fig. 161 B). Various names were given to the different types – *pique devant*, T-shape, *sugar loaf, swallowtail* (the latter divided).

Headdress

The high-crowned, rather stiff and narrow-brimmed beaver hat of the Elizabethan age continued in vogue until about 1625. The Cavalier or musketeer type dominated. It consisted of a medium-low crown, a wide, soft brim, and a feather or two draped about one side, the edges drooping over the brim (Fig. 156 D Fig. 160). The wide-brimmed hat was also worn without feathers (Fig. 161 B).

About 1640, the tall, high crown came back into vogue. It was even taller than the Elizabethan type (Fig. 156 B), had a medium-wide, rolling brim, and was decorated with a feather or a roll of material or beads. Van Dyck shows this type of hat on Charles I (Louvre) and on William of Orange and Mary Stuart (Amsterdam Museum). It is also seen in the portrait of Isabelle Brandt by Rubens (Alte Pinakothek, Munich). Hats were worn indoors as well as out. The tall, high-crowned hat was adopted by the Puritans (Fig. 161 A), who often wore a band with a large buckle, center front.

Ornaments and Accessories

Feathers, jeweled bands about the hats, buttons (of gold, silver, or jewels), rings, lockets, chains, jeweled points, jeweled rosettes on the shoes – these were some of the ornaments favored by the elegant gentlemen of the time. Men wore earrings, sometimes one only. The pear-shaped pearl-drop was the favorite style, like the one worn by Charles I in Van Dyck's portrait of him (National Gallery).

The lace Vandyke collars and cuffs (Fig. 165 C), the jeweled dagger, the sash about the waist or shoulders, the gloves – all characterized the man of fashion. In this century he began carrying a timepiece, a thick watch with one hand only (Fig. 165 A). For disguise, he wore the nose mask (Fig. 165 F). For walking, he used a waist-high, gold-headed cane. A long sword was worn at the left side, fastened to the sash (Fig. 161 B), or to a baldric of leather (Fig. 160). The sword was worn with civil as well as military dress. Muffs were occasionally worn by men.

Make-up

Men of fashion saw that their hair was well curled, perfumed, and adorned, that

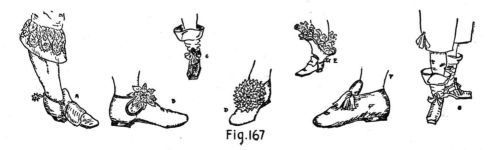

Fig. 167

their mustaches and beards were trimmed to a fine point, and that their hands were well kept.

Military Dress

The soldier wore the buff jerkin, with or without a steel corselet. The corselet had large, rounded pauldrons on the shoulders. Occasionally, full suits of plate armor were worn, but this was more generally true of Germany than of England and France, probably because of the Thirty Years' War. A steel pot-helmet, however, close and round, was worn, and sometimes a steel cap was worn under the high-crowned hat. A gorget was worn about the neck; often the gorget was worn without the corselet.

A *bandolier,* or leather strap, was worn over the shoulder. From it hung a row of canisters containing powder; a flask and touchbox (a receptacle for fine gunpowder, used for priming), for use with the musket or *harquebus,* was also carried. *Tasses* and cuisses might cover the thighs for protection against sword blows. The sword, long and straight, hung at the left side. A dagger or a pistol might be worn behind it.

The use of a colored scarf to indicate the regiment was an innovation introduced at this time. For instance, Hampden's men (Roundhead) wore green sashes; Sir Bevil Grenville's men (Cavalier) wore blue and white sashes. Musketeers (such as d'Artagnan and his comrades) wore buff jerkins, long breeches, boots, morions, and bandoliers. In 1645, the whole Roundhead army under Sir Thomas Fairfax was clad in red; from that time, the predominant color of English army uniforms was red. As Fairfax's family color was blue, his regiment wore blue facings.

Puritan Dress

In general, the Puritans wore the costume of the times, but simplified. The materials were plain woolens, linens, or cottons; no ribbons or laces were used, though not all Puritans were equally austere; collars and cuffs were plain linen or lawn, and low necks were not worn by Puritan women. A general opposition to the ruff first led to the adoption of the falling band; then, when the falling band grew to "worldly" proportions, the Puritans adopted a narrow band. As opposed to colored hose, they wore black or white; instead of square toes, they wore rounded toes; instead of long, curling hair, they wore short hair, as if cut under a round bowl (see below).

Puritan women wore the same styles as other women, but, like the men's clothes, theirs were simplified and devoid of ribbons, laces, and other ornaments.

Yet Puritans, in spite of their religious prejudices against adornment, were the feather-makers, bugle-makers, and starchers of the community. And a surviving bill of a New England seamstress shows that scarlet petticoats and silver buttons were worn. Indeed, the Pilgrims, while in Holland, quarreled seriously over the dress of Dame Thomasin Johnson, wife of the Reverend Rencis Johnson, pastor of the exiles. Her brother-in-law berated her for "showy hats, whalebone, ruffs, musk, and rings and a showish velvet hood." The watchman and rattleman said the quarrel in the meeting lasted until "past ten of the clock." Ill feeling continued and almost broke up the group; the *Mayflower* might never have set sail from Plymouth!

Cromwell was described by Sir Philip Warwick, in 1640, thus: "A gentleman very ordinary apparelled, a plain cloth suit which seemed made by an ill country tailor. His linen was plain and not clean. His hat was without a hat band; his sword stuck close to his side."

Ecclesiastical Dress

Catholic vestments continued the same. Clerics, however, adopted the small, pointed beard and mustache of the laity (even with the tonsure), and they wore the moderate ruff, or falling band. Protestant vestments were simple. A moderate ruff, or falling band, adorned the collar of the knee-length black cassock.

Champaigne's portrait of Richelieu (Louvre) shows him in red cassock, white cotta (or surplice) lace-trimmed, with lace cuffs, plain falling bands, large enveloping cape, and square *biretta* in his hand.

Full breeches to the knee, silk hose fastened with points or ribbons, and a soft, moderately trimmed hat sufficed for everyday wear out-of-doors. In church a white surplice with falling bands and a small close cap of black silk or velvet was used. Nonconformists dispensed with the surplice over the cassock and wore instead the *Geneva gown* (like a loose robe or dalmatic) with full, open sleeves, and open down the front. Plain falling bands were worn with this, and a close-fitting black cap or coif.

COSTUME FOR WOMEN

Types of Dress

Until about 1625, the type of dress worn in the Elizabethan age continued in use. The point of the bodice was as long as in Elizabeth's day, but was rounded at the end, sometimes with a frill of lace outlining the rounded end. In some parts of Germany, the point of the bodice was squared at the end.

In France, the gowns of the court ladies were very rich and stiff. Gabrielle d'Estrées, mistress of Henry of Navarre (Henry IV), wore a brocade and velvet dress so loaded with gold, silver, and precious stones that she had to be supported by gentlemen at either side.

It is said that the sultans in Constantinople thought English ladies deformed, on account of the low, pointed bodices and wide wheel farthingales worn by the wife of Sir Peter Wych and her retinue. The wheel accentuated by a wide ruffle about the waist was still favored. Sir Roger de Coverley called it "standing in a drum." The ruff was stiff, edged with lace, and now called the *rebato* (Fig. 163). The high, wired, de' Medici collar was also used. Bodices were cut low, immodestly so in some cases, as is attested by the papal bull issued at this time. This type of costume continued in vogue in Holland and Germany much longer. Rubens, Rembrandt, and others show us many examples of this type of dress. Isabelle Brandt (Rubens) wears the very exaggerated, long, curved stomacher popular in the Netherlands.

1. About 1625, the bodice became less stiff and padded, and the point in front was lessened. The high de' Medici collar was flattened; the sleeves were left full, but not stuffed or bombasted (Fig. 163). The bodice might have a fairly deep V stomacher in front, but it was not as stiffly boned as formerly (Fig. 163). The bodice was laced across the front, beneath the stomacher (Fig. 163, pattern). A collar and cuff pattern are shown in Fig. 163, and also a bodice pattern.

The sleeves were full, with stripes or slashes. They might be either long or short (to just below the elbow); either length had deep lace cuffs attached (Fig. 163).

The skirt was full, over a moderate farthingale, and was parted in front over a kirtle of another color.

2. Another type of dress, popular from about 1630 on, is shown in Fig. 164. The bodice was soft, high-waisted, and cut high or low on the neck. The high-necked

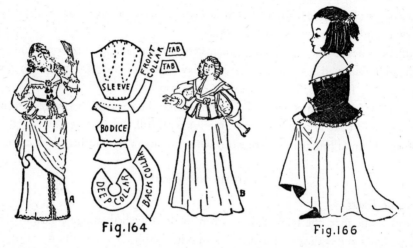

Fig. 164   Fig. 166

bodice is shown in Fig. 164 B. It was fastened down the front to the high waistline. Below this, tabs formed a skirt to the bodice (see pattern), or else the skirt, or flare, was in one piece (pattern). The sleeves were in wide strips, gathered in at the wrist or halfway up to the elbow. A ribbon, with bow or rosette, outlined the high waist.

About the neck was worn a Vandyke collar and the deep, wide "falling band" (see pattern). It had deep points in front, and might be either plain or edged with lace. Deep cuffs were turned back on the sleeves, which reached halfway from elbow to wrist.

A full skirt, over a kirtle, was worn with this bodice. The skirt could be parted down the front if desired.

The low-necked bodice was cut round (Fig. 164 A). A lace edge covered the front, and the back had a deep, lace-edged collar extending over the shoulders to the front (Fig. 164 A). The bodice was fastened down the front with buttons or ribbon bows. A ribbon sash encircled the waist. The skirt to the bodice was in one section or in tabs.

The sleeves were long and full, with deep lace (Vandyke) cuffs. (Short sleeves, also, were worn in 1645.) The skirt was parted, or in one piece, over a kirtle, which showed when the skirt was lifted (Fig. 164 A).

Sometimes a deep lace collar extended all the way around the low-necked gown. It might be graduated toward the front (Fig. 165 G). Also, bows or rosettes of ribbon might extend at intervals along the waistline. Ruffs were wired until 1630. The collar or falling band was still called *peccadillo;* but a newer name was *tiffany whisk*.

Van Dyck's pictures show this era at its peak. His portrait of Lady Sussex (for which he received £50) shows her in a rich gown and "leaner than I am – and fairer and rich in jewels; but 'tis no great matter for another age to think me richer than I was!"

These rich dresses lasted a lifetime and were often bequeathed to the next generation.

Trains were seldom used, except by royalty, or on formal occasions.

3. The Puritan gown was essentially the same dress as that worn by the Cavalier lady, except for the plainness of cut and material. The type shown in Fig. 164 B, if made with no trimming, no tabs, a plain skirt to the bodice, a plain white collar, and deep white cuffs, might have satisfied the stern regulations of the Puritans. Often a large white apron was added, and a kerchief about the neck. Often, also, the outer skirt was tucked up in loops about the waist. A high-crowned hat was worn by women as well as by men.

4. The Spanish seventeenth-century dress did not follow the general trends. The bodice was stiff, with pointed stomacher, as in the style of the sixteenth century. However, the rounded neckline, with low, falling band or collar about it, and the full sleeves, with slashes or straps over full white undersleeves and with deep lace cuffs, show the seventeenth-century characteristics. The skirts were very wide and full, worn over a side-pannier farthingale, which held the material out at either side, but not so much in front. An overskirt, or deep extension of the waist to the edge of the fall of the farthingale (like the wide ruff over the wheel farthingale, but not pleated) was often in evidence, emphasizing the long-waisted effect. Velásquez' many portraits show these details excellently.

Cloak

For outdoor wear, women wore long, circular cloaks with attached hoods. For extra warmth these cloaks were lined. In summer they were made of black taffeta. In very cold weather, fur cloaks and fur hoods were used.

Footwear

Women's shoes were similar to those worn by the men (Fig. 167 B D). Heels were fairly high, and toes were rounded or bluntly pointed. Rosettes were a favorite decoration (as shown in Hollar's engraving of "Winter").

Hair

The hair was worn curled. There was a fringe or row of ringlets across the forehead, or else the hair was brushed straight back (Fig. 156 C). A portion was kept on either side the face; this portion was curled, braided, and tied with ribbons like the lovelocks of the men; the hair might, however, hang loose on the sides (Fig. 165 G). The rest was gathered back into a circular knot at the back of the head, high off the nape of the neck.

Headdress

Hats, similar to those worn by men, might be worn with or without feathers. However, veils (Fig. 165 D) and scarves were more in favor; the hoods of cloaks were thrown over the head out-of-doors (Fig. 165 E). It was not unusual to see a lady in public bareheaded; however, she wore a *vizard,* or mask, to hide her features from public view. This was either a small, black nose mask (Fig. 165 E F) or a rectangular fan mask mounted on a stick (Fig. 165 F). Puritan women wore close-fitting hoods of white lawn, like those long in fashion, with a fold back from the face. Middle- and lower-class women wore the hood under the hat, and upper-class women, when traveling, did likewise.

German women wore, about 1640–45, a peculiar type of headdress. It consisted of a long veil or cloak, shaped like a triangle or a segment of a circle. The point was attached to a round plaque varying in size from two to five inches in diameter. This plaque rested over the forehead. Stuck upright in it (therefore thrust forward diagonally over the face) was an ornament about five inches long, ending in a tuft, or pompon, of feathers. At first (1640), the plaque was large and the veil was therefore draped over the head and shoulders. Toward 1645, the plaque became quite small, and was attached to the veil by a cord, so that the veil hung from the back of the head only, and the plaque was suspended over the forehead, where it held its position as if by magic.

Ornaments and Accessories

Rings, necklaces (pearls were most popular), brooches, jeweled buttons, and jeweled rosettes were some of the ornaments in demand. Earrings, of the pendant variety, came back into high favor.

Perhaps the little dog, the "King Charles spaniel," might be classed as an accessory; he was carried by ladies in their muffs, or he pranced about, clipped like a lion.

Gloves (Fig. 165 B), ribbons, rosettes, Vandyke collars and cuffs, handkerchiefs, mirrors, reticules, veils, muffs, gold and silver bodkins – all were part of the costume. Rosettes and bows were added wherever fancy dictated to heighten the informal, feminine effect. Buttons of silk-covered metal, precious stones, ivory, pearl, etc., were used everywhere; there were even handkerchief buttons to fasten handkerchiefs to the costume. The folding fan made its appearance at about this time (Fig. 165 F). First seen in portraits of Spanish ladies painted by Coello and other Spanish artists, it crept over the Pyrenees, and was in fairly common use among the nobility by 1630. At first these fans were of satin, ivory, or leather, but gradually the painted paper fan won highest regard.

Other accessories of the time are shown in an engraving of a store by Abraham

Bosse. In the store are displayed round lace collars, deep lace cuffs, gloves, neck ribbons, rosettes and bow knots, masks (vizards), round dressing caps, necklaces, and laces.

Although round whisks or oval feather fans were still used, as Hollar clearly shows in his contemporary engravings, the flag-fans began to go out of fashion. Italians made paper fans quite ingeniously. They were oval or shell-shaped, with scenes – of contemporary life, etc. – painted on them. Occasionally they were what we now call fan-shaped.

Make-up

Pencil-lined eyebrows, curled hair, paint, and patches were the marks of fashionable beauty. The patches were black, cut in stars, crescents, and many fantastic shapes.

Mourning

Black, both in body garments and in cloaks, was the mark of mourning. Poor people used black capes, if unable to afford whole suits of mourning. Well-to-do people left mourning rings to relatives and friends, as well as gloves and scarves. Women wore black gowns and hoods with crepe trimmings, cuffs, and veils. Children wore black clothes for near relatives, and for a time tied black ribbons on their clothing and in their hair. Servants in well-to-do households dressed in black when the head of the household died.

In prosperous and noble families in England, a *hatchment* was placed over the doorway at the death of a member of the family.

Costume for Children

Children wore simplified versions of their elders' garb (Fig. 162 Fig. 166). The girls wore aprons and caps (as shown in Van Dyck's portrait of the children of Charles I). The boys wore short breeches and doublet (Fig. 162) and plain collar. For children's portraits of the time, consult Rubens's "The Painter's Two Sons," Van Dyck's "Charles I's Family" and his "Balbi Children," Hals's "Nurse and Child," Rembrandt's portraits of Titus, Ter Borch's "Helene van der Schalke," Velásquez' "Don Baltasar Carlos," "Las Meninas," and his "Infanta Margarita." All these portraits show a growing interest in children, and reflect the mature styles still in vogue for children.

Costume for the Lower Classes

Men wore full breeches, plain cloth or leather doublet or jerkin, wide-brimmed hat, and low, round shoes with tabs. The women wore plain bodices with no flares or tabs, full skirts looped one upon the other and tucked into the waist, aprons, kerchiefs about their necks, and snug caps. Hollar's engravings depict the styles of the middle as well as the upper classes.

Another type of hat worn by both men and women was the *Monmouth cap,* a woolen or knitted stocking cap, with its brim rolled back and its pointed end falling over the side. This cap, in linen or knitted material, was also used for a nightcap. The type of shoe worn by the lower classes is shown in Fig. 167 F.

1600-1625

1600-1625

1625-1650

1625-1650

PLATE VII   CHAPTER X

1660-1675

1660-1675

1675-1700
FRENCH

1675-1700
SPANISH

PLATE VIII   CHAPTER XI

CHAPTER XI

THE SEVENTEENTH CENTURY
(Continued)

COSTUME

1660–1700

GENERAL CHARACTERISTICS

The Puritan influence in England and the restraint put upon French fashion by Mazarin and Anne of Austria were lifted when, in 1660, Charles II was restored to the English throne and when, in 1661, Mazarin died and the twenty-three year old Louis became, in very deed, "the State." For some twenty years, dress was sumptuous, beribboned, puffed, and furbelowed, with men's fashions more eccentric than women's. Coats (or doublets) were shortened, sleeves were fuller and more accentuated, breeches were very full and reached their apotheosis in the petticoat breeches flaunted by Mascarille in *Les Précieuses Ridicules*. Hats acquired wider brims and more plumes; boots receded in favor of silk hose and low shoes; the falling band was folded together or discarded altogether for a loose scarf, and soft, natural wigs began to be worn. However, in the reigns of James II and his conservative successor, Dutch William III, English dress became more formal and severe; in France, due to the pious influence of Madame de Maintenon (and to his own advancing years), Louis XIV decreed fashions and lines that upheld decorum and rheumatic joints – long, semi-fitted coats, stiff, three-cornered hats, vests and cravats that covered the chest well, and wigs that grew to imposing proportions.

The same cycle prevailed in women's styles. In 1660, gowns were full and puffed, beribboned and gay; by 1680, a tightly corseted figure was draped in stiffened bodice, stiff, weighted skirts, and formal overdrapings. The hair, soft and loosened about the face in ringlets in 1660, was tucked up primly with a towering headdress in 1680, as is shown in Largillière's painting of the family of Louis XIV (Wallace Collection).

Materials

The same kinds of cloth were used as in the first half of the century. For formal wear, satins, silks, and soft velvets were preferred in the period 1660–1680; stiff velvets and brocades, in the latter part of the century.

Linen of all qualities was still in demand, and dimity and calico (from Calicut, India) were finding favor, especially in the colonies. For heavy, durable wear, woolens and canvas were employed.

Colors

The light, lustrous materials favored in 1660 ran the gamut of bright hues. Red, crimson, ruby, sapphire blue, sky blue, yellow, orange, and emerald green were all popular. Later, around 1680, colors began to shade into the more sedate hues of garnet, wine, brown, russet, deep blue, olive green, and the like. Combinations of colors were much in favor.

COSTUME FOR MEN
1660–1680

Jacket

The doublet shrank to a short jacket, almost like a vest or Eton jacket (Fig. 169, pattern), with square or rounded corners; it reached barely to the waistline, or even stopped short of it (Fig. 169). The jacket was fastened at the neck, and had a row of buttons and buttonholes down the front, but these were seldom buttoned all the way, except by less modish folk. The edges of the jacket were often accented by braid or embroidery. The sleeves were usually quite short, above the elbow, and might be finished with a ruffle of lace. Occasionally the sleeves were long, fairly full, and slit from armhole to waist. The shorter sleeve might also be slit, with a row of buttons and buttonholes to fasten it together again. The shorter sleeve might also have a deep cuff, turned back and buttoned. A slit sleeve was occasionally used (Fig. 169, pattern). Knots of ribbon in various places added their decorative note.

Shirt

With the short jacket was worn a very full shirt of fine linen, cambric, or silk. The sleeves were also very full, and were caught in at the wrists and once or twice up the arms with ribbons, so that the sleeve was a series of puffs (Fig. 169). A frill of lace about the wrist gave a finish to the sleeves. The shirt was buttoned down the front; the front opening was accented by a band edged all about with a ruffle of linen or lace (perhaps "Venetian point") about two inches wide.

The neck was finished with a falling band less wide on the shoulders than in the preceding era (Fig. 168 A   Fig. 169) and drawn together in front; it was often in pleats, and oblong rather than round (Fig. 168 A   Fig. 169). It was made of linen or lace, or lace-edged linen.

The shirt was bloused very full over the low waistline.

Breeches

With jacket and shirt were worn the new *petticoat* (or *Rhinegrave*) *breeches.* These were made in several ways:

(1) Some were plain, gathered, or pleated skirts, to the knee, often edged with tabs of ribbon about the bottom and also about the waistline (Fig. 169, picture and pattern). These loops of ribbon were sometimes arranged in an inverted pyramid directly in front. Bows of ribbon were attached at the sides, or, it seemed, anywhere else that fancy dictated. When, in 1664, Louis sent six thousand of his men to help the Emperor Leopold against the Turks, the Grand Vizier, seeing the petticoat breeches,

ribbons, lace, and feathers, laughed scornfully at the "young girls," but the "skirted ones" won the day.

Under the petticoat were worn moderately large breeches, usually with deep lace ruffles at the knee. These ruffles, however, might be worn below the knee, independently of the breeches; they were, in effect, boothose tops that had survived the eclipse of boots for ordinary civil wear.

(2) Another type of petticoat breeches had full bloomers, or breeches (Fig. 170 A C), attached to the inner bottom edge of the petticoat by eyelets; a row of ribbon tabs marked the junction. The bloomers were gathered at the knee, often with a deep ruffle of lace, making, in effect, a divided skirt. A lace ruffle might be added to the edge of the skirt, thus making the effect still more elaborate and effeminate (Fig. 170 C). Samuel Pepys wrote on April 6, 1661: "Mr. Townsend put both his legs through one of the knees to his breeches, and went so all day"! Only the voluminous petticoat breeches could have given such an opening!

(3) Sometimes the breeches were so full and blousing that they gave the appearance of petticoat breeches. With the short jacket (usually the square-pointed variety) were also worn the loose open breeches, edged with ribbon tabs, shown in chapter X, Fig. 161 A. These plain, straight breeches were, however, usually decorated with the pyramids of ribbon tabs at the waistline.

The long, straight coat shown in chapter X, Fig. 161 A, was also worn for a while, but was soon discarded – to return in another form later. This was probably the basis for the *casaque,* a type of coat which Charles, anxious to outdo his cousin across the water, designed *à la Perse.* When the new fashion was brought to Louis's notice, he immediately ordered copies of the style for all his lackeys!

Cloak

The cloak was still circular, but fairly long and full (Fig. 170 B C), with or without a collar. Its purpose was to cover the body in cold weather or to disguise the wearer should need arise.

Footwear

Boots, still worn for active military duty, went out as part of civil garb. Long silk stockings and low shoes took their place. The stockings were fastened above the knee with garters, or with points or buttons attached to the breeches. The garters were camouflaged with ribbon loops, lace rufflings, and puffs of material until they seemed an extension of the breeches. Boothose tops, as stated above, were used over the stockings, and fell about the knees over the garter.

Shoes were of soft leather, brown or black, with square toes, high red heels, and a tongue of the leather upright over the instep. Often the heels were painted with landscapes, etc. Louis XIV had a pair painted by Van der Meulen with scenes of his Rhenish victories. Pepys wrote that he walked "wearily, and in great pain from wearing new shoes too tight for him." (Every age sympathizes with Pepys's discomfort!) A wide bow of lace, wired to hold it out, was worn over the instep (Fig. 181 G). Another type of shoe, less ornate, had a buckle over the instep.

Hair

Men still wore the slight mustache, pointed upward, of the Cavalier days. It dwindled to a wisp at each corner of the mouth and, after 1680, gradually disappeared. The beard was reduced to a mere tuft on the lower lip, and then it, too, disappeared.

The periwig took the place of the long, flowing locks of the previous era. Louis XIV, whose abundant chestnut locks had been admired since his childhood, put off wearing a wig until nature thinned his locks. Then, about 1673, he had wigs made so artfully that what remained of his own hair could be shown through holes made in the wig. He continued using wigs of this sort until at last a whole wig had to be used. But his wigs always had the shape of his own hair, piled high on the forehead as he had worn it (Fig. 170 C). The proper type of periwig was made of natural hair, curled and waved, parted in the center and hanging down on either side below the shoulder (Fig. 168 A   Fig. 169   Fig. 170 C   Fig. 171 C). The hair of Flemish women was especially prized for wigs. A perruquier's sign of the time showed a picture of Absalom hanging by his hair from the tree and David, below, weeping and exclaiming:

> O Absalom, O Absalom!
> O Absalom, my son!
> If thou hadst worn a periwig,
> Thou hadst not been undone!

Though Samuel Pepys says that Charles II did not adopt the periwig until 1663, it seems to have been in general use in England. Perhaps Charles, too, was proud of his own locks. In 1665, during the Great Plague, Pepys was much perturbed: "It is a wonder what will be the fashion after the plague is done, as to periwigs: for nobody will dare to buy any hair, for fear it had been cut off the heads of people dead with the plague." However, it took more than an epidemic to stop a fashion; wigs continued in vogue. To comfort Pepys and other timorous customers, perruquiers announced that hair from a dead person did not take curl. Periwigs were shortened for military campaigns into *dildoes,* or short bobs, which were twisted back and tied with ribbons. These were forerunners of the later *pigtails*.

Headdress

The broad-brimmed hat (chapter X, Fig. 156 D   Fig. 160) was still worn in 1660. However, it was soon superseded by a very wide-brimmed, low-crowned hat of felt or beaver. The best shapes were made in Flanders. Many feathers were placed about the brim in seeming disorder (Fig. 168 A   Fig. 169). The feathers were of several colors; occasionally the hat was "cocked" or rolled up at the side or behind. For traveling, a snug cap of felt or fur was worn.

Ornaments and Accessories

Jeweled buttons, ribbons, and lace knots of all kinds were used everywhere on the costume, and a sword knot decorated the hilt of the sword.

Men wore fair-sized, rectangular muffs hung on a cord about their necks. The muffs were often decorated with ribbons and laces; sometimes the entire muff was

VEST

SHIRT

SLEEVE CAP

SLEEVE

PETTICOAT BREECHES

2.5"

72"

Fig. 169

CAPE

COLLAR

B

PANTALOONS

A

C

Fig. 170

B

D

A

C

Fig. 171

JABOT

B

C

D

A

E

Fig. 175

COLLAR

BODICE

OVERSKIRT

FRONT

SLEEVE

FRONT

SKIRT

APRON

A

B

Fig. 172

COMPLETE

A

FRONT HALF-DRAPED SKIRT

A

B

gather

cut

C

40"

D

B

C

SLEEVE

D

BODICE

A

Fig. 180

made of padded silk. Fairly tall canes of ebony or malacca were carried (Fig. 169). They were often taller than those of Charles I's time. They were looped with ribbons or tassels, and often had gold heads.

Snuffboxes of gold or silver, jeweled and enameled, were also carried; tobacco had come into vogue. Beautiful combs were carried and used in public by the fops and gallants. Lace-trimmed and tasseled handkerchiefs were carried, as also were perfumed and embroidered gloves. Patches were carried in beautifully decorated boxes (Fig. 181 E).

The sword was worn on a handsomely embroidered baldric slung over the right shoulder. Money was carried in a pouch tucked into the waistband.

Umbrellas began to be used, but as yet only rarely. John Evelyn mentioned seeing them used in Italy as sunshades in 1664. Men carried them, but women had servants to hold the umbrella over them. Le Brun (1639) shows an umbrella, and Van Dyck's portrait of Lady Grimaldi shows one held over her head. Umbrellas folded up and sometimes had a loop at the end of the handle. They were made of oiled silk, and even of leather.

Make-up

The fops and beaux of the time used paint and powder; they waxed the corners of their infinitesimal mustaches and wore patches to attract the ladies' eyes. Perfume and civet were regularly used; orange blossom, civet, musk, and pulvilio were favorite odors. The beaux combed their hair with large combs of tortoise shell or ivory in the theater, on the Mall, and everywhere. At the theater, the custom of "combing" became especially distracting, for the fops of the time insisted upon parading across the stage whenever they pleased, combing and fondling their locks. Of the gallant of this time it was said: "He is made up of compliments, cringes, knots, ribbons, laces, fancies, perfumes, and a thousand apish French tricks." And yet these seemingly effeminate men fought many a gallant fight. Like the Scots in their kilts, they could sweep more than their skirts before them.

Military Dress

There was no standardized military uniform. Usually the buff jerkin and breeches, with a sash to denote the regiment, were enough. Charles II first chose certain colors for certain regiments. Helmets could be worn, but were worn only rarely; the same might be said of gorgets. But muskets and cannon made plate armor useless.

COSTUME FOR WOMEN

1660–1680

Bodice

The soft bodice of the Cavalier time was retained, with a few changes. There was a decided point in front and also, sometimes, in back. The bodice was cut low, and rounded (Fig. 172 A, pattern). A chemise of lace or a deep collar of lace all about the neckline, or a fold of material draped about the edge, added to the effect (Fig. 172 B). The bodice was fastened up the front or back. If it were fastened up the

Fig.168

Fig.173   Fig.174   Fig.177   Fig.178

Fig.176   Fig.179

front, a row of ribbon bows hid the opening (Fig. 172 A). One type of bodice still had tabs at the waistline (Fig. 172 B). For cold weather, or when a high neck was required, a scarf or a fur collar was worn.

Sleeves

The sleeves were short (halfway to the elbow) and full. With them were usually worn white linen or silk undersleeves, puffed two or three times with ribbons, and reaching below the elbow. These were called *virago sleeves*. Sometimes the dress sleeves were longer, halfway to the wrist, and full, edged with a ruffle of lace or a turned-back cuff (Fig. 172 A).

Skirt

The skirt was long and full, gathered or pleated about the hips. Usually it was left open down the front over an elaborate petticoat (Fig. 172 A). The top skirt was looped back with ribbon bows, pins, etc. It often had a train (Fig. 172 B). When it was looped over other skirts, the different layers were given names. The outer, looped-back skirt was called "modesty"; the inner skirt (petticoat, not seen) was called "the secret"; the underskirt, over which the overskirt was draped, and which was between the over and the inner skirt, was called "the cheat." The overskirt "modesty" could be looped back with bows of ribbon or small gold chains, with which the skirt could be lowered or raised at will. The length of the train depended on the rank of the wearer. Duchesses could wear five-yard trains; the queen wore trains fifteen yards long!

With the skirt was worn a short apron of linen, lace, or silk (Fig. 172 A). It was purely for ornament, and continued in vogue for some time.

Robe

A style which found favor in the colonies consisted of a robe falling from the shoulders, sleeveless, fitted in the back, and open down the front, showing the bodice and skirt of the dress. It was unbelted or else belted high with a ribbon. This style was particularly favored by the wives of the Dutch patroons.

Cloak

The long circular cape, with or without a hood, was still worn by women for warmth, for traveling, or for disguise. It was of taffeta for summer, of wool or velvet for winter, and was sometimes lined with fur.

Another type of wrap was the *samare,* or jacket of velvet, frequently outlined with fur (usually white rabbit). It was a loose sacque, with full sleeves, and fastened at the neck only. Ter Borch and others of the Little Dutch Masters show the Dutch ladies in samares, or "Dutch jackets," as others called them.

Another type of wrap was the shoulder cape worn with the low-necked dress for out-of-doors. It was adapted from the short circular cape which, as Racinet shows, was worn by ladies in their bedrooms. It was fastened at the neck in front. For winter, it was made of velvet trimmed with fur, or entirely of fur; for summer, it was made of taffeta or lawn, trimmed with lace.

Footwear

Women's shoes followed, in general, men's styles. The heels were fairly high; the leather or silk or velvet came up over the instep and fastened with a button, buckle (Fig. 181 D), or bow (Fig. 181 F). Tongues appeared in some models (Fig. 181 F). Other types, more dressy, used a ruffle of lace around the top (Fig. 181 B). The shoes came up quite high and snug about the ankle. Bedroom slippers without heels ("mules") were also used, as shown by Racinet. In England and her colonies shoes were called *pattens*.

Hair

The hair was worn in a soft, becoming fashion. Across the forehead was a row of curls or a wave of bangs. Clusters of curls (*confidantes*) framed the cheek; other clusters on the sides were called *heartbreakers* (Fig. 168 B). The rest of the hair was drawn into a knot, high up on the back of the head (Fig. 168 B). A ribbon might be worn around the head with a bow or rosette at the top or side. This type of headdress was called *touffes à la Mancini*. Ninon de Lenclos affected a style in which the hair was parted in the middle, partly confined by a loose veil on the back of the head.

Headdress

Women wore hats much like men's. The wide-brimmed felt or beaver hat, with or without feathers, the brim worn flat or turned up, was always in favor. It was usually black, but dark blue, red, dark green, and other colors were used. The feathers were of varying colors.

Caps and hoods were still worn. In fact, they were often worn under the hats, especially for traveling. Colonial women used them long after they had ceased to be fashionable in Europe. Hoods of Alpine blue were in favor; they were called *Mazarin hoods*.

Ornaments and Accessories

Rings, pins, necklaces (simple strands of pearls close about the throat were much favored), ribbons, bows, rosettes, and bands were used about the arms, neck, waist, bodice – anywhere it was possible to place them. Earrings were rarely worn, as the loose ringlets at the side of the coiffure hid them. Shoe buckles were of gold, silver, or steel. Patches were in high favor (Fig. 168 B). They were of various shapes and were called *court plasters* or *court patches,* possibly because they were first used at

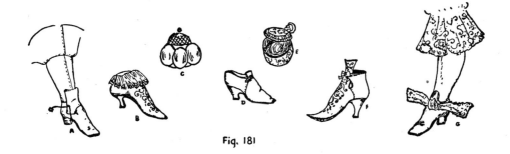

Fig. 181

court. They were in the shape of diamonds, crescents, flowers, and even human figures; one picture shows a coach and four. Names were given the patches placed at various places on the face. Placed near the eye, the little black patch was called "assassin"; near the mouth, "discreet"; on the chin, "gallant"; by the dimple, "sprightly"; on the forehead, "majestic."

Vizards (masks) were in high favor. Folding fans superseded the round or whisk variety. They were of paper, with charming designs painted on them by Mignard and others. The handles were of ivory or wood. Other accessories included muffs and pocket mirrors, the latter elaborately jeweled and encased in leather, tortoise shell, gold, etc. These were often worn attached to the girdle by a ribbon or chain. Pomanders, or *musk-balls,* were in great favor because of the plague, and contained musk, ambergris, myrrh, iris, or violet. India balm, essence of roses, cloves, citron, cinnamon, rosemary, marjoram, and anise were also used. Sometimes the pomanders were in filigree holders.

With the shorter sleeve, long gloves were used. These were essentially the same as the long kid gloves used today (Fig. 180 D). A reticule or purse, with fastening (Fig. 181 C), was carried by ladies of quality.

Make-up

Make-up was freely used, even in public. In *Sir Fopling Flutter,* we are told that a lady's "powdering, painting, and patching never fail in public to draw the tongue and eyes of all men."

Costume for Children

A little girl of the upper class is shown in Fig. 173.

Costume for Men

1680–1700

The change in men's fashions from the petticoat breeches to the long frock coat and vest (a garment in use today after more than two hundred years), was a gradual one, beginning with a lengthening of the jacket. By 1675, it had developed into a coat, fitted somewhat to the figure. The vest followed later.

Coat

A typical costume for men, around 1680, is shown in Fig. 175 A E, patterns B C D, and in Fig. 176. The coat was cut snugly to the body (pattern B is the outline, not allowing for fitting, darts, etc.), with a slight flare at the hips. It came just short of the knees. The coat had buttons and buttonholes all the way down the front; it might be buttoned to the waistline and left unbuttoned below, or left unbuttoned to the waistline and buttoned below, or buttoned all the way down. The coat had wide lapels (Fig. 176) or was buttoned close to the neck, with or without a narrow band, or collar. The falling band had now developed into a *cravat* or neckcloth of soft linen or lace. (The name *cravat* came from *croat* or *Croatia,* where a wrap-around tie was used.) It was pleated or gathered on a band, and fell over the front of the coat, in length about five to ten inches (Fig. 175 A E and pattern Fig. 168 C Fig. 176). Another type of cravat was the *Steinkirk*, fashionable after the battle of Steinkirk, where French officers, aroused hurriedly, had twisted the neckband negligently about the neck and caught the ends through a buttonhole of the coat.

The coat had pockets, one on either side, far down, toward the lower edge, well below the waistline. These were made on the coat, with slits to outline them (Fig. 175 E), and sometimes buttoned; or they had deep over-flaps, also buttoned, usually with three large buttons (Fig. 175 A). These were called "forage pockets," as soldiers used them to store the loot or food they collected on foraging trips.

The sleeves were fairly snug-fitting, but ended in very wide cuffs. The three large buttons which held back the cuff (Fig. 175 A E Fig. 176) show that the origin of the cuff was a turned-back piece of the sleeve. The sleeve was also cut somewhat flared toward the bottom, a style which continued in use after the cuff had become a separate piece. The three buttons are retained by tailors today, but merely as a vestige with no practical use. The large cuff (sometimes it measured twelve inches deep and eighteen inches wide) was often of a contrasting color to the coat, and was braided or embroidered. The pattern is shown in Figure 175 D.

The back of the coat was slit to the waist for riding. About 1690, the sides were slit to the waistline to accommodate the sword, worn before this on a baldric slung over the right shoulder. Buttons at the waistline were used to hold the skirts of the coat back; these buttons remain on the back of modern frock coats, another vestige of bygone usage and custom. About 1690, also, pleats were put into the sides of the coat, and the garment was flared and stiffened about the bottom edge. The more elaborate coats were ornamented with braid and embroidery. Louis XIV is pictured in gorgeous velvet and brocade coats with gold braid, with linings embroidered and braided, and with gold buttons inlaid with jewels. A knot of ribbon on the right shoulder, for formal occasions, was the last remnant of the many bows and rosettes of ribbon used in the earlier era.

A plainer type of coat was buttoned up the front; with the buttons on the pockets and sleeves, the total number of buttons might range from twenty to thirty (Fig. 175 E). However, there was no trimming, and the sleeves were quite plain. A Quaker gentleman might wear this type. The cravat would be of plain linen.

Vest

Beneath this long coat were worn a vest and a fine linen or lawn shirt. The vest was only an inch or so shorter than the coat, and for normal wear was elaborately braided and embroidered. In front it was cut very much like the coat, but was more form-fitting and was sleeveless; the back extended only to the waistline and was of plain lining material, as it was not visible. The vest was buttoned all the way up the front like the coat. It was usually of contrasting material and often of brocade.

Shirt

The shirt was made very full, gathered in a neat bow at the neck (with no collar, as we think of collars); it had full sleeves with ruffles at the wrists. Louis XIV had silk and taffeta shirts. (It took seven noblemen to help him put on his shirt at his daily ceremonial levées.)

Breeches

With the coat and vest, full breeches were worn (Fig. 175 E). These were fastened about the knee with ribbons tied in a neat bow at the side, or they were buckled.

Coat and breeches did not necessarily match in color, and the vest seldom matched. A coat might be red, the breeches blue, the vest orange. Louis forbade the wearing of purple or gold braid to all but royalty.

Cloak

The long, full cloak was still worn. It could be draped in various ways (Fig. 170 C Fig. 171 A).

Footwear

Shoes showed little change from the preceding era, except that the upstanding tongue was less in evidence (though not discarded) and a rolled top effect was used about the instep, with a buckle over the instep. Silk stockings were in high favor; they did not necessarily match the costume.

Hair

The natural-looking periwigs of the 1660's were now superseded by the towering, elaborately curled masterpieces of the wigmaker's art. A "full-bottomed" wig of this time was quite heavy, but was balanced by an ingenious equal distribution of the weight, before, on either side, and behind. The curls were rather stiff and rose in a thick cluster high over the forehead, with a simulated part (Fig. 168 C Fig. 171 D Fig. 176). It is said that Louis XIV, in his old age, had dozens of wigs to choose from daily.

Quakers and other dissenters wore their own hair, but wore it long, making that much concession to fashion. Beards disappeared entirely; so did mustaches. Clean-shaven faces had now come into vogue, to last until well into the nineteenth century. There were square *cavalier wigs* for country gentlemen. The Spanish first took to powdering wigs "to appear old, so as to be taken for wise." Later the fashion was to become general.

Headdress

The broad-brimmed, beplumed hat gave way to a stiffer type of felt or beaver, cocked up on all three sides, called the *tricorne*. It was ornamented with a spray of ostrich feather all about the brim (Fig. 171 A). Often a cockade or rosette of ribbon was attached at one side of the front, usually the right side.

As the wigs were very high, hats were not worn except when necessary, but instead were carried under the arm; this custom led to their being called *chapeaux bras*. (Before this time, men had worn their hats indoors as well as out, except in church or in the presence of the king; sometimes, as a royal favor, men were allowed to wear hats in the king's presence.) This fashion of men's uncovering their heads indoors has lasted into our times.

Quakers and other dissenters wore the plain, wide-brimmed hat with the low crown. However, the Quakers turned the brim up in a curve at the sides.

Ornaments and Accessories

Ornaments worn on the person were essentially the same as before.

Watches, now egg-shaped as well as round, were worn in pockets as well as suspended from the neck. Long canes were indispensable; loops to hold them by were run through slits in the staff. Tassels, ribbons, etc., ornamented the handle; the head was of gold or ivory. Large muffs, round or flat, and frequently decorated with ribbon bows and lace, were carried by men of fashion (Fig. 171 A Fig. 175 A).

Make-up

Make-up was much the same as in the previous era.

Military Dress

It is said that Louis XIV, who first developed real military uniforms, put different regiments in different colors so that he might distinguish them in battle. In 1667, he had the musketeers in gray-white, gray-brown, or maroon, with epaulets and appointments of various colors. When they went against the Dutch in 1672, the entire army was put into one color. After 1675, the uniform was standardized. The colors were neutral, relieved by facings of various shades. There were medium-sized breeches, high, stiff "jack" boots, frock coat (faced and perhaps buttoned back), and crossed straps, bandoliers or cartouches. The three-cornered hat was worn over the wig. Sometimes a steel corselet was worn beneath the coat. An ordinance passed by Louis XIV in March, 1672, forbade to all officers and even generals the use of lace, galloons, fringe, and gold and silver trimming on their uniforms – a rule which was not very strictly observed. By 1698, however, a regular type of uniform had been evolved.

The King's bodyguards were called *Les Grands Mousquetaires*. They wore blue cloth coats embroidered on the chest and back with a silver cross surrounded by gold rays and the king's cipher, *Le Roi Soleil*.

After 1685, English troops began to wear distinguishing uniforms. In 1661, the Horse Guard ("Earl of Oxford's Blues") wore blue uniforms. In 1665, the Third Buffs were so called from their buff jerkins. In 1662 the Yeomen of Charles II wore a scarlet habit very much like that of the Beef-Eaters. Cromwell's "Ironsides" wore a uniform costume consisting of buff jerkin, broad-brimmed hat, crossed bandoliers, straight breeches, boots, and gauntlets. Their hats, like those of other soldiers, usually had an iron skullcap inside, as did also even the feathered hats. By 1695, the coats and breeches of ordinary soldiers were gray. Epaulets, the last remnant of chain mail, survived merely as shoulder knots worn on the coats of the time.

The famous Coldstream Guards originated shortly after the Restoration. Charles II organized three regiments, with General Monck head of the second. But the general demurred at being second to any one, whereupon Charles organized the Coldstream

Guards, "second to none" – *nulli secundus*. Besides their regular uniform, members of the Coldstream Guards are privileged to wear a small Union Jack, as Monck was Admiral of the Fleet also.

Soldiers at this time were mostly pikemen and musketeers. Pikemen wore thin steel corselets and carried a pike, sometimes eighteen feet long (see "The Surrender at Breda" by Velásquez). The musket had to be supported on a rest when it was fired. Powder was kept in receptacles on the bandolier.

In France, pikemen and musketeers formed the larger part of the army until 1640. Grenadiers were added as an innovation in 1632, although, according to Evelyn, they were not organized in England until 1678. They threw grenades; there were four grenadiers to each company. The uniform of the French grenadier, in 1696, was a blue coat lined with red, red stockings, a pouch for grenades, a three-cornered hat, and a red bow on the right shoulder. They carried little hatchets as well as grenades. In England, grenadiers wore furred caps with coped crowns. The first fusiliers were organized in 1670 in France. Sieur Martinet, colonel and inspector-general of infantry (so strict that today his name stands for severe discipline), introduced the use of bayonets, first as a hand weapon, later fixed on the musket. Gustavus Adolphus of Sweden used bayonets also, calling them "Swedish plumes." The cartouche was introduced in 1683, taking the place of the heavy, awkward bandoliers.

A typical officer's outfit is shown in Fig. 177. The frock coat was of buff leather or woolen cloth, with a sash about the waist (instead of over the shoulder). The high boots had a flare at the top ("jack boots"). There was a baldric over the right shoulder for the sword (though the fashion of buckling the sword onto the belt at the left side was superseding this style). The hat had a wide brim, turned up in the front, and it was adorned with feathers. It might also flaunt a ribbon cockade. The regimental colors were worn on the turned-up brim. The sword was of the new type with the knuckle-bow hilt, instead of the cross guard that had been used for so many centuries.

Ecclesiastical Dress

There were no important changes in the garb of the clergy from that last described.

COSTUME FOR CHILDREN

Children wore a simplified type of the older people's dress (Fig. 178).

COSTUME FOR WOMEN
1680–1700

Bodice

The dress of the last quarter or so of the century showed a stiffening of line and material (Fig. 179), perhaps because men tailors now fashioned women's clothes. The bodice was very snug, and was worn over a tight corset of whalebone or steel (Fig. 180 B C). The bodice was high in the back and low in front, with a square neckline.

The front of the bodice might be a V of different material; it might be a row of ribbon bows or a lacing of ribbon over a lace or silk vest (Fig. 179). This V was still called, from its original type, a stomacher. The point of the stomacher extended down over the skirt. The belt, however, followed the natural waistline.

Sleeves

The sleeves, sewed into the bodice, were tight to the elbow, ending in a large, turned-back cuff – like those on men's frock coats (Fig. 180 A), or a ruffle of lace (Fig. 179).

Neck

About the neck, a soft scarf or lace might be draped, or a triangular kerchief, called a *fichu*. After the Battle of Steinkirk (August, 1692), ladies adopted a long, narrow strip of lace, folded negligently over the bosom with the ends tucked or pinned at the side (Fig. 168 E).

Skirt

The skirt was long, and was often worn over a second skirt, lined or even padded. A row of lead weights sewed into the hem held the skirt in place. The skirt was of brocade, satin, silk, or velvet, and might be trimmed with two or three rows of deep Chantilly lace. Over this was worn an overskirt, draped back into a bustle, with the ends falling to the ground or in a train (Fig. 180 A, pattern); or the material of the overskirt could be folded over, the ends falling in a sort of cascade.

The lace or silk apron was worn with this type of dress also (Fig. 179).

Cloak

The same type of cloak was used as in the previous era.

Footwear

Shoes were pointed, had high heels, and often (as shown before) had a ruffle about the ankle for dress wear.

Hair

The hair was worn in a knot high up on the head. The hair over the forehead was frizzed and curled. Curls at the side of the face and loose, flowing hair had gone out of style. The total effect was prim, erect, and rather neat.

Headdress

The most interesting development at this time was the high headdress, known as *la Fontanges, Cornette, commode,* or *tower.* The origin is traced to Mademoiselle de Fontanges who, while out riding one day with King Louis XIV, lost her hat. Down tumbled her hair. She whipped off her ribbon garter and bound up the unruly tresses, tying the bow on top of her head. The king admired the charming effect so much that next day every lady at court appeared with a coiffure *à la Fontanges.* This soft, informal arrangement was the immediate ancestor of a high crest of ribbons and lace, starched and wired (Fig. 171 B). It grew higher and higher, and inclined forward over the brow. Streamers of ribbon, or a veil, descended behind it, and helped hold it in place (Fig. 168 D E   Fig. 179   Fig. 180 A).

Ornaments and Accessories

The earring came back into great favor. Rings were used on all fingers, even on the thumbs. Necklaces – the choker type (Fig. 179), a few bracelets, pins, hairpins, jeweled ribbon-knots, and the like were used.

Long gloves, large flat muffs, silk, lace, and paper fans (the folding sort), reticules, watches, comfit boxes, pomanders, and gold-headed walking canes (Fig. 180 A) were among the articles necessary to complete the fashionable outfit.

The corset (Fig. 180 B C) was of whalebone or steel, stitched into tabby cloth, and was lined with flannel that had *tackers* or "modesty pieces" at the top. At this time, brushes "of gold or silver for making clean the teeth" appeared.

Make-up

Patches were no longer so popular as before, but a few were used. Powder and some rouge were also in demand; but the trend was rather toward disuse of many cosmetics than indulgence. The Dutch Stuarts were rather staid, and Madame de Maintenon was getting old!

Women did, however, wear "plumpers" of wax, or other substances, in their cheeks to fill them out.

Mourning

For mourning, women wore black muslin crepe.

Costume for Children

Children wore simplified adaptations of adult costume. Little girls wore plain, high- or low-necked bodices, full, gathered skirts, aprons, hoods, and sometimes kerchiefs. A little girl of the bourgeois class is shown in Fig. 174.

Costume for the Lower Classes

Bourgeois men of Louis XIV's time wore clothing of stout cloth – ratteen or barranca (woolen or cotton cloth of a dark color). The men wore small wigs, round or square, not curled very much. Their shoes were plain, with thick, wooden soles; stockings were of black or gray wool.

Bourgeois women wore woolen or cotton dresses, usually gray (whence *grisette* came to be a stock name for the "maid" type in light comedies). They wore no lace or ribbon, but always wore the looped-back overskirts. They wore aprons of cotton, linen, or grosgrain.

Peasant women wore a laced bodice, kerchief, full skirt, apron, and hood or flat hat. Peasant men wore jerkins, laced or buttoned, leggings, square-crowned, wide-brimmed hats, and their natural hair.

Running footmen wore fringed jacket petticoats and breeches of leather, somewhat like those of red Indians. They carried five-foot sticks topped with knobs, which had hinged tops. In these knobs messages were placed.

Ladies had little black boys as house-pages. They were dressed elegantly in silk or satin frock coats, breeches, stockings, and large, swathed turbans, which gave them the look of dwarfed Oriental potentates.

In general, the lower classes in any era wore the clothes of the preceding era or decade; in other words, the cast-off clothing of the fashionable world was inherited by the lower classes. If their clothes were of their own manufacture, they still tended to follow old-fashioned styles.

Modern Adaptations

For dresses of the seventeenth century, taffeta is preferable. For the 1625–1680 period, use rayon taffeta; for the 1680–1700 period, use pure silk taffeta; sateen, panne satin, or moiré may also be used. For heavier materials, velveteen, cotton-backed velvet, and satin can be used. Cotton laces, starched or unstarched, can be stiffened as described before. Old lace shawls can also be used for dresses, veils, etc.

Felt or beaver hats can be adapted to resemble the wide hats of this period. They can be trimmed with ostrich or cock feathers.

For ribbons, use ten-cent-store stock; cross-grained moiré and velvet are excellent. The cheaper satin ribbons are better than the more expensive ones, as they are stiffer and will make up better into rosettes and bows.

Stiffen cuffs and coats with canvas, not buckram.

Many petticoats, ruffled or plain, should be used with the dresses of this period to give the required bouffant effect.

Shoes can be adapted from modern footwear by adding rosettes and buckles strapped with elastic to ordinary slippers. A bow or buckle can be added, and the heels can also be lacquered red for the later period.

Headdresses can be arranged with extra false curls, etc., as indicated in drawings.

Patterns

For men's Cavalier costumes (chapter X, Fig. 158), use pajama coat and trouser patterns. For the closer fitting coat (Fig. 160), use a shirtwaist pattern and fit it snugly in at the waist. The trousers can be fulled or bagged as necessary.

For Fig. 163 and Fig. 164, use a bodice (*Vogue* pattern), but shorten the waistline. Use a full bishop sleeve pattern for the sleeves.

Collars should be of organdy or of good quality muslin, and edged with lace, if the costume calls for it. Even Indian head can be used for collars, especially for Puritan types, as it lasts much longer than the others and takes starch well.

For 1660 styles, use a tight bodice pattern for women's dress and a bloomer pattern for men's breeches.

For the short jacket, use a Spanish bolero or Eton jacket pattern, or else use a pajama coat pattern, shortened at the waistline. For long coats (Louis XIV style) use a "Benjamin Franklin" or frock coat pattern, and make appropriate changes. A pattern for women's gymnasium bloomers (of the 1905 era) is a good guide for the men's full breeches of the seventeenth-century style. For the full shirt – Cavalier or d'Artagnan type – with full sleeves, use a fancy dress Spanish shirt (bullfighter pattern).

CHAPTER XII

THE EIGHTEENTH CENTURY

IMPORTANT PEOPLE AND EVENTS

FRANCE

Rulers

Louis XIV
(1643–1715)
Louis XV
(1715–74)
Louis XVI
(1774–93)
The First Republic
Directory (1795–99)

Artists

Jean Antoine Watteau
Nicolas Lancret
Jean Marc Nattier
Jean Siméon Chardin
François Boucher
Jean Honoré Frago-
nard
Jean Baptiste Greuze
Vigée Lebrun
André Charles Boulle
Jacques Caffieri
Jean Henri Riesener
Pierre Gouthière

Writers

François de Voltaire
Montesquieu
(Charles de Secon-
dat, Baron de Mon-
tesquieu)
Jean Jacques Rousseau
Denis Diderot
Chateaubriand
(François René, Vis-
count de Chateau-
briand)
Beaumarchais
(Pierre Augustin
Caron)

Notable People

Anne Robert Turgot
Jacques Necker
Mirabeau
(Honoré Riquetti,
Count de Mirabeau)
Jean Paul Marat
Georges Jacques Dan-
ton
Maximilien de Robes-
pierre
Charlotte Corday
Mme Roland
Mme de Pompadour
Marie Antoinette

RUSSIA

Rulers

Peter the Great
(1689–1725)
Catherine I
(1725–27)
Elizabeth
(1741–62)
Peter III
(1762)
Catherine II (the
Great)
(1762–96)

GERMANY

Rulers

Frederick I
(1701–13)
Frederick William I
(1713–40)
Frederick II (the
Great)
(1740–86)
Frederick William II
(1786–97)

Frederick William III
(1797–1840)

Composers

Johann Sebastian Bach
Georg Friedrich Han-
del
Christoph von Gluck
Franz Joseph Haydn
Wolfgang Amadeus
Mozart
Ludwig van Beetho-
ven

Writers

Friedrich Klopstock
Gotthold Lessing
Johann von Goethe
Johann von Schiller
Jean Paul Richter
Immanuel Kant
Georg Wilhelm Hegel

ENGLAND

Rulers

William and Mary
(1689–1702)
Anne
(1702–14)
George I (Hanover)
(1714–27)
George II
(1727–60)
George III
(1760–1820)

Artists

William Hogarth
Sir Joshua Reynolds
Thomas Gainsborough
John Constable

George Romney
Benjamin West
Sir Thomas Lawrence
William Blake

Writers

Jonathan Swift
Joseph Addison
Richard Steele
Lord Chesterfield
(Philip Stanhope,
Earl of Chesterfield)
Alexander Pope
Henry Fielding
Oliver Goldsmith
James Boswell
Dr. Samuel Johnson
Edward Gibbon
Edmund Burke
Laurence Sterne
Samuel Richardson
Horace Walpole
(Earl of Oxford)
John Gay
Thomas Gray
James Thomson
Richard Brinsley Sher-
idan

Notable People

David Garrick
Margaret (Peg) Wof-
fington
Nance Oldfield
Thomas Chippendale
George Hepplewhite
Thomas Sheraton
Robert and James
Adam
John and Charles Wes-
ley

Adam Smith
James Hargreaves
William Pitt
John Churchill
  (Duke of Marlbor-
  ough)

UNITED STATES OF
AMERICA

Presidents
George Washington
  (1789–97)
John Adams
  (1797–1801)

Notable People
James Otis

Patrick Henry
Thomas Paine
Alexander Hamilton
Thomas Jefferson
Benjamin Franklin
John Paul Jones

Artist
Gilbert Stuart

AUSTRIA
Rulers
Maria Theresa
  (1740–80)
Joseph II
  (1765–90)
Francis I
  (1792–1835)

FRANCE

1713, Peace of Utrecht ended War of the Spanish Succession; a French prince (House of Bourbon) placed on Spanish throne. . . . 1720, John Law and the Mississippi Bubble; financial panic. . . . 1761, potatoes planted in France. . . . Age of Voltaire; he and Jean Jacques Rousseau dominated the thought and philosophy of Europe. . . . Rococo court atmosphere of Louis XV. . . . 1783, Montgolfier's hot-air balloon. . . . Mesmer and Cagliostro intrigued the courts of Louis X and Louis XVI. . . . 1789, storming of the Bastile (July 14); beginning of the French Revolution. . . . Tricolor adopted. . . . Establishment of republic. . . . Reign of Terror. . . . Charlotte Corday killed Marat, "the friend of the people." . . . Louis XVI and Marie Antoinette guillotined. . . . Directory, Consulate. . . . Napoleon Bonaparte sent to Italy and to Egypt. . . . Battles of the Pyramids, of the Nile.

ENGLAND

1701–14, War of the Spanish Succession; Duke of Marlborough won great victories at Blenheim, etc. . . . 1701, Act of Settlement, by which the Electress Sophia and her descendants became heirs to the throne of England. . . . Captain William Kidd, the famous pirate, hanged in London. . . . 1707, union of England and Scotland. . . . 1713, Gibraltar ceded to Britain by Treaty of Utrecht. . . . 1715, uprising in behalf of James Stuart. . . . 1720, bursting of the Mississippi Bubble. . . . 1721, Lady Mary Wortley Montagu introduced inoculation against smallpox. . . . 1745, uprising for Charles Stuart, the "Young Pretender." . . . 1752, Gregorian calendar adopted. . . . Age of Pope, Addison, etc.; "Spectator Papers." . . . 1753, British Museum founded. . . . 1755, expulsion of Acadians from Nova Scotia (cf. *Evangeline*). . . . 1756, Black Hole of Calcutta. . . . 1757, Clive's victory at Plassey, India. . . . Seven Years' War began in Europe and America. . . . 1763, Peace of Paris; England gained large slice of America. . . . 1767, Hargreaves invented the spinning jenny. . . . 1769, James Watt patented the steam engine. . . . 1771, first edition of the *Encyclopaedia Britannica*. . . . 1776, Adam Smith's *Wealth of Nations* published. . . . American Revolution began. . . . 1781, Robert Raikes founded Sunday schools to teach the "three R's" to working children. . . . 1787, trial of Warren Hastings. . . . 1789, mutiny on H.M.S. *Bounty*. . . . 1796, Jenner discovered vaccination serum. . . . 1799, Rowland Hill's postal reforms. . . . Great classical age in literature – Pope, Dr. Samuel Johnson, etc. . . . Later, political writers and historians. . . . Age of letter-writing. . . . Great age of portrait painters – Reynolds, Gainsborough. . . . Famous cabinet makers, Chippendale, Sheraton. . . . English stage represented by David Garrick, Mrs. Siddons, Nance Oldfield. . . . Coffeehouses, clubs, watering places were centers of fashion. . . . Houses became more comfortable; interior decoration was studied; chairs, wallpaper, mirrors, lighting added to general charm.

GERMANY, PRUSSIA, AUSTRIA

1724, Pragmatic Sanction obtained by Charles VI to secure Maria Theresa's succession to the Habsburg dominions. . . . 1740, Frederick the Great seized Silesia. . . . 1748–1832, "Golden Age" of German literature – Goethe, Schiller, etc. . . . 1772, first partition of Poland; 1793, second partition; 1795, third partition. . . . Frederick the Great imported workmen from Dresden to Prussia, developed great porcelain industry – Dresdenware, etc. . . . His court at Sans Souci became the center of intellectual Germany, with Voltaire the presiding spirit. . . . Great age of music – Bach, Beethoven, Mozart.

OTHER EUROPEAN COUNTRIES

Italy: 1710, Cristofori invented the pianoforte. . . . Goldoni, dramatist. . . . Great age of Italian opera. . . . *Russia:* 1703, Peter the Great built St. Petersburg. . . . Era of the Czarina Elizabeth and of Catherine the Great; Catherine developed the country, exploited Siberia, and imported European culture to her court. . . . *Portugal:* 1755, great earthquake in Lisbon killed fifty thousand people. . . . *Switzerland:* 1798, Swiss Confederation became Helvetic Republic.

UNITED STATES OF AMERICA

1701, Yale College established. . . . 1718, New Orleans founded. . . . 1733, colony of Georgia founded. . . . 1735, trial of John Peter Zenger established principle of freedom of the press. . . . 1746, College of New Jersey (Princeton) founded. . . . 1752, Franklin's electrical experiments. . . . 1754–63, French and Indian War. . . . 1765, Stamp Act. . . . 1773, Boston Tea Party. . . . 1775, Battle of Bunker Hill. . . . 1776, Declaration of Independence. . . . 1777, Articles of Confederation. . . . 1779, John Paul Jones's first naval victory. . . . 1783, Peace of Paris. . . . 1783, first daily newspaper established, *Pennsylvania Evening Post.* . . . 1787–89, Constitutional Convention. . . . 1789, Washington inaugurated as president. . . . 1793, Eli Whitney invented cotton gin. . . . 1793, Neutrality Proclamation. . . . 1794, John Jay negotiated treaty with Great Britain. . . . 1797, inauguration of John Adams. . . . XYZ episode in France. . . . 1799, naval warfare between England, France, and America.

We see the eighteenth century through the rose-colored glasses of a Sentimental Journalist; and yet it was an Age of Reason, in which thoughts led logically to deeds. It had the important yet lumbering pace of a coach and four; like this pompous and gilded equipage, it sank deep into the established ways.

Traveling gets one places, but always at a price. Progress had to be paid for, especially when there were so many first-class passengers with excess baggage who traveled duty-free.

In England, the dashing, hard-riding Stuarts reluctantly surrendered the reins to their Dutch relations, and these, in turn, made way for the dull and distant Hanoverians.

In downtrodden Russia, Catherine the Great, as she dashed over dangerous ground, cracked her whip over subjects and lovers alike. But Catherine's vision was keen and her hand was sure, and so Russia forgave the mistress her lovers for the mastery she had over men.

Frederick the Great at Sans Souci carefully studied the Baedeker of empire, marking new itineraries that included Silesia, Saxony, Poland, and other contiguous way stations. Maria Theresa, in Austria, cautiously maneuvered her vehicle by Pragmatic Sanction along the Power-infested highways.

George Washington, resisting the tax on foreign-built bodies, fashioned an independent vehicle for the American trade. The velvet and gold coaches of the French kings protected them from the muck of reality. At last, however, the wheels of privilege locked at Varennes with the wheels of progress, and the coach made way for the tumbril.

The eighteenth century was a woman's age, from throne to hut. Anne ruled in England, Catherine in Russia, Maria Theresa in Austria, Marie Antoinette (not in title, but in power) in France. Where women held the silken reins, gossip rode beside. In France, the salons of Madame du Deffand and others buzzed with philosophy and pseudo-philosophy; in England, Bath (christened by Anne in 1703) became the rendezvous of Sarah, Duchess of Marlborough, Kitty Clive, Mrs. Siddons, the Duchess of Devonshire, and others who mixed venom with wit. Boucher and Fragonard, Reynolds and Gainsborough gave to these rococo elegances the dignity of art.

Scenes were well set, and situations cleverly contrived. Beaumarchais' Suzanne dusted a Caffieri commode or a Falconet statuette, smoothed a Beauvais tapestry, or peeped into Mercier's *Journal des Modes*. Sheridan's Lady Teazle drank tea poured from a Wedgwood urn, fanned herself with a copy of the *Spectator,* or hid behind a Chippendale screen. Powers rose and fell; battles were won or lost at Blenheim, Quebec, Plassey, Yorktown; but an atmosphere of domestic intimacy prevailed.

Yet the day of reckoning came. Marie Antoinette, as dainty as one of her own Dresden shepherdesses, was broken in the fall of the Bourbon dynasty. A true daughter of the Caesars, she died a queen. The swish of her silken hoops was echoed by the hiss of the guillotine.

The happenings in France and in America obscured another revolution which got its momentum through the single turn of a wheel in Hargreaves's spinning jenny. Watt added power to the movement; and mass production began. The real guillotine of polite fashion was the mechanical cutter in the factory.

COSTUME

GENERAL CHARACTERISTICS

This century was devoted more single-heartedly, perhaps, than any other to Mistress Fashion. It saw a revolution in dress as complete as that in politics. The long, full frock coats of Louis XIV and the stiff, bustled gown of Madame de Maintenon gave way to the rococo daintiness of Louis XV's court, where bouffant skirts, trim bodices, and soft, powdered hair bedecked the women; and pastel satins and brocades of trim cut dressed their attending gallants. As time went on and fashion dolls were sent from Paris to European centers, with Mercier's *Journal des Modes* affirming the modish details, French taste was established as the criterion of the world's styles. Lancret, Watteau, and Greuze left enduring records of the sacques, the panniers, and the mobcaps of this feminine age. Marie Antoinette raised the powdered headdress to its height, and the mock simplicity of her straw hats, hoopless printed lawns, and full fichus became a real and enduring fashion.

Men, now politely in the background, were steadily becoming standardized in dress. The full frock coat was trimmed and shortened. The waistcoat was fitted until the silhouette was reduced to the slim-tailed, high-waisted figure of the Directory. Democracy took its toll by substituting long, striped trousers or culottes for the elegant knee breeches, though these lingered awhile, genteel hangers-on of fashion. In 1792, however, a sense of security was attained and held in place by – suspenders!

Materials

Nankeen, fustian, plush, everlasting or durant (made of worsted and used for breeches), and Dutch blanket cloth were some of the materials for coats and breeches of this period. Ticklenburg linen (or *ticking*) was used for workmen's clothes. Plain and flowered silk, gold and silver gauze, Irish holland, linen cambric, flowered dimity, drugget, kincob (cloth of gold interwoven with colored silk), and paduasay were also in demand. "Pompadour" or flowered silks were made popular by Madame de Pompadour. Cotton dresses (*indiennes*) owed their popularity to Marie Antoinette. They were manufactured at Jouy by Oberkampf, who had learned the art abroad. Jacquard striped silks were equally favored by Madame de Pompadour, Marie Antoinette, and the revolutionists – a true catholicity of taste! Chintz was very much in demand. The Revolution brought about the use of brilliantly striped materials, in both silk and wool.

Colors

Scarlet, buff, green, blue, crimson, white, sky blue, claret color, and Isabella (an Elizabethan pure yellow) were used throughout the period.

Delicate, pastel shades were favored by Marie Antoinette and her court – pinks, blues, citron, corn yellow, pale greens, and the like. However, dark brown had a certain vogue, and "puce," or flea color, was a great favorite, as was also mouse color. Apple green and marigold were combined frequently; so were pale blue and rose.

The revolutionists inclined toward brilliant colors and combinations of colors.

Underclothes

As this era was one in which dress was an art, even underclothes were chosen with great care, and were of comparatively fine linen and cambric materials.

Men wore long night robes and tasseled nightcaps on retiring. Under their daytime outer garments they wore cambric undershirts and drawers.

Women, on retiring, wore long nightgowns and fulled caps. Under their daytime outer garments they wore a sleeveless chemise (or shift), a corset (Fig. 185 A Fig. 189 B D), knee-length drawers, a short petticoat, and several long, full petticoats, besides the hoop-petticoat. A short bed-jacket was used on first awaking, and a dressing sacque was thrown over the petticoat and corset when a lady was receiving in her boudoir, during the long and complicated process of dressing and arranging the coiffure.

COSTUME FOR MEN

1700–1770

Coat

The frock coat was reduced in size and weight; sometimes (1720–50) the beaux wore skirts flared out with whalebone or buckram. The ultra-fashionable affected several full pleats in the skirt, smoothly wadded and stiffened with buckram, but the usual skirt to the coat was more moderate in width than formerly. Though the

Fig. 182

coat still had buttons all the way down the front, it was seldom buttoned, except perhaps at the waistline only (Fig. 183 A B and pattern).

After 1750, the wide, flared skirt disappeared, and the skirt was cut on scanty lines, with fullness toward the rear. The edge of the coat was embroidered or braided in colors or in gold or silver. The back slit of the coat was still provided with buttons and buttonholes, and there were also hip buttons, now placed nearer the center back. The pocket, near the hem in the seventeenth century, crept nearer the waist about 1720, and by 1745 was just below the waistline.

The sleeves were often short, halfway up the forearm, or above the elbow, though long sleeves were also worn. The deep cuff, with three large buttons, continued in fashion. After 1750 the cuffs diminished in size until, by 1775, they were modest bands about the wrist. The collar on the coat was a mere strip of material, and was surmounted by a piece of linen or lace wound about the neck several times and ending in a loose loop or tie.

As the century advanced, variations of the neckcloth appeared. Around 1725, linen cambric for the neckcloth was closely pleated and fastened in the back with a silver or steel buckle. By 1740, a small black cravat-bow in front was worn over the white neck-cloth. Sometimes this black ribbon was attached to the wig bag in the back (Fig. 183 D) and then brought around to the front and tied. The black cravat was usually worn with a ruffled shirt front, called a jabot (single or double ruffle).

The first *redingote* appeared in 1786 and came into general use at the time of the Directory (French Revolution).

Vest

The vest slowly but steadily grew shorter. In 1700 it was still only an inch or so shorter than the coat and had the same low pockets. By 1740 it was at least six or eight inches shorter and the pockets were just below the waistline. The vest was usually (though not always) of another color and material than the coat. Silks and flowered brocades were in great favor. Sometimes a silk braid, or one of gold and silver, edged the vest, which, like the coat, was stiffened with buckram or whale-bone and stood out at the sides.

A type of vest for informal wear at home or for exercising, dueling, etc., was plain, with snug-fitting sleeves of the same material. It was mid-thigh length, or a little less, and had buttons and buttonholes down the front.

BREECHES · WAIST COAT · POCKET · CUFF · SLEEVE · COAT · BACK · Fig.183

A · B · C · D

Fig.184 · A · B

Fig.187 · VEST · COAT

Fig.193 · A · B

B · c. Fig.186 · D · A · B · Fig.185 · C

Fig.186 · A · B · BODICE · C · Fig.189 · A · D · E

Vest, coat, and breeches did not have to match; for instance, one might wear canary-colored breeches and a grass-green coat with a pink and buff vest.

Shirt

Beneath the coat and the vest was the shirt, of fine linen cambric, or coarser weave (as the rank of the wearer varied). It was cut very full, gathered about the neck, and bloused full at the waist. The sleeves were full and long, with a deep ruffle, plain, lace-edged, or all lace, at the wrist. The shirt was held in at the neck with a narrow band which sometimes served as a collar about which the cravat was tied.

About 1740, down the front of the opening of the shirt, for a distance of about ten inches, was gathered a single or double ruffle, called a jabot. This fell in a cascade over the unbuttoned vest (Fig. 182 A   Fig. 183 A).

Breeches

Breeches grew steadily more shapely, especially about the knee. They were very short above the crotch, and, as suspenders were unknown, they had to be held up by the hips. They were buttoned on either side, with no front fly. Occasionally they were also buttoned over at the center back to insure a better fit. After 1740, the belt was widened and heightened and fitted to the body, making a more comfortable garment and one more easily kept in place.

The knees of the breeches were slit at the sides for about four inches and finished with a narrow band, which at first was tied and later buttoned or buckled at the side; the slit at the side was usually provided with buttons and buttonholes. Breeches might be black, white, or other colors; velvet and, later, satin were used, in delicate shades. It was not necessary to match the breeches to the coat or vest, just as it was not necessary to match the vest to the coat.

Cloak

For outdoor wear, the *roquelaure* (or *roquelo*) was used. This was a semicircular cloak often trimmed with fur, having sometimes a deep turnover collar (see chapter XI, Fig. 171 A). A heavy topcoat, similar to the regular coat, but longer, was also occasionally used.

Stockings

Stockings were of cotton, wool, or silk. Silk was only for dress wear. The stockings were worn under or over the knee breeches, being held up by garters underneath the breeches, or by garters or ribbons below the knee-bands. Occasionally cross-garters were used, but generally the gartering was hidden by the tight-fitting knees of the breeches (Fig. 183 A).

Knitted stockings of gray, black, or white were worn for everyday use; for dress occasions, silk stockings of various colors were fashionable. These latter were often clocked in gold, silver, or black silk embroidery thread.

Footwear

After 1720, shoes became rounded in the toe, rather than square (Fig. 183 A).

Tongues were still rather high, buckles fairly large. Red heels were still worn. By 1740 shoes had become pointed, and buckles varied widely in size and shape. By 1760 tongues had receded to the instep, and buckles were large squares or ovals of steel or silver (Fig. 195 A C). For dress occasions the buckles might be set with brilliants. Heels were fairly low; on dress shoes red heels were still not uncommon.

Boots were used only for riding or military purposes. Top gaiters, buttoned up to the knee, became popular around 1720 (Fig. 184 A Fig. 194 H); calf-length boots had stiffened tops turned down in a cuff; they were drawn on with loops fastened to the tops of the boots (Fig. 194 A). High jack boots extended sometimes halfway up the thigh; they were cut down back of the knee.

Hair

The large, full-bottomed, high periwigs, though still used by the more conservative, by professional men, and by provincials, gradually went out of fashion. After 1720, powder was used on wigs; then the front mass of curls began to be drawn back and tied at the nape of the neck with a black ribbon (Fig. 182 A), a custom learned from the soldiers. The front of the wig, instead of being massed in two mounds of curls, was smoothed back from the forehead, *à la Pompadour* (Fig. 182 A); the curls were retained at the side of the head, either in wavy masses called "pigeons' wings" (Fig. 182 A), or in clusters of distinct curls (Fig. 183 A B C).

To hold the curls at the nape of the neck, wig bags, like Tom Jones's (so often askew), came into favor (Fig. 183 D).

These wig bags were of black silk or taffeta, drawn together with a drawstring and ornamented with a black bow (Fig. 183 B D).

The *Ramillies wig,* first worn in honor of Marlborough's victory at Blenheim (1704), continued in favor past 1730. It had a braided queue down the back (sometimes two) tied at the top and bottom with a small bow of black ribbon.

Around 1760, a Mr. Papillon advertised, in *The Grand Magazine,* perrukes "with an ecclesiastical air" for churchmen; *tie wigs* for the lawyer; military *smarts; short bobs* for the country gentleman (a short bob was an allover mass not extending to the shoulders and without a queue); and, for impecunious young lawyers, *full-bottomed wigs* (for professional use), the ends of which could be tucked into wig bags for social occasions. He further stated that he could dye the natural hair on the head any tint desired.

Headdress

The cocked hat, laced with gold or silver galloons, and sometimes trimmed with a fringe of feathers (Fig. 194 F), was still in high favor. The everyday cocked hat was made of soft felt or beaver; the broad brim was sometimes caught up by three loops of cord to a button on the top. One side, or all sides, could be let down for protection against rain or sun. In saluting a lady, the hat was removed. When not in use, it was carried under the arm (like the *chapeau bras* – Fig. 183 B). A ribbon cockade or ornament was occasionally used.

Negligee

A kimonolike morning gown, of lined and padded silk, was worn; for summer wear it was of calico, and was sometimes called a *damask banyan*. With this was worn a turban, such as that shown in Hogarth's self-portrait and in many of his pictures.

From 1750 to 1775, the change in costume, as described above, was merely a matter of making the coat still scantier, the pockets smaller and higher, the breeches more close-fitting. The wigs were arranged symmetrically, with horizontal rows of curls at the side; queues, or pigtails, were in general favor. The pigtail, instead of being braided, was wrapped with narrow black ribbons and tied top and bottom (Fig. 182 E Fig. 184 A).

Costume for Women

1700–1770

Bodice

A. The bodice was snug, worn over stays ("a pair of bodices"), which were boned and very stiff, with or without straps over the shoulders (Fig. 185 A). In 1715, the bodice was cut with a rounded neck, up over the shoulders, and parted down the front, where it was laced across a white underbodice, or stomacher. The waistlines were straight, not pointed. This type is seen in the portraits of the Duchesse de Maine (who brought patches back into fashion) and the Duchesse de Luxembourg. The curve of the bodice about the neck and down the front was emphasized by embroidery or lace. The sleeves were plain at the armhole and loose toward the elbow, at which they were turned back in fairly deep cuffs (about six inches), showing white, lace-ruffled undersleeves beneath. (This type of sleeve is shown in Fig. 186 C.) Sometimes the white undersleeve was turned back over to make a cuff somewhat like the man's deep coat cuff.

Skirt

A. With the type of bodice described above was worn a fairly full skirt, sometimes looped up (Fig. 186 C) and fastened with ribbons or ropes of jewels. The hair was worn soft, with a few ornaments – ribbons, bows, or flowers (Fig. 185).

In 1711, Selby invented the *hoop,* or *hoop-petticoat,* which Sir Roger de Coverley compared to a gocart, and others to an inverted funnel. This funnel shape, about 1720, gave way to the rounded or cupola shape; about 1740, it was flattened at the front and back and widened at the sides. Hogarth shows the hoop denuded of its finery in "Death of the Earl" from his *Marriage à la Mode* series. In "Taste in High Life" the hoop is shown in full expanse, both on and off the figure, lifted up at the side, draping a statue, etc.

Bodice

B. Over the hoop, after 1720, was worn a sacque called after the artist who so often depicted it, the *Watteau sacque* (Fig. 186 A C D). It hung from the shoulders and was cut low and square in the neck, before and behind (though the back neckline might be higher). The front was frequently opened over a bodice or stomacher and a flowered, quilted, or brocaded petticoat. It was draped over a full hoop, or a half hoop. The width was sometimes excessive (Fig. 186 C). The back of the sacque was arranged in several box pleats (Fig. 186 A), sometimes held in place over a laced-in lining. When stitched into the formal box pleats, the gown was also called *à la française*. The fullness in the back might be gathered or pleated straight across. The fullness was often looped up at the back into a puff like a bustle (Fig. 186 A). The Watteau sacque was especially popular in the American colonies from 1720 to the Revolution. For variation, the sacque was shortened to hip length and often edged all around with a ruching or with fur. It opened down the front, and was, in fact, a short oversacque, though it was also worn for balls, as shown in Saint-Aubin's pictures, notably "Village Fete." With the Watteau sacque was generally worn the mobcap (Fig. 182 D Fig. 186 C). Watteau's "Minuet" and "Embarkation for Cythera" show these types.

Skirt

B. Skirts, since the ascendancy of Madame de Maintenon, were trimmed with furbelows, flounces, or ruchings, and were pleated, slashed, or puffed. These further added to the bouffant effect of the full skirts.

Bodice

C. A third type of dress came in about 1725 (Fig. 185 C). In this the bodice was fitted very smoothly over stiff stays, which gave a conelike shape to the body. The bodice had a low, rounded neckline (Fig. 185 C) – often softened with a fold of white lawn or lace – and a deep front. From the right shoulder diagonally down the front to the waistline was often draped a garland of flowers; otherwise the bodice was undecorated, as is shown in Lancret's portrait of Mademoiselle Camargo (formerly in the Wallace Collection; also compare Varin's picture of Mademoiselle Aïsse). This style was adopted later by the English, who further emphasized the diagonal crossing by an edging of contrasting color (as in Reynolds's portrait of the Marchioness Camden) or by a fold of contrasting material (as in Gainsborough's portrait of Mrs. Siddons). Perhaps this diagonal fold led to the use of the crossed fichu.

Nattier painted the same type of bodice, but often decorated the front or stomacher with lace pleated in designs, bouquets of flowers, or else a diagonal ribbon (as in the portrait of Mademoiselle de Chateaurenaud). The paintings of Gainsborough, Reynolds, and Lawrence show many examples of this type of bodice.

Skirt

C. With this type of bodice the full, gathered skirt was worn, often split in front and draped over a petticoat of another color (as in Gainsborough's "The Honorable Mrs. Graham") or over a quilted one (as in Reynolds's "Nellie O'Brien"). Skirts usually cleared the floor an inch or so and seldom had trains. They were ornamented with festoons of lace, flowers, and ribbons, except for house negligees or formal dress. The quilted petticoat was most favored in the American colonies, almost superseding other styles.

The sleeves worn with this type of dress were smooth at the shoulder line, were elbow length or just below, and were trimmed with several ruffles at the elbow or rows of double ruffles up the arm. Sometimes the sleeves were of sheer white muslin or puffed silk.

With these dresses, rich point lace or Brussels lace was much used. Short aprons of allover lace (shown in Nattier's portrait of Isabelle de Bourbon) were very fashionable. This picture shows the tendency, after 1730, of hoops to be wider at the sides and flatter at front and back.

Bodice

D. Around 1745, the square, low-in-front neckline was in universal favor. Madame de Pompadour, then at her zenith, established this style. The stomacher was adorned with ribbons, braid, or lace, with bows down the front (*échelles*), or with garlands and bouquets of artificial flowers. Colonial ladies sometimes made these flowers themselves, when delivery from England was slow.

With this rather low-cut bodice was often worn a frill, or ruffle, of lace close about the throat, tied with a bow of ribbon under the chin (as shown in Boucher's portrait of Madame de Pompadour). A short string of beads was also used, or a black velvet ribbon, close about the throat.

Skirt

D. Skirts were still very full, worn over a hoop about a yard wide at the sides and flat (about twelve inches in all) front and back. This type was called the *pannier* (after the baskets hung on either side of a donkey carrying provisions to market). After 1750 panniers were often divided into two frames, with provision for pockets in the frames. The loose panniers, as worn from the early part of the century, perhaps evolved from the pinned-up skirts of the lower classes.

This pannier type was more generally used in France and the American colonies than in England. The effect was obtained by overskirts looped and puffed at the sides. Sometimes a Watteau sacque was draped in this manner.

Sleeves

Sleeves were still moderate in size, and elbow length, finished with one or more lace ruffles. Long, tight sleeves, however, were also used (Fig. 185 B).

Apron

Aprons were still worn, short and lacy for dress wear, long and plain for home use.

At about this time an affectation of pastoral types, both in dress and behavior, swept over France and, in less degree, over England. Boucher exhibits the pastoral vogue in all its effulgence – imitation shepherds and shepherdesses in pseudo-rustic garments and surroundings, and the scene ornamented with scrolls, flowers, birds, and other rococo details. Madame de Pompadour, his good patron, and Madame du Barry encouraged this artificial style in art and dress, and Watteau, Pater, Van Loo, Lancret, and others glorified it on canvas.

Negligee

The night rail or nightgown corresponded to a modern dressing gown. It usually consisted of a sacque (long or short) over a skirt. In the "Breakfast Scene" in *Marriage à la Mode,* Hogarth depicted the wife in a short sacque. A circular sacque, gathered about the neck like a cape, is shown in the "Toilet Scene" of the same series, and in Pater's "La Toilette." The full-length sacque, gathered at the neck in back, is shown in Lancret's "Winter."

A loose gown called a *tabby* was used, especially about the house. Colonial women adopted it. George Washington, in 1759, ordered one for his wife.

Cloak

Cloaks are noted below in connection with hoods. Beside those mentioned (cardinal and capuchin), there were also the roquelaure (used very early in the century) and the *pompadour,* popular about 1750. The pompadour was a short cloak made of satin or velvet, black or some dark shade, and lined with a bright color, with slits for the arms. It was often edged with fur. An attached hood, like a monk's cowl, could be worn on the head, or thrown back; the cloak was hip length.

Footwear

Shoes lost their square toes, except for clogs (or undershoes) and the shoes of the lower classes. They were now made with fairly sharp-pointed toes; they fastened high up over the instep with crossed straps (Fig. 194 G) or with buckles made of brilliants, cut steel, or plain metal.

Shoes might be made of leather, brocade, silk, satin, or velvet. The high heels matched the material of the shoes, or were painted red. Some shoes were ornamented with spangles, square buckles, and heels three and one-half inches high. After Madame de Pompadour made striped silks popular (around 1745), striped materials for shoes were in demand.

Hair (1715–1770)

The *commode,* or *Fontanges,* went definitely out about 1715. In France, because the king had grown tired of this style, it had already disappeared around 1700. In place of the decorated headdress, the hair was brushed back soft from the forehead, with slight puffs and sometimes curls at the side (Fig. 185 C   Fig. 186 C). The hair was caught in a small knot at the back. A single artificial flower, or a small bouquet, or a row of pearls caught with a flower, was usually placed toward the front center of the low coiffure (Fig. 185 C). This type of headdress, popular for so much of the eighteenth century, was called "Pompadour" after the mistress who swayed the court from the time she was established at Versailles in 1745 until her death in 1764.

For formal occasions, one or more long curls were let fall from the knot down the nape of the neck, and were usually draped over the shoulder (Fig. 185 C). A few stray curls were allowable about the ears and at the back of the neck.

Powdered hair was always in fashion for dress occasions and often for ordinary dress also. Funnels or masks were placed over the face when powdering the hair.

Powdered hair was never generally worn in England except for ceremonial occasions, although it was popular for a brief period from 1760 to 1776.

French curls, fashionable in 1745, resembled eggs strung in orderly fashion on a wire and tied about the head. They could, however, be of the natural hair. *Italian curls* were like marcel waves. In the style called *tête du mouton,* the hair was tightly curled over the back of the head.

Toward 1760, the hair was arranged over a cushion, with curls on either side and a cap perched on top (Fig. 182 D). This was the beginning of the high headdresses. In many instances, the hair was bobbed or cut short, and arranged in tight curls about the head or at least behind.

The Dauphiness of France, Marie Antoinette, led the fashion toward the high headdress. As, however, this style did not develop fully until between 1770 and 1785, its details will be considered in the next division.

Headdress

Caps were retained after the *Fontanges* disappeared. Sometimes they were merely small bits of lace and lawn perched atop the head (Fig. 186 A C); sometimes they had side lappets tied under the chin (as shown in Eisen's picture, "The Comet"). These lappets were sometimes folded up over the head.

The mobcap was a round, full, puffed affair, with a ruffled, frilled edge, placed on top of the head or covering it like a bonnet (Fig. 182 D Fig. 190 C). This type remained in style, even into the nineteenth century, for home use – and around 1910, it was revived as a *boudoir cap.* It was worn under the large hats or hoods.

Hats had come back into fashion by 1715, and were black, white, or other colors. They were made of beaver or felt faced with colored silk, and were often trimmed with silver or gold lace. The crowns were higher than those of the tricornes of the seventeenth century, and the brims were wider. Around 1725, a type of riding hat with a low, round crown and a very wide brim was used. A ribbon passed over the top and tied under the chin held the hat on. This type of hat was often worn over a cap. It was particularly used with the "shepherdess" type of dress affected after 1725. Continuing this idea, straw hats, like peasant hats, were adopted around 1740 and called *gypsy hats.* They were worn like the broad felt hats, tied under the chin.

The *hood* was especially in favor, and was used intermittently for many years. Its simplest shape was a rectangle of material, gathered together to form a bonnet in the back, and folded back in a cuff from the forehead in front. As it was usually lined with material of a different color, the fold was quite effective. Cherry-colored hoods were popular around 1710.

A *cardinal,* a scarlet cloak with a hood, was used for outdoor wear. The cloak was hip length or longer.

Lace *tippets* or scarves were draped over the head; they were sometimes fastened together with diamond solitaires.

The *capuchin* came into favor about 1740. It consisted of a long, gathered, circular cloak, reaching the ground, with a cape over the shoulders, elbow deep. Over the

Fig.190

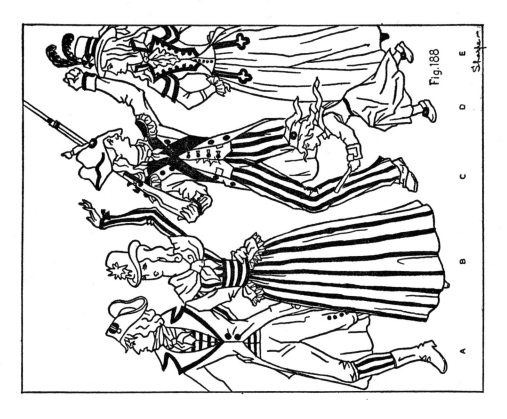

Fig.188

head was a large hood lined with a contrasting color, often edged with fur, as was the cape, which had a fur-edged slit in front for the arms.

The *calash* came in about 1765 and remained long in favor. It was a very large, wide hood, usually of green silk, shirred on hoops of whalebone or steel. These collapsed like the carriage hood of the calèche, or gig, after which it was named. To open and close these hoods, a cord, held in the hand of the wearer, was manipulated. The calash might be made of dimity, gauze, or other materials.

The *Quaker bonnet* evolved from the hoods of the day; it was simplified, sobered in hue, and shorn of ornament.

The *Venetian hat* for ladies was a black tricorne, with a deep lace veil fastened under the chin, gorget style.

Ornaments and Accessories

These are discussed at the end of the chapter.

COSTUME FOR MEN

1770–1790

About 1772, the "Macaroni" of London introduced a style of dress called after them. They were a group of young beaux, or dandies, who started the "Macaroni Club" as a rival to the "Beefsteak Club." They went counter to all prevailing styles: instead of low, smooth wigs, they wore tall, puffed ones with large knobs of hair behind; instead of long waistcoats and wide, full-skirted coats, they wore very short waistcoats and high-waisted coats, fitted very snugly. Their cocked hats were very small; their swords dangled about their heels; and their stockings were polka-dotted. These and other bizarre details drew much attention to them during the few years of their fame. A ballad about them was probably the forerunner of the "Yankee Doodle Dandy" tune. For a while men and women, and even the clergy, copied their styles.

Coat

About this time the frock coat became decidedly scantier. After 1750, the stiffened buckram in the full skirt of the coat and the wadding in the pleats began to disappear. The coat was cut away from the front, displaying the shortened waistcoat (Fig. 187 and pattern Fig. 195 A C). The back of the coat (knee length or a little shorter) had two slits reaching to the waistline, with a button at the top of each slit. Other buttons and buttonholes might decorate the edges of the slits. For a while the pleats were retained; about 1780, they seemed to have disappeared, and the whole effect of the coat was one of trimness. Buttons down the front were still used, but for formal or dress occasions they were discarded and an edging of braid or deep embroidery (colored silks or metallic threads) took their place. The coat was now definitely a cutaway, often not meeting over the chest (Fig. 195 A C).

The front of the coat frequently had a lapel faced with a lighter color (often of fawn or cream flannel) which turned back, giving a decorative touch to the coat

(Fig. 195 A). The lapel or facing followed the curve of the coat in front, and was retained well into the nineteenth century, and even later in military uniforms.

Pockets were at the natural waistline, and were smaller and less decorated than before. With the slender type of coat, a standing collar began to be used; sometimes the collar folded over, a forerunner of the Directory (*Directoire*) type.

Vest

The vest (or waistcoat) was shortened until it came to a mere four or five inches below the natural waistline. It was buttoned to the waist and tapered off from there.

Fig.195

A   B   C

Sharpe

The vest was frequently of flowered brocade or satin; around 1790, striped material was favored (Fig. 188 A   Fig. 195 C). Double-breasted, curved vests were sometimes used.

Sleeves

The sleeves were long and snug, with close-fitting cuffs of the same material, plain or edged with braid. The three buttons used to fasten back the huge cuffs of a former era were retained until about 1755. Thereafter the cuffs were frequently omitted and the plain sleeve was opened at the wrist for a few inches and buttoned up the opening with the three buttons (still retained in modern clothes). A moderate frill of lace or lawn showed beneath the cuff (Fig. 195 A C).

Neckwear

The neckcloth was folded about the throat. A modest jabot showed above the vest. The general effect about the throat was of neatness and simplicity (Fig. 182 E   Fig. 195 A C).

Breeches

Breeches were slenderer, if possible, than formerly, although fullness in the seat was allowed for. The breeches were buttoned at the sides and usually had several buttons on either side of the waist to hold them to an underbody. They extended over the knee and were fastened at the outside with several buttons (Fig. 188 A). A buckle or button held in the bottom edge, which might have a narrow band about it. Leather (chamois or doeskin) riding breeches were popular, both in the colonies and in England.

Stockings

Long silk stockings, white or light-colored, were worn for dress; woolen hose, in darker shades, were worn for everyday. They were gartered above the knee underneath the breeches (Fig. 187   Fig. 195 A C).

Cloak

A *greatcoat,* like the frock coat but longer and a bit fuller, came in about 1780 (Fig. 196   Fig. 198). It had a collar, and sometimes a cape or two over the shoulders. It was single- or double-breasted. Capes of the former era were, however, still worn.

Footwear

Shoes had lower heels and smaller tongues than formerly, but the buckles were a bit larger. Boots were worn for riding and by military men. Gaiters were also used (Fig. 194 H).

Hair

Wigs were still powdered, though wigs of natural-colored hair were now being used. Many dispensed with wigs altogether. (Franklin did this when at the court of Versailles in 1778.) The hair was brushed straight back and two or three curls were placed horizontally over the ear (Fig. 182 E   Fig. 195 A C). Another style won high favor, that of brushing the hair back until it stood out about the face, and was confined in a group of curls at the nape of the neck, or else left free. The face was still smooth-shaven.

Headdress

Cocked hats, edged with braid or plain, were still used; however, they were cocked in various shapes – tall behind, or low in front, or any of infinite ways (Fig. 188 A C).

A type of hat with high crown and moderate brim appeared about 1780. This type eventually supplanted the cocked hat.

Military Dress

Military dress of course varied in different countries; usually, it followed the fashion of the time. In fact, the officer's uniform was little more than civilian dress with some gold lace and small shoulder knots added. The epaulet, when gold, had a white strap; when silver, a yellow one.

English grenadiers, since the seventeenth century, had worn furred caps with coped crowns. The Scots Grays, favorite regiment of George II, wore gray uniforms until 1684; after that, they wore scarlet coats lined with blue, waistcoats and breeches of blue, and tall bearskin hats bearing the thistle and motto of St. Andrew.

Fig. 187 is not unlike an officer's uniform around 1775; a sash was often added. Fig. 184 A B shows the cross belt and the turned-back lapels of a lighter color facing the ordinary soldier's coat. Stockings were white, and the hair was powdered, or wigs were worn.

Variations in military dress are so many that, for accurate presentation, one must consult the books suggested for that purpose. Facings varied, not only with different regiments, but at different times, as Nevill's prints show. Facings were frequently buttoned back. Nevill notes that the gorget, last relic of plate armor, was retained. It was, however, only a small ornamental plate attached to the collar over the jabot. In this form it was retained until 1838 in England, and until 1881 in France, at which date epaulets for infantry officers were also abolished. The British "redcoats" and the "blue and buff" of the Continental Army are symbolic of these armies, though by no means accurate as descriptive terms; many of the colonials, at least, fought in their own local dress, even in the fringed buckskin garments of the backwoods.

George Morland shows many types of soldiers of the eighteenth century. Benjamin West's "Death of General Wolfe" shows the uniforms of 1759; Copley's portrait of Lord Cornwallis shows those around 1780; and Burbury's caricatures show the camp type of 1781.

Ecclesiastical Dress

French abbés (like Scarron) of the Louis XV period were of great importance socially and intellectually, and betrayed their worldly bias in their semi-clerical garb. An abbé might wear a black civilian frock coat with moderate sleeves and cuffs, black silk stockings, and a full, loose wig with small, round, black cap (covering the tonsure); over these garments he might wear a circular cape a few inches shorter than the frock coat.

Other Catholic vestments remained the same.

Protestant garb was similar to civilian dress, except that the colors were sober and the material plain. Instead of wearing jabots, the clergy wore plain, narrow bands. Anglican clergymen wore the regulation garments described in a previous chapter. Out-of-doors, they wore plain black frock coats and narrow bands. Quakers wore clothes similar in cut to those of the Anglican clergy, but somber in color and without ornament.

Some dissenting ministers wore the academic gown when preaching; some used ordinary dress. Hogarth has left many portrayals of the clergy of the time.

Fig. 196   Fig. 197

Wigs like those in the mode, but a bit more conservative, were worn by the ministry. Their hats also were more or less in the mode.

Costume for Women

1770–1790

This was the age of Marie Antoinette. Dress did not so much change as become artistic and elegant, under the deft fingers of Rose Bertin. Lancret and Watteau gave way to Greuze and to pastoral simplicity.

Bodice

The low, square-cut bodice (Fig. 189 C) was boned, the slim waist pointed, the snug elbow-length sleeves ruffled. The front, or stomacher (Fig. 189, pattern), was trimmed with ribbons, lace, and flowers; the sleeve, with lace ruffles and ribbons. Bodices were frequently laced up the back.

Skirt

A. The skirts were very wide, with panniers at the side. The top skirt was frequently divided in a wide, inverted V (V) over a petticoat (Fig. 195 B). For formal wear, as shown in Fig. 189 A and Fig. 195 B, the trimming on skirt and petticoat was most elaborate: it consisted of furbelows, shirrings, lace ruffles, puffs, ribbons, flowers, bows, and other decorations. The petticoats were frequently quilted, a fashion greatly favored in the English colonies in America. A train was used on ceremonial occasions, though often the dress had no train. A simpler version of this type had puffed panniers and a fichu; with this were used a straw hat and a shepherdess's crook.

B. For ordinary wear, a dress with moderate panniers and perhaps an overskirt looped over it was worn (Fig. 189 E Fig. 190 C). The skirt was divided over a petticoat and might be trimmed with ruchings and puffs. The custom arose of using several petticoats instead of the panniers; the awkward whalebone affairs were gradually superseded, except for formal occasions.

C. Another type of dress reverted to the Watteau sacque. It was called a *polonaise,* and though it was fitted in the back, it billowed out on the skirt in loops and puffs. Often the polonaise sacque was outlined with ruching or puffs to emphasize the lines of the garment. In some instances, the old Watteau pleats were used.

Bodice and Skirt

Another type of dress, called a *levite,* had usually a snug bodice, long, tight sleeves, and a fairly full skirt draped over another skirt. The top skirt hung straight, without looping or puffing; it left an opening varying from a modest panel in front (Fig. 190 B) to a breadth halfway around the figure (Fig. 197).

The bodice to the levite might have a snug, high neckline with a circular collar (Fig. 190 B) or collars (Fig. 197), with wide lapels down the front (Fig. 190 B Fig. 197). With this type the two watch fobs used by men were adopted by women. They were tucked into the belt. The bodice might also be adorned with the lawn fichu which had long been used by the middle classes (Fig. 188 B Fig. 190 C) and which was now adopted by ladies of fashion (Fig. 190 A). Toward 1790, it got very full and high, was called the *bouffant,* and made the wearer look like a pouter pigeon.

For this type of dress, the Jacquard striped silks and the Jouy prints were in great demand.

The general effect of the polonaise and the levite was to bring back again the bustle effect, and do away with the hoopskirt.

To disseminate the latest styles, dolls were dressed (*La Poupée de la Rue Honorée,* and others) and sent to England, Germany, Italy, Spain, and finally to America. This custom led to the founding of the first fashion magazine. The first number of *Cabinet des Modes,* edited by Mercier, was published in November, 1785.

Marie Antoinette each day chose her dresses from a book of colored dress plates by pricking the ones preferred with a pin. The name of the dressmaker was written above each drawing. Marie Antoinette had about twelve ordinary dresses, twelve ball dresses, and twelve supper dresses, besides cambric and muslin dresses, which, having been but recently introduced, were more expensive and therefore fewer in number than the silks.

Cloak

Cloaks remained about the same, except that shawls began to gain favor, and were draped sometimes like the fichus, also popular at this time – that is, crossed over in front and sometimes tied behind (Fig. 190 A).

Footwear

Shoes and stockings changed very little. For dress, shoes were very dainty, of satin colored in plain shades to match the dress, or flowered, or striped. Marie Antoinette had several pairs with rows of emeralds up the heel. She also had diamond buckles, and diamonds were worked into her stockings. Clocks up the side were embroidered in colored and gold threads. For ordinary dress, gray and white worsted stockings were used. The word *bluestocking* originated from the fact that ladies of Elizabeth Montagu's intellectual circle (about 1750) wore stockings of blue worsted instead of silk, to show their disdain of vain, worldly trifles. (A gentleman, Mr. Stillingfleet, however, gave them the idea!) A bluestocking either had or affected literary tastes and learning, and spoke of literature (no matter whether she knew anything about it or not) instead of playing cards.

Hair

This was the era of enormous and bizarre headdresses. Legros (founder of the Academy of Hairdressing) and Léonard, Marie Antoinette's own hairdresser, first combined ribbons, gauze, feathers, etc., with the headdress, and started a vogue in France for unique arrangements, which continued until about 1785 (Fig. 182 B Fig. 194 E Fig. 195B). The hair was rolled over puffs and pads of horsehair; then the artistic (?) urge led to creations seventy-two inches high, with names like *opera box, crouching dog, hedgehog, à la Montgolfier* (the balloonist), *à la harpy, La Bunkerhill* (cannon and all!), *à la Belle Paule.* The latter, in honor of a great French naval victory, represented a frigate in full sail atop monstrous waves of powdered hair (Fig. 194 C). The English, not to be outdone, had headdresses depicting a park, a coach and four with outriders (done in spun glass), and a lighted cookstove equipped with pots and pans! Garrick, caricaturing these styles, wore during one of his performances a structure with a crown of raw vegetables.

The hair was brushed up on a wire frame filled with cotton gauze. False hair and curls were added to whatever height might be desired. Pomatum held the structure together; the powder was applied last. Not only was white powder used, but also brown, flaxen, gray, and black – the last made of coal dust or dry Japan ink. White powder was mixed with flour, starch, and alabaster. To counteract the odor of these

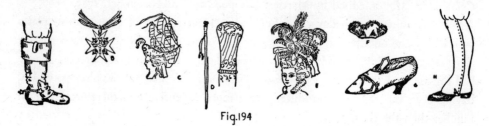

Fig.194

mixtures, perfumes were applied. Since it was an expensive process, heads were "dressed" only once in two or three weeks. The coiffure was not undone until the next dressing. No wonder the new fashion magazines carried many advertisements of insecticides! (See the end of this chapter for specific details of these coiffures.)

Caricatures of hairdressers sighting the top of the edifice with a telescope, working from an aerial seat near the ceiling, etc., did not undo the damage. Later, however, Marie Antoinette, after the birth of one of her children, cut off her hair, and wore it in short curls all over her head. This no doubt influenced the gradual return to normal coiffure, and the gradual abandonment of powder. The French Revolution (1789) put an abrupt end to the style in France; the American Revolution (1776) had modified the already modified version of styles which reached the colonies; and the powder tax (1794) in England definitely ended the fashion of powdering and opened the way for simpler headdresses. One may trace the variations of headdresses in France by studying the pictures of royalty; in England, portraits of ladies of fashion give the same information.

Gluck's opera *Iphigénie en Aulide* gave rise to the coiffure with veil. Suzanne, in *The Marriage of Figaro,* set the fashion for a certain type of large mobcap.

A poet of the time exclaimed thus:

> When he views your tresses thin,
> Touched by some French Friseur,
> Horsehair, hemp, and wool within
> Garnished with a diamond skiver;
> When he scents the mingled steam
> Which your plastered head is rich in,
> Lard and meal and clotted cream,
> Can he love a walking kitchen?

Headdress (1770–1790)

With the high, powdered coiffures, various headdresses were used. Besides the ribbons, plumes, gauze puffs, pearl chains, etc., woven in and out of the hair to make an "arrangement," there were caps of various kinds – a frilled bank about the head or tied under the chin; mobcaps, small or large, atop the edifice (Fig. 190 C), or with veils falling behind; bonnets barely covering the back of the head; or enormous hats (Fig. 190 B) of silk, lace, velvet, beaver, or straw, enveloping the head like a bowl, or perching on top of the full coiffure. In England the straw or *Leghorn hat* ("shepherdess") was very popular; these hats were first manufactured at Dunstable. Also popular in England was the black velvet or beaver hat, with moderate crown and wide brim, a bit turned up at the side, and trimmed with a bow or feathers. This type of hat, identified today as the *Gainsborough* (called after the English portrait painter), returned to favor from time to time, especially around 1910 (Fig. 182 C Fig. 190 A).

For riding, a plumed black hat with its brim turned up front or back was used.

When such hats were worn, the coiffure was lowered, at least in front, and the hat was tipped up behind.

Costume for Men

1790–1800

French fashion also suffered a revolution. In a world turned topsy-turvy, where radical changes were the order of the day, entirely new fashions were sought. As dress, however, had already gone to the extreme of exaggeration, the perfervid Jacobins could not reconstruct a complete code of customs and styles in a day. The simplest thing to do was to revert, as Renaissance men and women had done, to the source of classic inspiration and, fitly enough, to the source also of democratic ideas. The recent excavations at Pompeii and Herculaneum probably prompted the idea. Designers, therefore, studied the classic folds of Attic chiton and Latin toga. Except for the curled Alexandrian locks, however, men's dress did not follow the

Fig. 198

classic lines, but reflected, rather, the revolt from empty elegance and indolent affectation to matter-of-fact garments planned for doing rather than posing.

Coat

In 1789 the frock coat identified with the later Bourbons gave way to a long-tailed coat (Fig. 188 A C Fig. 196). This style was probably influenced by the English riding coat and was called the *redingote;* it was worn by both men and women. The Directory (1795–99) gave its name to a style distinctly masculine. The coat was single- or double-breasted, buttoned across the chest (Fig. 188 A) or left open (Fig. 196). It was sometimes cut straight across at or above the waistline and then tapered off to long tails (Fig. 196). The coat had a tall collar, which framed the back and sides of the neck and turned over. This was often separate from the revers, which folded out from the coat just below the collar (Fig. 196 Fig. 198).

Pockets, untrimmed and usually without buttons, were placed at the waistline, over the hips. The three or four buttons on either side of the waist of the coat were fairly large and of silver or cloth.

Sleeves were plain, with or without cuffs, as in the era immediately preceding. The ruffle at the wrist was seldom seen.

See also "1795," in Fig. 256 for the typical dress of this period.

Vest

The vest was short, to the waistline only, and was single- or double-breasted. It was often made of material with horizontal stripes (Fig. 188 A   Fig. 196   Fig. 198). The fashion of wearing two watch fobs continued (Fig. 188 E).

Neckwear

The white neckcloth continued to be worn; it was wrapped about several times.

Breeches

Breeches were smooth-fitting and buttoned just below the knee or extended down the leg to meet the new type of boots (Fig. 188 A   Fig. 196   Fig. 256). These boots were frequently short, to the calf only, with a stiff turned-over top of a different color or material, and with loops at the side for pulling on (Fig. 194 A).

Long, striped trousers were also worn (Fig. 188 C   Fig. 196). At this time, likewise, one of the most utilitarian of accessories was added to men's dress – suspenders (braces) for men came into use in 1792.

The *Incroyables,* a group of Parisian dandies, wore an exaggeration of this long-trouser style. The coat had a very high collar, very wide and exaggerated lapels, very high waistline, and very long tails (to the calf, in some instances). This group favored the Jacquard striped materials. Neckcloths were of crisp lawn, sometimes so high that they enveloped chin and mouth. The hair of the *Incroyables* was worn straight and stringy, or brushed forward from the nape of the neck to a ferocious-looking mass over the forehead. The hats were also unbelievable – either a hat with a very tall crown, or a cocked hat with two points only. The latter was worn with the points either front and back (English admiral style) or at the sides (Napoleon style). To show Revolutionary sympathies, a blue, red, and white rosette, or cockade, was attached in front.

Hair

At this period the natural hair was worn; it might be brushed up from the back and over the forehead, or confined in a small, loose mass at the nape of the neck (Fig. 196   Fig. 256). It might also be grown down over the cheek, in front of the ears (the later *sideburns*). However, a moderately short cut, with wavy locks about the face, was the usual mode.

Headdress

The cocked hat suffered a decline, and the tall-crowned, narrow-brimmed hat came into favor (Fig. 188 B E   Fig. 196). This was worn plain, or with a buckled band in front.

The type of cocked hat favored by the *Incroyables* was turned up front and back, with a cockade in front, Napoleon style (Fig. 188 A C   Fig. 196   Fig. 198).

Outer Coats

With the new era, greatcoats developed in favor. More capes and wider ones were added, and the collars were upstanding, with a deep turnover (Fig. 198). The coats reached almost to the ankle.

Footwear

Shoes were low-heeled, with flat buckles over the instep; sometimes rosettes were used, or even no decoration whatsoever. The high tongues had disappeared.

Boots came back into favor – a low one, to the calf of the leg (Fig. 188 A   Fig. 196   Fig. 256), and a higher one, to the knee (Fig. 198). Either variety might be straight or curved at the top; or either kind might have the stiff, turnover cuff, usually buff or of some lighter material. Loops with which to pull them on dangled over the top, in some styles (Fig. 194 A).

Stockings were long, and often striped (Fig. 188 A   Fig. 196   Fig. 198).

Military Dress

A typical soldier's dress of the Revolutionary era is shown in Fig. 188 C.

COSTUME FOR WOMEN

1790–1800

Bodice

The English riding coat influenced women's dress very much during this era. Women adopted the men's riding coat, and a dress known as the *redingote* (from "riding coat") became very popular, first for hunting, then for morning and church wear, then as a general style. The redingote was buttoned over in front, and might have a fichu (Fig. 188 B) about the neck, or else have revers, or lapels, and a tall, turnover collar (Fig. 188 E   Fig. 197). Sometimes two or more capes were added, similar to those on the greatcoat (Fig. 188 E   Fig. 197). About the neck might be worn a fichu or ruffle (Fig. 188 B). The neck might be also adorned with a folded neckcloth, tied in front in a bow (Fig. 190 B).

The skirts to the coat were short; or they might also be long, and looped or draped back to the rear. The redingote type of dress was adopted as a Directory mode.

A vest, with two pendant watch fobs or seals, was frequently worn with this costume.

The sleeves were snug-fitted, with cuffs and perhaps frills at the wrists.

Skirt

A full petticoat of the same or contrasting material was worn with this costume. Striped materials were favored. Hoopskirts were practically discontinued, except perhaps in the United States.

The redingote, or Directory style, was the forerunner of the tailor-made dress for women. Pursuing the new classic idea, women sought proper textiles and designs – Greek patterns of stars and sprigs, Greek and Roman borders, "wall of

Troy" and honeysuckle patterns. The himation and the Doric chiton were suggested by the drapings and the overfold; the sandal was revived.

"Greek" Gown

The *Nymph*, or the *Merveilleuse*, epitome of the licentiousness of the new era, wore a long, diaphanous gown, often slit to the knee or higher, in imitation of the Doric chiton (Fig. 199). For underwear, there was often nothing more than a skintight, flesh-colored silk garment. The waistline was high, just below the bosom. Often the crossed girdle of the Greeks was suggested, if the neckline were very low,

1795

Fig. 199

with a thin gauze piece scarcely covering the bosom. To reproduce the clinging lines of the classic model, the garment was soaked in water, wrung out, and plastered against the body. The Doric overfold was copied with variations. The hair was done in pseudo-Greek fashion, with ribbons wound about the curly coiffure (*à la Titus*); turbans were also fashionable (*à la Minerva*). Cameos held together the sleeves and the skirts, and were worn with necklaces and bracelets.

Shawls and scarves were innumerable in size, shape, and pattern. They were of black, white, orange, flame, and other colors, and were square, pointed, or oblong in shape. Silk, gauze, lawn, cashmere, and gray rabbit wool were favorite materials for these wraps.

Women like the fair Citoyennes Hamelin and Tallien led the caprices of this lightning-change period. This era of barefaced, unconfined license threw away the artificial stays of conventional propriety which had put some small restraint on the dissolute regime of the Bourbon monarchs.

Cloak

A greatcoat, similar to the men's, was used; the long, circular cloak with hood was, however, still the most favored type.

Footwear

Shoes were a bit more pointed, perhaps, but not very different (Fig. 188 B E Fig. 197). Stockings had clocks, stripes, dots, and other decorations.

Hair

The hair was no longer powdered, and the tall headdresses disappeared. Soft, natural curls about the face and a curl or so over the shoulder satisfied the most

Fig. 191　　　　　　Fig. 192

exacting for dress occasions. During the Reign of Terror it was, for a brief time, the fashion to cut the hair short (Fig. 199), but this fashion was short-lived.

Headdress

Turbans were made popular during this period by Madame de Staël and others of influence. Of plain, flowered, or striped material, they were wound about the head or poised on top of the hair (Fig. 199). Straw hats and big picture hats continued in fashion. The tall-crowned, narrow-brimmed hat was also in use; a feather or a buckle might be added to render it less severe (Fig. 188 B E).

COSTUME FOR CHILDREN

1700–1800

At the beginning of the century, children, both boys and girls, wore costumes after the fashion of the day. Little girls wore boned stays under the stiff, square-necked bodices, and hoops under the full skirts. Watteau sacques like those of their elders were favored, the usual material being chintz. A kerchief about the neck and a muslin hood added a simple note. Mobcaps, an adult item particularly adapted to children, were in common use around 1760 (Fig. 191 Fig. 199). In England, after 1760, little girls wore the simpler styles preserved today in the delightful Reynolds portraits of "The Strawberry Girl" (1773), "Miss Bowles" (1776), "Miss Crewe"

(1770), and the incomparable "Age of Innocence" (1785). One type of simple dress was of lawn or muslin, white-sprigged, and short-waisted, with a low, round neck often edged with a frill. The skirt was full, fairly long, and girded with a moderately wide sash in some pale shade. The hair, usually confined with a hood or cap, was, on ceremonial occasions, piled on the head, curled, and powdered.

After 1790, little girls wore the Directory type of dress, with a very high waist and long, scanty skirt, no sash, and low, round neck, as well as short, puffed sleeves (or none).

For wraps, little girls wore black, circular capes with hoods (little Miss Crewe, in Reynolds's portrait of 1770, wears a cape and a calash).

Gainsborough painted little Miss Haverfield in a large, mushroom-shaped hat with mobcap beneath. Wide-brimmed hats of beaver or straw were also used.

Shoes were flat and low, with moderate-sized buckles.

A little girl of the Revolutionary period, with red liberty cap and cockade, is shown in Fig. 188 D.

Until about 1760, little boys wore waistcoats, frock coats, and breeches patterned after their elders' clothes. Jabots, curled and powdered wigs, and tricorne hats were included, so that little boys looked like miniature gentlemen.

After 1760, simpler styles were adopted for boys also, at least in England. These included short jackets with two or three large pewter or silver buttons; long, loose trousers to the ankle or nearly so; a soft, frilled shirt, open at the neck, with a flat collar or frill; and a wide sash at the waist. Wide-brimmed, low-crowned hats of beaver, felt, or straw were used. The little Viscount Althorp, painted by Reynolds in 1780, wears this type of dress (Fig. 192).

Circular coats and low-heeled, buckled shoes, in the prevailing fashion, were worn by boys.

Though the American colonies promptly copied English fashions for children, the French were slower to change. Chardin's "The Blessing" and other genre pieces show the current costumes for children of the poor. The court painters have recorded the stiffer styles of the nobility. Marie Antoinette first adopted the short jacket and trousers for the Dauphin, but this sensible act received little credit at the time.

After the Revolution, however, French children reverted to the pseudo-Greek simplicity, along with their elders, as may be seen in pictures of Madame Lebrun and her daughter.

COSTUME FOR THE LOWER CLASSES

1700–1800

Of the lower classes, up to the time of the French Revolution, it is safe to say that they wore moderated versions of styles of the preceding period. In the time of Louis XV, for example, the men wore the long, full frock coat, very long vest, and baggy breeches of the Louis XIV era (Fig. 190 D Fig. 193 B). Around 1750–60, the coat grew a bit shorter and scantier. The vest grew shorter, the breeches more snug.

A plain bob wig (short hair, slightly curled) or a wig with queue was worn with a tricorne or a trimmed hat turned up behind or on the side. Shoes were of the old, high-tongued style until about 1750, when the tongue became inconspicuous and the heel low. Shirts of ticklenburg linen (ticking) and also trousers of striped ticking were worn by day laborers, as well as wide leather breeches, buttoned at the sides. Ticking or leather aprons were worn by laborers and tradesmen. (La Croix's "Aspect of Paris" shows many types of working garb.)

English sailors adopted medium-brimmed, flat-crowned, glazed leather hats about 1765. Their breeches, or "slops," were knee-length, wide petticoat breeches. The modern dress uniform of the English navy is said to have been copied from the blue riding habit with white facings worn by the Duchess of Bedford, around 1748.

Lower-class women wore plain, snug bodices, full skirts (often looped up about the waist), kerchiefs, hoods, caps, and low, flat shoes. Sleeves were usually elbow length, though long ones, turned back in a cuff, were worn (Fig. 193 A). Large, full aprons, colored or white, were worn indoors and out.

The very poor, both men and women, wore patchwork garments and went barefooted both winter and summer (thick-soled wooden sabots being a great luxury).

Miscellaneous Items

1700–1800

Make-up

Men used patches, hair powder, and perfume. The perfumes used by both men and women included musk, almond, civet, violet, and chypre. Attar of roses, though a favorite, was very costly, as it took about a hundred thousand roses to produce one ounce of the perfume.

From 1700 to 1780, make-up for women was most elaborate. French and English women struggled for alabaster complexions, using mixtures of red and white lead, bismuth, mercury, verdigris, and other dangerous ingredients. Death often followed the persistent use of such cosmetics. Skins became so sensitive that dairy creams had to be employed. Wash balls of rice flour, starch, and white lead were used, as today one uses soap. Lard was the basis of complexion salves.

Women slept in the tightly-boned corset (Fig. 189 B D) to preserve the slender waists necessary for fashionable dress. They also donned dogskin and chickenskin gloves at night to whiten their hands. Masks were used to protect complexions from sun and wind.

A complexion whitened and delicately rouged was enhanced by the court patches (called *mouches dans le lait*) made fashionable in the previous century. Patches had almost died out, when the Duchesse du Maine brought them back into fashion. As formerly, they were named "the gallant" when on the cheek, "the passionate" when at the corner of the eye, "the coquette" when near the lips, and other suggestive titles.

The powdering of the hair has already been described.

Ornaments and Accessories for Men (Fig. 198)

Lace, either as neckcloths or edging for cravats, jabots, wrist-ruffles, etc., continued in favor. Buckles were used to fasten neckcloths and breeches, and, plain or in ornamental forms, decorated the low-heeled shoes of the time. Buttons of cloth, pewter, or silver were used on the vest, on coat pockets, and on the breeches. Gold and silver braid, embroidery, and gold and silver lace were used to edge the vest and coat and to ornament pockets. Ribbon cockades were used on cocked hats, as were feather fringes. Powder was used on wigs. For this purpose, fashionable houses were equipped with niches, or recesses in the wall, holding powder, where the gentlemen could dip their heads for re-powdering.

Men wore patches on the face, signifying political affiliations.

Garters were less conspicuous than formerly, and were tied or buckled about the knee. Wig caps were in demand.

Muffs were worn by men – some were just big enough to admit both hands (these were called *muffties*); some were large and flat. Sometimes they were adorned with feathers and lace. Horace Walpole sent one of his friends a muff so small that it could be put in the pocket.

The sword was worn attached to a narrow sword belt underneath the vest; the hilt was thrust through the side slit of the coat. The hilt was now curved, with curving quillons. The sword knot was elaborate, and sometimes jeweled.

Snuffboxes were carried by men of fashion. They were of plain metal, gold, or silver, and might be adorned with precious stones or miniatures.

Canes of varying lengths were carried (Fig. 195 A); some were of oak, with ugly faces carved on them (as may be seen in many of Hogarth's cartoons of London life). They were also made of ebony, bamboo, and other woods, and were topped with elaborate gold heads (Fig. 194 D). A cord sometimes was attached, by which they could be carried hanging from the wrist (Fig. 194 D). An ingenious accessory for doctors was a scent ball, or pomander, inserted in the handle of the cane. On entering the sickroom, a tap of the cane scattered the scent or powder, thus providing a disinfectant.

Watches were worn in fob pockets, often with seals attached, but until the end of the century, they were not prominently displayed.

Rings, seals, and jeweled buckles were in demand.

Pipes were smoked, usually at clubs or at home, but seldom in public.

Handkerchiefs were very ornate, with gold, silver, or colored lace borders.

Spectacles came into general use after 1720; first, temple spectacles, and, later, "bridge spectacles" (pince-nez) were introduced, without side supporters, clipped on the nose only.

Perspective glasses (like lorgnettes with long handles, of silver or tortoise shell) were carried by beaux and dandies.

Gloves were used on occasions of ceremony or for riding or driving. For dress use, they were perfumed.

Royalty and the nobility wore various orders or medals attached to ribbons about the neck. The Order of the Ampulla (said to have been founded by Clovis in 511 A.D.) is shown in Fig. 194 B.

Ornaments and Accessories for Women (Fig. 199)

Furbelows, introduced by Madame de Maintenon, were intermittently popular in France until the French Revolution. As puffs, flowers, loops, etc., they decorated the various types of dress (Fig. 189 E   Fig. 190 C   Fig. 195 B).

Buckles of steel, gold, paste, and jewels were used on shoes (Fig. 190 C).

Laces of all kinds were used on bodices, sleeves, skirts, caps, and petticoats (Fig. 199). The lace was often pleated.

Artificial flowers, singly, in bunches, or in garlands, decorated hair, bodice, and skirt (Fig. 195 B).

Ribbons, particularly narrow black velvet ribbons, were worn at the throat and wrist (Fig. 189 A   Fig. 195 B). Ruchings of lace and ribbon, like ruffs, were worn close about the throat.

Embroidery in colored silks and in silver and gold thread was much in evidence on bodice and skirt, particularly along the edge and up the front of the skirt.

Patches were used, not only to enhance the beauty, but to denote political affiliation; Whig ladies wore them on the left side, and Tories on the right.

The muff, in 1715, was long and narrow, just fitting the hands. Later, it became larger and more rectangular in shape (Fig. 190 B). At times, it was round and fairly small.

The apron was used by the nobility as well as by the lower classes. For the former, it was made of fine cambric lawn or of handsome allover lace. Flowered materials and taffetas were also used. Around 1700, aprons were rather long. Aprons became short about 1740; afterward they grew long again.

Handkerchiefs were of cambric, lace, silk, and linen, plain or lace-edged. They were fairly large, like the modern costume handkerchief of chiffon.

Fans were indispensable. They were of paper, silk, or lace, and were hand-painted by Watteau and other artists of the rococo period. Pastoral, mythological, contemporary, and fantastic scenes were portrayed. Miniature heads, staves of music, calendars, and fortune-telling cards were painted or printed on the surfaces. Lacquered fans were popular. The sticks were of ivory, bone, sandalwood, mother-of-pearl, tortoise shell, or carved and gilded woods (Fig. 199).

Patches, so important in this era, were carried in patch boxes of ivory, tortoise shell, silver, and enamelwork. A small glass in the lid, like a modern "vanity" glass, aided in placing the patches.

Masks of black velvet were worn on the street, in the theater, and for purposes of disguise. For riding, a mask over the entire face was used.

An *etui,* or ornamental case, was worn suspended from the waist. It held scissors, scent bottle, thimble, and other necessaries.

The snuffbox, pouncet box (for perfumes), and also the pomander, with perforated lid, were used by women as well as men.

The wedding veil came into use after the fashion of wearing the hair loose over the shoulders had disappeared some time in the seventeenth century. In the eighteenth century, however (as Horace Walpole noted at his niece's wedding), veils were often dispensed with for the wedding ceremony, the hat being deemed sufficient covering. Perhaps Gretna Green runaway marriages may have had something to do with this.

Necklaces of gold or pearl beads, earrings, rings, and bracelets were all in use (Fig. 199). Cameos came back into favor for a while. Metal or stiffened and embroidered belts, jeweled and sometimes engraved, were used with the Directory type of dress for evening or formal wear (Fig. 199).

Reticules, embroidered and fringed, with a drawstring of ribbon through them, were carried throughout the century (Fig. 186 B). Flowered crepe shawls (from China or India) came into vogue toward the end of the century.

Parasols are shown in pictures of the time by such artists as Moreau, Boucher, and Lancret (Fig. 199). Jonas Hanway introduced umbrellas into England in 1771.

Gloves (perfumed for dress use) and mittens (Fig. 199, little girl) were used.

Servants' Dress

A woman servant wore a snug bodice, full skirt, fichu, and cap; Suzanne, in Beaumarchais' *Marriage of Figaro,* wore this type of dress with a mobcap when playing the maid. Another type of cap was the snug bonnet, or "baby cap," seen in Chardin's pictures. Gray was the usual color for women servants' clothing, hence the name *grisette,* or saucy maid.

A man servant wore a frock coat, knee breeches, and a vest, similar to his master's. The Louis XIV and Louis XV styles persisted, wig and all, and were adopted as more or less standard dress for footmen and, with variations, for other household retainers' formal wear (Fig. 190 D). Some of these costumes are worn by servants even today.

Mourning

Black was worn to funerals and for the mourning period, which varied from six months to two years. In the period of powdered hair, it was customary to powder the hair black during mourning.

Modern Adaptations

For the eighteenth century, up to the late Marie Antoinette period, use satins and taffetas, chiffon velvets, and brocades. Sateen and rayon silks are good substitutes; so are velveteens. Furniture brocades are particularly good for the Louis XV period, and so are flowered chintzes or shiny flowered percales.

For men's coats, use flowered chintz (or brocade), sateen (or satin), and velveteen (or velvet); stiffen the coats with canvas. Corduroy may also be used.

The pannier hoops can be made of heavy wire, wrapped and taped (for details, see page 238). Two tapes fastened to the lower front wire, about ten inches apart, passed through the crotch and fastened in the back, will prevent the frame from swinging when the wearer walks across the stage. It will also keep the frame (and the full skirt) from tipping up in front.

Use *Vogue* period patterns, or "Martha Washington" and "George Washington" patterns. The women's patterns should have tight bodices. The Watteau pleat type is usually easy to procure and to make.

If none of these patterns can be secured, use a plain lining pattern for the woman's bodice and a pajama coat pattern, lengthened and fitted, for the man's coat; the tight breeches can be shortened from the pajama trousers. The required Watteau pleats and other embellishments and drapings can be added to the plain foundation.

The following is a detailed description of a court costume of the time of Marie Antoinette (Fig. 195 B):

Materials for the Dress:
  15 yards of Japanese taffeta (light blue or similar color)
  14 yards of 1″ lace (white)
  14 yards of 5″ lace (white)
  3 yards of featherboning
  1⅓ yards lightweight muslin (white)
  ½ yard chiffon (deep rose or similar color)
  1 yard silk net (white)
  2 yards, 2 inches, satin ribbon (deep pink or similar color)
  ½ yard taffeta (light green or similar color)
Materials for the Hoop Petticoat:
  4 steel or wire hoops
  10 yards lightweight unbleached muslin
  12 yards of silk net (white)
Materials for the Wig:
  1 heavy bathing cap (white)
  1 old silk opera hat
  1 sun helmet (white)
  6 packages of spun glass
  2 rolls of cotton
  2 jars of mucilage
  2 ostrich tops (light blue or similar color)
  3 tall plumes (deep rose or similar color)

The ensemble of a court costume for Marie Antoinette's period consists of a light-colored taffeta dress with wide panniers worn over a hoop petticoat, and completed by a very tall white wig surmounted by plumes.

Hoop Petticoat

The hoop petticoat is made in the following manner:

Nearly any lampshade shop will order for you four very heavy wire or steel hoops. These hoops should be oval in shape with a decided depression in the front. They should graduate in size from the largest (which is 50″–52″ wide to 23″–25″ from front to back) to the smallest (which is 18″ wide and 12″ from front to back). These sizes may be varied slightly, depending on the size of the person who is to wear them. Wind each of the hoops securely with unbleached muslin so that each one is well covered. As the hoops are quite heavy, it is necessary to make a substantial waistband from which to hang them. Cover a piece of buckram 2″ or 3″ wide with unbleached muslin; fit it very securely around the waist of the person who is to wear it; hook it in the back, and fasten it. It is necessary to hang the hoops either on a person or a form. The hoops are hung by strips of tape, one in front and one in back, and three on either side. Sew the smallest hoop firmly to the front and back tapes, about 2 inches below the waistband. Adjust the length of the three tapes on either side so that there is a perfect balance between both sides of the hoops. Proceed with the rest of the hoops in the same manner, placing each one 2 inches below the one above in front and back, and adjusting the sides accordingly; the entire petticoat is made over this frame of hoops. Gather a skirt 6–7 yards wide of unbleached muslin, which reaches within about 5 inches of the floor, onto the bottom hoop. Cover each side of the exposed hoops with a long rectangular piece of muslin, gathered in at the waist and tacked to the hoops. Sew two net ruffles around the bottom of a net skirt 12 yards wide, and gather it over the hoops so that it just touches the floor all around. Instead of net, any lightweight white material may be used and trimmed with lace ruffles. Also, if desired, one or two more skirts may be added and sewn to the base of the hoops and muslin.

Dress

The dress is made from 12–15 yards of a light-colored Japanese taffeta or similar material, trimmed with pink ribbons and flowers (or a similar color) and white lace. The bodice should be made first. Cut it in three sections so that it may be fastened down the front. The back is cut rather high in the neck and fitted to the normal waistline; the two front pieces are cut with a very low, square neckline and with a point coming down below the center of the normal waistline for 2–3 inches, which gives the effect of a stomacher. The sleeves are perfectly plain, short, cap sleeves, reaching three-quarters to the elbow. They are trimmed with three graduating ruffles of white lace about 2–5 inches deep, which are first sewn onto a net foundation. The bottom ruffle is about 3 yards wide, and the other two ruffles 1½ yards each. The collar is made of the same lace as the sleeves, and is pleated around the neckline, graduating from ¼ inch wide across the front to 4–5 inches wide across the back. A double ruffle of 1″ lace, preferably the same pattern as the wider lace, runs straight down the front of the bodice from the neckline to the base of the point. There should also be a row of featherboning down each side of the front fastening, and the entire bodice should be generously and stiffly boned. The front panel of the skirt is cut in a triangular shape, 10 inches across the top and about 1 yard wide across the bottom, which touches the floor; this is not gathered, but is put on straight at the waistline, with the point of the bodice sewn on over it. The lower part of the panel is trimmed with a deep panel of white lawn or lightweight muslin, which is covered with white net and edged with 1″ lace; it is covered with garlands of deep pink (or a similar color) chiffon roses with leaves of pale green taffeta. Over this front panel is sewn the rest of the skirt, which is about 12 yards wide and is gathered to the bodice; it is cut diagonally down the front and left open, exposing the front panel and giving the effect of an under- and overskirt. The top skirt is sewn along the outer edge of the panel, and gradually lengthens from floor length in front to a slight train in back. It is rather difficult to fit the skirt on because of the shape of the hoops; the skirt must, of necessity, be very long in the front and back before it touches the floor on the sides, due to the wide panniers. This discrepancy can be taken care of in the hem. On either side of the front panel, a panel of white lawn, net, etc., trimmed with garlands and edged with lace, etc., is sewn on the top skirt, gradually deepening from 3 inches at the point of the bodice where the two panels meet to 10–12 inches at the bottom of the skirt. The last touch is three 2″-wide pink satin ribbon bows, one on either sleeve, and one on the front of the bodice.

Wig

The wig (Fig. 182 B Fig. 195 B), which completes the costume, is made in the style of the eighteenth century. Put a heavy, white bathing cap (the type that is waved like hair and has a chin strap) on the head of the person who is to wear the wig. Tuck all hair out of sight and remove the chin strap. Cut a slit in each side just large enough to pull the ears through; then cut the front of the cap into the desired hairline. Next, take an old opera hat, remove the brim, and fill the inside with cotton until it fits securely on the head over the bathing cap. On top of this place something round, such as the crown of a cork or cardboard sun helmet, and fit it trimly on top. Cover the whole structure with a thin layer of cotton; remove it carefully from the head and place it on a block the size and shape of the head. Pad it with cotton until it is of the desired shape and size. Purchase from any novelty store about six packages of spun glass. Start at the hairline of the cap, and cover the entire mass with spun glass, which should not be pulled or stretched out enough to spoil the wavy, hairlike effect. Now make three large rolls of cotton and cover them with spun glass. Place the largest roll on top at the back of the wig and extend it halfway around on either side. Place each of the other rolls in the same manner beneath, sewing and gluing them into place. Mucilage works beautifully with both the cotton and the spun glass; it holds them firmly in place and is almost invisible when it dries. The entire headdress, which should now look like a mass of beautifully waved and curled hair, should be finished with three tall, richly-colored plumes and two tiny, pastel-colored ostrich tips set on the top of the wig; also add two side curls of cotton and spun glass, one behind each ear.

Accessories

With the costume should be worn satin slippers to match the gown (or else white slippers), black ribbons at the wrists, and several beauty patches. If possible, a genuine Watteau fan, or a replica of one, should be carried.

CHAPTER XIII
THE NINETEENTH CENTURY
1800-1850

IMPORTANT PEOPLE AND EVENTS

ENGLAND

Rulers

George III
(1760–1820)
George IV
(1820–30)
William IV
(1830–37)
Victoria
(1837–1901)

Notable People

William Wordsworth
Robert Burns
Percy Bysshe Shelley
John Keats
George Gordon, Lord
Byron
Thomas Babington
Macaulay
Thomas Carlyle
Jane Austen
Mrs. Elizabeth Gaskell
Thomas De Quincey
Samuel Taylor Cole-
ridge
Charles Lamb
Charles Dickens
Charlotte Brontë
Emily Brontë
Edward Bulwer-
Lytton
Arthur Wellesley,
Duke of Wellington
Horatio, Viscount
Nelson
Beau Brummell
(George Bryan
Brummell)

Joseph M. W. Turner
Emma, Lady Hamilton
John Martin

FRANCE

Government

Consulate
(1799–1804)
First Empire
(Napoleon Bona-
parte)
(1804–15)
Restoration
(Louis XVIII –
Bourbon)
(1814–15 – 1815–24)
Charles X
(1824–30)
Louis Philippe (Or-
leans)
(1830–48)
Second Republic
(Louis Bonaparte)
(1848–52)

Notable People

Mme de Staël
(Anne Louise
Necker, Baronne de
Staël-Holstein)
Mme Jeanne Récamier
The Empress Josephine
(Josephine de Beau-
harnais Bonaparte)
Victor Hugo
Stendhal
(Marie Henri Beyle)
Alfred de Musset
Théophile Gautier

Alexandre Dumas
George Sand
(Mme Amantine
Dudevant, *née* Du-
pin)
Augustin Eugène
Scribe
Honoré de Balzac
Jacques Louis David
Jean Auguste Ingres
Hippolyte Paul Dela-
roche
Jean Louis Géricault
Ferdinand Eugène
Delacroix
Alexandre Gabriel De-
camps

UNITED STATES OF
AMERICA

Presidents

John Adams
(1797–1801)
Thomas Jefferson
(1801–09)
James Madison
(1809–17)
James Monroe
(1817–25)
John Quincy Adams
(1825–29)
Andrew Jackson
(1829–37)
Martin Van Buren
(1837–41)
William Henry Harri-
son
(1841)

John Tyler
(1841–45)
James Knox Polk
(1845–49)
Zachary Taylor
(1849–50)

Notable People

Washington Irving
Edgar Allan Poe
Nathaniel Hawthorne
Sidney Lanier
Ralph Waldo Emerson
Oliver Wendell
Holmes
Henry Wadsworth
Longfellow
John Marshall
Henry Clay
Daniel Webster
John Calhoun
Meriwether Lewis
William Clark
Robert Fulton
William Lloyd Garri-
son
Sam Houston
Charles Willson Peale
Thomas Sully

GERMANY

Rulers

Frederick William III
(1797–1840)
Frederick William IV
(1840–61)

Notable People
Wilhelm Richard
  Wagner
Jakob and Wilhelm
  Grimm
Heinrich Heine
Karl Marx
Jean Paul Friedrich
  Richter
Peter von Cornelius
Johann Friedrich Over-
  beck

Karl Maria, Baron von
  Weber
Felix Mendelssohn

ITALY
Rulers
Napoleon I
(1805–14)

Notable People
Camillo Benso, Count
  de Cavour

Giuseppe Mazzini
Giuseppe Garibaldi
Charles Albert (Carlo
  Alberto)
  (Sardinia-Piedmont)

RULERS PUT ON THRONE
BY NAPOLEON I
Eugène Beauharnais,
  Viceroy of Italy, 1805
Louis Bonaparte, King
  of Holland, 1806

Joseph Bonaparte, King
  of Naples and Sicily,
  1806; in 1808 he was
  transferred to Spain
  as King
Joachim Murat, King
  of Naples, 1808
Jerome Bonaparte,
  King of Westphalia,
  1807
Jean Baptiste Berna-
  dotte, King of Swe-
  den, 1810

GENERAL SURVEY

By the Congress of Vienna, 1815, Europe was reconstructed along autocratic lines. This policy of suppression led to revolutions. In 1830, there were revolutions in France, Belgium, Poland, Italy, and Germany. In 1848, there were revolutions in France, Germany, Hungary, and Italy. These upheavals had various results in the various countries. In France, a more democratic government was developed. In Italy, the process of unification was hastened. In Germany and Poland, emigration to other lands followed.

Communication and transportation developed to meet the changing and expanding world. Railroad trains, postal service, and steamboats speeded up communication. Machinery speeded up production. Increased city populations – an inevitable result of the demand for factory workers – gave impetus to the movement toward universal suffrage.

GREAT BRITAIN

1801, England and Ireland were united. . . . 1805, Lord Nelson defeated the French at Trafalgar, but lost his life. . . . 1815, Wellington crushed Napoleon's power by victory at Waterloo. . . . 1829, the "Bobbies," or "Peelers," a systematically organized police force, was founded by Sir Robert Peel. . . . 1829, Catholic emancipation achieved by Catholic Relief Bill. . . . 1830, first railroad built, between Liverpool and Manchester. . . . 1832, Great Reform Bill, sponsored by Lord John Russell, was passed. . . . 1833, all negro slaves in the British West Indies were freed by the Act for the Abolition of Slavery and their owners compensated. . . . 1838, Chartists attempted to gain their "Six Points." . . . 1839–42, Opium War in China. . . . 1840, through the efforts of Sir Rowland Hill, the penny postal system was established. . . . 1844, Factory Act was passed. . . . 1846, potato famine in Ireland brought about economic stress that resulted in the repeal of the Corn Law; Cobden, Bright, and Peel were leaders in this movement.

FRANCE

From 1800 to 1815, the Napoleonic era was marked by such events as the establishment of the empire, 1804; the Napoleonic Code and the concordat with the Pope; the dissolution of the Holy Roman Empire, 1806, and the Confederation of the Rhine; the Coalitions against Napoleon by other powers, notably England and Germany; the battles of Ulm, Austerlitz, Jena, Friedland; Napoleon's reconstruction of Europe and founding of vassal kingdoms; the Berlin and Milan Decrees and the Continental System; the Peninsular War in Spain; the Russian campaign and the retreat from Moscow, 1812; the Battle of Leipzig, 1813; the abdication of Napoleon and his exile to Elba; his return and the Hundred Days; his defeat at Waterloo, June 18, 1815, and his exile to St. Helena; the Congress of Vienna, 1815. . . . 1830, Algiers taken by the French; in the same year, the July Revolution. . . . 1836, Louis Napoleon attempted to gain the throne, but was surreptitiously sent by Louis Philippe to America. . . . 1848, the brief revolution took place. . . . 1848, Louis Napoleon made president.

UNITED STATES OF AMERICA

1802, West Point founded. . . . 1803, Louisiana purchased from France for $15,000,000. . . . 1804, Aaron Burr killed Alexander Hamilton in a duel. . . . 1804, the Lewis and Clark expedition started to explore the source of the Missouri River. . . . 1807, Fulton built the first practical steamboat, the *Clermont,* which was launched on the Hudson River. . . . 1812, war began with Great Britain, and the United States won many brilliant naval victories under Perry, Hull, and others in ships such as the *Constitution,* the *Wasp,* etc.; war ended with the Battle of New Orleans, under Andrew Jackson. . . . 1819, the *Savannah* was first steamship to cross the Atlantic. . . . 1820, Missouri Compromise settled the slavery area; Mason and Dixon line established as a dividing line. . . . Important decisions of Chief Justice John Marshall, from 1801 to 1835. . . . 1823, Monroe Doctrine was expounded in a presidential address. . . . 1825, Erie Canal built. . . . 1828, the Baltimore and Ohio horsecar railroad was built; steam locomotion followed in 1831. . . . 1830, Joseph Smith founded the Mormon Church. . . . 1837, general panic followed the closing of the United States Bank by Andrew Jackson. . . . Abolition movement gained momentum under William Lloyd Garrison, publisher of *The Liberator.* . . . 1830, Webster-Hayne debate argued the principle of nullification. . . . 1832, South Carolina threatened nullification over the tariff. . . . 1836, Texan independence was achieved after the Alamo, under such leaders as Sam Houston. . . . 1842, the Webster-Ashburton treaty gained part of Canada for Maine. . . . 1843, first telegraph line strung between Washington and Baltimore and first news of Polk's election sent over this wire. . . . 1845, United States Naval Academy established at Annapolis. . . . 1845, annexation of Texas accomplished. . . . 1846–48, Mexican War resulted in acquisition of southwest territory, including California. . . . 1846, Oregon Boundary dispute. . . . 1848, gold discovered in California. . . . 1849, Astor Place riots, directed against Macready, an English actor. . . . Lola Montez startled Europe and America with her escapades.

OTHER COUNTRIES

1821, struggle for Italian unity began in Piedmont. . . . 1822, revolution in Portugal. . . . 1828, Russian war against Turkey. . . . 1830, revolutions in Belgium, Poland, Italy, Germany. . . . 1848, Charles Albert of Sardinia-Piedmont declared war on Austria. . . . 1849, republic established in Rome. . . . Cavour, Mazzini, and Garibaldi built up unity in Italy, aided by Napoleon III. . . . Revolutions of 1848 in Hungary (led by Kossuth) and in Germany, Italy, and France were partly the result of Metternich's reactionary policy.

The French Revolution cleared the way for a new system, social and political. The whir of machinery marked the advent of mass production. In the early nineteenth century the kings and queens of fashion no longer wore hereditary crowns. They were persons of momentary importance whose evanescent brilliance attracted public interest – Beau Brummell, Count d'Orsay, Mademoiselle Mars, and François Joseph Talma. Paris was the arbiter of fashion for women, and London for men. Small-town seamstresses "by the day" and local tailors followed the Paris and London decrees with an unquestioning obedience which the Little Corporal would have envied.

Europe, the *modiste internationale,* was busy turning and piecing her outworn and outmoded vestments. France, guided by the designing hands of Napoleon, recut almost the entire continental pattern, and combined new and old materials with a blithe disregard for taste or choice. To obtain these, thousands of men were sacrificed and millions in property destroyed. At the same time almost half a continent of fresh new material in America was sold on the bargain counter of expediency, without a forward glance.

Germany, the thrifty *hausfrau,* salvaged hundreds of scraps and basted them together with deft stitches to produce a serviceably stout fabric. Its mixture of material showed a touch of French smartness traceable perhaps to the Napoleonic impress on the Rhenish Confederation.

Fig. 200

England was too wise to snip scraps from the Continental crazy quilt, but she did not neglect to add tidy bits of Oriental and African garniture to her Georgian pattern. A domestic trimming, itemized in the Reform Bill, emphasized the British cut. In America there was also a trimming of borders along the Mexican line, with a Canadian fringe added at the top.

Down along the Mediterranean, patriotic hands were busy weaving the brilliant Venetian, Piedmontese, Neapolitan, and Roman stripes into the glowing national scarf that was to be United Italy. Everywhere there seemed to be fusion or confusion, and the destiny of Europe was pieced out of the scrapbag of past finery.

Vienna was responsible for more than the waltz. The Congress of 1815 forced Europe to dance to the Pied Piper of autocracy. But the spell was soon broken, and the peoples sought in revolutions, or in new countries, the leaders which the new rhythm of life demanded.

COSTUME

General Characteristics

Fashion, in the nineteenth century, underwent evolutions as swift as those of the wheels in mushroom-growth factories. Out of the chaos of the French Revolution and of the Directory era that followed, the turn of the century brought a certain restraint and simplification in dress.

During the first fifty years, fashions for men showed the following general characteristics: The coat was cut on increasingly plain lines. The collar, loath to lose its flamboyant curves, gradually subsided, and by 1840 lay snug about the neck. The lapel suffered a similar collapse. The waspish waistline of the 1800's disappeared only when the slender tails of the coat were replaced by the shapeless skirts of the frock coat, which also came in during the 'forties. The stock, ennobled by Beau Brummell in the early years of the century, flattened into the low, turnover collar, accompanied by the flat bow tie. The elegance of knee breeches lasted well into the second decade, but long trousers were, by 1820, an accepted and general fashion.

For women, the silhouette gradually expanded from a long, narrow one in 1800 to a full, bouffant one in 1830. The waistline, by the end of the second decade, dropped from a high bustline to its normal place. The length of skirts varied gradually from ground level in 1800 to high ankle length in the 'thirties, but from 1840 on, the feet were covered. Sleeves expanded from a small puff in 1800 to a very wide, full sleeve in 1820. The long sleeve became general in 1840.

Fig.203

COAT

1800

Fig.205

1812

Fig.206

VEST

COAT

1810

Fig.210

1821

Fig.211

Fig.208

1813

1821

Fig.212

1823

Fig.219

1830

Fig.216

1840

Fig.221

1812

Fig.222

Fig.223

Fig.217

1805

Fig.225

1842

1825

1815

Fig.224

1832

Materials

For winter use, silk, damask, *gros de Tours* (wreaths of flowers on a ribbed ground), rep, crepe lisse, taffeta, chintz, satin, *gros de Naples,* velvet, and varieties of woolen cloth were in demand. For party wear, gauze, satin, and the thinner silks were used, though velvet was never discarded altogether. However, the general taste during the first half-century favored thin, sheer materials.

For summer wear, printed muslins, chintzes, cambric, brilliantine, batiste, mousselaine, tissue bayadere, barège, and taffeta were used. Plain calicoes and the heavier cotton prints and chintzes were used by Americans in the country or in towns remote from metropolitan fashions.

Colors

Throughout this half-century, the general tendency was toward the use of light colors. Especially in the first two decades were all the light shades in demand for both daytime and evening wear. After 1820, there was a wider range, and in the 'thirties, colors became decidedly definite and deep in tone. In the 'forties, drab grays, slate gray, dun gray, deep blues, browns of various types (such as snuff brown, russet brown, and the like) were in the ascendant. Dark backgrounds with small, flowered patterns were most popular.

Among the colors listed at various times in this period are Eau de Nile, levantine, smoke, snake green, brown biscuit, Vesuvius lava, frog green, flea gray, camelopard. The last shade was in honor of a giraffe presented to Charles X of France by the Pasha of Egypt – to offset, perhaps, the agitation caused in Paris at this time by the slapping of the French consul by the Dey of Algiers.

Costume for Men – 1800–1810

Materials

Nankeen was a favorite for trousers as well as for coats. Cashmere, velveteen, broadcloth, and kerseymere (a fine knitted fabric) were favored for all seasons. In summer, trousers were often made of piqué, linen, and other heavy washable fabrics.

Colors

Pale colors were used for pantaloons, such as dove, fawn, buff, gray, dun, white, and drab. Coats were of darker shades – gray, bottle green, Spanish blue, bright blue, Vandyke brown, chestnut brown, and similar shades. Greatcoats were of olive green, brown, dark blue, or maroon.

Coat

The coat was cut in sloping lines to the rear. The tails had a pleat toward the center back, with a button emphasizing each pleat at the waistline; the pleats reached a bit below the knees. The coat was buttoned up close to the throat, and had a tall, turnover collar. This style, with certain variations, remained the model for dress wear, even to the present day (Fig. 256).

The front of the coat might also be double-breasted, in which case the coat was cut straight across at the waistline (Fig. 201   Fig. 203). For court functions, the coat was cut in a long, slanting line from the chest to the tails, and was often embroidered with gold lace along the front edges. This style was adopted later for footmen's wear.

Collar

The coat collar was cut high in the back, and turned over usually in a deep roll. The revers were usually separate, or divided from the collar by a deep notch. Napoleon favored a high, rolled-over collar with revers of a contrasting color.

Vest

The vest was waist length, or slightly longer, so that it showed beneath the coat. The bottom edge was cut straight across, or else had shallow V's in front. It was

Fig. 201

single- or double-breasted, with or without revers. The vest was made of plain cloth or silk, or of material horizontally striped, or embroidered, or quilted (Fig. 201).

Shirt

The shirt was of fine linen or lawn, fairly full, with snug sleeves. It had no frill at the cuff, but had a double frill, or jabot, down the front.

Neckwear

The collar to the shirt was high and stiffly starched. Wound about it was a full, wide cravat, or scarf, of fine linen or lawn, starched or folded in many pleats, and usually tied in a small bow in front. For the first five years of this decade, the pleats or folds were massed high about the chin. Then they decreased in size and were folded about the lower part of the collar.

Breeches

Knee breeches were in general use for formal wear until 1815, and are still correct for formal court ceremonials in European countries. The breeches were cut snug to the figure, and were buttoned or buckled below the knee, or fitted with invisible fastening (Fig. 256).

Pantaloons

Pantaloons, introduced during the French Revolution, grew rapidly in favor. The long, striped pantaloons were succeeded by a type which reached only to the calf of the leg, and were skintight. Gradually they grew longer, until they were strapped under the instep. Very tight ones were buttoned up the outer side of the leg, like gaiters. There was no fly, but two almost invisible slits on either side of the front provided an opening. Two watch fobs covered these openings. To one of these was attached a real watch, and to the other, a *fausse montre,* or dummy watch. Two small pockets at the waistband held the watches (Fig. 203).

Cloak

The *topcoat* had a high, turned-over collar, several overlapping capes, and full, long skirts. It was single- or double-breasted (Fig. 203). This coat, warm and snug, continued in favor for many years, and was adopted by coachmen and other men whose work exposed them to the elements.

Footwear

Shoes were plain and varnished, with square or pointed toes. They were flat-heeled, low at the sides, and buttoned or strapped across the instep.

Boots to the calf of the leg – *Hessian boots* – higher in front than behind, were favored, even for indoor wear. Beau Brummell is often shown wearing this type. Another boot had a snug turnover cuff of contrasting color, usually buff or gray (Fig. 201).

Gaiters were also used over the low shoes.

Stockings

White or light-colored stockings – silk for dress occasions – were worn with knee breeches or pantaloons. Dandies, however, affected striped stockings in gay colors.

Hair

The hair, in 1800, was worn an inch and a half to two inches long. It was brushed forward over the eyes and in front of the ears. A style called *à la Titus,* after the Roman emperor, emphasized the classic influence, and was an exaggeration of the above type. Powdered hair was still worn on formal occasions. Wigs were worn only by elderly gentlemen or by those with bald pates. The queue was generally loosely tied, with a few curls escaping over the ears. The side curls of the eighteenth century continued to influence hairdressing for a long time, and eventually were standardized as side whiskers (Fig. 256).

Headdress

Hats were of two types: (1) the *tricorne,* relic of the eighteenth century, still used by older men on formal occasions, or by country gentlemen; (2) the *top hat,* a variation of which is still in use today.

The tricorne, or the *cocked hat,* as it was now called, might be either three-cornered or folded into two points. The three-cornered type was plain or edged with ribbon, or with a trimming of feathers (Fig. 201). The two-pointed hat was also trimmed in this way. It was worn with the points front and back, as officers in the navy, certain court functionaries, and members of the Masonic order still wear it. Napoleon wore this type of hat with the points at the sides (see chapter XII, Fig. 188 Fig. 198).

The top hat curved outward toward the top, and the brim was slightly rolling (Fig. 201 Fig. 217). Occasionally a narrow band of ribbon was put about the crown, but no buckle was used. A variation of the top hat, used around 1805, was flatter and wider in the crown (Fig. 201 Fig. 203). Still another type had a tall crown which narrowed at the top (Fig. 201).

Ornaments and Accessories

Heavy watch fobs were usually worn in pairs – one of the watches being a dummy – hung at either side, in front. Signet rings, short canes of malacca or bamboo, and gnarled and twisted walking sticks were in fashion.

Snuffboxes, eyeglasses, gloves, and an occasional pin in the shirt frill were the usual appurtenances of the well-dressed gentleman. Though Lord Byron extolled the cigar, it did not come into use until about 1830, and then only when men were in gatherings away from ladies. Cigars were, however, manufactured at South Windsor, in Connecticut, in 1801.

Military Dress

The Napoleonic wars brought out a variety of uniforms in the various countries. For the most part, military styles followed the customary cuts of the times. Separate revers of contrasting color were utilized to indicate regimental divisions. Officers favored gold braid, cutaway coats, and very high collars. The navy, in England and America, clung to this style for dress wear for many years. Ordinary soldiers used civilian-type coats of a standard color and trimming, with crossed straps.

A *dress sword,* with or without baldric, was worn by officers. For active service the saber, hung at the waist, was used. Sashes about the waist added an ornamental touch on dress occasions. The epaulet, remnant of chain mail, was of gold braid and heavily fringed.

Since the variations of military dress are legion, in each country, the above generalizations are only indicators; for individual costumes, one must consult specific authorities.

Ecclesiastical Dress

Protestant ministers wore long, fairly full frock coats, with stock and *tab* of white linen or muslin. With these were worn knee breeches or snug pantaloons. Some of the clergy wore the cutaway coat of the day, in somber colors.

Bishops of the Church of England wore the frock coat, knee breeches, gaiters, and an apron, and the broad-brimmed, low-crowned hat mentioned above.

In this era, two men stand out as dramatic subjects – Napoleon and Beau Brummell. Napoleon (1769–1821), whose *Book of Ceremonial* is an interesting guide to the manners and customs of the day, was most particular about his dress. His clothing had to be of fine quality and fit perfectly but comfortably. His breeches were always white – of piqué in the summer, and of swanskin or cashmere in winter. The coat was of chestnut brown or dark blue, the buttons of silver. He always wore white silk stockings, flannel vest, neckcloth of fine muslin, and a black silk stock. Josephine, it is said, wanted him to wear a lace stock. An *N* was embroidered on his linen shirts and on his suspenders. His hat was very light in weight, lined with silk, and wadded. It had no tassels or plumes, but had an edging of narrow silk braid and the tricolored cockade. Napoleon habitually carried a handkerchief, a snuffbox, and a tortoise-shell box filled with anise seed and licorice ground fine. He used a boxwood toothpick dipped in opiate, and he carried a plain silver repeater watch made by Meunier. For decoration he wore the Legion of Honor – created by him in 1802 – on a red ribbon, or the Iron Cross. He wore soft riding boots or English half-boots with pantaloons. For military duty he wore the chasseur or grenadier uniform, favoring the latter. In winter he wore flannel underwear, and habitually he wore suspenders.

George Brummell (1778–1840), the *arbiter elegantiarum* of England in the days of the Prince Regent – later George IV – brought into general favor the long, snug-fitting pantaloon. It was first opened up the leg over the instep, and fastened by loops or buttons. A strap under the instep held the tight pantaloon leg in place. Later, the opening was made on the outside of the pantaloon leg, at the bottom edge, with loops or buttons for fastening. The Beau favored a dark blue coat, of conservative cutaway style, black or brass buttons, a light-colored waistcoat (perhaps two, overlapping), buckskin pantaloons, and Hessian boots, or, for variety, top boots. A beautifully clean and starched stock, so wide that it hid his face when it was unfolded, was wound about the collar in careful folds until it just touched the tip of his chin.

For evening wear, he favored a blue coat, white waistcoat, white stock, black trousers buttoned at the ankle, striped silk stockings, low, heelless slippers, and a top hat. It is said that it took three men to dress his hair, which was worn carefully brushed forward in curls about his forehead and in front of his ears. Two firms made his gloves – one, the thumbs, and the other, the fingers. Lord Byron characterized him as having "an exquisite propriety," and did not hesitate to follow his dictates in dress. He set up an enduring standard for masculine good taste and conservative styles, for subdued coloring in clothes, for clean linen, and for daily baths.

COSTUME FOR WOMEN – 1800–1810

Among the exiles driven from France by the Reign of Terror was Rose Bertin, modiste to Marie Antoinette. She settled in London and from this vantage point dictated modes for the feminine world. For the first time, costume *à l'Anglaise* dominated fashion. In France, the leaders of the salons still held sway – Madame Récamier, Madame de Staël, Madame de Rémusat, and others. The Revolution, however, brought to the front such persons as Madame Tallien and Mademoiselle Mars. After 1804, the Empress Josephine and the Bonaparte family created vogues that were interesting, if not always in the best of taste. America, always a bit behind the times (because of poor facilities for communication), modified the styles with common sense and good taste.

The discoveries at Pompeii and Herculaneum still exerted a pseudo-classic influence, and, as usual, the Greco-Roman example was a safe one to follow in times of universal uncertainty. Napoleon's Egyptian expedition added an oriental suggestion, in turban and swathed body line, to the styles of the day.

Materials

Muslin led in popularity. As Jane Austen wrote in 1801, when ordering some new clothes, "I had rather they were different, [but] they must be cambric muslin." Even pelisses, open down the front, were made of cambric muslin. Barège, chintz, and brilliantine were also used. For variety, there were gingham, tissue, gauze, lace, crepe, satin, brocade, velvet, damask, *gros de Tours, gros de Lyons,* and challis.

Colors

Lavender, dove, fawn, pale blue, pink ("Levantine"), blue and pink checks, and other combinations led in favor. Yellow (favored by Mademoiselle Mars), smoke, rose, Nile green (Napoleon's influence), mouse color, olive green, lilac, and Parma-violet were also recorded in the fashion books.

Underclothes

Women wore chemises; long, sheathlike corsets (not to reappear until 1909) which encompassed the figure from a high bust line almost to the knees; a narrow, sheathlike petticoat (or none); and scanty drawers which covered the knees.

Women and men wore long, woolen underwear in the winter. Advertisements around 1808 emphasized "drawers and vests all in one, of real lambs' wool, warranted never to shrink in the wash." (This boast has not varied in a hundred and thirty years.) In this same year appeared, in *La Belle Assemblée,* an advertisement for Pear's Soap.

Types of Dress

1. The *costume antique* with which Madame Récamier shocked London consisted of a low-bosomed gown with a very high waistline – little more than a bust confiner. This dress is preserved for us in Jacques Louis David's portrait of the lady. It was so diaphanous that, when a gown of similar style was introduced by Madame Jerome Bonaparte ("Glorious Betsy") in Philadelphia, "no one dared to look at her but by stealth." The bodice at its widest point was only eight inches deep; the bust was generously exposed; the skirt was extremely narrow, to the ground, without a pleat or gathering. There were no sleeves (though a tiny puff was added to some gowns). The material was the thinnest sarcenet and white crepe, through which the form was distinctly visible. The Greek overfold, or peplum, was often added to this type of dress (Fig. 202).

2. Another type of dress had a low neck, cut moderately square in front, and was buttoned or laced down the back. The skirt was scantily gathered, with most of the

fullness in the back. A fold or a frill concealed the very low bosom line. For the conservative, a yoke of thin lawn or silk, gathered up about the neck into a ruche, was added. The sleeve was a small puff at the shoulder line. Another variety consisted of a long, tight sleeve with a puff at the armhole (Fig. 257).

3. A high-necked dress, buttoned or looped down the front, was designed for cold weather. It had a high waistline, long sleeves with puffs at the top (or plain), and a narrow, gored skirt trimmed with bands or cords about the bottom edge. Sometimes

Fig. 202

a full sleeve, gathered top and bottom, was used; the sleeve was usually made of thin material.

4. A high-waisted bodice, V-necked, with crossed fichu or surplice, continued in favor for several years. The skirt was plain, with a puffed or narrow ruffle about the hem. It had short or long sleeves.

5. The so-called "Empire dress" (1804–15) had a square neckline, low bosom, short waistline, puffed sleeves, and gored skirt gathered slightly in the back. It often had a panel down the front, or an overdress of satin or velvet which opened down the front to show the underdress. In the back it often extended into a train, especially for evening wear. The square neck frequently was embellished with a frill of lace, which increased in width at the back of the gown (Fig. 257).

6. The redingote, or English riding-coat type, made popular during the Directory, still retained its favor. The coat portion, single- or double-breasted, was also used as an outer jacket.

To most of the above types, the Grecian overskirt, with classic border draping, can be added. The overskirt was of varied lengths, and was draped evenly or diagonally (Fig. 202).

Hair

Short curls, in wanton disarray, were fashionable during this era. A ribbon was wound about the head, or a turban, oriental style, was draped over the coiffure. Lord Byron's Greco-Turkish adventures made this style popular in England, and Napoleon's Egyptian campaign gave impetus to the same style in France. Dolly Madison, in America, carried its popularity beyond the seas (Fig. 202).

Later, the Greco-Roman and Oriental influences called for a knot at the nape of the neck, and for dangling curls.

Headdress

Caps were worn indoors by older women. They were of the baby cap style, with a frill about the face, or they were modified mobcaps.

Turbans (Fig. 202) were in great demand. They were perched on top of the head, wound about, draped and tied in intricate arrangements, and augmented with plumes, flowers, and ribbons (Fig. 221).

Hats of the tall, stiff Directory style, like men's top hats, still continued in vogue, with or without buckle, plume, or ribbon (Fig. 202). A new style, however, called the *poke bonnet* (Fig. 200   Fig. 202   Fig. 257), swept all countries, and assumed exaggerated forms. There was the round, close-fitting poke, with or without side feather; the long poke, well over the face; the wide poke, worn over a cap, with a round, flat piece behind; and the moderately large poke, with gathered or shirred crown behind.

The tall *shako hat* of the soldier, with plume in front, was adopted for horseback riding.

A flat, wide-brimmed straw or chip hat, gypsy style, was also worn. It was plain, and was tied down about the cheeks with ribbons. Sometimes it was trimmed with flowers and lace. One variety of this was called the *Lavinia*.

Veils, of gauze or silk, were carelessly draped over the hat, or over the bare head.

Cloak

For outdoor wear or for extra warmth, a short jacket, English riding-coat style, was used. It fitted over the very short bodice, and was single- or double-breasted (Fig. 202). A *spencer,* resembling a jacket without tails, was buttoned up the front to the throat and had a high collar, upright or rolled. The collar might be rolled from high in the back to a low, deep V in front.

The pelisse was a long cloak with high neck and long sleeves, the sleeves puffed or gathered slightly at the armhole. The skirt of the cloak was plain in front, but pleated in the center back (Fig. 202).

The redingote had a skirt attached to it, very long and somewhat full. The Empress Josephine had a fur-lined redingote. Another style was edged with fur.

A mantle, with hood attached, was also used, especially for evening wear. Square scarves and long, narrow scarves, plain, flowered, fringed, and embroidered, were in great demand. They were draped about the shoulders and almost touched the ground in front.

Shawls were silk, mohair, cashmere, Persian, and many other varieties. The Empress Josephine had between three and four hundred shawls in her wardrobe. Shawls were to continue in style until 1870, and even after that, for older women.

Stockings

Light-colored or white stockings of silk or lisle were pulled up over the knees and held by garters. Clocks of embroidery or lace ornamented the outside of the stocking leg.

Footwear

Shoes were without heels, very thin and low, laced across the instep and over the ankle, *à la grecque*. A small rosette might be added at the toe. Shoes matched the gown in color, or were delicately tinted to harmonize with the toilette. Light pastel shades were preferred; apple green was a favorite shade.

Ornaments and Accessories

The *yoke*, or *guimpe*, of muslin or gauze, with or without attached sleeves, was a useful adjunct to the wardrobe. Sometimes the sleeves were made in a series of puffs down the arm.

Pin tucks, cording, narrow ruffles, puffs, embroidery, pearl and bead designs, were some of the decorations used. Embroidery and beading were used on the bodice, but most of the decoration was at the hem of the skirt.

Muffs of chinchilla, beaver, or swansdown were in great demand, and an occasional long piece of fox, mole, gray squirrel, or other fur was used. Leopardskin was in demand for muffs and for short jackets.

Ruffs of lace or silk were worn about the neck, even with very low gowns. They were gathered or pleated. Reticules, called "indispensables," were hung over the arm by a long cord or ribbon. They were embroidered or spangled for dress wear.

Locket watches were also worn for dress wear. Men's fobs were used with the redingote type of dress or coat.

Gloves of kid, dull or glacé, reached from fingertip almost to the shoulder. Some were made with a triangular piece over the hand, and no thumb, so that all the fingers were left bare. *Lace mitts,* not covering the fingers, or only halfway covering them, came partly up the forearm.

Parasols, sunshades, and eyeglasses were carried by those who wished to be considered fashionable. Tall Spanish combs were also used.

For jewelry, cameos were most popular, and were especially favored by the Empress Josephine. Garnets were next in favor, then diamonds, emeralds, and other stones. Jewelry came in sets, including brooches (to pin up the Grecian-type sleeves and overdress), earrings, necklaces, bracelets, chains, and other pieces. Serpent bracelets emphasized the Greco-Egyptian styles.

Mourning

Bombazine or crepe was used for mourning dresses which were, at this time, most elaborate. Black gossamer satin or lawn was also used. Men used black broadcloth or dull-finished materials for mourning.

The Empress Josephine dominated fashion in this period, although Pauline, Napoleon's sister, tried hard to outdo her sister-in-law. Once, when Pauline had ordered a vivid green dress for a party given by Josephine, the Empress, hearing the news, had the reception room done over in deep blue, thereby killing the effect of Pauline's gown.

In keeping with Napoleon's determination to further French industry was his order to the Empress to use silk, woven at Lyons, instead of the linen and muslins she favored. Josephine's unwilling obedience to this decree led to a vogue for silk ball gowns, which has continued to the present day.

The Empress, however, had more than two hundred white muslin dresses, in spite of the Emperor's decree. These were only a fraction of her extensive wardrobe. She changed clothes four and five times a day. It is not remarkable, then, that she owned several hundred dresses, 558 pairs of white silk stockings, 520 pairs of shoes (she never wore a pair but once), 500 lace-trimmed chemises, 252 hats, and 400 shawls. She spent three thousand francs a year for rouge and thousands more for perfumes, but she had only two flannel petticoats and two pairs of drawers. Her campaign for beauty, however, led eventually to defeat. An Austrian queen preceded her in power. An Austrian queen succeeded her in power. After Versailles came Malmaison. No artifice can stay the hand of fate.

COSTUME FOR MEN – 1810–1820

In this period, which witnessed the restoration of the Bourbons under Louis XVIII in France, and the growing power of America under the "Virginia dynasty," men's dress varied only in minor details (Fig. 256).

Coat

In 1810, coattails were shortened till they reached barely to the knees in the back. The collar had a deep, padded roll, which was extremely high in the back. It was set several inches away from the neck. The notch between collar and lapel was deep, and was placed far down in front, over the chest (Fig. 204 Fig. 205). Sleeves were moderately full, and were gathered into the armhole. The sleeve extended well over the wrist and had no cuff.

Vest

The vest was cut with a high, upstanding collar which was left unbuttoned toward the top in order to show the stock and shirt frill. Another style of vest was made double-breasted, with large, pointed lapels flaring out over the coat front. Flowered brocade and horizontally striped material were in demand for vests.

Fig. 204

Shirt

The shirt was made of fine linen or lawn, and had a moderately full sleeve with a modest cuff attached. The shirt front had a plain band down the center, with buttons or jeweled pins. For more elaborate effects, ruffles of linen or lawn, varying in width from a half inch to an inch and a half, were added to the central band. The shirt sometimes had a series of four or five tucks vertically placed at either side of the center.

Neckwear

Stocks were moderately high, and were of white or black linen, silk, or satin. A frilled jabot was added to the plain stock, if desired (Fig. 204). It was also customary to twist a fold of the material about the stock and tie it in a loose knot in front, with the pointed ends hanging down.

Trousers

Knee breeches were still in use, though long trousers, or pantaloons, predominated. The latter were usually made of *stockinet,* a knitted material which fitted the figure closely. The pantaloons were fitted into calf-length boots for semi-military occasions or for hunting.

For formal occasions, a coat with standing collar and with embroidery down either side was used, together with a light-colored or flowered vest, knee breeches, white hose, and low slippers. The stock was white, with a jabot or frill, and the shirt was ruffled (Fig. 206).

Cloak

Topcoats or greatcoats were cut full-skirted; pockets were hidden in the pleats in the rear (Fig. 205). The collar was tall, commonly of velvet, and usually surmounted one or more capes over the shoulders. Silver or brass buttons fastened the coat in front, in either single- or double-breasted style. Plum, purple, and bottle green were the colors preferred; the material was some smooth woolen fabric like broadcloth.

Footwear

After 1815, *Wellington trousers* were popular. They were long and form-fitting. With them were worn *Wellington boots,* of calfskin, reaching almost to the knee. The trousers were pulled down over them and fastened by a strap under the instep. Shoes (or boots) were of black leather and were pulled on with straps. Plain or embroidered gaiters were fashionable.

Hair

Hair arrangement remained much the same as in the previous decade, curls piled high over the forehead being still the predominant mode (Fig. 222).

Headdress

Hats varied in shape. Some had very low crowns with curved brims; some had very high crowns, wider at the top, with drooping, narrow brims. The high-crowned hats were more generally used. A cockade, with a feather, was adopted by certain fashionables of the time. The two-pointed cocked hat was still in general use.

Costume for Women – 1810–1820

The silhouette followed its logical trend. Bodices were cut with lower waistlines; skirts were made fuller about the bottom edge and a trifle shorter; shoulders became broader and sleeves acquired a larger puff than in the previous decade (Fig. 257).

Bodice

High necks returned to favor, after the extreme décolleté of Revolutionary days and their aftermath. Bodices were cut high about the neck, and fastened in the back. If a low-cut bodice were worn, it often had an additional neck cape of the same material, or of some suitable stuff, which was cut plain, or with ruffles, puffs, or frills (Fig. 206 Fig. 207 Fig. 208). Bodices were trimmed with braid, embroidery, lace, and ribbons. Flower embroidery in silk was most fashionable. Sleeves were short and puffed, or long and tight, though some more elaborate patterns showed sleeves which consisted of a series of puffs (Fig. 207). Deep cuffs, or ruffles, extended well over the hand. The slightly lowered waistline was accentuated by a narrow ribbon, tied in front; this style was adopted usually for party dresses.

Skirt

The skirt was cut in gores, fuller about the bottom edge than in the former decade. Varying trimmings were used about the bottom. Pleats, tucks, points, ruffles, puffs, and bands of fur were common; embroidered bands were used on the finer dresses. The row of trimming became two or more; these crept higher up the skirt until, by 1820, they reached the knee. In France, this trimming was employed to reflect political affiliations. To show allegiance to Louis XVIII, ladies wore eighteen tucks about the skirt. To show Orleanist leanings, ladies wore a bunch of royal purple violets.

An overskirt, reaching almost to the hem of the dress skirt, came into fashion. It did not ape the Grecian peplum, or overfold, as formerly, but was cut like the skirt beneath, with a straight, even hem (Fig. 208 Fig. 257).

Cloak

The spencer, frequently fur-trimmed, continued popular, but sometimes vaunted a short peplum. The long pelisse, buttoned or looped down the front, and the *witzchoura* were also in demand. The latter, fashionable around 1817, was a very handsome long wrap, lined with fur; it had a cape over the shoulders and, in some instances, a hood

Fig. 207

was attached for extra warmth. The *canezou*, a short jacket with muslin sleeves, was used for a light wrap in mild weather.

Footwear

Shoes, with high sides, buckled on the outside of the leg, were worn instead of the half-boots, which were used only in cold weather when low slippers were not desirable.

Hair

The hair continued to be arranged *à la grecque,* but the knot was placed on top of the head. Loose curls dangled at either side of the face. Feathers, strands of pearls, and other ornaments were used to accentuate the coiffure for formal occasions.

Headdress

The poke bonnet was still the rage, but in this decade it acquired a fairly large, curved brim and a very deep tall crown (Fig. 207 Fig. 208). It was adorned with feathers, ribbons, and flowers, and was called by such names as *chapeau spencer* and *Henry IV* (the latter name bestowed because of the white plume that bedecked it).

One type, called the *English drawn bonnet,* had a lace veil which could be drawn across the face by means of a pulley. (This is the bonnet worn by Miss Henrietta in *Quality Street,* which so intrigued Captain Brown.)

Plaids were fashionable for small hats or caps. Caledonian bonnets or caps, of various tartans or plaids trimmed with feathers, were popular with young women and girls. Turbans were fashionable with married women, especially the Turkish style of turban with a feather or aigrette.

Caps were used primarily for indoor wear, except by the very young. Some caps were fastened under the chin; some had frills about the face; some were draped on the back of the head; and some were perched on top of the head, like the *cornet cap.* Muslin, lawn, lace, ribbons, flowers, wheat ears, streamers of ribbon – all of these decorations, singly or in combinations, added to the attractiveness of the caps. Until late in the nineteenth century, married women and ladies "of a certain age" continued to wear caps indoors. In *Cranford* there is drawn the delightful picture of Miss Matty wearing two caps, the "company" one atop the other. Jane Austen, in 1813, expressed a desire for a white satin cap with a white flower over the left ear, "like Harriet Byron's."

Ornaments and Accessories

These included, in addition to those already in vogue, the snuffbox. It is related that Dolly Madison offered Henry Clay her snuffbox during a social function and that the box was made of precious metal, delicately tinted. A long feather or fur boa was another innovation.

During this era, outdoor sports became the vogue, and consequently riding habits, bonnets with visors *à la jockey,* and riding crops became a regular part of the wardrobe.

Costume for Men – 1820–1830

By 1820, men's dress had acquired a dashing air. "Three-bottle men" exchanged stories over port and walnuts around the polished mahogany table. Clubs were fashionable; Almack's, in London, had a carefully chosen roster and excluded even the Duke of Wellington from a ball when he failed to wear full evening dress. The waltz (introduced into England in 1813), the polka, the quadrille, the galop, and the lancers held society in their rhythmic embrace and made dancing dress an important item.

Coat

The coat had a rolling collar, padded and very high in the back. The collar was frequently of velvet and blended into the deep revers which tapered off into the lower point of the coat in front (Fig. 210). A row of buttons from the armhole to the waist added a decorative touch. The tails to the coat were rather narrow and very long. The *Jean de Bry,* a fashionable evening coat, had extremely long tails, and was made of very fine material. The "Uncle Sam" of popular conception wears a coat of this type.

Fig. 209

Sleeves

The sleeve gathered into the armhole continued in vogue; there was even a slight puff to emphasize the fullness. The wrists were well covered by the plain cuff (Fig. 256).

Vest

The vest was worn crossed over, surplice style, with plain or rolled revers; it was either single- or double-breasted. Often two vests were worn, one over the other (Fig. 256).

Shirt

Shirts of fine linen or lawn were made plain, tucked, or ruffled, though the last style was most favored. The cuffs were attached to the sleeves and were fastened with two buttons.

Neckwear

The stock (white or black, though white was preferred) was draped smoothly about a high, standing collar with starched, upright points at either side of the chin. The ends of the stock were folded over and puffed under the chin. A pearl pin was sometimes used to hold it in place (Fig. 209   Fig. 256).

Trousers

The trousers were fashioned somewhat full about the waistline, but they were very long in the leg, extending well over the instep, and were fastened by a strap under the foot.

Cloak

The full, long cloak with rolling collar and deep revers often had a cape attached, which was lined with a silk of brilliant hue; this cloak was worn for evening or dress wear as well as for daytime (Fig. 209).

Hair

The hair was worn rather long and curly, and brushed high over the forehead, with curls in front of the ears (Fig. 223). Beef tallow and bears' grease gave the necessary luster to the locks.

Headdress

The crown of the hat curved out widely at the top, and had a rolling brim. A ribbon band encircled the crown about the bottom, and was fastened with a buckle placed center front. Beaver and felt were the materials most commonly used for hats. Low-crowned hats were also worn, especially by country squires (Fig. 211).

This period of dress is best exemplified in America by such outstanding figures as Andrew Jackson, Henry Clay, Daniel Webster, John C. Calhoun, and the western pioneers like David Crockett. The essential details of their dress are summed up in the costume of "Uncle Sam," eliminating its patriotic coloring. Webster, it is said, made of dress an active ally when delivering his famous speech for the Constitution in 1830. He wore the old blue and buff dress, relic of the Revolutionary days, and in this way aroused the patriotic fervor of his audience.

COSTUME FOR WOMEN – 1820–1830

Bodice

The waistline almost reached normal during this period. The bodice, which was buttoned either front or back, had a wide, drooped shoulder line accentuated by bretelles, ruffles, or other drapery (Fig. 211 Fig. 212). The slightly raised waistline was emphasized by a sash of plain, embroidered, flowered, or plaid ribbon, which was tied in the front in a bow, with long streamers. Belts of ribbon or silk were also fastened in front with a buckle or garniture (Fig. 211 Fig. 212 Fig. 213). All fullness was drawn down from the shoulders toward the waist, and held in by the belt or sash (both fairly wide). This added to the trimness of the figure, and emphasized the wide shoulder line and slender waistline (Fig. 257).

The neckline was round and close-fitting; a ruching, single or double, an inch or two in diameter, added a touch of relief (Fig. 213).

Sleeves

The long sleeve with a puff at the shoulder was popular in the early 'twenties; toward the end of the decade, the sleeve became much fuller, increasing in size toward the low shoulder line; the fullness was held in at the wrist by a tight band or cuff.

Skirt

The skirt grew steadily wider and shorter toward the end of the decade; the long skirt was still in vogue for formal wear. All trimming was applied toward the bottom of the skirt. The gored skirt, in general use around 1820 (Fig. 211), gave way to the gathered skirt toward the 'thirties.

Cloak

The short shoulder cape continued fashionable; it usually had a turndown collar, with a bow and two long streamers or panels down the front (Fig. 213).

Footwear

Shoe styles varied little from those of the past decade. Stockings were also of the same kind as formerly.

Hair

The hair was elaborately arranged at this time. It was parted in the middle, with curls on the forehead and down either side of the face. The back hair was gathered

1820

Fig. 213

in a knot high up on top of the head. For dress wear, it was arranged in artificial loops, wired to stand upright, and adorned with ribbons, feathers, wheat ears, and other decorations (Fig. 213   Fig. 257).

Headdress

Colored bonnets were the rage. A cottage style, tied under the chin, frequently had a broad *blond,* or strip of lace, edging it (Fig. 211). Leghorn and other chips and straws were very fashionable. Black hats also were returning to favor; they were made of silk, cloth, or straw (Fig. 211   Fig. 212   Fig. 213).

Ornaments and Accessories

These reflected the taste of the former era.

Materials

Highland tartan, striped silks, and satins, plumed velvet, rep, and sprigged muslins were among the most frequently chosen fabrics. Plaids were very popular, and lace in many varieties was used for trimming. Dark-hued and black materials were more in use than formerly.

During this time classic and historic styles were aped, but not with any degree of accuracy. Fanny Kemble, famous English actress, in 1829, played Juliet in a fashionable ball gown of white satin with a long train, a girdle of brilliants adding the sole theatrical touch. Brilliants and spangles, incidentally, had been almost indispensable for theatrical costume since the days of the Restoration, as the indoor theaters of the time were so poorly lighted that some artificial decoration was needed to make the costumes stand out. Tinsel and spangles were metallic aids to light up the costumes. This gave rise to the expressions "tinsel" and "spangles" used in connection with the stage and with actors. Even in Shakespeare's day a material called *tylsent,* or *tinsell,* was recorded time and again in the lists of garments for players.

COSTUME FOR MEN – 1830–1840

In Europe, this was the romantic era; in America, it was the eloquent era. In Europe, men were fighting for national and political freedom on the battlefields; in America, they were fighting for freedom with equal ardor, if not with equal danger, in state and federal halls. The legal strategy of John Marshall bulwarked the Constitution, and the eloquent booming of Daniel Webster held internal war at bay for more than two decades.

Coat

The coat was cut to fit snugly into the rather low waistline. The coattails were curved sharply away from the hips and fell to the knees behind. The coat collar was rolled to a high peak at the back of the neck and had deep, sloping revers which curved out to show a wide expanse of shirt front. At either side of the coat in front, two buttons were placed vertically. The sleeves were gathered into the armhole. The general effect of this coat was to give to the figure a slender, almost effeminate appearance (Fig. 256).

Another type of coat had straight lines. The waist was only semi-fitting, and the skirts to the coat lapped over in front. This type was also used for a topcoat.

Vest

The vest (or waistcoat, as it was called) was rich, plain, or flowered. Count d'Orsay, one of the leaders of Continental fashions, favored white waistcoats. The vest was made single- or double-breasted, with or without revers. The waistcoat, like the coat, was buttoned either high or low (Fig. 214).

Shirt

The prevalent style of deep revers on waistcoat and coat allowed for a wide expanse of shirt front. Pleated and frilled shirts, of fine linen or lawn, were a matter of pride

Fig. 214

with those who were meticulously groomed. Sometimes a black silk shirt was worn (Fig. 214).

Outer Coat

The greatcoat was very full and long. The skirt to it was gathered in large pleats in the back (Fig. 214). The high rolling collar was of velvet or fur. The front of the coat was adorned with fancy frogs or large, round buttons of silver. A deep cape to the hip line was often attached to the coat.

Neckwear

The stock, wrapped neatly about a very tall, upstanding collar, was tied in a wide bow in front.

Trousers

The trousers were cut very full about the hips. They were close-fitting about the leg for dress wear, but more loosely cut for daytime wear. They were fastened under the instep.

Hair

A very exaggerated high pompadour was in fashion, brushed forward over the forehead, with side whiskers in front of the ears. These were sometimes extended about the chin in a beard.

Headdress

Very tall, straight hats were used – the "chimney pot" style. Sometimes these sloped in toward the top. Beaver was the favored material, gray or white for daytime, black for evening. Caps were used, especially in winter, when they were frequently fur-lined (Fig. 214).

Costume for Women – 1830–1840

Types of Dress

In this romantic period, women's dress emphasized curves in billowing repetitions. Enormous balloonlike sleeves gave fictitious value to shoulders which were genteelly unfitted to bear the slightest burdens (Fig. 257).

Bodice

The dropped shoulder line of the bodice was accentuated by crescent-shaped cushions, ruffles, or caps extending over the sleeve (Fig. 215). A trim belt or sash

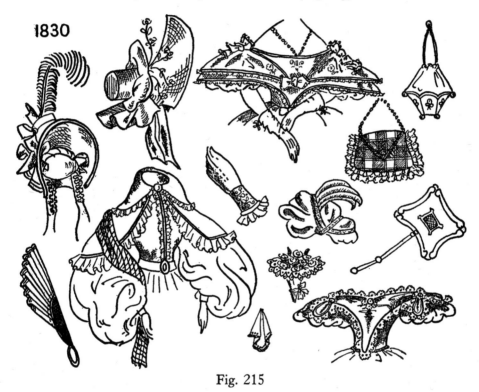

Fig. 215

confined the waist. Horizontal pleats across the bosom added to its apparent width, and a similar effect was achieved by the fitted-in waistline (Fig. 216).

Sleeves

The sleeves overshadowed all else (Fig. 215 Fig. 257). Large, balloonlike puffs which, in extreme cases, actually rubbed against each other behind, gave to the figure a grotesquely wide appearance, which the full skirts emphasized. Elbow sleeves were in fashion also, and another style used had a full puff above and a tight sleeve below.

As previously mentioned, the excessive width of the shoulder was further emphasized by ruffles, shoulder caps, and crescents; a curve of trimming was also used, beginning at the center front of the waistline and extending over the wide, dropped shoulder line of the sleeve.

Skirt

The skirt was usually gathered, though gored skirts were still used. The width was about three yards, though it might be four yards or more. The length depended on the age of the wearer; young women wore skirts ankle or even "shoetop" length; older women wore them ground-length. The trimming consisted of bands of ribbon or ruffles about the bottom edge. Panels down the front were also used, in imitation of the sixteenth-century panels or those favored by Marie Antoinette.

Cloak

The canezou was still worn, as were also the various types of long cloak, like the Wickla and the Algerian *burnoose,* which could be easily draped over the full, wide sleeves.

Scarves, however, and shawls were most in demand. The *bayadere* was a long, narrow, silk or lace scarf, sometimes fringed at the ends (Fig. 215). Chinese crepe shawls were popular, but the cashmere shawl was most in demand, a vogue that continued for thirty years at least.

Hair

The styles of the previous era, with the knot *à la chinois,* continued in vogue. A revival of Renaissance styles was also attempted. The hair was parted in the middle and smoothed back over the ears, with a ferronnière, or jeweled band about the forehead *à la da Vinci.* A filmy veil was also draped over the back of the head, *à la Botticelli.* Another style is shown in Fig. 224.

Headdress

In order, perhaps, to balance the wide sleeves, the hats were very broad of brim, with elaborate decorations of large bows, feathers, flowers, and ruffled lace edgings about the brim. The materials were cloth, velvet, silk, rice-straw, and other straws. In width of brim and sweep of decoration, hats were not to be so elaborate until the twentieth century (Fig. 257).

Caps were still worn, but only for indoor use. Poke bonnets, with very wide, flaring brims and towering ornament, continued in style. Turbans also maintained their vogue (Fig. 215).

Ornaments and Accessories

Aprons, of dark blue or black silk, gathered full about the waist and reaching to the knees, were in demand, especially in America. During the Jackson campaign, ladies who championed the cause of "Old Hickory" wore aprons with his portrait upon them.

Fans, long gloves, mitts, and small, square, flat pocketbooks were in common use. Sets of brooches, fastened at the neck and down the front of the high-necked bodice, or at intervals across the wide edge of the low-necked gown, were in great demand.

Fur, including mink, kolinsky, and that of other short-haired animals, was used for long, narrow boas or scarves, and also for trimming.

Harriet Martineau, visiting America about this time, carried her stockings, scarf, mitts, jewelry, and soft silk shoes in the pockets of her dress. These pockets, whose vogue increased with the advent of the full, gathered skirts, were long slits, to which were sewn great pouches on the inside. The gathers hid the openings. If Miss Martineau could carry so much in her pockets, it is strange that she overlooked the added capacity of her sleeves. What a wealth of treasure-trove she could have stored in their capacious depths!

Harriet Martineau brought her fashions on her back, so to speak; but America was developing fashion ideas worth expressing and preserving. The vehicle for this expression was a new magazine, published by Louis A. Godey of Philadelphia, and called *Godey's Lady's Book*. The first issue appeared in 1830.

Costume for Men – 1840–1850

Until 1840, men's clothes reflected a fairly wide range of color, though by degrees the shades subsided into soft fawns, grays, blues, and soft greens. After 1840, however, somber hues predominated. Coat and trousers were still of different colors, but darker shades for trousers came into use.

Coat

The coat, though still cut on the general lines prevalent since the beginning of the century, was squarer in outline, and the shoulders had less slope. The tails to the coat were short and broad, with several pleats at the back topped by buttons. The collar was fairly low and snug, with a slight roll. It joined the lapel, which tapered gradually toward the waist. A notch marked the joining. Sleeves were set in smoothly at the shoulders, with few gathers (Fig. 256).

Another type of coat had a narrow, turnover collar, narrow lapels, a row of buttons down either side of the front, snug, smooth-fitting sleeves, and a waistline that curved in sharply to the figure. The skirt to the coat, unlike earlier styles, was cut in one piece with the waist. This led to the long, straight frock coat of the next decade (Fig. 218).

Vest

The vest, as usual, followed the line of the coat and was low in the waistline. It was snug-fitting and single- or double-breasted. The material was often a plaid or a check. It was sometimes worn with the lower button at the waistline left unbuttoned.

Shirt

Shirts were starched, pleated, frilled, tucked, or shirred. The generous expanse was marked with fancy buttons or studs down the front.

Trousers

Trousers in this decade were slightly gathered about the waist for dress occasions; plain, moderately full trousers were in common use for daily wear. Dark shades, plaids, and checks of subdued patterns were preferred, though fawn, tan, and gray trousers were still worn with plain dark coats for formal wear. For evening wear, black or gray trousers were proper. The trousers were cut narrow for the full length of the leg, and were still fastened under the instep. It was during the 'forties that the

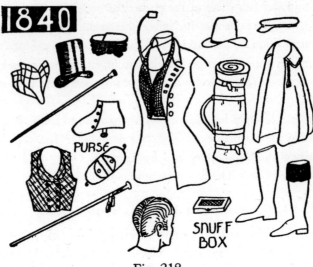

Fig. 218

modern trouser opening was standardized, the front flap, or *fly,* taking the place of the double slits or side openings.

Neckwear

Collars were quite high, curved out in front under the chin, or with points protruding upward at the sides (Fig. 256). A tall, turned-down collar was also correct for daytime wear. The points of this collar folded over the stock in front (Fig. 225).

Though the white cravat was still draped about the collar, or stock, and tied in front, black satin and taffeta cravats superseded it in favor. These were folded loosely about the stock, or puffed in front. Another style of black cravat consisted of a band about one and one-quarter inches wide tied in a flat bow in front, with pointed ends. The knot of the bow lay flat and square (Fig. 218). White cravats were still correct for dress wear.

Footwear

As in the former era, shoes had rather narrow, pointed toes. In addition, *spats* became very popular. Boots were used for riding.

Outer Coat

The topcoat, fashioned much like the suit coat, had a moderately high collar, which fitted snugly against the neck. The coat was usually worn buttoned high at the neck. A breast pocket for the handkerchief, straight or diagonal in line, appeared. Pockets were also placed in the moderately full skirt of the coat. The topcoat was often shorter than the suit coat, disclosing the tails of the coat behind.

A circular cape, with broad, turnover collar, like the Cavalier cape, was used for evening wear; it was tied at the throat with cords, and reached just below the knees (Fig. 218). It was frequently lined with a brilliant crimson, purple, or green satin.

Hair

The hair was worn parted on the side, brushed in a wave over the forehead, curled over the ears, and long and curly on the nape of the neck (Fig. 225). Pointed mustaches of moderate size were worn, with or without a closely trimmed circle of beard. Toward the end of this decade, side whiskers were worn, with clean-shaven chins. Sometimes the part in the hair extended from the forehead line to the nape of the neck in back (Fig. 218).

Headdress

Hats were tall and perpendicular, with moderately wide, dipped brims (Fig. 218). They were made of gray or black beaver. If a band were used, it was very narrow, without a buckle. Occasionally a slanting crown was seen.

Ornaments and Accessories (Fig. 218)

Canes, snuffboxes, eyeglasses, gaiters, gloves, and other gentlemanly appurtenances were in demand as accessories.

This was the period of revolutions in Germany, Italy, and elsewhere, of the gold rush in California, and of the Mexican War. Rough and ready wear began to take the place of fashionable dress. The covered wagons that crawled across the western plains of America were filled with men wearing plaid or checked shirts, canvas, corduroy, or denim trousers, wide, flopping hats, straight top boots, and serviceable leather belts with holsters attached. Even in Europe, men turned to plainer styles, to squarer lines, as evidence of a serious and practical trend. The age of elegance was vanishing; the age of progress and business expansion was at hand.

Costume for Women – 1840–1850

Types of Dress (Fig. 219   Fig. 220   Fig. 257)

Bodice

The long waist, common in men's costume, was added to that of women. It often had inner lacings, to insure a smooth fit; boning was also used for the same purpose. The line of the waist dipped modestly in front, in a V. This narrow V was accented by pleatings or folds gathered in at the dip and spreading out, fan-fashion, over the bust and to the shoulders. A dropped shoulder line emphasized the long, narrow waist. The neck of the dress was cut round, and was moderately low, even for afternoon and daytime wear. Bretelles, narrow at the waist, curved out in a wide band over the deeply-dropped shoulder line. High-necked bodices were worn by older women. These had low, turnover collars fastened with a brooch in front.

To fill in the low neck, a chemisette was used; it was of lawn, lace, or net, puffed, or ruffled, or tucked, and variously trimmed. It continued in vogue for over a half-century.

Sometimes the back of the bodice also was pointed at the waistline. If the waistline were straight around, a ribbon belt or buckled band was used.

For evening wear, the bodice was cut quite low, with a V dip in front. The neck-line was rounded, or straight across. It was trimmed with a deep ruffle, or *bertha,* with puffs or bias folds.

Sleeves

Sleeves subsided to modest proportions. Though a gathered sleeve was also used, in one or more puffs along the arm, the tight sleeve prevailed; a cap, or one or more ruffles at the top, emphasized the dropped shoulder line, together with the bretelles,

1840

Fig. 220

which extended over the shoulder. Toward the end of the decade, an oversleeve appeared, open below the elbow to show a full white undersleeve.

Skirt

The skirt was quite full, held out by *crinoline,* a fine horsehair weave (*crin* means "horsehair"), and, as the word indicates, it was combined with linen. The word later denoted the garment made of this material, or even a hoop skirt, when hoops of whalebone were used instead of horsehair. Deep ruffles, puffs, fur bands, soutache braid, or passementerie (appliquéd embroidery) decorated the bottom of the skirt, which might be four or five yards in diameter. Sometimes there was an overskirt, with the front panel variously decorated (Fig. 257). The full skirt trimmed with three or more ruffles appeared at this time (Fig. 219).

Cloak

Shawls were still in demand, cashmere, Persian, lace, knitted, and crocheted. Wraps, semi-fitted in the back and over the hips, with two long front panels (Fig. 220), vied in favor with a narrow bayadere scarf or with a deep, circular cloak, semi-fitted in the back. This cloak reached to the knees and had a deep, turned-down collar. Sometimes it was fashioned of fur and had a rounded muff to match.

A new jacket called the *Kasaveck* was waist length, close-fitting, with wide, bell-shaped sleeves. For warmth, it was made of wool or wadded cashmere. Another variety similar to this, but reminiscent of the Zouave type, was also worn.

Footwear

Shoes were narrow, with blunt tips. A varnished leather shoe came in at this time.

Hair

The hair was worn parted in the middle and smoothed down over the temples. It was puffed slightly at the sides and fastened in a knot low on the nape of the neck. Two or three curls might be worn at either side of the face or nestled against the neck at the sides. This style was especially used for evening wear. A bandeau of rosebuds or a cluster of several flowers over the ears was adopted for formal dress. Coronets of hair, braided or twisted, were made fashionable by Queen Victoria. Hair nets were worn over the side puffs and also over the knot behind (Fig. 220).

Headdress

The poke bonnet was again in the highest favor. In general, the shape was a wide, curved scoop like a coal scuttle, well over the face, with a round disk at the back about the size of a small saucer. Lace ruffles sometimes edged the face or lined the hood. Feathers, lace, flowers, and ribbons trimmed the bonnets in endless varieties of arrangement. The bonnets were usually tied with fairly wide ribbons under the chin, at the side (Fig. 219   Fig. 220   Fig. 257).

Caps, of many shapes and arrangements, were draped far back on the head, with lappets, or streamers, at the side. They were worn even by young married women and, in fact, by all women "over a certain age," the "certain age" being very uncertain! However, the caps were very becoming, and the "dear Queen" favored them; so they were in great demand.

Hats were still used, especially the leghorn, with a wide, flapping brim, trimmed with ribbon tied in a long bow at the back. A small hat of velvet, felt, or straw was also designed at this time; it had a narrow brim that dipped front and back; the sole decoration was a small bouquet of flowers at center front.

Ornaments and Accessories (Fig. 220)

Mittens of lace, as well as short and long kid gloves, were in constant use. The short gloves had turnover edges, and were laced up the wrist. Also, the sunshade or parasol was indispensable; it was a small silk affair, with the handle in sections, adjustable at various angles. Green and black were the favorite colors for sunshades.

Long *pantalettes* had come into general use by this time, and were used by grownups as well as by children. They were trimmed with lace, ribbons, and other frills, and showed quite a variety of styles.

Brooches, miniatures, clusters of garnets, mosaics, and lockets of all descriptions were worn. Seed pearl jewelry, sewed with white horsehair, came in sets of earrings, brooches, necklaces, and bracelets. (See Fig. 220 and Fig. 257 for further illustrations of the period ornaments and accessories.)

Equestrian Dress

Horseback riding was fashionable among young ladies. An equestrian costume was made of black, dark green, or blue broadcloth. The coat was cut snug to the figure, with long, tight sleeves fitted into a normal armhole. A slightly rolling collar and lapels of satin added a contrasting touch. The coat was not buttoned together, but was left open to show a white cloth or linen vest which could be buttoned from neck to waist, but which was usually left unbuttoned part way down the front. The skirt, cut to allow for sitting side-saddle, was full and so long that it almost swept the ground when the lady was seated on the horse. The hat had a tall, straight, stiff, round crown, and a narrow brim, which was slightly dipped in front. About the brim was draped a diaphanous flowing veil that hung to the waist behind (Fig. 220).

Mourning

Among the better classes, mourning was very elaborate. Jane Austen tells of wearing bombazine and crepe, with a pelisse lined with black ("I shall take my cloak for the lining," she added).

Costume for Children – 1800–1850

Children wore clothes cut on the lines of their elders'. Little boys wore long trousers, full about the waist, and frequently gathered into a fitted band which had a dip front and back. By 1840, the trousers were buttoned down the front. Shirts were cut full, with tucks and ruffles, and followed the general lines of women's waists rather than those of men's shirts. Hats had very wide or very narrow brims. Caps with pointed visors were popular.

Little girls wore the same types of dress as their mothers, though they were made more plainly. Pantalettes were used throughout the half-century (Fig. 207   Fig. 213).

Costume for the Lower Classes – 1800–1850

Workers, servants, and the lower classes in general wore garments similar in cut to the styles of a former decade – in other words, they usually wore the outmoded garments of their employers or else clothes cut on old-fashioned or conservative lines. For men, plain tail coats, or skirted coats, with medium-full trousers were usual; for women, plain bodices, along the general lines suggested by a previous era, but with no ornamentation, and skirts full enough and short enough for working purposes were used. Caps were of the mobcap variety, with fairly wide, full ruffles about the face. As these varied, however, only a general idea can be given.

1805

1825

1835

1845

PLATE IX   CHAPTER XIII

1856

1866

1876

1896

PLATE X   CHAPTER XIV

CHAPTER XIV

THE NINETEENTH CENTURY
1850-1900

IMPORTANT PEOPLE AND EVENTS

ENGLAND

Rulers

Victoria
(1837–1901)

Notable People

Robert Browning
Elizabeth Barrett
    Browning
William Makepeace
    Thackeray
George Eliot
    (Mary Ann Evans
    Lewes Cross)
John Ruskin
Herbert Spencer
Dante Gabriel Rossetti
William Morris
Algernon Charles
    Swinburne
Alfred, Lord Tennyson
Robert Louis Stevenson
George Meredith
George Du Maurier
Holman Hunt
Sir Laurence Alma-
    Tadema
Sir Edward Burne-
    Jones
Sir John Everett Millais
George Frederick
    Watts
Julia Arthur
Edmund Kean
Fanny Kemble
Sir Henry Irving
Ellen Terry
Nellie Melba
    (Nellie Armstrong,
    née Mitchell)

Lillian Nordica
    (Lillian Norton)
Sir William S. Gilbert
Sir Arthur Sullivan
Joseph Lister
Cecil Rhodes
William Ewart Glad-
    stone
Benjamin Disraeli
Charles Darwin

FRANCE

Government

Second Empire
    (Napoleon III)
    (1852–70)
Third Republic
    (1870–)

Notable People

Guy de Maupassant
Émile Zola
Gustave Flaubert
Victorien Sardou
Jean Baptiste Camille
    Corot
Jean François Millet
Jean Louis Meissonier
Édouard Manet
Claude Monet
Paul Cézanne
Vincent Van Gogh
Paul Gauguin
Sarah Bernhardt
Alfred Dreyfus
Louis Pasteur

RUSSIA

Notable People

Ivan Turgeniev

Leo Tolstoy
Feodor Mikhailovich
    Dostoievsky
Anton Chekhov
Nikolai Gogol
Petr Ilich Tchaikovsky

ITALY

Rulers

Victor Emmanuel II
    (first king of united
    Italy)
    (1861–78)
Humbert
    (1878–1900)

Notable People

Gabriele D'Annunzio
Eleonora Duse
Pope Pius IX
Pope Leo XIII

UNITED STATES OF
AMERICA

Presidents

Millard Fillmore
    (1850–53)
Franklin Pierce
    (1853–57)
James Buchanan
    (1857–61)
Abraham Lincoln
    (1861–65)
Andrew Johnson
    (1865–69)
Ulysses S. Grant
    (1869–77)
Rutherford B. Hayes
    (1877–81)

James A. Garfield
    (1881)
Chester A. Arthur
    (1881–85)
Grover Cleveland
    (1885–89)
Benjamin Harrison
    (1889–93)
Grover Cleveland
    (1893–97)
William McKinley
    (1897–1901)

Notable People

Robert E. Lee
William T. Sherman
Thomas ("Stonewall")
    Jackson
Horace Greeley
Alexander Graham
    Bell
Cyrus McCormick
Samuel F. B. Morse
Thomas Alva Edison
Luther Burbank
Clara Barton
Susan B. Anthony
Herman Melville
Harriet Beecher Stowe
Mark Twain
    (Samuel Clemens)
O. Henry
    (Sydney Porter)
Walt Whitman
Henry James
Bret Harte
Edward MacDowell
Mary Baker Eddy
John Hay
James G. Blaine

Elihu Root

William Jennings
Bryan

Mary Anderson

Laurence Barrett

Edwin Booth

Helena Modjeska

Lola Montez
(Eliza Gilbert)

Fanny Davenport

Timothy Cole

George Inness

SCANDINAVIA

Notable People

Hans Christian Ander-
sen

Henrik Ibsen

Björnstjerne Björnson

August Strindberg

HOLLAND

Queen Wilhelmina
(1890–   )

GERMANY

Rulers

Wilhelm I
(King of Prussia,
1861–88; Emperor of
Germany, 1871–88)

Wilhelm II
(1888–1918)

Notable People

Heinrich Schliemann

Arthur Schopenhauer

Hermann Sudermann

Gerhart Hauptmann

GREAT BRITAIN

1850, Clayton-Bulwer treaty concerning the Panama Canal. . . . The Crystal Palace exhibit was opened. . . . Gladstone and Disraeli struggled for parliamentary supremacy. . . . 1854, Crimean War. . . . Florence Nightingale. . . . Charge of the Light Brigade. . . . 1854–55, gold rush in Australia. . . . 1855, safety match invented. . . . 1857, Sepoy Rebellion in India. . . . 1859, Darwin's *Origin of Species* published. . . . 1861, death of Albert, Prince Consort of England. . . . 1867, Second Reform Bill, sponsored by Disraeli, passed. . . . 1875, the Suez Canal passed under control of the English. . . . 1876, Queen Victoria made Empress of India. . . . 1877, Charles Stewart Parnell, leader of the Irish party. . . . 1881, the Irish Land Act was passed. . . . 1884, Gladstone secured passage of Third Reform Bill. . . . 1893, Gladstone introduced the first Home Rule Bill for Ireland. . . . 1895, Jameson raid into the Transvaal led toward Boer War. . . . 1896, Kitchener led Sudan Expedition to avenge General Gordon. . . . 1897, Queen Victoria's Diamond Jubilee. . . . 1899, Boer War started. . . . Annexation of Sudan, Rhodesia, East Africa, Nigeria. . . . Cape to Cairo railway completed northward to Rhodesia.

FRANCE

1852, Louis Napoleon became Emperor Napoleon III by a coup d'état. . . . 1854, France joined England against Russia in Crimean War. . . . 1857, France joined Italy against Austria. . . . 1862, Napoleon III made Maximilian Emperor of Mexico. . . . 1867, Maximilian executed by Juarez in Mexico. . . . 1870, Franco-Prussian War; France lost Alsace-Lorraine. . . . 1871, Commune in Paris; establishment of the Third Republic. . . . From 1894 to 1899, Dreyfus case rocked military and political France. . . . By 1900, France had annexed Algiers, Tunis, Morocco, Senegal, French Sudan, and Madagascar.

UNITED STATES OF AMERICA

1850, Jenny Lind gave her first concert at Castle Garden in New York City. . . . 1852, Lola Montez danced at a celebration of the American stage in New York. . . . 1853, Perry opened trade relations with Japan. . . . 1855, first attempt to lay Atlantic cable. . . . 1857, Chief Justice Taney handed down "Dred Scott" decision. . . . 1859, John Brown's raid. . . . 1859, first petroleum wells bored at Titusville, Pennsylvania. . . . 1860, the Prince of Wales (later Edward VII) visited the United States. . . . 1860, South Carolina seceded from the Union. . . . 1861, War between the States began with bombardment of Fort Sumter. . . . Bull Run. . . . Mason-Slidell affair. . . . *Monitor-Merrimac* engagement. . . . Emancipation Proclamation. . . . Gettysburg. . . . Sherman's march through Georgia. . . . Lee's surrender at Appomattox. . . . Lincoln's Gettysburg Address. . . . 1865, Lincoln shot by John Wilkes Booth. . . . Thirteenth Amendment abolished slavery. . . . 1866, Ku Klux Klan was organized. . . . 1867, first successful Atlantic cable was laid. . . . Alaska purchased from Russia for $7,500,000. . . . 1869, a gold spike at Ogden, Utah, marked completion of first transcontinental railroad. . . . 1871, great fire devastated Chicago. . . . 1874, Charley Ross kidnaped and never found. . . . Boss Tweed jailed. . . . 1876, the Centennial Exposition opened at Philadelphia. . . . The Custer Massacre at Little Big Horn River in Montana. . . . Edison perfected electric light. . . . 1881, American Federation of Labor organized. . . . Assassination of President Garfield. . . . 1883, Brooklyn Bridge opened. . . . The growth of Big Business and capitalism became factors in industry and politics. . . . Pendleton Civil Service Act passed. . . . 1887, Interstate Commerce Act passed. . . . 1893, financial panic. . . . 1897, gold rush to the Klondike began. . . . 1898, annexation of Hawaii. . . . 1898, Spanish-American War began. . . . Theodore Roosevelt at San Juan Hill, Cuba. . . . Admiral Dewey's victory at Manila Bay. . . . Santiago Bay. . . . Acquisition of Puerto Rico, Philippine Islands, Guam, Wake Island, etc., by the Treaty of Paris.

OTHER COUNTRIES

1854, Roman Catholic Church adopted (by the Bull *Ineffabilis Deus*) the doctrine of the Immaculate Conception. . . . 1861, Czar Alexander II of Russia emancipated the serfs by imperial decree. . . . 1867, Dominion of Canada established. . . . In Japan, Shogun power was abolished and Mikado's power restored. . . . 1870, Rome was seized by Victor Emmanuel; the Pope became a voluntary "prisoner" in the Vatican. . . . Vatican Council proclaimed "infallibility of the Pope." . . . Ems dispatch; Bismarck maneuvers war against France. . . . Battle of Sedan. . . . German Empire established. . . . 1878, Congress of Berlin called to prevent a general European war. . . . 1882, Koch discovered tuberculosis germ. . . . 1882, Triple Alliance between Germany, Austria, and Italy. . . . 1896, Ethiopians defeated Italians at Adowa. . . . 1897, Andrée made unsuccessful attempt to reach the North Pole by balloon. . . . 1899, Hague Peace Conference called by Czar of Russia.

In science, Louis Pasteur (French) formulated the germ theory of disease. . . . William Morton (American) had discovered the use of ether (in 1846) as an anesthetic, and James Simpson (Scottish) had used chloroform for the same purpose; the latter half of the nineteenth century put these two discoveries into common use. . . . Lord Lister (English) introduced antiseptic measures in surgery. . . . E. von Behring (German) discovered antitoxin for diphtheria in 1892. . . . Elias Metchnikoff (Russian) discovered relative values of red and white corpuscles. . . . Wilhelm Konrad Röntgen (German) discovered X-rays in 1895. . . . Madame Curie and husband (Polish-French) discovered radium in 1898, and disclosed its benefits in curing cancer. . . . Gregory Mendel (Austrian monk) formulated the Mendelian law of heredity. . . . Luther Burbank (American) developed plant breeding to an astonishing degree. . . . Michael Faraday (English) experimented with electricity and magnetism (in 1862), leading to many inventions. . . . Albert Michelson (American) determined the velocity of light. . . . Thomas Alva Edison (American) perfected the incandescent electric light, the phonograph, the moving picture. . . . Cyrus Field (American) and Alexander Graham Bell (American) perfected the telephone in 1876. . . . Guglielmo Marconi (Italian) perfected the wireless in 1897.

The wheels of fashion, in the latter half of the nineteenth century, followed closely in the track of travel, and the rapid changes in styles kept pace with the increasing speed of transportation. Rapid communication, by both land and sea, and the ability of factories to turn out material hour after hour opened the realm of fashion to a democratic majority. In catering to this larger but less selective public, the styles became more complicated, elaborate, and involved, but not more artistic.

Factories upon a thousand streets exuded masses of smoke, which dulled the midday brightness of textiles and necessitated dust ruffles and other soot-catching ingenuities.

Science and invention kept pace with the increasing demands for speed. Over thin wires came messages ticked off by a magic key, came the human voice, came light. From circling scratches on a gutta percha tube or on a flat disk, came music; at last, over the land rolled the horseless carriage. Like an Olympic victor, it broke down tradition's wall, and crashed through to a new, daring, and speed-maddened world.

Frightened at these innovations, fashion, upholstered in its passementerie and jet, picked up its skirts and – decorously – ran.

COSTUME

COSTUME FOR MEN – 1850–1860

The outstanding tendency in this decade was to lengthen the waistline, to fit the coat, including the collar, smoothly to the figure, and to use plaids for trouser material.

Coat

The body of the coat was carefully fitted to the figure. The shoulder line resumed its normal place, and the waistline dropped below normal about an inch or two. The collar lay snug against the neck, and a fairly deep notch divided it from the flat, moderately wide lapels that ended near the chest line (Fig. 226   Fig. 256).

The skirt to the coat fitted trimly about the hips, and the edges met in front or

Fig. 226

were curved out toward the bottom. The usual length of the coat was to a point midway down the thigh.

A short sack coat, single-breasted, with pockets placed low and with braided edges, came in at this time, and was slowly to win favor. At first it was used for sports, and also by the lower classes; Bill Sikes, in *Oliver Twist,* wore this general type of coat (Fig. 230 A).

Many of the coats of this period showed a breast pocket for the handkerchief. Other pockets were hidden in the tails of the coat. Some coats had a concealed opening down the front.

Vest

The vest was also long-waisted, with a breast-deep opening and flat revers. It was made of plain, checked, plaid, brocaded, quilted, embroidered, or flowered material, linen, satin, or velvet. Small pockets were sometimes added, just above the low waistline.

Fig. 227
1852

Fig. 228
1855

Fig. 229
A
1855

B
C

A Fig. 230 B 1853

Fig. 240
1869

Fig. 231
1855

A

B

C

D 1850 Fig. 233 1860 E

Fig. 234 1850

C

SLEEVE

Fig. 239
A 1863

Fig. 236
1865

B

A 1860

Fig. 238
1861

A Fig. 242 B C
1870

Fig. 243
1870

Fig. 245

BUSTLE
C

BODICE D

BACK gather OVER SKIRT
FRONT

A B 1870

Shirt

The shirt was pleated or tucked and starched. For dress wear a frilled front pleat was used.

Neckwear

The standing collar was quite high, and starched, with points either side the chin. A turnover collar was used for informal wear. A colored or black stock with pointed ends was wrapped about the neck, an inch or so below the top of the collar, and tied in a medium bow in front. For dress wear, the white stock was used. White ties were also good form for dress wear.

Trousers

Trousers were narrower than in 1840. Dress trousers were still looped under the shoe, but for everyday trousers the loops were now discarded. Plaids and stripes were in great demand (Fig. 227 Fig. 256). The trousers did not necessarily match the coat. Light shades found favor for dress wear, but darker shades became the accepted mode for everyday. The smoke of the factories cast its shadow over the landscape and over the color wheel of the dress designer.

Outer Coat

Topcoats were short. Some were form-fitting, fashioned like the suit coats. Others were loose, and flared at the bottom, with wide, bell sleeves. For evening, the long, lined cape was used (Fig. 226 Fig. 227 Fig. 228 Fig. 229 A).

Footwear

Shoes were blunt-tipped, with moderate heels. Lacing, or elastic insets at the sides or front, kept them snugly in place. For dress wear, low slippers with bows, and striped socks, were used (Fig. 226).

Hair

The hair was parted on the side, waved over the forehead and curled forward over the temples. The parting down the back was still used, but the hair was somewhat shorter on the nape of the neck. Bears' grease and Macassar oil were used to smooth down the hair and give it elegant luster. (From the habit of using hair oil arose the necessary "antimacassars" to protect upholstery!) Very small mustaches were worn by some men, and side whiskers with a smooth chin by others (Fig. 231 Fig. 256). In 1858 a play, *Our American Cousin,* established the long, wavy, "Lord Dundreary" type of side whiskers (Fig. 228). A short, rounded beard was also in fashion, and some long, full beards were to be seen.

Ornaments and Accessories

Hats were very tall and cylindrical (Fig. 226). The "stovepipe" style, in gray, fawn, tan, or black beaver, was in most demand. A very narrow band with a small bow (side or back) was the only trimming. The hat had a fairly straight, narrow brim, though a slight roll was also used (Fig. 227).

A low, flat-topped hat was used for sports (Fig. 226). The soft felt with wide brim, made popular by Western pioneers, grew in favor. A low, rounded dressing cap, with a button on top (Fig. 226), was used with a loose dressing gown.

Ornaments and Accessories

Canes, eyeglasses or monocles, link watch chains that looped over the vest, and gloves added elegance to the costume (Fig. 226).

COSTUME FOR WOMEN – 1850–1860

Bodice

The general fashion emphasized in 1840–50 continued to be worn. The waistline showed the V in front, especially for evening wear (Fig. 232). However, a

Fig. 232

rounded waistline was also used, with a ribbon or a belt buckle confining the trim waist, which looked even trimmer because of the yards and yards of skirt below.

The bodice had a rather low V neck, or a rounded one. A lace or tulle fichu filled in the V neck. A high-necked bodice, fastened down the front, was also modish. This type had a narrow, turned-down collar of linen or lace, fastened around the throat with a brooch (Fig. 232). Feminine allure was accentuated by a high waistline and an off-shoulder droop.

A new type of garment was the *basque,* fashioned on the lines of the early seventeenth-century Spanish bodice, immortalized by Velásquez. The bodice was tight-fitting, high- or low-necked, and had a short skirt, peplum, or tabs about the waist (Fig. 232). In this respect it was like the seventeenth-century dress worn by the Cavalier lady (Fig. 257). It was made of velvet or some dark color, and was often worn over a light-colored skirt.

Another type of bodice consisted of a separate blouse worn tucked into the skirt band. In honor of the Italian patriot, it was called the *Garibaldi blouse*. The colors, in remembrance of outstanding Italian victories, were *Magenta* and *Solferino*.

For evening wear, bodices were sleeveless, or had small puffed sleeves off the shoulders. The low bodice had a horizontal neckline which dropped low off the shoulder. A deep lace bertha often edged the neckline (Fig. 232 Fig. 234).

Sleeves

The sleeve, plain or very slightly fulled, was sewed into the drop shoulder opening. The open bell, or pagoda, sleeve became popular (Fig. 233 D). From elbow to wrist, a fulled white undersleeve was used (Fig. 229 B C Fig. 255 C).

Skirt

The skirt was gored, gathered, or pleated. The gored or gathered skirt sometimes had three or more deep ruffles, one above the other (Fig. 230 B). The Empress Eugénie had a ball gown, the skirt of which had two thousand yards of tulle ruffling.

The skirts were long, touching the ground. Formal dresses had trains. Summer dresses, or sports costumes, for such strenuous games as battledore and shuttlecock, croquet, and drop-the-handkerchief, were shortened to ankle length. The summer dress was usually made of muslin, with embroidery ruffles or bands. The skirt often opened down the front, over a panel or another skirt.

Skirts were looped up over an underskirt, the loop caught with passementerie and tassels. Rosettes, lace ruffles, bands of velvet ribbon, and flowers were used for trimming.

Fullness was attained by the use of crinoline over several starched skirts. About 1855, a hoop skirt of steel wires, or whalebone in tiers, was used (Fig. 233 A B). In spite of caricaturists, the hoop skirt persisted for almost twenty years, principally because it was so much lighter than the wadded and starched skirts. It weighed less than a pound, and one petticoat over it was sufficient. Skirts were fullest about 1858 (Fig. 233). At this time some skirts measured eight yards about the bottom edge.

Crinoline entered politics in Paris. Bonapartists wore full skirts ten or twelve yards around; Legitimists wore flat skirts.

About 1851, Mrs. Amelia Jenks Bloomer of Seneca Falls, New York (an advocate of dress reform – principally in regard to tight corsets or stays and the crinoline and hoop skirts), designed a costume called a "Camilia," consisting of a full, loose tunic, short, knee-length skirt, and long, full pantalettes. Though we pay due respect to her good intentions, we must say that the costume was more striking than thrilling.

Cloak

Cloaks had to be quite full, to fit over the wide hoop skirts. Shawls of all kinds were in high favor; cashmere shawls were common, but black or white lace Spanish shawls or *mantillas* were most in demand (Fig. 232). They were made popular by the Empress Eugénie's example, and were worn over the head and shoulders, or around the shoulders only. Fur capes, circular in shape, were fashionable. They were also cut along the line of current style. Sealskin was the favored fur.

A type of *mantillette,* cut narrow and fitted at the shoulders, was worn with décolleté dresses, to cover the bare shoulders. The mantilla had deep points in front.

Stockings

White stockings of cotton, lisle, or wool were usual. Silk stockings were rare.

Footwear

There was very little change in shoes. Evening slippers had thin soles and flat heels. Shoes for daytime wear (ankle boots) were laced up the front or the inside, or else had elastic sides. They had low, curved French heels, and were adorned with tassels at the top.

Hair

Hair was worn smooth and parted, with a knot at the back; a few curls at the side were added for variety (Fig. 234). The knot was long, and arranged in a large loop, confined in a net. Bangs were occasionally worn over the forehead, and long curls over the shoulder. For evening wear, bandeaux of ribbons, flowers, and feathers were worn. Tall Spanish combs, also, were made fashionable by the Empress Eugénie, of Spanish birth.

Headdress

The poke bonnet was still worn. It was now smaller, however, and was pushed back from the face, making a becoming frame. It was edged and lined with rows of lace, and tied with long ribbon streamers (Fig. 230 B Fig. 233 D Fig. 257). Long, flowing veils were draped over the hoods. Matrons wore caps placed well back on the head, and beautifully made, with elaborate lace and ribbon ornament (Fig. 232 Fig. 255 F K).

A wide-brimmed leghorn hat trimmed with a ribbon band or knots of flowers was worn by younger women (Fig. 232). A variant of it, in felt or velvet, was worn for riding.

Ornaments and Accessories

Cameos, coral beads, bracelets, necklaces, earrings, and brooches were in great demand; so also were hair jewelry of all kinds, and lockets. Sunshades, muffs, combs, reticules, and eyeglasses were also popular (Fig. 232 Fig. 255).

Underclothes

About this time, underwear consisted of a chemise, a corset, long drawers or pantalettes, a short flannel or knit petticoat for winter wear, and two or three long, plain or embroidery-trimmed petticoats.

Directly over the hoop skirt was worn a petticoat with puffs, wadding, or crinoline trimming. Over this was a lace-trimmed one. The corset (Fig. 255 E) was fitted to the figure, and laced up the back, curving out at the high bust line and around the hips and abdomen. It extended down over the abdomen and over the back for some distance, but was short on the hips.

Equestrian Dress

Riding habits made *à la basque* were much in favor. Others were fashioned like the Louis XV frock coat, with wide, deep cuffs to the sleeves.

Bathing Dress

A bathing suit typical of the time is shown in Fig. 255 G. It has long, bell-shaped sleeves, a skirt in two layers of ruffles, pantalettes to the ankles, and a straw hat tied under the chin. Bathing shoes and stockings complete the unquestionably modest costume.

1860–1870

This decade, momentous in world history, developed no startling new lines in dress, but rather elaborated those already established. The full crinoline and steel hoop of the 'fifties still held sway, though as early as 1863 rumors of their collapse were rife. These rumors, like the hoop skirts, were greatly exaggerated. The Empress Eugénie, who had glorified the vogue, and her Bonapartisans, clung tenaciously to these artificial aggrandizements. The Legitimists, opponents of the regime, withdrew these supports from their ranks, and flattened skirts became their outward and visible sign.

Victoria, blessed with a great sense of decorum but no taste, blandly augmented her wardrobe with crinoline and garnitured creations of impeccable stiffness. To make assurance doubly sure, she ordered her dresses in pairs, two alike.

America, in the midst of internal war, was more concerned with procuring enough clothes than with whimsical variety. Southern belles, deprived by the blockade of even necessary cloth (since the domestic factories were in the New England states), resorted to strange makeshifts, such as lace curtains, velvet portières, calicoes, bedspreads, mosquito nettings, and other unusual stuffs. Covered or painted wooden molds and melon seeds were used for buttons.

The general characteristics of this age were the continued use of crinoline and hoops, though these distinctly diminished after 1865. Other details were the low bertha for evening, the tight bodice, with coatee tails or side pannier-ribbons, the use of Zouave and other small sacks and jackets, the use of shawls, the use of triangular bonnets and caps, and the use of Scotch plaids and Scotch fashions. Rich and somber materials prevailed. The influence of Garibaldi, of the Empress Eugénie, and of the new French designer, Boberg, lent distinction to the period.

Materials

Among the woolen materials for winter use were cashmere, mousseline, drugget, poplin, ottoman, velours, astrakhan, merino, rep, and a material called Mozambique. Alpaca became very popular, and continued so for many years.

Among the silks, crepe, thulle (tulle), gauze, and tarletan were the thin fabrics used for warm weather. Among other light materials were grenadine, muslin, organdie, chintz, piqué, dimity, chambray, and cambric. Many figured materials were used – sprigs of flowers, stars, chevrons, and other geometrical designs were placed on plain or grayish backgrounds.

For heavier silks, moiré or watered silks, brocades, Jacquard stripes, grosgrain, and poplins were in great demand, as the styles called for materials which "would stand alone."

Velvets included many varieties of weave – uncut velvet, velours épinglé, Terry velvet, brocaded velvet, and others.

Colors

With the advent of the factory a common grayness spread its pall over the color range. The War between the States further dulled the colors used by Americans to slate grays, drabs, browns, and other somber shades. In England, the influence of Queen Victoria restrained fashion to a respectably drab range of colors. However, Paris fashion still delighted in such hues as crimson, fuchsia, cerise, garnet, rose, green, violet, wine, brown, maroon, and deep blue. The light shades included peach, Nile green, pale blue, mauve, and lilac. For evening wear, all countries lightened and brightened the range of colors.

Carnavale, the French Beau Brummell, was a "Symboliste." He changed his clothes according to the weather, the color of his thoughts, or the performances at the Italian opera. For *The Barber of Seville,* for instance, he wore a canary-colored coat; for *Lucia di Lammermoor,* he wore a sky-blue costume.

Costume for Men – 1860–1870

Coat

Men's styles, in 1860, almost achieved a standard pattern. The frock coat, cut on very straight lines, dominated fashion. It was of black or some dark color, with a modest turndown collar and rather high lapels. A straight edge ran from the lapel to the hem, which was about knee length. The skirts of the coat had a pleat on each side of the slit in the back, and two buttons at the waistline. Sleeves were plain (Fig. 256), cuffed, or cuffless, and set in the armhole without noticeable gathers.

The cutaway was worn for formal daytime affairs, and was of dark woolen material with the edges bound with braid. For sport or business wear it was of tweed or some light mixture.

The sack coat came into still greater favor. It was short (hip length), with square or rounded edges. It had a modest, flat, turned-back collar, and high lapels buttoned together with a single row of buttons. The pockets were at the waistline (Fig. 236 B).

For evening dress, the tail coat, with normal waistline, cut straight across the front, and with moderately long tails, was worn.

Vest

The vest was usually of the same black broadcloth material as the coat, or of satin, though white waistcoats were also used. The vest was usually cut low with a flat revers. It could be single- or double-breasted. Sleeves were slightly fulled into the armhole and had no cuff.

Shirt

Shirts were pleated and starched or plain and starched. Ruffled shirts disappeared, except on very conservative gentlemen. Studs were used with the stiff-bosomed shirt. These were merely ornamental, as the shirt usually fastened up the back. The stiff-bosomed front was held in place by a tab with a buttonhole, which fastened over an inside button at the trousers top.

Neckwear

The collar was a low, turnover, starched affair or else a standing collar with moderately tall points on either side of the chin. This left a gap between, which

Fig. 235

was filled in by a black bow tie with fairly long ends (Fig. 256). The same type of tie was worn with the turned-down collar. Most of Lincoln's pictures show the turndown collar, black bow tie, black vest, long frock coat, tubular trousers, and tall stovepipe hat (Fig. 235).

Trousers

Trousers were made on straight lines, tubular, and loosely hung at the ankles. The strap under the instep, except for the tightly-fitting evening trouser, was generally dispensed with. No cuffs as yet appeared on trousers (Fig. 236 B   Fig. 256).

Outer Coat

An overcoat, or topcoat, made on the general lines of the frock coat, but a bit longer and fuller and with a wider collar, was the usual extra garment. The knee-length cape (often with a velvet collar) was still used for evening wear. In addition, the loose-hanging coat with cape sleeves or open bell sleeves was also in use. It was at this time that the *Inverness coat* was introduced, especially for traveling. Men also wore a plaid shawl (as Lincoln did) wrapped about the shoulders. A short topcoat is shown in Fig. 235.

Stockings

Plain black or white socks, or striped ones, were worn. They were of cotton or silk.

Footwear

Shoes with elastic sides were in great favor. Toes were rather blunt. For evening wear, the slippers were more pointed. *Congress gaiters* with elastic inserts at the side were in unusual favor in America. Boots (or shoes) were varnished. Laced-up shoes were also worn.

Hair

The side parting, wavy curls over the temple, and a moderately long haircut were still fashionable. Small, pointed mustaches were the rule, though many men were clean-shaven. The side whiskers were narrow at the temple and full at the jaw (Fig. 236). They were called *mutton chops* or *sideburns* (after the Union general, Burnside). A large, drooping mustache, curled to a point at the ends ("Simon Legree" style), was called "Texas longhorns."

Full beards were also worn, as pictures of Lincoln, Grant, Sherman, Robert E. Lee, and others illustrate. The round type of beard was called a *horseshoe.* The long goatee on the chin was dubbed *Uncle Sam.*

Headdress

The tall, cylindrical "stovepipe," with narrow, straight brim, was universally worn. It was of beaver with a fuzzy nap, or of "silk" beaver, brushed smooth. Black was most common, but gray or beige was occasionally seen. Cloth hats were also favored. Those for sports had low crowns. The *derby,* or "bowler," with low crown, was occasionally seen, but it was not really fashionable.

Southerners and artists affected the wide-brimmed, soft-crowned, black felt hat. This same shape, in a straw or panama, was used for summer.

Ornaments and Accessories

The umbrella and cane (with curved handles), steel-rimmed spectacles, watch fobs, seals, heavy gold chains, muffler, small round muffs, and small round skating caps were among the fashionable foibles of the day. Ice skating was made popular by the Empress Eugénie (Fig. 235).

Cigars were in fairly general use in Paris after 1820, and in Germany, England, and America after 1830 (thanks to Lord Byron's praise of them). Men used cigars from then on, though not in the company of ladies, heaven forbid! Pipes were used by the lower classes or by the master of the household in the privacy of his own sitting room – when his wife allowed it. However, it was not until the War between the States that General Grant's cigars made history. He emancipated the slaves, and he also freed the "filthy weed" from its social stigma. Snuff was not used, except by very old-fashioned gentlemen and (whisper it!) very old women – including old "ladies."

Eyeglasses, including a monocle for the fashionably inclined, gloves, and heavy "hunter" and "repeater" watches were carried. Handkerchiefs were tucked into the upper breast pocket or into the pocket in the tails of the frock coat or cutaway.

Military Dress

This varied with every country and from year to year. In general, however, it was trim, standardized, and plain, though gold braid and brass buttons still abounded for officers. The War between the States saw blue uniforms adopted by the North, gray by the South. In this hard-fought contest, men paid little attention to nattiness; daguerreotypes of the time show uniforms with the coats half buttoned down the front, caps at all angles, various types of shirts and collars. In general, the coats were plain, hip length, and without pockets.

Costume for Women – 1860–1870

Types of Dress (Fig. 237)

Women continued the mad vogue of hoop skirt and crinoline. Thanks to the sewing machine, yards and yards of ruffling could be run off and gathered in tiers over a foundation. The lower circumference sometimes measured six or eight yards (Fig. 236). Pantalettes, with ruffles of embroidery or lace, were indispensable adjuncts.

Bodice

The bodice was cut on moderate lines. It was boned and fitted over a tight corset. The waist was belted or pointed in front, and often had a basque. The dropped shoulder was still used, especially for evening, but it was somewhat modified for daytime use. The snug neckline was set off by a small, round collar of lace or embroidery, pinned with a brooch (Fig. 255 D). Occasionally a slight V neck was seen, filled in with small lace ruffles (Fig. 239 A   Fig. 257). A bodice of parallel rows of puffing, with strips of ribbon or lace between, was found becoming by young women. A wide black velvet girdle, like a Swiss peasant's laced bodice, was sometimes worn with the waist. Wide ribbon belts with long streamers were also used to add a festive note (Fig. 237).

The evening bodice was cut low off the shoulder, with a deep bertha or ruffle flounce, a row of bias folds, or other trimming about the shoulder line (Fig. 233 E).

Sleeves

The sleeves, set in without gathers at the shoulder opening, expanded to a full puff at the wrist. The pagoda sleeve superseded all previous styles. It was full and open, like a bell, about midway between elbow and wrist (Fig. 237). Underneath it was worn a white lawn or cambric undersleeve, or half-sleeve, full and gathered at the wrist and tied above the elbow. These sleeves were of many styles, with plain cuff, turned-back cuffs, ruffles, and other variations (Fig. 237   Fig. 255 C).

The pagoda sleeve flared very full at times, the edge being turned back to form a cuff; or perhaps it was cut short, above the elbow, and slit up the outside (Fig. 237 – pattern of pagoda sleeve, Fig. 239 sleeve).

1860

Fig. 237

Neckline

The daytime dress had a high neckline, with a moderately high standing collar or a low round collar, fastened at center front with a brooch or button. The evening bodice had a very low, horizontal neckline, straight across to a point off the shoulders (Fig. 233 E).

Skirt

The crinoline and steel hoop were still very much in vogue (Fig. 233), despite rumors, from 1863 on, that they would be discarded. By 1865, the hoops were narrowed except in the back, where they flared out, and the waistline was moved upward (Fig. 240). This is clearly shown in an advertisement of Bradley's "Duplex Elliptic" skirt frame. However, it took several years to do away altogether with the wide, full skirts. "Pride of the World" was another type of hoop advertised "for Assemblies, railroad cars, carriages, church pews, arm-chairs, promenades and house dresses."

Skirts were variously fashioned (Fig. 233 E Fig. 236 A Fig. 239 A Fig. 240 Fig. 257). Rows of wide ruffles (seven to twenty narrow rows), puffs, drapings, and other embellishments set off these imposing creations. Wide ribbon bows and festoons, soutache braid, and passementeries of various sorts, vied with simple gathered skirts of plain, watered, moiré, checked, or plaid materials. Scotch plaid was very popular, due to Queen Victoria's sojourns at Balmoral; a kind of high-topped, betasseled "boot" (or shoe) was named after this Scotch castle.

In this era, the Zouave jacket continued in style. Also very popular was the Garibaldi blouse, which much resembled the modern shirtwaist. It was either red (the "red shirts") or "Solferino" or "Magenta" colored, in honor of these battles.

A short jacket, cut square in front and reaching just below the waist, with high lapels and low collar, like a man's coat, was favored by young women. It had wide, open sleeves, and was called a *Kasawaika* coat (Fig. 237).

Cloak

This was a great era of cloaks, wraps, mantles, and shawls (Fig. 237 Fig. 240). The types and styles were legion. The enveloping *pardessus* was popular; so was the *Valencian,* an opera or ball mantle, long, circular, and looped over into a semi-hood in the back. There was also the *Garibaldi,* a type of long cloak, semi-fitted in the back, with full, open sleeves.

A more elaborate development of the pardessus and pelisse was a princess style, fitted to the body smoothly from neck to hem, and trimmed with passementerie or fur. There was also the basque cloak, with the skirt or tabs elongated below the knee. The Algerian burnoose with attached hood was very popular. The *Patti sack* was a loose, hip-length coat with sleeves, fastened at the neck only.

Indian, Chinese crepe, Spanish lace, Chantilly, cashmere, Persian, crocheted, and knitted shawls, square and diagonal in shape, were in great demand (Fig. 238).

The *coatee* was a type which harked back, for its origin, to the long-tailed frock coats worn by men around 1800 and perpetuated, in lesser degree, by the riding habit. The bodice, whatever its general design, had two long tails added which curved away from the hips and down the back, over the crinoline, like long streamers. They were used with evening gowns, as well as with daytime dresses.

Stockings

As in the previous era, white cotton stockings were used for all ordinary occasions. For evening or for very dressy affairs, silk stockings in paler shades were donned.

Footwear

Women wore low, heelless slippers of silk, moiré, or satin, in delicate shades, for evening dress. For daytime wear, high boots (or shoes), buttoned on the side or laced up the front or with elastic sides, were used. The front of the shoe curved up and was decorated with one or two tassels. High heels became the rage. This was another fashion accredited to the Empress Eugénie, who was, willy-nilly, sponsor to a certain walk, blond curls, shawls, crinolines, and other vagaries of dress.

Hair

The hair was worn parted in the middle, waved back over the ears, and arranged in a long, low knot, or *chignon,* at the back of the head. The chignon was usually encased in a net. Braids, loops, and other intricate arrangements added variety to the coiffure. Pads were used to puff out the hair at the sides.

Curls were at the side, over the ears, for evening wear. Long curls were arranged over the shoulder. Flowers, bands, ribbons, and other ornaments were arranged coronet style at the sides or across the back of the head. Nets of all kinds were worn over the knot or *waterfall* in the back (Fig. 255 J). These were appliquéd with steel or gilt spangles or crystal beads. Those who had little hair wore a bag of bright silk or velvet, stuffed with horsehair, fastened at the back and held in place by a comb (Fig. 255 L).

False hair was in great demand – puffs, switches, braids, curls, hair nets. Toward the middle of the decade, the hair in front was arranged *à la pompadour,* often with a part in the middle. Fanciful names were given to hairdresses, such as *Marie Stuart, à la Valois* (a pompadour with wreaths of flowers), *Druid, Naiad, Leda, Proserpina* (with leaves about the head), and many others.

Headdress

The poke bonnet dwindled still further in size. It sat back on the forehead, but was raised rather high in front (Fig. 237). Wide ribbons were tied under the chin. Feathers, lace, and flowers decorated the bonnet.

A flat, low-crowned, fairly wide-brimmed leghorn hat, trimmed with a ribbon (the streamers down the back) and perhaps flowers or feathers at center front, was often seen in summer wardrobes.

A round "pillbox" toque, tilted forward over the eyes, was worn winter or summer, but for winter use fur toques predominated.

Another hat, similar to the "pillbox" had a small, round, upcurved brim, bound with narrow ribbon about the edge. A flower or tips of feathers decorated it at front or side.

A Scotch bonnet with a ribbon about it, the streamers hanging behind, also found favor. It was made of plaid woolen cloth. The shape was also reproduced in straw.

Another hat, used especially for riding, was a low-crowned felt, with a fairly wide brim, which dipped front and back. It had a plume at one side, which curved down at the back (Fig. 237 Fig. 239 Fig. 257). This is the hat which returned to favor in 1932 as the "Eugénie" hat.

Hats, toward the end of the decade, were shaped like half a kerchief, a sort of triangle. They were trimmed with a ruffle across the back of the head. The point of the triangle came over the forehead (Fig. 237).

Straw hats, like sailor hats, were popular for the seaside or for yachting. They were trimmed with ribbons about the brim and with streamers at the back (Fig. 237).

Bonnets were fashionable for married women. These had flaring brims, and were arched high over the forehead in front. Wide streamers tied them under the chin. The bonnet was often heart-shaped, or dented in the center, like the Mary, Queen of Scots bonnet of a previous era.

Veils were draped over the wide brims of the hats. They added a certain allure and helped to shade the face.

Opera or evening bonnets of lace and ribbons were most elaborate. Opera hoods (for formal parties) were also used.

Caps of all descriptions were worn. These were perched on the back of the head.

They were trimmed with ribbon, lace, flowers, wheat ears, and other fanciful items. Married women and older women habitually wore caps in the house (Fig. 255 F K).

A bandbox was used to carry the party cap, which was adjusted, on arrival, with great ceremony.

Ornaments and Accessories (Fig. 237)

Wide ribbon sashes were important items of dress. They were tied in large bows with the ends hanging almost to the hem of the skirt.

Undersleeves of lace or lawn, to wear beneath the wide pagoda sleeves, became an important accessory to the wardrobe. They were puffed, frilled, and fashioned in dozens of ways.

Chemisettes, or underbodices, were also necessary. Girdles (the "Marguerite" and others) of black velvet, pointed and laced in front like a peasant's bodice, grew in favor.

Reticules and knitted and beaded purses, either square or rectangular, were carried. The stocking "miser" bag was very popular.

The sunshade, a small black parasol with a folding handle, was carried for walking or for riding in open carriages – such as the barouche or landau. The parasols were square-canopy or round in shape. They were often lined with white silk and were trimmed with lace, tassels, fringe, marabou feathers, or goffered ribbon. Larger parasols were used at the seashore. These were made in bright colors, trimmed with ribbons, lace, or frills. Serviceable black cotton or silk umbrellas were used for rainy days.

The crinoline, with its wide breadth of skirt, set off lace flowers and ruffles admirably, and it is not surprising to find that many types of lace were in demand.

Point lace (rose point was very fine), Brussels, Valenciennes, Chantilly, and needle point were used. Queen Victoria, in order to revive the handmade lace industry, had her bridal gown made of Honiton lace, costing a thousand pounds; Empress Eugénie had in her trousseau a gown with Alençon lace flowers, which cost twenty-two thousand francs.

Ribbons were also used in bows, loops, streamers, and studied decorations. These ribbons were wide or narrow, plain or plaid, shining satin or moiré antique, and of every shade from pale ivory or pink to deep garnet or black.

Fringe of various types, wide, narrow, plain or knotted, edged the expansive hems of skirts, or draped bodices, or adorned parasols.

Braid, soutache, and silk bands, plain or arranged in patterns, decorated both men's and women's clothing.

Passementeries, particularly of jet, had a certain vogue. (Passementerie is a trimming of braid, cord, beads, tinsel, jet, or other materials arranged in a running pattern, usually in openwork or cutout style. It is appliquéd to the garment.)

Furs were increasingly used – Russian sable, mink for street wear, ermine for evening wear, and sealskin for almost every occasion. Nations had not yet restricted the killing of seals. Chinchilla was much in use for children's dress and wraps. Muffs, collarets, and tippets, as well as long, circular, semi-fitted capes, were fashioned of this fur.

Another accessory was the necktie, to accompany the high bodice with the round, low collar. The necktie was of ribbon or of knitted material, and the ends were embroidered, braided, or otherwise trimmed. It was tied in a big, flat bow in front.

Embroidery was used on bodices and sleeves and occasionally on skirts. It decorated reticules and other personal belongings, and added the feminine touch so much desired in the Victorian era.

Aprons were demurely donned by housewife and working woman. The housewife, for sewing or other household tasks, wore a black sateen apron, with pockets. It might also be made of lighter material and shade, and be decorated with lace, embroidery, and ribbon. Saleswomen and schoolteachers wore black sateen aprons, sometimes with bibs. Cooks wore gingham aprons with bibs; parlormaids wore white aprons for waiting on table, answering the door, and performing other duties. A plain bodice and full skirt, without hoops, was worn by servants and saleswomen. Women teachers who wished to appear "genteel" wore hoops.

Gloves and mittens were regular accessories. Short gloves, some with ornate tops, some banded with a bracelet, were worn with very short sleeves for evening wear. Long gloves were seldom seen. Pale colors were chosen. White was the favorite choice for evening wear. *Josephine* and *Mathilde* gloves – the latter bordered at the wrist with a row of leaves – were frequently seen on the hands of the belles of the 'sixties.

Mittens of black, white, or colored silk, or of cotton lace, were commonly used, and were frequently knitted by the ladies themselves.

Fans were charmingly displayed by ladies at home or at parties. Small, circular, folding fans, round Chinese fans, and large feather fans were equally popular.

Jewelry came in "sets" – necklace, brooch (or "breastpin"), earrings, locket, bracelet, and ring. These were usually of gold, often ornamented in black enamelwork, with settings of garnets, seed pearls, coral, jet, or human hair. The coral was beaded or carved in the shapes of lilies, roses, and miniature heads. Cameos were again in fashion, and large ones were used for breastpins. Seed pearls were strung on white horsehair in twisted strands for necklaces or bracelets, or they were fashioned into earrings and brooches. Long ropes of twisted gold, and beads of coral, jet, amber, or gold were much favored. Human hair was braided, woven, or twisted into watch fobs, bracelets, rings, and other trinkets. They were fashioned into vari-colored flowers, or else coiled in lockets, or laid under glass for pins or rings. The hair of deceased persons was made into mourning rings and brooches for near relatives. Godey printed this touching advertisement in 1861: "Hair is at once the most delicate and lasting of our materials and survives us like love. . . . With a lock of hair [of the deceased] we may . . . look up to heaven . . . and say: 'I have a piece of thee here, not unworthy of thy being.' "

Coiffures, consisting of silk or velvet bands shaped to the head, ornamented with pearls, feathers, lace, etc., were used for evening wear.

Ribbon belts, with sashes or long streamers placed at intervals about the waist, were commonly-used garnitures. Belt buckles were made of gilt, jet, mother-of-pearl, and other ornamental materials.

A *parne* of flowers was a favorite accompaniment for evening dress. It might be used as a wreath for the hair, a bouquet for the corsage, or a decoration for the skirt.

Combs of ivory, coral, silver, gold, and tortoise shell were placed at the nape of the neck, above the "waterfall."

Spiral studs, for fastening muslin habit-shirts, chemisettes, and delicate lace fabrics, were used in place of ordinary buttons.

Make-up

Women blushed more easily in those days, or else were unusually crafty in the art of make-up, for in spite of the fact that paint and powder were decried – in fact, held up as the mark of "fast women" – cheeks showed charming coloring, and brows were white "as was the snowdrift." Lips, though innocent of lip-salve, were bitten by the owners' little teeth until they pulsated with a ruddy glow. No advertisements of paint or powder were countenanced; yet druggists did a brisk business in selling a red, chalklike substance called *carmine,* which, when powdered and dusted ever so lightly, tinted the cheeks delightfully. Rice powder and prepared chalk, two other indispensable druggists' wares, were also sold to maidens who superimposed alabaster overtones on their fair complexions.

Mourning

Men and women wore black for varying periods of time. Women of high social standing went into deep mourning for two years. The outward and visible signs were black crepe dresses, black crepe bonnet, and very long crepe veil, black mourning jewelry, black gloves, and other habiliments of woe. Men wore black broadcloth for the funeral and for state occasions thereafter, and black or very dark suits for ordinary wear. Little girls wore silk or wool mourning dresses, and little boys wore black for a short while. For summer, black lawn, organdie, and grenadine were chosen.

It is noteworthy that mauve and royal purple were combined with black, not only for half mourning but for full mourning. Gray, however, was the usual color for half mourning. Half mourning lasted from six months to a year after the period of full mourning. The French fashion – initiated by the Empress Eugénie – of white ruchings and white edgings on black, was but slowly accepted in the United States.

Equestrian Dress

A typical riding costume consisted of a round-brimmed straw or beaver Spanish hat, with or without a plume. The hair was dressed low, and gathered in a net at the back. Long stockings and morocco boots with heels, or low shoes and gaiters, were worn. Long cloth trousers matched the habit. They were cut full and gathered in at the ankle by an elastic band. Over the breeches there was a short petticoat of light flannel. The habit was of broadcloth, velvet, or some other closely woven wool material. Over a sleeved chemise of light flannel, a tight bodice was worn. It buttoned up the front to a snug neckline, and had long, tight sleeves and a full skirt one-third to one-half a yard longer than that of an ordinary walking dress. Braid and buttons ornamented the bodice.

Horseback riding grew in popularity in America due to the development of this sport in the new "Central Park," in New York, whence the vogue spread over the country.

Bridal Dress

The custom of wearing white seems to have been followed by brides of this decade, for all formal weddings; informally – as in wartime weddings – the traveling dress might be used.

French brides wore bodices with high necklines and long, tight sleeves. American brides began to copy this fashion, though the low-necked, short-sleeved bridal dress was still used.

Veils were worn back on the head, the long folds falling behind. They were usually held in place by a small knot of orange blossoms at center front, or by a bandeau, a coronet, or other ornamental wreath. Only toward the end of the decade did the custom of draping the veil over the face find favor in America.

A filigree flower holder, of silver or gilded metal, held the bouquet, which was arranged in a paper-lace cone. At one end of the holder was a ring through which the handkerchief was slipped or by which the bouquet could be held while the bride was shaking hands.

COSTUME FOR CHILDREN

Baby dresses were very long and elaborately embroidered and trimmed with ribbons and lace. It was a general boast that the christening robe swept the floor when the baby was held in the sponsor's arms. Many flannel bands, petticoats, skirts, and embroidered petticoats were wrapped and pinned about the baby until it was almost as tightly imprisoned as in the days of swaddling clothes.

Very young children, both boys and girls, wore long pantalettes and a sort of tunic, or overdress. Up to six or seven years of age, a little boy wore a skirt, a Garibaldi blouse, and a Zouave jacket. Another costume featured a Scotch plaid jacket with slight peplum and full or pleated skirt.

Boys

After about seven, a little boy wore loose pantaloons which ended below the knee. These were usually edged with braid and had a wide waistband, which dipped in a point at the front and at the back. With them he wore a shirt with a low, round collar and a loose jacket, bolero or Zouave style, just reaching the waist, or perhaps a bit longer, with square or rounded edges. The pocket was usually fastened.

For boys the materials used were poplins, flannel, mohair, serge, and similar durable materials. Plaids were very much favored. For summertime, white linen and other substantial but cool materials were used. An embroidered or scalloped edge in red or some other color was placed about the pantaloon edge, the wide, pointed waistband, and the shirt.

Older lads wore trousers to the ankle, with a wide skirted coat, belted about the waist. *Renfrew caps,* with visors, were much in favor. Other hats used were the *Washington,* the *tourist hat* (which had a soft, round crown and turned-up brim), and the page's cap. Knickerbockers were sometimes worn instead of long trousers.

The Russian dress for boys, such as that worn by the Prince Imperial, son of Napoleon III and the Empress Eugénie, consisted of a long jacket waistcoat and long, full trousers gathered below the knee.

Girls

Little girls wore pantalettes, full skirts, and low-cut bodices. For winter, or when a high-necked dress was desired, chemisettes (called *Swiss bodies*) of lawn or of thicker cloth were used. Separate sleeves were also added to short sleeves, or placed under the bell-mouthed oversleeve.

A belt or sash confined the waist. Bretelles over the shoulder were common. The skirt, though occasionally gored, was usually gathered over a hoop skirt. Sometimes it was ornamented with braid and ribbons, lace, or rows of ruffles (Fig. 237).

Children's styles were copied after grown-up fashions; even their hat styles followed those of their elders, though the "pillbox," the Scotch cap, and the Tudor hat with plume were the favorite styles.

Shoes were cut high, had heels, and were polished and tasseled. They were buttoned on the side. Cloth gaiters were worn over shoes in the wintertime for extra warmth.

Both little boys and girls wore black aprons over their good clothes. Girls of ten and in the early teens wore aprons of black or white, silk or muslin, elaborately trimmed and decorated.

COSTUME FOR THE LOWER CLASSES

Workingmen wore rather shapeless garments, including loose trousers, sack coat, unstarched shirt, and cap. Tradesmen aped their "betters," and the frock coat or morning coat came to be the mark of elegance.

Aprons of leather were worn by blacksmiths, shoemakers, and certain other tradesmen.

Workingwomen wore tight, fitted bodices with high necks and narrow, round, turnover collars. The sleeves were tight-fitting, and the skirts were full, gathered without hoops. They wore hoods or caps indoors. As previously stated, aprons of black sateen were used by sewing women, saleswomen, and teachers. White aprons were worn by maids; gingham aprons, by cooks and cleaners. The aprons were fairly large and enveloping, with capacious pockets.

1870–1880

This decade, ushered in by the collapse of Paris (and the crinoline), was distinctly a transition period. The crinoline, subsiding fitfully since 1865, left as its heir the bustle, which confined its operations to the rear of the figure. With Eugénie an exile in England and Victoria immersed in her grief after Prince Albert's death, fashion turned for inspiration not toward royalty but toward outstanding social leaders and fashionable beauties like Madame MacMahon, the Marquise de Charette (Antoinette Polk of Tennessee), the Princess Troubetskoi, Lady Algernon Lennox, and Lady Asquith, whose "routs," "crushes," "assemblies," and "kettledrums" were famous. It also copied the styles of theatrical stars like Lillie Langtry (Lady de Bathe) and Adelina Patti. Monet and the Impressionists influenced color and line.

The general characteristics of dress for women were (1) the bustle, (2) the short-waisted bodice, (3) the modest high or V neck, (4) the low square neck for extreme décolletage, (5) the coatee bodice with tails in the back, (6) the use of heavy materials, contrasting materials, ruchings, and bows, (7) the dressing of the hair high on the head with loops and curls behind, coiled in loops at the nape of the neck, and (8) the preference for very small hats tilted on the head. The bustle was largest about 1875.

For men, fashions did not materially change, except that it became customary to reserve the frock coat for formal daytime wear. The cutaway, or sack coat, was in general use for everyday. The shoulder line was broad and square, or sloping. The bowler or derby hat almost supplanted the top hat, and a soft cap was universally adopted for traveling.

Underclothes

Men wore long underdrawers and undershirts. In winter, these were of wool; in summer, they were of light cotton. Socks were of cotton or wool, rarely of silk. Dark gray and black were the accepted colors.

Women wore an elaborate series of garments underneath the outer dress. Underclothes were of linen, cambric, muslin, or flannel. Silk underwear was not tolerated in respectable society. In dressing, a chemise, with a square yoke and underarm ruffles, was first donned; a corset, boned and curved to fit the fashionable figure –full bust, narrow waist, curved hips, and arched stomacher–was next put on; open drawers, ruffled, embroidered, and often having additional pantalettes reaching to the ankles, followed; then came a short flannel petticoat, a corset cover, and several more petticoats to complete the modest array. The petticoat was most important. It was made with crinoline ruffles in the back.

Stockings were white cotton, or lisle, for daytime wear; silk stockings, in white or pale shades, were used for evening wear and for formal occasions.

A nightdress, which was hip length only, like a sacque, became fashionable. All nightdresses had high necks and long sleeves. They were trimmed with pleats, lace, and embroidery.

Costume for Men – 1870–1880

Coat

The frock coat still retained its popularity, though it was reserved for formal occasions except by older men, who preferred its dignified lines to those of the more informal sack coat. The skirt of the frock coat was somewhat shorter than formerly, and was fitted in more snugly at the waistline. The lapels were fairly wide, and had deep V's, in contrast to the lapels of the cutaway and sack coats. The collar was often of velvet.

In this, as in other coats of this decade, the shoulder line was very broad and square, or sloping, and the armhole was placed off the shoulder. There was no attempt at padding the shoulders.

The coat sleeve was set smoothly into the armhole. The sleeve was cut fairly full, especially at the elbow, and was made with or without a rather deep cuff of the same material. The white shirt cuff showed slightly below the sleeve.

The waistline was conservatively low. Coats and trousers did not have to match.

Fig. 241

The cutaway coat was made with wide, deeply-notched lapels, sloping in a wide V to the waistline. It was buttoned with two or more buttons down the front to the waistline. From this point, the skirt of the coat curved away to the back, where it was split down the center, with two (false) pleats, one on either side of the opening. A button was placed at the top of each pleat. The same somewhat sloping shoulders and full sleeves were used. A braided edge often set off the garment. For formal daytime functions, the coat was of black broadcloth; for less formal occasions, it was of checked, plaid, or rough-woven woolen materials.

The sack coat now tended to supersede all others for everyday use, being almost universally adopted by business and working men. It was cut with wide, short lapels; it buttoned high; and frequently it had breast and hip pockets. The sleeves were moderately full, with sloping shoulders. It was not as snugly fitted as the frock coat. The front lower edges of the coat were usually rounded (Fig. 256).

The riding coat or sportsman's jacket was cut low-hip-length, with the back slightly gathered in to a belt buttoned at either side of the back. This was the first belted coat since the seventeenth century.

The evening coat, as shown in Du Maurier's drawings, was cut with sloping shoulders and broad lapels, faced with silk and folded deep. The coat was cut square in front, at a low waistline, ran straight back to the hips, and had long tails behind (Fig. 241 Fig. 242).

Vest

Vests for the frock coat were high, with small revers, or plain. However, low-cut white vests were also worn. Vests for evening dress were low cut, and of black broadcloth or brocade (Fig. 241).

Shirt

The shirt was invariably white and stiff-bosomed; pleated bosoms, as well as plain, were worn. The plain bosoms were for evening dress; at least two, sometimes three, studs, usually with spiral points, fastened them down the front, though sometimes the front opening was false, and the shirt opened down the back. Cuffs as well as collars were stiffly starched and detachable; cuff links were important accessories. Sometimes cuffs were clipped to the shirtsleeves. The stiff bosom was held in place as formerly.

Neckwear

Collars were of two kinds: (1) the standing collar with points in front, almost meeting and straight or folded out at the tips (wing collar); (2) turnover collars with straight points or diagonal opening. Both sorts were worn with evening dress, as well as with daytime suits.

The black tie (bow) was seen with all types of daytime wear, but the white bow tie was used for formal dress. A narrow string tie was also favored, especially by men who wore beards (for instance, General Grant, Garfield, etc.) Artists, like "Taffy" in *Trilby,* wore soft *Windsor ties* of black silk. The four-in-hand, at first narrow, became quite wide toward the end of the decade, and superseded the bow tie in favor; it was of black or some dark shade. By 1874, the wide white four-in-hand was also used for evening dress; it was somewhat wider than that for day wear, and was tied under a low, turndown collar (Fig. 241).

Trousers

In this decade, trousers were fairly full, long, but not strapped, and without creases. The opening was by means of a fly in front. Plain, checked, and striped materials were equally favored. Suspenders were used to hold the trousers in place.

The increasing popularity of sports – tennis, baseball, archery, and cycling – caused a sports trouser to creep into fashion. The first games of baseball, as portrayed in the Currier and Ives prints, were played in fairly full long trousers gathered about the ankles, like the old Gallic braccae. Later on, the trousers were shortened until, like the Russian full breeches worn by young boys, they were gathered just above or just below the knee. In time they came to be called "knickerbockers" after Washington Irving's imaginary historian of the early Dutch settlers. (One cannot suppose men copied the suggestions of Mrs. Bloomer and her feminist knickers!)

Outer Coat

The overcoat, fairly short, was about knee length, and cut with wide lapels; it was single- or double-breasted.

A raincoat of Scotch plaid, with a cape over the shoulders, called an *Inverness,* found favor, along with the *McFarlan coat.*

Footwear

Long stockings of Scotch plaid or plain wool were worn with the short sports knickerbockers, but otherwise socks, usually black or dark gray, were worn. Silk socks were worn for evening.

Shoes were ankle height, and frequently had elastic pieces at the sides – Congress gaiters – and straps with which to pull them on. However, front-laced shoes were also made for men as well as for women.

For evening, the low, flat pump, with medium heels, was used. Both shoes and pumps had narrow, rounded or square-tipped toes.

Gaiters, buttoned at the side, were used for outdoor sports and walking.

Tall, snug-fitting boots were used for riding; they had to be pulled off with a bootjack.

Hair

Sometimes the hair was parted from the middle of the forehead in front to the extreme nape of the neck in back. In this decade, men wore their hair parted, but usually it was parted on the side, with a slight wave over the forehead and over the temples (Fig. 241). Sometimes the hair was brushed back in a pompadour. The mustache was fairly full, sweeping and pointed; if a beard were worn, it might be either the deep, full beard (Fig. 243), sometimes parted in the middle (familiar to us in pictures of Grant, Hayes, and others of the time), or side whiskers (mutton chops), or very long and flowing whiskers, of the effulgent "Lord Dundreary" type. Both of these types are depicted in Du Maurier's drawings in *Punch.* Sometimes beards, especially "chin whiskers," were worn without mustaches, and mustaches without beards.

Headdress (*Fig. 241*)

The tall silk hat was worn for daytime as well as for evening; the sides were slightly curved out toward the top; there was a narrow silk band about the bottom. The stiff felt derby, with low round crown, was very much in vogue, as was the softer felt with a dented crown and deep rolled brim at the sides; this style was usually worn by sporty gentlemen or by young boys.

A light-colored (gray or tan) felt hat, with squared crown and rolling brim, was also correct for the street and for sports. Also, a very low-crowned hat with a wide brim was worn by the middle and lower classes.

The wide-brimmed, soft, black felt used by Southern plantation owners was still a favorite in the North, the South, and the fast-growing West (Fig. 243).

Straw hats were occasionally worn, but felt caps with visors were usually used for traveling.

Ornaments and Accessories (Fig. 241)

The watch fob was fairly heavy, of gold links, braided leather, or black gun metal; it might have a seal attached. It was fastened to the vest button with a small cross-bar. Watches were large and thick, of gold, silver, or gun metal; the "hunter" and "repeater" types were favorites.

Gloves were mauve, or tan; white gloves were used for evening.

Canes were slim and fairly long, with small knobs of ivory, gold, or silver; walking sticks were heavy, with curved handles.

Handkerchiefs were white, and quite large; initials were large, elaborate, and embroidered in white thread. Silk handkerchiefs were carried for evening.

For jewelry, men wore shirt-studs, cuff links, watch chains, and heavy rings, usually seals of onyx or severely set stones.

Spectacles had curved pieces over the ears. Eyeglasses were worn on ribbons about the neck.

The umbrella was carried for rainy weather. The handle ended in a slight bulb.

Military Dress

Uniforms tended toward plainer lines. The Franco-Prussian War saw the shorter tunic adopted, as well as the low, visored forage cap familiar to us since the War between the States. The French wore vivid, full, red trousers, and the English, red coats. Khaki, though used by British troops in India in 1849, and again at Peshawar in 1857, was not yet adopted for general use. In America, dark blue tunics and trousers were used by Indian-fighters like Custer, and probably proved almost as good targets for Sitting Bull and the other savages as the red coats of General Braddock's men had been to the Indians at Fort Duquesne.

Ecclesiastical Dress

Little change occurred. Most Protestant ministers wore frock coats and black or white ties.

Mourning

Men wore black for funerals, and dark, somber colors for varying periods afterwards. A crepe band on the hat was an additional sign of grief, but was not adopted universally.

COSTUME FOR CHILDREN

It was about this time that Kate Greenaway began to influence children's dress. It was later said that she "dressed the children of two continents." From a drawing of hers (December 30, 1879), it was evident that she copied the styles of Reynolds and of the 1800's.

Very little boys still wore dresses with pantalettes showing beneath. Boys from two to five years old wore little jackets which buttoned straight down the front or slantwise over the chest. With these were worn pleated skirts. Scotch styles were still very popular for children. A turned-down English collar and a sailor hat completed the costume. Boys of seven or more wore knickerbockers and a blouse either hip or thigh length, fastened down the front and belted; the blouse had a diagonal opening.

Boys from five to twelve wore the Russian trousers gathered about the knee, loose jacket crossed in front, and sailor hat, or a small cap, with or without a peak. Boys of twelve or more wore knickerbockers and a shirt with round or wing collar. Knickers were either open at the knee or gathered in to elastic bands at the bottom edge. With them were worn a shirt, vest, and sack coat, buttoned down the front or secured by a top button at the neck only. Horizontally striped stockings were a new style, worn with rather tall shoes. Hats were round, with rolling brims, or the Scotch cap style, with streamers behind.

Garibaldi and Cossack suits were popular. Velveteen, black or brown, trimmed with silk braid, was very much in demand for boys' suits.

COSTUME FOR THE LOWER CLASSES

The working classes wore, for Sunday best, cheap imitations of the garments of their "betters." Loose, baggy trousers, with a shirt and vest, often sufficed for daily wear. If a coat were worn, it was either a loose sack coat or an outmoded frock coat. A nondescript cap with visor, or a felt or sailor hat was worn.

It was about this time that the "aesthetic" craze swept England, and affected France and even America. Oscar Wilde is credited with starting the vogue of "art for art's sake." As a devotee of beauty, Oscar Wilde wore purple velvet coats, soft collars open at the throat, flaming ties of orange and other "moodish" colors. His trousers were of delicate mauve or pearl gray, and his hair was elaborately curled and perfumed. He carried a lily, a sunflower, or a green carnation, and affected drooping, effeminate postures that led to his being caricatured in Gilbert and Sullivan's *Patience* in 1881. His influence upon fashions was not, however, as important as his influence in other channels. However, the objection of the sturdy 'nineties to artists and all Bohemian and pseudo-Bohemian groups may be traced to Wilde's "aesthetic" mauves and lavenders, and his gestures against the general drab ugliness of his times.

COSTUME FOR WOMEN – 1870–1880

Hoops and crinoline, having reached the height of their vogue about 1867, were still in use in 1869, but finally were superseded by the bustle type. Along with the bustle came high waistlines, plain-cut sleeves, trains, hair piled on the head and cascading down the back, and hats tilted forward over the forehead. The "Grecian bend" walk seemed a fair accompaniment to the bustle and the high shoes.

Materials

In general, materials were thicker, heavier, and more durable than formerly. Velvet, brocade velvet, shot velvet (which is a changeable weave of black and another color such as green or ruby, like a hummingbird's breast), velours, and plaid were used, but uncut velvet was the most elegant. Silks of all sorts, grosgrain, *satin de Holland,* silk rep, crepe, silk grenadine, and other weaves were used. Among woolens, one could buy cashmere, poplin, serge, tartan or Scotch plaid, merino, and other twilled goods, besides broadcloth. For summer wear, there were piqué, cotton grenadine, lawn, cambric, chambray, chintz, and striped lawns. In thin stuffs, there were gauze, tulle, and tarletan.

Colors

Deep, somber colors were used for winter or daytime dress; very light, pale colors for evening; light colors and white for summer.

Black was popular in 1870, following the Franco-Prussian War; then, in 1873, emerald green became the rage. However, white was always good, especially for evening.

For daytime wear, cuir (leather color) was a prime favorite. Bottle green, russet, bronze, steel, scarlet, maroon, and deep blue were also popular. Algerian stripes and Scotch plaids were very popular, in combination with plain materials. Street dresses were of several colors and materials; skirts and waists did not necessarily match. House dresses were usually of one color only.

The collapse of the Second Empire revived memories of the French Revolution. In honor of this, there were revivals of the Marie Antoinette fichu, the Watteau sacque, the Corday bonnet, and even the powdered headdress. Edouard Manet, the artist, influenced dress; William Morris and Oscar Wilde also gave thought to the significance of line in dress.

Bodice

Steel backboards were used to train women for the erect carriage necessary for these types of dresses. The bodice was snug-fitting, with a round, fairly high waistline (Fig. 245, pattern). High-necked bodices were the rule, though variations occurred (Fig. 257). If a low or a square neck were used, a chemisette of lawn or other thin material was worn underneath to fill in the uncovered area. A rounded neckline, or a very modest V neck were among the variations from the high-necked bodice. The collar of this high-necked bodice was usually finished with a narrow ruching, gathered or pleated. This ruching also outlined the round or V neck (Fig. 245).

In the early part of the decade, the Watteau bodice prevailed (Fig. 245). In this type, the back had inverted box pleats, or gathers, which spread out over the bustle behind to make a puff; joining it on either side were panniers of material, also puffed. For stout people who disliked the voluminous puffs there were simulated panniers and puffs made of large, wide, silk tabs edged with ribbon, lace, or fringe.

The ordinary bodice was short-waisted, with fairly sloping shoulders, and plain, snug, long sleeves. The neck had a fairly high collar attached, which was buttoned or fastened in front with a brooch. The neck might also be V-shaped, or modestly rounded. A band of trimming was sometimes used, which extended from center

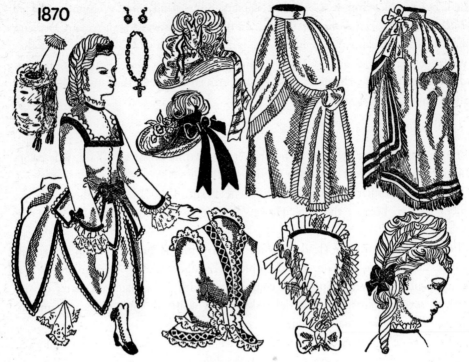

Fig. 244

front to center back and was caught at the sloping shoulder line. The band might also be put on in a curve about the shoulders to simulate the low neckline.

A bodice, with tails in the back – postilion effect – was very popular from 1870 to 1876. The tails were short and square, or pointed, or arranged in loops. They lay out over the bustle, accentuating the silhouette. After 1876, the tails became very long, ending in square or rounded points.

There was a bodice which was fitted in to the figure, and extended below the waistline in front (Fig. 244). The skirt, or peplum, was cut in points or tabs, and usually edged in braid or ribbon. Another type copied the long basque effects. In addition, it often had an apron draping in front. Other drapings on the sides and toward the back built up the bustle effect (Fig. 244 Fig. 245 B).

After 1875, the tendency was to cut the bodice more strictly in princess style, tightly fitted in at the waist, and extending over the skirt to form a deep peplum, ending at a low hip line (Fig. 246 B C). Variations of this showed a deep point of the peplum, front and back, with a curve upward over the hip.

For evening wear, the bodice was cut with a fairly deep V, or a low, square neck; both of these, however, were partially filled in with deep ruchings. Toward the end of the era, the pointed peplum style, very plain and resembling a corset worn on the outside, came into fashion. This was to continue into the next decade.

The bodice was buttoned down the front with jet or molded buttons. It was further embellished with pleated lace, net, lawn, or silk ribbons, fringe, puffs, tassels, jet, passementerie, bugles, embroidery, and braid. In fact, the embellishments of costume were as many and varied as the lines of the costume.

Sleeves

Sleeves were snug and fairly plain in cut and trim. They were usually long or a moderate bell shape, with pleating at the edge. Under the bell-shaped sleeve, an undersleeve (or a deep cuff, or ruffles) was used. Ruching at the wrist became extraordinarily popular toward the end of the decade.

Skirt

Around 1870, skirts were full, long, and frequently trained. They were worn over a frame (Fig. 245 C), or over wired hoops, flat in front but bulging high behind. Stiff crinoline ruffles also gave the desired effect.

Often the bottom edge of the skirt was edged with a deep ruffle and drawn back. An overskirt was looped up over this skirt in panniers at the side and arranged in a high puff at the back. This overskirt simulated an apron rounded, squared, or pointed in front (Fig. 244 Fig. 245 and pattern). All fullness was drawn toward the rear of the skirt. Additional drapings of material were smoothed over the front and curved upward toward the back to be affixed underneath an overdrape of one sort or another.

After 1875, the bustle diminished in size and dropped lower in the back. Skirts became layers of varying materials, colors, and patterns, and, though narrowed almost to normal width by 1879, they still presented a bewildering spectacle (Fig. 246).

A very extreme type of skirt around 1879 was so tight at the ankle and knees that ladies could scarcely climb steps.

Cloak

Sealskin continued to be most fashionable, especially the rare golden seal, the natural light tan, dyed. Sacques and long boas of this fur were used, and also collarines or pelerine capes, slightly pointed front and back. The sealskin cloak had sleeves, standing collar, and pockets. The boas were short or long, the latter being stylish. Ermine, Hudson Bay sable, Russian sable, mink, astrakhan, Persian lamb, Angora, and the like were used. Muffs were round and small for evening, and flat for skating and shopping (Fig. 244 Fig. 255 B).

Cloaks were short, about knee length, but varied in the decade.

Pelerines, or shoulder capes, were still in use. The *paletot,* or tight-fitting cloak with sleeves, was also popular.

A waterproof wrap of tweed or tartan could be worn over the outer cloak.

A *mantelet* was worn over the very full panniers. Toward 1880, a long velvet or cloth coat, princess style, was used. It was sometimes split up the back to the hip line.

Shawls of lace, wool, and silk continued in use.

The *Carrick,* a mantle of velvet with cape sleeves and fur trimming, was fashionable.

Footwear

Shoes were slender with rounded toes, high heels, and buttons in scallops on the sides (Fig. 255 A). They also laced up the front (Fig. 255 H), or had side elastics and loops for pulling them on. Slippers for evening wear had rosettes in front, high on the instep.

A quilted, laced shoe was also used for winter. Over this, a carriage shoe of silk, fur-lined and fur-edged, was worn en route to parties.

Charles IX shoes were very fashionable; they had long, pointed toes, high heels, and were of glacé kid with a bow in front. Walking boots with cloth tops to match the costume were very fashionable.

Hair

Around 1870, the hair was worn parted in front, waved back in pompadour style on the sides, caught up on the crown of the head, and twisted into a chignon, and allowed to fall in puffs, braids, twists, or curls down the back of the head. For evening, several long curls rested on the shoulder. Much false hair was used.

In or about 1875, the hair was arranged in curls across the front (bangs or fringe); the pompadour was higher in front, and the twist or rolls of hair down the back continued. Two long braids, *à la Marguerite,* were looped in the back.

Throughout this time the hair was brushed back from the ears, exposing them to view. Coronets of ribbon, flowers, jet, etc., decorated the hair for evening. Ribbons were woven in and out of the masses of hair.

Headdress

Hats, though more elaborately trimmed, were similar in size and shape to those of the 'sixties; bonnets were probably more in general use.

Bonnets and straw hats were in demand for summer wear. The hats frequently tipped forward over the forehead, and were tilted high up in the back. Bows and streamers in the back hung down on the elaborate hair arrangement. The bonnets had strings at the sides, tied under the chin to hold them in place. Feathers, lace, flowers, jet ornaments, and other additions decorated both hats and bonnets. The hats were usually not larger than a fair-sized pancake; the bonnets tilted forward and in shape looked like wired and decorated triangles.

Around 1875, bonnets and hats grew larger, with upturned rolled brims and festoons of feathers or flowers. The hat was often placed back on the head. Crowns grew higher and higher toward 1880.

Lace caps were still worn indoors, but were falling into disuse. Ribbons in knots and bows tended to be used instead.

Ornaments and Accessories (Fig. 244)

Jet jewelry predominated, with cameos and coral still popular. Short, round necklaces, with bells or other ornaments, were worn. Earrings were long and massive, always for pierced ears; bracelets were much as they had been in 1860. Lockets were in great favor, and so were brooches at the neck. Black India rubber ornaments of many varieties were popular.

Fig. 246

BODICE
BODICE YOKE
DRAPED SKIRT

1879

Fig. 249

BODICE
FICHU

1888

1890

1890 1890 1890 1891 Fig. 253 1896 1897 1898

Fig. 255

Bathing dress 1850

Fig. 252

Fig. 250

Pockets were made on the outside of the skirt, or inserted invisibly in the folds. In addition, aumonières, or bags, were carried; they were made of jet, beads, or of embroidered and lace-trimmed silk.

Gloves were short, even for evening, though long kid gloves with twenty to twenty-four buttons were also used.

Fans were often of heavy satin, embroidered and edged with feathers or fringe.

Parasols and sunshades were very similar to those of the preceding decade. Parasols were quite small, with long handles and very long tips.

Collar and cuff sets, plain or frilled, round or V-shaped, were used, as were chemisettes and inner sleeves.

Combs continued in use. Eyeglasses and spectacles were much in use. Liberty and Japanese silks were in great demand. There was a growing vogue for Oriental things.

Bridal Dress

White grosgrain silk was a favorite material for the wedding gown. A veil was draped over the face, and held in place by small rosebuds or orange blossoms. Formal bouquets of flowers were generally carried.

Equestrian Dress

High hats were usually worn, with bands of velvet and long veils flowing behind; but low hats were used by those to whom this style was unbecoming. The *Louis XV tricorne* was used in Paris. Straws with plumes were used for summer.

Habits for ladies were of cloth; jacket and skirt were of the same material. The jacket was worn open at the throat, displaying a white habit shirt. The tight coat sleeve had deep cuffs. Gloves and gauntlets were worn with the costume.

Mourning

Imperial serge, bombazine (silk and wool), Thibet merino, Empress cloth, poplin alpaca (with demi-luster), Henrietta cloth (a silk-warped cashmere), and all-wool delaine were some of the materials used for mourning.

Purple and gray were not used for half mourning, though purple bows on hats and at the throat were permissible. Crepe was removed and replaced by silk ribbon, black and white ruchings, etc., to signify the approach to the end of mourning.

A crepe veil, which might be as much as one and a half yards long, was worn over the bonnet; the length varied with the closeness of relationship to the deceased. Only widows wore the white crepe ruche in the bonnet.

Handkerchiefs for mourning had a two-inch hem of deep black. Massive jewelry of jet, onyx, or hard India rubber, made into earrings, brooches, chains, bracelets, and rings, were used by those who affected fashion, even at this time. Generally speaking, very little jewelry was worn during mourning.

COSTUME FOR CHILDREN

Girls from ten years on wore high-waisted dresses, replicas of adult styles. Coats, even for the very young, were modeled after the grown-ups' styles. The polonaise

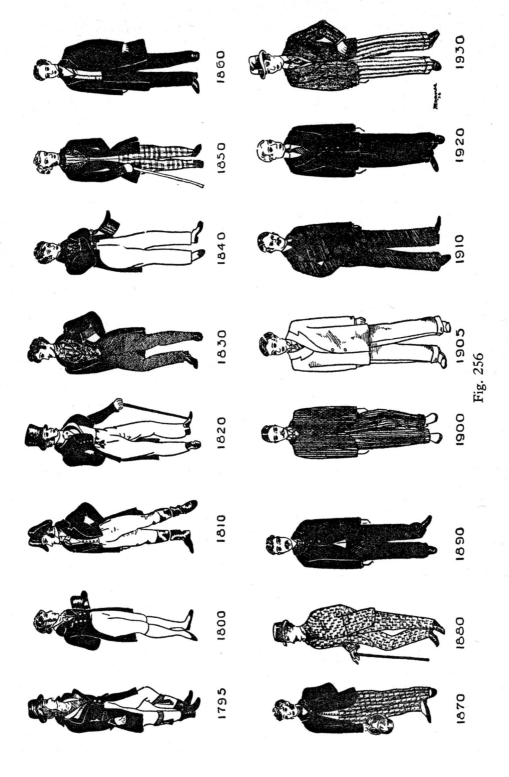

1795 1800 1810 1820 1830 1840 1850 1860

1870 1880 1890 1900 1905 1910 1920 1930

Fig. 256

and short sack coat were most used. The only great difference was that skirts were short, to the calf of the leg, and styles were simpler.

Rather high shoes with heels were fashionable.

The hair was smoothed back from the forehead, and tied on the crown, or let fall behind in braids, or loose. Hats were small, dipped forward over the forehead, with a trimming center front or side, and with streamers down the back. A rolled brim or turban was also worn, as well as glazed leather, patent leather, and sailor styles.

"Page caps" were popular with young girls.

For rainy weather, a coat with ample cape was used.

Little girls about ten years old wore a peplum, attached to a low bodice with chemisette of cambric, tight sleeves (often with a fluting along the outer seams), and an overskirt or paletot, looped at the sides and back. Sometimes straps or bretelles were placed over the shoulders.

Costume for the Lower Classes

Plain basques or rounded bodices, made high or with a very modest V neck, full skirt without a bustle, and an apron – these were sufficient for the workingwoman's costume. A white collar added some adornment to the dress. Sleeves were plain.

1880–1890

General Characteristics

The characteristic feminine silhouette of the decade showed princess lines, with wasplike waists. Tall bonnets, tight sleeves, and vertical trimming added seeming height to these Tennysonian, Pre-Raphaelite ladies, "divinely tall and most divinely fair." For men, the frock coat, the cutaway, and the sack coat were snugly fitted; shoulders were square, and trousers creaseless and narrow.

Materials

The materials were very much the same as those of the former decade. For men, tweeds, pepper-and-salt mixtures, and heavy twills were much in demand. For women, heavy, rich silks, satins, brocaded velvets, and allover lace were popular. For evening, thin silks, crepes, mousseline de soie, mull, tulle, foulard, and gauzy fabrics of all kinds were fashionable. For ordinary wear, "ladies' cloth," cambric, chambray, piqué, dotted Swiss muslin, gingham, sateen, mohair, surah, nuns' veiling, alpaca, grenadine, flannel, and the Jersey elastic cloth (or stockinet) were in demand. Rope or braid trimming – soutache braid was very popular – fringe, bows, velvet loops, and ribbons were used for decoration. Passementerie and embroidery were standard embellishment, and heavy jet trimming also led in popular fancy. Ruchings of various sorts, both narrow and wide, were used about the neck, throat, and sleeves, as well as about various drapings on the skirt. Folds of satin or lace, flowers, puffs, and ruffling and fur in long strips were included among the trimmings of the day.

Colors

For daytime wear, dark shades were still in order, especially a deep violet, and heliotrope. For evening, pale shades, particularly shell pink and pale blue were correct. Lotus blue, Vandyke red, loutre, and mandragora were named among the fashionable shades.

Underclothes

In this decade the same amount of coverage was used to clothe the female form divine. The foundation consisted of essentially the same layers as before. The corset was of a different shape, to give the desired princess effect. Drawers and petticoats were fastened with drawstrings or buttons. The petticoats, or underskirts, were form-fitting in front, but gathered at the back; frequently three or more deep ruffles in tiers across the back emphasized the bustle effect; sometimes a drawstring, about knee height, held in the skirt to the fashionably constricted slenderness about the knees demanded by the hobble-skirt style of dress. Nightgowns returned to ankle length. Negligees were made with Watteau-like pleats in the back.

"Thomson's glove-fitting corset" and "Patti's skirt band" for lengthening the waist were among the advertisements in *Godey's Lady's Book*.

Costume for Men (Fig. 247)

Coat

The frock coat had slightly longer tails than the 1870 type, with small lapels buttoned close about the neck. It was usually buttoned down the front with four buttons; the skirt of the coat was sometimes made separate from the waist, which was long and smooth-fitting. The straight frock coat was still used. The cutaway was fastened high with one or two buttons; from this fastening, the line of the coat curved sharply toward the back.

A business coat was cut along the lines of the frock coat, with a low waistline

Fig. 247

and high lapels. The skirt to the coat was attached separately, and curved away in a diagonal line. Deep pockets with flaps were placed at the waistline at the sides. There were five buttons up the front (Fig. 256).

The sack coat was long, but scant. It was fastened with two or three buttons, though the bottom of the coat was often left open. The adoption of deep pockets led to the habit of thrusting the hands in the pockets. As this custom put undue strain on the buttons, the coat was often worn open, and the few buttons were placed high.

Vest and Shirt

Vest and shirt for this decade showed only minor variations. The ultra-stylish vest was cut quite low in front. "Dress suit" vests were of black broadcloth and cut quite low, with three buttons down the front.

Neckwear

The type of collar most in use was a standing collar, with wings placed wide apart in front, so that the Adam's apple was freely exposed. The collar was only moderately high, rising but a half-inch or so above the snug, low-lying coat collar.

The Ascot tie and the wide, flat four-in-hand were becoming very popular. A tie pin was used in the fold of the Ascot tie.

Trousers

These were somewhat narrow, plain, striped, or of a mixture like tweed. No crease was used. The trousers were smoothly fitted about the hips, and often baggy at the knees.

Outer Coat

Topcoats were cut along the same general lines as in the preceding era. Linen dusters were favored for summer outings.

Footwear

Shoes were much the same as in the preceding decade. Socks were still conservative in color.

Hair

The hair was trimmed close to the head, but still brushed forward at the temples. Rather heavy mustaches drooping over the lips were worn, but, except for older men, there were no beards; side whiskers were still affected by men of dignity and position.

Headdress

Tall stovepipe hats, derbies, black felts, or toppers were in demand. Soft plaid traveling caps had a front visor, or two visors, one in front, one at the back – the Sherlock Holmes type. Striped jockey caps were worn for tennis, cycling, and the like. The British preferred the top hat for most occasions, including business wear.

Ornaments and Accessories

Accessories and ornaments showed little change. The heavy watch chain and fob were still in evidence. Tie pins were more generally used, whole pearls being particularly favored. Gold links fastened the watch chain into a vest buttonhole; the watch was usually placed in the left-hand vest pocket. The cuffs were also fastened with links. A cane with a loop was used. Pipes, cigars, large, fine cambric handkerchiefs, and billfolds were numbered among gentlemen's accessories (Fig. 247).

Costume for Children

Boys wore jersey coats or striped blazers, and visored caps. Flannels were very popular for the boarding-school age.

Costume for the Lower Classes

The sack coat, derby with low crown, and loose-fitting trousers marked the man of lower social rank.

Costume for Women

Bodice

The bodice (called a *basque* at this period) was fitted smoothly and tightly from neck to low hip line. The princess line was emphasized. Sometimes the bodice was cut as part of the skirt. Sometimes it was cut separately. When made separately, it showed a decided dip front and back, with short sides, so that it presented the appearance of a corset worn outside of the dress (Fig. 248). A *jersey,* or tight-fitting basque of elastic fabric (like stockinet), achieved great popularity at this time, due, it is said, to the influence of Lillie Langtry, "The Jersey Lily." A low hip line was also used; the garment was tightly molded to the figure. Patterns of this day were made in many gores and with numerous darts. All garments were lined and interlined, and the seams about the waist were heavily boned.

The bodice was buttoned either front or back. Cloth, jet, or steel buttons usually the size of a pea were set close together down the front or back and gave a trim touch to the garment.

It was customary to make the dress with a vest of gathered or pleated material, extending from the neck to the waistline. Bands of trimming or ruffles bordered the vest. Passementerie, embroidery, shirrings, fur, and ribbon garnitures trimmed the bodices.

Sleeves

Sleeves were tight and long, and fitted into the small armhole with a slight puff. A cuff was frequently added, with a ruching about the wrist. Elbow-length sleeves were also used for a dressy effect or for summer costumes. For evening wear, elbow-length sleeves or very small puffs at the shoulder were used, though some bodices had no sleeves at all.

Toward 1887 the three-quarter-length sleeve was stylish. It frequently had a cuff of pleated material with a wide ruching underneath.

Neckline

For daytime the neckline was high. Usually a fairly tall collar was sewn to the bodice and fastened either front or back, according to the fashion of the bodice. A velvet collar was most fashionable. The moderate V-shaped neck was also used, with a ruching outlining the V (Fig. 248).

For evening wear, the bodice was cut low, outlining the bust, and often with no ornamentation whatever about the neckline. Garnitures of artificial flowers added a festive note to the costume at times (Fig. 249 A).

Skirt

In 1880 the skirt was draped tightly about the princess silhouette, with any fullness looped up toward the back. The overskirt was still fashionable, though it was much

1880

Fig. 248

longer, almost touching the ground in front. Many variations of the overskirt were seen. It was cut in loops or layers or segments, but always followed the general line – a deep dip in front and a curve upward at the back. Some dresses were so tightly fitted to the figure that the walk was little more than a hobble. The foundation skirt beneath the overdrape was usually finished with one or more pleated ruffles or other embellishments. Wide sashes tied in bows, or fringe, draped the bustle in the back. Some dressmakers crisscrossed layers of material over the skirt until it presented a puzzling appearance (Fig. 248   Fig. 249   Fig. 257).

About 1885 the bustle increased in size until it stood out in the back at least a foot from the figure. The rear view of a woman looked like the back of a centaur. By 1890, however, the bustle had decreased to a moderate puff.

The postilion type of dress still continued fashionable. In this the basque extended over the bustle with long tails in the back. The *polonaise,* buttoned down the front, was also a favored style.

For evening wear, the overskirt was draped over lace or a ruffled foundation skirt. Sashes and garnitures of flowers were used for decorative effect. Trains a yard or more in length added dignity to a creation already imposing (Fig. 249 A).

The length of skirts varied; the walking skirt cleared the ground, but the full evening dress swept the floor, and frequently ended in a long train behind.

The skirt, like the bodice, was lined and interlined. One or more dust ruffles lined the inner edge. Weights sewn into the hems were often used to hold the skirts in place. Paper cambric was a favorite lining material, though silk and other fabrics were also used.

With such complexity of pattern and such wealth of material, the cost of women's clothes advanced to a considerable figure. Most costumes called for ten or twelve yards of material, and frequently more was necessary. Dressmakers, even those local seamstresses who were paid by the day, asked high prices for making these intricate creations.

Cloak

The cloak was made of cloth or velvet, or of sealskin or other furs. It was semi-fitted, and cut to be worn over the bustle (Fig. 248). A *visite* was made with semi-detachable sleeves and a long panel in the front. Long coats to the ground were also made in pseudo-princess style.

Circular shoulder capes trimmed with fur of various kinds were worn. Shawls were in great demand, especially for parties or for receiving in the home.

Stockings

Cotton stockings were the usual wear, with silk stockings reserved for evening, as in the former decade.

Footwear

Shoes were narrow and had blunt toes. A high shoe with seven or eight buttons and a curving heel was in general use. For evening wear, a low slipper with a bow or rosette over the instep was used; it was made of kid dyed a pale color to match the gown.

Hair

Except for bangs across the forehead and a cluster of curls above the ears, the hair was drawn back quite simply into a knot placed high on the head. Tendrils of small curls were adjusted in front of the ears and lay against the nape of the neck. Women blessed with large amounts of hair coiled and twisted the loops or braids into intricate patterns on top of the head; these sometimes extended down the back of the head to the nape of the neck. A few combs or ornaments were placed in the coils to add a touch of decoration to the coiffure. The high headdress further enhanced the tall, slender silhouettes of the period.

For evening wear, a wreath of flowers, a bow, or aigrette was worn in the hair (Fig. 249 A).

Headdress

Bonnets still led in favor. They were worn on the back of the head, the raised brim in front framing the face. The trimming was placed toward the front and built high to a peak.

Hats, however, gained favor during this decade. They were of two types. One was shaped like a modified poke bonnet with the crown on top of the head and the brim curved about the face in a more horizontal position than that of the original poke bonnet (Fig. 249 B). A wide ribbon frequently held the hat in place; it was tied in a large bow under the chin (Fig. 248).

Another type of hat was fashioned with a very tall, sloping crown, and a narrow, rolling brim which sometimes dipped sharply in front. An ornament of feathers or ribbon was placed either directly in front or at the side. This type of hat was very mannish and added to the trim effect of the costume. Birds' wings were used as a trimming and dotted veils were draped about the hats and bonnets (Fig. 250).

The use of caps was confined to elderly women.

Ornaments and Accessories

The fan was very large, of satin, double-faced, with an ostrich fringe or a lace-ruffled edge to accentuate its size. It was often painted with flowers or landscapes; sometimes it was embroidered in various designs. The fan was frequently so large and heavy that in order to keep it shut a ring was attached to the end of the ribbon or cord and slipped over the folded fan when it was not in use. Feather fans were also fashionable. The large fan was called a "fire screen." Another type of fan used was the circular, flat, Chinese paper fan with round bamboo handle.

Gloves were long, twenty-four-button length for evening wear, and made of kid in white or delicate shades to match the gown. For daytime wear they were short and were fastened over the wrists by cords crisscrossed over metal tabs.

Parasols had long handles and very long tips. Umbrellas were small and were rolled tightly and strapped when not in use.

Ties and ribbon bows were used with the high, tight bodices. Buckles of steel or gilt fastened the plain, wide belts which ornamented some of the basques. Tortoise-shell combs were used; those for evening wear were set with brilliants.

Muffs were small, round or flattened, and bows decorated those carried for dressy occasions. Bags, rectangular in shape, and sometimes beaded, held the large, sheer, linen handkerchief and other simple accessories carried by the ladies. Skirts, however, were still fashioned with capacious pockets hidden in the folds; in these pockets were carried many trinkets dear to the heart of femininity. Calling cards were carried in flat cases of silver or tortoise shell.

For jewelry, earrings were in great demand. The ears were pierced, and the earrings screwed in. Small rosettes, solitaire diamonds, and single pearls were in the height of style for these earrings. A few drop types of earrings were seen. Rings and bracelets were necessary additions, as was the round or flat breastpin, quite small in size, used at the throat or to mark the deep V of the basque. Necklaces and beads were worn in short strands close about the throat. Gold chains in long loops added richness to the costume.

Make-up

A suspicion of rouge or powder was used, but lipstick was unknown, except on the stage. The hair was oiled and brushed until it shone, fifty strokes to each side of the head being the standard.

COSTUME FOR CHILDREN

Little girls wore costumes in the styles of their elders. The very long waistline was the most outstanding characteristic. High collars, pleated skirts (draped in the fashion used by older women), and high-crowned hats similar to those worn by their elders typified the dress of the young misses of this era.

1890–1900

GENERAL CHARACTERISTICS

During this decade, men's dress continued to emphasize the tendency away from the formal frock coat and toward the general adoption of the short sack coat. Trousers were narrow, and the front and back crease appeared. Dark colors were preferred, with striped designs; thick, closely-woven materials were particularly popular. The bowler hat, or derby, was used, especially in America.

Women's dress still showed the bustle, in very reduced form. However, the huge leg-of-mutton sleeve eclipsed in interest all other points. Skirts were many-gored, but usually were without trimming or draping. Hats were mixtures of many ornaments.

COSTUME FOR MEN

Coat (Fig. 251   Fig. 252   Fig. 253)

The frock coat still held its own for formal daytime use. For the races, promenading, afternoon teas, "gallery openings," and the like, it was indispensable. Frock coats were of gray and fawn, as well as black, though Americans preferred the more conventional black (Fig. 253). It was fitted to the body snugly, with a slight flare at the bottom. Lapels were buttoned together high on the chest, or they flared in a deep V to the waist. Coats were single- or double-breasted. Lapels and collars were frequently of velvet.

The cutaway or morning coat was the correct garb for certain functions, particularly those which took place before noon. The tails of the fitted cutaway were somewhat shorter than in the previous decade (Fig. 251).

The sack coat was still buttoned high on the chest. The bottom was rounded, and there was a definite fit to the garment (Fig. 256). The loose sack style was popularized in the blazer, the bicycle coat, and sports garments in general.

OVER COAT   BOY'S FAUNTLEROY SUIT

Fig. 251

The *blazer* was of flannel, plain or striped. If plain, it was usually edged with braid. It was appropriate for tennis, for boating, bicycling, picnicking, racing, and the like.

The *Norfolk jacket* began to be worn, especially in the country, for hunting, fishing and like pursuits. It was of plain or plaid material with box pleats front and back on each side, and it had a broad cloth belt laced through the pleats and buttoned in front. Capacious pockets added to its usefulness.

The full dress evening coat was cut with tails much shorter than formerly. The lapels were often faced with satin.

The *Tuxedo,* or English dinner jacket, was named after the American summer resort. It was used for stag affairs, for home dinners, but not for formal occasions, if ladies were present.

The smoking jacket was of velveteen or cloth, faced with a satin or quilted collar and lapel of black or a contrasting color. These jackets were affected by "Bohemian" painters, who also wore the Vandyke beard, a black wing tie, and a sash about the waist. The smoking jacket was similar to the morning robe of 1870.

Sleeves

The sleeve did not materially change in this decade.

Vest

Full evening vests were of white piqué, but toward the end of the decade they were also made of black broadcloth or silk brocade. Vests for daytime wear were of plain or figured cloth. If worn with sack suits, they often matched the suit. They were made single- or double-breasted, with or without lapels.

Shirt

Dress suit shirts were stiff-bosomed, held together with studs down the front; they also opened down the back and were fastened at the neck. Cuffs were very stiff and detachable, and showed almost an inch beyond the coat sleeve. Reversible cuffs, advertised extensively, were used by the thrifty.

Everyday shirts were pleated or plain. Shirt bosoms, collars, and cuffs were stiffly starched. White shirts only were worn by all classes except industrial workers.

The shirtwaist came in with the growing interest in bicycling and other outdoor sports. This type of shirt often had a soft collar and cuffs attached; the bosom was plain, not pleated, and had little or no starch. It had no tab at the front waistline to hold it in place. It was worn without a vest, with a sack suit, Norfolk jacket, blazer, or the like.

Workmen's shirts were usually of coarse, dark blue materials. They were plain in cut, with attached collars and cuffs.

Neckwear

The "white collar group" were very caste-conscious. The high stiff collar was a veritable fetish. The standing collar was used for everyday wear as well as for formal occasions (Fig. 251 Fig. 253). It had straight edges brought close together in front, or points slightly bent back. The stiff, winged collar and a stiff, high turnover were coming into general favor (Fig. 251). The soft, low, turnover collar was used only rarely, mainly for sports (Fig. 252).

The four-in-hand was still large in the knot and flat. The Ascot tie, favored by Edward, Prince of Wales, at Ascot and other famous race courses, was a large puffed arrangement, with a stickpin in the center to hold its folds. The bow tie was still worn, and the string tie was favored by old men and politicians.

With the dress suit, the white organdie bow tie was proper. With the newly introduced Tuxedo, a black bow tie was preferred.

Trousers

Throughout this decade, trousers were very narrow in cut, particularly dress trousers. By 1891, the crease in the trouser was an established custom, though not a universal one. It was used for dress trousers and those worn with frock coats and cutaways; by the end of the decade, it was almost a general custom.

Dress trousers were of black broadcloth, matching the coat. For the frock coat and cutaway, trousers were usually dark gray and striped. For the sack coat, they either matched the coat or were of plain or striped material. However, striped trousers and occasionally plaid trousers were also worn with odd coats. The formal type of trousers had no cuffs, but cuffs began to appear on the trousers of business suits and sometimes on flannel trousers.

Knickers of plain cloth, tweed, or plaid became increasingly popular. They were scant of cut, and fastened below the knee. Toward the end of the century, they were more generous in cut. Long golf stockings were worn with the knickers.

Outer Coat

Overcoats followed the lines of the frock coat. They were long, scant in cut, with short lapels (frequently of velvet – Fig. 253). The coats were usually fashioned of heavy black or dark green cloth. Irish frieze, beaver, melton, and kersey were among the materials used for overcoats.

A covert coat, straight cut, with an invisible fastening down the front, was very fashionable. Dandies and sportsmen favored a short, tan box coat flared at the bottom, with wide sleeves and large buttons.

For the races, there was a very long tan or plaid coat, neatly tailored to the figure, with several pleats in the back to give fullness.

The Inverness, with a cape over the shoulders, was still worn for traveling. The *ulster* was another type, similar to the Inverness. A rubberized raincoat known as the *Mackintosh* or *stormcoat,* fashioned like the Inverness or ulster, was worn in inclement weather. (The Mackintosh – named for Charles Mackintosh, inventor of a process for waterproofing cloth – had been used in England since the 'forties; but the name, at least, was not adopted in America until a much later date.

A *duster,* fashioned like a plain overcoat, with a turnover collar buttoned close about the throat, was also worn for traveling.

Socks

Socks in this decade were still conservatively dark in hue. Knee-length woolen golf stockings were worn with men's knickerbockers.

Hair

The hair was worn fairly short and well-trimmed. Though the center part was favored, many parted the hair on the side, and the pompadour was also used.

Mustaches were usually rather full and drooping; some, however, were worn with ends curled up, in imitation, perhaps, of Kaiser Wilhelm II. Sideburns, mutton chops, chin whiskers, and full beards were favored by older men, professional men, and clergymen. The Vandyke pointed beard was adopted by artists, as has been mentioned, and also by doctors.

Headdress

The top hat, or "tile," was stylish and the correct wear for formal occasions. A collapsible silk opera hat was used for the theater.

The derby became increasingly popular. It was of black, brown, or tan felt, and was made with a high crown and a curved brim. The soft felt hat also was seen. The Vandyke, a fedora of felt or velours, affected by artists, had a wide, rakish brim and a soft crown.

The round tam-o'-shanter was also used by artists, as well as by the general public for country use and for golfing. A flat cap with a visor was used for boating and cycling. The two-visored cap, fore and aft – the Sherlock Holmes type – was proper for traveling, or for wear on ocean voyages.

For summer, the straw hat became a common choice. It had a low crown, and early in the decade the brim was narrow. Later the brim became fairly wide, and the crown was decorated with a wide hatband of striped colors, horizontal or vertical. A cord looped about the crown was attached to the lapel buttonhole of the coat to hold it on in windy weather, or when riding on the bicycle, the street cars, the tallyho, or the houseboat.

Ornaments and Accessories (Fig. 251)

Canes were used both for daytime and for dress use. For evening, they were short and slender; for daytime, they were long and thick.

Gloves of gray, fawn, mauve, or tan were used with the morning coat or frock coat; white gloves were used with the dress suit. Doeskin, chamois, or pigskin gloves were worn for driving or for everyday street wear.

Eyeglasses on a ribbon were worn by professional men; spectacles were worn by all classes; the monocle on a ribbon identified the dandy and the Englishman.

Watch chains were still fairly heavy and fastened to the vest button. The sash-vest and the *Gordon sash* were favored by younger men, artists, and the aesthetically inclined.

Special Costume for Men

Clergymen, for daily wear, wore frock coats, or the cutaway. The clergyman's collar was close, high, and fastened behind. In addition, dickies of black silk were worn inside the frock coat.

Upperclassmen at colleges and universities wore the cap and gown; the cap was a square "mortarboard"; the gown was a full-cut garment with a square yoke and full, open sleeves.

For lounging, men wore a smoking jacket, bath robe, dressing gown, or kimono made with a pleated, deep roll collar, and a rolled pad about the bottom edge.

Work shirts and overalls with bibs identified the workman. Tradesmen wore full-length aprons with detachable sleeves.

Chamois vests, single- or double-breasted, were worn under or over the outer vest for driving, riding, etc. A *chest protector* was also used for cold weather, and a dress vest, of quilted satin, was worn over the immaculate full dress, with stiff-bosomed shirt front.

The jersey pull-over sweater was used for bicycling and other outing events. It was either in plain colors or in brilliant horizontal stripes.

COSTUME FOR CHILDREN

Very little boys – two to five years old – wore dresses with pleated skirts, attached waists, and deep square collars with ruffled edges. Boys from five to eight wore short, knee-length trousers, jackets buttoned down the front, and shirts with deep square collars, ruffled about the edge, deep ruffled cuffs, and ruffled shirt fronts – the "Little Lord Fauntleroy" style (Fig. 251). Eton jackets were also popular; they were made of cloth or velvet. Sailor suits were worn by boys up to ten or twelve; older boys wore knee-length trousers and sack coats or Norfolk jackets.

The *reefer* – a double-breasted short overcoat – was very popular for boys. For extra wear out-of-doors, the covert coat, with invisible fastening up the front, was also used.

Wide sailor hats or peaked caps were favored. The sailor hats had ribbon streamers behind. The Scotch cap was also used.

Costume for Women (Fig. 253 Fig. 254)

This decade shows several changes in the silhouette.

Bodice

The figure in 1890 showed the long, slender waistline of the late 'eighties. The bodice was snug, with a decided point in front. Revers or bretelles accentuated this

Fig. 254

deep V effect in front. For daytime, the bodice had a high neck with a standing collar to accent the line. For evening, the bodice was cut low, and was square, round, or a deep V. A full décolleté dress was often sleeveless, with just a lace bow, a ribbon knot, or a bouquet of flowers decorating the shoulders.

A basque extending below the waistline was occasionally used, but was confined to the coat type of bodice, with revers.

Sleeves

The sleeves began to show a puff at the shoulder, though they were tight-fitting to the wrist. An elbow-length sleeve was also used, with a slight puff or ruffle at the elbow. A three-quarter-length sleeve was occasionally used.

Skirt

The skirt, though slightly draped across the front, flared out full behind. Though the bustle had subsided to modest proportions, it was still quite evident.

1895

Bodice

By this time the wide shoulder line was accentuated by very full sleeves and a slender waistline (Fig. 257). The hourglass figure attained its height in 1896. Above the waistline there were huge leg-of-mutton or balloon sleeves, deep bretelles over the shoulders, a deep bertha in front, and much trimming of lace, velvet, ribbon, passementerie, and jet. Below the waistline was a full radiation of stiffly-gored skirt. The waistline was squeezed between the two to most modest proportions (Fig. 254).

The evening waist was made with a deep square neck; a deep V or a rounded neck was also used. The sleeve was a very large balloon type, elbow length. A small puff at the shoulder was also fashionable. The waist and skirt were separate, though a princess effect was sometimes used. Wide, sharply-pointed bretelles, like detached wings, often decorated either side of the front of the blouse. A short peplum was also added to some models; a bow or knot of ribbon gave an additional touch.

The shirtwaist came into vogue for bicycling, golfing, and other sports. The distinguishing features of the shirtwaist were its plainness, its being made of percale and other washable materials (though it was occasionally made of silk), its yoke in back (also sometimes in front), its buttoned front opening, its collar (standing or turndown, but very high), its buttoned cuffs, and its waistband. With it was worn a four-in-hand tie. Full sleeves or modified leg-of-mutton sleeves were used.

A short tea jacket was used. There was also a dressing sack, hip length, with lace and ribbon trimming. These were worn with a ruffled or lace flounced skirt.

A Norfolk jacket with basque was worn with the shirtwaist or divided skirt.

The tailored suit consisted of a jacket and skirt of the same cloth. The jacket was fitted in to the slender waistline, and flared out in a short peplum over the hips. It often had wide revers and a vestee, or front. Sometimes a regular vest, buttoned up the front, and a tall white standing or turndown collar with bow tie or four-in-hand were used. The jacket also buttoned up the front; it was at times left open with the buttons at each side to suggest a closing.

Sleeves (Fig. 254)

This was the age of the sleeve. Human ingenuity was taxed to the utmost to create variations of the high, wide, and handsome effect deemed fashionable. The balloon sleeve was what its name implied: a huge puff to the elbow, and a tight sleeve to the wrist. Sometimes this puff was tacked at intervals, like a wadded quilt. The *butterfly sleeve* consisted of a puff divided in two parts, with a long, tight sleeve below. The *mushroom puff* draped over the tight sleeve, mushroom fashion; the *empire puff*, with mousquetaire or wrinkled sleeve below, was also called the "Bernhardt" sleeve. There was a *double mushroom puff*, and the sleeve, in sections of puffs, graduated from a small one at the wrist to a huge one at the shoulder.

There was the *bishop sleeve,* full from the shoulder to the wrist, confining the fullness at the wrist.

There was the leg-of-mutton sleeve, which was full at the shoulder, and drawn in tight from the elbow down (Fig. 253 Fig. 254); sometimes the tight sleeve extended above the elbow; sometimes the tight part was wrinkled, mousquetaire style. There was the leg-of-mutton with one, two, or three circular caps, or with handkerchief-pointed caps.

There was the leg-of-mutton or bishop shirt sleeve, with deep, buttoned cuff, to be used with the shirtwaist.

There was the short puffed sleeve, lace-ruffled, and the frilled cap sleeve for evening wear.

These represent only a few of the hundred variations.

Skirt

The skirt was also at its zenith in 1895. It was cut in many gores, ranging from five to nine; eleven gores were not unusual. The gores were set smooth about the waist and flared out to tremendous sweep at the bottom; a patented "skirt extender" of pliable hoops held the back gores in regular folds.

Hip pads and a slight bustle in the back gave the required roundness to the figure, and the long, sweeping folds in the back were graceful. Gores flared out toward the bottom, making the width around the lower edge four to six yards. An ordinary five-gored skirt took eight to ten yards of thirty-six-inch material. Skirts were lined with cambric and sometimes interlined, with dust ruffles and velvet edging at the bottom inner edge. Skirts ordinarily touched the ground.

Trains were usual, from very slight ones for daytime use to long, square-edged ones for formal afternoon or evening. Some of these measured eight and a half yards about the lower edge, and trailed over a yard on the floor. A dress of this type required about fifteen yards for the skirt alone, as the back gores were pleated (Fig. 254). The bodice with leg-of-mutton sleeves required about six yards more.

For bicycling, a short skirt (high shoetop length) was worn. It was made with full bloomers and gaiters, and measured about three and a half yards about the bottom edge. A divided skirt with bloomers was adopted by the more daring. A wide panel discreetly hid the division in front.

For gymnastics, ladies wore calf-length bloomers and a blouse with high neck, long sleeves, and a sailor or "Byron" collar.

For horseback riding, ladies wore knickerbocker drawers – also recommended for traveling and outing use – of the same cloth as the outer skirt. Long equestrian trousers were also permitted by fashion – *mirabile dictu!* With the knickers were worn long gaiters buttoned up the outer leg. The skirt was cut full and fashioned to fit the position in the side saddle. The equestrienne adjusted the extra fullness of the skirt, when walking, by a loop fastened over a button on the hip. The riding skirt was not as long as formerly; it now cleared the ground when the lady stood. A double-breasted basque with high-collared chemisette was worn with the skirt.

Fig. 257

For bathing, ladies wore blue serge or mohair suits, consisting of knickerbockers gathered with a ruffle below the knee, a bloused waist gathered to a square yoke, a sailor collar, long – or elbow length – sleeves, a full skirt reaching below the knees, and a belt. White braid trimming outlined collars, cuffs, belt, yoke, and the hem of the skirt. Over this revealing costume were worn a long circular cape and hood. A large straw hat tied under the chin kept off the prying sun.

A tea gown or a Mother Hubbard wrapper worn in the house let one relax, for a while, from the tightly laced corsets and boned dresses. The tea gown, or similar dress, was made princess or empress style, or it might be fashioned on a yoke, with fullness front and back. Often the fullness in the back was arranged in a Watteau double pleat. It was confined by a ribbon belt or sash, though it was equally fashionable to wear the garment unbelted. A fitted lining gave the negligee shape and form. Negligees were often very elaborate, of silk brocade and lace, and they often had trains.

1898

Bodice

A change came over the silhouette of the hour. By this year, the bodice or waist distinctly showed the shirtwaist influence. Separate silk bodices of warm colors were worn with cloth or silk skirts, black taffeta or satin skirts being most popular. The yoke line, square or rounded, was accentuated with braid, ruffles, jet, or passementerie. The waists were fashioned with slight blouses at the waistline and dips in front. High, boned collars, with a bow or pleated ornament in front or in back, finished the neckline (Fig. 253).

Belts were fashioned of velvet folds with cut steel buckles. Ribbon belts with a bow at the side, the front, or the back, were also used.

Evening bodices were cut very low and usually square. The bodice was sleeveless, with straps over the shoulders. Elbow sleeves were, however, also used for evening wear.

Sleeves

Sleeves were tight and long, with a V extending down over the wrist. The V was frequently accentuated by a ruffle or ruching. A slight leg-of-mutton fullness, or a modest puff at the shoulder, relieved the slender effect (Fig. 253).

Skirt

Skirts were still gored, but there were not quite so many gathers or pleats in the rear gores. The resulting trimness gave a bell shape to the skirt. Ruffles and other trimming were re-introduced around the bottom edge of the skirt as a relief from the plain lines of the former skirts.

Cloak

The favorite cloak was circular and knee length, with short cape collar, similar to those worn by Queen Victoria. A short, rippled cape was favored by younger women; another type popular with them was the small, circular, French (or "Bernhardt") cape, made on plain lines, or a more elaborate type of the same, made with one or more ruffles or flounces, with a full ruff about the neck of the cape. For evening, the long, circular cloak was preferred. Around 1895, the shoulders were built out to allow for the huge leg-of-mutton sleeves beneath.

The Inverness cape coat, Mackintosh, ulster, or duster was used for traveling. Toward the end of the decade, a fitted coat with princess lines was added to the wardrobe. At this time a French cape, circular in shape, with Vandyke or Cavalier collar, came in. A small, circular sealskin cape or sealskin basque was very fashionable. Short separate jackets, Eton, Zouave, bolero, or basque style, were also used. Long, full, bell sleeves were used on some jackets or cloaks. Serge, cheviot, tweed, etamine, broadcloth, and velvet were the materials principally used for jackets, cloaks, and capes.

Hosiery

The hosiery matched the shoes, black and brown, in cotton or lisle, being the regular colors for daytime wear. For evening, tints to match the gown were permissible, but women of taste wore black or white silk stockings only. In 1897, long opera hose were worn by women for horseback riding instead of the trousers underneath the skirt. Openwork hosiery in lisle or silk, with lace appliqué or embroidery, were used for weddings, balls, and other special occasions.

Footwear

The long, slender, pointed "Trilby" shoe, with cloth, velvet, or jersey knit top, buttoned or laced, held sway throughout the decade. Toward 1897, the shoe became broader, but the toe was still pointed. Patent leather was favored for full dress, at least for the lower half of the shoe. Russet or bronze shoes were also popular.

For evening wear, slippers of patent leather, satin, and bronze were in favor. V-shaped or cross straps with rhinestone buckles or rosettes added a fancy touch to the slippers. French heels, of the height today called "Baby French," were in vogue.

Hair

In 1890, the hair was worn in a long twist up the back of the head and low on the neck. A frieze of bangs decorated the forehead. The coiffure was pinned close to the head.

The hair, in 1895, was worn parted down the middle, fluffed out at either side, and elaborately curled. There were bangs over the forehead and tendrils before the ears and at the nape of the neck. The knot was a loose, full one, placed quite high on the head, but not directly on top, except for evening wear. A *Psyche knot* was favored then; it was twisted high, with an ornament of feathers, aigrettes, or wired ribbon, braid, etc., to emphasize the height. In 1898, the hair was drawn up evenly about the face and forehead in a moderate pompadour (over a pad or *rat*), smoothed up in the back, and arranged in a Psyche knot on top of the head. A few tendrils escaped about the ears, the nape of the neck, and either side of the forehead (Fig. 253). For evening, the hair was more softly arranged; the Psyche knot was taller, and ornaments similar to those described above were put into the knot or in front of it. Spangled butterflies were fashionable as ornaments.

Headdress

In 1890 hats were as wide of brim in front as they had formerly been high of crown. The brim projected over the face, and the rear of the hat tilted up behind. Bonnets were quite small, perched on top of the head, with bows or ornaments upright (Fig. 253). They were often tied under the chin with moderately wide ribbons. Dotted veils, favored by the Princess Alexandra, were worn with bonnets and sometimes with smaller hats. Caps and tam-o'-shanters (with two stiff feathers jauntily affixed at the side) were used for outdoor sports.

By 1895, bonnets were almost discontinued, and those that lasted were almost as large as hats. They were adjusted flat on top of the head, without bonnet strings, but they were held on with the aid of dotted veils.

Hats, in 1895, were medium in size, and were perched on the wide, fluffy coiffure. Ribbon, lace, feathers, birds, or bird wings and other creations decorated the hat. The back of the hat was turned up and trimmed with flowers, lace, velvet, etc. Plain or dotted veils were worn, loosely draped over the face and hat.

In 1898, hats were designed to perch upon the Psyche knot. They were shaped of velvet or felt, with upright ornaments of feathers and bows wired in infinite variety of shapes. Bird wings were widely used, in pairs or singly, and full, loose veils enveloped all.

With the bicycle and outdoor sports, the sailor hat came into use. It had a small, low crown and a very wide brim; a velvet band often encircled the crown. Long hatpins, singly or in pairs, held it firmly anchored to the Psyche knot. The soft felt or fedora hat was also used. With a stiff feather added at the side, it became an *Alpine,* or *outing hat.*

Other types of headgear were the Inverness, capuchin, Irish peasant, golf, and Red Riding hoods; the sunbonnet, with hood and curtain (one style was called "Kiss-me-quick!"); the nightcap (like a sunbonnet without the curtain); and the bathing or dusting cap, like a mobcap.

Ornaments and Accessories

Women wore hair ornaments of feathers, rosettes, spangled butterflies, wired velvet ribbon, and other arrangements. Combs with brilliants were also popular.

Fans were indispensable for formal wear. They were not as large as they had been in the 'eighties, but they were still imposing. They were carried in the hand.

Gloves for evening were long and slightly wrinkled on the arm. Short gloves were donned for daytime use. For sports, chamois or kid gloves were proper.

Parasols were long and slender and could be wrapped, as could umbrellas. The parasols had ruffled edges, and were frequently lined.

Around 1898, the chatelaine bag became a regular adjunct to the toilette. Made of beads, leather, or velvet, it hung from the waist by a chain. It was square, round, or oval in shape, and fastened with a clasp. It remained in style for several years.

Veils, plain or dotted, were usually black, though white lace veils were also used.

Collars, cuffs, ties, fichus, ribbons, and stocks (or separate collars) of ribbon, lace, and velvet were worn.

Muffs were melon- or spool-shaped, and fairly small. Sealskin and Persian lamb were the furs most used.

Relatively little jewelry was worn. Rings, perhaps, and bracelets for evening were in good taste. Occasionally a necklace, preferably of pearls, was worn.

However, trimmings showed no such restraint. Ruchings, lace, ribbons, velvet, passementeries, furs, buckles – every type of trimming was used, alone or in combination.

The bustle, and hip pads, used under the gored skirts, were made of flexible wire mesh, of pads stuffed with horsehair, or of quilted or padded cotton forms. Tapes fastened them about the waist.

Make-up

Ladies still did little in the way of make-up. Professional beauties, actresses, singers, and the like were allowed rouge and even eyebrow penciling, and no doubt some lip rouge was used.

Mourning

The types and gradations of mourning customary in the preceding eras were continued.

Costume for Children

Very little girls wore short dresses, yoked bodices, full skirts, and bonnets tied under the chin. Older little girls wore short, full skirts, and waists with yokes. Girls ten years old wore Eton jackets, blouses, and gored skirts, or else they wore dresses with square or round yokes. Sashes were much used, and aprons of black sateen covered the dresses during playtime. The aprons were made with yokes and straps with ruffled capes over the shoulders. The full skirt of the apron fully covered the dress. White aprons were used on Sundays or semi-dress occasions.

Older girls wore the fashions of their elders. Sunbonnets were used on children in the summertime; sailor hats were favored for the older girls.

Costume for the Lower Classes

Workingwomen wore dresses of gingham or percale; in cold weather, they used serge and coarse woolen. Dresses were made along the lines of the shirtwaist and skirt type, with plain, full waists buttoned up the front, a plain collar, full sleeves with cuffs, full gathered skirt, and long apron. Maids' caps were very frilly and set back on the head. Skirts were made long, or at least they just cleared the ground.

Modern Adaptations

In this century, all sorts of cotton materials can be used – gingham, percale, dimity, organdie, chambray, dotted swiss, marquisette, and other weaves of this type. Silks are very good, either very light, thin silks, or dark, dull, heavy silks, ribbed (like rep or silk peplum) or brocaded. Sateen, rayon, poplin, and cotton rep are good substitutes; also chintzes with small flowered patterns and dark brown or gray backgrounds can be used to create the proper atmosphere. Woolen cloth or a substitute, dyed unbleached muslin, corduroy, or duvetyn can be used for daytime costumes or for men's clothes. Colors in general are dark – slate gray, olive green, maroon, garnet, deep navy blue, and similar shades.

Men's waistcoats can be of chintz, flowered brocade, plaids, or striped material. Coats can be made of duvetyn or flannel in deep blues, browns, grays, and greens, maroons, and black. The trousers should be of a dark color, and plain, except where the fashion of the period indicates checks or plaids.

Patterns

For the 1800 type of gown, use a brassière pattern for the bodice. For the skirt, use a gored pattern without fullness. For 1805, use an empire pattern. The waist can be gradually lengthened from 1805 to 1830. Until 1825, all skirts were cut on a gored pattern. Again, in 1840, the gored skirt pattern can be used, though the full, gathered skirt was never totally relinquished from 1825 through the 1860's. With the bustle, from 1870 to the end of the century, the gored skirt pattern is again a basic necessity.

From 1800 to 1830, a puff sleeve pattern can be used, very small at first, but larger as the century advances. For the 1830's, use a bishop sleeve pattern, or a full shirtwaist sleeve pattern, made much wider and fuller. For the pagoda sleeves of the 'sixties, use a shirtwaist sleeve; cut it fuller and shorter, shaping and slitting the bottom edge. For the 'seventies and 'eighties, use a tight lining sleeve pattern for the basic pattern. For the leg-of-mutton sleeve of the 'nineties, use a *Vogue* period pattern (or the *Pictorial Review* "Gay Nineties"). A leg-of-mutton pattern or puffed sleeve pattern can be obtained at most pattern departments, though these should be enlarged to obtain the best effect. The puffs and larger types of sleeves should be lined with crinoline and sometimes reinforced with unbleached muslin.

Bustles must be draped on the figure. It is best to drape the bustle with a piece of heavy unbleached domestic or canvas; then cover with the costume material. This holds the bustle out and prevents waste of material. A wire bustle frame can be made, or a series of featherbone loops covered with canvas can be fashioned to give the proper effect. In an emergency, or where strict economy must be practiced, newspapers crushed and fastened to a tape around the waist make a fair substitute. An old skirt can be used as an overskirt with passable effect.

To make a hoop skirt, use a gored pattern, cut very large; make facings about 12″ apart around the skirt in parallel rows, and run wire or featherboning through them. The latter is preferable, as it is flexible and can be stitched at the endings. A ruffle finished the bottom edge. At least two other petticoats should be worn on top. Otherwise the hoops show through.

Pantalettes, edged with ruffles or lace, are made tubular and attached above the knee with elastic bands. Use a pajama pattern for the legs, and add the desired rows of ruffles.

For poke bonnets, old straw, velvet, or satin hats can be used, and even fishing and beach and sun hats. Cut off the back part, tip up, curve, and fasten in place. Tie under the chin with a ribbon.

For heelless slippers, use ballet or bedroom slippers and lace up the ankles with narrow ribbons.

The drop shoulder effect on women's dresses, in vogue from 1820 to 1870, is achieved by elongating the shoulder seam out over the arm and tapering in from this outer point to a lower armhole line.

The fitted basque (1820–1870) should have the front and back cut in three pieces or more, with the seams curving out to the shoulders and tapering in to the waist.

For men's coats from 1800 to 1840, use a "colonial" or "George Washington" pattern as a base, and make the proper alterations in sleeve, collar, etc. A dress suit can be used, if necessary, by covering collar, lapels, and cuffs with velvet, rolling the collar, and other slight changes. The wide collar and lapels of the Directory period and of the early part of the century can be made of colored flannel (blue, mauve, etc.) and tacked into the suit.

For the high-buttoned sack coats, take any fairly modern coat, steam out the creases in the lapels, fold them over as high up as desired, press, and sew a button where the lapels meet. If no buttonhole is desired, pin the coat together. The modern coat may also have to be shortened about the bottom.

To make modern trousers narrow, take in the seams along the inner side of the leg. For the early eighteen hundreds, the trousers are almost skintight. A piece of black braid sewed along the outer seam of the trouser leg adds an effective touch. For the cutaway coat, if a real one is not available, take a frock coat and turn the front edges back under, on a slant or curve.

CHAPTER XV

THE TWENTIETH CENTURY

IMPORTANT PEOPLE AND EVENTS

ENGLAND
Rulers
Edward VII
  (1901–10)
George V
  (1910–36)
Edward VIII
  (1936)
George VI
  (1936–)

Writers
Thomas Hardy
James M. Barrie
Rudyard Kipling
George Bernard Shaw
John Drinkwater
John Masefield
H. G. Wells
John Galsworthy

Notable People
David Lloyd George
Herbert Henry Asquith
  (Earl of Oxford and
  Asquith)
Ramsay MacDonald

Theatrical Personages
Gordon Craig
Noel Coward
W. Somerset Maugham
John Millington Synge
William Butler Yeats
Lady Isabella Augusta
  Gregory
Lord Edward Dunsany
Donn Byrne

SWITZERLAND
Adolf Appia

GERMANY
Rulers
Wilhelm II
  (1888–1918)
Paul von Hindenburg
  President, 1925–34
Adolf Hitler
  (Leader-Chancellor,
  1934–)

Notable People
Hermann Sudermann
Max Reinhardt

RUSSIA
Rulers
Nicholas II
  (last Romanoff czar)
  (1894–1917)
(Leaders of Soviet
  Union)
Nikolai Lenin
  (1917–24)
Leon Trotzky
  (1924–27)
Josef Stalin
  (1927–)

Writers
Konstantin Stanislavski
Richard Boleslavski
Maxim Gorky

FRANCE
Writers and Artists
Paul Bourget
Marcel Proust
Romain Rolland
André Maurois
Maurice Barrès
Anatole France
J. K. Huysmans
Pierre Loti
Raymond Poincaré

Edmond Rostand
Sarah Bernhardt
Auguste Rodin
Jean Cocteau

ITALY
Rulers
Victor Emmanuel III
  (1900–)
  (Emperor of Ethio-
  pia, 1936–)
Benito Mussolini
  (Premier, 1922–)

Theatrical Personages
Eleonora Duse
Luigi Pirandello

UNITED STATES OF
  AMERICA
Presidents
William McKinley
  (1897–1901)
Theodore Roosevelt
  (1901–09)
William Howard Taft
  (1909–13)
Woodrow Wilson
  (1913–21)
Warren G. Harding
  (1921–23)
Calvin Coolidge
  (1923–29)
Herbert Hoover
  (1929–33)
Franklin D. Roosevelt
  (1933–)

Writers
Jack London
Upton Sinclair
Theodore Dreiser
Sinclair Lewis

Edith Wharton
Willa Cather
Robert Frost

Notable People
Robert La Follette
Charles Evans Hughes
Orville and Wilbur
  Wright
Robert E. Peary
Richard E. Byrd
Glenn Curtiss
Charles A. Lindbergh
Andrew Mellon
Russell Sage
John D. Rockefeller
J. Pierpont Morgan, the
  elder
Andrew Carnegie
Henry Ford

Theatrical Personages
Norman Bel Geddes
Robert Edmond Jones
Eugene O'Neill
Maxwell Anderson
George Pierce Baker
David Belasco
Charles Frohman
Richard Mansfield
Minnie Maddern Fiske
John Drew
Marie Dressler
Ernestine Schumann-
  Heink
Enrico Caruso
John Barrymore
Lionel Barrymore
Ethel Barrymore
Katharine Cornell
Helen Hayes
Alfred Lunt
Lynn Fontanne

BRITISH EMPIRE

1901, League of Empire established; Cape-to-Cairo Railway projected. . . . 1903, wireless communication between England and America. . . . Labor Party gained foothold in Parliament, scoring a major victory in the general election of 1906. . . . Budget. . . . Woman Suffrage agitation. . . . Popularization of all kinds of insurance. . . . 1909, Irish Question and Home Rule. . . . July 25, 1909, Louis Bleriot flew across English Channel. . . . 1909, Admiral Peary discovered North Pole. . . . 1912, *Titanic* sank – 1,635 lost. . . . 1914, World War began with assassination of Archduke Franz Ferdinand of Austria at Sarajevo, June 28. . . . Battle of the Marne. . . . Ypres. . . . 1915, naval battles between Germany and England at Dogger Bank. . . . *Lusitania* sunk. . . . Edith Cavell executed. . . . 1916, Verdun. . . . Sir Roger Casement hanged for treason. . . . Naval battle of Jutland. . . . Submarine warfare. . . . Battle of the Somme. . . . 1917, Cambrai. . . Jerusalem captured. . . . 1918, Battle of the Aisne. . . . The Argonne Forest. . . . Armistice, November 11, 1918. . . . 1919, Peace Conference, Lloyd George, Wilson, Clemenceau, Orlando. . . . Sir Oliver Lodge and "psychic" messages from "Raymond." . . . Arthur Griffith and the Sinn Feiners. . . . The Black and Tans. . . . England on the dole. . . . Labor government installed. . . . Youth movement. . . . "Jazz Age." . . . *The Young Visiters*. . . . 1920, League of Nations formed. . . . 1922, Irish Free State established. . . . 1924, Prince of Wales made American tour. . . . 1925, Locarno Pact ratified. . . . 1926, general strike, coal miners leading. . . . 1932, Gandhi fasted and passively resisted British control of India. . . . 1936, death of George V. . . . Dionne quintuplets born in Canada. . . . 1937, Mrs. Wallis Warfield Simpson divorced. . . . Edward VIII abdicated, received title of Duke of Windsor. . . . Succeeded by George VI, his brother. . . . Coronation, May 12, 1937. . . . Duke of Windsor married Mrs. Simpson, June 3, 1937. . . . Ramsay MacDonald died, November 9, 1937.

UNITED STATES OF AMERICA

1900, Dr. Walter Reed proved yellow fever transmitted by mosquitoes. . . . 1903, Wright Brothers flew first successful airplane at Kitty Hawk, North Carolina, Dec. 17. . . . Iroquois Theater fire, Chicago, Dec. 30, 1903. . . . 1904, Great fire, Baltimore. . . . St. Louis Exposition. . . . United States occupied Panama Canal Zone. . . . April 18, 1906, San Francisco earthquake. . . . June 25, 1906, Harry Thaw killed Stanford White, the architect. . . . 1910, Los Angeles *Times* dynamited. . . . 1911, United States ordered Standard Oil combine dissolved. . . . 1912, R. C. Fowler made first transcontinental airplane flight, Jacksonville, Florida, to San Francisco, California. . . . 1913, parcel post established, leading to a large mail-order business. . . . 1914, World War began. . . . 1916, Preparedness Day bombing – Tom Mooney imprisoned. . . . "Watchful waiting" on the Mexican border. . . . 1917, Eighteenth Amendment. . . . 1919, Peace Conference. . . . Boston police strike settled by Calvin Coolidge. . . . I.W.W. gained headway. . . . "Red" scare. . . . Woman suffrage gained. . . . The flight of the NC-4 across the Atlantic. . . . Popularity of tea dances. . . . Advent of prohibition – and the jazz age. . . . 1920, League of Nations formed – United States refused to join. . . . Sacco-Vanzetti case. . . . 1922, "Teapot Dome" scandal. . . . Ku Klux Klan. . . . Radio first introduced into the home. . . . Newly established tabloids exploited bathing beauties. . . . Tutankhamen's tomb discovered in Egypt (November 4), and modernized Egyptian costume popularized. . . . 1923, Mah Jong became popular. . . . Day by day Dr. Coué got better and better. . . . Flaming youths and reckless maidens took to parked cars, gin, cigarettes, rolled stockings, lipstick, rouge, night clubs, petting parties. . . . "Gate-crashing." . . . Saxophones, sex magazines, motion pictures – and Freud. . . . 1924, case of Leopold-Loeb-Frank. . . . Girls allowed to smoke at Bryn Mawr. . . . Diphtheria serum taken to Nome, Alaska, by dog-sled, in heroic race against death. . . . 1925, dirigible *Shenandoah* crashed. . . . Scopes anti-evolution trial in Tennessee. . . . 1927, Mississippi floods. . . . Lindbergh's flight across Atlantic. . . . 1929, Stock market crash. . . . Admiral Byrd's Antarctic trip. . . . Bootlegging, racketeering, and gangster warfare, led by hoodlums like Al Capone, terrorized society. . . . 1931, Lindbergh baby kidnaped; other kidnapings followed. . . . 1933, Bank "holidays." . . . Gold retired from circulation. . . . Long Beach earthquake. . . . Epidemic of gangster hold-ups. . . . Capture of Dillinger and other public enemies. . . . 1934, Philippine independence granted. . . . Longshoremen's strike. . . . 1935, Will Rogers killed in Alaskan airplane crash. . . . 1936, soldiers' bonus granted. . . . Ohio-Mississippi floods. . . . Bruno Hauptmann electrocuted for Lindbergh baby murder. . . . President Roosevelt's trip to South America. . . . 1937, Industrial "sit-down" strikes. . . . CIO agitation. . . . Supreme Court reorganization controversy. . . . Amelia Earhart lost, July 2. . . . Quarrel between A. F. of L. and CIO (October). . . . Business recession (November). . . . U. S. gunboat *Panay* bombed by Japanese in Yangtze River; three Americans killed (December 12).

OTHER COUNTRIES

1900, Paris Exposition opened. . . . Boxer Rebellion in China. . . . 1901, Marconi signaled "S" across Atlantic; first radio message. . . . 1902, eruption of Mt. Pelée at Martinique. . . . 1904–05, Russo-Japanese War. . . . First Russian Duma. . . . 1912, Balkan wars. . . . 1914, World War. . . . 1916, Rasputin killed in Petrograd. . . . 1917, Bolsheviks, under Lenin, seized power in Russia. . . . 1918, Czar Nicholas and family executed by Bolsheviks. . . . June 28, Treaty of Versailles signed. . . . Motor races. . . . Suzanne Lenglen's tennis. . . . November 9, workmen and soldiers took over German government. . . . Bulgaria became a republic. . . . Kaiser abdicated; Germany became a republic under control of Friedrich Ebert, first president. . . . 1922, Premier Mussolini, "Il Duce," assumed control of Italian affairs. . . . Soviet Union formed. . . . 1929, Papal State re-created. . . . Tacna-Arica treaty. . . . 1931, Revolution in Spain. . . . 1933, Leader Chancellor Hitler took over dictatorial power in Germany. . . . 1934, King Albert of Belgium killed in mountaineering accident. . . . 1935, Italo-Ethiopian war. . . . 1936, army mutiny in Japan. . . . German troops occupied Rhineland. . . . "Sit-down" strikes in France and elsewhere. . . . 1937, John D. Rockefeller, Sr., died, May 23. . . . Eight Russian generals shot for treason. . . . Chino-Japanese War. . . . Guglielmo Marconi died. . . . Japanese entered Peiping, July 28. . . . Shanghai bombed by Japanese, August 20. . . . Japan, Italy, and Germany formed triple alliance, September 17. . . . Premier Benito Mussolini visited Chancellor Adolf Hitler, September 25. . . . 1938, Hitler reduces Austrian Republic to a German province, March 13.

When Freedom, from her mountain height, volplaned into the twentieth century, she was soon forced down into No Man's Land. However, she found the postwar delirium more devastating than all the filth and terror of the trenches. The Nineteenth Amendment emancipated women, and in the Reconstruction Era that followed, morals were loosened and often discarded along with the corset. Stockings were rolled in public, and so were cigarettes; the hair was shingled, and the sex-obsessed youth was not; the speed limit of the automobile was exceeded by the rumble-seat petters; gin was no sin.

Dress barely kept up with the swiftness of communication; the high noon of Paris fashion was hurled instantaneously to the breakfast table of America. The forgotten man wore the obsolete style of yesterday afternoon. The curve of fashion skyrocketed with the stock market; and with the crash, down came dress.

Italy has its Mussolini and Germany its Hitler, but the dictators of the world of fashion are the "movie stars" of Hollywood. What they wear, from shorts to zippers, the rest of the world obediently dons the day after. Thus dress follows the celluloid trail, and the shadow of today screens the silhouette of tomorrow.

COSTUME

GENERAL CHARACTERISTICS

The machine age, with its resulting mass production, definitely affected styles. An original and exclusive design became, almost overnight, available to hundreds of thousands, by way of steamship, railway, automobile, parcel post, airplane, and radio. The printed word, in increasingly attractive advertisements in newspapers and magazines, was augmented, in the 'twenties and 'thirties, by fashion talks over the radio. Where style was concerned, there were no secrets kept from women.

Mass production and swift distribution influenced prices, materials, and patterns or styles. These had to meet the requirements of general purse and general taste, which had never run to caviar. At last there was real democracy in dress.

Prices dropped from two, three, and even four figures (for original creations of the great Parisian designers and dressmakers) to as little as ninety-eight cents for mass-produced reproductions. An amazing number of acceptable dresses and styles could be procured for sums less than ten dollars. Dressmakers fought against the overwhelming competition of factory-made clothing, but to no avail. The wheels of the fashion-gods ground on, eight hours a day.

Materials met the budget with the aid of science's laboratories. Wool and cotton mixtures, thin silks so woven as to seem heavier, cotton and silk mixtures, and a cellulose product which proved acceptable as a silk substitute, even to the most discriminating, were placed on the market at attractively low prices. The age of synthetic cloth unrolled.

Patterns, cut in lots of hundreds of thousands, were simplified to the fewest possible details, with dangerous lines and curves avoided. Fashion followed the exigencies of the cutting machine, and also of its great general public. Even underclothes were slimly designed as unobtrusive foundations for the sheathlike outer garments.

Styles, too, must please all the Judy O'Gradys as well as the Colonels' ladies. Women, lured by cheap prices and the ease of acquiring "store-bought" wardrobes, stifled the urge to be different, and cheerfully saw themselves and their clothes duplicated a thousand times on as many varied forms.

The yardage shrank more amazingly than the woolen shirt denied a certain soap's beneficent cleansing. Earlier dresses required ten to twenty yards of material; the twentieth century reduced this quota to a mere five or ten yards. In the 1920's, indeed, the lowest minimum requirement – three yards – was frequently touched.

Material was not only scant but light in weight. Woman's outer dress and also her underclothing reflected the comfort and warmth of steam-heated houses and closed cars. Men's underwear also became less lengthy but more admirable. The street car, bus, and motor car called for simple and mobile styles; the airplane demanded sheer fabrics and no excess trimming.

Finally, air-conditioned houses with even temperatures influenced a discontinuance of seasonal styles and increased the need for thin, all-purpose materials. Underclothing was reduced almost to the vanishing point, but not quite; for, thanks to the ubiquitous and artful advertiser, the intimate facts of man's and woman's next-of-skin were displayed with truly tropical ardor.

Dress, in truth, was no longer the individual expression of a creative art; it was being reduced to an industry, with the millions for its market.

Materials

Materials included brocade (silk and cotton), brocatelle, buckram, cambric (and paper cambric for lining), cellophane (and other synthetic transparent materials), chiffon, china silk, chintz, ciré, crepe, crinoline, cut velvet, duvetyn, etamine, faille, georgette, jersey (cotton, wool, and silk), lamé, metaline, monk's cloth, net (of many types), nun's cloth, organdie, Osnaburg, plush, panne velvet, ratiné, raw silk, rayon (silk substitute), sateen, satin (many types), silk (many types), silkolite, silkaline, taffeta (many types), tarletan, tinsel, tricotine, velvet (many types), velveteen, and voile.

Colors

Black, blue, and brown led for the darker colors. Many in-between shades were evolved, such as russet, beige, midnight blue, ashes of roses, Copenhagen blue, Yale blue, and the like. Light colors were used for daytime as well as for evening wear. Indeed, there were no set rules as to colors; there was only infinite variety. Prints and gay patterns always lent added cheer to the color range. In general, however, colors were clear and bright, and showed the influence of more sanitary streets, air-conditioned buildings, and other factors which did away with the necessity for durable – and dull – colors.

1900–1910

Costume for Men

General Characteristics

Men's dress reflected the turn of the century in certain details, such as the definite choice of the sack suit and the derby hat for business wear. Shoes for business wear were pointed.

Underwear

Men wore long woolen union suits (Fig. 259) in the winter, and long, porous-knit cotton ones in the summer. Short underdrawers of checked nainsook were also used. Socks were varicolored, and of cotton, lisle, or silk.

Coat

In 1900 the sack coat had rather narrow lapels buttoned high. The single-breasted coat was preferred, buttoned down the front with three or four buttons. The bottom edge was rounded off at medium hip length. Sleeves were set snugly into a normal shoulder line. Coat, vest, and trousers usually matched (Fig. 256).

In 1905 the sack coat was long, hip length, rather boxlike in appearance, and the lapels were wide and deep. The shoulders were padded, furthering the boxlike effect, and sleeves were loose and long, with or without cuffs. The double-breasted coat had a great vogue. Vests of another material were sometimes worn with these coats (Fig. 261).

The cutaway coat was worn more and more on formal occasions in place of the frock coat. With it were worn striped trousers and a pearl gray vest. It might also be worn for business use, especially in England. American cutaways were sometimes fashioned of rough tweed or similar weave.

Correct full dress for evening consisted of black broadcloth "tails," creased trousers, and a white vest, with white tie, although a black vest was permissible. The Tuxedo grew in favor; in 1901 *Vogue* had to warn against using the dinner coat for any occasion after six o'clock at which women were to be present. As *Vogue* said, the dinner coat was for occasions when men only were present, at "stag" dinners, hotels, and clubs. Men liked Tuxedos, however, and by 1912 or 1914 they had almost

Fig. 258

superseded the full dress coat except for weddings and the most formal affairs. A black vest and black tie were worn with the dinner coat.

Vest

Vests usually matched business suits; with cutaways a pearl gray vest, single- or double-breasted, was correct. With the frock coat, a black or gray vest was proper. With the full dress coat, a white piqué or black vest was worn. With the dinner coat, a black cloth vest was correct.

Shirt

The dress shirt did not change much until toward the end of the decade, when pleated bosoms came to be used, first with dinner coats, then with full dress suits.

Ordinary shirts were cut along plain lines; little starch was used. The cuffs were attached to the shirt; the stiff collars, however, were separate. Suspenders were used less and less; belts took their place. Colored and striped shirts came in at the close of the decade.

Neckwear

The collar was snugly fitted to the neck, with wide-spread wings, or a deep turnover.

The four-in-hand had a smaller knot than previously, and was tied more closely to the collar. The bow tie was also used. The ascot was proper with a cutaway, and for daytime dress occasions.

Sweater

Sweaters grew in popularity, turtle-neck or pull-over, the kind that buttoned up the front, and the V-neck (Fig. 258   Fig. 259). College boys and girls wore their college letters or class numerals on the front of pull-over sweaters made in the college colors.

Trousers

Trousers were growing wider, were creased, and business suits and sport flannels, in particular, had cuffs. The sport trousers grew short toward the end of the decade.

Fig. 259

For bicycling and golf, knickers were used, moderately full, buttoned below the knee. Golf stockings were worn with them. Long trousers, when used for bicycling, were folded about the ankle and held secure by flexible metal trouser-clips. Flannel trousers, plain white or cream, or with pin stripes, grew in favor, and were worn with the soft shirtwaists and with plain blue or pin-striped blue coats. The Palm Beach suit made its appearance, to hold its place until today, by virtue of its coolness, comfort, and clean appearance.

Outer Coat

The long straight topcoat did not greatly change. A short, light tan topcoat, called the covert coat, and the raglan coat were also used for sports or traveling; the *cravenette* was for rainy weather; the duster (Fig. 259) was donned for the adventurous automobile trip. Overcoats were usually made of broadcloth, kersey, or Merton cloth.

Socks

Socks were black, brown, blue, or other colors. They were plain, striped, or dotted (Fig. 258). For evening, black silk socks were correct. White socks were worn with white shoes.

Footwear

Shoes were made with medium thick soles and toothpick toes. Button shoes were in common use, but laced shoes were also adopted. Patent leather button shoes or pumps were proper for evening wear. The oxford low shoe came in about this time, and grew steadily in favor.

Tan, brown, and "ox-blood" oxfords and high shoes came into fashion about 1905, but their vogue was restricted to the less conservative members of society. After 1905, white oxfords were the acceptable footwear for summer.

Hair

Men parted their hair on the side or in the middle, or they brushed it back pompadour style. The side part grew in favor toward the end of the decade. Between 1905 and 1910, the hair was worn slightly long, particularly over the forehead.

Mustaches were small, thin, and pointed at the ends. Young men usually went clean-shaven. Professional and older men wore conservative beards.

Headdress

Hats showed a slight change of brim and blocking. The silk hat was used for formal wear with frock coat and cutaway; the folding silk opera hat, for the theater; a fedora, felt, or derby, for everyday wear; a soft felt slouch hat or a tweed cap, for golfing; a straw hat, for summertime. In 1905, and for a few years after, the straw hat had a wide, low crown and very wide brim; a felt hat had a fairly low crown and a wide brim curved down on one side in a slanting line (Fig. 259). The Panama hat, with low, wide crown, and wide, curled brim, was most popular (Fig. 260).

Costume for Women

Women wore chemises, corsets, drawers, petticoats, stockings, and corset covers. The round-necked chemise helped to confine the bust. The corset was very carefully cut to the figure (Fig. 264). In 1900, it had a straight military front, curved hips, and a low bust line. It showed the contour, a slope over the hips, a dip of the curve at the waist. The hips, on the sides and behind, were well padded.

As the decade went on, the straight front was accentuated and the length grew until 1909, when a very long corset became stylish. It was heavily boned, very low in the bust, and had many elastic supporters to hold the bottom edge down in the back and at the sides. The hips were slim and the waist somewhat large; a perfect princess line was attained (Fig. 265).

Petticoats of taffeta silk, in black, or plain or changeable colors, were in fashion. They were gored, and sometimes put on a yoke, with pleats or gathers, and a ruffle at the bottom. This ruffle measured four to eight yards about the bottom edge. A new fitted petticoat, called the *Anna Held,* became popular in 1905, and was fashionable for the next five years. In 1905, *The Theatre Magazine* advertised it as follows: "The sensation of the Fashion World. Clinging closely to the form from the waist over the hips and down to the deep flounce without a pucker, it presents an ideally smooth surface upon which the closest fitting gown of today's fashion will hang without a wrinkle. And yet – here's the genius of it – *it positively does not bind,* all through a clever trick in the making. Best quality silk taffeta, black and all colors. Cut circular, fastens at the back with glove snaps, has deep flounce fashioned in various styles." Stockings were of lisle, silk, or lace. Drawers were made circular and full, with embroidery or lace trimming about the bottom edges.

Waist

The smooth silhouette of 1900, with the low dip in front, padded hips, and bustle, continued until about 1904 (Fig. 262). Around 1900, the evening bodice was cut very low across the bosom and held up by very narrow shoulder straps. A heart-shaped outline was favored for the top of the bodice, and extreme styles dispensed altogether with shoulder straps, relying on the boned and built-up lining to hold the bodice in place. The separate bodice shared favor with the princess style of dress, in which waist and skirt were one. A sheathlike contour was followed, in both styles. About 1902, the so-called *Gibson waist* came in. It had a wide pleat over the shoulder and down the sides, front and back. This pleat made the shoulders seem broad and the waist narrow. The favorite material for this waist was white linen, stiffly starched (Fig. 264).

About 1903, the deep dip, center front of the waistline, was exaggerated (Fig. 262). The lingerie waist of thin muslin, nainsook, or handkerchief linen, came in. This type of shirtwaist had a high, boned neck, long sleeves, elaborate embroidery, fine tucking, lace insertion, and lace edging. Occasionally it was buttoned down the front, but was usually fastened with two dozen or more very small lingerie buttons set close together down the center back. The lingerie shirtwaist remained stylish for several years (Fig. 263 "1906" Fig. 264 Fig. 265). In 1907 it was made with eyelet embroidery, cut work, or other openwork design, and called the *peekaboo waist.*

In 1907 and 1908, the wide line over the shoulder was emphasized by a series of pleats, or by cap sleeves (Fig. 263 "1908" Fig. 265).

Sleeves

In 1900, sleeves were rather plain, tight, and slightly fulled at the armhole (Fig. 262 "1901" "1902"). The *Renaissance sleeve* appeared; it was slightly gathered at the armhole and had a full puff, or bag, at the wrist. The puff was usually confined by a narrow cuff (Fig. 262 "1903" Fig. 264). The evening bodice might have no sleeves at all, or short puffed sleeves. After 1908 the kimono sleeve was used.

Skirt

Skirts showed the tendencies of the times more than any other article of dress. Bicycling made popular the "safety" skirt, plainly gored and ankle length. Lawn tennis and ping-pong also encouraged a shorter skirt. Basketball and other college athletics led to the adoption of bloomers, very full and long, but giving some freedom of movement.

"Rainy-daisy" skirts, also ankle length, with three or more rows of stitching about

Fig. 260

Fig. 261   1900   1901   Fig. 262   1901   1902   1903   1903

1904   1905   1906   1907   1908   1909

Fig. 263

1913   1913   1914   1914   1914   1915

Fig. 270

the lower edge, were made of cravenette or some durable material. By 1902, women were riding horseback astride, clad in divided skirts and breeches.

Yet the long, flowing, dust-catching skirts still held sway for ordinary use. In 1900, they fitted snugly about the well-padded hips, smoothly to the knees, and flared out four yards or more about the bottom, which had a "brush-binding" – perhaps to brush the streets. The fold of the skirt was gracefully held in one hand.

1900

Fig. 264

When the Flatiron Building in New York was completed in 1903, observant gentlemen crowded the corner to watch the frantic manipulations of the ladies as they vainly attempted to hold the situation well in hand against the opposing winds (Fig. 262   Fig. 263   "1900" through "1908").

Fullness about the bottom edge was also achieved by circular or pleated flounces, or smoothly-stitched tucks and pleats attached to smoothly-fitted yokes (Fig. 262   Fig. 263   "1903"   "1904"   "1905"   "1906"   Fig. 264).

In 1909, a decided change in the silhouette occurred. The so-called "Empire" or "Directoire" or "princess" style (Fig. 265) came in. It had a high waistline, bolero-type waist, smoothly-fitted princess waist, long, slender hip line, and narrow skirt. It was also called the *sheath gown*.

The tailored suit for 1909 had a smooth coat cut on princess lines. The coat reached a low hip line, about twelve inches below the normal waistline, and was smoothly fitted about hips, bust, and neck. The skirt had a slight flare at the bottom.

Evening skirts were gathered, shirred, or pleated to a smooth yoke. Passementerie, openwork embroidery, and lace outlined the yoke and were arranged in patterns on the skirt.

Cloak

Around 1900, a loose, semi-fitting cloak, with or without a yoke, was fashionable. It reached to the knees. Tan was a particularly good shade for cloaks. A short, tight-

1905

Fig. 265

fitting coat of fur, with wide and deep revers, was also used. Large, round muffs were carried with this type.

Around 1905, the cloak grew longer; in 1907, it almost reached the ground (Fig. 263 "1907"), and had a flare toward the bottom. In 1909 and 1910, the coat was cut on straight lines, neatly tailored, and with little or no flare at the bottom. With this type the very large, flat, *pillow muff* was used.

Hosiery

Black stockings were used for daytime wear; silk stockings were still a rarity. Stockings with silk lace inlay or openwork (Fig. 264), in stripes or solid color, were fashionable for party wear. The silk or lace frequently extended only to the calf of the leg; the upper part of the stocking was of cotton lisle.

Footwear

In 1900, shoes had pointed toes, vamp, and extension soles. Around 1905, laced and twelve-buttoned shoes with Cuban heels were favored for daytime wear; oxfords or slippers with two to five buttons or buckled straps for afternoon wear, and also low pumps with long vamps and a flat bow; for evening wear, the evening dress slipper was worn with French heel, short vamp, and a small bow or buckle.

Patent leather was very fashionable; glacé kid, and velvet tops to high shoes were used.

Hair

In 1900, the hair was piled high on the head in a pompadour. Pads or "rats" held up the puffs. The knot was placed on the crown of the head. Another style placed the knot in a loop at the nape of the neck. A black taffeta bow was frequently placed over the knot, either on top of the head or at the nape of the neck (Fig. 264).

About 1905, the pompadour or puff extended in a continuous circle around the head, and was waved or "marcelled." The knot was usually in the center of this hairdress. Ornaments – combs, bows, aigrettes, and the like – added variety to the coiffure. Hairpins were purchased by the box.

Headdress

With this type of hairdressing, hats were necessarily large (Fig. 262). Wide brims, tilted forward over the face, were worn in 1900. The hat was pinned on, at the back, with very long hatpins. A hat with a rolled brim, ornamented with plumes at the side, was very fashionable at this time (Fig. 262). The musical comedy *Floradora,* with its famous sextette, appeared in 1901. Its 547 performances in New York made the *Floradora hat* famous throughout the land. This hat had a very wide, tilted brim, ornamented with feathers (Fig. 262 "1901"). A dotted veil was frequently worn with this creation, which was reminiscent of the (equally becoming) "Gains-borough" hat of the eighteenth century. Another style of hat had an upturned brim, like a sugar scoop, tilted forward and upward over the face and high pompadour; it was plain or ornamented with feathers. This type was popular around 1904 (Fig. 260 Fig. 263 "1904" "1905" Fig. 264).

In 1908, the high, deep-crowned *peach-basket hat* had a brief vogue. It was superseded in favor by a hat with a very wide, drooping brim, sometimes fifteen to twenty inches in diameter. The crown measured about ten inches in diameter, and was from two to five inches deep. This general type of hat was called the *Merry Widow,* after the musical comedy of that name. Extremely long hatpins, with fanciful heads, were thrust through the crown from either side (Fig. 265). A willow ostrich plume, ten to twenty-five inches long and five to fifteen inches deep (Fig. 260), frequently draped this structure (Fig. 263 "1908" "1909"). The drooping, cuplike brim was sometimes bent up in a V-point front and back (Fig. 260).

Beaver hats, of the general 1908 style, became popular. They were dyed various colors and trimmed with feathers and ribbons.

Horsehair braid and straw were used for summer hats. All hats were worn resting on the high pompadour.

Ornaments and Accessories

The automobile brought in many styles for both men and women. Caps, dusters, gauntlets, veils, and goggles were used by both men and women; long green veils, swathed over the hats, were worn by the women. The long (!) twenty-five-mile jaunts over unpaved roads were so punctuated by jolts and jars that they were recommended "for the liver." It is said that from this imputation Henry Ford's super-jolter got its nickname, "flivver."

For jewelry, the fashionable trinkets were rings, pins, necklaces, and bracelets. The latter were round, and chased or plain. Several were worn at one time. Turquoises, pearls (plain and baroque), and amethysts were much used in all types of jewelry.

In 1900, the long feather boa was most fashionable; in 1902, the long, boalike neckpiece was worn with a round muff; the silk and chiffon neckpiece and muff were also stylish. In 1909, a flat, capelike, fur neckpiece, with tails, and a large, flat pillow muff to match, were in vogue.

Large, full veils were used throughout the decade.

Pocketbooks were flat and rectangular, with a chain or cord attached, and closed with a clasp. Shapes and sizes varied. If a muff were carried, a small coin purse only was used.

Gloves, slender rolled umbrellas, parasols, and fans with a ribbon or cord to slip about the neck, were other common accessories.

Jabots of lace, attached to stocks, or separate, came in toward 1910. Chemisettes and stocks, of embroidery and lace, were indispensable to the dress of the period.

Switches, puffs, and curls came in with the large pompadour. Fancy-headed hatpins, eight to twelve inches long, were necessary to anchor the huge hats.

Link bracelets, with charms dangling from each link, were the rage around 1900–05 (to reappear in 1936). There were hearts, clovers, etc., engraved with the donor's initial, making an interesting display, and attesting to the recipient's popularity.

1910–1920

Costume for Men (Fig. 266)

Around 1910, the suits had broad shoulders, wide trousers ("peg tops"), sometimes gathered about the hips and with deep cuffs at the bottom of the trouser legs (Fig. 266). Flashily striped silk shirts and striped socks were worn. Lapels were fairly long and medium large (Fig. 256).

Coat

Coats were still fairly long. They were, however, more snugly fitted. The shirt (or "shirtwaist," as it was frequently called) was plain, with attached cuffs. Collars were still separate, though they were of material matching the shirt. Trousers were quite long, with deep cuffs. The shoulders were padded to a squared outline. The loose, box coat was much in demand (Fig. 266). Tuxedos or dinner jackets were now used for most occasions – formal or semi-formal.

Collars were very high. The deep turnover collar with rounded edges was preferred. With it was worn a tie with a small knot; the wing collar was also used. After the war, collars were lower and more comfortable. The four-in-hand tie was most favored, though the ascot and string tie were frequently seen.

The war broke many traditions. The khaki uniform, the khaki shirt and blouse, led to shorter coats and brown shirts, to soft, attached collars and attached cuffs, to tighter trousers and a general trimness. Wrist watches and an almost universal preference for brown shoes also echoed wartime habits. Even dress shirts, though occasionally stiffly starched, were made with pleats, only slightly starched; and dress shirts of soft silk or soft, fine cambric were proper.

After 1918, men's clothing varied only slightly from year to year as to lapel, pockets, and minor details.

Coats were belted across the back, or about the waist. This style was favored for informal wear (Fig. 266). Sack suits (business suits) were made with vests to match.

Fig. 266

Coats for summer wear were unlined. White piqué vests were used in the summer, if a vest were thought necessary, but frequently no vest at all was used with the "shirt-waist." Vests were also used with "tails" when these were donned; in the winter, white piqué or silk vests were used with "tails."

Trousers

Trousers matched the coat, except for summer wear, when plain or striped trousers of cream, white, or gray were used with a blue or gray coat. Flannel and serge were the favored materials for separate trousers. Peg-top trousers had a brief vogue (from 1910 to 1912), but were soon discarded; only the wide cuffs to trousers lingered on.

For golf and other outdoor games, knickers were worn with plaid woolen stockings; for riding, breeches with puttees were used.

Outer Coat

The loose, box overcoat was favored; it could be of tweed or of a mixture. For dress wear, a black overcoat was worn. Raglans were belted. The belted coat grew in favor after the World War, because the trench coat, invariably belted, had been the daily wear of millions of men.

Socks

These were of many brilliant colors, striped, dotted, and variously designed. Plain black socks, of silk or lisle, were worn by older or more conservative men. They were, of course, the only proper wear for formal evening dress.

Footwear

Brown oxfords were very popular, though black shoes were used by the conservative element. In 1910 the *bulldog shoe,* with thick soles and high, rounded toes, was popular with the young, sporting crowd. Black was obligatory for dress wear; white canvas or buckskin shoes were worn for summer. Black pumps were still correct for evening, but black oxfords were quite acceptable. High, laced shoes were preferred in winter. Spats were worn until 1914; after that they were rarely donned, except with cutaways.

Hair

The side part was in general favor, but the pompadour was also common. Trimmed mustaches were seen on older men; young men went clean-shaven. Some professional men and many older Frenchmen still favored the pointed beard.

Headdress

The felt slouch hat led in popularity. The straw hat, or panama, was donned in the summer. The top hat was reserved for very formal occasions; the collapsible opera hat almost disappeared from use.

Caps were used for sports, traveling, and outdoor use (Fig. 266). They were gathered slightly into a band about the head, and had a short visor.

Ornaments and Accessories

Wrist watches, on leather or gold bands, with luminous dials, came into use with the World War.

Handkerchiefs were colored as well as white, and were worn in the upper left-hand pocket.

Gloves were of chamois or pigskin.

Canes were small and straight. The "swagger stick" of the wartime officer was echoed in peacetime styles.

The *beret* was adopted from the French, for outdoor motoring wear. Sweaters grew in favor. At first they had been used only by college boys; due to their wartime usefulness, they became a general part of costume for golf, riding, etc. The pull-over sweater and the coat sweater were equally in favor.

The war influenced the adoption of neck scarves and mufflers as a regular accessory, and not alone as an occasional cold-weather addition to the costume.

Military Dress

The World War brought the greatest changes in uniform ever experienced. The French discarded their baggy red trousers and blue coats for horizon-blue uniforms. The Germans adopted a dark gray (*feldgrau*); the English, who had adopted khaki from the Hindus, made it universal in their army. The Americans discarded the old army blue uniforms altogether for olive drab (khaki), which had been in use for field service since the Spanish-American War. Khaki was also adopted by other nations for army use – by Poland, Belgium, Japan, and some lesser states; blue-gray and gray-green were used by other nations; so that the general color tone of most armies is very much the same. The reason for the adoption of these neutral shades is the need for low visibility, due to trench fighting, guerilla warfare, and air attacks. Wide riding breeches with wrapped puttees took the place of long trousers for most of the regulation uniforms. Officers and dispatch riders generally wore leather puttees.

The trench cap superseded the wide khaki felt hat. The Sam Browne belt, with the accompanying automatic pistol, distinguished the commissioned officer. The sword was rarely carried.

Decorations were many and varied. For America, the highest award was the Distinguished Service medal; in England, the Victoria Cross; in France, the Légion d'Honneur was the highest award, with the Médaille Militaire and the Croix de Guerre with palms or *étoiles* (stars) next in order; in Germany, the Iron Cross was the highest award.

Officers wore a visored cap on ceremonial occasions, but on active duty a trench cap with the insignia of rank pinned on it was considered sufficient. In the American army, a general had four silver stars embroidered on each shoulder strap; a lieutenant general had three stars; a major general, two; and a brigadier general, one. A colonel had a silver spread eagle; a major, a gold oak leaf; a captain, two silver bars; a first lieutenant, one silver bar; and a second lieutenant, one gold bar.

Costume for Women

In this decade, the skirt was the important item of dress. Its variations are noted under the heading "Skirt."

Waist

The waist followed a general bolero or Eton jacket trend. It was fitted closely at the neck. The kimono or wide-shoulder effect was emphasized by folds, pleats, and deep flounces. A surplice, cross-over style, of flounces, with the deep V-front and back filled in for daytime use, was very popular, especially from 1912 to 1916 (Fig. 269 "1910" Fig. 270 "1914").

Influenced by the war, the waist was cut on plain, boxlike lines. Cross straps, or berthas of flat, pleated ruffles, added a decorative touch. The neckline was V-shaped, rounded, or square (Fig. 268 Fig. 270 "1914" "1915").

The very high waistline of 1910 dropped to a slightly raised waistline in 1914 (Fig. 269 Fig. 270 Fig. 278). In 1916, the waist showed a decided blouse front and back. The *Russian blouse,* another echo of the war, also had a vogue. The *middy blouse* put in an appearance about this time and was soon adopted by the younger generation. The normal waistline was attained in 1920 (Fig. 268 Fig. 272 Fig. 278).

Shirtwaists of allover lace – Irish lace was very much in demand – were used with tailored suits. The kimono blouse was also used with a separate skirt (Fig. 270 "1914").

The tailored suit in 1916 (Fig. 271) had a fitted bodice, full, flared skirt, and high, turnover collar (Fig. 268). In 1917 the loose box coat was favored (Fig. 271).

Sleeves were fairly plain in cut; long sleeves predominated, but short, elbow-length sleeves were also used. The three-quarter-length sleeve was favored in 1912. The

Fig. 267

kimono sleeve was used from 1908, with variations, for many years. It was especially favored for cloaks and coats (Fig. 267 Fig. 269 "1912").

Skirt

The skirt began its long "Upidee" climb, upward and outward. In 1910, the "princess," "empire," or "moyen âge" style, with its long, unbroken line from waist to knee, tended to increase the apparent size of the waist and to decrease that of the hips (Fig. 267 Fig. 269). Even bathing suits and house aprons followed these lines; front panels emphasized the slender effect. Draping became important; the skirt was gathered into a narrow band at the bottom (Fig. 269 "1910"), or folded over ("1911"); it was gathered up on the sides, pannier style, or in front ("1912" "1913"), or behind ("1912" "1914"). The *harem skirt,* slit in front ("1911" "1914") or on the side, enjoyed a brief vogue. The *lampshade skirt* ("1914") also caused a ripple of interest.

In 1911, skirts made a feeble attempt to leave the ground, but the flight was not sustained. In 1914, ankles were definitely revealed, and in 1916, the curve of the calf appeared. From this time until the present day, the skirt line has been an active skirmish line, with many ups and downs.

Around 1915, the wide, short skirts were often trimmed about the bottom edge with a wide band of contrasting material (Fig. 271 "1916" Fig. 278). A broad belt was sometimes added (Fig. 268). Tiers of ruffles, reminiscent of 1850, were favored (Fig. 271 Fig. 278). In 1917, a narrow string belt with looped ends was tied about the waist. A type of skirt with simulated deep, open pockets at the side (Fig. 268) and narrow bottom edge definitely reflected trench coats and the wartime breeches tucked into trim puttees.

Trains were used on evening dresses until 1916, and again in 1920.

1915

Fig. 268

Fur banding trimmed the bottoms of skirts, as well as coats and collars.

Petticoats, as well as the one-piece *teddy-bear* (Fig. 268), were full and flaring about the bottom.

Coat and Cloak

The coat followed the general lines of the dress. Around 1910, the kimono sleeve, surplice opening in front, and long, narrow skirt were favored. The neckline had a high turnover collar folded in a deep revers (Fig. 267 Fig. 269 "1912"). Any fullness was draped toward the front. It was fastened with one button at the waistline.

After 1914, coats were cut on the "swagger" or trench coat lines, with boxlike squareness at the shoulders, flaring skirts, high turnover and snugly-fitted collar, military belt, and deep, capacious "trench" pockets (Fig. 268). Fur cloaks were made along similar lines.

Muffs were large, flat, pillow-shaped, with collar or scarf-piece to match.

Fig. 269

Stockings

Silk stockings became almost a necessity with the steadily shortening skirts. Black was still the regulation color, but dark blue and brown silk stockings made their appearances. Lace stockings were used for evening wear.

Footwear

Low oxfords and pumps almost entirely superseded the high buttoned or laced shoe. The Cuban heel led in favor, except for evening slippers. Black, brown, bronze, and russet were the colors most used for footwear.

Hair

The hair was worn in a full pompadour all over the head, and around the face; the knot was on top. Frequently a band of ribbon or velvet confined the hair in an even puff about the face (Fig. 267). After 1914, the pompadour flattened, the rat disappeared, and the hair was arranged snugly over the head, with only a puff pulled forward over each ear. In 1914, also, Irene Castle, exponent of decorous ballroom dancing, bobbed her hair. Nurses and other wartime workers found this style both comfortable and sanitary. The style slowly gained headway, and eventually women everywhere bobbed their hair – in as many shapes as there were heads.

Headdress

In 1910, hats were very large, with wide, curved Gainsborough brims and large, deep crowns (Fig. 269 Fig. 270), or mushroom-shaped, completely enveloping the head – and the pompadour (Fig. 267). Soft, fuzzy beavers were in great demand. Swaths of

Fig. 271

velvet or satin, plumes, birds of paradise, and the like, added to the size and weight of the hats. The Plumage Acts of the United States (1913) and similar acts in Great Britain (1921) led to the gradual discontinuance of aigrettes (egrets) and birds of paradise as milliners' trimmings.

Very large, long hatpins were used, with fancy heads – such as jewels, golf sticks, birds' heads, etc.

After 1914, when bobbed hair came in, the hats became perceptibly smaller. The brim was narrowed or turned up in front. The head of the wearer fitted snugly up into the crown (Fig. 268   Fig. 271   Fig. 272   Fig. 278). The tall, conical hat with vertically-

Fig. 272

placed ornaments appeared, along with the tricorne or Napoleonic upturned brim. The small toque was worn low on the forehead, tipped over one eye.

Ornaments and Accessories

In the midst of wars and rumors of wars, women stopped to powder their noses. A round "vanity" box made its appearance. It contained loose powder, a little puff, and a mirror conveniently placed in the top of the box. Wrist watches were used by Tommies, Yanks, and others to time the "zero hour" (when to go over the top); they were also used by nurses and stay-at-home Red Cross workers to mark the leaden hours of waiting, to signal the moment of the doughboys' return. The Breton beret, worn by the Chasseurs Alpins and many other French poilus, was adopted by civilians after the war as a convenient cap for sports and motoring. Hollywood moving picture stars popularized this style, and still carry it on.

Pocketbooks were carried by handles or by cords looped over the wrist. A rectangular type was preferred.

Cigarettes were a staple with the soldier; the wartime worker acquired the habit, and soon society women were seen smoking in public. As early as 1910, Alice Longworth had created a sensation in social circles by publicly smoking a cigarette. In 1914, however, public smoking by women was still a misdemeanor, in most cities of the United States, and the culprit was arrested and fined. With the growing popularity of smoking among women came the cigarette case, of metal or leather; men likewise used the cigarette case.

Scarves, mufflers, gloves, canes, leather pocketbooks, and address books were some of the items carried by men at this time.

1920–1930
Costume for Men

Men's dress was consistently well cut. The loose sack coat was of medium length; the lapels were medium width, and tapered down to a fairly deep V in front. Sleeves were set in the armhole, and without fullness. There might be breast or hip pockets, or both. Belts were increasingly used – an echo of the war.

Silk shirts, plain or striped, had an astonishing vogue for a few years; workingmen even wore them to work. However, by 1925, cotton shirts returned to favor. They had

CUFF LINKS STUDS   SILK SHIRT   BILL FOLDER

Fig. 273

attached collars and cuffs, which were moderately starched. Toward the end of the decade, the points of the collars were fashioned with grooves in which little bone or celluloid stays could be inserted to hold the collar stiffly in position. The tie, which was fastened in a small, tight knot, was held in place by a small clip. The spring clip had been used since 1915; around 1930 a slip clip, monogrammed or in ornate form, was used. The trousers were of medium width, with conservative cuffs and trim creases.

Colors were conservative; dark blue and brown predominated. Invisible pin stripes and pepper-and-salt mixtures were also good.

Serges, tweeds, cheviots, and the rougher weaves were favored. Shoes, hats, and other accessories changed very little (Fig. 256   Fig. 273). Palm Beach suits, of a wiry cotton weave, were favored for summer wear.

Bathing suits followed the trend toward simplification. Other details are shown in Fig. 273.

In 1920, the Prince of Wales (then the indisputable leader of masculine fashion) appeared on the golf course in a *jumper*. From that time, the jumper took its place in the gentleman's wardrobe. The Prince, at this time, also popularized the short-waisted, double-breasted waistcoat, wide trousers pleated at the waist (reminiscent of the 1830's) and the diamond-patterned dress shirt with figured waistcoat to match, wide-winged collars, and stiffly-starched bow ties which stood out like butterflies.

Another indisputable Prince Charming, in the early part of this decade (until his death in 1926), was Rudolph Valentino, who definitely influenced men's fashions. Along with the tango, he brought the dashing dress of the Argentine – black, broad-brimmed hat, wide colorful sash, full white shirt, smooth black trousers, slim-hipped but flaring widely about the ankles. Even staid business men set their proper hats at a rakish tilt, and trotted to work in dashing, bell-bottomed trousers.

In 1924, the wide trousers called *Oxford bags* appeared. They measured twenty-six inches at the knee, and twenty-four inches about the cuffs.

In England, the war killed the silk hat and morning coat for ordinary office workers' wear. Henceforth they, too, wore the sack coat, which had long been customary attire in the American business world.

Around 1928, the oilskin coat and Cape Cod hat were adopted for wear in rainy weather.

Costume for Women

Underclothes

The strange figure made by fashion's decree was molded in a long, shapeless corset, which began below the normal waistline and ended at the knees (Fig. 274). Garters held it in place, and served to keep surplus measurements under control. Girls of dancing age "parked" their corsets at dances, claiming that the boys refused to dance with them unless they did so. A single straight slip – combining vest and open drawers – or a separate vest and scant, elastic-topped panties were worn beneath the corset. The top of the vest or combination was cut straight across, with straps to hold it over the shoulders. The petticoat was cut on slim, tubular lines. A wrap-around skirt, to give a certain fullness, made its appearance.

Pajamas, long-waisted, sleeveless, and gaily colored, became the accepted fashion for night attire. There were bust-confiners (or brassières) as a visible means to support the bust that, generally speaking, was not visible. To mankind in general, as to all mankind before Columbus's day, the world seemed flat, not round (Fig. 274).

Waist

This was the decade of the one-piece dress. In 1920, the waist vied for importance with the skirt. A rounded or square-necked blouse (the Russian revolution possibly being responsible for its origin) set the trend of the style. It had long, wide, open-cuffed sleeves which frequently were attached kimono-fashion to the blouse. A surplice, fold-over style, was also favored. A waist of one shade, with sleeves of another, was also being used. The blouse remained a regular feature.

Gradually the waistline slipped from the normal to a low waistline, until in 1925 the belt (if any) was draped about the hips. The progress of the waistlines can be studied in Fig. 274, Fig. 275, and Fig. 278.

Around 1925, the open V neck, with turnover collar, came into general use, remaining a constantly recurring style to the present day. Berthas over the shoulders, reminiscent of seventeenth-century Puritan styles, added another note to costume. In 1925 (and until 1930) the low, draped blouse, with irregular, slanting hip-waist (!) line, proved very popular. A long, narrow tunic blouse, knee length, and frequently slit up

1920

Fig. 274

the side, was also favored (Fig. 275 Fig. 278). Panels down the front were also used. Sleeves, when used at all (sleeveless dresses were the most popular), were long and close-fitting, or bell-shaped and open, or above elbow length.

Evening blouses were made with round or V necks, with an occasional slight draping at the shoulder. A large flower at shoulder or hip was used for ornament. Belts were of ribbon or velvet, with bows or other ornaments. Evening blouses were generally entirely sleeveless; a slight cap could be used by women who disliked the bared-arm effect.

Skirt

The skirt, like the woman it sheathed, could not make up its mind as to length, width, or draping. In 1920, the skirt was generally fairly full, with ruffles or loops about the waist. Scallops or pointed edges were frequently used on silk skirts. In 1921 a panel or cascade at the side was used. The draping usually extended below the level of the skirt hem (Fig. 274   Fig. 278). Tiers of ruffles, side pleats, and diagonal layers were introduced, for variety, in 1922, 1923, and 1924 (Fig. 275   Fig. 278). An evening skirt was made in layers of petal-like diamonds or scallops (Fig. 274).

In 1925, the skirt was very tight and narrow, but fairly short. One or more over-skirts were used, and side drapings also (Fig. 275). Diagonal lines were also followed.

In 1927, the skirt reached a new high. It was frankly above the knees, and some women went further in their display of (one hopes!) shapely limbs. For daytime, the

Fig. 275

skirt was narrow and plain, with, perforce, at times, a pleat or two. For evening wear, it was finished with scallops, drapings, or the like (Fig. 275   Fig. 278). The uneven hem was in evidence everywhere.

In the years 1928 and 1929, skirts became a bit longer and a bit fuller; and there was promise of a return to the normal waistline (Fig. 278).

Suit skirts and coats followed the trend of the dresses throughout this period. Allover beaded dresses were desirable for evening wear. Figures 274, 275, and 278 give skirt lengths and other details in graphic form.

Coat

These followed the general line of costume. They were quite short, scanty, with high, snug collars, or deep, flat revers. An ensemble coat became very popular around 1925 (Fig. 278). It was cut like the deep tunic blouse, but open down the front, and usually worn unbuttoned or fastened with one button at the low waistline.

The one-piece and two-piece costumes of this decade were usually fashioned of satin or silk. Cassia cloth was frequently chosen for the coat or ensemble styles. Bands of fur were also used.

Stockings

The perfection of silk substitutes led to a tremendous vogue for silk stockings. About 1924, flesh-colored stockings became standard equipment for the "sport-model" woman. Brown stockings, or occasionally black, were worn by the conservative, with dark dresses and suits.

Footwear

The oxford still led in popularity. A dress shoe, with two or more straps across the ankle, came into fashion around 1920. In 1925 the more shapely pump, with pointed toe and Cuban or French heel, returned to favor.

Hair

In 1920 the hair was arranged in soft waves or puffs about the face. A fight to the death was on between the long-hair and the short-hair adherents. The bobbed-hair devotees wore the hair clipped "page-boy" length, with bangs across the forehead.

In 1925, the "boyish bob" led in fashion. A wisp of hair was looped up over the cheek (Fig. 275). Bobbed hair in 1928 had a slight fluff and a long sweep of wave across the forehead. Toward the end of the decade the "windblown" bob came into great popularity.

Headdress

In 1920 hats were turned up in a deep, rolled brim in front, and were pulled low over the eyes. They were of medium size. In 1925, hats became very small and tight, with strange flares about the face. They extended down over the nape of the neck to hide the shaved base of the hair.

The small hat, with minor changes, has continued in vogue until the present day.

Ornaments and Accessories

The scarf about the neck came into vogue around 1925. Artificial flowers, earrings, locket-necklaces, and large pocketbooks were some of the accessories of the time. *Bandeaux* were worn in the hair, for evening dress.

About 1922, the Lido gave the world of fashion the beach-pajama suit, which eventually progressed from shore to drawing room (Fig. 274).

Clothing in general became, if not rich, rare and racy. The Charleston and other dance crazes led to scantier and scantier clothing. Thirty ounces of cloth could sheath the woman's slim, curveless figure – "as streamlined as a racing-car."

1930 –

COSTUME FOR MEN

Men's dress showed the influence of sports on everyday life. Colors began to loom importantly in the scheme of things. No longer were black and blue the criteria of good taste. Deep and brilliant shades appeared for everyday wear, and plaids were most popular. The coat often showed an action back, and pleats over the shoulders. Belts and capacious pockets, both regulation and pouch, or "Gable" pockets, with pleats, were popular around 1935. Lapels were fairly deep, long, and wide (Fig. 256 Fig. 276). Sleeves were medium large, and shoulders were padded. Coats were slit up the side back seams about five or six inches, instead of the center slit.

Summer suits were gray crash or alpaca, in dark or light colors. Shirts and trousers matched. Congo cloth was much in demand in 1937. Palm Beach cloth was still good.

For evening wear, Tuxedos were fashioned of blue cloth, especially midnight blue, and also of white. Short *mess jackets* in white became the vogue, particularly with

Fig. 276

young men. Sashes of black or plain colors were worn with Tuxedos (Fig. 276).

Trousers became wider, and were pleated about the waist. The belt, sewed directly on the trousers, became important, and was fashioned in various ways, lapped over, buckled, and clasped. The zipper was popularized by Edward, Prince of Wales. By 1935, tailors and the general public were beginning to adopt it for fastening the trouser-fly, the necks of polo shirts, work shirts, leather jackets, and sports garments in general.

Trousers also showed side pleats. The cuff was moderate, and the width of the trousers at the ankle was also moderate. Suits generally were sold with two pairs of trousers, but both pairs did not necessarily match the coat.

Shorts were worn for certain sports, for sun baths, for tennis, canoeing, and the like (Fig. 276).

Shirts were plain in cut, of blue or other shades. Polo shirts in all colors were in great demand for sports and even for everyday wear (Fig. 276).

Ties showed patterns of plaids, diagonals, Persian designs, dots, and the usual mixtures. Wool ties became popular in 1936.

Shoes were conservative, although white shoes and sandals were acceptable for sports. Oxfords patterned in white with toes and heels of black or brown leather became popular.

Socks of dark colors were used with light shoes. At the beginning of the decade, men (especially younger men) went garterless, allowing flopping sock-tops to dangle over the shoes. Toward the end of the decade men adopted socks with elastic bands built into the top; such socks were called *ankle socks*.

Hats of the established types were still used, but more and more they were dispensed with for sports wear. College men, in the 'twenties, had started the vogue of going hatless, even on city streets. By 1935, this custom was general among young people.

Overcoats were cut generously full, belted, and equipped with capacious pockets. Reversible topcoats, gabardine on one side, coat-cloth on the other, were in demand for all-around wear.

Sweaters, in a variety of styles – knitted slipover and coat sweaters, and sweaterlike jackets of chamois and other leather goods or substitutes – continued steadily to gain favor.

Clip-suspenders or braces, chain tie-guards, patent collar stiffeners, Hollywood scarves and gaily-colored handkerchiefs, plaid woolen ties, wrinkle-proof ties, gum-soled shoes, and raw-cord soled shoes, and sandals, were among the recent additions to man's wardrobe.

Underwear for men was carefully considered as to cut, material, and color. Undershirts (if and when used) were of thin cotton lisle, or silk in a variety of colors. Shorts were of broadcloth or silk, plain, striped, or patterned, with pleats, and patent clasps. Other varieties of men's shorts were fashioned of elastic webbing fitted to the figure.

Costume for Women

Colors became quite subdued. Black, dark blue, and dark brown predominated for street wear. Evening gowns had a more catholic range of shade. The one-piece dress was all-important in this era.

For the sports dress, the one-piece, and the shirtmaker style, plain, lightweight woolens and silk-wool mixtures were used. Silk rayons, prints, and crepes were still preferred for most models of everyday dress. For evening or formal wear, nets, allover lace, satin, and velvet were used.

After 1930, a gradual return to the normal figure was visible. The bust was allowed to display its normal curves. About 1935, and after, bust forms were sold, to insure an erect, pleasing contour.

Soft, elastic-webbed corsets, with built-up busts, zipper fastenings, and two-way stretch, aided in the molding of the figure into pliable, gracefully curved lines.

In 1930, skirts dropped suddenly to about ten inches from the ground. They were conservatively narrow, with pleats or a slight flare at the bottom. The natural waistline returned. The bertha grew in favor, and acquired a deep dip in the back. The skirt might be high in front and low in the back, particularly for evening wear; another style showed tiers of ruffles gathered to a yoke. The blouse was sleeveless (Fig. 277   Fig. 278). Evening dresses showed a tendency to return to long skirts.

For daytime, the shawl collar, or bertha, was most in use. The waistline was occasionally emphasized by shirrings at the side. Ensemble coats were three-quarter length, straight cut, open in front. They carried out the long line.

In 1931, skirts were tailored with pleats or a slight flare. Coats were hip length,

Fig. 277

belted, buttoned or unbuttoned, and often had a capacious hip pocket. Suits came back into favor.

Evening dresses were cut with backless effects, the skirt touching the floor, and flaring full about the bottom hem line. A hip flare might be added. A low bertha over the shoulder was often added (Fig. 277).

Neck scarves of various shapes were fashionable with the daytime blouse. Prints were much in demand.

1932

The long skirt and the normal waistline continued in fashion. Sleeveless dresses were in good taste even for daytime wear.

The wide lounging pajamas (originating on the Lido) were definitely a part of the wardrobe, along with shorts and slacks (Fig. 277). Skirts were now about eight inches from the floor.

A new type of dress was made with a wide, draped V point in the blouse in front.

A peplum extended to hip length (Fig. 278). Sometimes the skirt was shirred on each hip. Short, puffed sleeves, or long ones with elbow or wrist puffs, were used.

Separate blouses with starched collars were in fashion.

Suits with hip-length coat, a scarf about the neck, and buttoned at the waist only, were in style. Knitted suits were very much in demand.

For evening, sleeveless dresses, low under the arm and in the back, were fashionable. A high Directoire waistline was noted in most sheath-style evening gowns.

Swim suits were one-piece, scanty of cut, without a skirt (Fig. 277).

1933

The shoulder line was interesting. A partial return to the full, puffed leg-of-mutton was attempted. It gave the figure a square-cut, masculine appearance (Fig. 278).

The vogue for knitted and sport suits continued. Capes and cape coats came in. Trim scarves, tied in front, softened the contour. The waistline was a trifle high, and trimly belted. Skirts were conservative in length and cut. In silk dresses, a certain amount of flare was obtained by a grouping of pleats or gathers at the center back.

1934

The draped collar line, the normal, belted waistline, a moderate skirt, pleated or flared, for daytime, with a coat, low hip length, added, was the usual type of dress. Separate blouses, belted, and extending to the hip length, added variety. Evening dresses were long-skirted, with occasional trains, long sleeves, and deep V's in the back.

1935

Suits came back into vogue, with hip-length, belted coats. Collar and cuffs were of white material, frilly or plain. Blouses were in great demand. Evening gowns had long, slim lines and backless effects. The one-piece dress still held sway. The pseudo-Greek draped neckline was very much in vogue. A round, turndown collar, a bow collar, or a scarf was also used to finish off the round or V back. Renaissance richness was reflected in gold, silver, and brocaded materials and in the soft, draped lines of the costume.

1936

Sports influenced American styles tremendously in this year. Perhaps the Olympic Games, held in the United States at Los Angeles, had some influence. The shirtmaker type of dress for daytime wear emphasized plain lines, conservatively short skirts, and open collar. For evening wear, long, sheathlike dresses of simple design were used, and a shirtwaist type, buttoned from neck to waist with small, brilliant buttons, was very fashionable. Slacks, shorts, and sun suits were part of the abbreviated wardrobe. Zippers for fastening became very popular, and proved extremely convenient for dresses, girdles, handbags, and many other articles of dress. Dresses were also fastened with rows of buttons down the back (Fig. 277).

1937

The same tendency toward simple clothes and plain materials continued. Color became increasingly important. Desert cloth, in gay shades, was used for slacks, beach coats, shorts, culottes, and similar garments. Skirts for street wear became very short; an attempt to shorten evening dresses was also made. Rubber swim suits of the scantiest proportions took the eye (or rather, only half an eye) of the beach promenader. Peasant handkerchiefs were draped over the head, for evening or sports wear.

1938

Chamois-weave materials were very popular for shirtmaker dresses. Slim, pleated, or flared skirts held sway. The return of the many-gored skirt, widely flared at the bottom edge, echoed the late 'nineties. The two-piece knit dress continued to be in excellent taste. The short bolero jacket was also revived from the archives of the early nineteen hundreds. The *hostess gown,* cut princess style, and frequently fastened by a zipper up the center front from neck to hem, was a pleasing innovation. It was made of corduroy, desert cloth, India print, and other modish materials. The *house coat,* worn with skirt or pajamas, was another comfortable garment. The *cocktail dress* and the short *cocktail jacket* emphasized the importance of this highlight in the day's routine.

Hair

The short, bobbed head had become a standard form of hairdressing. However, those who preferred long hair found many charming arrangements of waves and curls placed close to the contour of the head. The wave was indispensable to the well-groomed head. It was "set" with water, the curling iron, or the patented curler. The "windblown" bob continued to be popular with the younger set – and with those who liked to appear young.

Headdress

In 1930, hats were small, set off the forehead in front, and resting low on the nape of the neck. They were usually of felt or velvet. In 1931, they were still close-fitting, but a slightly wider brim was used. Uneven shapes were popular. In 1932, the *Eugénie hat* made its appearance. It was small, with a peak in front, and often an ostrich feather placed at the side, the tip curving gracefully down in the back. Its excessive popularity hastened its downfall. Although it had the most charming and graceful lines, its adoption by fat and lean, tall and short, old and young, destroyed its delicate appeal and sped its journey into the limbo of forgotten vogues (Fig. 277   Fig. 278).

In 1932, the small beret type also appeared. This year saw the elevation of the hat from the close confines of the cranium to the jaunty position on top of the head.

In 1933, 1934, and 1935, various small shapes were used, designed to be worn aperch a trim coiffure.

In 1936, hats were quite dashing, set on the head at a rakish angle. Small or large, they were distinctly saucy.

In 1937, designers went to the Tower of Babel, the spire of Chartres, the Leaning Tower of Pisa, Rockefeller Center, and other dissociated peaks for strange variations of vertical headgear. Women walked about, for all the world like acrobats or French poodles, balancing strange edifices on their uneasy heads. Circular veils, draped loosely over the peaks, covered all with a filmy charity. These veils were also adopted, with

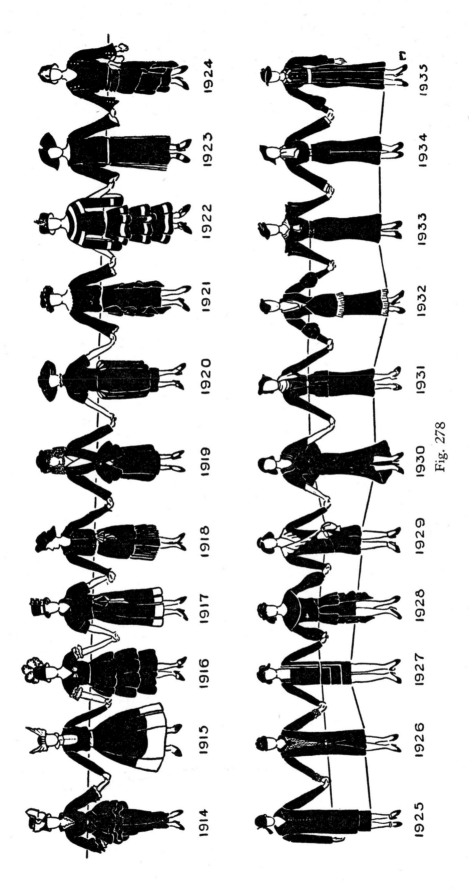

Fig. 278

the addition of flowers and ornaments, for the evening coiffure. This style extended into 1938.

Coat

Swagger coats, ensemble coats, and others which followed the general lines of the costume were developed in materials rough rather than smooth. High turnover fur collars were frequently added. The sleeves were neatly tailored. Circular capes regained great favor in 1937.

Stockings

The new departure in stockings, during the last few years, includes a definite tendency toward neutral gray-browns, cocoa-browns, cinnamon, beige, sun-tan, and other adaptable colors. The popularity of sun baths, with resultant sunburn, is shown in the range of shades for stockings. Garter-top stockings came in around 1935; the garters were stitched into the stocking tops, and were adjusted below or above the knee. Sheer black stockings were favored by the ultra-smart.

Ankle socks were used for tennis, golf, and other sports. Bare legs (seen on the street as well as on the athletic field since 1927) were still in order for young schoolgirls – and the inveterate tennis, badminton, or golf enthusiast. Bathing stockings took their place as museum pieces, along with "rats" and bustles, about the time of the Harding administration.

Footwear

Changes in shoe styles were very noticeable. Plain pumps and strapped slippers gave way to ornate styles. Even the oxford became a thing of two-toned leather; a white shoe had brown or black toes, heels, and instep patches.

Evening slippers first showed the influence of the sandal. Instead of being a decorous covering, they followed the open sandal, cross-strapped styles. In 1934, this type of evening slipper was well established. In 1935, daytime pumps followed these lines – and the open-toed shoe made its appearance. In 1936, 1937, and 1938, variations were legion: the medieval (center seam, running high up the arch), the Deauville sandal, the perforated shoe, the wrap-around, the multi-colored, the sport opera pump, and finally, the clog with solid, thick cork soles.

Underclothes

Underclothes reached a minimum of material and a maximum of comfort. "Scanties," step-ins, and feminine shorts were a graceful gesture to modesty. The combination still served the more conservative. Girdles were of two-way elastic, but very scant of dimension. Slips were bias or straight, princess-line models in pink, white, or black silk (or silk substitutes), or jersey. Gowns were princess type, of silk or jersey, and pajamas were of a variety of materials and patterns. Brassières were worn with the scanties or other nether garment, or with the girdle. Pink was the most usual color for underwear.

Ornaments and Accessories

Modern innovations followed one another with the speed of a sixteen-cylinder auto-mobile. Transparent raincoats, hats, and umbrellas, and zippered overshoes were fashionable for rainy-day wear. Zipper fastenings appeared on all types of clothing. Rubberized and quilted swim suits came into fashion.

Lace collars and jabots were revived around 1936. Flat pocketbooks in odd shapes, of oilcloth, rubber, and suede, were initialed and fitted, even to cigarette cases. The latter were also made separately, in various shapes and sizes. The vogue for initials extended to brooches, scarves, and other accessories. Costume jewelry usurped the place of real jewelry.

Vanity boxes included rouge, powder, lipstick, and eyebrow pencil. Handkerchiefs were gaily colored and patterned, and worn draped in an upper left-hand pocket.

Peasant scarves were draped about the neck, shoulders, or head. Linked and meshed metal belts – of gold, silver, steel, or gun metal – were used as accessories to street dresses, as well as to evening gowns. Rhinestone clasps, clips, and pins were used singly and in pairs. The 1937 circular veils have been mentioned.

Tinted fingernails, in general fashion since 1925, had a definite range of colors and lusters. Frequently the nails matched the lips in color. False eyelashes, eyebrows plucked to a thin line, and heavy eye shadow were the mark, no longer of the demi-mondaine, but of the ultra-fashionable woman, old or young (and her imitators). The virus of the motion picture beauty technique infected womanhood, and the marks are still upon her.

CHAPTER XVI

THE TWENTIETH CENTURY
(Continued)
1937-1950

IMPORTANT PEOPLE AND EVENTS

UNITED STATES
Franklin D. Roosevelt
Dwight Eisenhower
George C. Marshall
Douglas MacArthur
John L. Lewis
Albert Einstein
Herman "Babe" Ruth
Wendell Willkie
Orson Welles
Huey Long
Judith Anderson
Thomas Wolfe
Eugene O'Neill
Harry S. Truman
Maurice Evans

GREAT BRITAIN
King George VI
Winston Churchill
Bernard L. Montgomery
Archibald Wavell
Clement R. Attlee
Anthony Eden
Laurence Olivier
Evelyn Waugh

GERMANY
Adolf Hitler
Hermann Goering
Paul Joseph Goebbels
Heinrich Himmler
Joachim von Ribbentrop
Erwin Rommel
Rudolf Hess

ITALY
Pope Pius XII
Benito Mussolini
Pietro Badoglio

FRANCE
Henri Philippe Pétain
Léon Blum
Pierre Laval
Jean Darlan
Charles de Gaulle

RUSSIA
Joseph V. Stalin
Vyacheslav Molotov
Andrei Gromyko
Grigori K. Zhukov

OTHER COUNTRIES
China
Chiang K'ai-shek
T. V. Soong

Japan
Hideki Hirohito

Spain
Francisco Franco

Norway
King Haakon VII
Vidkun Quisling

Yugoslavia
King Peter II
Joseph Broz (Tito)

Rumania
King Carol II
King Michael I

India
Jawaharlal Nehru
Mohandas Gandhi

Philippines
Manuel Quézon

Recent Plays
Wilder's "Our Town"
Lindsay-Crouse's "Life with Father"
Kauffman-Hart's "The Man Who Came to Dinner"
Saroyan's "The Time of Your Life"
Williams' "A Streetcar Named Desire"
Miller's "Death of a Salesman"
O'Neill's "The Ice Man Cometh"
Rodgers-Hammerstein's "Oklahoma"
Logan-Mitchner's "South Pacific"

World's Fairs in New York and San Francisco. . . . Pin-up girls, swooner-crooners, sun-bathing, radio quizzes, "name" bands, song hits, publicity "stunts," capture public's fancy. . . . China's struggle against Japan. . . . Bombing of Barcelona and other open towns in Spanish revolution. . . . Russo-Finnish war. . . . Edward VIII abdicates, becomes Duke of Windsor, and George VI crowned King of England. . . . Hitler's New Order annexes Austria, Danzig. . . . Sept. 1, 1939, World War II begins with Third Reich's blitzkrieg invasion and conquest of Poland (divided with

Russia), Denmark, Norway (first transportation of troops by air), Belgium, the Netherlands, Northern France. . . . Luftwaffe bombs London, Coventry, other cities in "Battle of Britain." . . . Lend-Lease from United States. . . . U.S. Selective Service Act; women inducted into military service. . . . Japan's sneak-attack on Pearl Harbor, Dec. 7, 1941, forces entrance of United States into war. . . . Remarkable wartime industrial and military production, wartime restrictions, rationing. . . . Invasion and conquest of North Africa, Italy, France, Germany. . . . Disappearance of Adolf Hitler during thousand-plane bombing of Berlin. . . . V.E. Day, May 8, 1945. . . . U.S. invades and conquers Japanese South Pacific strongholds. . . . Atomic bombing of Hiroshima, August 6, 1945, results in V.J. Day, August 14, 1945. . . . A few places on history's map – Dunkerque, El Alamein, Hill 606, Stalingrad, Anzio, Bastogne, Remagen, Berchtesgaden, Attu, Lidice, Battle of the Bulge, Bataan, Guadalcanal, Iwo Jima, Dachau, Buchenwald. . . . V-mail. . . . Alphabet organizations. . . . Scientific contributions to war – radar, bombsight, jet and robot planes, plastics, plastic surgery, blood banks, sulfa drugs, nylon fabrics, compressed rations, powdered foods, lighter, better military clothing and equipment, improved transportation, communication, and care of men on land, sea, and air. . . . Foundation of postwar reconstruction laid at Atlantic Charter meeting, Dumbarton Oaks, San Francisco (where the United Nations was formulated), Potsdam, Casablanca, Teheran, Yalta. . . . MacArthur's reorganization of Japan. . . . G.I. Bill gives thousands of men and women veterans a chance for college educations. . . . Housing shortages. . . . Rise in prices after wartime restrictions lifted. . . . Race riots. . . . Strikes. . . . Jewish Nation established in Palestine; Ralph Bunche's fine work there. . . . India wins independence. . . . Negroes win vote in Mississippi. . . . International war criminals tried and sentenced (Goering commits suicide). . . . Marshall Plan for Europe's need. . . . Cold War with Russia. . . . Bikini experiment. . . . Asserted appearance of "flying saucers." . . . Russia claims secret of atom bomb. . . . Princess Elizabeth's marriage blessed with birth of son, Prince Charles. . . . Socialist Government in England. . . . Drives against infantile paralysis, cancer. . . . Congressional "investigations." . . . Commercial development of television. . . . Queen Wilhelmina of Holland abdicates in favor of daughter, Princess Juliana. . . . Russian-spy trials in United States, spy trials in Communist European areas. . . . Alaska, Hawaii are candidates for statehood. . . . U.S. announces possibility of hydrogen bomb. . . . Korean "police action" by U.N.-U.S. forces.

The atomic bombing of Hiroshima set off an explosion in man's mind more terrible than the physical detonation. The famous Krakatoa eruption and dissolution in 1883 was heard three thousand miles away, and spread atmospheric disturbance over five continents. Through radio's magic, the atomic bomb's sound waves enveloped the earth, and its impact shook the soul of man.

This fissile power of isotopes and neutrons spread its chain reaction to other areas. In the thirteen fateful years between 1937 and 1950, there were minor explosions in the laboratory of fashion – the creation of synthetic fabrics, the compression of styles to all-purposes and all-seasons. With the war years, scientific formulae were applied to military dress and equipment, to make it light, comfortable, and expedient.

The postwar years saw minor explosions of the gossamer threads and rainbow hues of popular taste. Already the variable stars of Hollywood have shown a decline in light years. From radio, emanates an invisible influence over the ecstatic bobby-soxer. Television, in chaps and sombrero, "Hop-a-longs" the small fry's lethal trail.

Facts, like flying saucers, flash and vanish before the naked eye of scientific inquiry; new discoveries may bring a New Look to fashion, and a New Outlook to man's mode of life. Korea already emphasizes the responsibility for peace.

COSTUME

General Characteristics

The mobile years, geared to intensity by the high friction of war, stamped official approval on synthetic fabrics, simplified styles, and saturated hues. Textiles, woven of the elements, fashioned for round-the-clock use in round-the-world places, traced the mazes of modern art in puzzling patterns and dazzling colors.

The total war effort was felt particularly in women's dress. For the first time, fashion designers like Mainbocher created uniforms for women serving in military zones of operation. Women factory workers found action-freedom in zippered coveralls, "Levi's," and slacks. Women at home shortened skirts, eliminated metal accessories, accepted substitutes, and otherwise conformed to OPA and L-85.

Men in the armed services found their equipment geared to the minutest exigency – for parachute-jumping, for icy mountain-scaling, for crossing desert sands. Myriads of pockets, zippered and snapped; light and comfortable fabrics proofed against water, wind, cold and heat, and camouflaged against detection were designed with a minimum of yardage and weight and a maximum of adaptability.

Even in the high tension of conflict, man must relax. Sportswear became increasingly important – slacks, sweaters, coats, shoes. The beaches of Miami and Malibu called for swim suits, beach togs, boating costumes. The snowy slopes of Sun Valley required trim, warm ski outfits. The dude ranches of Tucson and Cheyenne turned out frontier shirts, chaps, "Levi's," sombreros, and boots. Fashion, which once made its formal bow to the decree of kings, now straddled the rail fence of cowboy corrals.

The "One World" idea was accepted in the Norwegian peasant shoe; the Breton peasant's beret; the Spanish fisherman's pull-over; the Russian peasant's kerchief; the Mexican peasant's sandal, full skirt and ruffled blouse; the American Indian's patterns, colors, and fringed jacket; the South Pacific native's wrap-around of gaily blocked colors.

Not nations, but individuals, are, first and last, the most interesting sources of inspiration and influence in the world of dress. The Duchess of Windsor (formerly the American Wallis Warfield Simpson) not only turned the course of history, but also added to fashion's silhouette the inflated shoulder and the trim tunic. Mrs. Harrison Williams made the simple black evening dress a standard item of the wardrobe. Brenda Frazier popularized the white face and the full skirt. Betty Co-ed introduced Sloppy Joe and blue jeans into the college curriculum. Mary Martin gave the cue for crew-cut hair. The Duke of Windsor sponsored the tab collar, the Windsor tie, the roll lapel, the Fair Isles sweater, the snap-brim hat, and other items. Sinatra brought back the bow tie, and Crosby, the loud sport shirt. Fashion communiqués from the war zone included General Eisenhower's jacket, General Montgomery's beret, and General Issue's pouch with shoulder strap.

In this age of name-bands, name-products, and name-calling, women preferred articles properly tagged with such names as Alix, Dior, Schiaparelli. In this alphabetical age, there were special costumes for the WAC, WAVE, RAF, OGPU, KKK, NAZI, and others. But the rarest satisfaction, in dress and in daily living, will be found in the initials U.S.A.

Materials

In addition to the established materials, there were many which had been processed by pre-shrinking and wrinkle-proofing. The usual wools and worsteds became lighter in weight and wider in color range and in variety of weaves; gabardine, wool jersey, flannel, and alpaca held high favor. Silk fabrics included the newer weaves of jersey, moiré, sharkskin, faille, and metallic combinations. Cottons attained high popularity (and at a high price), and covered a wide range of new and old favorites, such as chintz, velveteen, canvas, and burlap. The most important development was seen in synthetics; out of the laboratory came rayon, nylon, and other multi-filaments, chemically mixed and spun fabrics.

Colors

Among the colors winning favor in the 1937–1950 era, might be cited ice blue, spice tan, palomino beige, desert sand, sienna, rust, Bimini blue, shocking pink, dusty pink, kelly green, garnet red, cherry red, oatmeal tan, macaw blue, pelican pink, canary yellow, parrakeet green, finch aqua, flame, chartreuse, gold, cigar brown, burgundy, dubonnet, ginger, silver grey, RAF blue, khaki brown, field grey.

1937–1950

COSTUME FOR MEN

GENERAL CHARACTERISTICS

The silhouette of man's garb reflected wide shoulders, slim waist, and trousers wide at top and tapering toward the bottom. Predominant in the wardrobe were sport clothes – slacks, coats, shirts, sweaters, shoes. There was an increasing popularity for double-breasted coats with square, padded shoulders; for pleated trousers; for shirts with attached collars. Fashion noted the return to favor of the raglan outer coat, and the discard from favor of the vest. Other highlights of masculine dress were the snap-brim hat; the Windsor knot and bow tie; the short, snug sock; the comfortable shoe, such as saddle, loafer, and moccasin; the development of accessories, such as tie bar, key chain, folding wallet, cigarette case.

Underwear

Men's underwear, since 1937, became slim, snug-fitting and light in weight. Pajamas were attractive in gay colors and designs. Lounging robes, with shawl collars and deep pouch pockets, were made of cotton, silk, rayon, and wool. Shorts, favored by George VI and the Duke of Windsor, were well cut; some, of elastic, were snugly fitted. Undershirts, with the low, round neck, were prevalent around 1937; by 1947, few men wore undershirts – and many also discarded pajamas.

1937-1950

Fig. 279

Suits, daytime, 1937–1941

The year 1937 saw the double-breasted suit in general demand. There were two- and three-button models, knuckle-long, with fairly wide and deep lapels. After 1935, the sleeve was cut smooth and rounded at the shoulder seam and tapered to a narrow cuff. Trousers sometimes had a single pleat on either side, front; the legs were fairly wide and long, with cuffs, and showed a slight break over the instep.

A ridiculous fad, extending only to a small group of youths, was the "zoot suit," with the "reet pleat" and the "drape shape" – the long, knee-length coat, wide shoulders, finger-tip length sleeves, trousers pleated full about the waist and tightened about the ankles, adorned with a keychain that swept the ground. This style, fortunately, was as short-lived as the "hit-tune."

The usual suit had wide, square, padded shoulders, tapering waist, loose, English drape. The business suit had a breast pocket, two flap pockets at or below the waistline; the dressy suit might omit the flaps. Two pairs of trousers usually accompanied the suit, one of which might be of a different color or weave. Trousers increased slightly in width up to 1941. Materials in demand were worsteds, coverts, cheviots, with flannels, gabardines, and Palm Beach weaves for summertime. Warm weather also influenced use of the single-breasted suit, unlined, loosely fitted, and less padded in the shoulders.

Suits, daytime, 1941–1945

Wartime restrictions were imposed on men's wear, in the matter of fabric, style, range of color, and variety of choice. OPA and WPB issued regulations which governed, for civilians, the size of lapels, length of coat, width of trousers. It eliminated trousers cuffs, pleats, and vests with double-breasted suits – indeed, vests never came back into general favor afterwards. Wool, needed for uniforms, had to depend on domestic supply alone, as England used her entire domestic and colonial supply. Civilian trade, therefore, had to put up with various mixtures of wool, cotton, rayon, and other materials. Clothes were not rationed, but they were limited in type and appeal; it was difficult to purchase suits, particularly, though high prices were held in line by government regulation.

Suits, daytime, 1945–1950

After the war, restrictions were slow in lifting; however, America reacted with its usual resilience, and men's suits became fuller; with wider shoulders and lapels, with cuffs, and two pleats, either side, added to the trousers. By 1947, tweeds and other good worsteds returned. By 1948, the "Bold Look Go-With" was emphasized – to go with a brown suit, for instance, there was a brown homburg, a tan shirt, a brown dotted tie, brown brogues, brown braces, a brown-edged handkerchief. Even the jewelry could be brown leather studs and tie bar.

For single-breasted models, the curved lower edge to the coat was preferred; for the double-breasted, a straight edge. The one-button, long-roll, double-breasted coat became very much in demand. Brown was the choice color, with dark blue and medium gray close seconds. Along with tweeds, coverts, gabardines, tropical worsteds, and various rayon and nylon mixtures became accepted fabrics.

Suits, evening, 1937–1941

By 1937, the use of midnight blue for dinner clothes was well established. In general, dress clothes, up to 1941, had broad, wide shoulders, full chest, slender waistline, long, hip-hugging "Surrey" tails, falling below the knees, and peak lapels. In 1938, a dinner jacket of red, with red bow tie, carnation, and maroon cummerbund, were introduced. Double-and single-breasted models, with the one-button fastening favored, were fashionable; the trousers had a wide satin stripe down the sides.

With dress clothes was worn a white silk shirt, having a three-inch center box pleat, and fastened with one or two studs. A bow tie and patent leather oxfords were worn with the dinner jacket; a white lawn tie, and patent leather pumps, with the full dress suit.

Suits, evening, 1941–1950

During the war, evening clothes almost disappeared from the wardrobe; those that remained in use showed little change. Postwar elegance expressed itself in the continued use of midnight blue, maroon and red, for dinner jackets; white was adopted for summer dinner jackets. The rolling peak lapel tended to replace the shawl collar;

the tails to the full dress suit were shortened; and the cummerbund, of white twill, became popular.

Coats

The "mixed suit" appeared in 1930, with unmatched coat and trousers. This probably led to the separate sports coat, though the old Nineteenth-Century blazer and Norfolk jacket had pointed the way. The sports coat, usually unlined, grew swiftly in popularity, and proved a most useful addition to man's wardrobe, especially during the war years, when styles and materials were restricted. It was designed along loose lines: with wide lapels, patch pockets, of long, knuckle-tip length, wide, square shoulders, and full sleeves. The cardigan type, without collar, was also in demand. For a time, the back had an inverted pleat over the shoulders in back, for free action, but this disappeared during war years. Tweeds and checks were very popular for sports coats; of late, flannel is bidding for favor. Today, the sports jacket has the loose, English drape, and wide shoulders; some late models have the collar and cuffs lined with contrasting material. Sports coats of canvas, leather, and wool, for fishing and other outdoor activities, have zippered fastenings and zippered-in linings.

During the war, in 1943, the Eisenhower jacket (perhaps suggested by the lumberjack coat) made its appearance, and this style continued on for civilian use after the war.

Trousers

Slacks were the outstanding innovation in trousers in the thirties and forties. Though the war years narrowed the leg-width, eliminated cuffs, and limited pleats, the separate slacks proved a boon to those unable to procure suits to their taste. Solid colors were preferred, and the tendency, in late years, has been toward soft, pastel shades. The belt is now usually sewed to the trouser top. After the war, the two front pleats reappeared, and pockets, slanted forward, were added. Gabardines, twills, flannel, and rayon mixtures led in desired fabrics, and blue or blue grey led in color. The zippered fly, with a snap fastening at the top, the narrow belt, of fabric or belting, and the gripper inside the waistband (to prevent slipping) were useful additions to fit and comfort.

Shirt

The shirt acquired a soft collar in 1920, due to Van Heusen's studies in shirt styling. The next step, taken by Sanford Cluett, was the pre-shrinking of cotton cloth, the most important textile discovery since fast dyes and mercerizing, around 1905. Today, over ninety-eight per cent of all shirts have attached soft collars, due to the added discovery, in 1947, of a finish that made cotton more wrinkle-resistant than other materials.

Rayon first made its appearance as a shirting in 1928, and has steadily increased in favor. Since the war, nylon is being used more and more for shirts, and is especially valued for travel and sportswear, as it needs no pressing. Shirts are still made of broadcloth, cord, and other weaves, with soft, plain colors preferred. The attached collar has varied slightly as to height, but more in the shape of the points, which are buttoned down at the tips, the deeper V points being stiffened with boning. Cuffs, attached to the shirt, changed very little until 1947, when the turned-back French cuff, long discarded, returned, and with it, the French cuff links.

Neckwear

Ties, in 1937, had small, narrow knots, were narrow in width, about forty-eight inches long, and when tied were lifted up and forward. After the war, the tie became wider and the knot thicker and wider. The Duke of Windsor introduced the thick, wide knot, in the fifty-inch length tie. Materials for ties included foulard, satin, taffeta, madras, worsteds (plaids and stripes) rep and knitted fabric, and other materials. Colors included all shades, from pastels to brilliant oranges; designs included plaids, stripes, large floral and abstract patterns. Bing Crosby made the wide, hand-painted tie, with startling designs and colors, a fashionable item. In 1949, the Tremlett shape – slim, two inches wide and fifty-two inches long – was favored.

The bow tie, associated with Frank Sinatra since the swooning forties, was used for daytime, informal dress, and also for the dinner jacket, in black, blue and maroon. The white bow tie is still correct for full dress.

Sportswear

The tremendous interest in sports, which arose with the development of such playtime resorts as Palm Beach, the California coast line, and mountain resorts – Sun Valley and others – led to a variety of "dress-up" sportswear, from complete outfits for special occasions, to individual accessories. A skiing outfit, in 1938, consisted of a single-breasted loden jacket, standing military collar, blue gabardine downhill trousers, headband, and ski boots. A wind jacket, or a blazer, might be substituted. Shalom gaiters and wool or leather gloves were worn with the costume.

For golf, there were coats, belted in the back; or sweater coats, with collar, or of the cardigan type; some sweaters were held in at the waist with a knitted band. Shirts for hunting, fishing and other sports were designed with two to four patch pockets, buttoned, snapped or zippered, in flannel, canvas, or worsted (plaids preferred); of late, the pockets are slanted and zippered.

The sports shirt, first appearing in 1927–1928, and made popular in 1935–1938, presented such novel features as the open collar, short sleeves, and short, eight-inch front opening. They were made of broadcloth, cotton knit, twill, cord, rayon, nylon, and other weaves. White was favored at first, though pastel shades, stripes, and mixtures were soon added. Bing Crosby and others popularized the primitive, gay floral patterns of the South Seas.

The "in-and-out" shirt, worn inside or outside the trouser belt, appeared about 1938, and was well established by 1940. It had a front yoke and an open, overlapping V neck, requiring no collar or fastenings. Sometimes two pockets were added at waist level. After 1947, this style was made with a diagonal closing in front. Snap fastenings, off the market during the war, returned in 1945, for use down shirt front openings, on cuffs, or pocket flaps.

The other shirt in constant use, particularly by young men, was the tee shirt, with rounded crew neck and short sleeves, of cotton knit, white or colored, plain or horizontally striped.

The many varieties of sports shirts, besides those mentioned, included the striped Basque shirt, with crew neck; the shirt-jacket, of sharkskin suiting, with four patch pockets and open collar; the dinghy shirt of blue denim; the tweed blazer, worn with white foulard scarf; the Shetland jacket; the terry cloth shirt; and gaily colored and printed washable rayon shirts, worn in or out of the trouser belt.

The "western" shirt became very much in demand about 1945. These shirts were of flannel, gabardine, seersucker, cotton, or even silk and satin. The "pioneer" shirt was designed with a yoke front and back, a piping of contrasting color, a flaring open collar, piped breast pockets, deep, piped cuffs, and pearl snap buttons down the front and up the high cuffs. The rest of the "pioneer" outfit consisted of trousers cut very tight and figure-fitting, with horizontally-slanted piped pockets; a large "Stetson" hat, with high, six-inch crown, and wide, five-inch brim, sharply rolled up at the sides, a carved leather band, and made of felt in black, red, maroon, green, or other colors; a "rodeo" tie, knotted four-in-hand, with very short ends (about eight inches), in gay colors, usually hand-painted; a carved leather belt; cowboy boots, hand-stitched and hand-carved, with high heels, in black, green, red, and other colors. This pioneer costume was made up in many materials, usually gabardine for the trousers, and gabardine, silk or satin for the shirt; it also appeared in "faded blue" denim, with pearl snaps and contrasting piping, about 1948.

Sweaters have become a must in every wardrobe. From 1937 on, the V neck leads in popularity, though the crew (round) neck and even the old turtle-neck (for winter sports) are in demand. It was the (then) Prince of Wales who introduced the Fair Isles sweater, with horizontal stripes in different patterns, which led to variations of design and color. In 1949, cashmere was the favorite material, in pastel shades, and the V neck the favorite type.

Denim, both dark blue and faded blue, was in demand for "Levi's," first favored in the West, but now accepted in the East, especially by the younger college set.

In addition to all types of slacks, in various materials, men used riding breeches and jodhpurs for horse-back sports. Shorts were adopted for walking, bathing, golfing, beach wear, and other moments of relaxation and exercise. These shorts were pleated, belted, and made of such materials as terry cloth, canvas, gabardine, cotton and rayon mixtures. Bathing suits included a shirt, cut low, with crab back, in 1937; by 1940, the tops had disappeared, and the bathing shorts were frequently made of elastic. Beach coats were donned for lounging on the sands.

It used to be said that "everybody talks about the weather, but nobody does anything about it." In the last fifteen years, men have sensibly adopted thin, light suitings, thin underwear, thin, open-collared sports shirts, short socks, light-weight shoes. Even hats, straw and felt, have become lighter in weight. The Tyrolean hat, complete with feather, is a fixture for sportswear.

Top Coats

This type of clothing has varied little in the last fifteen years. The straight, con servatively cut top coat, with set-in sleeves, single- or double-breasted, still leads, though the raglan type (unavailable during the war) returned to favor, especially for inclement weather; in 1939, it acquired a matching hat. The top coat, with full back, took hold of public favor, and held it. For formal wear, the top coat is usually of black or dark gray worsted, or cheviot, with concealed buttons under a fly front. Tweed, worsted, and wool gabardine lead for the informal type; fine worsteds for the formal type. The raglan is made up in gabardine, rainproof cloth, wool and camel's hair. Short raincoats and short suede coats appeared in 1949. In 1937, the top coat was usually belted, but belts were discarded during the war, and are just returning. The new idea in top coats is a double-duty garment, of light fabric, with additional lining, of flannel, sheepskin, or other warm material, which can be zippered in for cold weather (a sewed-in plaid lining had been used since 1939). Fur coats and fur collars, though still used, are not as popular as in the days of the raccoon coat.

Socks

Since 1937, socks have tended to become shorter in length and easier to hold up. Garters have given way to the elastic top, used from 1935 to the war, and to the later narrow, knit top. Rayon socks became very popular, but, since 1943, the demand has been for pure wool Argyle socks, in large, diamond-shaped patterns and gay colors. Heavy, ribbed socks come next in choice. For formal evening wear, black silk is still the correct thing. Golf socks, in loud plaids, or ribbed, are available, but the prevalence of shorts has led to the adoption of the short sock.

Shoes

Loafers, developed from the Norwegian moccasin, were being worn in 1937. A little later appeared the saddle shoe, of white buckskin or calfskin, with black or brown saddle strips. Brogues, espadrilles, and many types of sandals came into ordinary usage, especially for sportswear. Thick crepe and rope soles were used on these sports shoes. A new type of shoestring was the ghillie tie. For conservative use, the Oxford straight tip shoe, in black or brown, was correct; later, the wing tip equaled it in popularity. The patent leather pump was correct for full dress wear, the patent leather oxford for dinner wear. The chukker boot, with high sides, evolved from World War II. Materials for footwear included fine leather, calfskin, buckskin, canvas, rope, and straw; the last three were especially in use for sandals, espadrilles, and general beach and yachting wear.

Hair

From 1937, the side part in the hair, usually on the left, was favored. The hair was waved over the forehead, cut short on sides and back, and held smoothly in place with hair tonic. After the war, about 1947, the crew cut became the college man's idea of tonsorial elegance.

Hats

The felt hat, with welt- or bound-edge brim, continued in favor. This was worn with the brim curved, or upturned, and the crown indented in a single center crease, or in a pork-pie, around-the-edge crease, or in a telescope crease. The Homburg was the conservative type, worn off the face, with the center crease sometimes pinched in front or sides. Other varieties used since 1937 include the velour, the Borsalino, the Tyrolean (with feather). The snap brim, with welt- or bound-edge brim, was introduced by the Duke of Windsor, and is at present the most popular type, especially with the younger men. For summer wear, the straw hat continued standard, though the Panama was reintroduced by the Duke of Windsor. Cocoanut straw, with puggaree band, was an innovation for summer wear. A rain hat, of canvas or other cloth, was brought in, about 1939, to accompany the raincoat. The Montgomery beret was copied by civilians, about 1942. However, there is a growing inclination, especially among the younger generation, not to bow, but to bare the head, to the decrees of the crown – with brim.

Accessories, Jewelry

Gloves were fashioned of pigskin, deerskin, capeskin, suede, cotton, and nylon; some were furlined, for cold weather. Suspenders were made of elastic, then of plastic. In 1937, they were narrow, but became wider after the war. The free-swing, swivel-action back, and gripper fastener, are new features. Mufflers, for daytime use, were of cashmere or wool; evening scarves were of silk. Belts, of leather, fabric, silk, rubber, and plastic, sometimes had monogrammed buckles. An inner belt, with rubbery traction, held the shirt down and trousers up. The handkerchief, folded in points, for the breast pocket, was white or colored; plaid designs were used for the colored type; the border could be up to one and a quarter inches wide. Loafer socks, with soles attached, were a comfortable accessory for a lazy hour.

The zipper (actually dating back to 1891) took forty years to reach its valued place in men's and women's dress. First used on men's raincoats, it was later applied to their jackets, trousers, pockets, and linings. In 1917, 20,000 zippers were used, mostly on money belts; in 1949, 8,000,000,000 zippers were used.

The billfold, of pin seal or sharkskin, was a favorite accessory; it was usually zippered. The shaving or traveling case, of pigskin or calfskin, was another choice item. Cigarette cases were made thin and flat, of leather or plastic. Tobacco pouches were of pliofilm, with zipper fastening. Patent lighters completed the smoker's outfit. The cummerbund added an Eastern touch to dress wear.

Jewelry, in 1938, ran to matched sets, and it has continued to follow this pattern, though single items are also in good taste. The earlier sets consisted of shirt studs, cuff links, tie bar, and, perhaps, belt buckle; the later sets have added French cuff links, collar bar, and key chain. The long watch chain, with a knife on the end, popular around 1937, was followed by the long key chain fastened to the waist band. The wrist watch is, today, a standard item of men's dress; it has a leather, fabric, plastic, or metal-linked band.

COSTUME FOR WOMEN

GENERAL CHARACTERISTICS

The thirteen eventful years between 1937 and 1950 marked outstanding events also in the world of dress. There was the introduction of nylon, for stockings and light-weight materials; the uplift sole to the shoe; the handbag with shoulder strap; the hat without a crown; the swing-back top coat; the strapless evening gown; the padded shoulder; the slanted pocket; the abbreviated pantie and the built-up bra; the use of slacks, shorts, western regalia; the New Look in longer skirts; the use of unusual materials such as burlap and suede; the finely-varied shades of make-up, with accent on sun-tan colors. New materials, new ideas, and new trends made this an interesting era, in spite of the routines of war and the perils of peace.

1937-1950

Fig. 280

Materials

Among the most-used fabrics were worsteds, flannel, jersey (wool, silk and cotton), gabardine (wool, silk and cotton), tweed, flannel, alpaca. Other silk (including rayon and nylon silk weaves) materials were faille, crepe, foulard, bemberg, chiffon, satin (including slipper satin), marquisette, shantung, moiré, grosgrain, taffeta (including paper taffeta), bengaline, surah, pongee, sharkskin, tulle, velvet, brocade. Among the desired cottons were batiste, gingham, organdy, dotted Swiss, velveteen, twill, percale, piqué, chintz (plain and glazed), muslin, lawn, duvetyn, canvas, corduroy, and burlap. Irish and handkerchief linen returned to favor, also laces, em-

broidery, and chenille. Metallic and fancy weaves included lamé, metallic taffeta, and
matelassé; leopard, panther, python and ostrich imitation weaves. Synthetic fabrics
were made, in imitation of many standard weaves; the rayon and nylon types were
most in demand. Styles in weaves were waffle, basket, two-faced, besides the usual
plaids, checks, herringbone, print, paisley and batik.

Colors

Colors ran the gamut of the rainbow, with the accent on the gay and brilliant, the
earthy and regional, the bizarre and striking, especially in the combinations used.
Some shades reflected in dress and accessories, not mentioned earlier, were mustard
tan, vanilla ice cream, coquette blue, shoe leather black, poison green, chablis, bitter-
sweet, sunset grey, tangerine, and Bermuda red.

Underwear

Light materials and adaptable styles were carried out in foundation corsets and
girdles. Net, satin, lace, crepe de Chine, silk and rayon tricot, English broadcloth, and
batiste were generally used, though the elastic yarn materials took precedence over all
else, if not for the whole garment, then for insets and gores. Brocades and heavier
fabrics were reserved for those who needed more support. The two-way stretch in
corset and girdles provided flexibility and ease. Garters for the stockings and zippers
for the fastening, side, back, or front, proved important items. The corset and girdle
were straighter in silhouette and shorter in length, in 1937, than they were in 1947,
when the waist was drawn in and the length was increased.

With the girdle, was worn the brassière, or "bra." It was made of the various materials mentioned, reinforced, and moulded to the bust. Toward the end of the era,
the bra was stiffened, built up and out to give prominence to the bust (perhaps the
Jane Russell influence). For evening wear, the strapless bra was invented, held up by
ingenuity.

In the brief category of women's underthings, the pantie and bra held strategic, if
reduced, position. The short, loose-legged pantie was varied by an elastic type, snug to
the leg; it also served as a girdle. Jersey or silk was used for panties, though black
chiffon, trimmed with lace, was desirable for dressy occasions.

The slip (or petticoat), in 1937, was made on the bias, with a sunpanel and bandeau
top. Later, the bias gave way to the straight cut, and the high empire waist dropped
to a normal waistline. Jersey and crepe were the usual materials. In 1947, along with
the New Look, rounder hips and smaller waists were featured; embroidery, lace, and
ruffles added length to older models. For the varying hemlines in the wardrobe, slips
were trimmed with hemstitched bands, or ruffles, which could be snipped off at the
required length.

Nightgowns appeared in many styles, long or short (just below the knees) with
high or low neck, fitted or flowing lines, gathered or plain, trimmed or untrimmed,
strapless or backless; materials ranged from sheer chiffon to brushed flannel. The only
common denominator was that they were all designed for horizonal wear.

The housecoat was made long, or in three-quarter length (for use with pajamas).

Though the flannel type, tailored, piped, and belted, held high place, there were other styles, zippered and buttoned, in thinner materials, and in heavier weaves, such as corduroy, quilting, and terry cloth. The negligée, in myriad designs, draped and trimmed, was made of the thinner silks, usually in pastel shades.

Suits

The two-piece mannish suit for women was universally popular; in 1937, the jacket was fairly short, single-breasted, straight-lined, with small, high-placed lapels, four or five buttons down the front, and few, if any, pockets. The skirt, cut in two pieces, and moulded to the figure, reached just below the knee. By 1938, shoulders were padded to give the horizontal effect; the one-button coat was a favorite, as was the waffle weave material. By 1939, the popularity of gabardine rose; lapels were longer, pockets were featured, and the three-piece suit – jacket, skirt and topper – became a standard outfit. In 1940, suits of contrasting materials were introduced – such as a plaid coat with plain skirt. In 1942, the box-pleated skirt reappeared. The inverted pleat in back had been in for several years.

With the war years, suits suffered restrictions in material, cut, and trim. Jackets had to meet specifications as to lining, pockets, and buttons; for the latter, plastic, wood, and self-fabric buttons replaced prewar types, particularly metal buttons. The waist was defined with one or two darts. The cardigan jacket, without collar or lapel, was designed to meet restrictions in cloth. The skirt had to achieve fullness with one or two kick pleats, or a slit up the sides. The shawl collar, yoke top, and diagonal pockets added new notes to wartime styles. Another innovation, urged by wartime conditions, was the suit-dress, a jacket and skirt combination without blouse, which combined the smarter features of a casual dress and a trim suit; it was made up in woolen, silk, and cotton materials. For women who shunned the formality of long dinner gowns, there was the dinner suit, of silk, satin, moiré, velveteen or velvet, cut suit-fashion, with short, slim skirt, short jacket, and dressy blouse of satin or metallic weave.

With the lifting of restrictions after the war, materials and styles became more varied. Skirts acquired more pleats, belts appeared again, deeper and wider pockets were added to the somewhat longer jacket. The real change, however, came in 1947, with the New Look; shoulders were sloping and narrowed, the waistline was small (nipped in with "waist-corsets"), the curved hip was emphasized, and the skirt descended to within twelve inches of the floor. Many ingenious means were employed to lengthen the old skirt to meet the New Look – by the addition of yokes, or bands at bottom and above the hem, by ruffles, pleatings, or ribbon loops. When all else failed, a new longer skirt, of contrasting shade, was worn with the original jacket. Jutting, flared patch pockets appeared on the slender skirts, giving a "lamp shade" effect. Black faille was the favored material for dressy suits, with moiré a close second.

The bolero, popular since 1937 retained its favored place throughout this era, for use with suit skirts and blouse, as well as with daytime and evening dresses. In contrast to the short bolero, featured in late fashion notes, there is the mid-thigh length jacket, single- or double-breasted, with shawl collar, sloping shoulders, pinched-in waist, and long, slim skirt (with back pleats for fullness). The jacket sometimes had a peplum, flared in the back, and stand-away pockets, to give variety to the silhouette. Taffeta vied with faille for dressy wear.

Dresses

From 1937 on, the trimly tailored shirtmaker style of dress held first place, except for afternoon dress wear. This all-purpose, shirtwaist style, in 1937, emphasized the shirtwaist collar, open or closed; the plain sleeve, with cuff; the front fastening, with buttons – to waist or to hem of skirt – and pockets. The silhouette for all dresses was straight, with emphasis on a natural waistline; skirts were plain and short. For dress wear, the neck was cut in a V, or rounded; the surplice and shawl collar were also used. The torso effect was emphasized by a wide sash or corselet girdle. The bolero dress, made fashionable by Mrs. Harrison Williams, featured a printed blouse and sash with the plain cloth bolero and skirt. A circular skirt, ballerina length, was sometimes used with the bolero. Sleeves became gathered at the armhole (suggesting the old leg-o-mutton type) and shoulders were padded.

In 1938, a neckline appeared, consisting of an upright banding, tied in a bow in front. Front fastenings were of studs, with appropriate birthstones. The action sleeve appeared, for the shirtmaker type; the criss-cross short sleeve, for dressier types. After-noon dresses were usually fastened in the back, zippers being the favored fastening. Other necklines featured were the draw-string type, pulled in like a miser's bag, and the tie-drape, held in by clips. Skirts acquired a slight fullness, with kick pleat, swing, knife, or umbrella pleats, and the circular cut; they were also a bit longer.

The war years induced the return of the short tighter skirt, short sleeves, and in-genuity of cut and trim. Drapes on blouse and skirt made up for scantiness of cut; but-tons and pockets were multiplied. The neckline gained attention; a high, rounded neck, plain or nicked in front, sometimes finished with a turnover collar, fastened be-hind, found favor. The middy blouse was reintroduced, also the yoked shirtwaist. The effect of fullness was achieved in the skirt by bell-shaped gores, center-front gathers or pleats, and a yoked, circular style.

The real transition in styles, as mentioned earlier, came in postwar days, with the New Look, in 1947. Dior's emphasis was on the long, slender silhouette, feminine in contour, with freedom of line. Sloping shoulders replaced the horizontal padded type; the small, hourglass waist was accented by tightly drawn belts. A flared peplum gave the free look; the button-basque, bolero with torso sash, draped bodice with yoke, suggested feminine softness. The long raglan sleeve carried out the sloping shoulder line; the sculptured open collar, the shawl collar, "chin-up" neckline, or halter neck-line, added interest to the blouse. The skirt, twelve inches from the floor, varied in width from pencil-slim to full circle width. Pleats were unstitched, unpressed, cartridge-shaped, or inverted. Draping followed the peg-top style, but side and diagonal drap-ings were also used. Fullness was lured to the rear, as seen in the fish-tail back. Pouch pockets, on the slant, protruded from blouse or skirt.

Late developments in dress styles include the return of the Gibson Girl silhouette, the descending waistline, the cascade drape, the peplum gathered or draped over the skirt, the built-up neckline – keyhole, horseshoe, and bateau types – the snug cummerbund to accent the wasp waist, the deep yoke with circular or pleated skirt, the sleeveless blouse, the tiered skirt, and the new length, twelve inches from the floor.

In general, interest in dresses, in the last thirteen years, centered on the skirt, shoulder, neck, and waist. All-time, all-purpose dresses vied with ensembles, suit-dresses and draped models; but the general effect was simplicity.

Skirts

The skirt held the spotlight throughout most of this era. In 1937, the separate skirt was short, slim, and plain in cut; the separate evening skirt, however, was frequently cut gored, or circular. In 1938, the peasant dirndl, full gathered, won favor for sport and playtime wear; fullness in other skirts began to be achieved by pleats and fan tucks, or by pleats and gathers, in center front. The New Look gave the longer skirt, tubular-slim, or circular-full. Hips were emphasized by pannier pockets, as well as by peg-top, unpressed, and inverted pleats. The ballerina circular skirt reached the ankles. The latest style in skirts hints at shorter length, panels, fan pleats, diagonal, flared pockets, and the use of such unusual materials as drapery cloth, burlap, and suede. The full circle skirt, woven in one piece, with circular design, is the latest sports fashion.

Blouses

The blouse, necessary as it is, was decidedly an adjunct to the suit or separate skirt, and was frequently omitted, during these years, in favor of a jacket or sweater top. The jacket-top became part of the suit-dress, or accompanied the long dinner or evening skirt; in which case, it was made, like the dinner blouse, of lamé, velvet, brocade, or the like. Made popular by the Duchess of Windsor, this type was frequently ornamented with embroidery, spangles, or appliqué. The cut of the blouse, in 1937, was very plain, with interest focussed at the neckline. For the suit, there was a preference for the shirtwaist blouse, of batiste, linen, crepe, broadcloth or chiffon, with trimming of tucks, pleats, ruffles, and stitching. Stud-buttons, in 1938, added interest. Vest-blouses, of piqué, and sweater-blouses, in black, white or beige, gaily embroidered or spangled, added charm to wartime outfits. In 1947, the lingerie blouse appeared, along with the feminine appeal of the New Look; insertions of lace and embroidery gave a delicate air to the white creation. A late development in blouses is the very deeply pointed collar, the back-buttoned blouse with high collar, and the low, round neckline trimmed with ruffles.

Evening Gowns

The one-piece evening gown vied with the separate skirt and blouse (or jacket) in popularity; the latter type was dedicated to dinner parties, and semi-formal affairs. In 1937 (the Coronation year, in England), the one-piece evening gown was cut with a plain or bandeau top, or surplice, or with the Empire or Regency high waistline, gathered or draped at the neck. A separate bolero jacket, with square or rounded edges, was frequently worn with the low gown, especially if it was backless and sleeveless. The skirt was cut slim and long, with a slit to ease up the hobble hem. Some skirts had a hem up in front and down in back, reminiscent of the early 'thirties. Another type of skirt, usually of net or bouffant material, was cut very full and gathered.

In 1938, the shirtwaist gown came in; it was made of chiffon, net or allover lace; the blouse was fashioned like a shirtwaist, with yoke, collar, full, long sleeves with cuff (or short, puffed sleeve), and front buttoned opening, which extended to the waistline, or down to the bottom of the hem, the buttons being fashioned of small brilliant clusters. The skirt was usually full. This year reflected the Winterhalter influence – the romantic off-the-shoulder bodice, with ruffle, and full, tiered skirt. A classic Greek type was designed of clinging jersey, with draped halter neck, center-front drape, and flowing sleeves. The Mittel-Europa influence was reflected in the full dirndl skirt with black velvet bodice. Giant flowered materials became the vogue. In 1939, the ballerina length circular evening skirt was used.

During the war, bodices were simply cut, and skirts were sheathlike, with side drapes; a back bustle bow added an extravagant touch. The strapless gown focussed public interest and still holds its place. The separate evening blouse became important, with a skirt that was long, or ballerina length, or short.

In 1947, the short, ballet-length skirt (to ankles) led in popularity. All evening skirts became fuller; Dior fashioned one of tulle, containing one hundred yards of fabric. The bustle back and side drape gave a simulated width to the more sheathlike skirts. The nation-wide vogue for the square dance gave popularity to the square dance dress, which was short, full, of a plaid, checked, or flowered cotton material, with low, rounded bodice trimmed with a wide ruffle.

Outer Coats, Wraps

Especial attention was paid to outer coats, wraps, capes, sports coats, fur coats, and evening wraps. In 1937, the conservative coat was cut with straight lines, mannish collar and lapel, and button fastening – one or many. Fur coats were in demand, either full length or hip length. Some of the furs, used for entire coats, or for collars to cloth coats, were fox, mink, broadtail, opossum, beaver, ermine, kolinsky, Persian lamb, leopard, and guanaco.

In 1939, the fitted coat had wide revers. A redingote type showed a row of buttons all down the front. Capes, with wide, padded shoulders and slits for arms, were lined or unlined. For sportswear, there was the swagger coat, of tweed or plaid, cut knee length. Fur coats showed high collars and full, gathered sleeves. Evening cloaks were of velvet or full-gathered chiffon.

During the war years, coats were trimly cut. Sports coats, with deep pockets, decorated with very large plastic or synthetic buttons, and casual coats, knee length, in checks, plaid, and tweed, filled the need for variety. However, wartime industry lined these deep pockets, so the demand for fur coats reached an all-time high; it was no unusual event to see a woman war worker, in overalls or slacks, shopping – and buying – not one, but two fur coats, of real, not imitation pelts. Raincoats also took on a martial note, being fashioned like the WAC raincoat, double-breasted, with deep pouch pockets, double yoke, high, turned-up collar, detachable hood, and a belt, tied or snapped. Elkskin was a favored material for these.

In 1947, the New Look established its freedom, in coats, by the flared, swing-back; a detachable lining, of wool or fur, zippered in, added warmth when needed, and did not add weight when not needed. Deep pouch pockets, cut on the diagonal, gave free storage space. The balmacaan sports coat found great favor. A late type of jacket, short, waist length, was cut with kimono-like sleeves – it was called the "batwing," and emphasized width of sleeves and height of collar.

Sportswear

The variety of items, and the importance of sportswear increased in the years between 1937 and 1950. The interest in home and near-home play-spots, – due partly to the unsettled condition in Europe – and the craze for sun-tan, influenced new and daring styles in the bathing suit, beach dress, ski suit, riding togs, slacks, golf and tennis outfit, play suit, sun suit, and western outfit. In 1937, the one-piece bathing suit, with V or rounded neck, or with straps over the shoulder, prevailed; cotton, jersey, sharkskin, rubber and elastic weaves were the materials used. By 1938, the separate bra was worn with tight shorts, usually of elastic. A rubber swim cap, fish-net sandals, tabi socks or pool shoes, and swim goggles, were worn with the bathing suit. War shortages appeared also in scantier shorts and narrower bra. A halter neck appeared on a one-piece suit. In 1948, the Bikini suit appeared, a miniature shock of a small kerchief tied diaper-fashion about the waist and hips, and a bandeau like a disappearing atoll.

The 1937 beach dress consisted of a short-sleeved blouse, with bare back, shorts, and hip-length cotton coat. In 1938, a long shirt, worn outside the shorts, was favored. Toward the end of the era, the Hawaiian influence appeared in brilliant, large floral patterns. The ski suit consisted of a double-breasted jacket, plus fours, cap, and fur-lined shoes and gloves. Later, the long slacks, gathered or tucked into boots, became customary; the jacket was hooded; however, a sweater, with high neck, was preferred by some. For horse-back riding, jodhpurs were favored, with shirt, sweater, or jacket, and derby hat.

Slacks, of all types, rose to great popularity; front pleats and an attached waist-band gave trimness and flexibility. Flannel and corduroy were the usual fabrics. Pedal pushers, reaching about midway between knee and ankle, were designed for bicycle riding, hiking, and other sports.

The play suit, attributed to Helen Wills, was used for tennis, golf, sun-bathing, and other outdoor sports, by both participant and spectator. The tennis shorts, with blouse cut low and square in back, was a favorite. A three-piece suit – shirt, shorts, and skirt – appeared early in this era, and led to many different designs. Toward 1948, the kiltie-culotte shorts appeared; and another ingenious outfit, consisting of seven pieces, formed a complete weekend beach wardrobe. It consisted of a gaily colored bra; two pairs of shorts, one to match the bra, one of black jersey, with cuffs; two sport shirts, one of white cotton, and a sleeveless one of black jersey; a full, ankle-length skirt, and long, narrow stole, to match the bra. These seven pieces, in various combinations, made up a swim suit, beach suit, play suit, beach cabana dress, and dinner dress.

Western clothes increased in favor. The closing of European resorts, swift transportation, dude ranches, and western pictures (screen and television) led to the adoption of "faded denim" outfits (first introduced in 1937), of "Levi's" (in 1938), of cowboy shirts and trimming (piping, nailheads, and the like) and, in 1947, of the "pioneer" outfit, similar to the men's, described previously. The true ranch woman (not a "dude rancher") wore narrow, denim slacks, with horizontal pockets, a round-up jacket, shirt, or sweater, a wide-brimmed hat, and boots. She disdained all trim except the copper or silvered nailheads.

Certain specific items annexed a geographical flavor. There was the Bermuda beach dress, the Russian peasant blouse, the Swiss breeches with Edelweiss jacket, the Algerian beach coat with burnoose-type hood, and the South American gaucho boots and leather bolero.

Hose

Ever since the mid-twenties, when short skirts raised the question of appropriate hosiery, interest in this item of attire had increased. By 1937, sheer hose, in varying lengths to fit the height of the wearer, appeared. A diamond or round mesh also was designed, with an elastic weave, guaranteed not to run – but it did, alas, break into holes. The lighter shades of beige, tan, rust, and copper prevailed toward the beginning of the era; but toward the end, the dark, gun-metal shades, the rust and brown tinges took precedence. Sheer black and dark blue were used for evening wear, by 1941.

The real addition to hosiery history was the development of the nylon stocking. Research on this substance had begun in 1928; by 1938, the name nylon was adopted. In 1939, it was first made into stockings, and by 1940, was introduced on the market, just in time to become a wartime restriction, one of the most painful ones suffered by patriotic women, who had to content themselves with cotton, rayon, and lisle substitutes. However, with the lifting of wartime regulations, sheer nylons, with reinforced toes and heels, with seamless backs, and with peerless texture, slid back into circulation. Leg make-up, an innovation first for beach wear, proved a kind of substitute for stockings during the war, and is still used on occasion; it was made in shades matching hosiery colors. A loafer sock, of knitted wool, with padded soles of glove leather, was adopted for lounge wear. Socks were voguish for informal or sports wear.

Shoes

The major development in shoes, as is dress, was for sportswear. Two important trends were the diversity of materials and the adding of the uplift sole and heel. In 1937, the regular type of shoe and pump was varied by the use of perforated holes in decoration and the open toe in design. For evening wear, the plain opera style pumps, in patent leather, suede, gold, or silver were most in favor, and have continued so throughout the era. For sportswear, the huarache was used, around 1937; then came the raffia sandal and brogue oxford.

The important year in shoe history was 1938. Ferragamo of Florence created a radical shoe style, with uplift sole, inspired, perhaps, by the Roman caligula, the Greek cothurnos, and the Mediterranean sandals. The high soles of cork, leather, and other materials, were applied to daytime shoes and sandals and to evening sandals as well. Perugia, the same year, designed the Padova shoe; and, in quick succession, came the wedgie, the platform, Valkyrie, "freesoling," clogs, and other types. Ghillie laces gave a new touch, as did the Renaissance tongue, the wood-block heels, and the Indian moccasin boots. Felt, crepe, and rubber soles appeared on sports shoes; gabardine, python, and canvas became interesting materials.

By the time war was declared, certain shoes had become standard – the spectator, in white with black or brown trim; the loafer (from the Norwegian peasant shoe), the slot in which was used to store small change; the saddle shoe, with brown or black saddle strip; and platform and uplift shoes of all kinds. As shoes were rationed during the war, even these kinds were difficult to obtain, and few new models appeared. However, variety was achieved by the use of unusual (and unrationed) materials such as straw, plastic, animal and reptile skins (alligator, lizard, and the like), satin, moiré, and felt. Evening sandals, with criss-cross straps, were made of transparent plastic, like Cinderella's slippers. Bedroom slippers used synthetic soles and fabric tops – silk, wool, felt, quilting, and crochet work.

Late developments in footwear included the sling-back pump, the Napoleon, high-hugged heel, the empire back, bracelet and ribbon bands on evening sandals, the use of cobra and ostrich skin, and the refinement of design in the spectator, loafer, and saddle shoe. A rain boot, zippered and lined, brought comfort to inclement days.

Hair

A woman's crowning glory, like all regal things, was cut and twisted to bow to the democratic will of the day. In 1937, the hair was shortened (but not bobbed), brushed, and curled close to the head, with a new upswing in back. Sometimes the whole head was capped with inverted cinnamon-bun curls. For variety, the swirl in back was brushed to one side. Brenda Frazier, the Glamour Girl of 1937, made the page-boy bob popular, briefly, for the younger set. By 1939, the upsweep included the hair above the ears, in a smooth vertical movement. The side part and Stuart roll was still favored by some. During the war, curls seemed to give way to smoothly brushed hair styles, with the knot on top, or in a neat bun at the nape of the neck. In 1943, the three-inch shingle was popular, smoothly moulded to the head. Hair was even worn shoulder length, braided or pinned into buns or rolls. For evening, a mass of curls on top of the head was preferred. The page-boy bob also returned to favor.

Late hair styles returned to favor the blossom bob, the Mary Martin crew cut, and the cap cut; the latter resembled the old-fashioned porridge-bowl shearing, straight-edged and skull-fitted. Some preferred the feather bob, brushing the bobbed hair in many directions, giving a wind-blown effect. Small evening caps were designed to wear with the short bob, the curled ends being brushed up over the edges of the cap. Hair styling depends greatly on personal preference and looks, so the variations were legion. Young girls affected pigtails, and Gretchen braids were used, coronet-fashion, by others. The introduction of the cold wave (machineless) permanent wave, about 1945, led to inexpensive home wave sets in the following years; consequently softly curled locks were within the reach of any woman whose nimble fingers had the artistic touch.

Hats

Some one has said that there are only two kinds of hats – becoming and unbecoming. Unfortunately, a careful inventory unveils many kinds and varieties. In 1937, small hats were most in demand – the toque, the pillbox, and the beret. Crowns were very high, for the smaller hats, and sometimes, for the larger types; frequently they resembled a truncated stovepipe. The larger hat had a very wide brim and, usually, a low, wide crown; the brim was stiff, or soft and curved, in a tilt over the face. Felt, velvet, fur, metallic fabrics, were used, with the addition of straw and horsehair for summer wear. The new idea in hats, introduced in 1938, was the open crown, for both large and small hats. The pancake model, a flat disk of felt, also came in about 1938, a year which saw the greatest popularity of the turban. Some turbans had a high peak in front; some were twisted close about the head, with a clip center front; some were wound halo-fashion, with open crown. Small toques composed of bunches of tulle, flowers or feather, perched over one eye, proved alluring and, therefore, fashionable. Coq and bird wings, singly or in pairs, were a favored trimming, and veils became attached to wide brims as well as to the small toque.

During the war, the beret, pillbox, hood, and turban held their place at the top of popular choice; the cloche was revived, from the 'twenties, but worn back from the forehead. Tulle and veiling were twisted into many shapes, for dress wear; for evening wear, a bandeau of flowers, feathers or tulle ruching served as headdress. To hold on the hats of this era, bands of felt or elastic were attached to the sides of the crown, and fitted to the back of the head. Plastic straw and synthetic felts were another wartime invention.

After the war, the small hat still held first place – models like the bowler, the Dutch bonnet, the cannon shape, the sunbonnet type, the shell, the cocarde, and the bicorne. Late styles include the candy Breton, the chalk-white Toyo, the shadow cloche, the crescent bicorne, and the ever-popular sailor. The very narrow brim, fashionable during the first part of the era, was supplanted, after the war, by a normal-sized brim – if any hat can fit normal specifications. With the steady increase of interest in outdoor sports and occupations, which would seemingly demand an increase also in sun-shading hats, the opposite trend arose; the sun-worshiper of today bares the head to the golden idol, and the custom of wearing hats is more favored in the breach than in the observance.

Make-up

Once a closely-guarded secret, make-up has become a scientific process, openly arrived at. This is a healthy change from the earlier mysterious concoctions of paste, Paris green, and noxious acids. Today, the formulae for creams, lotions, powder, paint, and salve are laboratory-tested and adjusted to the needs of all textures of skin, shades of color, and even bone structure. During the thirteen years since 1937, many kinds of face creams, lotions, and astringents have been perfected. Rouge, once a necessary addition to the bloom of youth, was discarded by Brenda Frazier, who made the white-faced maiden fashionable. However, rouge is still sparingly applied by some, especially for evening make-up.

The interesting development of these years, from 1937 to 1950, has been the gradation of make-up items to fit individual types. Powder is made in many shades, from dead white to deep tan; a pancake powder has been perfected which requires but one application a day. Lipstick salve may be obtained in many shades, from purple to light rose; one type of lipstick is guaranteed not to smear or vanish under the most strenuous conditions. Eyes were brightened with eye wash, darkened with mascara; eyebrows were even dyed, and shaped by plucking out uneven hairs; Marlene Dietrich is credited with the vogue for a finely shaped and arched eyebrow.

Fingernails were shaped with pointed tips, and painted in shades varying from a translucent white, through a silver sheen to a deep red, and even to a purple and a black. Toenails, after the introduction of the open-toe shoes, were also painted to match the nails.

Along with scientific aids to beauty (which even included mud masks and wrinkle and chin plasters), there developed new styles in the shape of eyebrows and lips. The brows were arched, widened, or curved outward; the lips were widened, from the bee-kissed pout made fashionable in the 'twenties by Mae Murray, to the broad, full contour introduced by Joan Crawford. Of late, the style is to follow the natural line of the lips, but to accentuate it in the most flattering direction. Indeed, the make-up of today, though it has a scientific base, tends to follow the natural lines, planes, and colors of the face. Even the sought-for deep tan is accented by cleverly simulated powders which aid and abet nature. Indeed, modern woman puts her best complexion on, publicly, and with scientific exactness; her charm is her secret, the one formula not available in chain drug stores.

Accessories and Jewelry

It would be impossible to classify the thousands of items which became "necessary" accessories to woman's costume, during the years 1937 to 1950. Three types stand out as leading in number and in use – the handbag, gloves, and costume jewelry. The handbag was made in all sizes and shapes, though, in general, the medium-sized, envelope, or rectangular shape led in popularity. By 1938, the zipper was a regular fastening, and with the years, zippered pockets and fastenings increased in number, on the individual bag. A bag, with several covers, of different colors and materials, added variety to the wardrobe. For evening wear, the small bag, of silk, satin, beaded or metallic, was used. Billfolds, in colors to match the bag or costume, were introduced. The matching sets – handbag, gloves, shoes, and belt – were made popular in the first years of this era, and continued in favor. In 1940, the pouch bag with shoulder strap was introduced, and became part of the uniform of the WACS and WAVES; it was not discarded after the war, but has become a staple fashion in accessories. The round bandbox variety of bag appeared about 1943, and the large gathered pouch, like a huge "reticule" of great-grandmother's day, made of felt, linen, or silk, has been adopted by those who like a carry-all for cosmetics, knitting, and other needs. Needle-point bags, as well as gold leather and jeweled cloth evening bags, added color to the dress costume; these were small, post-card size, or of some similar shape. Day-time handbags were made of calfskin, suede, pinseal, crocodile, alligator, antelope, and patent leather. During the war, when leather was restricted, bags were made of plastic, straw, braid, and fabrics. The cordé bag became popular, and continues its vogue.

Gloves were of many kinds, for day and evening wear, for sports and for work. In 1937, the short top was fashionable; these were made of suede, doeskin, calfskin, silk and cotton jersey, lace, and the ever-popular pigskin. Long evening gloves, ornamented with flowers, bows, and jewels, became fashionable. During the war, the gaily knitted or crocheted mitten, embroidered in colored worsteds, appeared; evening gloves were made of velveteen and jersey. Recent styles feature the back fastening, usually the favored zipper; gauntlet types, in silk and lace, have reappeared.

Costume jewelry, in myriad forms, has held its vogue since the thirties, and even earlier. The clip was designed in various styles, and sets of costume jewelry to match included the earrings, the clips, the necklace, the large pin, and sometimes a bracelet, ring, and watchband. In 1940, novelty animal pins had a vogue. During the war, costume jewelry became large and bulky, and plastics were fashioned into colorful shapes. Charm bracelets were revived, and some of the charms, though miniature in size, were huge in price. French cuff links have been introduced of late, and match the studs, used in the beginning of this era.

Belts of gold and silver leather, of natural leather, and of patent leather, vied for favor with crochet, silk, and plastic varieties. Belts were wide, or narrow, and followed no particular fashion.

Veils and scarfs differed from former times in being more colorful. The circular Dietrich veil appeared, about 1938. The peasant scarf, in bright colors, was folded diagonally, draped over the head, and tied under the chin; it was called the "Babushka." A long scarf, or stole, to match the dress, was adopted in 1947. Veiling became a part of the hat, draped over and around it, from about 1939 on.

Eyeglasses, formerly a necessary evil, boldly took their place as companion pieces to every-day wear. Swim goggles and sun glasses, of many hues, appeared. The blue, rose, green, amber, grey, and other shades which might be procured, were rimmed with plastic in such colors as white, brown, and red. The "harlequin" sunglasses appeared, during the war, slanted upward like the eyes of the Oriental; a further note of fantasy was the decoration of these plastic rims with colored paste jewels.

Handkerchiefs were seldom plain white, though this type was considered the best taste; flowered and figured handkerchiefs, in gay colors, accompanied most costumes not strictly evening wear, when the white linen handkerchief, lace-edged or embroidered, was required.

Neckwear included all shapes and styles of linen and silk wear, in collars, jabots, ruffles, folds, vests, and revers. Piqué, lace, net, and chiffon were also used for these dainty adjuncts to the costume.

Among the accessories dear to women, the "vanity" or "compact," for cosmetics – which might include powder, eyebrow and eyelash mascara, lipstick, and, rarely, rouge – and the cigarette and lighter cases, hold high place. Though many plastic models were shown during the war, the usual type continued to be made of metal, gold, or silver finish, and decorated with enamel, jewels, or carving. Leather, fabric, and straw have also been used for these handy aids to everyday charm and comfort. Slave anklet chains were a fad for the adolescent girl.

The recital of women's vanities is a tale without an end; nor can custom stale its infinite variety.

MILITARY UNIFORMS World War II

General Characteristics

Two World Wars in one generation have emphasized how much the destiny of civilization rests in the hands of the uniformed men. Events have proved the need for, and importance of, well-designed uniforms which can be adapted to all tasks and all climates, on land, sea, and air. The signal deficiencies of World War I uniforms were noted and eliminated. World War II uniforms, for all branches of the armed services, were made of the best materials, in various weights and textures; they were well fitted, no longer justifying the gibe formerly leveled at them, of "two sizes, too large and too small"; they had pleasing, comfortable lines; they were designed in unique cuts to fit the highly specialized tasks or unusual temperatures.

The most outstanding improvements in uniforms, in general, were the adoption of the turned-down coat collar with lapels, instead of the stock collar; the long trousers; the small overseas cap; the well-cut, comfortable shoes.

The most spectacular development was the creation of regulation uniforms for women, due to their induction into the regular armed forces. Although World War I had inducted women into certain organizations – the Marinettes, Women's Motor Corps, Army Nurses Corps, Navy Nurses Corps, Signal Corps, Red Cross, Navy Yeomanettes – these, with rare exceptions (the nurses' corps, the Red Cross, and the French-speaking women in the Signal Corps) were not sent overseas. The organizations in World War II which accepted women for active duty were the WAC (Women Army Auxiliary Corps); the WAVES (Women Appointed for Voluntary Emergency Service); the WAFS (Women Auxiliary Ferrying Squadron); the Army Nurses Corps; the Navy Nurses Corps; the Marine Corps, Women Reserve; the AWVS (American Women Voluntary Service); the Red Cross; and the

Factory Guards. In comparing the women's uniforms of World War II with those of World War I, it is evident that skirts were shorter, hats were smaller and trimmer, shoes were neater, uniforms were tailored to the lines of the body, and cosmetics, in moderation, were approved; a neat handbag, with shoulder strap, was added, to hold the necessities for an attractive appearance.

Men's Uniforms, Army

The service uniform for winter was as follows: For officers, it consisted of a jacket and/or shirt and trousers. The jacket was of wool, elastique, barathon, or whipcord, in olive drab; it was single-breasted, with three gilt buttons, four pockets, and a leather belt. The shirt was of wool – plain or twill weave – or of cotton – broadcloth, cotton khaki, poplin – in olive drab or khaki shade. With the shirt was worn an olive-drab tie, four-in-hand; the service shirt might be worn without the jacket, in which case, it bore the insignia of rank. The trousers were of wool, elastique, barathon, or whipcord, in olive drab, or the lighter shade, called "pinks." A service cap, or garrison ("overseas") cap, brown shoes, khaki-colored socks, and overcoat (of olive-drab poplin or twill, wind resistant, water repellent, with removable wool lining and detachable hood) completed the outfit. A raincoat, like the overcoat, but waterproof, was also used.

The winter outfit for enlisted men consisted of a jacket, and/or shirt and trousers similar to the officers', except for the overcoat, which varied as to material and cut.

The summer outfit for officers consisted of cotton khaki shirt, trousers, and service cap (or cotton garrison cap, of khaki), or fatigue clothing, with necktie, brown shoes, khaki-colored socks. The enlisted men wore similar garments.

The dress uniform for winter was as follows: For officers, it consisted of a dark green wool coat, or a blue dress, blue mess, or evening dress coat (for very formal occasions), with trousers of the "pink" wool shade, or blue to match the blue coat. Enlisted men wore, for dress, a wool serge coat, khaki color, or jacket, shirt, trousers (same as coat), dark green tie, brown shoes, service cap (or garrison), and overcoat. The summer dress uniform for officers consisted of a tropical worsted khaki coat and trousers, service or garrison cap, khaki cotton shirt, olive-green tie; or else a white dress or white mess jacket outfit.

In addition to the regular items of dress, there were the combat boots, held in place above the ankle by two straps; steel helmets; gloves, of leather or wool; the waist-length "Eisenhower" jacket, belted and buttoned; and the several kinds of special-purpose suits, such as the ski-trooper's, the tropical field uniform, the rubberized double-texture suit for extremely wet climates, the cold-weather uniform, furred and lined, the paratrooper's uniform, the outfit for snowshoe troops, overalls, and many other types. Insignia were worn by officers and enlisted men, to signify rank; orders and decorations – ribbons, medals, pins – were awarded for special services rendered. Among the outstanding awards were the Distinguished Service Order, the Purple Heart, and the Silver Star.

Aviators were distinguished by their winged insignia, their fitted leather helmets, and other special equipment. Their uniforms followed the regulation types described above. It is understood that there were slight variations in the above outfits, but these do not constitute serious divergences.

Men's Uniforms, Navy

The service uniform for winter was as follows: For officers, it consisted of a blue double-breasted sack coat, of broadcloth, three gilt buttons down each forepart, seam back, no vent, semi-fitting, one left hand breast pocket, two hip pockets, peaked rolling lapels, left hip sword slit; with the coat was worn a shirt of blue chambray, blue flannel, or gray cotton, a black silk four-in-hand tie, tailored trousers to match coat, black shoes and socks. The cap was of blue to match the uniform. A blue overcoat or raincoat was used in cold weather.

The winter outfit for enlisted men ("gobs") consisted of a jumper of blue Melton cloth, loose, with square sailor collar trimmed with three stripes of white tape on the edge and a white star in each lower corner. The sleeves had two buttoned cuffs, trimmed with the three white stripes. The neckerchief, of black silk or rayon, was tied in a square knot, leaving ends from four to six inches long. The trousers of blue Melton cloth had a broadfall opening, with thirteen black buttons, and a laced placket, with gusset, in the back. This uniform is steeped in tradition. It is said that the collar was devised to protect the uniform from the greased pigtails of the eighteenth-century sailors; that the black tie is for mourning adopted at the death of Lord Nelson; that the three white stripes were for Nelson's three greatest victories; that the thirteen buttons on the broadfall represent the thirteen colonies (the English sailors used seven buttons, for the seven seas). The cap was blue, with raked crown and flared side; the band trimmed with a ribbon bearing the embroidered insignia, "U.S. Navy." Black shoes and socks were used.

The summer outfit for officers consisted of a coat, either of white, grey, or khaki tropical lightweight fabric, or cotton; single-breasted, with roll collar, notched lapels, three buttons, four patch pockets with pocket flaps, two-inch belt of same material as coat, and an (optional) bi-swing in side seams of back. The trousers and cap matched the coat. The shirt was of grey, white, or khaki cotton. Shoes were of black (for the grey), brown, or white, to match the outfit, and stockings matched the shoes.

The summer outfit for enlisted men included a white bleached cotton twill jumper, with square plain white sailor collar, open at the neck, without cuffs (though these were used early in the war), the same black neckerchief, white trousers like the jumper, with fly front and top pockets, and white hat of bleached cotton twill with rounded crown and full-stitched brim. This hat, worn with upturned brim, was said to be adopted from that of the Chinese pirate. The short overcoat, or "pea-jacket," with deep, turned-down collar, double-breasted, four-button front, and two vertical side pockets, received its name from the "pea-soup" fogs of London town.

The winter dress uniform, for officers, might consist of a long frock coat, full dress, with gilt epaulets, belt and sword, or an evening-dress coat with long tails, like the civilian full-dress coat, except for the blue broadcloth material. However, dress clothes, for both army and navy, were almost abandoned during World War II. The summer dress coat, or mess jacket, was white.

Navy aviators, like those in the army, followed, in general, the uniforms of their branch of the service with certain deviations and additions, as noted above.

The Marines (soldiers of the sea) adopted gray-green uniforms, patterned after those of the army, in lieu of the older blue type with white belt and trim, which were usually reserved for dress wear. The marine cap was of gray green with a brim much larger and higher than the army service cap.

Women's Uniforms, Army

The WAC officer's winter uniform consisted of a brown khaki wool jacket, single-breasted, four-buttoned, with four patch pockets, roll collar and lapels, a gored "pink" wool skirt, a brown cloth vizored cap with square crown, a shoulder-strap bag (brown), brown oxfords with low heels, beige stockings, khaki cotton or wool shirt, khaki four-in-hand tie. The enlisted women wore a similar outfit, but the skirt was of brown khaki; all skirts were short, about two or three inches below the knee. The gold insignia represented Pallas Athene. A brown khaki wool overcoat was included in the outfit. The overseas cap was favored by both officers and enlisted women.

For summer, a blouse and skirt of drab cotton could be worn by both officers and enlisted women; the insignia of rank was then worn on collar and shoulder.

The army nurse wore a uniform similar to that of the WAC, except that the cap had a curved brim, and the insignia was that of the regular U.S. Army. A blue cloth cape, skirt length, was worn for an outer wrap. The indoor white uniform was similar to any regulation nurse's uniform, with the proper insignia added.

Women's Uniforms, Navy

The WAVES officer's winter uniform consisted of blue wool cloth double-breasted jacket, with two rows of three buttons each, shawl collar and lapels, four pockets, no belt, blue gored skirt to match (two or three inches below the knee), blue cap with white crown and blue rolled brim, a shoulder-strap black bag, black, low-heeled oxfords, beige stockings (silk or rayon), blue chambray, or white cotton shirt, black four-in-hand silk tie, and the corps insignia on the hat as well as on designated places on the jacket. As with the men's uniforms, insignia of rank were placed on the sleeve in winter, on the shoulder, in summer. The enlisted WAVES wore similar uniforms, but the cap was like that worn by the "gob" with the "U.S. Navy" ribbon about the band.

The Navy nurse wore a dark blue double-breasted coat, like that of the man, with skirt to match, blue chambray or white shirt, black tie, black shoulder-strap bag, black shoes, beige stockings, and regular service cap, or overseas cap. For summer, a white linen, duck, twill, or tropical lightweight fabric might be used for the uniform. The indoor uniform was similar to the regulation nurse's uniform, with the proper insignia added.

1905

1927

1935

1947

PLATE XI   CHAPTERS XV, XVI

1917-1919

1941-1945
INFANTRYMAN

1941-1945
W.A.C.

1941-1945
AVIATOR

PLATE XII   CHAPTER XVI

APPENDIX

RANDOM PRODUCTION NOTES

MATERIALS

Silk is a fibrous substance woven from cocoons. That for manufacturing purposes is produced from the mulberry silk moth of China, *Bombyx mori*. Silk is called *si* in China, *soi* in Korea; ancient Greeks called it *ser*, the Romans, *sericum;* the French call it *soie*, the Germans, *seide*.

The silk industry originated in China. According to native records, it has existed from a remote period. Empress Si-Ling, wife of Emperor Huan-Ti, 2640 B. C., encouraged the cultivation of the mulberry tree, and is credited with the invention of the loom. The Chinese guarded the secret jealously. Through Korea silk reached Japan about 250 or 300 A. D. Eggs carried to India by a Chinese princess in the lining of her headdress, when she was married to a Hindu prince about 350 or 400 A. D., carried the industry to that country.

Herodotus (448 B. C.) believed silk to be a plant fiber. The philosopher Aristotle, tutor of Alexander the Great, concluded about 304 B. C. that it came from the fleece of animals, or was the product of trees or flowers. It is said to have been first spun from cocoons on the Island of Cos, by Pamphile, daughter of Plates. It was the famous "Cos vestis" tissue, very thin and revealing.

Silk was rarely used in Greece or Rome, because of its high cost: a pound of silk was literally worth its weight in gold – until about the first century B. C. By the first century A. D., Roman emperors and wealthy men and women used silk extravagantly, though sumptuary laws passed by the Roman Senate prohibited the use of silk to men on the grounds of effeminacy. Heliogabalus (220 A. D.) clothed himself entirely in silk.

Up to 550 A. D. all silk in Europe was woven from raw silk brought from China, either in bales or fabric, which was unraveled so that threads of pure silk might be rewoven into a linen or silk mixture. In 550, during Justinian's reign, two Nestorian monks from Persia brought some silkworms wrapped in mulberry leaves and hidden in hollow bamboo staffs to the court, and so began the culture and manufacture of silk in Europe. By the twelfth century, the Sicilian manufactories were famous for their brocades, which employed many Saracen patterns.

Silk weaving was begun at Tours in 1480, under Louis XI. Francis I brought silkworms from Milan to Rome. Colbert encouraged the industry in the reign of Louis XIV. Henry IV encouraged it in England in 1425. Flemish weavers took it up in 1585. Cortez introduced it into Mexico in 1522.

Cotton Lace

Cotton lace can be starched (Medici ruff), dyed, gilded, etc., for various effects. Lace curtains so treated can be used for whole costumes.

Padding

Cotton in rolls is best for *padding*. To simulate fat men, build padding onto an old vest which has been split down the back. For a very fat effect, a wire frame should be used, as a vest is too hot and heavy.

Lions

Lions' manes may be made of hemp rope stitched on a hood in rows and shredded, giving a very good effect. For a tail, hemp rope frayed at the end is good. For dogs, etc., cotton yarn, dyed and stitched, can be used.

Cotton Yarn

Cotton yarn makes a fair imitation fur.

Ermine

Ermine can be simulated with cotton flannel or eiderdown, to which tails of fur or yarn are sewn.

Caracul

For *caracul* the strips of yarn should be left in strips, instead of cut.

Wigs

For *wigs,* use yarn or silk floss, rope, spirals, metallic shavings, gold and silver Christmas ribbons, tin cans, etc., in addition to the materials mentioned before. (See section on wigs, page 17.)

Fantastic Figures

Fantastic figures may be made of cellophane, oilcloth, felt, heavy duck, etc. (For playing cards, use spring steel at the edges to hold the shape.)

Flitter

Flitter is invaluable for decoration. It shines very brightly.

Rain

Capsules strung on white cord will give costume a rain effect.

Rope

Cotton cable cord braided or woven, after having been dyed, will serve for *rope.* It is lighter than rope and can be sewn easily.

Tassels

For large *tassels,* fringe rolled up, or cotton yarn, clipped, gives a good effect.

Feathers

Use old *feathers* from discarded hats, or arrange cotton string on buckram.

Quills

To make *quills,* use a double thickness of crepe paper glued together and wired down the center.

Claws

For *claws,* use old gloves. Cut buckram in claw shapes and stitch to gloves.

Dyeing

To dye or dry shoes quickly, use oil paints diluted with cleaning solvent. To dye designs without running, melt crayons the same shade as the design, outline the figure with melted wax, and dye the inside. Glycerine helps to set the color of the dye.

Decorative Relief

Water putty, plastic wood, and sealing wax should be used to decorate shields, crowns, etc. They take paint well, but will crack in time.

Jewels

Gumdrops, large and small, are a satisfactory makeshift. They should be glued on with shellac. Metal paper, as mentioned before, is excellent. Sealing wax is also acceptable. Soft copper wire (it can be obtained inexpensively secondhand) is excellent for ornamental coils and belts for soldiers and the like. Button molds, painted, or covered with sealing wax, putty, or tinfoil (chewing gum wrappers are stiffest), make fine effects. Milkbottle caps can also be covered. Soft drink bottle caps give the effect of medieval armor. Tin pans make effective halos.

Chain Mail

The method for making *chain mail* has already been described (page 105).

Tights

Mercerized *tights* are less baggy than cotton ones. To hold tights more smoothly, use elastic at belt of tights, twist about a button (or penny) and roll down several times.

EFFECT OF COLORED LIGHTS ON COLORED MATERIALS

Color of Light	Effect on Materials
Straw	Used with little loss of light to tone down harshness of white light. For full sunshine effect.
Middle Pink	Bad for greens.
Light Pink	Good for all colors except greens.
Salmon Pink	Tends to darken blues.
Dark Pink	Same as above, but more pronounced. Turns blues to purple; turns greens to blue.
S 39 (Lavender light)	Flattering; preserves and heightens natural shades.
Dark Amber	Completely spoils greens and blues. Poor for reds.
Light and Dark Red	Turns yellows to orange or red. Bad for greens and blues. Good for reds.
Magenta	A very useful and vivid color. Will bring out blues and purples. All light colors are completely wiped out.
Violet	Spoils most colors as colors, but often produces new and pleasing colors, as in the case of greens. Good for some reds.
New Blue	Darkens some reds.
Middle Blue	Spoils no colors – good for some.
Dark Blue	Good for most colors. Tendency to turn red to black. Used for general lighting or moonlight scenes.
Purple	Bad for greens. Good for reds and blues.
Dark Green	Spoils all colors except green. Seldom used in acting area.
Light Green or Moonlight Green	Good with all colors, especially greens.

Lavender or (pale)
Transilene   Excellent for complexions. Heightens reds, pinks, etc. Natural tints toned up.

Bastard Amber   Clearly reproduces colors.

SOME PLAYS OF THE PERIOD

Egypt – Plays based on Egyptian themes:
Lord Dunsany: *The Golden Doom, The Queen's Enemies.* . . . Allison Gaw: *Pharaoh's Daughter.* . . . William Shakespeare: *Antony and Cleopatra.* . . . George Bernard Shaw: *Caesar and Cleopatra.*

Mesopotamia – Plays based on Mespotamian themes:
Marc Connelly: *The Green Pastures.* . . . James Elroy Flecker: *Hassan.* . . . Thomas Preston: *Cambises.* . . . Lew Wallace: *Ben Hur.* . . . Franz Werfel: *The Eternal Road.*

Greece – Contemporary plays:
Aeschylus: *Agamemnon, Choephoroi, Eumenides, The Persians, Prometheus Bound, Seven against Thebes.* . . . Aristophanes: *The Birds, The Clouds, The Frogs, The Knights, Lysistrata, The Wasps.* . . . Euripides: *Alcestis, Electra, Hippolytus, Iphigenia at Aulis, Iphigenia in Tauris, Medea, Orestes, The Trojan Women.* . . . Sophocles: *Antigone, Ajax, Electra, Oedipus Coloneus, Oedipus Rex.*
Plays based on Grecian themes:
William Shakespeare: *A Midsummer Night's Dream, Pericles, Timon of Athens, Troilus and Cressida.* . . . Robert Turney: *Daughters of Atreus.*

Rome – Contemporary plays:
Plautus: *Amphitryon, Aulularia* (*The Pot of Gold*), *Captivi* (*The Captives*), *Menaechmi* (*The Twins*), *Miles Gloriosus* (*The Braggart Captain*). . . . Seneca: *Medea, Octavia, The Phoenicians, Thyestes.* . . . Terence: *Maid of Andros, Phormio, The Self-Tormenter.*
Plays based on Roman themes:
Joseph Addison: *Cato.* . . . Jean Giraudoux: *Amphitryon 38.* . . . James Sheridan Knowles: *Virginius.* . . . John Masefield: *Pompey the Great.* . . . Eugene O'Neill: *Lazarus Laughed.* . . . William Shakespeare: *Coriolanus, Julius Caesar, Titus Andronicus.* . . . Robert Sherwood: *The Road to Rome.* . . . Henryk Sienkiewicz: *Quo Vadis* (dramatized by Marie Doran). . . . Julian Thompson: *The Warrior's Husband.*

Dark Ages – Plays based on the period:
Maurice Maeterlinck: *Pelleas and Melisande.* . . . (Operas): Edna St. Vincent Millay: *The King's Henchman* (music by Deems Taylor). . . . Richard Wagner: *Die Walküre, Götterdämmerung, Parsifal, Siegfried, Tristan und Isolde.* . . . All others based on Norse sagas or eddas or Arthurian legends or legend of Tristan and Iseult.

China – Contemporary plays:
The Chalk Circle, The Hundred Plays of the Yuen Dynasty, *The Little Orphan of the House of Tchao, The Sorrows of Han, The Story of the Magic Lute, The Western Chamber, Autumn in the Han Palace, The Moon Pavilion, The Romance of the Guitar, The Peony Pavilion.*

Japan – Contemporary plays:

The Noh plays; the Kabuki plays. . . . Takeda Izumo: *The Pine Tree.* . . . Kiyotsugu: *The Maiden's Tomb.* . . . Miyamasu: *The Battle of Kikusenya, Eboshi-Ori, Hachi-No-Ki, The Magazine of Faithful Retainers.* . . . Monzayamon: *The Soga Revenge.* . . . Motokiyo: *Kayekiyo.*

India – Contemporary plays:

Bhavabuti: *The History of Rama.* . . . Criharsha: *The String of Pearls.* . . . Kalidasa: *Shakuntala.* . . . King Sudraka (attributed to): *The Little Clay Cart.*

Middle Ages and Renaissance – Contemporary plays:

Liturgical plays: *Magi, Pastores, Quem Quaeritis, Sepulchrum.* . . . Craft cycles: Chester, Coventry, Wakefield, and York cycles. . . . Plays from other cycles: *The Creation of Eve, The Fall of Lucifer, The Harrowing of Hell, Noah, The Sacrifice of Isaac, The Second Shepherd's Play.* . . . Non-cycle plays: *Conversion of St. Paul, Mary Magdalene.* . . . Moralities: *The Castle of Perseverance, Everyman.* . . . Folk plays: *Revesby Sword Play, Robin Hood, The Saint George Play, The Shetland Sword Dance.* . . . French plays: *Jongleur de Notre Dame, Robert the Devil, Sister Beatrice.* . . . Gringoire: *The Prince of Fools.* . . . Farces – Hans Sachs: *Caligula, The Wandering Scholar and Exorcist.* . . . *Master Pierre Patelin, The Wash Tub, The Women Who Have Their Husbands Remolded.*

Plays based on Medieval and Renaissance themes:

George Henry Boker: *Paolo and Francesca.* . . . Gordon Daviot: *Richard of Bordeaux.* . . . T. S. Eliot: *Murder in the Cathedral.* . . . Anatole France: *The Man Who Married a Dumb Wife.* . . . Stephen Phillips: *Paolo and Francesca.* . . . William Shakespeare: *Hamlet, Henry IV, Parts 1* and *2, Henry V, Henry VI, Parts 1, 2,* and *3, King John, King Lear, Macbeth, Richard II, Richard III, The Winter's Tale.* . . . Alfred Tennyson: *Becket.*

Sixteenth Century – Pre-Shakespearean plays:

R. Edwards: *Damon and Pythias.* . . . Robert Greene: *Friar Bacon and Friar Bungay.* . . . Thomas Kyd: *The Spanish Tragedy.* . . . John Lyly: *Campaspe, Endymion.* . . . George Peele: *The Old Wives' Tale.* . . . Sackville and Norton: *Gorboduc.* . . . William Stevenson: *Gammer Gurton's Needle.* . . . Nicholas Udall: *Ralph Roister Doister.*

Elizabethan plays:

Beaumont and Fletcher: *The Faithful Shepherdess, Henry VII, The Knight of the Burning Pestle, The Maid's Tragedy, Philaster.* . . . Thomas Dekker: *The Honest Whore, The Shoemaker's Holiday.* . . . Thomas Heywood: *A Woman Killed with Kindness.* . . . Ben Jonson: *The Alchemist, Every Man in His Humor, Sejanus, Volpone the Fox.* . . . Christopher Marlowe: *Doctor Faustus, Edward II, The Jew of Malta, Tamburlaine.* . . . Thomas Middleton: *A Trick to Catch the Old One.* . . . William Shakespeare: Complete Works.

Seventeenth Century – English contemporary plays:

William Congreve: *Love for Love, The Way of the World.* . . . John Dryden: *All for Love.* . . . George Farquhar: *The Beaux' Stratagem.* . . . John Ford: *The Broken Heart.* . . . Philip Massinger: *A New Way to Pay Old Debts.* . . . Thomas Otway: *Venice Preserved.* . . . James Shirley: *Hyde Park.* . . . John Vanbrugh: *The Provok'd Wife.* . . . John Webster: *The Duchess of Malfi.* . . . William Wycherley: *The Country Wife.*

French contemporary plays:

Pierre Corneille: *The Cid*. . . . Molière (Jean Baptiste Poquelin): *Le Bourgeois Gentilhomme, Les Précieuses Ridicules, Tartuffe*. . . . Jean Racine: *Athalie, Phèdre*.

Spanish contemporary plays:

Pedro Calderón de la Barca: *Life Is a Dream*. . . . Lope de Vega: *The Star of Seville*.

Eighteenth Century – English contemporary plays:

Joseph Addison: *Cato*. . . . David Garrick: *The Clandestine Marriage*. . . . John Gay: *The Beggar's Opera*. . . . Oliver Goldsmith: *The Good Natured Man, She Stoops to Conquer*. . . . George Lillo: *The London Merchant*. . . . Richard Sheridan: *The Critic, The Duenna, The Rivals, The School for Scandal*. . . . Richard Steele: *The Conscious Lovers*.

French contemporary plays:

Pierre de Beaumarchais: *The Barber of Seville, The Marriage of Figaro*. . . . François Voltaire: *Merope, Zaire*.

German contemporary plays:

Johann Wolfgang von Goethe: *Egmont, Faust*. . . . Gotthold Lessing: *Emilia Galotti, Minna von Barnhelm*. . . . Johann Schiller: *Don Carlos, Mary Stuart*.

Italian contemporary plays:

Carlo Goldoni: *The Coffee House, The Fan, The Mistress of the Inn*.

American contemporary playwrights:

Thomas Godfrey, Jr., Royall Tyler, Mrs. Mercy Warren.

Nineteenth Century Playwrights:

American: George L. Aiken (dramatized *Uncle Tom's Cabin*), George Henry Boker, Charles Burke, William Gillette, James A. Herne, Bronson Howard, Charles H. Hoyt, Mrs. Anna Cora Mowatt, John Howard Payne, Augustus Thomas.

British: Dion Boucicault, Edward Bulwer-Lytton, W. S. Gilbert, James Sheridan Knowles, Thomas Robertson, Tom Taylor, Oscar Wilde.

French: Alexandre Dumas *fils,* Victor Hugo, Victorien Sardou, Eugène Scribe.

Italian: Gabriele d'Annunzio, Sem Bennelli, Giuseppe Giacosa.

Norwegian: Björnstjerne Björnson, Henrik Ibsen.

Swedish: August Strindberg.

Russian: Anton Chekhov, Feodor Dostoevski, Nikolai V. Gogol, Aleksandr Pushkin, Alexei Tolstoi, Count Leo Tolstoi.

Spanish: José Echegaray.

Twentieth Century Playwrights:

American: George Abbott, George Ade, Zoë Akins, Maxwell Anderson, John Balderston, Philip Barry, S. N. Behrman, David Belasco, Guy Bolton, Witter Bynner, George M. Cohan, John Colton, Marc Connelly, Frank Craven, Rachel Crothers, Owen Davis, Edna Ferber, Clyde Fitch, Martin Flavin, Zona Gale, Susan Glaspell, Paul Green, William Hodge, Sidney Howard, George S. Kaufman, George Kelly, Sidney S. Kingsley, Charles Klein, Clare Kummer, Lawrence Langner, Charles MacArthur, Percy MacKaye, Edward Justus Mayer, Langdon Mitchell, William Vaughan Moody, Clifford Odets, Eugene O'Neill, Paul Osborn, Samson Raphaelson, Elmer Rice, Lynn Riggs, Edward Sheldon, Robert Sherwood, Booth Tarkington, Dan Totheroh, Eugene Walter, Thornton Wilder.

Belgian: Maurice Maeterlinck.

English: Rodney Ackland, C. L. Anthony (Dodie Smith), William Archer, James

M. Barrie, Arnold Bennett, Rudolph Besier, Noel Coward, Clemence Dane, Gordon Daviot, John Drinkwater, Ashley Dukes, John Galsworthy, Harley Granville-Barker, Henry Arthur Jones, Edward Knoblock, Benn W. Levy, Frederick Lonsdale, John Masefield, W. Somerset Maugham, A. A. Milne, Louis N. Parker, Stephen Phillips, Arthur Wing Pinero, J. B. Priestley, George Bernard Shaw, R. C. Sherriff, John Van Druten.

French: Henri Bernstein, Édouard Bourdet, Eugène Brieux, Paul Claudel, Jean Cocteau, Jacques Copeau, François de Curel, Maurice Donnay, Jean Giraudoux, Sacha Guitry, Georges de Porto-Riche, Romain Rolland, Edmond Rostand.

Austrian: Vicki Baum, Hugo von Hofmannsthal, Arthur Schnitzler.

Bohemian: Karel Capek.

German: Leonhard Frank, Max Halbe, Gerhart Hauptmann, Hermann Sudermann, Ernst Toller, Franz Werfel, Christa Winsloe.

Hungarian: Ferenc Molnar, Ernst Vajda.

Irish: Paul Vincent Carroll, Lord Dunsany, St. John Ervine, Lady Gregory, Denis Johnston, Sean O'Casey, Lennox Robinson, John Millington Synge, William Butler Yeats.

Italian: Marco Praga, Gallarati-Scotti, Luigi Pirandello.

Norwegian: Hans Wiers-Jenssen.

Russian: Leonid Andreyev, S. Ansky, Maxim Gorky.

Spanish: Jacinto Benavente, Gregorio Martínez Sierra, Serafín and Joaquín Álvarez Quintero.

BIBLIOGRAPHY

Abrahams, Ethel B. *Greek Dress*. Murray, London, 1908.

Airne, C. W. *Britain's Story*. 7 v. Sankey, Hudson, Manchester, no date.

Alexander, William. *Picturesque Representations of the Dress and Manners of the Chinese*. M'Lean, London, [1805?].

Alexandre, Arsène. *L'Art décoratif de Léon Bakst*. Brunoff, Paris, 1913.

Allen, Frederick L. *Only Yesterday; an Informal History of the Nineteen-Twenties*. Harper, New York, 1931.

Allom, Thomas. *Character and Costume in Turkey and Italy*. Fisher, London, [1845?].

Anderson, Rasmus B. *Norse Mythology*. Scott, Foresman, Chicago, 1907.

Aretz, Gertrude. *The Elegant Woman* (translated by James Laver). Harrap, London, 1932.

Aria, Mrs. E. D. *Costume, Fanciful, Historical, and Theatrical*. Macmillan, London, 1906.

Ashdown, Charles H. *British and Foreign Arms and Armour*. Jack, London, 1909.

Ashdown, Mrs. Charles H. *British Costume during Nineteen Centuries*. Jack, London, 1910.

Barthez, Ernest [Antoine Charles Ernest]. *The Empress Eugénie and Her Circle* (translated by Bernard Miall). Brentano, New York, 1913.

Barton, Lucy. *Historic Costume for the Stage*. Baker, Boston, 1935.

Belloc, Hilaire. *Marie Antoinette*. Putnam, New York, 1924.

Blakeslee, Fred G. *Uniforms of the World*. Dutton, New York, 1929.

Block, Maurice. *François Boucher and the Beauvais Tapestries*. Houghton, Boston, 1933.

Boehn, Max von. *Die Mode: Menschen und Moden im achtzehnten Jahrhundert*, etc. Bruckmann, München, 1909.

Boehn, Max von. *Die Mode: Menschen und Moden im Mittelalter*, etc. Bruckmann, München, 1925.

Boehn, Max von. *Die Mode: Menschen und Moden im neunzehnten Jahrhundert*, etc. Bruckmann, München, 1907–19.

Boehn, Max von. *Die Mode: Menschen und Moden im sechzehnten Jahrhundert*, etc. Bruckmann, München, 1923.

Boehn, Max von. *Die Mode: Menschen und Moden im siebzehnten Jahrhundert*, etc. Bruckmann, München, 1913.

Boehn, Max von. *Modes and Manners* (translated by Joan Joshua). 4 v. Harrap, London, 1932–35.

Bonnard, Camille. *Costumes historiques*. 3 v. Lévy, Paris, 1860–61.

Boswell, James. *Boswell's Life of Johnson* (edited by George Birkbeck Hill). Clarendon Press, Oxford, 1887.

Bott, Alan. *Our Fathers (This was England) (1870–1900)*. Doubleday, Garden City, N. Y., 1931.

Bott, Alan. *Our Mothers (1870–1890)*. Gollancz, London, 1932.

Boutell, Charles. *The Monumental Brasses of England*. Bell, London, 1849.

Boutet, Henri. *Les Modes féminines du XIXe siècle*. Société Française d'Éducation d'Art, Paris, 1902.

Boutet de Monvel, Roger. *Beau Brummell and His Times*. Lippincott, Philadelphia, 1908.

Bradford, William. *Sketches of the Country, Character, and Costume in Portugal and Spain,* etc. Booth, London, 1812.

Bradley, H. Dennis. *The Eternal Masquerade*. Boni and Liveright, New York, 1923.

Breasted, James Henry. *Ancient Times*. Ginn, New York, 1916.

Breasted, James Henry. *A History of Egypt,* etc. Scribner, New York, 1905.

Brockhaus, F. A. *Iconographic Encyclopedia*. Iconographic Publishing Co., Philadelphia, 1886.

Brooke, Iris. *English Children's Costume since 1775*. Black, London, 1930.

Brooke, Iris. *English Costume in the Age of Elizabeth*. Black, London, 1933.

Brooke, Iris. *English Costume of the Early Middle Ages*. Black, London, 1936.

Brooke, Iris. *English Costume of the Eighteenth Century*. Black, London, 1931.

Brooke, Iris. *English Costume of the Later Middle Ages*. Black, London, 1935.

Brooke, Iris. *English Costume of the Nineteenth Century*. Black, London, 1929.

Brooke, Iris. *English Costume of the Seventeenth Century*. Black, London, 1934.

Brown, Henry Collins. "In the Golden Nineties," in *Valentine's Manual of the City of New York*. Valentine, New York, 1928.

Brown, Henry Collins. "New York in the Elegant Eighties," in *Valentine's Manual of the City of New York*. Valentine, New York, 1927.

Budge, Sir E. A. Wallis. *Amulets and Superstitions,* etc. Oxford University Press, London, 1930.

Bulfinch, Thomas. *Bulfinch's Mythology* (The Age of Fable, The Age of Chivalry, The Age of Charlemagne). Modern Library, New York, 1934.

Bulfinch, Thomas. *The Golden Age of Myth and Legend, Being a Revised and Enlarged Edition of The Age of Fable* (edited by George H. Godfrey). Stokes, New York, 1934.

Calthrop, Dion Clayton. *English Costume Painted and Described*. Black, London, 1923.

The Cambridge Ancient History. 11 v. University Press, Cambridge, 1928–36.

The Cambridge Medieval History. 8 v. University Press, Cambridge, 1911–36.

The Cambridge Modern History. 13 v. University Press, Cambridge, 1912–20.

Campan, Madame de (Jeanne-Louise-Henriette Genet). *Memoirs of Marie Antoinette*. Nichols, London, 1895. (Numerous other editions.)

Carlyle, Thomas. *Sartor Resartus*. Dutton, New York, 1924. (Numerous other editions.)

Carr, Lucien. *Dress and Ornaments of Certain American Indians*. Hamilton, Worcester, 1897.

Carus, Paul. *Chinese Life and Customs*. Open Court, Chicago, 1907.

Carter, Howard, and Mace, A. C. *The Tomb of Tut-Ankh-Amen,* etc. Cassell, London, 1923.

Cellini, Benvenuto. *The Autobiography of Benvenuto Cellini* (translated by John Addington Symonds). Garden City Publishing Co., Garden City, N. Y., 1932.

Chalif, Louis H. *Russian Festivals and Costumes for Pageant and Dance*. Chalif Russian School of Dance, New York, 1921.

Challamel, Jean B. M. A. *The History of Fashion in France*. Marston, London, 1882.

Chalmers, Helena. *Clothes: On and Off the Stage*. Appleton, New York, 1928.

Chambers, Robert. *The Book of Days.* Chambers, London, [1906?]; first edition, 1862–64.

Chancellor, Edwin B. *Life in Regency and Early Victorian Times.* Batsford, London, 1926.

Chaucer, Geoffrey. *Canterbury Tales.* (Various editions, especially Clarendon Press, Oxford, 1894.)

Chesterfield, Philip Dormer Stanhope, 4th Earl of. *Letters to His Son.* Dutton, New York, 1935. (Everyman's Library.)

Child, Theodore. *Wimples and Crisping Pins,* etc. Harper, New York, 1895.

Church, Sir Arthur Herbert. *Color: Elementary Manual.* Cassall, New York, [1908?].

Clinch, George. *English Costume from Prehistoric Times to the Eighteenth Century.* Methuen, London, 1909.

Coate, Mary. *Social Life in Stuart England.* Methuen, London, 1924.

Collier, John, and Lang, Iain. *Just the Other Day,* etc. Hamilton, London, 1932.

Colman, Edna M. *Seventy-Five Years of White House Gossip (from Washington to Lincoln).* Doubleday, Garden City, N. Y., 1926.

Constant, (known as) Louis Constant Wairy. *Recollections of the Private Life of Napoleon* (translated by Walter Clark). Saalfield, Akron, 1904.

Cotman, John S. *Engravings of Sepulchral Brasses in Norfolk and Suffolk.* Bohn, London, 1839.

Cutts, Edward L. *Scenes and Characters of Middle Ages.* Virtue, London, 1872.

Dabney, Edith, and Wise, C. M. *A Book of Dramatic Costume.* Crofts, New York, 1930.

Davis, Henry W. C. (editor). *Medieval England* (a new edition of *Barnard's Companion to English History*). Oxford University Press, London, 1924.

Davis, William S. *Life in Elizabethan Days.* Harper, New York, 1930.

Davis, William S. *Life on a Medieval Barony.* Harper, New York, 1923.

Dayot, A. D. M. *Louis XIV.* Flammarion, Paris, 1909.

Dearmer, Percy. *Everyman's History of the English Church.* Mowbray, London (c. 1900).

Debrett, John (compiler). *DeBrett's Coronation Guide.* Dean, London, 1911.

Demmin, Auguste F. *An Illustrated History of Arms and Armor,* etc. Bell, London, 1877.

De Quincey, T. *Toilette of the Hebrew Lady.* Mitchell, Hartford, 1926.

Ditchett, S. H. "Costumes of Bygone Centuries Still Inspire Great Fashion Designers," *Dry Goods Economist* (New York), April 3, 1920, pp. 37–47.

Doran, John. *Knights and Their Days.* Bentley, London, 1856.

Doran, John. *Habits and Men,* etc. McKay, Philadelphia, 1890.

Druitt, Herbert. *A Manual of Costume,* etc. Jacobs, Philadelphia, 1907.

Du Chaillu, Paul. *The Viking Age.* Scribner, New York, 1889.

Ducros, Louis. *French Society in the Eighteenth Century* (translated by W. de Geijer). Bell, London, 1926.

Du Maurier, George. *English Society.* Harper, New York, 1897.

Earle, Alice M. *Two Centuries of Costume in America.* 2 v. Macmillan, New York, 1903.

Eden, Hon. Emily. *Portraits of Princes and People of India.* Dickinson, London, 1844.

Edwards, Amelia A. B. *A Thousand Miles up the Nile.* Routledge, London, 1889.

Eichler, Lillian. *The Customs of Mankind.* Doubleday, New York, 1924.

Einhard (or Eginhard). *Early Lives of Charlemagne* (translated and edited by Professor A. J. Grant). Chatto, London, 1922.

Encyclopaedia Britannica. Eleventh edition. 29 v. London, 1910–11.

Encyclopaedia Britannica. Ninth edition. 24 v. Scribner, New York, 1878.

Encyclopaedia Britannica. Fourteenth edition. 24 v. New York, 1937.

Encyclopaedia Britannica. Thirteenth edition. 28 v. London, 1926.

Evans, Sir Arthur. *The Palace of Minos,* etc. 4 v. Macmillan, London, 1921–36.

Evans, Maria. *Chapters on Greek Dress.* Macmillan, London, 1893.

Evans, Mary. *Costume Silhouettes.* Lippincott, Philadelphia, 1923.

Evans, Mary. *Costume Throughout the Ages.* Lippincott, Philadelphia, 1930.

Evelyn, Sir John. *Diary (1641–1705).* 2 v. Dunne, Washington, 1901.

Fairholt, F. W. *Costume in England; a History of Dress to the End of the Eighteenth Century.* 2 v. Bell, London, 1916.

Fales, Jane T. *Dressmaking; a Manual for Schools and Colleges.* Scribner, New York, 1917.

Falke, Jakob von. *Kostümgeschichte.* Spemann, Stuttgart, n. d.

Farington, Joseph. *Farington Diary* (edited by James Grieg). Doran, New York, 1923.

Faure, Élie. *History of Art.* 5 v. Harper, New York, 1921–30.

Ffoulkes, Charles. *Armour and Weapons.* Clarendon Press, Oxford, 1909.

Field, Marshall. *Man and His Wardrobe.* Marshall Field and Co., Chicago, 1920.

Fischel, Oskar. *Chronisten der Mode.* Müller, Potsdam, 1923.

Fischel, Oskar, and Boehn, Max von. *Modes and Manners of the Nineteenth Century,* etc. 4 v. Dent, London, 1909.

Frazer, Sir James G. *The Golden Bough,* etc. 12 v. Macmillan, London, 1911–27.

Froissart, Jean. *Chronicles,* etc. Bohn, London, 1849.

Furnivall, F. J. (editor). *The Babees Book.* Chatto, London, 1923.

Giafferri, Paul L. de. *The History of the Feminine Costume of the World,* etc. 2 v. Foreign Publications, New York, 1926.

Giafferri, Paul L. de. *The History of French Masculine Costume.* Foreign Publications, New York, 1927.

Giafferri, Paul L. de. *Millinery in the Fashion History of the World: from 5300 B. C. to the Present Era, etc.* Illustrated Milliner Co., New York, 1927.

Glanville, S. R. K. *Daily Life in Ancient Egypt.* Routledge, London, 1930.

Gloag, John, and Walker, C. Thompson. *Home Life in History.* Benn, London, 1927.

Goodwin, Mrs. Maud (Wilder). *Dolly Madison.* Scribner, New York, 1896.

Graves, Charles L. *Mr. Punch's History of Modern England.* 4 v. Cassell, London, 1921–22.

Grimball, Elizabeth B., and Wells, Rhea. *Costuming a Play,* etc. Century, New York, 1925.

Guhl, E. K., and Koner, W. D. *The Life of the Greeks and Romans,* etc. (translated by F. Hueffer). Appleton, New York, 1876.

Gulick, Charles B. *The Life of the Ancient Greeks,* etc. Appleton, New York, 1902.

Gummere, Amelia M. *The Quaker: a Study in Costume.* Ferris, Philadelphia, 1901.

Haire, Frances H. *The Folk Costume Book.* Barnes, New York, 1926.

Hammerstein-Equord, Hans F. von. *Trachten der Alpenländer,* etc. Reichner, Wien, 1937.

Hammerton, J. A. *People of All Nations.* Educational Book Co., London, n. d.

Hannah, Ian Campbell. *Christian Monasticism,* etc. Macmillan, New York, 1925.

Harriman, Florence (Jaffray) (Mrs. J. Borden). *From Pinafores to Politics.* Holt, New York, 1923.

Hartley, Dorothy R., and Elliot, Margaret M. *Life and Work of the People of England,* etc. 6 v. Batsford, London, 1925–31.

Hartley, Dorothy, and Elliot, Margaret M. *Life and Work of the People of England (The Eleventh to Thirteenth Century – A. D. 1000–1300).* Putnam, New York, 1931.

Hartley, Dorothy, and Elliot, Margaret M. *Life and Work of the People of England (The Eighteenth Century).* Putnam, New York, 1931.

Heffner, Hubert C., Selden, Samuel, and Sellman, Hunton D. *Modern Theatre Practice: a Handbook for Non-professionals.* Crofts, New York, 1936.

Hefner-Alteneck, Jacob. *Costumes illustrés du Moyen Age.* Mannheim, 1850.

Hefner-Alteneck, Jacob. *Costumes illustrés des 17. und 18. Jahrhunderts.* Keller, Frankfurt-am-Main, 1879.

Hefner-Alteneck, Jacob H. von. *Trachten, Kunstwerke und Geräthschaften vom frühen Mittelalter,* etc. 10 v. Keller, Frankfurt-am-Main, 1879.

Hegermann-Lindencrone, Fru Lillie (Greenough). *In the Courts of Memory.* Harper, New York, 1912.

Helyot, Pierre. *Album ou collection complète et historique des costumes de la cour de Rome, des ordres monastiques, religieux, et militaires,* etc. Camerlinck, Paris, 1862.

Herodotus. *Herodotus, a New and Literal Version,* etc. (translated by Henry Cary). Harper, New York, 1858.

Heuzey, Léon A. *Histoire du costume antique d'après des études sur le modèle vivante.* Champion, Paris, 1922.

Hewitt, John. *Ancient Armour and Weapons in Europe,* etc. 3 v. Parker, Oxford, 1855–60.

Hill, Georgiana. *A History of English Dress from the Saxon Period to the Present Day.* 2 v. Bentley, London, 1893.

Hinton, Henry E. *Select Historical Costumes,* etc. Wynkoop, New York, 1868.

Hoes, Mrs. Rose G. *Catalogue of American Historical Costumes,* etc. United States National Museum, Washington, 1915.

Holding, Thomas H. *Uniforms of the British Army, Navy and Court.* The Author, London, 1894.

Holme, Charles. *Peasant Art in Austria and Hungary.* Studio, London, 1911.

Holme, Charles. *Peasant Art in Italy.* Studio, London, 1913.

Holme, Charles. *Peasant Life in Sweden, Lapland, and Iceland.* Studio, London, 1910.

Homer. *The Iliad* (done into English prose by Andrew Lang, Walter Leaf, and Ernest Myers). Macmillan, London, 1907.

Homer. *The Odyssey* (done into English prose by S. H. Butcher and Andrew Lang). Macmillan, London, 1881.

Hone, William. *The Everyday Book and Table Book.* Tegg, London, 1826–27.

Hone, William. *The Year Book of Daily Recreation and Information.* Tegg, London, 1849.

Hope, Thomas. *Costume of the Ancients.* 2 v. Miller, London, 1809.

Hottenroth, Friedrich. *Le Costume chez les peuples anciens et modernes.* Guérinet, Paris, 1896.

Houston, Mary G., and Hornblower, F. S. *Ancient Egyptian, Assyrian, and Persian Costumes.* Black, London, 1920.

Hughes, Talbot. *Dress Design; an Account of Costume for Artists and Dressmakers.* Macmillan, New York, 1913.

Hugon, Cecile. *Social France in the Seventeenth Century.* Macmillan, New York, 1915.

Hutt, Henry. *The Picture Book.* Century, New York, 1908.

Imbert de Saint-Amand, Arthur Léon, baron. *Marie Antoinette and the End of the Old Régime* (translated by Thomas Sergeant Perry). Scribner, New York, 1890.

Jackson, Holbrook. *The Eighteen Nineties.* Richards, London, 1913.

Jameson, Mrs. Anna. *Sacred and Legendary Art.* Osgood, Boston, 1875.

Johnson, A. E. *The Russian Ballet.* Houghton, Boston, 1913.

Johnston, Harold W. *The Private Life of the Romans.* Scott, Foresman, Chicago, 1903.

Jones, Inigo. *Designs for Masques and Plays at Court,* etc. (Walpole Society Publication, Twelfth Annual Volume.) Oxford University Press, London, 1924.

Jusserand, Jean A. A. J. *English Wayfaring Life in the Middle Ages.* Unwin, London, 1920.

Kelly, Francis M., and Schwabe, Randolph. *Historic Costume, a Chronicle of Fashion in Western Europe (1490–1790).* Batsford, London, 1925.

Kittredge, George L. *A Study of Gawain and the Green Knight.* Harvard University Press, Cambridge, 1916.

Klarwill, Victor (editor). *The Fugger News-Letters* (translated by Pauline de Chary). Lane, London, 1924.

Klarwill, Victor (editor). *The Fugger News-Letters; Second Series.* [Special emphasis on England – Queen Elizabeth, 1568–1605.] Translated by L. S. R. Byrne. Putnam, New York, 1926.

Koehler, Carl, and Sichart, Emma von. *A History of Costume.* Harrap, London, 1928.

Kommissarzhevskii, Fedor Fedorovich. *The Costume of the Theatre.* Bles, London, 1931.

Krause, Gregor. *Bali.* Duchartre et Van Buggenhoudt, Paris, 1930.

Lacroix, Paul. *Costumes historiques de la France,* etc. 8 v. Administration de Libraire, Paris, 1852–60.

Lacroix, Paul. *The Eighteenth Century, Its Institutions, Customs, and Costumes.* Scribner, New York, 1876.

Lacroix, Paul. *Moeurs, usages et costumes au Moyen Âge et à l'époque de la Renaissance.* Firmin-Didot, Paris, 1874.

Lacroix, Paul. *Vie militaire et religieuse,* etc. Didot, Paris, 1877.

Lamballe, Marie Thérèse Louise de Savoie Carignan, Princesse de. *Secret Memoirs of Princess Lamballe* (edited and annotated by Catherine Hyde). Universal Classics Library, Washington (c. 1901).

Lawrence, A. W. *Classical Sculpture.* Cape, London, 1929.

Lay, J. S. *History in Pictures.* Macmillan, London, n. d.

Lester, Katherine M. *Historic Costume,* etc. Manual Arts Press, Peoria, Illinois, 1925.

Librairie Hachette. *Histoire du costume en France.* Imprimerie Crêté Corbeil, 1924. Encyclopédie par l'Image.

Linati, C. *Costumes civils, militaires et religieux du Mexique.* Sattanino, Brussels, 1828.

Linthicum, M. Channing. *Costume in the Drama of Shakespeare and His Contemporaries.* Clarendon Press, Oxford, 1936.

Logan, James. *The Clans of the Scottish Highlands.* 2 v. Willis, London, 1857.

Luard, Col. John. *A History of the Dress of the British Soldier.* Clowes, London, 1852.

Luchaire, Achille. *Social France at the Time of Philip Augustus.* Holt, New York, 1912.

Lukiesch, Matthew. *Color and Its Application.* Van Nostrand, New York, second edition 1921.

Lutz, Henry F. *Textiles and Costumes among the Peoples of the Ancient Near East.* Heinrichs, Leipzig, 1923.

Mackay, Constance d'Arcy. *Costumes and Scenery for Amateurs.* Holt, New York, 1932.

MacQuoid, Percy. *Four Hundred Years of Children's Costume from the Great Masters, 1400–1800.* Medici Society, London, 1923.

Mahaffy, Sir John P. *Social Life in Greece from Homer to Menander.* Macmillan, London, 1877.

Mann, Kathleen. *Peasant Costume in Europe.* Black, London, 1931.

Marshall, Frederic. *International Vanities.* Blackwood, Edinburgh, 1825.

Mason, Amelia G. *The Women of the French Salons.* Century, New York, 1891.

Mason, George H. *The Costume of China.* Miller, London, 1800.

McClees, Helen. *The Daily Life of the Greeks and Romans,* etc. Metropolitan Museum of Art, New York, 1924.

McClellan, Elizabeth. *Historic Dress in America, 1607–1800,* etc. Jacobs, Philadelphia, 1917.

McFall, C. Haldane. *Beautiful Children Immortalized by the Masters.* Dodd, Mead, New York, 1909.

Meller, Walter C. *A Knight's Life in the Days of Chivalry.* Greenberg, New York, 1924.

Menpes, Mortimer. *The People of India.* Black, London, 1910.

Metropolitan Museum of Art. *The Egyptian Expedition, 1918–1920.* New York, 1920.

Metropolitan Museum of Art. *The Egyptian Expedition, 1921–1922.* New York, 1922.

Metropolitan Museum of Art. *Shapes of Greek Vases.* New York, 1922.

Metropolitan Museum of Art. *Sporting Prints and Paintings.* New York, 1937.

Meyrick, S. R. *A Critical Inquiry into Ancient Armor,* etc. 3 v. Bohn, London, 1842.

Mills, Dorothy. *The Book of the Ancient Greeks.* Putnam, New York, 1925.

Mills, Dorothy. *The Book of the Ancient Romans.* Putnam, New York, 1927.

Mills, Dorothy. *The Book of the Ancient World.* Putnam, New York, 1923.

Minnigerode, Meade. *Presidential Years (1787–1860).* Putnam, New York, 1928.

La Mode Féminine (1490–1920). Éditions Nilsson, Paris, 1926.

Monstrelet, Enguerrand de. *The Chronicles of Enguerrand de Monstrelet* (translated by Thomas Johnes). Smith, London, 1840.

Morse, Harriet K. *Elizabethan Pageantry,* etc. Studio, London, 1934.

Nevill, Ralph Henry. *British Military Prints.* Connoisseur Publishing Co., London, 1909.

Norris, Herbert. *Costume and Fashion,* etc. 3 v. Dent, London, 1924.

Northrup, Belle. *The Story of Costume Told in Pictures.* Art Education Press, New York, 1935.

Palencia, Isabel de. *The Regional Costumes of Spain,* etc. Batsford, London, 1926.

Parsons, Frank A. *The Psychology of Dress.* Doubleday, Garden City, N. Y., 1920.

The Paston Letters. (Edited by John Ferris; re-edited by Mrs. Archer-Hind.) Dent, London, 1924.

Pauquet, Hippolyte and Polydor. *Modes et costumes historiques étrangers.* Pauquet Frères, Paris, 1864.

Peel, Dorothy Constance. *A Hundred Wonderful Years . . . 1820–1920*. Lane, London, 1926.

Pepys, Samuel. *Diary and Correspondence of Samuel Pepys*. 10 v. Dodd, Mead, New York, 1885.

Percival, MacIver. *The Fan Book*. Unwin, London, 1920.

Perleberg, Hans Carl. *Historical Russian Costumes, XIV–XVIII Century*, etc. Perleberg, New York, 1923.

Petrie, W. M. Flinders. *The Arts and Crafts of Ancient Egypt*. Foulis, London, 1910.

Piton, Camille. *Le Costume civile en France du XIII ͤ au XIX ͤ siècle*. Flammarion, Paris, 1913–15.

Planché, James R. *Costumes of Shakespeare*. Miller, London, 1823.

Planché, James R. *A Cyclopedia of Costume; or Dictionary of Dress*, etc. 2 v. Chatto, London, 1876–79.

Planché, James R. *History of British Costume from the Earliest Period to the Close of the Eighteenth Century*. Knight, London, 1836.

Poland, Franz, Reisinger, E., and Wagner, R. *The Culture of Ancient Greece and Rome*. Harrap, London, 1926.

Potter, John. *Archaeologia Graeca, or the Antiquities of Greece*. 2 v. Stirling, Edinburgh, 1818.

Power, Eileen. *Medieval People*. Methuen, London, 1924.

Pratt, Margaret Swain. *National Costumes of the Slavic People*. Woman's Press, 1920.

Price, Julius M. *Dame Fashion*. Low, London, 1912.

Quennell, Marjorie and C. H. B. *Everyday Life in Roman Britain*. Batsford, London, 1924.

Quennell, Marjorie and C. H. B. *Everyday Things in Archaic Greece*. Batsford, London, 1931.

Quennell, Marjorie and C. H. B. *Everyday Things in Classical Greece*. Batsford, London, 1932.

Quennell, Marjorie and C. H. B. *Everyday Things in Homeric Greece*. Batsford, London, 1929.

Quennell, Marjorie and C. H. B. *A History of Everyday Things in England (1066–1799)*. 2 v. Scribner, New York, 1918.

Quicherat, Jules E. J. *Histoire du costume en France*, etc. Hachette, Paris, 1877.

Racinet, Albert C. A. *Le Costume historique*. 6 v. Firmin-Didot, Paris, 1888.

Rawlinson, George. *The Five Great Monarchies of the Ancient Eastern World . . . Chaldea, Assyria, Babylon, Medea, and Persia*. 4 v. Murray, London, 1862–67.

Rawlinson, George. *History of Ancient Egypt*. 2 v. Dodd, Mead, New York, 1882.

Rawlinson, George. *The Seventh Great Oriental Monarchy . . . the New Persian Empire*. Longmans, London, 1876.

Rawlinson, George. *The Sixth Great Oriental Monarchy . . . Parthia*. Dodd, Mead, New York, [190–?].

Renan, Ary. *Le Costume en France*. Quantin, Paris, 1890.

Rhead, George W. *Chats on Costume*. Stokes, New York, 1906.

Robida, Albert. *Yester-year: Ten Centuries of Toilette* (translated by Mrs. Cashel Hoey). Scribner, New York, 1891.

Rohrbach, Carl, and Kretschmer, Albert. *Die Trachten der Völker*, etc. Bach, Leipzig, 1882.

Rosenberg, Adolf. *Geschichte des Kostüms*. 2 v. Wasmuth, Berlin, 1905.

Rothfeld, Otto. *Women of India*. Simpkin, London, 1920.

Sage, Elizabeth. *A Study of Costume,* etc. Scribner, New York, 1926.

Saint-Simon, Louis de Rouvroy, duc de. *Memoirs of Louis XIV and the Regency* (translated by Bayle St. John). Dunne, Washington, 1901.

Salzman, Louis F. *English Life in the Middle Ages.* Milford, London, 1926.

Sardou, Victorien. *Costumes du temps de la Révolution,* etc. Lévy, Paris, 1876.

Saunders, Catharine. *Costume in Roman Comedy.* Columbia University Press, New York, 1919.

Sayce, Archibald H. *The Ancient Empires of the East.* Scribner, New York, 1889.

Schumacher, F., and Company. *The Development of Various Decorative and Up-holstery Fabrics.* Schumacher and Co., New York, 1924.

Seignobos, C. *The Feudal Regime.* Holt, New York, 1902.

Selden, Samuel, and Sellman, Hunton D. *Stage Scenery and Lighting,* etc. Crofts, New York, 1936.

Sergeant, Lewis. *The Franks,* etc. Unwin, London, 1898.

Seymour, Thomas D. *Life in the Homeric Age.* Macmillan, New York, 1908.

Shaw, H. *Dresses and Decorations of the Middle Ages.* 2 v. Pickering, London, 1843.

Shepherd, William R. *Historical Atlas.* Holt, New York, 1929.

Speltz, Alexander. *The Styles of Ornaments,* etc. (translated and revised by R. P. Spiers). Batsford, London, 1910.

Stephenson, Henry T. *The Elizabethan People.* Holt, New York, 1910.

Stone, Melicent. *The Bankside Costume Book for Children.* Saalfield, Akron, Ohio, 1913.

Strachey, Giles Lytton. *Queen Victoria.* Harcourt, New York, 1921.

Strutt, Joseph. *A Complete View of the Dress and Habits of the People of England,* etc. 2 v. Bohn, London, 1842.

Stuart, John S. S. and C. E. *The Costume of the Clan,* etc. Grant, Edinburgh, 1892.

Stylianou, Demetrios. *The Inner Life of Cyprus.* Apollo Press, Nicosia, Cyprus, 1931.

Sullivan, Mark. *Our Times; the United States, 1900–1925.* 6 v. Scribner, New York, 1927–35.

Symonds, John A. *Renaissance in Italy.* 5 v. Murray, London, 1921–30.

Taine, Hippolyte Adolphe. *The Ancient Régime* (translated by John Durand). Holt, New York, 1885.

Tappan, Eva March. *When Knights Were Bold.* Houghton, Boston, 1911.

Tenison, E. M. *Elizabethan England* (*Being the History of this Country "In Relation to all Foreign Princes"*). 10 v. Issued for the Author at the Sign of the Dove with the Griffin, Royal Leamington Spa, in the County of Warwick, England, 1933.

Thorndike, Lynn. *A Short History of Civilization.* Crofts, New York, 1936.

Tilke, Max. *Orienthalische Kostüme in Schnitt und Farbe.* Wasmuth, Berlin, 1923.

Towne, Charles H. *This New York of Mine.* Cosmopolitan Book Co., New York, 1931.

Traill, Henry D. *Social England,* etc. 6 v. Cassell, London, 1893–97.

Traphagen, Ethel. *Costume Design and Illustration.* Wiley, New York, 1918.

Trendell, Henry A. P. *Dress Worn at His Majesty's Court.* Harrison, London, 1912.

Tuberville, Arthur Stanley. *English Men and Manners in the 18th Century.* Clarendon Press, Oxford, 1926.

Tucker, Thomas G. *Life in Ancient Athens,* etc. Macmillan, New York, 1930.

Tuer, Andrew W. *The Follies and Fashions of Our Grandfathers (1807).* Field and Tuer, London, 1886–87.

Tyack, George S. *Historic Dress of the Clergy.* Andrews, London, 1897.

Uzanne, Louis Octave. *Fashion in Paris,* etc. Heinemann, London, 1901.

Victoria and Albert Museum. *Guide to the Collection of Costumes.* Board of Education, London, 1924.

Viollet-le-Duc, Eugène E. *Dictionnaire raisonné de l'architecture française,* etc. 10 v. Morel, Paris, 1861–75.

Viollet-le-Duc, Eugène E. *Dictionnaire raisonné du mobilier français,* etc. 6 v. Morel, Paris, 1871–75.

Wagner, Leopold. *Manners, Customs, and Observances.* Macmillan, New York, 1895.

Webb, W. M. *The Heritage of Dress,* etc. Richards, London, 1907.

Weigall, Arthur E. P. B. *The Life and Times of Akhnaton,* etc. Butterworth, London, 1922.

Wharton, Grace and Philip. *The Wits and Beaux of Society.* Routledge, London, 1873.

Wilkinson, Sir John G. *The Manners and Customs of the Ancient Egyptians.* 3 v. Murray, London, 1878.

Wordsworth, Christopher. *Greece: Pictorial, Descriptive, and Historical.* Orr, London, 1839.

Wright, Thomas. *The Romance of the Shoe,* etc. Farncombe, London, 1922.

Wright, Thomas. *Womankind in Western Europe,* etc. Groombridge, London, 1869.

Yaggy, Levi W., and Haines, T. W. *Museum of Antiquity,* etc. Law, Chicago, 1885.

Young, Agnes Brooks. *Stage Costuming.* Macmillan, New York, 1927.

Zimmern, Sir Alfred E. *The Greek Commonwealth,* etc. Clarendon Press, Oxford, 1924.

Zur Geschichte der Kostüme. (Edited by Louis Braun, W. Diez, Ernst Fröhlich, I. Gehrts, C. Häberlin, M. Heil, A. Müller, and F. Rothbart.) Braun and Schneider, München, 1909.

Periodicals

Antiquarian, The (1923–)

Art and Archaeology (1914–)

Art et la Mode; Revue de l'Élégance (Paris) (1853–)

La Belle Assemblée (London) (1806–1810)

Le Bon Ton and *Le Moniteur de la Mode* (Paris) (1853–)

The Connoisseur (merged with *International Studio* in 1927) (London) (1901–)

The Delineator (1873–)

Gallery of Fashion (London) (1794–1802)

Gazette des Beaux Arts (Paris) (1859)

Gazette des Salons, Journal des Dames et des Modes (Paris) (1797–1838)

The Gentleman's Magazine (London) (1731–1907[?])

Godey's Lady's Book (1830–1898)

Good Housekeeping (1885–)

Harper's Bazaar (1867–)

L'Illustration (Paris) (1843–)

Illustrated London News (London) (1842–)

International Studio (1897–)

Journal des Dames (London) (1817-19)

Judge (1881–)

Ladies' Home Journal (1883–)

The Lady's Magazine (London) (1749-1753)

Lady's Pocket Magazine (London) (1824-40)

Life (1883–)

London Repository (London) (1809-15)

London Tailor and Record of Fashion (London) (1876-1914)

Magazin des Modes (Paris) (1851-58)

McCall's (1870–)

La Mode Illustrée (London) (1869-73)

Le Moniteur de la Mode (Paris) (1843-1903)

National Geographic Magazine (1889-)

Peterson's Magazine (1840-1898)

Petit Courier des Dames (Paris) (1836-1868)

Puck (1877-1918)

Punch (London) 1841-)

Revue de l'Art (Paris) (1897-)

Saturday Evening Post (1821-)

St. Nicholas (1873-)

Scribner's (1870-)

Simplicissimus (Munich) (1896-)

The Studio (London) (1893)

Vogue (1892-)

Woman's Home Companion (1873-)

SUPPLEMENTARY BIBLIOGRAPHY

Davenport, Millia. *The Book of Costume.* Crown, New York, 1948.

Norris, Herbert, and Curtis, Oswald. *Costume and Fashion.* 6 v. (The Nineteenth Century). Dutton, New York, 1933.

Wilcox, R. Turner. *The Mode in Costume.* Scribner, New York, 1942.

Periodicals

Esquire (1937-1950)

Flair (1950)

Christian Science Monitor, Magazine Section (Dec. 12, 1942), pp. 10-11

Men's Wear (1937-1950)

Saturday Evening Post, Magazine Section (May 29, 1943), pp. 26-27

Vogue (1937-1950)

U.S. Army Uniform Regulations, # 600-40 (1944)

U.S. Navy Uniform Regulations, NAVPERS 15665 (1947)

Women's Wear (1937-1950)

In addition to these specific references, it is well to consult contemporary periodicals and newspapers.

The study of contemporary art, particularly portraits and genre subjects, is most valuable for correct detail.

The costume of any given time is also reflected in bric-a-brac, vases, and other objects worthy of study in this connection.

Frequently the outstanding fiction of each era, as well as the best biographies, gives much valuable information as to dress and its details. Consult also letters of the times. *Letters of Fanny Brawne to Fanny Keats* (Oxford University Press, London, 1936) not only offers charming descriptions of Georgian costumes, but also has crude sketches of Fanny Brawne's own dress patterns.

INDEX

INDEX

(As the text material is arranged chronologically, this is a subject index to the principal garments and developments covered. Suggestions for making costumes for the various periods appear at the end of most of the chapters. Bold-face figures refer to illustrations.)

413

Date Due